CW01375961

The Origin and History of the Primitive Methodist Church Volume 1

You are holding a reproduction of an original work that is in the public domain in the United States of America, and possibly other countries. You may freely copy and distribute this work as no entity (individual or corporate) has a copyright on the body of the work. This book may contain prior copyright references, and library stamps (as most of these works were scanned from library copies). These have been scanned and retained as part of the historical artifact.

This book may have occasional imperfections such as missing or blurred pages, poor pictures, errant marks, etc. that were either part of the original artifact, or were introduced by the scanning process. We believe this work is culturally important, and despite the imperfections, have elected to bring it back into print as part of our continuing commitment to the preservation of printed works worldwide. We appreciate your understanding of the imperfections in the preservation process, and hope you enjoy this valuable book.

THE ORIGIN AND HISTORY
OF THE
PRIMITIVE METHODIST CHURCH

THE ORIGIN AND HISTORY

OF THE

PRIMITIVE METHODIST CHURCH

BY THE

REV. H. B. KENDALL, B.A.

Vol. I.

London:
EDWIN DALTON, E.C.

ACKNOWLEDGMENT

THE Author hereby sincerely thanks those many friends who have materially assisted in the preparation of this work by giving information or supplying illustrations His acknowledgments are especially due to the Revs J. W Chappel, J. T Gooderidge, and Sydney A. Barron for the labour they cheerfully undertook in making researches into the early history of our Church in Staffordshire, Nottinghamshire and Leicestershire, respectively, and for the loan of portraits and documents

H. B. K

INTRODUCTORY.

IN an important document recently discovered, and never, up to this time, quoted, William Clowes passes certain strictures on the first official History of the Primitive Methodist Church. "I must confess," he says, "though I never said so to anybody in my life, that I did not approve of its being drawn up in the way it was." To William Clowes, the history of the Primitive Methodist Church began when the Camp Meeting Methodists and the Clowesites came together in 1811 to form one united Church. He furthermore maintained that Hugh Bourne, William Clowes, James Steele, James Nixon, and Thomas Woodnorth, should be recognised and honoured as the real founders of our Church.

As though to confirm the view of Clowes, the historical preamble to the Deed Poll of the Primitive Methodist Connexion—its document of highest official authority—sets forth the origin of the Connexion, and finds it in the fusion of the Clowesites and Camp Meeting Methodists. Having mentioned the societies at Ramsor, Wootton, Stanley, and Tnustall, this carefully-drawn legal instrument proceeds:—

"And the said several societies and classes, together with other congregations, societies, and classes, in several parts of England, were afterwards closely united and connected, and the whole thereof under the care of the said Hugh Bourne, James Bourne, William Clowes, and James Steele, were formed into one general community or Connexion, known and distinguished by the title or denomination of 'The Primitive Methodist Connexion.'"

Undoubtedly, then, William Clowes is right in his main contention, viz., that the Primitive Methodist Church began in 1811, and, therefore, that the proper history of the Church must also begin with that date. It is an anachronism to speak of Primitive Methodism before 1811. Any incidents which took place prior to the union effected in this memorable year, must be regarded as incidents and episodes belonging to a revivalistic movement, or series of revivalistic movements, locally differentiated, proceeding on early or primitive Methodist lines, partaking, therefore, of the nature of a revival,

All this may appear very obvious when stated, and to amount to little more than a question of words. But words, unless carefully chosen and kept in their right place, have a way of confusing thought and raising a false issue. The view of Clowes, endorsed as it is by the Deed Poll as to the origin and foundership of the Connexion, may be plain as a pikestaff when pointed out, but had this very obvious truth been always kept in mind, it would have made impossible much useless discussion as to whether this or that event which occurred anywhere between 1799 and 1811, is to be regarded as the beginning of Primitive Methodism—whether it be the conversion of Hugh Bourne in 1799, the conversation-sermon and revival at Harriseahead in 1800, 'the camp-meeting without a name' in the same year, Mow-Cop camp-meeting in 1807, or the taking over of Stanley class in 1810. All these events, important as they were, belong to the preparatory movement, and not the denominational period. Another result would have followed: disputes as to who was the true founder of the Connexion would soon have had the heart taken out of them. For "Who was the one founder of the Connexion?" is seen to be a question quite beside the mark, as soon as we recognise the true state of facts. How could there be but one founder when there must have been as many founders as there were heads and leaders of the various revivalistic agencies which in 1811 became as the Deed Poll puts it, "closely united and connected"? Who was the founder of the Camp Meeting Methodists, or of the Dowites at Rizley, or of the Clowesites? are questions relevant enough. But who was the founder of the Primitive Methodist Connexion? is like asking, What was the name of Isaac's son? or What did they call Solomon's wife? The enquirer must re-shape his question, or stand down. We have had founders in the plural, but no one man can lay exclusive claim to that distinction, as Clowes knew, as the Deed Poll deponeth, and as this history, we hope, will clearly show.

And now we fear that, like Dr Faustus when he preached his too moving sermon in the market-place, we have proved our point too much. We have laboured to make clear the fact that Primitive Methodist history properly so called, begins in 1811, and yet, straightway, we shall proceed to dwell with some minuteness and care on men who lived and events that happened in the twelve years previous to 1811. And it should, moreover, be admitted that we shall do this despite the opinion and judgment of William Clowes himself, as recorded in the document aforesaid, recently brought to light. In the strictures passed upon the first "History" of 1823, he expresses the opinion that in drawing up that History, there was no need to write of events so far back as the conversion of Hugh Bourne, or of the Tunstall revival in which Clowes himself was converted. We cannot go with him in this opinion. On the contrary, we make bold to say, and the truth of the statement is not less assured because expressed in a paradoxical form. The most important part of the history of Primitive Methodism relates to what occurred in 1800—11, when, as yet, there was no Primitive Methodism. William Clowes lived in the pre-evolutionary days, before the advent of the relative spirit by which our methods of writing history and biography have been largely modified. Under the influence of this pervasive spirit, neither man nor institution can now be regarded as a true "absolute", separate and self-contained, independent of what went before and unrelated to what is around. It is felt that

that subject—be it individual or institutional—cannot properly be understood unless we know something of its parentage and antecedents as well as of the contemporary forces which have gone to shape and modify it. Thus history has become largely biological, and biography the analysis of a product as well as the telling of a human story. True, there is danger that too much may be yielded to the exacting demands of the relative spirit—as we can see in such a work as Buckle's "History of Civilisation,"—yet, within limits, its claims are just and reasonable. No one can ignore the sources and streams of the Jordan because they do not bear that name until their confluence; neither do men begin to write of the Oxford Movement by describing the publication of the 'Tracts for the Times.' The 'movement,' as its originators and abettors loved to call it, had been some seven years in progress before that "portentous birth of time," and the explanation of that movement must be sought in the character and aims of the three men who gave it its inspiration, impulse and direction. To understand the confluent stream, you must survey its tributaries and trace them to their source. To understand movements, you must know something of the men who gave them their momenta and direction.

It is such considerations as these that induce—yea, that compel us—to include within the scope of this history a survey of the formative period prior to 1811 and especially to consider the training of Hugh Bourne and William Clowes, and how they acted upon the movements of their time, and were in their turn, re-acted upon by those movements. Let the reader not begrudge the space needful for dealing at all satisfactorily with so difficult and necessary a task.

BOOK I.

SOURCES AND ORIGIN

PRIMITIVE METHODIST CHURCH.

CHAPTER I.

THE HARRISEAHEAD REVIVALISTS.

Hugh Bourne's Conversion.

HUGH BOURNE first saw the light at Fordhays Farm, in the parish of Stoke-upon-Trent, Staffordshire, April 3rd, 1772; his second birth took place in the summer of 1799. For the first sixteen years of his life— that is to say, during the period when the deepest and most permanent impressions are made—Hugh Bourne lived on a solitary moorland farm. The farmstead is still standing, though it has been raised, and its roof is no longer thatched. Those who knew the original building well have left us a description of it which might almost seem to have been taken from "Wuthering Heights."

"As a residence, there could hardly be anything more bleak, desolate, and lonely. In the whole neighbourhood of this moorland there were only some two or three other houses, and beyond these was the wide stretch of the moor. There was no road, public or private, not even a foot-road to the house or anywhere near it, and to complete the isolation and loneliness, the only access to the house was over a wide brook upon a plank, and often for weeks together, the family saw no one beyond their own circle, and of the great outside world they knew but very little."

If the bleak Yorkshire fells are needed to account for the sombre genius of the Brontë sisters, so it needs Fordhays Farm fully to account for Hugh Bourne. To the very last his moorland origin stood confessed. His native environment had its counterpart in his strong, rugged nature, and especially in that bashfulness which was so marked a feature of the man. Nor need we wonder at this, for he must have enabled him to overcome the steady pressure and influence of such an environment as that amid which the most plastic years of life were passed. But he was also constitutionally shy and serious, and it was inevitable that a timidity inborn and ingrained should be deepened by the solitary aspects of his early life. To such an extent was this the case that he became, to use his own words, "so bashful as is seldom seen." We cannot but admire that, handicapped as he was by this temperamental thorn in the flesh, in its very despite this diffident moorland youth of few words eventually got so far and did so much. After all, he must have had considerable reserves of doggedness and moral courage to draw upon, and there must have been rigorous self-discipline and the habit of reliance.

"But, perhaps," it may be said, "even Fordhays had its compensations. When the plank over the brook was crossed, and you entered the farm-kitchen, there might be enough light and cheerfulness within to make up for the gloom without and to people its solitude. It might be the abode of piety—of 'plain living and high thinking.'" Scarcely; for the master of Fordhays— Joseph Bourne, farmer, wheelwright, and timber-dealer —was no good liver, though his days were long in the land.* He was passionate, a drunkard and dissolute, a derider of Methodism and dissent, and yet withal a stiff Churchman. Sometimes in his convivial moments he would boast that "he had a bishop and two parsons at home" (alluding to his wife and sons); but if so, the parsons had to do their priest's office in the attic or anywhere they could out of sight and hearing of the violent and churlish man. All the time, Joseph Bourne had an angel in the house had he but known it—a thrifty, long-suffering woman who did her best to keep together the gear he did his worst to scatter. She, and not he, the husband, was the true stay and band of the house. Partly to save expense, and partly from the love of the work, she taught her children to read as she sat busy at the spinning-wheel. Ellen Steel—let us give her maiden name so that two of that surname may honourably figure in the history of our Church—early taught her lad to fear God and walk righteously, though she could not bring him into the joy and peace of assurance, and, indeed, did not herself enter therein until Hugh, her son, showed her the way.

Hugh Bourne's own papers reveal that as a child he was uncommonly serious, and knew something of gloom and even of terror. Early might it have been said of him:

"Shades of the prison-house begin to close
Upon the growing boy."

But he kept his sorrows and struggles to himself, hiding them even from his mother.

HUGH BOURNE.
(From an old Circuit Plan).
Circa, 1848.
"This side-view portrait struck us as an exceedingly good one, and worthy of being published in a more permanent form."—
REV. J. WOOD, D.D.

* He is said to be nearly a hundred years of age.

FORDHAYS FARM AS IT WAS. HUGH BOURNE'S BIRTHPLACE.

FORDHAYS FARM AS IT IS. BACK VIEW.

Of this period he afterwards wrote pathetically:—

"Oh, that I had had some one to take me by the hand and instruct me in the mystery of faith and the nature of a free, full and present salvation! How happy would it have been for me! But like Bunyan's Pilgrim I had to make my way alone. The Lord neither gave me guide nor companion in the way to the Cross. I was painfully convinced of sin when I was but a small boy, and this without the aid or knowledge of any man, and during my twenty sorrowful years I went through much moral and religious readings."

This period in Hugh Bourne's life left its mark upon him to the end. Familiar to all is that peculiarity in his character and ministry—his constant practice of taking kindly notice of children. He did this not merely to please their parents, or because he himself was, as the phrase goes, "fond of children." He did it on principle, because, as he knew from his own experience, they had affinities with the Kingdom of God, and rightly belonged that Kingdom. So it was his invariable custom to preach short, simple sermons to the children, and to insist upon others doing the same. There lay behind this practice of his, as its sufficient reason and justification, his own experience when as a child he walked in darkness and had no light. What sore travail might have been missed, and how much earlier might he have been won for the Church, had some good soul but broken in upon his solitude and led him, child as he was, into the fold of Christ! So, as he had suffered when a child from the wrong ideas or indifference of others, he was determined to do his part to save other children, who might even now be before him, from the like experience.

We shall see, when we come to consider Hugh Bourne as author and editor, what he did in this same period towards self-culture. If we refer to his reading now it is only because by reading, and by reading alone, he was led into the light. It was not by the means of grace as ordinarily understood, or by the living voice of preacher, teacher, or friend that a new direction was given to his life. His conversion was not directly traceable to any living personal influence whatever. On the contrary, the influence exerted upon him by the lives of many around was rather such as to perplex him and hinder his progress. If ever there was a conversion brought about through the instrumentality of books it was in the case of Hugh Bourne. All that men did for him was to lend him the books for which he asked. They neither chose his reading for him, nor asked the question Philip put to the eunuch, "Understandest thou what thou readest?"

In 1799 he found rich spoil in a volume of varied contents borrowed of a Methodist neighbour. Between the covers of this book were the Life of Fletcher of Madeley, Jane Cooper's "Letters," the lives of T. Taylor and John Haime, early Methodist preachers, Alleine's "Alarm to the Unconverted," a Treatise on the Articles and Homilies of the Church of England, etc.—truly a library in a volume. Amongst the sermons of Wesley was the one on the Trinity (1 John v. 7), which made it clear to him that he had been pursuing a search foredoomed to failure in trying to find a perfect form of religion, perfectly expressed. He was now "delivered from laying stress on opinions," ' " ' ' ' ' ' of the heart was alike in all." How much Hugh Bou   We   broad Catholic teaching may be inferred from the fact that he has incorporated a weighty paragraph from this sermon in the first History of the Primitive Methodist Connexion, published in 1823. That quotation rightly stands where it does in the History since, but for it, he might have continued to hold aloof from any and every organised religious society. On this ground, Wesley's sermon on the Trinity, and particularly the excerpt given by Hugh Bourne, may be viewed in the light of a document belonging to our sources, and for this reason might quite properly have had insertion here.

In the early part of this same year—1799—he

> "Read the books of the first Quakers—great examples of patient suffering, zealous for open-air worship, mighty in faith. They would exercise faith even in silence, until they moved whole neighbourhoods by so doing. I was much edified in reading of the faith, patience, and sufferings of the primitive Quakers. . . . . I was enabled to see a little more clearly into the mystery and power of faith. truly their trials of faith were great."

BIDDULPH MOOR.

Next, sundry volumes of the "Arminian Magazine"—eldest of our religious serials—fell in his way; and now, for the first time, he learned that the Arminians, whom he had once thought of seeking out in the West of England, were the same people as the Methodists at his very doors! After this we can quite believe him when he avers that he "knew but little of the Methodists," and that on account of the conduct of certain inconsistent professors in his neighbourhood, he had gone the length of "thinking the Methodists a fallen people." Assuredly, he much needed at this juncture the offices of a candid and well informed friend

As Wesley had broken down barriers

John Fletcher was instrumentally the means of completing the work — of ending the twenty long years of conflict and giving him sure-grounded peace. It will be well to let Hugh Bourne describe in his own naïve way that experience which was at once the end of a dreary journey, shot by only occasional gleams of brightness, and the beginning of a new and fuller life.

"One Sunday morning (in the spring of 1799) in my father's house at Bemersley, I sat reading in Mr. Fletcher's 'Letters on the Spiritual Manifestation of the Son of God,' and realised the blessing named in John xiv. 21, where Christ says, 'I will love him, and will manifest Myself to him'; and He manifested Himself to me, and I was born again in an instant! yea, passed from death unto life. The naughty was taken out of my heart and the good put in. In an instant I had power over sin, which I had not before; and I was filled with joy and love and glory which

BEMERSLEY FARM, THE HOME OF THE BOURNES.

made a full amends for the twenty years' suffering. The Bible looked new; creation looked new; and I felt a love to all mankind; and my desire was that friends and enemies and all the world, if possible, might be saved."

Hugh Bourne could, one thinks, have written a good article on "Books that have Influenced me." And, indeed, from his own incidental references to his indebtedness to books, we have endeavoured to put together such a chapter. Well might he believe in the power of the Press, who was himself a living witness of its power, and humbly follow the example of Wesley in making use of the Press as an instrument in advancing the Kingdom of God.

for 1822 the six letters of Fletcher, in which Bourne maintains the thesis—regarded as "unscriptural, enthusiastical, and dangerous" by some—"That the Son of God, for purposes worthy of His wisdom, manifests Himself sooner or later to His sincere followers in a spiritual manner which the world knows not of." Soon, we shall find John xiv. 21, the very heart and centre of the written account of his own conversion he drew up for the edification of others, and the text of his first conversation-sermon.

Elsewhere we have written—"Hugh Bourne was the child of *primitive* Methodism." This is no question-begging phrase. We use it without prejudice or thought of any ulterior argumentative advantage to be gained thereby. As the dictum stands it is historically and psychologically true, and further reflection only serves to deepen our conviction of its truth: only, the statement needs to be somewhat enlarged. Hugh Bourne *was* the child of primitive Methodism, but there was also a strain of primitive Quakerism in his blood. He was the product of Methodism, but not of the Methodism of his own day. He knew but little, and could know but little of that. The Methodism of which he was the product, the Methodism he was to do his best to revive and make a living force, was the Methodism of John Nelson, and of the other early preachers whose lives he had read. As we have shown, Methodism reached him first of all through the media of books. Very illuminating are his own words written of a time two or three years subsequent to his conversion:—"As my information had been mainly acquired by reading it was chiefly primitive—I may say unconsciously primitive." The remark shows acuteness of self-discrimination; Methodism of the early type was at first imbibed unconsciously. Presently it became his set deliberate purpose to revive it, and he found himself in association with others of like mind and purpose, and an active participant in a movement which locally was afterwards to differentiate itself. But a word as to the Quaker element in Hugh Bourne's Methodism: the reading of the large volumes containing the annals of the first race of Quakers left its mark—its indelible mark upon him, and to a certain extent upon the denomination he helped to found. To his somewhat narrow, intense, sombre nature there was much in the primitive Quakerism of George Fox—with its mystic sympathies, its openness to receive and be guided by impressions and dreams with its tendency to give a severe and ascetic interpretation to the injunction "be not conformed to this world"—there was much in all this that was congenial to Hugh Bourne, and to which he readily responded. The law that stood so long on the statute-book requiring travelling-preachers to wear their hair in its natural form, witnesses to the influence which Quakerism in its least vital and attractive form exerted upon our fathers. But though its lower workings might be seen in enactments prescribing the mode of wearing the hair or the cut of the coat, its higher workings wrought results of much more permanent value. In truth, primitive Methodism and primitive Quakerism made a good blend, one which England at the turn of the century was all the better for having offered to it.

After his conversion, Hugh Bourne was still in some perplexity as to what Church he should join; for that it was his duty to join *some* Church he was quite convinced. The question in debate within his own mind was whether he should cast in his lot with the Methodists or Quakers. he thought that he would be better off than the

14   PRIMITIVE METHODIST CHURCH.

BIDDULPH PARISH CHURCH.

KNYPERSLEY FIELD FARM, RESIDENCE OF FARMER BIRCHENOUGH.

Apostle, and that he had likewise drawings to the Quaker-Methodists, who formed a kind of *tertium quid*. With each of these he had affinities and sympathy. There is no evidence that he ever seriously thought of making his home in the Established Church, though up to the time of his conversion he and his mother regularly attended the Sunday morning service at Biddulph parish church. He seems to have had some weeks of hesitancy. He felt himself "in a dilemma"; that is the phrase he uses to express the difficulty he experienced in making up his mind, and he resolved to take no decisive step until the Lord should make known His will.

Deliverance from his perplexities was brought about in an odd and unexpected way. Of lovefeasts, Hugh Bourne had read in Wesley's Life, and was wishful to see one for himself. But, in his innocence and unfamiliarity with Methodist procedure, he did not know that the ticket he took from the minister's hand was not only a passport to the lovefeast to be held at Burslem on the wake-Monday, but actually made him a member of the Church. But farmer Birchenough, in whose house the travelling-preacher was writing the tickets, knew. He, shrewd man, harped upon the value of the ticket as an open-sesame to the lovefeast, but was discreetly silent as to its higher value. He doubtless wished to put an end once for all to Hugh Bourne's dubieties and hesitancies, and to commit him to a definitive course by a little well-meant guile. Next day, Hugh Bourne learned the truth, but resolved upon now going through with the business and attending the lovefeast, since if it were not the Lord's will that he should be a Methodist, he could still draw back. The superintendent—the Rev. John Brettell—led that Burslem lovefeast, and so much was Hugh Bourne's heart stirred that, despite his timidity, he was near rising to speak, and at the close he gratefully acknowledged that God had indeed made known His will. "I was," says he, "heart and hand a Methodist." The next Sabbath, June, 1799, Hugh Bourne and his mother both joined the class at Ridgway. Thus by a singular coincidence Hugh Bourne was both made a member of the Church and nine years afterwards dismembered without at the time being privy to the fact.

REV. JOHN BRETTELL.

MOW COP THE MOUNT OF BEGINNINGS.

By the beginning of 1800, Hugh Bourne had become his own master, and business affairs required him

RIDGWAY-HALL FARM.

A VIEW OF MOW COP.

He had speculated in timber at Dales Green between Harriseahead and Mow Cop, and, naturally, he had to be on the spot to take over and prove his purchase.

As Mow now becomes for a time the chief centre of interest, a word as to this rugged district and its, then, equally rugged inhabitants will not be out of place. The moorlands and heights of North Staffordshire are part of the Pennine range which like a spine runs down from the Cheviots to the Peak of Derbyshire. Mow is a spur or outlier of that range to which Cross Fell and Ingleborough also belong, and forms the south-western extremity of the range. On the north-west, the ridge of Mow presents a somewhat steep and abrupt face to the plain of Cheshire, but on the Staffordshire side its descent is more gradual, and it sinks in terraces into the valley of the Trent—the great central plain of England. As its name signifies, Mow Cop is the highest point of the south-westernmost ridge of the aforesaid Pennine range, which here, as if to make the very most of its proportions, thrusts itself up some 1091 feet above the level of the sea and attains almost to the dignity of a mountain.* The traveller on the London and North Western Railway between Manchester and London, must surely have lifted his eyes from his newspaper to notice the extended ridge, bordering the counties of Cheshire and Stafford, and crowned by the picturesque structure known as the Tower, which, though erected only in 1754, not unsuccessfully puts on the aspect of hoary antiquity. This is Mow Cop.

We cannot but think that Primitive Methodism was happy in the *locale* of its origin, and that there was something even of prophetic significance in what the Northumbrians call its 'calf-yard'—the place of its nativity. The north-midland county of Staffordshire here epitomises many of the physical and industrial features amongst which so much of the success of the denomination was to be won. The wealth and population of Staffordshire aggregate round its two coal-fields. The northern one, where the coal-measures which run through Lancashire and Cheshire end in the hilly district of the county, is the chief centre of the manufacture of earthenware. Here, too, are moorland shepherds, and miners, and iron-workers as well as the still more numerous potters. The southern coal-field, separated from the northern one by the purely agricultural valley of the Trent, is given up to ironworks and hardware manufactures, and is known to everybody as the Black Country. Candid friends of our Church will tell us that right along the course of our history we have worked amongst peasants and potters, pitmen and puddlers. If so, we have been true to our origin, for we began among these classes of workers and, the physical geography of Stafford and the industrial life of its crowded population being what they were, we could not well have begun among any other, nor could we have begun our work among any sections of the community that more needed a rousing evangelism.

---

* Though "Mow," we are told, was formerly written 'Mole," we need not infer that the name was given in irony or to express a fancied resemblance to a mole-hill though such a derivation is possible enough. Mow may be the slightly disguised Celtic "Meol" or "Mel" a bare chalk-hill, or it may, more probably, be the Saxon "Mow a stack or heap as in barley-mow and as "Cop" is the good old word for the top summit or crest Mow-Cop will be in that compound, but a pure Saxon double designation denoting the loftiest point of the ridge

18 PRIMITIVE METHODIST CHURCH.

SOURCES AND ORIGIN. 19

Red Hall Farm, Dales Green.

The Old Class Meeting House.

Harding's House.

Mow's Highest Point Rising up to the Left.

The Mow Cop of a century ago was very different from the Mow Cop of to-day. It requires an effort of the imagination to picture it as it would appear to Hugh Bourne in 1800, when his lot was cast there. It was a region rugged and bleak, dotted here and there with a few grey roughly-built cottages, that might have been the outcrop of the rocky ground, so well did they correspond in form and hue with their environment. And the morals and manners of the people who lived in these cottages and wrought the quarries or won coal in the adjacent pits, were in keeping with the physical aspects and conditions amid which their lives were spent, being rough and rude. But they were worse than rough and rude; for those who lived nearer those days speak of the district as though it were an enclave of heathendom. One biographer of Bourne records his opinion that the Kidsgrove and Harriseahead colliers were quite as ignorant and

KIDSGROVE COLLIERY.

debased as the Kingswood colliers of Wesley's and Whitefield's day. Drunkenness, cock-fighting, bull-baiting, poaching, pugilism, midnight marauding, and profanity were rife. Crimes of violence were common enough to give the stranger, or even the belated native who was compelled to cross the mountain, an unpleasant feeling of uneasiness, and he walked warily, as one who knew he ran some risk. It was, indeed, one of the dark places of the land; for, with the exception of one small chapel of ease (New Chapel - where Brindley, the great canal engineer, lies buried), there was no place of worship to be seen for miles on the Staffordshire side of Mow. Here, however, it ought to be observed, lest a wrong impression be made, that, bad as the people of Mow were, they were not, after all, "sinners above all that dwelt" in England at the opening of the nineteenth century. Though special attention, like a searchlight,

SOURCES AND ORIGIN.

NEW CHAPEL CHURCH.
(Brindley's Grave is the Monument on the left).

has been turned on this particular corner of North Staffordshire, with the result of disclosing sad spiritual destitution and deplorable morals, yet the light only needed to be concentrated elsewhere with equal intensity, in order to reveal a spiritual destitution just as great and morals not one whit better. Of this abundant evidence could be given were this but the time and place to give it. Let us think of Mow as one of many similar

MOW COP CHAPEL, (SIDE VIEW).
The foreground is past the site of the first Camp Meeting of 1807.

benighted districts that in 1800 sorely needed evangelising.

But what conspicuous changes the years have brought! In few parts of England is

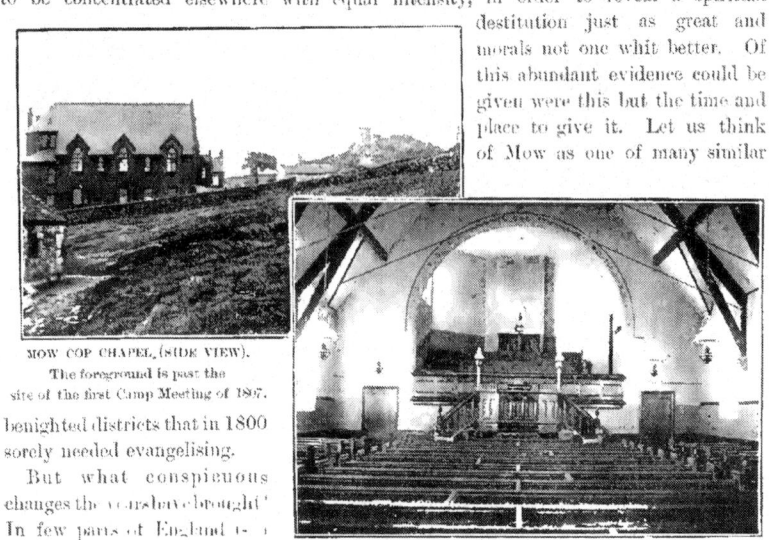

MOW COP CHAPEL (INTERIOR).

more striking contrast between the state of things prevailing in 1800 and 1900 afforded than in the neighbourhood of Mow. Ironworks and other industries now give steady and remunerative employment to an increased population. The conditions of material well-being are everywhere to be seen. On hill and in dale neat cottages abound—the homes of thrifty, self-respecting, and God-fearing men and women, and the country is dotted with sanctuaries and Sunday-schools—at once the sign, cause, and effect of the improvement the century has witnessed. No wonder that one of ourselves should have broken out into a jingle:—

"Upon the mossy brow
Of the venerable Mow
There stands a chapel now,
Upon a hill."

FIRST PRIMITIVE METHODIST CHAPEL
MOW COP
BUILT ANNO DOMINI 1841

THE CHRISTMAS-DAY CONVERSATION-SERMON.

But we revert to 1800 and to Mow as Hugh Bourne looked upon it in the early part of that year. His first feeling was not "What a fine field of usefulness is here!" but rather "Woe is me, that I sojourn in Mesech, that I dwell among the tents of Kedar!" He recalled with a twinge of self-condemnation how at Ridgway he had thought the means of grace .... but now, as if to punish him for his undervaluing of opportunities, there was an absolute famine of the Word of Life. In this mood Mow was to him as the hill Mizar, the hill of longing and of wistful memories. With this regret for what he had lost, there was mingled the more acute feeling of fear for himself lest he should succumb to the dearth of means and the evil examples all around him. He wished the timber were all won and he free to return to more congenial surroundings. But, instead of loosing him, providence proceeded to tie him more tightly to this barren spot by a double cord of business engagements. First he was asked to undertake the woodwork of a mountain farm, and then to do the same for Stonetrough Colliery, nor did he see how he could, with any show of reason, refuse either contract.

It is with the beginnings of the Christian life in the renewed heart of the individual as it is with fire and water. The fire needs fuel to feed it and air to fan it, so that it

STONETROUGH COLLIERY.
Showing shops where Hugh Bourne worked.

may gather strength and subdue other material to its own nature ; and the water must be let flow so that it may find its way and keep itself fresh by running, and join with kindred drops and streams. Should it be hindered of its way, the fire will die down, and the water, perchance, turn into a noisome puddle. In like manner, the new life in Christ must seek to express itself or it will soon be repressed. So it was well for Hugh Bourne that soon the instinct, so elemental in the Christian life, to tell to others what he himself had experienced, began to force its way through the regret and fear for his own spiritual safety, and even to master that morbid shyness which kept him from having any dealings, save unavoidable business ones, with the hill-dwellers so different from himself.

As yet—and we would emphasise the fact—we are a long way from the first conscious efforts in Church-founding or proselytising. We have not even reached the stage when testimony is borne to what is regarded as primitive Methodism as against a Methodism not primitive. This stage will be reached by-and-by. At present we have to do with something more primitive than primitive Methodism, viz., the primal instinct and impulse of the renewed soul such as prompted Andrew to bring his brother to Jesus. As that incident, so true to the elemental, abiding facts of the Christian life, stands on the first page of the Church's beginnings, so we are glad that the first incident which after Hugh Bourne's conversion can distinctly be related to the chain of causes and effects which led to the formation of our own Church, irresistibly reminds us of Andrew's deed. Better so than that something more showy or cataclysmic marked our beginning. Better the tiny streamlet trickling from the heart moved with compassion than the breaking forth of the waters of strife.

The story of how the shy moorland carpenter spent the Christmas Day of 1800 has often been told, but it must be told once more, for it is entirely honourable to Hugh Bourne and to the denomination that claims him as one of its founders. Moreover that incident stands as an object-lesson pointing out the way of hope for the conversion of the world—each man seeking to save his brother. Individual reproduction is the law of the Christian life. With that law Primitive Methodism is accordant, and in obedience to that law it had its birth.

Workers in wood naturally have frequent business relations with workers in iron. So Hugh Bourne, the carpenter, was occasionally found at the village smithy. On one of these visits he so far broke through his habitual reserve and bashfulness as to broach the subject of experimental religion, and finished by putting into the hands of Thomas Maxfield, the smith, a written account of his own conversion.* This would probably be in the autumn of 1800, as the MS bears the date August 17th.

Now, the smith had a crony who was a man of some note in the neighbourhood, not, however, because of his virtues, for he was a ringleader in wickedness, a champion boxer, an adept rabbit-snarer, a card player and hard drinker. There was something Titanic about Daniel Shubotham. When his vehement temper was on him he could do nothing by halves, but did it, as it were, with both hands. But these hot fits were apt to be succeeded by what, in comparison, looked like cold ones. There were intervals of listlessness and inactivity between his outbursts of energy. Because when he willed he willed strongly, Daniel was a man to be reckoned with, but the fitful character of his energising was in danger of giving his life the appearance of a patch-work discontinuity. Daniel's father had been a man of some position and property, and had given his son what would be considered at the time a very fair education, and had started him with hopeful prospects. But Daniel had squandered all but a remnant of his patrimony, and was now reduced to the level of a working miner.

At the time of which we write Daniel Shubotham was intermittently under conviction of sin. It was brought about in this wise. One evening he and others were, by invitation, making a night of it with a moorland farmer. When inflamed with his potations Daniel surpassed himself in profanity. His oaths were loud and deep and various, so much so that the farmer-host, himself a proficient in profanity, was shocked, and administered a severe rebuke. Quoth he, "Thou art the worst curser and swearer, Dan, I ever heard in my life! I am quite ashamed of thee!" Daniel was cowed and in silence sat self-condemned; and from that time the habit of profane swearing, which he had worn as a garment, seemed to have fallen from him. Bouts of drinking alternated with seasons of poignant conviction. When the latter were upon him he would throw down his pick, and, to seek distraction and comfort, make his way to the smithy, where he would sit on the smithy hearth, kicking his heels and talking as he listed. On one such "idle day" Daniel's splenetic humour led him to rail against his cousin, Hugh Bourne. 'What a timid, bashful fellow he was; no company for any one, and he had no comfort of his life!' "Aye, lad! but he's a safe mon!" was the smith's quick retort, for he had read Hugh Bourne's written statement, and knew the real worth of the man. These few words in the vernacular, spoken on the impulse of the moment, produced a startling effect on Daniel as though a finger had pressed a secret spring. "I'll be a safe man, for I'll go and join him," cries Daniel, leaping to his feet from the smithy hearth on which he had been ensconced. Maxfield, astonished at the effect of his own words, would have recalled them, or at least have discounted their influence, for he feared lest Daniel should make good his threat and he should lose his boon companion. But the words had gone home and done their work. The kinsmen, so dissimilar, did come together. Daniel lost no chance of having speech with his cousin, and often would the two forgather, and the one be seen squatting, miner-like, "on his hunkers," hearing and asking the other questions concerning the deep things of God. But all these conversations were but preparatory leading up to the memorable meeting on Christmas Day morning of 1800, which meeting we will let Hugh Bourne describe in his own words. Only, let the reader note (as accordant with what has already been said of the primitive sources of Hugh Bourne's present enjoyed experience) the reference to the reading from the book of Robert Barclay, the Quaker; the written statement of his conversion put into his interlocutor's hand; and, above all, the conversation-sermon on the text—'I will love him, and will manifest Myself to him.' The scribe who had been made a disciple to the kingdom of heaven brought out of his treasure things new and old.*

"*Christmas Day, Thursday, December 25th 1800.* Last night I lay down in sorrow, and this morning I arose in sorrow; the main cause of my grief was my kinsman not being born of God. My natural timidity pressed upon me so that it was a task to go, but my mouth had been opened before the Lord, and to have drawn back would have been awful; so off I set, taking with me a book written by R. Barclay, the Quaker; and I took the written account of my own conversion and experience. It was a sorrowful journey; but I found Daniel waiting for me, so my introduction was easy. Having never prayed in public, and judging myself not capable of it, I did not pray with the family; but, knowing him to be hindered by an erroneous notion, read him a piece out of Barclay with which he declared himself satisfied; so the way was open. Next followed a little general conversation. I then rose up to go, requesting him to accompany me a little way. I was full of sorrow; but so soon as we were in a suitable place, I set to preaching the gospel to him with all my might; and, taking up John xiv. 21, where the words of Jesus Christ are, 'I will love him, and will manifest Myself to him,' I told him that Jesus Christ must be manifested to him, or else he would never be born again, and then he could not go to heaven: and, being all the time in deep sorrow, I laid open the gospel of Jesus Christ, showing him of being justified by faith, and having

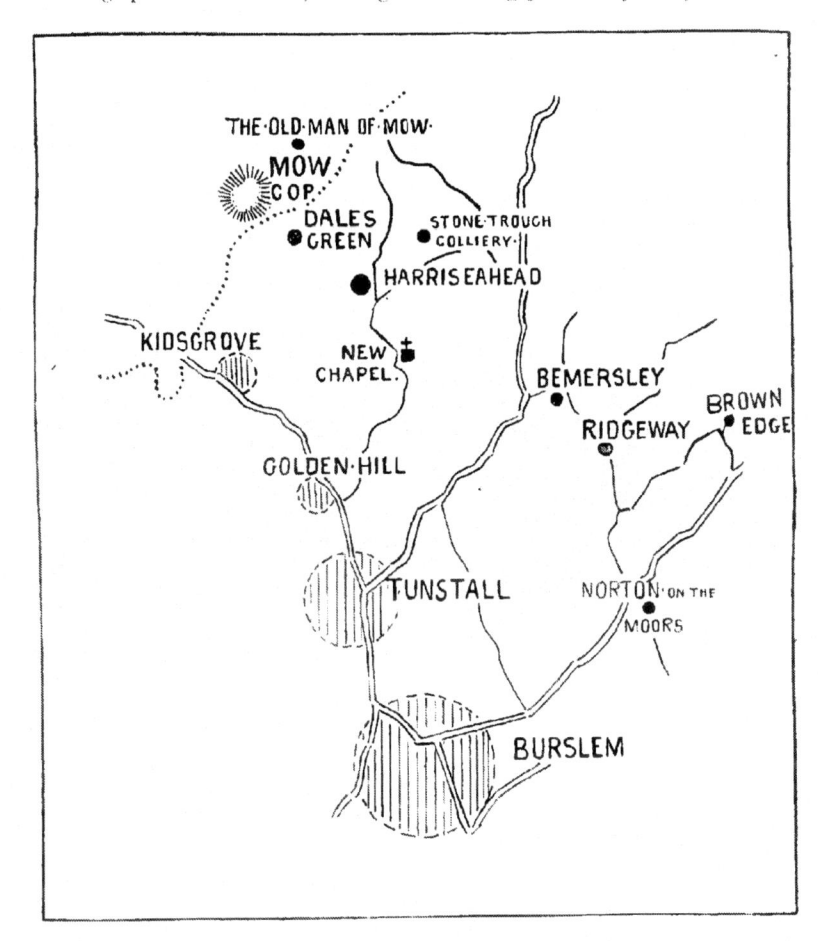

peace with God through our Lord Jesus Christ; and I dwelt very fully on the manifestation of Jesus Christ unto him. At parting I put into his hands the full account of my own conversion and experience. I then took leave, but parted from him in sorrow, fearing he did not take sufficient notice, and I passed the day in sorrow. But God's thoughts were not as my thoughts, for Daniel afterwards told me that when I was talking to him that morning, every word went through him."

One could fain linger on that scene in the miner's cottage, and on the walk and talk by the way, when one humble soul brought to another sorely needing it the true Christmas message—the manifestation of the Christ. And one could linger all the more willingly upon it, remembering that just then, the year 1800—perhaps the gloomiest year of the fast-dying century, was itself fleeting away with its grisly attendant shapes of war, famine, and tumult, into the "dark backward and abysm of time." It would be easy, under the stress of the notion of the dignity of history, to

HARRISEAHEAD VILLAGE.
The second building from the left-hand side is the Chapel built by Bourne, and now used as Wesleyan Sunday Schools.

cavil at the introduction of such an incident into this book and grudge the space devoted to its narration. But events are trivial or important as they are or are not related to what is of abiding significance. Adjudged by this standard the Christmas-day conversation-sermon at Harriseahead was not trivial. That incident was the beginning of beginnings—a runlet which fed the stream itself destined to be a tributary of the broad river tending to the sea. Humanly speaking, the revival at Harriseahead and much else came of that incident. Meanwhile, let sticklers for the dignity of history ponder what good Cotton Mather has said :—" A little man may do a great deal of harm ; and pray, why may not a little man do a great deal of good ? It is possible that 'the wisdom of a poor man' may start a proposal which may 'save a city'— a nation ! A single hair, applied to a flyer that has other wheels depending on it, may eradicate an oak or pull down a house."

The Harriseahead Revivalists and Some of Their Methods.

In the good old town of Driffield, in Yorkshire, there is a clear chalk-stream which bears, and doubtless for more than a thousand years has borne, the name of "Waterforlorns"—the issuing forth of the water. We think of this graphic and appropriate name as we take note of the revival of religion that followed and was largely the result of Daniel Shubotham's conversion. In that morally dry and sterile region, God's prophetic Word had its fulfilment:—"In the wilderness shall waters break out, and streams in the desert." Now and onwards Mow Cop was to be, in a double sense, the birthplace of streams. In a natural sense it had long been so; for on Mow, as on any other part of England's "Great Divide," the presence of running water is distinctly felt.

THE WATER-FORLORNS, DRIFFIELD.

"A tricklet here at the bottom of a crag, or a trickle there from the top of it, is always making one think whether this is one of the sources of the Trent, or rootlets of Mersey, or beginnings of distant Severn."* Thoughts similar to these, though relating to higher things, occur to us as we watch the progress of the revival that "broke out" at Harriseahead like a stream from the well-head. That time of revival may belong to "the day of small things," but the small things are beginnings which, like the rills trickling down the sides of Mow, are destined to last and go far. Knowing what they will become we cannot "despise the day of small things." Mow has had its part to play in the wondrous hydraulics of Grace as well as Nature. It may be but a coincidence, but whether or not, it is worth noting that Primitive Methodism and the river Trent

* Ruskin: 'Praeterita' i. ix. The quotation is adapted.

SOURCES AND ORIGIN.

THE MOW COP SOURCE OF THE TRENT.
The stream rises under the wall shown at bottom of right-hand corner of illustration.

are inseparably associated; for both have their head-waters near Mow Cop* (as any good map will show), and in its early progress Primitive Methodism followed the course of the Trent.

Daniel Shubotham was soundly converted. He escaped the snares his old companions

THE JUNCTION OF THE TWO STREAMS FORMING THE TRENT.

* One of the sources of the Trent is on Mow, under the wall shown in our first picture. The other is on Biddulph Moor. These come together near the Arbo... Farm, Milton.

set for him, and began at once in his turn to capture others for Christ. He was not the man to do anything by halves, and soon his conversion and the change it had wrought in him, became the talk of the country-side. Daniel's zeal acted as a stimulus to the shrinking piety of Hugh Bourne. The two colleagues were soon joined by another collier, who was to do yeoman service. This recruit, whose name was Matthias Bayley, had been converted, as Hugh Bourne is careful to inform us, through the instrumentality of Thomas Allen, the only open-air preacher on the Burslem plan. The moorland carpenter and the two colliers became like a threefold cord.

"H. Bourne's timidity stood in his way. But Daniel would not allow this to be a reasonable objection. H. Bourne had talked to him to purpose, and why not

CONGLETON EARLY IN THE 19TH CENTURY.

to others. And he saw no reason for talking in a doubting, hesitating way about religion. Daniel and Matthias spoke and spared not. And their plain, strong way was NEW (sic) to H. Bourne. In that one conversation H. B. was fully brought out of his former way. He saw at once the excellence of Daniel and Matthias' way, and fully entered into it; and in that respect fully entered on a NEW course. And from that hour to the present, H. Bourne has laboured with all the diligence in his power to promote that course; and, through the mercy of God, it has great root in the Connexion." (H. B. in *Magazine*, 1836, pp. 178, 9).

"And, really, in a short time, we were like two flames of fire. I had never in my life noticed anything that equalled this—it really was primitive Methodism indeed."—(*Early Journal*.)

No wonder that a revival broke out which soon changed the face of things in Harriseahead and neighbourhood. One trophy of the revival was a collier who had been the first of a newly-organised gang of poachers, and the gang was broken up. Not only was Harriseahead "moralised" (to use Hugh Bourne's expression), but from this point as a centre the revival spread, until by the time of Congleton May Fair (1801), much of the country lying on the slopes and under the shadow of Mow, as well as Mow itself, felt the influence of the evangel. It reached the colliers in the vale of Kidsgrove over whom Hugh Bourne felt called upon to exercise some degree of oversight. He not only visited them in their homes but established a society class. For him the revival meant more work and more care. He could not escape responsibility; for his reputation as "a safe man," and one gifted with book-learning, naturally led his colleagues to rely on his judgment and look to him for guidance. "We had," says he, "to establish order and maintain discipline, keep up the converting work, and promote piety."

Historically, the revival at Harriseahead in the opening year of the 19th century merits close attention. We may think that if we know one revival we know all revivals, and may ask, "What, then, was there about this Harriseahead revival that makes it unlike any other within our knowledge and experience?" Well, it had its own peculiar features and its special meaning. It set a type. It moved on early Methodist lines; and yet for a time it was unattached, or but slenderly attached, to the official Methodism of the locality. Indeed, some of the features it presented, and the methods of carrying it on most in favour were, to say the least, not the ordinary conventional ones in use and repute at the time in official circles.

One of the methods of evangelism mainly relied on and most successful in results was Conversation-preaching—we need the word to mark off the thing. What Hugh Bourne had done on Christmas Day everybody seems to have been expected to do. Never, perhaps, was a revival carried on with less preaching of a formal pulpit kind, and yet preaching was everywhere going on. The preacher was always ready, and his congregation never far to seek. On the pit heaps, in the "delf," by the wayside, the new converts talked religion. They did it both by impulse and on principle; not in a general abstract kind of way, but in the way of direct personal appeal. "All at it, always at it," seems to have been the watchword of the time. So characteristic of the Harriseahead proceedings was this button-holing Conversation-preaching that the revivalists might have been called Conversation-preaching Methodists.

Soon after the revival began, a weekly cottage prayer meeting was established at Jane Hall's—for long the only Methodist at Harriseahead. At the first meeting held here, Hugh Bourne "broke through splendidly." He had attempted to pray at Ridgway the previous Sunday, but the result was not encouraging. From this time, he notes, "he was fitted to be a public praying labourer." The prayer meetings thus instituted were not of the ordinary kind. Here, again, everybody was expected to take part, and liveliness was the characteristic. "The people got to be, in a great measure Israelitish," says Hugh Bourne, which we find, being interpreted, means—noisyish. He quotes Ezra iii. 12, 13. "And all the people shouted with a great shout . . . . and the noise was heard afar off." This was strictly true of the "Israelitish" prayer meetings held at Jane Hall's, for Hugh Bourne tells how, the door of a house on Mow Cop happening to stand open, Elizabeth Baddeley, a miner's wife, who was given to the use of profane language, distinctly heard the sound of prayer and praise coming from Harriseahead a mile and a half off, and was convinced of sin and set out for heaven. The praying company were exercising with all their hearts and minds, and with all their voices striving to "get into faith." H. B. says drily: "Any one that could distinguish his or her own voice must have had a pretty good ear!" Yet it would be wrong to describe these lively meetings as lawless. That they could not well be if Hugh Bourne had anything to do with them. "Our rules," says he, "were strict." Every one must keep out of sin, and none were allowed to use improper expressions,*

OLD JANE HALL'S HOUSE, HARRISEAHEAD.

and the meeting was not to continue beyond the hour or the hour and a half at the longest, lest they should be unfitted for their morrow's labours, and their good be evil spoken of. To the stringency of this last regulation we owe a homely saying of Daniel Shubotham, which for years men kept in mind, and is likely to be recalled as often as the history of camp meetings shall be written. One night when the allotted hour and a quarter seemed all too short, and the praying labourers rose from their knees with an appetite for more prayer, and expostulatory voices were heard—"Would that the meeting had gone on longer! Why did you break it up so soon?"—then it was that Daniel, prophet like, spoke words of wider reference than he himself knew at the time. Wishful to mollify those who felt as though they had been put off with short-commons,

* "H. Bourne showed them a sermon of Mr. Wesley's, that disallows fondling expressions as 'dear Lord,' 'sweet Lord.' So these were put away, and sound and clear expressions were cultivated." *Magazine* 1836.

he promised they should have their fill some one day. "You shall have," said he, "a meeting upon Mow some Sunday and have a whole day's praying, and then you'll be satisfied." Daniel's proposal was novel, yet seemed eminently suitable. So acceptable was it to the people that it was repeated the next Sunday. The twice-given assurance did not fall on heedless ears, but "the people began to take it up, and months and years after they conceived that the first proposal of a day's meeting was providential."

Another fixed and favourite idea of Hugh Bourne's was "variety in class leading." He maintained that this method of multiple leadership also was quite in accordance with the practice of early Methodism, and he refers for corroboration to Wesley's expressed views in the Minutes of 1744. We are not sure whether, in his view, the ideal class would not have been one in which every member should take his or her turn at "leading." Be this as it may, he believed in variety in class leading, and, as far as lay in his power, practised it too. The class which Hugh Bourne first joined at Ridgway was conducted on these lines, and when Daniel Shubotham was made leader

JOSEPH POINTON'S HOUSE ON THE SIDE OF MOW COP.

of the Harriseahead class, he would not consent to act unless he were assisted. So Hugh Bourne, Matthias Bayley, and T. Cotton would lead in turn, and sometimes others. When a class was formed at Norton the same course of procedure was adopted, and we infer that the class at Kidsgrove was similarly conducted.

To this same revival time—the time of beginnings—belongs also what is known as

"THE CAMP MEETING WITHOUT A NAME."

So far, Hugh Bourne had never, to use his own quaint phrase, "stood up in the pulpit way," though he had, despite his shyness, become an adept in talking salvation-sermons. But in the Midsummer of 1801 he was pressed to preach. It was thought a man who knew so much and had done so much could do still more. Reluctantly he consented. The service was to be held at Joseph Pointon's house on the Cheshire side of Mow, where there was a small Sunday morning class and a fortnightly preaching service.

It was arranged that Hugh Bourne should preach on July 11th, advantage being taken of its being an "off" Sunday on the plan. He himself had wished that the service might be held out of doors; but Joseph Pointon was no believer in open-air worship, and vetoed the proposal. But held in the open air the service was, after all; for the fame of the revival, and the announcement that the man was going to preach who, according to Thomas Maxfield had driven Daniel Shubotham crazy, drew such a number of people together from far and near that the house could not hold them. "*Then it's like to be out of doors,*" said good Joseph Pointon. The words, in his use of them, simply expressed a physical necessity; but to us, who see them in the light of after events, the words convey the hint of a moral necessity as well. There was a needs-be for out-of-door religious services, not so much because chapels were always full, as because

HUGH BOURNE PREACHING HIS FIRST SERMON.

they were so often nearly empty. So we have here, in Joseph Pointon's "Then it's like to be out of doors," another of those homely sayings in the vernacular which the reader of our history occasionally meets with as he passes along—sayings in which he cannot but find a deeper meaning than may have been felt at the time even by those who first uttered them. Two, at least, of these *voces populi* we have already noted, and others will challenge attention as we follow our narrative.

Hugh Bourne stood up and took for his text Heb. xi. 7, which speaks of the faith of Noah. He preached with his left hand before his face—fingers outspread—like one who looks forth from a barred window. The attitude was very characteristic of the man when conversing or addressing an audience, and was noted as a peculiarity to the end. Behind this fleshy screen did diffidence entrench itself, not suffering the searching glance of men to get within its guard."* Hugh Bourne tells us he was "soon at a loss" in preaching, but recovered himself somewhat when he bethought him of speaking before many as though he were addressing but one. Exhausted with the nervous strain of this effort he withdrew for rest, but soon returned to join in the exercises of prayer and exhortation which followed the sermon.

Assuming as we do the fact of the importance of this first open-air service on Mow Cop, we must be careful lest we emphasise its importance in the wrong place. We shall be wrong if we magnify it as the first camp meeting or celebrate it as the birthday of Primitive Methodism. And yet men have fallen into this double error, and may fall into it again. This may be shown by a concrete case. In a twelve-page

POINTON'S FARM, AND FIELD OF FIRST CAMP MEETING.
With Mow Cop Chapel in the distance.

pamphlet published in 1854, now lying before us, the anonymous author, in a truculent and scornful fashion, repudiates the claim of William Clowes to be regarded as a founder of our Church simply on the ground that when the founding took place

* "Occasionally in preaching, almost constantly in conversation, his open left hand elbow of that arm resting the while in the palm of the right hand was put up like a shutter before his face and eyes, but unlike a shutter in this respect that he could watch, through the interstices formed by the fingers being spread out a little, the effect of his words upon the person or persons with whom he was conversing, without their being able to obtain any satisfactory view of his countenance. In this posture, the left shoulder (that of the "shutter" arm) keeping up a kind of motion like that of a perpendicular piston in action, he would express his thoughts in terse and suitable phrase." Rev. J. Wenn's MSS

William Clowes was not Methodistically born, that is to say, the repudiation of William Clowes' right to be called a founder can be made good only by antedating the origin of the Connexion by some ten years and five months, and the establishment of camp meetings by close upon six years. Then, by a daring adaptation of the sublime question which the Eternal is represented as putting to Job out of the whirlwind, the pamphleteer pictures Hugh Bourne demanding of William Clowes "Where wast thou when I laid the foundations of English camp meetings on Mow Cop in 1801?" And we are left to imagine how, when he hears this demand, William Clowes is covered with shame and confusion, and buries his face in his mantle. All this is very amusing though smacking of irreverence, and the foolish pamphlet is only unearthed for a moment in order to point the lesson—How history can be perverted by the misreading of the plainest facts when looked at through partisan eyes. And now, to earth again with the exhumed pamphlet!

In sober truth, the service in Joseph Pointon's field, so far as Hugh Bourne's part in it was concerned, was but a halting exhortation, by the veriest chance delivered out of doors. Wherein then lies its significance? for it must be confessed that, looking back upon it in after years, Hugh Bourne regards it as of outstanding importance. To him, July 12th, 1801, was "this great Sabbath", "this extraordinary day", "it may be called a camp meeting without a name." And, in a sense, Hugh Bourne is right, as he so often is. Though, only proleptically—in the light of subsequent developments—could it with any shadow of propriety be called a camp-meeting, yet it was of importance, from the influence it exerted upon the mind of Hugh Bourne in leading him to develop on principle what others had struck out casually. It suggested a modification of field-preaching, in harmony with Hugh Bourne's ruling idea of variety, and the co-operation of the many in evangelistic work. In this respect it was in close analogy with the other methods adopted by the Harriseahead revivalists, to which reference has been made—conversation-preaching, the participation of all in prayer meetings, variety in class leading. The fine saying of Moses—"Would God that all the Lord's people were prophets, that the Lord would put His spirit upon them!" seems to have been the ideal they were instinctively groping after; and this is the ideal we must still set in front of all our work and steadily pursue and contend for, whatever may be the changes a hundred years may have brought about in our methods. How Hugh Bourne came to regard this camp meeting without a name is shown by the following remarks concerning it, made in the retrospect:—

"Mr Whitefield, Mr Wesley, and others practised field preaching; but here on Mow Cop the Lord caused open-air worship to be commenced on a broader foundation." "On this day, July 12th, 1801, the Lord enlarged our ideas. He, in His mercy, opened out a dispensation of sacred and divine worship, consisting of a text and sermon accompanied with a camp meeting movement, performed or carried on by more persons than one; and this order of proceeding exhibited a newness or enlargement in Methodism. In the union of preaching and praying services, the Lord, in His providence, set forth an example for holding future camp meetings."

Within

deputation of the Harriseahead miners waited upon Hugh Bourne with a project for building a new chapel, for which Daniel Shubotham had promised a corner of his garden as site. They themselves promised to do what they could towards the erection. Hugh Bourne looked upon the proposal favourably and undertook, for his part, to provide the timber necessary for the building. It is clear that none concerned were much versed in chapel building, or quite knew the right way to go about the work. The miners, probably as the result of their former thriftless and dissipated habits, were poor, and after digging out the foundations were at the end of their resources, which were muscular rather than monetary. It seemed as though, once more, the parable in the gospel of the man who "layeth the foundation and is not able to finish" was about to be enacted. To save the situation, Hugh Bourne was again appealed to, with the result that he had to shoulder the responsibility and bear the chief expense of seeing the business through. "Materials had to be brought from a great distance, and the roads in general were not good, and in some parts very bad; and there was no one to lay on a hand, or advance a single pound, and it was difficult at times to get materials carried." Worse was to follow—one of the gables was blown down and the roof fell in. "I hope the Lord will have mercy on any one who has to pass through such scenes of trouble," is the prayerful comment of Hugh Bourne on this, his first, experience of chapel building.

But the movement, such as has been described, was not to be allowed to go on without check or conflict. Hitherto the work in the Harriseahead district had met with opposition springing only from the unregenerate human heart, just as is the case when the gospel is making its way in a region as yet unchristianised; but we have now reached a period at which, describing it in his *Journals*, Hugh Bourne has to record how the views and practices he favoured came in conflict with views and practices of a different cast and type. The revival at Harriseahead was brought to a stand, we are told, mainly through the influence of two Goldenhill potters* who began to attend the meetings. The Moorland carpenter and the Goldenhill potters were quite at issue. They claimed to be old standards in Methodism, and regarded Hugh Bourne and his coadjutors as innovators, as men who 'were in a new way, a new cause, and new proceedings." He, on the other hand, believed himself to be moving on the lines of primitive Methodism, and saw in them the representatives of modern Methodism. Hugh Bourne expresses his sense of the contrariety or divergence between himself and them very clearly when he says: "Modern Methodism, by these two potters, said we were all wrong and should soon ruin all by our proceedings." Now, the potters it seems, could mould men as well as clay, for they succeeded for a time in impressing their views on both Daniel Shubotham and Matthias Bayley, and, as we

---

* Goldenhill is a village three miles from Mow. Since the above paragraph was written we have come across a passage in the *Magazine* for 1846, in which Bourne still more strongly puts the fact of the controversy thus early showing itself. He says: "When the Lord began to own their labours there was soon an outcry made, that they were going on in a NEW (sic) course. This outcry was raised by Methodists who came from a distance, and who called themselves 'old standards.' But Hugh Bourne and his fellows were not conscious of any NEW course, any more than were Mr Wesley and his fellows at Oxford."—p 174.

have said, the revival received a check, until the two miners, seeing how they were being manipulated and turned, "laid hands on the potters, and got rid of them by passing them on to Newchapel village, where they soon ruined the cause, and then forsook the place and Daniel and Matthias learned a lesson which for years they did not forget."

We are not attempting to judge between Hugh Bourne and the potters, and to decide who were the innovators and who inquired for the old paths. The former naturally looked upon the two latter very much as Paul looked upon Hymenæus and Alexander, the coppersmith, who did him much evil. But, doubtless, the two potters stood not alone; they were types and representatives—very unworthy ones, it may be—but they *were* representatives. They had their point of view, and had something to say for taking their stand where, and viewing things as, they did. On a small scale they precipitated a conflict between divergent views and practices which was going on elsewhere on a much wider scale.

We believe the history of Primitive Methodism as hitherto written, so far as that history claims to have to do with the yeasty formative period of the first decade of the nineteenth century, has not sufficiently taken account of the fact that what was going on in North Staffordshire was but part of a larger movement, similar in character though marked by minor local differences. To be rightly understood and appraised, the Harriseahead Revivalism must not be isolated as though it were a Melchizedekian movement, with no traceable lineage or relationships. If the differences that showed themselves at Harriseahead were nothing but a petty local squabble, it were foolish to recall them. If the case stood on the calendar as "The Goldenhill Potters *v* Hugh Bourne," then the affair might be left to the local historian or, better still, be clean forgotten, as so many Church bickerings deservedly have been. But Hugh Bourne maintained that it was much more than that; it was no local, or temporary, or personal squabble. To him it stands docketed "Modern *v* primitive Methodism." The claim involved in the very title of the case at once lifts it into importance, and requires a change of venue. It belongs of right to the history of the Church at the beginning of the nineteenth century. Let us, therefore, take a wider survey, and inquire what ground there is for concluding that the description "Modern *v* primitive Methodism" does truly express the bearings of the case.

METHODISM—MODERN AND PRIMITIVE

We have just used the words primitive and modern Methodism. Is the use of these terms in their application to the religious life of the opening years of the nineteenth century defensible? Such is our opinion. These terms do not express a merely verbal, and therefore false, antithesis. They are not simply question-begging epithets. They were terms in current use, and they represented real distinctions.

And first of all, as a descriptive term, "primitive" Methodism was in use years before it was assumed as a denominational title. In 1792, a twopenny tract was issued by G. Whitfield at the Chapel, City Road, entitled "Sufferings of the Primitive Methodists at Wednesbury." This tract has nothing to do with the sufferings of the early missionaries of our Church as but for the date upon it, we might suppose to be the case but it narrates the sufferings undergone by the Methodists in 1743 Here, plainly, the word "primitive" refers to those who came first in order of time, and is used in its primary chronological sense

But here is the title of another book in which the word "primitive" is evidently used in a secondary and derived sense "Primitive Methodism Defended showing what means have been used to make a Division among the Methodists and to separate them from the English Church 1795' That the non-holding of preaching services in church hours, or, still more dependence upon the clergy of the Church of England for the reception of the sacrament was one form of primitive Methodism which was departed from—and rightly departed from—by modern Methodism, will not of course be denied It was just this defection—as it was deemed—from primitive practice which was made the ground of the secession of the Primitive Wesleyans in 1816

But the word "primitive" may stand for something else besides an attitude of subserviency to the Church of England and dependence upon its most sacred ordinance, as it does in the fervent ejaculation of a writer in the Methodist Magazine for 1802, who has been describing the revival resulting from the holding of camp meetings in America "What cannot the Methodist do through grace? Glory be to God! primitive Methodism shines in this country and through America" Needless to say it was in this sense Hugh Bourne was constantly using the term in describing the events of the period we are considering He does this when he says —

"I never knew a Burslem circuit travelling preacher perform what Mr Wesley calls 'field-preaching' all the time I was a member This then was and is modern not primitive Methodism, and I think there is a broad difference between the two'

Now though the phrase "modern Methodism" may not so frequently be met with in the literature of the time, yet in the very fervour with which a writer will avow his wish or determination to revive or maintain primitive Methodism, there is the tacit acknowledgment that some change of tone or modification in practice has taken place, resulting in what naturally and for the sake of distinction might be called modern Methodism Of course what may be called "the opposition" habitually use the term as might be expected It was to them an organised entity to be feared and withstood But even members of the government (to keep to our parliamentary figure) will betray their knowledge of the existence of the said entity For example, Mr Entwisle writes in a private letter of 1807 —

"The doctrines preached by Messrs Wesley, Grimshaw, &c, in the beginning, accompanied with the power of the Holy Ghost, did wonders And the same truths are now equally important, equally necessary, and may be equally efficacious Primitive Methodism I admire, and I think I come nearer than ever to that standard'*

A few weeks after Hugh Bourne had preached in the open air beside Joseph Pointon's

* The Life of Jabez Bunting D D, vol 1 p 290

house, Jabez Bunting, then a young man of twenty-two, but wise and already influential beyond his years, entered upon the third year of his probation in the adjoining Macclesfield Circuit—a fact in itself interesting and suggestive. It is more than likely that Hugh Bourne, who lost no opportunity of hearing the ministers of both the Burslem and Macclesfield Circuits, would occasionally hear Bunting on his visits to one of the preaching places not far from Bemersley. Bunting was already taking a keen and watchful interest in the "crystallisation of Methodism." His biographer sheds light on the conflicting diversities of Methodist life of which we have already seen the signs in Burslem Circuit.

REV. JOS. ENTWISLE.

"Mr. Lomas and Mr. Reece corresponded with each other, and with my Father, as to certain movements at Leeds and Manchester, on the part of the 'Revivalists'; a class which, about this period, again occasioned considerable uneasiness to the Fathers of the Connexion, and to the more intelligent and pious of the junior Preachers. William Bramwell, a man eminent for holiness, and for the gifts which, rightfully used, insure ministerial success, openly espoused the cause of this party, until their conduct ended in a miserable schism."*

Bramwell's biographer is somewhat reticent about the Leeds episode, but what he does say is significant:—

"Mr. Bramwell was, at this period, in danger of thinking that his brethren in the ministry who could not enter into all his plans of usefulness were opposed to revivals; he therefore yielded himself to gloomy forebodings, similar to those which distressed the mind of Elijah. . . . He for a time yielded to the temptation that the glory of God had departed from Methodism, and that it was his duty to separate from his brethren." †

JABEZ BUNTING.
The earliest portrait in existence.

* The Life of J. Bunting, D.D., vol. i. p. 147. The date is 1803.

† Memoir of William Bramwell by the Rev. Thomas Harris, pp. 111, 112. Bramwell was at Leeds 1801-2 with John Barber and Richard Reece as colleagues.

The painful experience glanced at in the preceding quotation is also referred to by William Dawson in the funeral sermon he preached on the occasion of Bramwell's death. In a highly rhetorical passage of this sermon Bramwell is once more likened to Elijah, who in a fit of depression betook himself to the wilderness, where his solicitous brethren find him. When they put the question: "What doest thou here, brother?"

"He might have answered with great propriety, 'I have been very jealous for the Lord God of Hosts. I fear a criminal love of the world is rivalling Jesus Christ in the heart of His Church, and therefore I thought my best course was to retire, and try what can be done by me in any other way.' But when his brethren softened down the distorted features of the detested object, which his trembling hand, at the instigation of his jealous heart, had drawn; when they took off the deep shades with which he had overcharged its countenance; when they drew the picture of the monster division; when they proved that, in the present state of the Methodist Body, the evils of a schism and division would be much greater than the evils which he lamented and deplored—and he then saw, in some measure, as they did; conviction, like a voice behind him, cried out, 'This is the way, walk thou in it.' He listened; he obeyed; he retraced his steps; he returned to his work; filled his station with credit to himself, and profit to the Church; and lived and died in union with his brethren." *

REV. W. BRAMWELL.

We may be sure that any cause Bramwell openly espoused would, in his judgment, be in harmony with primitive Methodism, though in conscientiously taking the line he did it is likely enough he may have fallen into some imprudences, crossed the inclinations of the majority, or even have infringed some recognised written or unwritten regulations of the Church. However this may have been, it is clear that he suffered greatly in the clash and impact of opposing ideals and tendencies, and was pained by not meeting with the sympathy and co-operation he desired. In a private letter of November, 1802, he laments :—

"I have not the help I want; I say sometimes, 'Woe is me! for I am a man beset with opposition from all the powers of hell.' You would be surprised to see what plans I have discovered to prevent the general crush."†

Why do we dwell on these things and press the distinction between primitive and modern Methodism? It is in no contentious spirit; with no desire to stir into flame

* Life. p. 113.   † Op. cit. p. 116.

the embers of strife that, left alone, would soon go black out. Our purpose is rather eirenic, to make it clear that revivalism of the early Methodist type such as Hugh Bourne and his fellow-workers were carrying on, was not confined to Mow Cop and its vicinity, but, allowing for local differences, was contemporaneously to be met with among the Band-room Methodists of Manchester, the Independent Methodists of Macclesfield, the Quaker Methodists of Warrington, the Magic Methodists of Delamere Forest, the Tent Methodists of Bristol (1820), the Revivalists of Leeds. The development and crystallisation of Methodism that took place after the death of Wesley and the Plan of Pacification of 1795 was no process superintended by Fate or due to accident or the working of natural law, but was a process directed and controlled by some of the wisest heads of those concerned for the future of Methodism. In this period of transition for Methodism, an ethos was acquired and a form assumed that involved the discountenancing and rejection of the methods of revivalism, although these were very largely the survival or revival of methods that characterised Methodism in its primitive and heroic period.

The two types of Methodism were at that day regarded as incompatible, and modern Methodism, in the person of its leaders, made its election and acted accordingly—thinking to serve the best interests of the Church by so doing. We have already shown what some of the heads of houses thought of Leeds revivalism and Revivalists. To illustrate still further what was the consistent attitude and policy of the influential leaders of Methodism with regard to the recrudescence of old-time methods of evangelisation, we give two quotations from contemporary letters—and private letters help us to the knowledge of the real thoughts of men, as official documents cannot. In 1803 Mr. Lomas writes to Mr. Bunting:—

"Divisions in the Church of Christ are awful, and I would do all I could, with a good conscience, to prevent them, but I think the time is come for the Methodist preachers to bestir themselves, and to do all they can for the honour of the religion of Christ, as taught and enforced among themselves. I think they must now 'arise or be for ever fallen.'"*

Then Bunting, writing confidentially to Marsden in December of the same year, lays down the guiding principle:—

"All persons enthusiastically or schismatically disposed are dangerous in our Connexion to its peace and permanency, and the more pious in their general character, the more dangerous."†

Does the reader ask, "And what is the bearing of all this on the beginnings of the camp meeting movement?" The answer is—"Much, every way." It—and the if implies no doubt, but is simply basal of inference—if what Hugh Bourne honestly believed was agreeable to Methodism in her pristine and palmy state, was just as honestly regarded by others as part and parcel of that troublesome Revivalism, which for the safety of Methodism must be discountenanced and disallowed, then separation sooner or later was inevitable—unless, indeed, one yielded to the other; and as neither was made of yielding stuff the inevitable happened—the earthen pipkin and iron pot clashed together—with what results we do not need to be told.

* Life of J. Bunting, D.D., p. 118. † Op. cit. p. 219.

The view we have endeavoured to set forth in this section—which may be summed up as the frank recognition of the working incompatibility between the two types of Methodism we have called modern and primitive—explains much that would else be inexplicable. For instance, most biographers of Hugh Bourne or those who have touched upon the history of the period 1800—7 are puzzled to understand why Hugh Bourne was never put on the plan; why he and his co-workers were so severely let alone; and how it was that, only after considerable delay, and by dint of importunity, the Burslem circuit authorities were prevailed upon to take over Harriseahead chapel and authorise Hugh Bourne to gather into classes the fruits of the revival. But surely, after what has been said, the reason is neither recondite nor far to seek. If Hugh Bourne's proceedings were regarded as of a piece with the proceedings of the Revivalists at Leeds and elsewhere, then the reason of the action or inaction of the authorities lies on the surface and it needed no prophet to foretell what would happen.

THE CONVERSION OF WILLIAM CLOWES.

The interdependence of events is seen in the fact that the conversion of William Clowes was the indirect result of that Revivalism which was endemic at the beginning of the century. By this statement more is meant than that Clowes was converted during a revival: for the said revival can be distinctly traced to the influence propagated by the Stockport Revivalists whom J. Clark, at his own expense, brought over to the September Lovefeast at Congleton in 1804. In his first History of the Connexion * Hugh Bourne refers to these people as REVIVALISTS, and by thus typographically distinguishing them, he evidently intended to convey the impression that they were a well-known band who had been made a link in the chain of events. Hugh Bourne and many of the Staffordshire Methodists were present at the Lovefeast. The services partook largely the character of what we should now call "a Holiness Convention." The

From the steel portrait of W. Clowes that formed the frontispiece to the minutes of 1819.

* 1823: the name is also so printed in the edition of 1835.

Revivalists "spoke much of being sanctified wholly." In prayer and testimony and conversation the distinction of Methodism as 'the doctrine of heart-holiness' was made emphatic and pressed home. The Staffordshire men were quickened and instructed. They were led to probe themselves with questions similar to those which by Wesley's direction were to be put to his helpers on the occasion of their being received:—"Have you faith in Christ? Are you going on to perfection? Do you expect to be perfected in love in this life? Are you groaning after it?"* The effect of all this was marked; for the next night a most remarkable prayer meeting was held at Harriseahead, at which "there was an extraordinary outpouring of the Holy Spirit"; and to the visit of the Stockport Revivalists Hugh Bourne attributes the origin of the second revival which was by no means confined to Harriseahead: "since their first coming many have obtained clean hearts, and the work has been great among sinners, and it has almost spread through the circuit."

DANE VALLEY, CONGLETON.

A second visit of the Stockport men to Congleton on Christmas Day, 1804, gave a still further impetus to the revival in its double aspect, and the work of grace amongst both saints and sinners rolled on. A Lovefeast at Harriseahead followed quickly the one at Congleton, and this is of special interest to us because Mr. James Steele, whose name stands on the Deed Poll of the Connexion, was present and took a leading part. Hugh Bourne speaks of this meeting in enthusiastic terms. He tells how the chapel was packed with people and "twenty souls prayed into liberty." He had evidently caught the spirit of the Revivalists, and it is curious how naturally the word seems to drop from his pen, and how important a matter it seemed to him

* Minutes of Several Conversations, &c., from the year 1744 to 1780. p. 34.

JAMES STEELE, TUNSTALL.
(From an old print.)

that James Steele should have been drawn consentingly into the movement. He writes:—

"Mr. Steele and others from Tunstall were converted into Revivalists. It was a mighty revivalist move, and the Lord enabled those from Tunstall to carry an increase of the revival fire and revival work to that place. The mighty outpouring of the Holy Ghost in Harriseahead chapel, in September, had reached Tunstall, and had made a gracious move; but on this Christmas occasion it increased to a gracious outpouring of the Holy Spirit. The Tunstall deadness, which had been proverbial for years, was done away, and Tunstall rose into revival notice, insomuch that shortly after this great Lovefeast, William Clowes, Thomas Woodnorth, James Nixon, William Morris, and others were brought to God, and became useful evangelists."

As William Clowes steps on the scene we experience something like a feeling of relief; just such a feeling probably as the portrait-painter will have when at last a bafflingly difficult subject is bowed out and another takes his place, whose facial lines and expression and natural pose can more easily be caught and transferred to the canvas. Mr. Gladstone, in comparing two men, both great, but very diversely great, once wrote—"The constitution of Dr. Döllinger's mind was simple, that of Newman's complex." We recall these words and the distinction drawn as we think of our founders: the constitution of Clowes' mind was simple, that of Hugh Bourne's complex. This radical difference between the two men can only be noted here. Meanwhile, in passing, we may remark it is not at all surprising, that a distinguished journalist who seems to have taken all knowledge for his province and who is a candid friend of our Church, should have admitted that William Clowes he thought he knew, but he was not sure that he had got to the true inwardness of Hugh Bourne. We judge that every one who has made a careful study of the mechanism and movements of Hugh Bourne's mind would have to make a similar confession.

Though no completer contrasts than Bourne and Clowes presented can well be imagined, their lives had certain points of coincidence. Both were true Staffordshire men—scions of families long rooted in that county. If, as has been repeatedly said, Bourne had Norman blood in his veins and came of a stock that once held considerable landed estates, so, on his mother's side, Clowes claimed kinship with a family of consideration that any one might be proud to belong. His mother was born Ann Wedgwood, and belonged to the family which did so much to extend and improve the ceramic art.

46 PRIMITIVE METHODIST CHURCH.

Who does not know the famous "Wedgwood" ware? Through his mother, Clowes could claim relationship with Josiah Wedgwood, the founder of Etruria, the bearer, by royal grant and the good pleasure of Queen Charlotte, of the title of "the Queen's Potter," the promoter of roads and munificent patron of the Grand Junction Canal, by which Trent and Mersey and Severn were linked together. Clowes' grandfather, Aaron Wedgwood, in partnership with his brother-in-law, Mr. William Littler, made costly experiments to improve the white stone-ware of the district, and afterwards won the distinction of producing the first china-ware at Longton, near Stoke-on-Trent.

The Clowes family had to be content with the reflected glory of their house, for nothing more substantial fell in their way as the result of their connections on the spindle-side. If Clowes could record with pardonable pride, how some of his forbears, in 1740, built the largest house in Burslem, "The Big House"—and, he might have added, owned also "Ivy House," to which Josiah Wedgwood brought his newly-wedded bride—he himself first saw the light—March 12th, 1780—in a workman's cottage in an obscure court, neat probably, thanks to the housewife, and at that time covered with flowers, yet a dwelling humble enough. Now, whether a child be born in a big house or a little one is really a matter of small concernment, as many a wise saying testifies. But in this case, as in so many others, the small house was part of a long, quiet domestic tragedy, just as it was in the Bourne household—a tragedy in which it falls to the lot of wife and child quietly to suffer what the husband and father, as the evil genius of the family, brings on or will not avert. Samuel Clowes never got to be more than a working potter, nor ever seriously strove to give his wife the position due to her. He was indolent and dissipated, and though he had been religiously inclined in early life, he was turned aside by the reading of a pernicious book and by yielding to temptation, and underwent no change until his last illness.

CLOWES' HOUSE AS IT IS NOW, BURSLEM.

Mrs. Clowes was a woman of good parts and amiable character, who bravely set herself to supply as best she could the deficiencies of her home. She had been brought up in the belief and practice of the Church of England, nor did she enter upon the rest of faith until after her son's conversion. And here another interesting parallel may be observed between the personal and family experience of Clowes and Bourne. Each pressed into the kingdom of God before the mother to whom each owed so much; soon each had the comfort of welcoming his beloved parent into the joy and peace of that kingdom; and each had well-grounded hopes, at the long last, that the father, though late, and while drawing near to the very margin of the grave, had truly repented and found mercy.

Still one other parallel between the two remains to be noticed. After that is pointed out, then, any comparison drawn between our two chief founders would yield contrasts rather than resemblances. This last point of coincidence between the youthful experience of Bourne and Clowes has in it instruction for the Church of to-day. It blazons the lesson—Shepherd the young! Whatever you do for the full-grown flocks, look after the lambs. The story of the shadowed and perplexed childhood of Hugh Bourne has already been told, and the biography of Clowes yields the same lesson. At ten years of age, he tells us, being at a prayer meeting, he wept bitterly, under the clear conviction of the sin of disobedience; and later, during a revival at Burslem he adds:—

CLOWES' HOUSE, BURSLEM, AS IT WAS.

"My convictions were such, that had an experienced Christian taken me by the hand, I have no doubt that I should at that time have been converted; but being young, I passed unnoticed, and soon lost those convictions."—*Journals*, p. 12.

The story of Clowes' life for the first twenty years, when, to use his own words, he was "in the wild olive-tree which is wild by nature," is edifying as a warning rather than as an example. It is just the old familiar story of a youth, who is richly endowed by nature, with abounding vitality and strong in social qualities, giving the reins to his lower propensities. And what wonder! His education was meagre in the extreme, and he had no intellectual interests. He was not inspired and directed by parental example and counsel, or restrained by wisely administered home discipline. Besides, the world seemed fair; pleasure allured, and youthful passion went forth to welcome it.

SOURCES AND ORIGIN. 49

When a mere child of ten years of age, he was apprenticed to his uncle, Joseph Wedgwood, of the Church Works Pottery. He soon became so expert at his trade that he could easily make up the twenty-one dozen plates which formed his daily tale of work. But what he could do was not always done; work was sometimes neglected for play, and then deception was resorted to in order to save him from censure or punishment. Next, he was apprenticed to Mr. Mear in order that he might acquire skill in another branch of the potter's art—"turning." In this he soon became so proficient that, as

OVEN-HOUSE, OR HOVEL.   THROWER, WITH THE OLD POTTER'S WHEEL.

a reward and encouragement, he was paid for all work done beyond what was due to his master. Whether he were saint or sinner, William Clowes was always a clever workman.

But his great accomplishment was dancing, for which he had a perfect passion. He became a prize-dancer, and "pride and vanity so inflated his heart" that he challenged all England to compete with him. But his favourite amusement reacted unfavourably upon his morals. It took him into questionable places and bad company. "Associated

E

with dancing was visiting public assembly rooms, where banquetings, gambling, and fighting ranked among the sins of my youth." To this black catalogue must be added drunkenness and profanity. What a scene that is which Clowes describes himself as taking part in at Leek in North Staffordshire during wake-week! We see Clowes (who has now a *young wife*) and his set holding a mock prayer meeting in the sanded parlour of the public-house. Their deep potations that have been going on for hours have brought them to this pitch of recklessness and profanity. This "extravagance of impiety" is

LEEK OLD TOWN HALL.

LEEK MARKET-PLACE FROM THE NORTH.

too much even for the not very squeamish tipplers who witnessed it, and the bacchanals are turned into the streets only to make their way to the Market Cross, there to finish their burlesque of sacred things. By Tuesday morning all their money is spent, but not their ardour to drink strong drink. One of their number pawns his watch; others borrow two guineas of a recruiting-sergeant of the 55th Regiment, and one guinea of a sergeant of the Royal Artillery, who advance the money on mortgage of their persons; for if the money is not returned by Saturday night the recruiting-sergeants will foreclose and the borrowers will belong to His Majesty's forces. With their pockets thus strangely replenished the orgie goes on until Thursday, and then "each one of us retired to his home." Whether the money-lending recruiting-sergeants got back their loan we are not told.

Between the close of his apprenticeship and his conversion Clowes flitted from place

SOURCES AND ORIGIN. 51

to place like a restless spirit—sometimes with his wife and sometimes from her and his mother-in-law. In 1803 he is in Hull working at a new Pottery, and able to earn, if the will is there, his pound a day. But whatever he earns it is put into a bag with

BARTON FROM WATERSIDE ROAD ONE HUNDRED YEARS AGO.

holes, and he cannot keep out of debt. It was the time when the press-gang was unusually active, and when the sight of it, or the merest rumour of its approach, was enough to spread consternation. Taking advantage of this feeling Clowes and his companions determine to play a practical joke upon the inhabitants of the quiet town of Barton-on-Humber. Attired in appropriate costume, and accompanied by fiddlers and hornpipe dancers, they take a boat and cross the broad

THE MARKET-PLACE.

BARTON FROM BEACON HILL 100 YEARS AGO.

river, and making the public-house their base of operations, they sally out to frighten His Majesty's lieges. Clowes, in his ma-

E 2

regenerate days, was something of a dandy, and he tells us how he was dressed on this occasion:—"I wore a coat and pantaloons of the best superfine, mounted with yellow buttons, which were made according to the orders that pride led me to give the tailor when I first came to Hull." Parenthetically, we may observe that imagination refuses to conceive the time when Hugh Bourne could have been "hail fellow well met" to those seated at the ale-bench, or when he with zest "tripped the light fantastic toe," or when he might have been seen dressed in a coat and pantaloons of the best superfine, with yellow buttons, made by a fashionable tailor—and not paid for. And yet it was Clowes, and not Bourne, who was afterwards the stiffer on the dress question. We take note of these contrasts and what they imply, and pass on.

A PRESS-GANG AT WORK.

The culmination of what may be called "the rake's progress" was reached soon after the Barton exploit. By what looked like the retributive irony of providence, Clowes was to make closer acquaintance with the press-gang. He was a noted bruiser, and one day was fighting in a drunken brawl which had originated in the "Dog and Duck" public-house, where certain officers of the press-gang were quartered. Some of these watched the fight with evident interest, but when it was over they claimed the combatants for His Majesty's Honourable Corps of Marines. While being escorted by the police, Clowes made a bolt for it, running down Grimsby Lane into Market Street, finally taking refuge in his master's china-shop. But for the intervention and appeals of the keeper of the tavern where the captain lodged, and of his own master, Clowes would undoubtedly have been pressed as a marine. The captain let the brawlers off, warning them "never to be out after nine o'clock at night." But thoroughly frightened, Clowes was off by nine o'clock next morning. He left Hull and his debts behind him, and tramped to Tunstall, paving the way with good intentions.

These dark passages in Clowes' unregenerate life are referred to with reluctance—with no thought of dishonouring the memory or sullying the reputation of one to whom our Church owes so much. The passages in question could not be omitted from any history of the Connexion worthy of the name; for, while they may serve to throw some light on the events, the manners and morals of the time, especially of the class which Clowes in the years to come was most mightily to influence and to which he himself belonged, they are referred to mainly here for the same reason that Clowes himself referred to them in his *Journal*—to magnify the grace of God in him. He showed how in his case sin had abounded, and did it relentlessly as though resolute not to omit the least detail or soften the darkest colours of the condemnatory picture; and he did this in order to show more triumphantly that "where sin had abounded, grace did much more abound." His fervid evangelism had a great "But I obtained mercy" at the back of it. Did any one in the hey-day of Clowes' folly and wickedness think and speak of him as "the graceless potter"? The judgment was a natural one and in a sense just; but in a higher sense it was vastly wide of the truth; for even when he ran to excess in riot and evil-doing grace was abounding to him, the chief of sinners, just as it was to the Tinker of Elstow before him, ere the tempest within his soul had been turned to calm. Indeed, in reading Clowes' experiences in these early years of his life, one is irresistibly reminded of Bunyan. Like him, paroxysms of passion were succeeded by paroxysms of conviction. Like him he made resolutions and even took vows on God's Holy Word to amend his ways; and like him both resolutions and vows were broken by the gusts of temptation like a web of gossamer.

So it was with him on his return from Hull. He was as 'a limed soul struggling to be free.' Here is a Bunyan-like account of the experience which antedated his conversion:—

"Under feelings of terror, I prayed that if God would carry me in safety to my native place, I would then serve Him; but no sooner had He preserved me safe to my journey's end, than among my old companions my promises were forgotten in acts of rebellion. Before my conversion to God, the internal misery of which I was the victim was in many instances almost insupportable. Sometimes I used to walk in solitary and unfrequented places, wishing that I was a bird or a beast, or anything else that was not accountable to the tribunal of heaven. Sometimes in sleep in the night I have been agitated with terrible dreams, and, starting up, I have been afraid of looking out of my bed, supposing the room to be full of devils and damned spirits. Occasionally I have broken out in strong perspiration, and wished for the light of day, in order that I might drown my distressing convictions with strong drink, and in singing the drunkard's song, which begins with the words:—

'Come push the grog about—strong beer drowns all our sorrows.'

GRIMSBY LANE, HULL.

"Well I remember how conscience used to lash me when I used to sing this song, and with what power and force those words were occasionally applied to my soul: 'For all these things God will bring thee to Judgment.'"

His anguish of soul became known to a friend, who took him to the House of God. Shortly afterwards he gained admission to a lovefeast (in a way we need not stop to describe) and, as if to better Hugh Bourne's innocency about the Burslem Lovefeast, when he saw the bread and water being carried round, he thought in his simplicity "This must be the sacrament of the Lord's Supper." Thus thinking, he had an access of terror, for he was fresh from reading the passage which solemnly warns against eating the bread or drinking the cup of the Lord unworthily. This, the unpardonable sin as he deemed it to be, he feared he was in danger of committing. The next morning he attended a prayer meeting, and while all was excitement and noise around him he wrestled as one alone with his Maker until he felt the bands which long had held him breaking. "What is this?" asked he of himself. This, he said "is what the Methodists mean by being converted; yes, this is it—God is converting my soul. In an agony me—then I believed he had saved me, and it was so." This notable event took place January 20th, 1805, some three weeks after the memorable lovefeast at Harriseahead before described.

Clowes' conversion was clear and convincing. Its catastrophic character was quite in keeping with the fervid nature of him who experienced it. His profiting soon appeared to all. His old associates, who had reckoned on soon welcoming him back to their fellowship, were both astonished and angry when they saw him taking long forward steps in his new-found path, and had to admit that they had lost him for good and all. His debts in Hull and Staffordshire were paid. He withdrew from the volunteer corps, officered by his master, much to the chagrin of the latter. He joined the class of Mr. James Steele, associated himself with the people of God, and made each Sabbath a day of unremitting yet gladsome toil. He threw open his house for the holding of prayer meetings, lovefeasts, and class meetings. The practical side of religion was not overlooked. He drew up strict rules for holy living, began to reprove sin, took part in efforts to suppress Sabbath breaking, and became an active member of a Tract and Bible Mission, and as such walked many miles and did real evangelistic work in the homes of the people. The members of this society, apostle-like, went two and two on their mission. Clowes' colleague was his like-minded friend, James Nixon, and, together, they visited the part around Alsager Heath and Lawton Saltworks in Cheshire, which was the district assigned them.

JAMES NIXON.

And so for Clowes the former internecine conflict—the sad duality of the 7th Romans was overcome, and his life could now flow evenly on in blessed simplicity and singleness. And here for a time we leave him.

CHAPTER II.

THE CAMP MEETING METHODISTS.

THE ABEYANT PERIOD.

OUR class tickets have long familiarised us with the statement—"First Camp Meeting held, May 31, 1807." Yet it was as far back as 1801 when Daniel Shubotham made his twice-repeated promise to give the Harriseahead converts a day's praying on Mow Cop. What is the explanation of this long delay? It is scarcely consistent with the assumption that there were many during those six intervening years consumed with longing to have a camp meeting, or surely they would have found a way to have one. If any were eager Hugh Bourne would be the most eager. But a careful reading of his *Journals* kept at the time, as contradistinguished from the historic and autobiographical memoranda written much later, does not leave the impression that even Hugh Bourne was possessed with the camp meeting idea so fully as we might suppose. The idea was there, and there as a cherished idea, but it was not so dominant or charged with such driving power as it afterwards got to be. The fact is, from 1801 to 1807 the Harriseahead Revivalists— and Bourne chief among them—were being led a step at a time, and the establishment of camp meetings was the outcome of a kind of evolutionary process. Still, we need further explanation with regard to this abeyant period, and as Hugh Bourne's is the only explanation forthcoming, let this be briefly summarised. He says, with reason, that the day's praying should have been arranged for, if at all, before the society and chapel at Harriseahead were taken over late in 1802, for after that, the plan with its two services a Sabbath—which says he "was overdoing it"—interposed an effectual barrier. Moreover, the redoubtable Daniel had veered round again, and was now in 1802 opposed to open-air worship. In this same year, and right on into 1807, the Methodist magazines contained stirring accounts of camp meetings on an elaborate scale which were being held in various parts of America and were attended by vast throngs who camped for two or three days together in the forest. The reading of these accounts increased the desire for a camp meeting, so that Hugh Bourne intimates that from 1802 to 1804 the burden of the Harriseahead people's prayer was "Lord, give us a camp meeting!" But in September of the latter year, the second revival breaking out gave them ample employment. The time was all too short for the work to be done; minds and hearts were full. Then the revival received a check; nor does Hugh Bourne hesitate to say from what quarter the check came. It was, he affirms, "modern" Methodism that quenched it. Even in the first official History it stands on record:—

"Early in the year 1806, owing, as it was thought, to some steps taken by the under ... the second travelling preacher, the revival at Harriseahead made a pause, which was cause of grief to many, and the more so as upwards of twelve months elapsed without a single conversion taking place. During this interval, many wished the day's meeting upon Mow to be held, hoping it would be a means to increase or revive religion."

In his journals, Bourne felt free to write more frankly. Nor is there any reason at this day why Mr. Miller's name should not be mentioned, for he was an able and eminently worthy man. Clowes was much attached to him, and has recorded an interesting interview he had with him at Leeds after Primitive Methodism had gained firm footing. Mr. Miller had his own views of Revivalism such as we have described it—or rather he shared the views of the leading ministers of his Church in regard to it—and when he came to the Burslem circuit, late in 1805, he made those views known and impressed them on the societies. This is what is meant when Hugh Bourne, evidently recognising the marked ability of Mr. Miller, writes :—

REV. ROBT. MILLER.

"Mr. Miller could do what no other preacher had been able to effect. He could talk on revivalism as no other travelling preacher had been able to do, and by so doing he could get hold of the people's minds, and bend them to his own views."

Daniel Shubotham—for whom, one thinks, Reuben Shufflebotham * would have been a fitter name, so impressionable and variable of mood was he—came under Mr. Miller's quiet but strong influence. He was induced to take the charge of the class at Harriseahead entirely into his own hands, for Mr. Miller did not believe in variety in class meeting; so that here, as in other places, variety gave way to uniformity. Daniel furthermore hinted that the prayer meetings too were " to be put in a different way by Mr. Miller." Hugh Bourne expostulated, but Daniel "had no ears to hear; neither had others; so the Lord might have said as in Jer. xii. 10—'Many pastors have destroyed my vineyard.' The preachers had made Daniel so unprimitive, that he was opposed to open-air worship."

So revivalism, or as Hugh Bourne and those who were with him would have called it, primitive Methodism, suffered a reverse at the hands of modern Methodism; "and it became a serious inquiry, Would not a camp meeting again raise the cause?"—shall we not, in short, re-introduce the old tactics in our campaign against sin. Thus we have now reached the point at which the Harriseahead Revivalists who, with

* This, it turns out, was his real name, though he had used . . . . Shubotham.

fluctuating fortunes, have been at work since 1800, will try to retrieve the day by giving body and actuality to what has long been before their minds as an ideal of religious enjoyment and a promising method of usefulness. The Revivalists of these parts will soon be differentiated as the Camp Meeting Methodists.

LORENZO DOW AND THE AMERICAN FACTOR.

What precipitated their resolve to have a camp meeting as well as pray for one, was a visit of Lorenzo Dow to the neighbourhood. We have not time to write Dow's strange biography, or to describe what had been the influence of his occasional visits to this part of the country——where his forefathers had lived——in fanning the revivalistic flame; nor shall we attempt a sketch of the personal appearance and dress of the man, which may best be judged of by the aid of the engraver. Suffice it to say——in words used elsewhere :——" It was the presence and writings and personal influence of Lorenzo Dow——unattached Methodist——whom no Conference or Bishop could hold or bind——a veritable comet in the religious world——who rushed flashing from America to England and Ireland and back again thrice over, astonishing and bewildering men——who had a record of labours and privations almost without parallel; whom many thought more than half madman and the rest knave, while others beheld in him more than half prophet and the latest apostle and discerner of spirits, and who hence was at once reviled and praised, shunned and followed, persecuted and kindly entreated; it was through Lorenzo Dow—surely one of the strangest earthen vessels that ever God condescended to use and honour, that the Camp Meeting movement was precipitated."*

We need not nervously set about trying to eliminate the Dow-factor from the origin of the English Camp Meetings, as though the admission of any indebtedness to him would detract from the originality of Bourne. There are few perfectly original things in this world; and, as Dr. Clifford says: " It is little, vain-glorious souls who are afraid of citing the works of others, lest somebody should presume to think they themselves are not absolutely original. Really capable minds, instead of shrinking from quotation, delight in it." Men and movements are very largely but multiplex quotations from other men and other movements, and the function of biography, and yet more the function of history, is to discover such quotations and trace them to their source. In this sense, Bourne himself and the first and succeeding camp meetings were quotations. John Wilkes once said that Hugh Bourne made him think of

LORENZO DOW.

* Quot... ... History of the Primitive Methodist Connexion, p. 21.

SOURCES AND ORIGIN.   59.

George Fox, the Quaker,* a certain Deist, fresh from a discussion with him, remarked "that he had just seen Lorenzo Dow's brother." There was a measure of truth in both observations, which were like the attaching of quotation marks to a human life. Undoubtedly, because of the influence he exerted on Bourne and others, Lorenzo Dow was one factor amongst several, of which Mow Cop Camp Meeting was the joint resultant. This and only this is meant by the statement "If there had been no Dow, there would have been no Mow." The few grains which, when added to the heap already in the scale, make the balance even, must not have all the credit for the equipoise gained.

While some would minimise our indebtedness to Lorenzo Dow in order, possibly, to magnify Hugh Bourne and the leaders of the Camp Meeting movement, others, apparently for the very opposite reason, would seem to have an interest in emphasising and exaggerating the fact of that indebtedness. To be able to prove a real connection between Dow and Mow Cop seems to be thought quite sufficient to compromise the latter, because Dow was a religious irregular, an itinerant evangelist, who broke bounds and made the world his parish, and "communicated his own spirit of self-superintendence to the leaders of the movement."† But one cannot but reflect—and the reflection brings with it a certain measure of relief and satisfaction—that all the terms here used of Lorenzo Dow could have been employed, and were employed, to describe John Wesley, to say nothing of Martin Luther. Those, therefore, who owe more than they can tell to the "irregularities," and world-parish outlook, and "spirit of self-superintendence of John Wesley," may be counted upon to look with complacency and appreciative interest upon our indebtedness to "the erratic American." There was nothing in Lorenzo Dow we are aware of that should make us anxious to repudiate any obligation we may be under to him. We acknowledge our debt, though it is not a large one, and we have heavier liabilities elsewhere. Still it is a debt of honour and not of dishonour.‡

On the eve of his second departure to America April, 1807, Lorenzo Dow paid a flying visit to Harriseahead, where Hugh Bourne saw and heard him for the first time. Dow spoke largely of camp meetings, observing—

"That occasionally something of a Pentecostal power attended them, and that, for a considerable time in America, as much good had been done, and as many souls brought to God, at the Camp Meetings as at all the meetings put together."

The same day Dow spoke at Burslem, and the next morning at five and nine o'clock he preached farewell sermons at Congleton, so abundantly did he labour down to the last moment. On each occasion Hugh Bourne was one of his auditory. Clowes, too, tells us how he walked the nine miles from Tunstall to be present at the five o'clock service, that he saw the two Bournes there, and noticed that Hugh bought some books of Dow. These were 'An Account of the Origin and Progress of Camp Meetings and

* John Wilkes was the legal adviser employed in the preparation of the Deed Poll
† The late Dr Gregory as quoted in *Methodist Times*
‡ It is a fact of some interest and significance that Lorenzo Dow preached in the Wesleyan Chapel Tunstall for the Primitive Methodists in 1818. See engraving of handbill

Tunstall Sunday School.

TWO SERMONS

WILL BE PREACHED

In the Methodist Chapel, Tunstall,

On Sunday, Aug. 16, 1818,

BY LORENZO DOW,

(From America)

When a Collection will be made after each Sermon, for the support of this Institution.

Afternoon service at half past two;—Evening Service at Six.

NUMBER OF SCHOLARS.

BOYS.		GIRLS.		
In Writing	80	In Writing	73	
Reading	133	Reading	134	Total 420
	213		207	

The friends of the Old Methodist Connexion having generously offered the use of their Chapel, by which a more numerous congregation may be accommodated, the Managers of the School respectfully solicit the attendance and support of its friends on the above occasion.

Printed by J. Tregortha, Burslem.

the Method of conducting them," written by himself, and "A Defence of Camp Meetings" by Rev G K Jennings, M A. Familiar as Bourne already was with camp-meeting literature, the reading of these pamphlets gave him new light, and decided him upon trying to introduce camp meetings into Staffordshire. The time and place were fixed upon, and the details thought out.

To Counteract the Wake

The wake or annual feast of Norton-on-the-Moors would be held in August. These feasts or wakes were quite a feature of the lower social life of England at the beginning of the century, and as such, and because we shall often meet with references to them as we proceed with our narrative, a word or two with respect to them will not be out of place. As the word 'wake' suggests, their origin was distinctly ecclesiastical, and, unlike the more modern statutes or hirings with which they sometimes became blended, that origin goes back to the far distant past. The wake was really at first a Feast of Dedication, commemorating the opening of the parish church for worship, which would take place on the festival day of the patron-saint of the church. At the first institution of the parish feast, the vigil or wake of the saint, on the eve of the day devoted to him or her, would be duly observed, and then would follow the feast, lasting several days, and, at the beginning, often held in the churchyard. So the annual return of the wake was a double anniversary—of the dedication of the church and of the patron-saint to whom it was dedicated. But in the long course of time the feast became secularised, and then almost paganised. The Church and Saint's Festival degenerated into a satanic revel—a time of licence—an annual saturnalia. We know how Clowes kept the wake at Leek before his conversion—the 'high old time," as modern roysterers might term it, he and his companions fancied they enjoyed while there. To many the local wake held out the prospect of such deplorable goings on as these. But after his conversion how different his attitude! Knowing that while the Tunstall wake was on, he would, as a young convert, be exposed to peculiar temptations, he shut himself up in his room during the day, and read and fasted and prayed, and then at night, when the carnival was at its worst, he went forth to warn and rebuke. Bad as the wakes were in North Staffordshire at this time, they were quite as bad in other parts of England during the early part of the century. The author of "Tom Brown's School Days" has written as favourably as he can of the "veasts" in the vale of the White Horse, in Herts, but he is forced to admit that the picture drawn by his friend, Charles Kingsley in "Yeast," of the low vice and nameless abominations that went on in the booths and amongst the shows of the village feast or wake, is all too true to life. At these recurring vanity-fairs many a youth and maiden were ensnared and ruined body and soul. At such times the devil seemed to have it all his own way, and the pious onlooker might have exclaimed, "This is your hour and the power of darkness."

It seemed necessary to say thus much, once for all, about the old-time wakes because a century has wrought many changes. The social perils of one age are not those of another. From some parts the wake has vanished altogether, and where it survives it often is but the shadow of its former self. What we have now to fear is the football field, the racecourse and the betting ring rather than the wake. But we want to make it clear that Bourne and his coadjutors were not fighting chimæras or wind-mills, but veritable early nineteenth century devils when they seriously set about to counteract the evils of the wake, and fell back on the camp meeting as the best means to do it. We emphasise the fact that the first-planned camp meeting "went for" the wake. As those who cared for public morals, and felt they were in special trust for the young and frail and inexperienced, they might well await the annual recurrence of the wake with apprehension. The wake justified the camp meeting regarded both as a defensive and aggressive instrumentality. Furthermore, the Norton Camp Meeting laid down the principle and furnished the example that was to be largely followed in the early history of our Church. This principle, illustrated by example both at Norton and at the second Mow Cop Camp Meeting, as well as at the one on the Wrekin, was that evil must be sought out and met on its own ground. Time and again shall we see this

VIEW OF MACCLESFIELD FROM BUXTON ROAD EARLY IN NINETEENTH CENTURY.
From an old print.

principle acted upon as we proceed. Enough here to state it, and to point out the significance of the fact that in the very first number of the Connexional Magazine published in 1819, there is an article on "Camp Meetings at the Times of Wakes," in which Hugh Bourne quaintly says: "Camp meetings at wakes have a peculiar beauty and propriety"—yes; the beauty of treating serious evils seriously, and of coming to closest quarters with them.

MOW COP CAMP MEETING.

But why was the camp meeting first sketched and determined upon, not also the first to be ... He ... termed in the strange variations—oscillations

SOURCES AND ORIGIN   63

we may even call them—of Daniel Shubotham's mind. He, too, had come under the influence of Lorenzo Dow, having heard him at Macclesfield, and now was all for camp meetings. So that when Hugh Bourne attended the class meeting at Harriseahead, in order to lay his Norton project before the members and secure their concurrence and help, he met with much encouragement. "Norton? Yes, by all means. You may rely upon us. But why not, in the meantime, have that day's praying on Mow, which has been our dream for these six years past?" Why not, indeed! It were feasible enough, but for that double appointment on the plan, thirteen Sundays a quarter, which like a dam bars the way! Hereupon Daniel took up the plan and examined it closely. Said he "Thomas Cotton is planned in this chapel on May 31st. *That's the camp meeting*," which homely utterance must be added to the other vernacular sayings we have already noted. It is strange how Daniel by virtue of his mere mass and bulk should have to be reckoned with at every turn, notwithstanding his tergiversations. He might be as easy to move as a rocking-stone, but he was formidable enough when he did move. After Daniel's *ipse dixit* the little company fell on their knees and devoutly prayed for the success of the two camp meetings.

The words of Daniel Shubotham might serve to express the feelings of thousands of our people with respect to Mow Cop camp meeting—"That's the camp meeting." It has the pre-eminence, and is likely to keep it, because, as the joint offspring of the eighteenth century field-preachings and American camp meetings, it was the first English camp meeting of the new century worthy of the name of which we have any record. Moreover its site was happily chosen—on the Cheshire side of Mow, in the same field and hard by the spot where Hugh Bourne had his open-air service ("It's like to be out-of-doors"). With Mow Cop for its site, sentiment has something to attach itself to, and imagination something to work upon, more so than in the case even of Norton which historically, was of much greater moment. Mount Zion appealed all the more strongly to the imagination of the devout Jew because of its physical eminence and because it was "beautiful for situation." Alumni of a certain northern university think all the more tenderly and proudly of their Alma Mater, as they recall her incomparable situation so appropriately set forth in the legend on her seal—"Her foundation is in the holy mountains." So no more ideal situation for the holding of the first English Camp Meeting than Mow Cop's "bleak and frowning summit" can well be conceived; and if it be in contemplation to commemorate the centenary of the establishment of camp meetings by the striking of a medal, no apter legend to place round its periphery could be chosen than these same words—"Her foundation is in the holy mountains." One can but wonder that Mow has not inspired verses worthier the theme. The subject is there, awaiting the poet's advent, but he tarries long. Meanwhile rhymesters give us of their poor best, and we have to rest content with such a stanza as this :—

> On the great mountain called Mow Cop
> God did His Majesty display
> A cloud of glory then rose up
> To shine unto the perfect day.

The morning of the 31st May broke cloudy and unpromising and many, no doubt, as they looked out from their door, concluded that no camp meeting would be held that day. Amongst these was Hugh Bourne, who intimates that the Harriseahead people had agreed that the holding of the meetings should depend on the weather's being favourable, and hence, he and others were somewhat late on the ground. Whether Clowes was aware of this understanding we are not told. He had stayed overnight with Daniel Shubotham in order to make an early start, and the unpropitious weather did not deter him from making his way to the rendezvous at an early hour. At six o'clock he found a small group singing under the lee of a wall. He threw himself heartily into the prayer meeting with which the day's proceedings were opened, and did not slacken his labours until nightfall. Shortly after six o'clock the clouds lifted and the day became more favourable. Soon, from various points, the people streamed to the field, which was a few yards from the dividing-line of the two counties, and, the better

FIRST CAMP MEETING ON MOW COP, MAY 31ST, 1807.

to guide them to the spot, at the suggestion of one Taylor, of Tunstall, Capt. Edward Anderson improvised "a sort of flag" to serve as a signal. Many who made their way up the steeps of Mow came from a considerable distance; for Lorenzo Dow's recent visit to the neighbourhood had aroused much interest in the camp meetings which he often so graphically described, so that when the news circulated that one of these novel meetings was actually going to be held on Mow, curiosity was stirred, and many came from Macclesfield, Congleton, Warrington, Knutsford, and other places where Dow had laboured and revivals had been going on.

As the day wore on, the multitude increased to such an extent that Hugh Bourne feels justified in describing it as "immense," "prodigious," and says that it presented a "sublime and magnificent spectacle." Even during the morning a second and third stand of stones were erected in elevated positions, and in the afternoon yet a fourth was found necessary in order to reach the vast assemblage, so that simultaneously "four preachers were dealing out their lives at every stroke."

Yet these four preachers multiplied we know not how many times over, are all but unknown to us, despite the fact that Mow Cop Camp Meeting has been so often described. Hugh Bourne published an account of it at the time which was widely circulated, and he also refers to it at length in his History. Clowes, too, describes it in his *Journal*, and his description has been incorporated by Mr Petty in his Connexional History. Successive writers have copied these accounts without being able to supplement them. We are thankful for the information we have but we would gladly have had more. Especially could we have wished to know the names, "persuasion" and antecedents of those who took a leading part in this memorable gathering. But names are sparingly given, and the distinction is not always drawn between those who preached and those who laboured in the "permanent praying companies which did not break up for preaching." It is clear, too, from Hugh Bourne's words that many gave a word of exhortation who were not officially recognised as local preachers:—

"At the first camp meeting, there were abundance of local preachers and praying labourers of the Old Methodist Connexion. These came from Macclesfield, Congleton, and many other places. From Tunstall there was a considerable number who were not preachers, but who laboured diligently, among whom were William Clowes and James Nixon. There were also several preachers of the Independent Methodists."

Two others, we may be quite certain were present to do their part—Thomas Cotton, none the less active because he was not in the Harriseahead pulpit, and James Bourne, calm, self-possessed, practical, reliable, ever ready to do his best without fee or reward, whether under or away from the eyes of men, who will be spared to be present "in age and feebleness extreme" at the Jubilee Camp Meeting on this same spot. Curiously enough we cannot be sure that Hugh Bourne was amongst the public speakers of the day.* We see him moving about the ground. Returning from the first stand he found a company praying with a man in distress. He got as near to the circle as he could and fain would have lingered, but "other matters called him away." Probably his organising bent found sufficient employment in directing and overseeing the proceedings. This is all the more likely from the fact that this huge camp meeting was not conducted according to a plan drawn up beforehand. "It was" we are told, "like Judges xxi. 25—Every man did that which was right in his own eyes." When men were wanted to address the people, men were forthcoming. The stringent rules afterwards in force as to how long a man should speak and what should be the staple of his discourse, do not seem to have been applied at Mow Cop first camp meeting. The result was an extraordinary variety marked the public utterances of the day. The various speakers assuredly succeeded, amongst them, in sounding the entire gamut of hortatory and edificatory speech; for there were exhortations, readings, the recital of experience, and the telling of anecdotes, nor was there wanting an example of the conveyance of truth through the medium of verse.

* "Brother H. B. was not there when we began the meeting in the morning, and I do not know that he preached at all that day."—*Clowes MSS.*

For instance, at ten o'clock, Clowes rose and began by narrating his Christian experience. He explained the reason of his presence and the motive urging him to take an active part in the day's proceedings, and he closed with an impassioned and powerful exhortation. Concerning the poet of the camp meeting, who was also its flag-hoister, a word or two may be permitted. Captain Edward Anderson's biography reads like a romance. His father was a farmer on the Yorkshire Wolds, and the youth's first business in life was tending his father's sheep. But the shepherd-lad early took to sea and poetry, for he had the knack of rhyming, and even wrote a poem called "The Sailor," which is said to have achieved a certain measure of popularity and to have run through several editions. During his sea-faring life he had many adventures and hair-breadth escapes. He suffered shipwreck at various times, was captured by French privateers, and, like Clowes, fell into the hands of the press-gang. But after all his sufferings and hazards he at last found safe anchorage. Lost to his friends, he one week-night wandered into Pitt Street Chapel, Liverpool; he heard his brother, whom he did not recognise at the time, preach a moving sermon from the story of the Prodigal Son. He united with the Methodists of Pitt Street, of which circuit his brother was a minister, and afterwards settled in Hull where, on Clowes' entry into that town, he joined the society in Mill Street. His name stood on the prayer-leader's plan; he was an anti-slavery advocate, a temperance reformer, and, to the extent of his powers, a favourer and promoter of all that was good. He died in 1843, and his body lies near the porch of the parish church of Kilham, his native place. On the Sunday before the holding of Norton camp meeting, August 16th, a camp meeting, attended by a vast concourse of people, was held at the secluded village of Langtoft-on-the-Wolds, near Driffield, in Yorkshire. During the day, allusions were made by the speakers not only to American camp meetings, but to those just held in Staffordshire. Though nothing permanent remained as the result of the Langtoft services, yet the fact of a camp meeting on such a scale being held in this part of England at this early date is worth chronicling—the more so, as, but for the meeting on Mow, it might never have been held at all. As Kilham is only a few miles distant from Langtoft, are we wrong in surmising that Captain Edward Anderson who, on May 31st, at Mow Cop Camp Meeting, told the story of his life in verse interspersed with sentences of exhortation,

CAPTAIN E. ANDERSON'S TOMBSTONE, KILHAM CHURCHYARD.

had something to do with the inception and carrying out of the great camp meeting at Langtoft-on-the-Wolds in August?

Spiritual and individualistic as were the aims of the promoters of the first camp meeting, there were some of the speakers from the waggons that day who, being far-travelled men, naturally could not refrain from dwelling, for purposes of edification, on experiences they had gone through and events they had taken part in in those days of "sturt and strife," and who by so doing imported a deeper meaning into the day's proceedings. Listening to these speakers, their stay-at-home auditory would find their horizon insensibly widening, and dimly perceive that to set down or set aside that

KILHAM CHURCH.
The Tomb of Captain E. Anderson and his brother is the second from the Porch on your left hand as you enter the Porch.

camp meeting as being nothing more than a faddist's freak or a glorified gigantic religious picnic, was a conclusion forbidden not only by the condition of their own souls that day, which was also the condition of multitudes of people in these parts, but that it was a conclusion yet more sternly forbidden by the condition of the sorely distracted and disjointed world they were hearing about. And we, coming across these allusions to current or recent events in the reports of that first camp meeting left to us, do not scout them as irrelevancies, but welcome them as timely and significant of much. For our founders and others being men of parts and ability to take a wider outlook, so far as world affairs were concerned and yet, being above all, men of such single purpose that they could have said "this one thing we do," they have not left us in their scanty journals many allusions to contemporary national or world events. They did the work that was before them, and saw not or recked not of the far-reaching references and influences of their work. But this does not absolve us from the necessity of constantly reminding ourselves what kind of a world it was into which they were thrust when they began their long day's work. Rightly regarded, those humble camp meeting stands were no more to be scoffed at than a park of artillery with unlimbered guns, for they marked the bringing up of fresh supports in the war of amelioration.

Yielding to such thoughts as these, we can appreciate the statement that one of the

LANGTOFT-ON-THE-WOLDS.

speakers at Mow Camp Meeting— an Irish lawyer and a convert of Lorenzo Dow—gave vivid details of the horrors of the late rebellion in Ireland he himself had witnessed, and in which to his own spiritual enrichment he had lost his worldly all. We can see the pertinence of his applications—"that we should praise God for our privileges as English Christians, improve them to the glory of God, and pity and pray for the poor and spiritually degraded Irish."

Largely autobiographic too was the address of another speaker—an ex-officer in the British army and ex-Deist who had recently been arrested and soundly converted under the instrumentality of Lorenzo Dow at Macclesfield. Though no name is given we know that this man was Eleazar Hathorn *alias* "Eleazar of the wooden leg"; for he had lost a limb in

SOURCES AND ORIGIN.

with a rhetorical exaggeration rather unusual to him, "seen death flying in every direction, and men falling slain on every side. He had walked in blood, over fields covered with mountains of dying and dead. He showed the happiness of our land, and the gratitude we owed to God for its exemption from being the seat of war."

So this day of labour and of blessing lapsed. At six o'clock there was but one stand, and towards the end the work was carried on by praying companies. At seven, Hugh Bourne tells us—and how characteristic this is—a work broke out amongst the children, some half-dozen of whom were converted, forming the last, though by no means the least, spoil of the day. We can picture W. Clowes, as exhausted with his incessant labours extending from six in the morning until eight at night, he left the field, feeling inexpressibly thankful as he reflected—"Myriads of saints and angels will everlastingly laud the Eternal Majesty on account of the day's praying on Mow Cop."

CAMP MEETINGS AND THE CONVENTICLE ACT.

It was not so much the holding of Mow Cop Camp Meeting that gave offence and roused opposition, as the fact that its success encouraged its supporters to arrange at once for the holding of a second and third. Had it stood alone—without a successor, like the one at Langtoft, its contemporary, it would have been a nine days' wonder nothing more. The first was borne with because it was expected it would also be the last. Such an impression might have been justified in 1801; it was quite erroneous now. Then, opponents might have said:—"Let them have their fling and you will hear no more of camp meetings. They will tire of them as a child of the toy for which it has clamoured." But what might have been true in 1801 was not true in 1807. The movement had acquired momentum; all the greater because it "had been let hitherto," and now that the propulsion given by Lorenzo Dow had been added, the movement was not to spend itself in one big effort, as some who had neither understanding of the times nor of men thought it would.

REV. JOHN RILES.

A conversation reported to have taken place between Hugh Bourne and his superintendent, Mr. Riles, before Mow Cop Camp Meeting, lets us see into the minds of both the promoters and the opponents of camp meetings. In Walford's "Life of Hugh Bourne," that conversation is made a foot-note, but it is too significant to be left in that obscurity, as though it had no bearing on the course of events. If that brief talk did not shape events it certainly throws light on them.

Mr. R.—"The forthcoming meeting will do hurt."

H. B.—"It will *not* do hurt."

Mr. R.—"Well, one meeting will 'satisfy' all people."

H. B.—"Very well, then, we'll have a second that is the first."

Mr. R.—"Very well."

Unless we are much mistaken, this very laconic dialogue discloses ready to our hand a clue worth following. Mr. Thomas Church has too hastily drawn a double inference from Mr. Riles' sentence. He concludes that "the official representative of the Wesleyan Conference not only sanctioned officially the holding of England's first camp meeting," but more than that—"his words conveyed a willingness on his part for camp meetings to be continued, should the first prove successful in its design."* We, on the contrary, take Mr. Riles' meaning to be that, as there was not likely to be a second camp meeting, this one should be tolerated—"sanctioned" is too strong a term. He saw no long series, no extended vista of camp meetings opening out before him. One, he thought, would satisfy all, opponents and favourers alike. "All people' included Bourne himself; therefore he would interpret Hugh Bourne's somewhat enigmatical utterance by his own thought. The forthcoming meeting would, at its finish, leave Hugh Bourne so satisfied with having had his own way that he would be quite willing to settle down, and avoid the trouble inseparable from organising further meetings, and the pain and discomfort of running counter to the wishes of the Methodist authorities. One camp meeting was to be suffered because it would have no successor, and there would be an end of it, and we are not sure whether Mr. Riles would not read acquiescence in this view of the matter into Hugh Bourne's reply. As to Bourne, whether there was to be a second camp meeting or not, was to be determined by the event. If that meeting left him "satisfied" that there had been more of the whim and will of man in camp meetings than he had suspected—well and good he would desist. But if by its success and manifest tokens of the divine favour the impression were deepened that camp meetings "should not die but live," then, in God's name, he would stand by them.

How, then, to use Bourne's phrase, did Mow Camp Meeting "leave it'? "The propriety and utility of camp meetings appeared to every one.' Adjudged by the criteria of numbers, good order and decorum, and spiritual results, there could be no doubt as to its success. 'Pious people were of opinion that more good was done at that camp meeting than had been done at all the preachings and meetings held at Harriseahead and Mow during the preceding twelve months." Its promoters were fully satisfied it was of God, and were resolved to continue this method of doing good. A public announcement to this effect was made on the camp-ground, and the penny pamphlet which was at once published and circulated by thousands, not only described the first camp meeting, but also advertised the second and third, and laid down certain regulations for the due ordering of the same.

This public advertising could not fail to be construed into a declaration of war—as tantamount to throwing down the gage of battle. The first camp meeting had been but "loathly allowed." Now, the permissive era was to give place to the prohibitive

---

* Thomas Church, *History of the Primitive Methodists*, 1870, p. 121. H. Bourne writing in 1836 on this conversation, recognises its importance. "It would seem Mr. Riles in his zeal was not fully aware of the import of his own words; for he, being the agent of the Conference in that circuit, did hereby in effect not only give the Conference sanction (as far as he was concerned) to that meeting, but to leaving the Camp Meeting cause or system, on the same footing as that meeting should have it. Neither was H. B. at the time aware either of his own words, or of those of Mr. R."—*Mo*

Henceforward the opposition to camp meetings became more pronounced, organised, and official in character, so much so, that some who in heart sympathised with this new mode of evangelism and had even countenanced and aided the first effort of the kind, now wavered and drew back. Handbills in opposition to camp meetings were published by the preachers of the Burslem and Macclesfield Circuits. This was fair and above-board; but there also crept forth from some quarter or other a handbill announcing that no camp meeting would be held. But it was bill against bill. A counter-placard drawn up and signed by H. and J. Bourne, D. Shubotham, M. Bayley and T. Cotton soon appeared, declaring that the arrangements already made held good, and that the camp meetings most assuredly would be held. How fared it with Hugh Bourne and the rest as the storm thus gathered? We shall be deceived if we regard him as absolutely tremorless—composed and comfortable as the storm hurtled around him. He was not so devoid of sensitiveness.* Indeed, there was one moment when the thought took him like a vice—"Put out a bill to say there will be no camp meeting and be at peace." But that moment was not, we may be sure, the moment when his eye first caught sight of the unauthorised poster, minus the printer's imprint, but rather the moment when by staring handbill it was brought home to him that the highest local authorities of his Church had declared against him.

After what has been said of the working incompatibility between modern and primitive Methodism, and the inevitability of a collision between them sooner or later taking place, we need not now stay to account for the opposition of official Methodism to camp meetings, much less to denounce it. However unwise and unfortunate we may now think it to have been, regarded from the standpoint taken at the time, it is quite understandable, and one may even say, natural. So here for the time we may leave it, always remembering whether it be referred to or not, that the opposition is there to be felt and reckoned with, like a strong head-wind, in the teeth of which the camp-meeting movement has to make its way.

There was, however, opposition to be encountered and provided against of quite another kind—of a kind, indeed, we find it hard to estimate the nature and gravity of, since it owed its being and force to the more intolerant laws under which Dissenters and Nonconformists then lived and in the shadow of which they had to do their work. True, there was the Toleration Act, but the Conventicle and Five Mile Acts were not yet repealed. They still stood on the Statute Book and could be invoked and set in motion to harass and injure. It was a time, too, when the growing influence of Dissent and Methodism was the cause of uneasiness and offence to many. Under the stimulus of this composite feeling, the provisions of the Toleration Act were very closely scanned, with the result, that the highest legal authority in the realm—Lord Ellenborough—presiding over the Court of Queen's Bench, threw doubt on the meaning and effect of the existing laws. What though a dissenter had got his licence as a preacher and teacher, it now began to be questioned whether that licence availed him anything, unless it could be proved that he was the minister of a separate and particular

---

* There is one place in his *Journals*, written some little time after this, where something very much like a moan escapes him that he who would like above all things to live at peace with all men seems cruelly fated to a life was with a time.

congregation—nay more, unless it could also be proved that he had been duly ordained by those authorised and competent to convey the grace of orders and confer legal status. But if the position of regular pastors and ministers of dissenting churches was thus called in question and made insecure, the position of lay preachers, and those "irregulars" who, like Bourne, carried on religious services in the open-air was rendered doubly precarious. There can be little doubt, with the strong disposition felt in certain quarters to strain the existing laws so as to make them bear hardly on dissenters, that not only the speakers at the first camp meeting but all those who attended and took part in it, might have been pounced upon and subjected to fine, and, in default of payment, to imprisonment, had any one bold and bad enough to take the needful trouble been forthcoming. That this is no extravagant fancy is clear from the provisions of the Toleration Act itself, and is established by such facts as these: £90 were recovered from persons found at a prayer meeting, and another man was fined £20 for offering

> I Charles Hurt Esquire one of his Majesty's Justices of the peace for the county of Derby Do hereby certify that William Taylor of Belper in the parish of Duffield in the County of Derby did this day appear before me, and did make take and subscribe the several oaths and declarations specified in an act, made in the fifty second year of the reign of King George the Third intitled "An act to repeal certain acts and amend other acts relating to religious worship and assemblies, and persons teaching or preaching therein."
> Witness my hand this ninth day of August 1822.
> Chas Hurt

up public prayer to the Almighty.* Again, on Sunday, the 14th June, 1812, the ancestor of an influential Primitive Methodist family now resident in Nantwich, Crewe, and Willaston, was made to feel the weight of the obnoxious laws. George Wood had taken his stand on a bank in the open air of the town of Audlem with a view to the holding of a religious service when he was assaulted and stopped by an attorney named Groom, acting under an alleged warrant which he never showed. Wood, on appearing before the Bench, was convicted in the penalty of £20, and, being unable or unwilling to pay the fine, he suffered the distraint of his goods. Fortunately he appealed to a higher Court, and the judges of the Chester Assizes awarded him £200 damages. The mortified defendant appealed to the King's Bench, but the verdict of the lower court

* Hebber "Short History of the Free Churche" p. 144

SOURCES AND ORIGIN.

was sustained.* Thus, locally, even as late as 1812 the Conventicle Act had power to annoy, and what the trend of the time was is clearly shown by Lord Sidmouth's bill for checking the facilities with which persons entered the dissenting ministry. This bill was brought in in 1811, the birth-year of Primitive Methodism. Lord Sidmouth complained that "cobblers, tailors, pig-drivers, and chimney-sweeps" had assumed the sacred office. The clause requiring the signatures of six respectable householders of the village belonging to the applicant's denomination might seem a harmless condition, but it was shrewdly suspected that the true billet of the bill, and especially this clause of it, was the suppression of local preachers and the extirpation of village dissent. The Nonconformists were up in arms; and historians do not fail to note the fact that, for the first time, the Wesleyans took a leading part in a political struggle, joining heart and soul in the resistance which was organised to the bill. On the day of its second reading there

THE LATE MR. JOHN WOOD.    THE LATE MR. THOMAS WOOD.

were lodged against it no less than 336 petitions—so bulky that they impeded the movements of "my lords." The bill had to be dropped, but its dropping was the immediate raising of the Protestant Society for the Protection of Religious Liberty, of which John Wilkes, who had to do with the preparation of the Deed Poll of our Church, was the secretary. The year 1812 saw the obnoxious Conventicle and Five Mile Acts wiped off the Statute Book.

We have said thus much in order to place the second camp meeting in its proper historic setting. That being done, certain special features of that camp meeting, which might easily be passed over as due to nothing but the personal idiosyncrasies of Hugh Bourne, are seen to have been the outcome of prudent foresight, and are full of significance. They have the Conventicle Act at the back of them. When we are told that it began to be whispered Hugh Bourne was a political ringleader, and most likely a traitor; that if he got his deserts he would be brought to justice and mulcted in heavy damages, or clapped in prison, we can see, in the light of what has been said, that these rumours were of sinister import. When, further, we are told how it was noised abroad that a man of standing and influence in the neighbourhood—

---

* "Religious Intolerance in Cheshire in 1812." Reprinted from the *Crewe and Nantwich Chronicle*, May 28th, 1887. Also "The Story of an Old Case of Persecution Retold," by Rev. T. Horne, *Aldersgate Primitive Methodist Magazine*.

a deistic master-potter named Stephenson—was threatening to crush camp meetings and get the leaders of them punished by means of the Conventicle Act, we can understand Hugh Bourne's movements. We can see he was not "frighted with false fire," or indulging a whim, but simply taking precautionary measures when, having secured the promise of the ground from a freeholder, he trudged to Lichfield and back in order to get the ground licensed for worship. He was told, however, that the licence could not be granted unless a building were erected on the site. Accordingly, at an expense to himself of some thirty pounds, he got a wooden tabernacle erected, together with two smaller tents. W. Clowes assisted him in the purchase of crockery; a stock of provisions for the expected strangers was laid in; then he got a preacher's licence for

AUDLEM.

himself from Stafford, and, having done all he could, he finished by affixing a public notice on a board, warning all and sundry that the ground and erections being duly licensed for worship, any one disturbing the worshippers would render himself liable to penalty.

Mow Cop second camp meeting was held on July 19th. As its design was to counteract the wake of the ancient parish of Wolstanton, which included Tunstall and district, it lasted three days. We need not describe the services further than to say that like those of   on be   ere largely carried on by auxiliaries from a distance. Clowes was present, but tells us he "laboured little." James Nixon, however, was not only on the ground but threw himself heart and soul into the services "I was, with many others," says Clowes, "greatly struck with the solemnity and power which attended his ministrations."

Camp meeting No 2 was, as we have seen, organised with a view to probable opposition of a quasi-legal kind. Its elaborate preparations were of the nature of a defence, as much so as are the parapets and stockades of a fort, and it is chiefly memorable to us from the way in which the threatened opposition showed itself and did little more than that. All eyes were fixed on the master potter—the champion of order and the Conventicle Act, who "breathed out threatenings." On that July Sunday afternoon, he endeavoured to make his threatenings good. Attended by one or two others, whose names, fortunately for themselves, have not transpired, Mr Stephenson rode on the ground just at the time penitents were being prayed with at one of the praying companies. Not succeeding in breaking up the company by riding through it, he asked for the person in charge, and was directed to Hugh Bourne. Mr Hugh Bourne had retired behind the hill and, because of the labour he had to perform, he had not yet endued his Sunday garments, so that he did not look much like the generalissimo of the forces. The two met—the representative of the Conventicle Act and the champion of camp meetings. Mr S was heated and spoke in a high tone, but H B, on the contrary, conversed with him "coolly and at large." The minister's licence was demanded and at once produced; then the licence for the buildings was asked for. That, he was told, was at home, but should be sent for if necessary. Upon this, Mr S went away, riding past the congregation. "Then," we are told, "the Lord interposed, and struck such a terror in him, that he stopped his horse and sent for H B, and seemed conscious of being in the wrong." Very probably, for as he rode off, in all likelihood his eye caught sight of the minatory board warning all would-be disturbers of a lawful assembly. Anyhow, his mood was changed. He was now more reasonable, and deist though he was, disposed to argue from the Scriptures as a common standard of authority. So he took his final leave, invoking a "God bless you" upon the bystanders, and the people present cried "God bless him." He who had come on the ground like a lion left it like a lamb.

We have referred to this instance of unsuccessful opposition because it was the first of its kind, though not the last by any means. And yet we may be permitted to doubt whether, if the opposition had only been more thorough and persistent, the existing laws might not have been so strained as in the result to make H B's two licences not worth the parchment they were written on—insufficient for his own protection, still less sufficing to screen the other speakers and praying labourers who had no licence. It must have been under the influence of the suspicion that after all, his proposed safeguards might prove worthless, that H B shouted to the people who were disquieted by the manufacturer's bluster and threats. 'Whoever is fined for attending the meeting I will pay." By these words of reassurance he sought to stay the beginning of panic.

The attempt to put down camp meetings under legal cover had in this case ignominiously failed, and this ... "If a man of

PRIMITIVE METHODIST CHURCH.

standing and substance like this, who ought to know the law if any one knows it, and how far it will let him go—if he has done his best, or his worst, and has failed, then it is not likely that any one else who may be bold enough to try conclusions with the camp meeting Methodists will fare any better. We may safely go. We run no risks." Considerations of this kind would induce many to attend camp meetings who might have been intimidated and kept away by the successful imposition of fines.

Camp Meetings and Conference. Norton, the Proclaimed Camp Meeting

Between the second and fourth camp meetings, what H. B. calls "a small camp meeting," was held at Brown Edge, two miles from Norton, on August 16th (the very day on which Langtoft Camp Meeting was held); but as this was really nothing more than a couple of open-air services held morning and evening we need not linger upon it, though it may by courtesy be called the third camp meeting.

Norton Camp Meeting bespeaks our careful attention in many regards. It had been arranged for long before the Conference of 1807 met at Liverpool. Until the Conference pronounced, the opposition of the ministers and the greater part of the officialdom of the circuit, though hard to withstand, might be partly discounted and, therefore, more easily braved, by its being regarded as local, and as not representing the deliberate, final judgment of Methodism. In such circumstances, a silent appeal might be made to a higher tribunal and the hope cherished that the local judgment might not obtain the endorsement of the supreme court. In vain, the Conference pronounced and pronounced adversely. The fateful words have often been written, but they must be written once more—

Q.—"What is the judgment of the Conference concerning what are called Camp Meetings?"

A.—"It is our judgment that, even supposing such meetings to be allowable in America, they are highly improper in England and likely to be productive of considerable mischief; and we disclaim all connection with them."

Compared with some fulminations of the Church, this Conference minute was mildness itself. If camp meetings were really so very bad—too bad to be let live—then one thinks the minute might very properly have been made more stringent and have been couched in stronger terms. It reads more like a recommendation than an anathema; its attitude to camp meetings is negative rather than positive, and that attitude is taken up more from expediency than on principle. For it is conceded—grudgingly, we grant—that camp meetings may "do good," and therefore be allowed in America, while in England they will be highly improper and must be disallowed. Hence it is reasonable to infer, that it is not camp meetings in themselves that are objected to, so much as the temper and habit from which they are supposed to spring—the self-willedness and ecclesiastical do-as-we-likeness which, in the thought of many, had come to be associated with Revivalism of which, probably, it was regarded as the latest and most flagrant manifestation. We do not condemn the Conference. It had a perfect right to take its own course, but we claim the liberty of expressing an

QUEEN STREET, BURSLEM.

QUEEN STREET, BURSLEM.

opinion whether the direction taken was according to precedent, or the genius of Methodism. The Minute of Conference marked a deliberate departure from the primitive policy and practice of Methodism. Several times during the course of his marvellous itineraries, Wesley had preached at Burslem in the open-air—the last time so recently as 1790, only seventeen years before. "I was obliged to preach abroad," says he, "such were the multitudes of the people. Surely the people of this place were highly favoured. Mercy embraced them on every side." The Conference minute, too, is in striking contrast with Wesley's farewell address to the preachers of the Chester Circuit given that same year—1790.

"Fellow labourers, wherever there is an open door enter in and preach the Gospel; if it be to two or three, under a hedge or a tree; preach the Gospel—go out quickly into the streets and lanes of the city, and bring in hither the poor and the maimed, and the halt and the blind; and the servant said, 'Lord, it is done as Thou hast commanded, and yet there is room.' He then lifted up his hands, and with tears flowing down his cheeks, repeated, 'And yet there is room!'"

If "Conference is the living Wesley," his views and practices must have undergone a great change during the short course of seventeen years. But even Dr. Bunting is witness that there are times when it is both right and expedient to take to the streets and lanes and fields and commons to preach the gospel :—

"When a superintendent told the Conference that the Warrenites had got all the chapels in his Circuit which were not upon the model deed, Dr. Bunting nobly told him to go out into the streets and lanes and fields and commons and preach the doctrines that our fathers preached, and in the way they preached them, and we should soon have as good chapels or better ones, or as big chapels or bigger."*

Dr. Bunting *did* speak nobly when he tendered such advice as this. Would that a voice equally potent had been raised in the Conference of 1807 in defence of camp meetings as an agency for reaching those whom no chapels, however good or big, could entice within their walls. If the "irregularity" of going into the open was justifiable in 1849 under the circumstances, then, *a fortiori*, it was still more justifiable as things were in the country in the earlier years of the century. However, it is not the unwisdom of the minute of Conference on which we care to dwell. Rather do we press the fact of the inconsistency of that minute with the views and methods characteristic of Methodism in its early heroic days. It is this fact—for fact it is, and no mere private opinion—on which the historian of the Free Churches has fastened; and we are quite content to leave the matter where he has left it:—

"The Primitive Methodists were established because the Conference, proving more conservative than Wesley himself, and forgetting the origin of their existence, set itself against the general practice of field preaching."*

If the Conference pronouncement had to be no mere *brutum fulmen*, it was the Burslem Circuit which must feel its effects. That circuit was the storm-centre of the camp meeting movement, and within its limits the issue between the promoters of the movement and the Conference would have to be decided. The circuit preachers, on their return from the Conference, took such a view of the action of Conference and of their duty in relation to it, that they could not allow the minute to remain a dead letter. The officials of the circuit were got together and required to declare themselves against camp meetings. This prompt and decided action on the part of the ministers had its natural effect. William Clowes was absent from Norton Camp Meeting, and was not seen at another for a period of thirteen months. For a time even James Bourne wavered; and then, one can well imagine Hugh Bourne would feel himself a terribly lonely man with a heavy burthen to bear. He had reached at one

BURSLEM IN 1800, SHOWING TOWN HALL.

BURSLEM WESLEYAN CHAPEL.

* Skeats' "A History of the Free Churches of England," 1868, p. 624.

and the same time the culminating point of his responsibility and the nadir of his loneliness. Had he, too, lost heart at this juncture the movement must have collapsed. But H. B. remained firm, and very soon his brother became convinced that it was his duty to stand by camp meetings, being, it would appear, largely brought to this conviction by a remarkable dream. This is all the more noteworthy because he was matter-of-fact, and we seldom hear of his dreaming dreams. Now he was ready to share the expense and labour involved in successfully carrying through another camp meeting of the American type—a type not destined to take root in England—with its booths and tents, its provision for worshippers, and lasting three days. All eyes were directed to the forthcoming Norton Camp Meeting—and with good reason. It was the crucial gathering; for it would decide whether camp meetings could go on living and

NORTON.

justify their survival, even in the state of outlawry created by Conference proscription. Had the movement given way at this point, just where the pressure was the strongest, and the power of resistance apparently the feeblest, then it would have mattered little that Captain Anderson had hoisted the flag of out-door evangelism on Mow Cop. The contest seemed a very unequal one. If it were not exactly "*Athanasius contra mundum*" it was Hugh Bourne flying in the face of the Wesleyan Conference and of his own circuit authorities. But he tells us how he had read that "General Councils may err, and sometimes have erred, even in things pertaining unto God," and was led to believe that this was just such an instance of aberration on the part of a grave and reverend assembly as Article XXI of the Church of England had recognised as possible. Thinking thus, he stiffened his will, and was emboldened to carry through what he had determined, as though he were right and the whole Methodist Conference wrong. Moreover, he believed the Conference had been misled by giving heed to hearsay reports, and "If and J Bourne knew that the Lord could turn the minds of the Conference or carry on the camp meetings by other means."*

The morning of August 23rd, 1807, broke unfavourably, and in other respects than weather the conditions were depressing. Not that the assembly was disappointingly small, rather was it unexpectedly large, and the labourers few in proportion to the multitude gathered together. Many, no doubt, were absent who but for the Conference edict would have been present, and whose presence would have stamped it as a local Methodist gathering. But, probably, the edict brought together more than it kept away. Those to whom the interdict did not apply, or for whom it had no terrors, would come out of curiosity to see what all the stir was about, and wherein lay the harm of such meetings. The promoters of the camp meeting had not looked further than the holding of a series of meetings of modest dimensions, yet sufficing with their praying companies to keep the young from being drawn away by the enticements of the wake, and, behold! a multitude brought together from far and near, and only four or five available for labour! Besides Hugh Bourne and his brother, there were James Nixon, "about as difficult to be persuaded from pursuing what he deemed a proper course as Hugh Bourne himself," † a man from Knutsford and another from Macclesfield. Later in the day Thomas Cotton would render good service, but he had to fulfil his appointments at Kidsgrove morning and afternoon. One can imagine Hugh Bourne's surveying the slender forces at his disposal and the work cut out for them, and the depression that would come upon him as he recognised how disproportionate they were in numbers and physical strength to the task before them. But help came unexpectedly. A stranger to the conductors of the meeting came upon the field and made his way to the centre. The stranger proved to be Paul Johnson, a physician from Dublin, staunch friend of Lorenzo Dow, whom his professional skill had saved from what seemed imminent death. He had laboured too with Dow in the recent revivals in Lancashire and Cheshire, and consequently would be known to many on the ground. He was "much in the Quaker way," and had come to the camp meeting by "impression, though at some sacrifice, and was moved to take a prominent part in the meetings. Being an excellent speaker, with a fine resonant voice which filled the field, he quite captivated the potters. His coming at that moment was regarded as exceedingly opportune, it was even looked upon as "an extraordinary interposition of Divine Providence," and turned the feeling of depression into one of hopefulness and confidence. They were satisfied that camp meetings were of the Lord, and taught by experience how faithless had been their fears, they resolved hereafter to trust less than ever in an arm of flesh.

The camp meeting went on until Tuesday evening, though on the latter day with diminished numbers, and marred by the appearance on the field of Daniel Shubotham to play the part of a protester! Henceforward Daniel will be absent from this history. Soon the tents were struck and the tabernacle taken down, and Norton Camp Meeting, fourth in order but first in historical importance, was a thing of the past. It had answered its immediate purpose—not one member was "drawn away by the vanities of the wake." More than this—"from that important moment the English camp meetings were established on an immovable foundation, and could never afterwards be shaken."

The "Shedding" of Hugh Bourne.

From Norton Camp Meeting follows in true historical sequence the expulsion, or, as it might more correctly be called, the dropping or shedding of Hugh Bourne. It was the next natural step to take after what had already been done. If camp meetings were proscribed, the man who more than any other was responsible for their forfeited existence, could not long be tolerated; if they were proclaimed un-Methodistic, he, their

NORTON CHURCH.
Where Hugh Bourne's parents are buried.

chief author and abettor, must soon be denied the character of true Methodist. And yet, one thinks, the authorities were not precipitate in their action; for the guillotine did not fall until June 27th, 1808—ten months after the holding of Norton Camp Meeting, so there was no indecent haste in making Hugh Bourne pay the penalty of his contumacy. But even during those ten months of respite he was not suffered to live under the illusion that the passing of the Conference minute had made no difference, and that things would continue on the old footing. True; opposition may be said to have spent its force at Norton, and after that time to have quickly moderated, yet, Bourne tells us, "the minute of Conference continued to be pressed," and the brothers "were made ... of ... " Whatever unpleasant form

SOURCES AND ORIGIN. 83

this pressure took, its indirect result was for the furtherance of the gospel. If it availed to close some accustomed doors, mediately it brought about the finding of fresh openings for evangelistic activity. The line of least resistance taken coincided largely with the line of most usefulness. Where they found themselves free to labour was just the spot where labour was most needed. Neglected neighbourhoods were missioned; open-air services were held and cottage prayer meetings established; the scantiness of religious ordinances here and there was supplemented. In addition to all this, conversation-preaching and family visitation went on continually. These, not the least effective methods of evangelisation, were under no ban, and could be followed anywhere. Moreover, when the vernal equinox of the new year—1808—was passed, the Camp

THE WREKIN.

Meeting Methodists, as they now began to be called, acting in conformity with their name, organised a series of camp meetings.

The first of the series, opening what may be called the camp meeting season, was held May 1st, 1808, on the singular isolated hill or mountain in Shropshire—the Wrekin, not far from Madeley, where John Fletcher lived and laboured. What made them pitch upon a distant mountain, 1320 feet high, for their camp meeting, was not the strangeness or the picturesqueness of the site, though in these respects the spot chosen was quite as remarkable as Mow Cop itself. What took them so far afield* was the knowledge that on this first Sunday in May, as had been the custom time out of mind, a vast multitude of people would come together to spend the day in unhallowed pleasure. True to their principle of coming to close quarters with vice and profanity, they resolved not to let this annual desecration both of the Lord's Day and of the Lord's mountain pass without protest. They would bear witness to the truth that "the heights of the hills are His also," and would see to it that the heights of old Wrekin should for once give back other echoes than those with which bad "old use and wont" had made them familiar in the long succession of years. So the sounds of praise and prayer and exhortation vied and struggled for the mastery with the sounds of revelry, lewdness, and profanity. Finally, and appropriately, they distributed their "Rules for Holy Living," and left the mountain and the results with God.

Three other camp meetings were held during what we have called the ten months of respite. These were Bug Lawton, in Cheshire, May 15th, a small one at Wootton, May 22nd, and the third Mow Camp Meeting, May 29th. These need not detain us from considering what is of much more importance—the formal exclusion of Hugh Bourne from the Wesleyan Methodist Society by the Burslem Circuit Quarterly Meeting of June 27th, 1808. The blow was in some measure anticipated. He tells us that as he was on his return journey from "a religious excursion" into Cheshire and Lancashire, it was painfully borne in upon his mind that he would soon be put out of the Old Methodist communion and that he would be more useful out than in. He did not rest passive under the impression, but strove and argued against it. Such an event was most unlikely, he reasoned,—he being a trustee, having been a considerable giver to the cause, a raiser up of societies, and "vehemently attached to Methodism." These were the grounds he went upon in this inward debate and with such considerations he sought to get rid of the impression, and because of its intrinsic unlikelihood ventured to conclude it had not a Divine source. Nevertheless the impression persisted, nor had he any peace until he let it sink into his mind and gave it credence and yielded is with a "Be it as the Lord will." On reaching home he found rumours flying about that his expulsion was intended. Whatever explanation may be offered of this mental conflict one obvious advantage resulted from it. He had reckoned with the event beforehand, so that its happening found him calm and prepared.

What was the charge or complaint preferred against Hugh Bourne by the Burslem Quarterly Meeting? No doubt the impression has largely obtained that a clear, definitive issue was raised—that of H B's insubordination to a circuit prohibition based on a Conference resolution. But there is no evidence for this. On the contrary, there is evidence that much lower ground was taken. In the Clowes MSS it is distinctly stated by Clowes himself:—

'I was at the Quarter Day at Burslem when H B was put out of Society as a private member, and the charge that was brought against him was for not attending his class. The leader said he had not been at his class for a long time, and they put him away.'

Thus what nearly all biographers of Hugh Bourne and Connexional historians had surmised, is now established—that the ostensible ground of Hugh Bourne's dismemberment was r   ' of ordinary discipline, much less any allegation of immorality or wrong doing, but the fact of infrequent attendance at his class. He himself has admitted the truth of the charge, and explained why it was true. How could he be present at Norton Class on the Sunday morning when, as a rule, he was pursuing his evangelistic labours miles away? Yet, in his absence, without being apprised of what was going to be done, or being allowed to plead anything in extenuation, he was dropped. The Circuit Steward, Mr Walker, we are told, spoke up on behalf of fairness to an absent man who, after all, was more than a private member. Whether any one else did so we are not told.

Does the new evidence available permit us to regard the action of the authorities more favourably? Scarcely. There were two questions involved in the unchurching of Hugh Bourne—the question of fact and of right whether he had or had not attended his class and whether the fact of non-attendance, supposing it proved, was a sufficient ground for expulsion. If, when the fact was proved that H B had not been at his class for some time—and if his leader were present it would not take long to prove *that*—it were then agreed to rule out all questions of why and wherefore, all considerations explanatory and exculpatory, and determine the issue on the simple matter of fact—then all that can be said is that such mode of procedure would have been the veriest travesty of justice, although one can easily see that such an easy method of barring out troublesome discussion and getting rid of a troublesome man would have its obvious advantages. If this were the course really taken—a thing in itself hardly credible—then such a statement as the subjoined is quite beside the mark —

"As he, Mr Bourne, definitely rejected the authority of the Leaders and Local Preachers Meeting they not unnaturally or ungraciously felt driven to disown all responsibility for his acts *

This view, we say, is irrelevant—it does not fit the facts—unless the question of the rightness or wrongness of the pre-occupation which kept Hugh Bourne from his class were duly considered and adjudicated upon. Doubtless this was the course pursued, and the decision reached was adverse, as we know. This being so, the "natural" and "gracious" course, surely, would have been to make H B's "irregularities," and Revivalistic methods, and especially his persistence in pushing camp meetings, the gravamen of the charge against him and, if sustained, the ground of the disciplinary measures taken. This, we admit (thus agreeing with Dr Gregory, who wrote according to the evidence available at the time) would have been the natural and logical sequence of the clash between Conference and Camp Meetings which was only part of the bigger clash between primitive and modern Methodism. That this was the real, though not the alleged ground of Hugh Bourne's expulsion may be regarded as confirmed by the President of the Quarterly Meeting himself. Soon after his expulsion Hugh Bourne met Mr J Riles in the street, and on inquiring of him the reason of that expulsion was told "that he had a tendency to set up other than the ordinary worship."

The best feature of this unhappy episode was the way the victim bore it. On the evening of this fateful day he called upon W Clowes, and the two attended a meeting of the Tract Mission. But it was not from Clowes' lips he learned the news of his expulsion. Clowes was freshly arrived from the Quarterly Meeting, and one might reasonably conclude the treatment his friend had received would be the thought uppermost in his mind and the one topic of conversation. His silence is significant, and makes us wonder as to its cause. Was the subject too painful to broach? If so, we get a glimpse of one of the small tragedies of life. It is not always that "out of the fulness of the heart the mouth speaketh." Next day, when the news reached him that he had been put out of the Methodist Society, Bourne simply said, "The Lord's will be done," and was thankful that he had been forewarned and prepared for the blow. He was neither disconsolate nor angry, fomented no division, paid his arrears of class money, and went on with his work as though nothing had happened.

CHAPTER III.

RAMSOR FOURTH CAMP MEETING AND AFTER.

CLOWES, A METHODIST LOCAL PREACHER.

FROM the time of the Conference declaration against camp meetings to September 4th, 1809—the date of the first Ramsor Camp Meeting—the story of Clowes' life belongs to Burslem Methodism, and therefore need not be told here in detail. After the official action taken in 1807 he could not have been a Methodist and an out-and-out Camp Meetinger without compromising himself, and it is clear to us that as yet he was not prepared to incur the penalty of exclusion from the society he loved. Still, even during this period of fifteen months, he has more than an incidental connection with this narrative. Clowes kept up his friendship with various members of the Camp Meeting brotherhood—notably with Hugh Bourne, with whom he had frequent intercourse. Often Bourne looked in upon his friend, and long and profitable talks ensued. Clowes notes it as an oddity in his visitor that he would invariably, as though on principle, decline all hospitality; he would neither bite nor sup, nor, however late the hour might be, would he accept the offer of bed or "squab," but insist upon returning to his own home at Bemersley. At such times the staple of their talk was the deep things of God. Theirs was no caucus, no hole-and-corner meeting. They did not forgather to canvass church affairs, but to seek after mutual edification. Nor, do we find from Hugh Bourne's *Journals*, that in the give and take of their nocturnal intercourse it was Bourne who was principally the giver and Clowes the receiver; that to the elder disciple naturally fell the rôle of teacher, inspirer, leader, while the younger was quite content to sit at his feet. It were a mistake so to conclude; for the records show that often the younger disciple left his impress on the elder. Thus early did Clowes' atmosphere tell. The animation and readiness of his speech, coupled with the fact of his rich and growing experience, gave him, almost from the beginning, an ascendency over colder and less vocal natures.

Sometimes, too, Hugh Bourne would lead Clowes' class, and together they made several excursions into Lancashire and Cheshire. But although all this betokens considerable sympathy with the aims and methods of the Camp Meeting Methodists, yet this sympathy and his friendship and company-keeping with Bourne and others like-minded were without prejudice to his standing and expectations as a Methodist. His name did not stand on any of their written plans—drawn up for the sake of convenience—as did the names of Thomas Cotton and James Nixon. It is reasonable to conclude that to Clowes the idea of the Church as an organisation making claims and conferring privileges appealed more strongly than it did to Bourne. To the latter the Church was more an ideal thing, and even the Methodism to which he had expressed himself as vehemently attached was also an ideal. It was Methodism as it had been and as it ought to be again, rather than the particular Methodism of the Burslem Circuit or of the Annual Conference that attracted Hugh Bourne. There are certain entries in his *Journals* bearing out these views. He records a conversation he had with James Nixon soon after his expulsion:—

"*Friday, July 8th,* 1808.— I went to Tunstall. J. Nixon discoursed with me about being out of the Society. I said, I ought to have had an opportunity to have answered for myself. He said, I should endeavour to come in again. I said, I had left it to the Lord. He said, *I should have more privileges.* I said, as it was I should have the privilege of doing the Lord's will. He said, if I did that I should be a happy man; nevertheless, he thought I ought to talk with —— about it, to prevent him acting hastily another time. We then talked of the deep things of religion."

RAMSOR COMMON.
The Site of the First Camp Meeting.

If James Nixon thought that Hugh Bourne missed many privileges by being outside the Methodist pale and hence should endeavour to get inside once more, we may fairly infer that William Clowes would still more decidedly be of this opinion; for hitherto his adhesion to camp meetings had not been so close and continuous as Nixon's. This attachment to the Old Methodist Society was strong, and he occasionally gave it as his opinion that H. B. would have more privileges, and might be more useful if he were in the Old Society. But in this W. Clowes soon found cause to change his opinion."

It is just here, no doubt, we find the explanation of the fact that after Mow Cop second camp meeting W. Clowes was not present at another for a period of fifteen months; or to put it in another way—out of seventeen camp meetings held from May 31st, 1807, until the establishment of Primitive Methodism in 1811 Clowes was present at five only. There is nothing specially puzzling in the fact as thus stated if we remember that Clowes' "time" as a founder of Primitive Methodism "was not yet come." He was a convinced and ardent Methodist, who, at the same time, believed in camp meetings. His belief went a long way. It cemented rather than dissolved the friendship he had formed with the promoters of the movement. It emboldened him to speak up in defence of camp meetings when he heard their utility called in question or the motives of their promoters impugned. The Conference pronouncement had made a difference; but it neither suppressed his convictions nor tied his tongue, though for a time it did avail to keep him from actively participating in what was disallowed, since participation would have meant severance from the Church he loved. This we take to be the meaning of Clowes' statement in regard to the second camp meeting on Mow:—

"I laboured but little at this meeting, but I felt equally interested in its success and defended it with all my might against its opponents."

This period of fifteen months in which William Clowes held aloof from camp meetings, while at the same time he held fellowship with camp meetingers, forms a short chapter this history cannot afford to omit. It bears witness to the fact that Clowes, at any rate, is not chargeable with holding low views of the Church or lightly esteeming its privileges. If after this interval of suspense and struggle during which he, too, felt the pressure of the Conference pronouncement, Clowes did after all put to hazard what was so dear to him and whole-heartedly throw himself into the new movement, it is a valuable tribute to the character and urgency of the movement itself; while at the same time it furnishes a guarantee that when the time shall come for the movement to organise itself into a denomination, the claims of the Church as against unchecked individualism will be safeguarded. The union of the Clowesites and Camp Meeting Methodists was to form an amalgam from which neither the Tunstall nor the Bemersley ingredient could be spared.

W. Clowes has left it in writing that he was present at all the Ramsor Camp Meetings, the first of the series being held on September 4th, 1809. The second held five weeks afterwards, is noteworthy to us because at it Clowes preached from his first text. Exhortations indeed, he had been in the habit of giving—powerful, effective and acceptable to the people, like the one delivered at Mow Cop first camp meeting—but, still from a homiletic point of view these were nothing more than exhortations, because wanting the formality of a previously-announced text and essentially hortatory in character, consisting of appeals based on the elemental evangelic facts and declarations of Scripture, as confirmed by personal experience. Perhaps this form of public address best suited Clowes' modest estimate of the range within which his own powers as yet could safely and efficiently work, while he deemed it more in keeping with his standing — that of a recognised exhorter who had not yet attained to the dignity of the plan. After considerable research the facts are still obscure. Probably usage has changed, and the exhorter and local preacher of that time might be separated by a sharper line than now obtains. But, however this may have been, it is certain that Clowes had received some kind of official authorisation to speak in public. Either he had a "note to accompany" an accredited local preacher, or he was empowered to fill a vacancy that might occur, or to conduct cottage services. It is equally certain that when at Ramsor Moor Camp

RAMSOR COMMON.
Ramsor Second Camp Meeting. New Chapel in background.

Meeting Clowes ventured to announce as his text, "He that hath the Son hath life," he had at the time no part whatever in what some one has called "the planetary heavens." He did not figure there even as a modest asterisk, much less had he the honour of having his name, or the initials of his name, emblazoned thereon. So it was something of an event when on October 9th, 1809, the Methodist class-leader and exhorter preached his first sermon. He did so well, we are told, that "the people encouraged him to go forward." Soon after this—precisely how soon we know not[*]—he was required to

* W. Garner, in his "Life of Clowes," gives October 9th as the date of the trial sermon. But that is, of course, an error, as October 9th was the date of the Ramsor Camp Meeting. "Very shortly after ... called upon to preach a trial sermon

preach his trial-sermon at Tunstall before the superintendent of the Burslem Circuit. At the close of the service the Rev. Jonathan Edmondson observed:—"You have done very well; but you will kill yourself." The non-predictive part of this sentence had weight as coming from one who in the pulpit was said to be "judicious, pithy, and practical," and who was the author of sermons once widely known.

It has often been noted as singular that Clowes' trial sermon, the indispensable step to plan-promotion, should have followed hot-foot on his active participation in the Ramsor Camp Meeting. It *is* singular, and remains so after all attempts at explanation. Assuming—what it seems unreasonable not to assume—that at the time of the trial sermon the superintendent was privy to Clowes' proceedings at Ramsor, we cannot but recall how different was the treatment meted out to Hugh Bourne after Norton Camp Meeting. He certainly was not rewarded as Clowes was by being invited to "go up higher." In his case the utmost that can be said is that "sentence" against what was regarded as "an evil work was not executed speedily." The fact is—and herein lies the best available and most concise explanation of the diverse treatment of the two men, and of much besides—Clowes was *persona grata* to the authorities of the Burslem Circuit and Bourne was not. The former, as we have seen, was attached, not only outwardly, but by true inward affection, to Methodism in the concrete; and up to this time the attachment was mutual. He stood well with both ministers and people, and was in a measure popular and successful. And yet, so far as the available evidence goes, the promotion which should have followed the trial sermon was no great one, and was tardily entered upon. We have, in facsimile, a Methodist Plan of the Burslem Circuit for the quarter August 6th—October 29th, 1809, on which after the names of the preachers follows the note:—

REV. JONATHAN EDMONDSON.

"N.B.—W. Clowes, Wedgwood, W. E. to be employed occasionally."*

Of course, being without a figure, no appointments are given to Clowes on this plan. More than this: Herod, while evidently unacquainted with this plan, states that identically the same note stands on the plan for the succeeding quarter, November 5th, 1809—January 28th, 1810. If it be unreasonable to suppose that after having had his figure with appointments given him, W. Clowes was afterwards reduced to the third part of an N.B., we are shut up to the conclusion that if W. C. ever were a local preacher on "full plan," it could only have been for two quarters, February 4th—July 29th, 1810, and before the plan for the second quarter had been worked out Clowes' plan was taken from him. The fact thus elicited is startling, but the evidence for it is strong. Was Clowes' complicity in Ramsor Camp Meeting after all not known when he preached his trial sermon, and does the evidence point to the fact that the authorities were dubious about him, and yet reluctant to take more drastic measures?

* Given by Thomas Church—Popular Sketches of Primitive Methodism, 1850, p. 34.

Omitting the third Ramsor Camp Meeting, May 21st, 1809, we come to the crucial fourth one of June 3rd, 1810. Prior to this meeting, there would seem to have been a conflict going on in Clowes' mind as to whether he should take an active part in it or not. Various considerations and opposing motives presented themselves. He wanted to attend, but, again——in short his mind lay balanced between "yea" and "nay" until, harassed by the suspense and anxious to end it, he made known his perplexities to Hugh Bourne and James Crawfoot. The latter had, since November, 1809, been employed as an itinerant evangelist, but, though he had gifts of no ordinary kind, they were not of the camp meeting order, and hence he seldom took part in such services. Ramsor fourth camp meeting, however, was to be an exception. Thus taken into counsel, Hugh Bourne "thought it would be better for Clowes not to attend." There is no sign here of any wish to compromise his friend with the authorities, and detach him from old Methodism. On the contrary, he recognised the delicacy of W. Clowes' position and sympathised with it. But when the appeal was made to Crawfoot, the "old man of the Forest" was ready with an answer that at once made the balance dip. Said he, "'Tis better to obey God than man." After this conference, his doubts being resolved and his mind made up, Clowes went with his friends to the camp meeting, which, on various grounds, is of note in our history. It was the first held after the refusal of the Burslem Circuit to take over the Stanley Society of ten members, and, therefore, was the first camp meeting held by the Camp Meeting Methodists after they became a distinct community. Then, too, it was the only camp meeting at which Crawfoot and the popular Mrs. Dunnell were present together. If, apart from Hugh Bourne, Crawfoot was the first itinerant preacher of the camp meeting community, Mrs. Dunnell cannot well be denied the distinction of having been its first female preacher. She wrought some good, but in the end the mischief and trouble she wrought outweighed the good, and she was not numbered amongst the first Primitive Methodists. To a woman in every way worthier than Mrs. Dunnell, was reserved the honour of being file-leader of the goodly array of female travelling preachers. We anticipate a little, but let it be noted here that Sarah Kirkland, of Mercaston, afterwards known as Mrs. Harrison, was, as Bourne tells us, "the first female taken out to labour as a travelling preacher in the Primitive Methodist Connexion. She travelled several years, and was the means of raising the character of female travelling preachers very high."

Ramsor and its neighbourhood, including Wootton-under-Weaver, Lexhead, Kingsley, and Farley, was from a very early date a favourite and fruitful field of missionary labour, at first as auxiliary to Wesleyan Methodism, and then, after the Stanley episode, conducted on independent lines. Here and hereabout were the substantial homes of several families, whose hospitality was freely ... ... by the missionaries as repeated references

DAVID BUXTON.

in the *Journals* of Bourne and Clowes serve to show. We are continually meeting with the names of the Heatons of Farley, the Sergeants of Kingsley, the Buxtons, the Critchelows, the Dreacotts, the Salts of Wootton, and, above all, the Brothers Horobin.

It was Francis Horobin who, on Hugh Bourne's first visit to Ramsor in May, 1808, pointed out half a dozen spiritually destitute villages, and promised help— a promise which he fully honoured. Of James Horobin, Bourne writes :—*November 24th,* 1810. "This man and his wife have been, and are abundantly kind to me and the cause of God. Oh, may God reward them ;" and of the Buxtons, in the same month— "At Wootton, I felt a love to David Buxton almost beyond measure. Well, in heaven our love will be perfect."

WOOTTON PARK FARM.
The Home of David Buxton.

Who Joseph Salt was and what his relation to the Wootton Society have faithfully been put down for us by H. Bourne in his *Journals* under date September 18th, 1808 :—

"Mr. Joseph Salt, a respectable farmer, of Wootton, was fully brought to God under Thomas Cotton's ministry. Before this, Mr. Salt had been awakened by a pious young female. [Why this periphrase, O Venerable Founder? Was not the "pious young female" one Mrs. Samuel Evans, better known as "Dinah Morris"?] Our Wootton people met in the Lexhead and Ramsor class ; but when it was judged proper to have a class at Wootton, Mr. J. Salt was made leader, and Mrs. Salt was a mother in Israel."

If Mrs. Salt was a mother in Israel, Elizabeth Salt seems to have been a fair daughter of Zion, of whom there were a good many hereabouts, as the *Journals* testify. Writing just after the September, 1811, plan was "out," and like a general casting about in his mind to see how many effective troops he could bring into the field, Bourne writes:—

"There are seventeen preachers on this plan, and three at Ramsor. One is raised up at Rocester, and two will shortly be raised up at Cannock Wood. And I suppose the Lord will raise up some women— Hannah Heaton, Dorothy Buxton, Sarah Scott, and Sarah Mace. Elizabeth Salt at Wootton bids fair to be useful. So there are nearly thirty in view, as Samuel Simcock has begun."

Clowes, who was in these parts in 1810, bears a similar testimony to the heads of these house-churches.

JOSEPH SALT.

"We did not limit the preaching to one place, but preached from house to house. We found the houses of Brother Crichley (Critchelow) and Brother Buxton very convenient; in the house of the latter five souls were converted to God. In this house I held a lovefeast, which began at eleven o'clock in the forenoon, being most suitable for the country people residing here. No sooner did the meeting commence than tears and bursts of joy took place throughout the lovefeast; great freedom was experienced in speaking of the glorious things pertaining to the Kingdom, and several, in giving expression to their religious feelings, declared that God had made me, His unworthy servant, an honoured instrument in His hands in the salvation of their souls. At the termination of the meeting, Francis Dricott (Dreacott),* a local preacher, prayed that the Lord would keep me humble, and save me from thinking too highly of myself. I felt thankful for the sentiment of the prayer, and responded to it from my heart, Amen and Amen. I was aware that 'God resisteth the proud, but giveth grace to the humble,' and that the devil's object is to inflate the hearts of preachers of the gospel with spiritual pride. Alas! how many have been thus deceived, and have said to their fellow-labourers: 'Stand thou by; I am holier than thou.'" (Clowes' *Journals*, 100-1).

GEORGE CRITCHELOW.

For long the Sunday services were held alternately at Lexhead, the home of the Horobins, and at Wootton Park Farm, the home of the Buxtons, and on the death of David Buxton were transferred to George Critchelow's home, where they were

---

* Proper names are frequently mis-spelled in Clowes' *Journals*. He evidently had few documents to . . . The form Dracott also occurs.

LEXHEAD FARM.
The Home of James Horobin.

continued until the new chapel was built, while the Ramsor week-evening services were held at the house of James Horobin up to the time of his death some forty years ago. Ramsor Circuit has had a long and creditable history. Though Cheadle and part of Leek Circuits have been carved out of it, it is still some twenty-five miles long and sixteen wide. Singular to say, through the greater part of its long history the village which gives its name to this historic circuit, was without its chapel; but the difficulties in the way of the accomplishment of this have at last been surmounted and now a neat chapel, opened 1890, ornaments the village.

As of old the Word of the Lord sounded forth from Thessalonica, so from Ramsor by means of this camp meeting, still further advances were made. Before the same month of June was over both Bourne and Clowes, with Mrs. Dunnell, under the direction of the former, were labouring at Boylestone, Rodsley, and Hollington in Derbyshire, where societies were formed with the prospect of still further extension. Ramsor, too, was one of the links in "the chain of circumstances" which led Hugh Bourne to pay a visit to Wyrley Bank and Cannock Wood in South Staffordshire. In response to a pressing invitation from Mr. David Buxton, a native of Stanton near Ramsor, Hugh Bourne walked thirty-four miles through the rain to Wyrley Bank, arriving there on July 27th, 1810. It was during this evangelistic tour that Bourne met with John Benton,

RAMSOR CHAPEL.

who was afterwards for several years a successful pioneer missionary. Bourne calls him "an extraordinary man," and he was such if for no other reason than that his sincere piety and zeal were able to triumph over all the disadvantages of illiteracy and natural defects. He had "little grammar and not much command of language," and hence he did not escape reproach and scoffs from both professors and profane. Said a local preacher to him on........ after....... him try to preach at Cannock Common :—" You are bringing a scandal on the cause of Christ, you have had no learning, you do not understand grammar." Benton's most effective answer was given some time after. He was preaching on a Good Friday afternoon from the text, "It is finished." The room was crowded with colliers, and he had got but half-way through his discourse when a large part of the congregation became strangely affected :—

> "Some groaned, others shrieked; some fell from their seats; and the whole assembly was thrown into consternation: he therefore closed the Bible, and went from his stand to pray for mourners; and when passing down among the people he saw his friend, the local preacher, standing and looking on with amazement Said Benton to him, 'This is grammar!'"

WYRLEY BANK.
Where Clowes, Turner, and Steele stood and missioned in 1813. This place is now a considerable village and better known as Cheslyn Hay.

The reply that came was almost identical in form with that of the astonished witnesses of Christ's wonder-working power: "We never saw it in this fashion." Now, though Benton, with his "little grammar and not much command of language," was far from being an Apollos, he was like him in that he needed fuller spiritual instruction. He could and did rouse the sinner; but he was at a loss what to do with him when he was roused. He could not complete the work he had so well begun. He had still to learn the secret: how to impart true evangelical peace. So Bourne conversed much with him on such high themes. Together they went to Essington Wood to meet a number of inquirers whom Benton had gathered into a kind of class. Bourne "spoke to the people and the Lord made bare His arm; six souls were immediately set at liberty, and Benton entered fully into the knowledge of a present salvation. His usefulness after this was greater than it had been before, and it kept increasing." Induced by what he heard, Benton resolved to attend the fifth Ramsor Camp Meeting to be held on May 26th, 1811. His experience there gave the finishing-touches to his spiritual education, and completed his equipment. Says he:—"At this meeting I received such a baptism of the Holy Spirit as I never experienced before, and I felt from this day it was my duty to be given up to the work of the ministry." So for a time we leave Wyrley Bank and Cannock Wood, where already can be discerned the germ of Darlaston Circuit in the Black Country; and we leave John Benton saying, "Here am I, send me," and ready to take the place of James Crawfoot soon to be vacant by his retirement.

But to return to Ramsor fourth camp meeting, and what we owe to it. Perhaps its chief indirect result was that it gave William Clowes to the movement. Nor must we, in any balancing of accounts as between James Crawfoot and the Primitive Methodist Connexion, omit to place as a considerable item on the credit side, the fact that but for him William Clowes could not well have been what he now must be—a conspicuous figure in this history. Clowes' expulsion was the direct, swift, retributive result of his share in that day's proceedings; and it was the brave, sharp, knot-cutting words of Crawfoot that decided his action. Let the credit item be allowed.

CHAPTER IV.

CLOWES' EXPULSION.

AT the June, 1810, Quarterly Meeting of the Burslem Circuit William Clowes' plan was withheld. That is the bare simple fact, soon told—a fact we need not labour, since no one disputes it or its cause. We have no circumstantial account of that Board's proceedings except the short account given by Clowes himself, which, on account of its importance, we will reproduce here, as well as one or two items from Bourne's *Journals* which suggest that it was a time of confusion and trial. These incidental allusions will prepare us for the fuller narrative:—

"*June 18th.*—I stopped with Clowes all night. He has been at Stoke-upon-Trent, and the Lord has made him very useful there; but the preachers at Burslem are raising up war against him.

"*July 8th.*—There is much confusion at Burslem. Mr. E—— rails hard, and many of the local preachers.

"*Wednesday 11th.*—I worked at home, and in the evening went to see Clowes. He is going on well, but they have put him out of the plan, and are seeking occasion against him. Nevertheless, he preached at Stoke Chapel last Sunday night. O Lord, bless him.

"*July 16th.*—Clowes came to our house, and I spent some time with him, and went with him to Kidsgrove, where he preached from Malachi iii. 6. I stopped with him at Tunstall all night. The local preachers are ashamed of their conduct towards Clowes in putting him out of the plan. O Lord, stand by him and strengthen him, through Jesus Christ our Lord, Amen."

And now for the fuller account given by Clowes in his *Journals*:—

"About this time, much uneasiness began to show itself among certain parties in the Burslem Circuit on account of the camp meetings, and my attending them. Accordingly, in the June quarter of 1810, my name was omitted on the preachers' plan. This proceeding excited a strong ferment throughout the country, especially amongst religious persons of different denominations, who in strong terms expressed their disapprobation of the preachers in carrying a measure of such an unconstitutional and intolerant character; hence, invitations from all parts of the country flowed in upon me, soliciting me to preach, and offering me every encouragement in the name of the Lord. The travelling preachers in the Methodist New Connexion urged me to preach for them. I preached once in their chapel, and one soul was set at liberty. One of the official persons invited me to join their body; but I observed I could do nothing as yet, but wait to lay my case fully before the Lord, for Him to direct me in my providential way."

But this was not the end; only the beginning. More stringent measures were to follow. Possibly, had W. Clowes forsworn his old camp meeting companions and become mute as a Trappist monk, instead of exhorting whenever and wherever he could during the next three months, he might have been forgiven and reinstated. It is much more likely, however, that the inevitable happened, that what we have long foreseen would take place, did take place, that the authorities deemed that the time had come to purge the Church of the virus of Revivalism before the whole body should be infected with the distemper, and now that a change of preachers had taken place and a strict disciplinarian was at the head of affairs, the time was thought opportune for effecting the purgation. It was this wider question, we will charitably

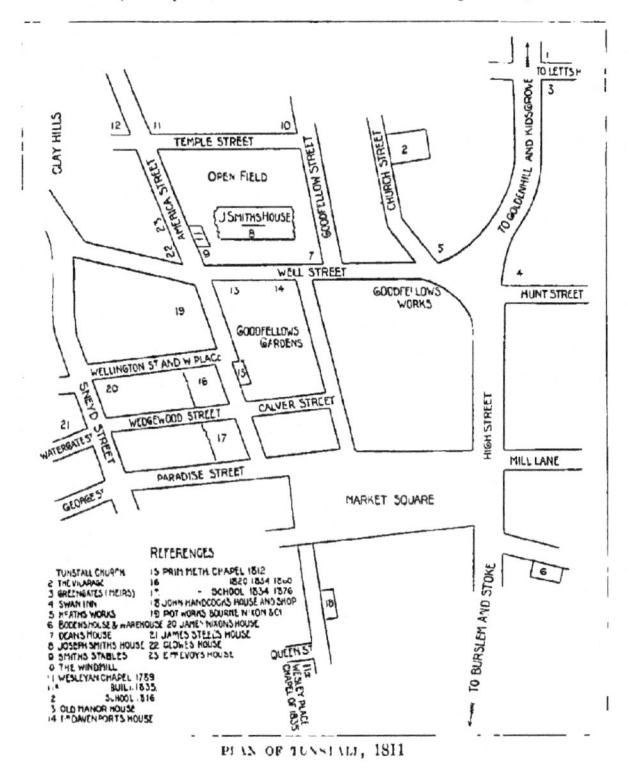

PLAN OF TUNSTALL, 1811

continue to believe, that was really at the bottom of the Tunstall troubles and not the single question of camp meetings. To our founders, Primitive Methodism meant more than camp meetings and to those who exercised discipline on our founders, camp meetings were only the last most pronounced symptom of that Revivalism, the very name of which was as distasteful to many at the beginning of the nineteenth century as the word Enthusiasm had been to the opponents of the evangelical revival in the century p[revious] ... our view, and that view is confirmed by the local Methodist historian who lived on the spot through all these stirring times, and in 1843 gave his version of the occurrences when old age should, one supposes, have brought something of the philosophic mind. This writer makes no reference to camp meetings, but he does say:—

"It was very evident their purpose was to form a party upon what they called the simplicity and uniformity of primitive Methodism; they maintained that Methodism had lost its original character, and its members were conforming to the world in spirit, manners, dress," etc.

We do not know that any serious exception need be taken to this way of stating the case. If the recovery of "the simplicity and uniformity of primitive Methodism" were indeed the prime aim of our founders, then they cherished no unworthy purpose. Nor was their purpose a futile one though worthy, for all reformations and revolutions have gone the way they took—by the way of the recovery of the past. Has not John Morley somewhere noted—"Simplicity is the key-word to every revolution with a moral core"? That generalisation the history of both Wesleyan Methodism and Primitive Methodism illustrates. These remarks, while they may have kept us from hearing the conclusion of Clowes' narrative of his "unchurching," may perhaps serve to remind us of the larger meanings and issues involved. Clowes proceeds:—

"At the September visitation my quarterly ticket as a member of Society was withheld. When Mr. Aikenhead, the travelling preacher, came to Kidsgrove to preach and renew the tickets, as the leader of the class I gave him my class-paper to call over the names as usual; but in calling over the names he passed by my name, which stood first on the paper, and called over the rest in order. In speaking to the people, he rebuked them for their liveliness in their way of worshipping and praising God; and remarked, he supposed they acted as they had been taught. The night following, the same preacher, who was in a great measure a stranger, having but recently come into the circuit, preached in Tunstall and afterwards called a leaders' meeting. I stopped at the meeting in my official character, and ventured to inquire of it what I had done amiss that my ticket had been withheld by the preacher, and my name left off the preachers' plan: for no charge had been officially brought against me. I therefore

REV. JOHN AIKENHEAD.
("The strict disciplinarian.")

wished to know the reason of such singular proceedings. I was then told my name was left off the plan because I attended camp meetings, contrary to the Methodist discipline, and that I could not be a preacher or leader amongst them unless I promised not to attend such meetings any more. I told the members of the meeting that I would promise to attend every appointment on the plan which should be put down for me, and to attend all the means of grace and ordinances of the Church; but to promise not to attend any more camp meetings, that I could not conscientiously do, for God had greatly blessed me in these meetings, which were calculated for great usefulness, and my motive for assisting in them was simply to glorify God, and bring sinners to the knowledge of the truth as it is in Jesus. I was then told that I was no longer with them; that the matter was settled. I therefore immediately delivered up my class-papers to the meeting, and became unchurched.

> 'Of my Eden dispossessed,
> The world was all before me where to choose
> My place of rest, and Providence my guide.'"

THE CLOWESITES.

The expulsion of Clowes meant virtually the withdrawal of many more. Attraction is a fact in psychology as well as in physics. Some men can never move alone; whatever their fortunes may be they draw others along with them. Clowes was one of such men. "Of his Eden dispossessed" he could not leave its gates unattended. Clowes was the leader of two classes—one at Kidsgrove, the other at Tunstall. To some of his members he was as a "father in the Gospel," while to all he had been a faithful instructor and guide. During the following week a goodly number of these waited upon him at his house. Distressed at what had happened, they expressed their unwillingness that the ties binding them together should be severed, and pleaded that he should still continue to be their leader. Though touched by this proof of their attachment, he pointed out to them that he had now no right in them or claim upon them, being as one ecclesiastically dead, and he besought them to choose other leaders, and to leave him to the watchful care of God. They listened, as Ruth listened to Naomi, and like her they remained unconvinced and unpersuaded, meeting each argument and entreaty with her—"Whither thou goest, we will go: where thou lodgest, we will lodge."

WILLIAM CLOWES.
From an Oil Painting in the possession of Mrs. W. Norman of Hull.

And a lodge—a fold where the little flock of thirty or forty might be sheltered and tended was ready to hand. How this had come about must now be told, and the more so, as the story links on to Norton Camp Meeting, and shows how one of the unexpected results of that gathering was to provide a home—"an asylum where the camp meeting fathers and revivalists could worship God in their own way."* Being at Tunstall on the Saturday, ready to take part in the Norton Camp Meeting, Mrs. Dunnell received a flattering invitation to take the appointments of the Superintendent in the Wesleyan Chapel, thus allowing herself to be intercepted, as it

Walford Memoirs of Hugh Bourne.

were, *en route*. True, the Conference was known to be just as much against female preaching as it was against camp meetings, but this time that difficulty was got over. The news that Mrs. Dunnell had failed him was brought to Hugh Bourne at six o'clock on the Sunday morning by E. McEvoy, and the news did not tend to raise his spirits for the day. Later on in the same year, Mrs. Dunnell was again at Tunstall, quite ready to take the pulpit once more as was desired by some, but this time she found it shut against her; for had not the Conference strong views on the subject of female-preaching? This exclusion of Mrs. Dunnell from the Tunstall pulpit gave great offence to those whom she had captivated. Among these non-contents were Mr. Joseph Smith and James Steele. The former was an old gentleman of eccentric habits, who owned considerable property in Tunstall. He had been bred a Methodist, and for twenty years or more had preached much in various parts of Cheshire and North Staffordshire; but on settling down in Tunstall his zeal had lost its fervency. Yet it was in the

TUNSTALL WESLEYAN CHAPEL, 1789.

dining-room of his house that the first Methodist services in Tunstall were held, and his family gave the site for the new chapel, concerning which Wesley wrote, April 29th, 1790:—"At nine I preached in the new chapel at Tunstall; the most elegant I have seen since I left Bath." Now Mr. Smith was in such high dudgeon at the treatment of Mrs. Dunnell that he determined to provide a place for preaching in his own house. Hugh Bourne, on the condition, which he pressed, that no class or separate society should be established, fell in with the proposal and procured a licence from the Bishop's court at Lichfield. So in Mr. Smith's kitchen preaching services, "accompanied by extended praying services," had been held on a Friday evening since March, 1808. The plan for these services was drawn up, we are told, by Hugh Bourne; yet, though R. Bayley, Thomas Knight, J. Bourne, J. Steele, and others, besides J. Crawfoot and Mrs. Dunnell, took their turn at preaching here, strange to say neither Bourne nor W. Clowes had yet officiated. The fact is, whether through his own motion, or as Clowes asserts, at the instigation of others, the old gentleman, although he liked Clowes personally, would not suffer him to preach on his premises. He might sing and pray, but the line was drawn at preaching; and because his friend was excluded, Hugh Bourne would not plan himself, nor did he preach in the kitchen until November, 1810, when the embargo had been removed. Mr. Smith was, we have said, eccentric, and he was somewhat autocratic in his whims. He promulged a sort of Public Worship

JOSEPH SMITH'S HOUSE, TUNSTALL.
The Kitchen of the House was Licensed for Preaching, 1808.

Regulation Act on a small scale, for the due regulation of the prayer meetings carried on in his kitchen, and what was more, he took care to be present himself to see that the regulations were duly enforced. Loud utterance was prohibited; the expressions "my God" and "send fire" interdicted; and no suppliant was to repeat any petition more than thrice, whether his petition had been answered or not. As a material help towards decorum, a chest of drawers was put on castors, supplied with velvet-covered book-board and swing brass candlestick, and thus ingeniously converted into a movable pulpit. Each one who gave out hymn or engaged in prayer was required to take his place behind the sacred desk. Such was the ideal, but, alas! like many other ideals it was not fated to be reached. The "camp-meeting fathers" wanted to worship God in their own way, and that way was not Mr. Smith's. On the first evening the new regulations were to come into force, James Nixon and W. Clowes were both in turn called upon to conform. The former stood up and remonstrated, while Clowes, after striking up a hymn, fell on his knees and repeated

FIRST PULPIT, TUNSTALL.

some twenty ... tipped, until ' all rose into the faith; a grand shout of glory followed, and the victory was declared for the faithful." Amid this extraordinary scene the old gentleman stood mute and helpless. After this opening night the dismantled rostrum stood with its back to the wall—a piece of furniture—nothing more.

On the morrow of Clowes' expulsion Mr. Smith was greatly excited, and went about the village making known to all and sundry that 'they had put Billy off the plan, but he could outpreach them all, and he should preach in his kitchen.' —

"And so it was; for Mr. Smith's kitchen became our preaching-place till the day of his death, and many will have to bless God to all eternity that it became, on many an occasion now well remembered, 'The house of God, and the gate of heaven.'" (Clowes' *Journals*, p. 86.) "Mr. Smith now invited William Clowes to preach at his house, and went about to publish it in the neighbourhood. This was a strengthening to W. Clowes' class, as there was constant preaching at Mr. Smith's on Friday evenings; and they began to look upon it as their proper place of worship."—Bourne's *History*, 1823, p. 33.

At the time these events happened, or soon afterwards, James Nixon, Thomas Woodnorth, William Morris, and Samuel Barber cast in their lot with the little company meeting in the kitchen, ere long to be known as "Clowesites." In fulfilment of a promise made at Ramsor fourth camp meeting, Clowes visited Ramsor, and in company with Bourne and Crawfoot had a turn in Derbyshire, where Mrs. Dunnell was labouring. Clowes notes that perhaps more good was effected in these parts by house to house visitation and prayer than by public services. Many of the people seem to have been as primitive in their notions as the Lycaonians, who thought the gods had come down in the likeness of men, for it was currently reported there were two men going about the country who could convert anybody; and accordingly the services of the converters were in great demand. Returning for a while to Tunstall to see that all was well, Clowes made a somewhat extensive excursion into Lancashire. He visited the family of the Eatons at London Bridge, 'the best-ordered family he had ever seen,' also Mrs. Richardson, of Warrington, in whose conversion he and Crawfoot had been instrumental. Mrs. Richardson was a West Indian proprietress, and by the act of liberating the slaves in whom she had the right of property, she evidenced the reality of the change wrought in her. But during this mission-tour Clowes made acquaintance with persecution and discomfort as well as with pleasant interiors. Thus he tells how one morning he awoke to find his bed well sprinkled with snow which had blown in through a half-broken window. Then followed breakfast on milk and water porridge, seasoned with the reproaches of a loud-voiced virago, who taunted him with being "after nothing but his belly." No wonder he took a solitary walk after breakfast, and had a sharp attack of home-sickness! But neither Lancashire nor even Derbyshire was his allotted sphere of labour—that lay nearer his home, to which he returned to find a serious proposal awaiting him. This was (December 1810) that he should give himself wholly to the work of a home missionary. At this time there was depression in the potting industry, so that Clowes was working little more than half-time; yet in the three or four and a half days which he figured on he could still earn £1 2s., and trade was "looking up," so that full work in the near future might reasonably be anticipated. Such were his circumstances, when James Nixon and Thomas Woodnorth, Clowes' brother-in-law, proposed that each should give him five shillings per week that he might be at liberty to open up fresh places and look after those already visited. After much fasting and prayer, with the full acquiescence of his wife—whose share in the self-denying arrangement should not be forgotten—Clowes agreed to the proposal. To the end he felt towards these two as Moses may be supposed to have felt towards Aaron and Hur when he remembered how they had held up his hands at Rephidim. He has even recorded his opinion that these two brethren should be enrolled amongst the founders of the Connexion on the ground of their self-denying liberality. And certainly, as soon as the distinction between arch-founders and founders is admitted, then James Nixon and Thomas Woodnorth may fairly claim the right to inclusion among the latter.

In regard to the time of which we are now writing—the beginning of 1811—two facts must be kept quite clear and borne in mind, viz. (1), that the Society, with its headquarters in Mr. Smith's kitchen, was separate and distinct not only from the Wesleyans, but also from any other organisation; and (2) that Clowes, as a paid home missionary, with this kitchen-church as his base of operations, and with the friends already named as his helpers, missioned and formed societies at several places chiefly in Staffordshire, so that the Clowesites soon had what might be called a circuit, with Tunstall as its head.

The Expulsion of James Steele.

Meanwhile, they were not, ecclesiastically, "the piping times of peace" at Tunstall. Sword was handled as well as trowel. There was "heavy war," says H. B., writing in January. Feeling ran high, and the village—for at this time it was nothing more—was much moved and divided in opinion. It looks almost as if rage had got the better of discretion and was striking out wildly when, on April 16th, it deposed James Steele. It was no light matter to unchurch such a man, and the needs-be for resorting to that extreme act of discipline should surely have been well considered beforehand. Abundant evidence is forthcoming to show that James Steele was no ordinary man. Local historians and Methodist annalists themselves are at one in their acknowledgment that he was a man of sense and unblemished character, and to whom considerable deference was paid. They are agreed, too, that he was a strong man, born to rule and to command, who wherever he might be, would have to be reckoned with. They insist upon regarding him as *the* man of the new movement. They know there are others who are active, but as if by one consent they fix their eyes upon him.

JAMES STEELE, TUNSTALL.

In their unacquaintance with our Church phraseology they fall back upon an unusual and even foreign word, and speak of him as having been the "directeur" of the young

JAMES STEELE'S HOUSE.

denomination until his death in 1827, and that then the reins fell, as a matter of course, into the hands of Clowes and the Bournes. Strange that the local and outside estimate of what James Steele was to the Connexion in those early days should contrast so markedly — so glaringly — with the accepted Connexional estimate of the part he played, and the place he should fill, in our history! If, locally, he has been over-estimated, Connexionally he has been under-estimated, or, to speak more accurately, the materials for estimating him not being easily available, he has been too much ignored. Though the work he did may remain, built up into the fabric of Primitive Methodism, it cannot now, after this lapse of time, be discriminated from the work of others so as to enable one to say admiringly, " He did this and that." Yet the fact remains, he was one of the early master-builders, yea, one of the founders of the Church we love.

MRS. JAMES STEELE.

At the time Mr. James Steele came under discipline he had been connected with Methodism twenty-four years, and superintendent of a large Sunday school twelve years; he was a local preacher, the leader of two large classes, a trustee and chapel steward. And the reason? What had he done or forborne to do? Well, on Good Friday W. Clowes had led a powerful lovefeast in Mr. Smith's kitchen, and the rumour ran that Mr. Steele had been present. Now, as he was the cousin of Mr. Smith and his bailiff, and in consequence of Mr. Smith's advanced age was much about the house and frequently conducted family worship, there would have been nothing very surprising

108   PRIMITIVE METHODIST CHURCH.

or criminal in his presence there on that occasion—though as a matter of fact he was not present. However, he was arraigned on the following Tuesday, not indeed on the specific charge of having been present at the lovefeast, but on the amended and more general charge of having taken part in the worship in the kitchen. A final knock-down blow was dealt on the Sunday following, when he was dismissed from his office of superintendent of the school. A trustee entered the chapel while Mr. Steele was fulfilling his duties and discharged him from his office. He quietly obeyed the

WOLSTANTON CHURCH (JAMES STEELE'S BURIAL PLACE).

injunction and withdrew, turning, as he did so, a tender and sympathetic look on those whom he was leaving. Recovering from their stupefaction, and helped probably by that parting look to comprehend what the withdrawal meant, a large number of the teachers and scholars followed their superintendent into the street. Mr. Steele had now to pass through the same experience as Mr. Clowes before him, and with the same result. H

BODEN'S HOUSE AND WARD HOUSE, TUNSTALL.

the Sunday school that they should let him go quietly and alone, fell on unwilling ears, and was not taken except by a small minority. There was a pause, a short period of seeming hesitancy, while Mr. Steele was surveying the situation and making up his mind what to do; so that for a brief while—the space of a few hours or days at most, there were the "Steelites" in addition to the "Clowesites" and Camp Meetingers. But the period of suspense did not last long; for under date *Friday, April 26th*, Bourne notes:—"I was at Tunstall. James Steele preached in great power. It was a glorious time. I spent much time in conversation . . . there is much confusion." Mr. Steele's adhesion to the nascent society gave it an element of strength and, one may even say, a prestige which was of great value. But what was gain to the new society was a serious loss to the Old Methodist Society; nor need we be surprised that hereafter efforts should be made to entice Mr. Steele back into the old fold.

The licensed kitchen, it was plain, could not be stretched to meet the present enlarged requirements; but during the week Mr. John Boden placed a large room, designed for the stowage of earthenware, at the service of the school—and the difficulty was temporarily met. Here, on the 28th April, the first services were held, and soon after it was arranged that the Sunday preaching services should also be held here, to be conducted by the brother who was planned in the kitchen on the Friday evening.

Clowes records that "he had the honour and delight, along with Richard Bayley, of opening Sunday preaching in Tunstall." Scarcely, however, had the room been used for services than steps were taken to secure a chapel. This was necessary, as Mr. Boden's room could not long be at their disposal, and was in its turn becoming too small. On May 13th a site was fixed upon; on June 11th the Bournes bought the land, and the "writings were signed;" on July 13th the chapel was opened by James Crawfoot. The size of the building, we are told, was—

"Sixteen yards long by eight wide, inside, and galleried half way. It was finished in a plain manner, the walls were not coated, and it had no ceiling. ['To my opinion a place of worship looks better without a ceiling than with one.'—*Journals*, July 20th, 1811.] It was much approved of on account of its plainness and neat appearance. In the erection of it, the house-form was chosen in preference to the chapel-form, so that, if not wanted, it would just form four houses, according to the plan on which houses are usually built at Tunstall. This cautious method was made use of because it could not be known whether the Connexion would be of any long continuance."—Bourne's *History*, 1823.

As hereafter the gentlemanly John Flesher was not above taking off his coat when Sutton Street Chapel, London, was a-building, so we can picture Hugh Bourne, James Crawfoot, and other of the fathers on June 11th "breaking ground," and the first-named later making window-cases "as the bricklayer wanted them," for this first chapel in the Connexion. This chapel owed much to the courage and generosity of the brothers, and was actually their private property until 1834, when it was legally transferred to trustees for the use of the Connexion.

TUNSTALL FIRST CHAPEL.

CHAPTER V.

THE PRIMITIVE METHODISTS, OR THE COMING TOGETHER OF THE CAMP MEETING METHODISTS AND THE CLOWESITES.

"THURSDAY, May 30, 1811, I ordered Tickets to be printed for the first time." So writes Hugh Bourne in his *Journals*. The credit of having urged and brought about the use, Methodist fashion, of class tickets mainly belongs to Ramsor Society. The objection that it would cost money was promptly met by Francis Horobin's offer to bear the expense of printing, and after the chiefs had consulted together on the important question involved, the measure was adopted. These class tickets were the sign and seal of the union of the Camp Meeting Methodists and the Clowesites. Unity amongst the different societies now drawn together there may have been before this, but this little piece of printed paper given to each member showed that now union had been consummated and a lowly denomination, with its name PRIMITIVE METHODIST already waiting for it, had unobtrusively slipped into the world. Many thought that this ticket would be the last as well as the first; that no more would ever be wanted. But, spite of misgivings, from that day to this, quarter by quarter the ticket has continued to appear.

From the typical examples given of our class tickets, the reader can judge for himself of the artistic character—or otherwise—of these vouchers of membership, and may trace the somewhat inconsiderable changes that have taken place in their form or subject-matter. Did we write the words "inconsiderable changes"? The words should be recalled or modified; for in the course of the years two innovations have been introduced—one in the nature of an addition, the other of an alteration. Not till 1829—and then probably without authority—did the ticket bear on its face the reference to the first Camp Meeting and "the first Class formed in March, 1810." This reference to Stanley and its class was unfortunate, because seeming to commit the Connexion to a particular view of its origin, which to say the least rests on a shaky foundation, and because probably pre-dating by twelve months the birth of our denomination. For the substitution of the word "Church" for "Connexion" recently made and by authority, satisfactory as the change is in itself, it is a pity the change was not made quarter of a century earlier. Perhaps we cannot well get on without the adjective "Connexional," but it was high time that "Connexion"—a word so suggestive of a mere mechanical connexion of parts such as the carpenter may achieve by help of nails or, if he be more skilful, by use of dovetail and mortise—should be displaced by a higher and more spiritual vocable.

MAY, 1811.

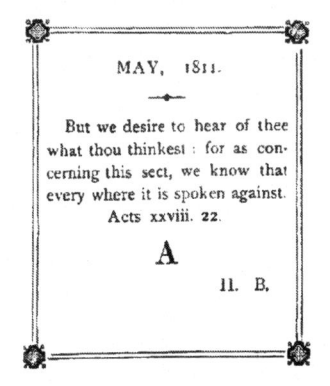

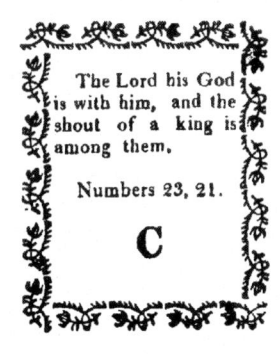

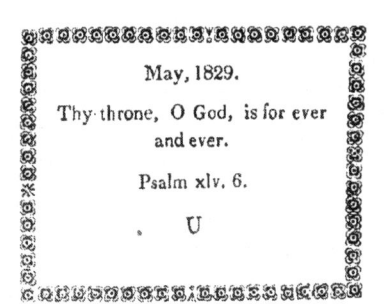

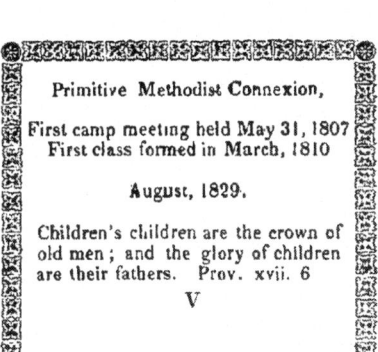

But we desire to hear of thee what thou thinkest: for as concerning this sect, we know that every where it is spoken against. Acts xxviii. 22.

A

H. B.

The Lord his God is with him, and the shout of a king is among them.

Numbers 23, 21.

C

May, 1829.

Thy throne, O God, is for ever and ever.

Psalm xlv. 6.

U

Primitive Methodist Connexion.

First camp meeting held May 31, 1807
First class formed in March, 1810

August, 1829.

Children's children are the crown of old men; and the glory of children are their fathers. Prov. xvii. 6

V

Primitive Methodist Church.

First Camp Meeting Held May 31, 1807.   First Class Formed March, 1810.

NOVEMBER, 1902.

"Be perfect, be of good comfort, be of one mind, live in peace; and the God of love and peace shall be with you."—2 COR. xiii. 11.

.... is at this date a Member of the above Church.

Minister.

	June.	July.	Aug.	Sept.	
1811	2 9 16 23 30	7 14 21 28	4 11 18 25	1 8 15	
Tunstall, 2 and 6	3 1 2 4	7 5 6 2	4 3 5	1 6 7 2 4	1. J. Crowfoot
					2. J. Steele
Bagnall 10, Badley Edge 6	13 15 7 11	5 9 11 12	5 14 15	6 13 14 7 9	3. J. Bourne
					4. H. Bourne
Stanly, 2 ; Brown Edge, 6	10 5 8 14 15	6 11 4 12	7 3 9	10 8 13 6	5. W. Clowes
					6. R. Bayley
Ramsor	3 8	12 9	4 7	3 8	7. W. Alcock
					8. T. Woodnorth
Lax Edge, 2, Gratten 4,	14 9	8 7	6 13	12 15	9. E. Macery
					10. W. Turner
					11. J. Nixon
					12. Mattison
					13. T. Alcock
					14. T. Hulme
					15. J. Marsh

When it happens a preacher does not attend, an endeavour must be made to supply.

If any other person be present whom the congregation wishes to speak, the wish of the congregation must be complied with.

Copy of the First Written Plan after the Amalgamation of the Societies, June—Sept., 1811.

[The spelling of the original as given by Peet has been preserved.]

From *Primitive Methodism:* A Sketch of the History, Doctrines, etc., of the Primitive Methodist Connexion, by Rev. James Peet, 1867.

On the authority of Clowes, we learn that a plan showing fifteen preachers and eight places was drawn up, to begin on June 2nd, 1811. But if such plan be extant it has not come in our way, but we are enabled to give what is said to be a copy of it. What others have called the first written plan, running from September 22nd to December 15th, has been secured and, notwithstanding its cryptic spelling and other obvious shortcomings is here given in facsimile. This plan shows seventeen preachers and the same number of places. By the help of this poor plan we can see what societies each section brought to the now united body. First of all we are struck with the fact that the societies of which Hugh Bourne was the acknowledged founder and head having place on the plan, are a mere salvage. They very inadequately represent the results of the evangelistic work which the Bournes and their helpers had carried on since 1801. On this plan there are really only two of Bourne's places Stanley and Ramsor. There is so little to show for the unflagging and, we might say prodigious, labour of several years that we must conclude either that the labour had proved very unproductive or that other Churches had reaped the fruit. Of course the latter alternative gives the true explanation. It is perfectly clear that if Bourne was cherishing through these years of itineracy the ambition to become a church-founder he had chosen the wrong way to gain his end. He had raised up societies at Harriseahead, Norton, Kidsgrove,

114   PRIMITIVE METHODIST CHURCH.

Tean, and Kingsley and these had been taken over by the Methodists. How much work, and at what an expenditure of time and toil, he had put into the societies of the Quaker or Independent Methodists, and the Society at Rizley that owed its

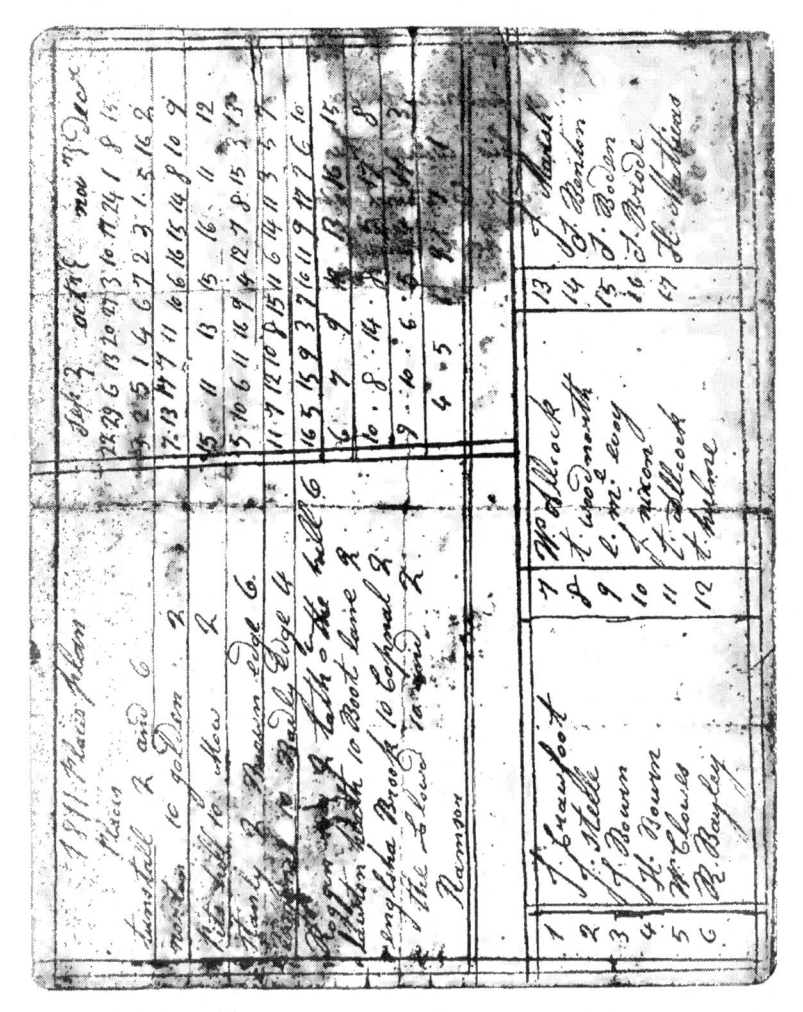

existence to Lorenzo Dow! and yet on the plan for September there is nothing to show for all this labour; though Rizley will be found on the first printed plan—that of 1812. We are prepared to learn that James Crawfoot, the missionary whom the

Bournes engaged, had instructions to counsel those who professed to have received good under his labours, to join some other Church. In fact, until the middle of 1810 the Bournes and their helpers were like men putting their wheat into other men's barns. Their labours were auxiliary to those of other Churches, in large part consisting of supplying preaching services on alternate weeks, as was the case at Ramsor from 1808 to 1810. The refusal of the Burslem Circuit to take over Stanley on the condition of a working arrangement of the kind described, its determination to have all or none, changed all this. What then precisely was the significance of this Stanley episode? The question is a difficult and disputed one and must be faced. If it could be settled once for all it would be well.

We do not enter into the question of the priority of Stanley class over that of Clowes which met in Mr. Smith's kitchen. The fact of this priority is not so assured as many think, but as, from our point of view, nothing of importance hangs on the fact of such priority we waive the discussion of dates. We may remark, then, the importance of the Stanley episode does not lie in the fact that *the members of the society had never belonged to any other Church* since Bourne distinctly says that Mr. Edmondson put it on the plan; that it had always been his intention to offer Stanley to the Wesleyans, and that he had only been anticipated in this by a forward man—one Brindley of Norton. If, then, Stanley were put on the Methodist plan for ever so short a time and then put off, technically at any rate it was a Methodist Society "cut off," as Bourne and Clowes were cut off.

Nor, again, does the importance of the Stanley episode turn on the fact that the ten members composing it were the *nucleus of the Primitive Methodist Church*. Certain rather unexpected conclusions will be found to follow from this harmless-looking and generally accepted thesis. A close examination of Bourne's autograph *Journals* day by day from March 14th, 1810 when Mrs. Dunnell preached the first sermon at Stanley, to May 22nd when the class is found meeting, discloses the fact that between these respective dates Hugh Bourne had never preached at Stanley nor organised a class. Neither does his name nor that of his brother occur in the list of ten members constituting the class of which James Slater was the leader. So that we find ourselves landed in the strange conclusion that if Stanley class were the nucleus of the Primitive Methodist Connexion then its reputed founder formed no part of it. Even if he afterwards joined the Stanley Society (of which there is no evidence), then he joined a Church already founded without him. Such is the pretty dilemma we find ourselves placed in by the acceptance of the current popular view that Stanley was the nucleus of the Primitive Methodist Connexion. The Rev. W. Garner, both in his "Jubilee of English Camp Meetings," and his "Life of the Venerable William Clowes" as also the Rev. John Morton before him, clearly appreciated this dilemma. Says the former:—

"Either the idea of the Stanley class being the base of the Primitive Methodist Connexion must be given up, or the foundership of Hugh Bourne be ignored, or at least doubted. To the former we have no objection, to the latter we cannot consent."

That is to say, Mr. Garner, being a sensible man and finding himself led straight to an absurd conclusion by the premise he started from—which in this case was the assumption that Stanley class was "the base of the Primitive Methodist Connexion"—will go back on his premise and deny it altogether rather than accept the absurdity its retention would involve. With Mr. Gaines's views we find ourselves in complete accord; but there still remains the interesting and not unimportant question—"How would Hugh Bourne have read the facts under discussion? What would have been his behaviour to the Stanley-Connexional-nucleus idea and the dilemma it creates?" Now there exists a preface to the General Minutes of 1832, remarkable on many grounds but chiefly so because it enables us to catch Hugh Bourne's point of view of the period ending in the union of 1811. We omit the first paragraph referring to the raising up of camp meetings, and the last, which glances at our history subsequent to 1812:—

> "And in His Providence the Primitive Methodist Connexion rose, undesigned of man. (It did not originate in any split or division from any other community—*footnote*.) *It was long composed of two members, Hugh and James Bourne*, who continued to expend their property and labours in promoting religion, the fruits falling into other communities, they not being willing to take further care upon them.
>
> "They visited new places; and in one of these, Standley, in Staffordshire, they, in March, 1810, raised up a class of ten members. These they attempted to join to the Wesleyans. But their design being frustrated, they, contrary to their inclinations, were necessitated to take upon them the care of a religious Connexion. This caused trial of mind. But the Lord soon manifested His will, and classes were formed at Ramsor and Wootton, and the work spread in different counties. And *towards the latter end of the same year, a class at Tunstall joined them.*"

The two passages we have italicised give us Hugh Bourne's point of view. He believed that he and his brother were "called of God to stand by camp meetings." They represented the Camp Meeting movement, disallowed indeed of men but chosen of God. They embodied and sought to propagate what they deemed to be primitive Methodism, long before Stanley class was thrown on their hands. Quite naturally, William Clowes could not take this high ground, and see things as Hugh Bourne saw them. So in his friendly strictures on the 'History' of 1823, he takes exception to the statement that, towards the close of the year 1810 "a class at Tunstall joined" the brothers. To him such a way of putting it seemed an upsettal of facts—a picture quite out of drawing. It was like saying that the mountain had come to Mahomet. To him it would seem plain as plain could be, that, from the close of the year 1810 onwards, everything was moving on Tunstall; that Tunstall was to be the goal and centre of the combined movement. But then, Clowes had not Bourne's point of view. To the latter, the fact that he now found himself at Tunstall, going in and out among the brethren was taken as a sign and proof of the advance of the cause he and his brother had stood by so long and sought to further. They had annexed Tunstall; they had not been absorbed by it.

Who shall decide between these two views—if, indeed, they are really divergent and not recon............. For our own part though strongly holding that, historically and externally, our Church had its birth in the coming together of the Camp Meeting Methodists and the Clowesites, we willingly concede that but for the austere enthusiasm, the ceaseless, dogged labour of Hugh Bourne, there would have been nothing to come together in 1811—no materials out of which to build a denomination. It is to the idiosyncrasies of Hugh Bourne and the course of life pursued by him during the preceding ten years, we must look to find the true inwardness of the movement. If we would understand the true "evangelical succession" of that movement it is indispensable we should closely watch the doings of Hugh Bourne, since he was the link between the past and the present. Moreover, it may be granted that in the coming together of the sections he played no unimportant part. His incomings and outgoings amongst the various societies were as the motions of a living shuttle, weaving them into one homogeneous tissue.

But the question still recurs—Wherein lies the importance of Stanley class? If it was not the nucleus of Primitive Methodism, what then was it? The answer must be that the declinature of Stanley by the old Methodist body marked and inaugurated a more decisive policy towards the camp meeting fathers. Just as Christianity for a time clung to the skirts of Judaism, and early Methodism to the skirts of the Establishment until she shook it off, so did the camp meetingers cling to the skirts of Methodism, and by the same analogy, the time almost sure to come had now arrived when the Mother Church gathered her skirts about her and said, in effect: This kind of thing has gone on long enough, and must now cease. Henceforth if you get any people converted it must be on your own ground, and you must look after them when they are converted, and not hand them over to us.* By so determining, the authorities were simply bringing their procedure into the line of logical consistency with the policy laid down by the Conference of 1807, and partially followed up to the present by the discountenancing of camp meetings, and the dismembering of Bourne, Crawfoot, and Thomas Cotton. Not even does Bourne find fault with this procedure; nor do we, but rather would we suggest that it might have been an advantage if a thorough understanding of this kind had been arrived at two years earlier; for then, Bourne's contribution to the amalgamation of 1811 would have been much more considerable than it actually was.

Thus, as though by the simple pull of a lever, the movement was switched on to an independent line of action. At a stroke, James Crawfoot became the salaried preacher, and the Bournes, Thomas Cotton, F. Horobin, and Thomas Knight, the voluntary preachers of a new Methodist community with its own classes and leaders, its camp meeting agency, and its regular preaching places, not only at Stanley and Ramsor with Wootton, but also at Tean, Calden Lowe, and Lask Edge, all of which places stood on the written plans which the Camp Meeting Methodists drew up for their own use. Nor must it be thought that this transformation of an unattached and irregular movement into an organised society was brought about by violent rupture and attendant heart-burnings. It was the result of no "schism" in the proper sense of that much-abused term; that is to say, there was no riving process, no rending asunder, no "split"

* "At first the societies which Bourne formed were allowed to go under the protection of the older body."—*Rev. H. B. Kendall, M.A.*

Rather was it the result of a clear understanding arrived at, like that between Abraham and Lot—an understanding, on the whole, honourably kept by both sides, not only at Stanley, but wherever the societies of the Mother Church and the Camp Meeting Methodists were conterminous. Such is Hugh Bourne's explicit statement with respect to the societies under his care:—

"There was cleanliness of hands on both sides. They did not take one member from us, and we did not take one from them—all was pure on both sides. There were various places at which we had laboured once a fortnight and they had done the same, but these we left without taking a member, and made our leaving as easy as it could well be; so in these instances we gave no cause of complaint, nor can we charge the Wesleyans with wrong in making a law to prevent their members from attending the camp meetings."

Stanley is a good historic name, it sounds well, and is familiar to us from being borne by the noble house of Derby. But the importance of Stanley in our annals was largely an adventitious and a dwindling one; and by 1814 its name disappears from the plan. Yet, two of its ten members should have passing mention. One—Samuel Simcock, was a young man of one-and-twenty when he joined the Stanley class, and in June, 1817, his course was run; but he lived long enough to become the leader of two classes, to prove himself a "useful and persevering" local preacher, and to assist in establishing a Sunday School at Hollington in Derbyshire. It takes time, we are told, for myths to grow, and so years after Samuel Simcock's demise, his name became associated with a myth that W. Clowes found it needful to track to its influential source, and to expose. The myth was to the effect that once upon a time Clowes and Simcock unaided and alone had held a camp meeting all through a summer's day; that Clowes, being 'tough as whit-leather," survived, but that Simcock died of that camp meeting. The obvious moral was—"Be short in your camp meeting exercises or swift retribution will follow.' But it was shrewdly suspected that the particular inference intended to be drawn from the myth was, that W. Clowes had killed Simcock by flagrantly violating the regulations for conducting camp meetings. The myth had grown to such formidable proportions that, at last, in 1833, it invaded Conference, and there had to be met and exorcised. Fortunately for Clowes, he had been a close reader of the magazines from the first, and he remembered Samuel Simcock's memoir in the volume for 1819, wherein it is plainly stated that he did not die of 'long preaching," but of pulmonary consumption brought on by overheating himself in a journey he took into Staffordshire to see his mother. It is not every one who attains the posthumous honour of figuring in a mythical story like this. But Samuel Simcock has much worthier and more durable claims to be remembered here, as the interesting memoir of him from the pen of Hugh Bourne bears witness; for we are told:—"He was like a fine musical instrument—always in tune a stream of pious conversation flowed from him in all places and upon all occasions; and his conduct ornamented the Christian character in his own neighbourhood." Clowes also adds his testimony to his character "With Samuel I was intimately acquainted. With him I often took sweet counsel, and was refreshed in spirit. I admired his piety and zeal in the good cause.'— *Journals*, p. 114.

Mary Slater, to whom Hugh Bourne was first cousin, once removed, outlived all the other members of the original class at Stanley. Her husband was its leader, and in their house the class was formed and met. She survived until December 3rd, 1865; and on the day of her interment in Willenhall cemetery, the interest naturally aroused by this sundering of a link with the past, coupled with the respect felt for the blameless character of this "old disciple," resulted in giving a semi-public character to her obsequies.

We come back again to the September Plan, 1811, of the amalgamated societies; for the significance of that ink-faded, ill-spelled document is not exhausted after Ramsor branch—as even already it may be called—and Stanley, have had the recognition their prominent mention in our Deed Poll demands. Looking closely at the places and preachers on this plan and comparing

BADDELEY EDGE CHAPEL.

them with those of the first printed plan of 1812, we notice that though John Benton's name has its place and figure, Wyrley Bank mission has not yet been taken over, though negotiations for its transfer are now afoot, and by 1812 the names of Cannock and Cannock Wood will show

GREYSTONE FARM.
OLD PREACHING HOUSE, BADDELEY EDGE.

they have proved successful. As for the Derbyshire mission, where we know a good work had for some time been going on in several places—the plan affords no evidence of the fact, the explanation being that clever and crafty Mrs. Dunnell had stolen away the hearts of the people and, much to the grief of some, set up for herself. But there will be an *eclaircissement*; her downfall is imminent; the societies will return to their first love and allegiance. These matters will be adjusted by the time the first printed plan appears, and we shall find on its list of places, Hollington, Boylestone, Rodsley, Roston, and Rocester—all destined to have a history. Another omission on this plan is noteworthy:—Rizley, in Lancashire, with its twenty members under the leadership of Thomas Webb, does not figure. Yet this society, which owed its existence to Lorenzo Dow, had accepted the overseership of Hugh Bourne and was regarded as one of his societies; over it he had expended a considerable amount of labour and even money, and he had a liking for it and its rather peculiar ways. It is interesting, as casting a sidelight on the contrasted tastes and bias of Clowes and Bourne, to compare their respective comments on the same proceedings of this Rizley society.

BROWN EDGE P.M.C.

OLD PREACHING HOUSE, BROWN EDGE.

"*April 23rd, 1809.* Here each one does that which is right in his own eyes. They stand, sit, kneel, pray, exhort, etc., as they are moved. *I was very fond of this way.*"—H. Bourne *Journals*.

"From Warrington we went down to Rissley, and found a people very singular in their notions and manner of worship, *which we did not at all admire*; nevertheless, the Lord made us useful among them, as we proceeded in our straightforward manner in preaching a present, free, and full salvation."—Clowes' *Journals*, p. 76.

Rizley, along with Five Crosses, will be found at the bottom of the first printed plan as the Lancashire outposts of the denomination.

To the Clowesite section must be assigned the places standing on the 1811 plan not already named. A definite answer to the general correctness of this attribution though it must be borne in mind there was growingly frequent intercourse and co-operation between the sections. Unfortunately, the *Journals* of Clowes are sadly wanting in just those details of the twelve months' evangelistic labours of Clowes himself and his colleagues we should like to have. We must do our best with the scant material at hand to represent to ourselves what was going on. Perhaps the combination-views of preaching-houses and chapels inserted here and there in the text may help us somewhat to realise what was the usual order of development in this preparatory period and in the one immediately to follow. At first, a village or hamlet would be "opened" by a service out of doors ; or advantage would be taken of the offer of a cottage or room from some kindly disposed person ; then the services would be held at regular intervals and the cottage would become the recognised preaching-house. As yet the progress made

LAWTON HEATH.
The highest building on the right hand of picture is the first preaching room.

does not carry us beyond this humble stage. We have not reached the chapel-building era, but we are close upon it—how close the unpretentious chapels of our Janus-like pictures serve to show. So, while the chapels anticipate by a year or two what is to come, they indicate that all this pioneer work has not been, and will not be in vain in the Lord ; the rude and feeble beginnings are preparing the way for something better : the cause will not lack continuity and development. These combination-pictures may render us another wholesome service :—they may check the swellings of pride as we look in these days on the costly, spacious, ornate structures springing up all over our land

and notice the legend "Primitive Methodist Church" inscribed on their front. Just as "Primislaus, the first king of Bohemia, kept his country shoes always by him, to remember from whence he was raised; and Agathocles by the furniture of his table confessed, that from a potter he was raised to be the King of Sicily,"* so here we have our humble monitors—our reminders of "the rock whence we were hewn, and the hole of the pit whence we were digged."

Some of Clowes' places are in Cheshire, though naturally still more are in Staffordshire, within comparatively easy reach of Tunstall. Among the former are Lawton Heath; Roggin Row, in the near neighbourhood of Buglawton, where the fourth camp meeting was held May 14th, 1808; Englesea Brook, in the graveyard of whose present chapel lie the mortal remains of Hugh and James Bourne and Thomas Russell; and more distant Coppenhall. These two places—said to have been missioned—the former by Thomas Woodnorth, assisted by "old Sarah Smith," the latter by William Morris—will provide the base for future extensive missionary operations.

Coming now to the Staffordshire places: it is interesting to find Talke on the list, thus early beginning its honourable career. "O' th' hill" indeed it is, and enjoys the advantages of its situation, for not only does it command a fine view of Mow Cop, but there also stretches out before the eye England's Vale Royal, which runs through Cheshire to the sea. But far different sights than those of the picturesque or of peaceful industry have occasionally been witnessed here; for, standing as it does in the midst of a populous mining district, colliery disasters on a large scale have now and again carried sorrow into many a home and made havoc of the church. We are anticipating a little, but before 1813 is over, Hugh Bourne will have built at his own expense a chapel here, standing on a site now covered by

ROGGIN ROW, BUGLAWTON, NEAR CONGLETON.
One of the places on the First Plan.

the present school. Some of the forms which he made are still preserved in this school, which was enlarged in 1857. The present chapel at Talke was erected in 1876 at a cost of more than £2,000.

Cloud, with its picturesque name, suggestive of a height that holds commerce with the skies, must not be passed over; for it, too, is on the 1811 plan, and is a place interesting in many regards. He who relishes a far-reaching prospect

ENGLESEA BROOK CHAPEL.
(Interior.)

will, if he can, make his way here: for, from its elevation, he can catch sight of the distant Flintshire hills, and discern the unmistakable contours of the Shropshire Wrekin, and on the other side the heights of Morridge and Weaver. Antiquaries too, know the Cloud well; for in the grounds of Mr. Abner Dale, a Primitive Methodist of long standing and influence, are the famous Druidical remains known as the Bride Stones. In the next period we shall have to tell the story of the building of Cloud Chapel, but at the time of which we are writing, the services

ENGLESEA BROOK CHAPEL.
(Exterior.)

were held at Woodhouse Green—a quarter of a mile off, in the big parlour of a farmhouse wherein the Baptists had been used to worship, until the society became so robust that the The other places on the plan, not as yet particularised, must be content to be visually represented through the medium of the engravings interspersed in the text.

Let us now turn for a moment to the seventeen preachers who have their names on the plan. With some of them, such as James Nixon and "precious Thomas Woodnorth" (as in one place Hugh Bourne calls him) we have by this time grown familiar. But there are others on the list who must have a word for identification and remembrance. Amongst these is Richard Bayley, whom also we have met with before, as one who since 1807 had taken his turn of preaching in Mr. Smith's kitchen. He shared the fate of William Clowes

TALKE SCHOOL.
(Site of First Chapel.)

in being expelled from the Old Body, and henceforward he was resolved on sharing his fortunes in the new denomination. We meet with many kindly references to him in Hugh Bourne's *Journals*; for Richard Bayley was one of those "old companions" with whom his last thoughts were pre-occupied, and whose shadowy forms seemed

TALKE CHAPEL.

TALKE: THREE OLD FORMS MADE BY HUGH BOURNE.

THE BRIDE-STONES.

WOODHOUSE GREEN PREACHING-HOUSE.
Services were held in Parlour.

BIDDULPH MOOR ROCKS. TROUGHSTONE HILL.

SOURCES AND ORIGIN. 127

round. Often, on his return from his long rounds, did Hugh Bourne slip over to Biddulph Moor to refresh himself by a talk with Richard, and they were friends to the last. No. 6 on the plan was quite a character in his way; and your local annalist likes "characters," and is caught by the odd and whimsical. So one local writer speaks of Bayley as—

"An eccentric old 'Biddle Moor' man, who used to speak in the broad accent of that peculiar district. A favourite text of Bayley's was: 'Sonner, tharst bin weight u'th bolance un' fund wonting.' Yet the Biddle Moor man was master of a good deal of rough eloquence in his way. In later years he used to preach in the first Primitive Methodist Chapel that stood where the Hanley Railway stands. It was only a small place of one storey, and was built about 1824." *

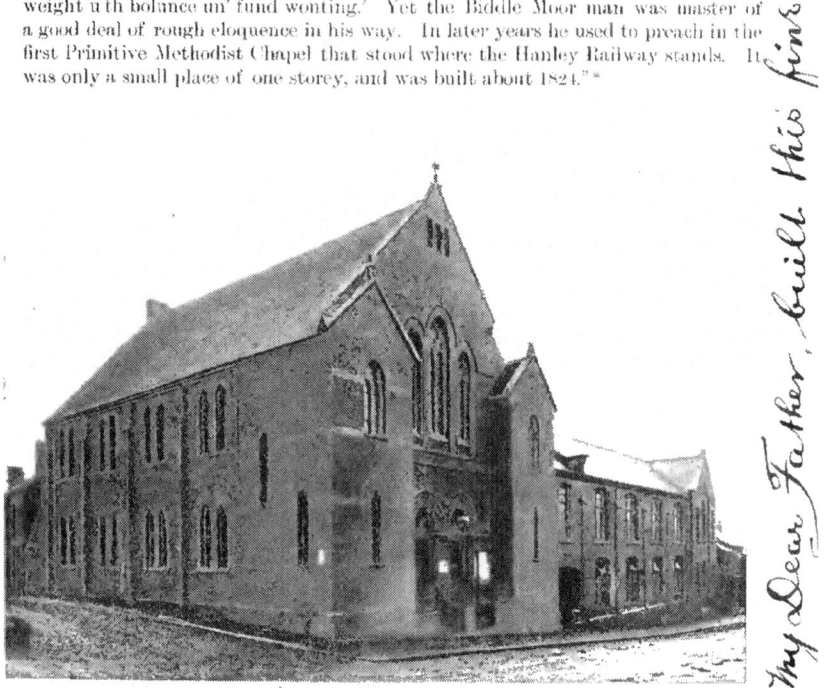

PITT'S HILL CHAPEL AND SCHOOL.
The original preaching-place was on the site of the present Schools.

William and Thomas Alcock, whose names stand on the plan Nos. 7 and 10 respectively, had their homestead at Latheredge, where the first preachers often found rest and refuge.† William was a *protégé* of Hugh Bourne, and from February 20th,

* Wedgwood: "Staffordshire—Up and Down the County," pp. 6, 7.
† October 1st, 1819:—"When I left Tunstall on Tuesday, about three o'clock in the afternoon, I had *forty* miles to travel to my Sunday's appointment. I had not walked far before it began to rain and become very thick, so that night came on by the time I arrived at the house of Mr. Alcock, at Ladder-edge. I stayed with him till the morning."—*Journal of Sampson Turner.* Ladder-edge is probably the correct form, though Latheredge is the form used by H. Bourne in his *Journals.*

1809, when the two first met, the *Journals* make repeated references to young Alcock. His first attempt at preaching in the presence of the camp meeting fathers seemed anything but promising. He made two attempts, and each time became "hard fast" soon after giving out his text. Perhaps the text had something to do with his poverty of ideas and abrupt failure of utterance, for the text was, "He had nothing to pay," etc. On standing up after prayer to make yet a third attempt, William Maxfield cried,

NORTON GREEN PRIMITIVE METHODIST CHAPEL AND SCHOOLS.

"Tell us your experience." This sensible piece of advice was at once acted upon with the happiest results. Falling back upon personal experience, William got "purchase" for a weighty exhortation, and even succeeded before he sat down in gripping his text. Hugh Bourne remarks:—"Upon the whole it was a very powerful time. At night I discoursed much with him in order to strengthen his hands and direct him. O Lord, bless him. I believe he will be a useful man." A little later, when he had an unfounded presentiment that his own life would be short, Bourne writes: "If it were God's will I should like to live till F. Horobin and W. Alcock are fairly yoked in preaching." His

OLD PREACHING-HOUSE, NORTON GREEN.
Here Bourne preached his last sermon.

prayer was answered; his prophecy fulfilled; his wish gratified. He *did* live to see his son in the ———— and laborious preacher of the Word. William Alcock gave himself more and more fully to the work. In 1818 we find his name standing No. 6 on the Tunstall circuit plan. Then he retired from the ranks and, it is said, located in Derbyshire, and lived to write a few words on the friend of his youth and prime, which found a place in Walford's "Life of Bourne."

Thomas Alcock, his brother, was spared to become one of the oldest local preachers of the Connexion, and was honoured by his portrait's appearing in the magazine. That portrait is here reproduced, and shows a stalwart form and prepossessing countenance. He was associated with the Society at Talke, and was "a man of faith and spiritual power, the memory of whose piety and usefulness is still fresh and invigorating." *

E. McEvoy and J. Boden have incidentally been mentioned during the course of this history; † and we catch increasingly frequent glimpses of the former during this time. On Christmas Day, 1810, he, Clowes, and James Bourne, on returning to Macclesfield, were lost; "so they called at an inn and had a most extraordinary time, the power of the Lord came over all."

About the midsummer of 1811 James Marsh comes on the scene. Bourne records how Marsh spoke at Ashmore House, the home of the Dakin's, in much power and with wisdom, though he complained of having "a short time."

THOMAS ALCOCK.

So this poor scrap of a plan has on it the names of some good and true men. We have done what little we could to rescue their names from oblivion, and can only regret that so much of their memorial has been carried down by the time-stream, and is now irrecoverable.

RUDIMENTARY ORGANISATION.

July 26th, 1811, and February 13th, 1812, are dates to be noted and remembered in any history of our origins; for by the proceedings of those two days the coping-stone and name-plate were put on the newly-raised fabric of the denomination. On the former, we were saved from Free-Gospelism: on the latter, we got our distinctive denominational title.

Yet the extant records of the meetings held on these two days are brief and bald as the first telegraphed summary of some important committee. You have the statement of what was done in its most condensed form. All verbiage has been pruned away; there is little by way of preface or explanation. Still what little we have suffices, especially as we know the proceedings were marked by unanimity, and the conclusions arrived at *nem. con.*

At the meeting held in Mr. Smith's kitchen on July 26th, two matters were discussed and settled—minor and incidental by comparison—which may have passing reference. Apparently by direct questioning, agreement was arrived at that preachers should be planned where best received and most likely to be useful, and that when planned they should not be free to pick and choose their appointments, but just go in the fear of God and fulfil them. Then it was asked whether friend J. Boden should be received as a local preacher, and the answer was "yes"; and accordingly his name will duly be found on the September written plan. But the one weighty piece of business, compared with which the other were trifles, and the business which had brought the fathers together, was the question as to the relation hereafter to subsist between preachers and people. Should there be men set apart to the work, and if so, how were they to be supported? By the regular contributions of one or two as heretofore, or by the collective body? In short, the business to be settled really resolved itself into the question whether Primitive Methodism should be, or should not be, a form of Free-Gospelism.

BUTT LANE CHAPEL, ON THE 1811 PLAN.

Nor was this question approached in a leisurely, indifferent, academic manner. The men who sat and talked in that kitchen were no doctrinaires, but a number of plain and very serious men, who had met under the impulsion of hard insistent facts, to see what had best be done. Even if the Brothers Bourne could go on providing subsistence-money for James Crawfoot, there was William Clowes and his maintenance to think of. For the simple truth was that James Nixon and Thomas Woodnorth had come to the end of their monetary ability, and, as trade now was, could no longer continue to do as they had done. Even as it was they had pinched and straitened themselves, and even wronged their families to keep William Clowes in the mission-field. What then was to be done? Truly a kind of crisis had been reached.

Now, it may seem to us that what wanted doing was obvious enough. But what is clear to us does not seem to have been so clear to the Primitive fathers. In truth, a good deal lay at stake that day. There was the danger lest the denomination should start wrong, and soon find itself swamped in the welter of the lower invertebrate forms of religious life.* The acceptance of the tenet of Free-Gospelism would have arrested

* "I have no time to write their entomology"! T. P. Bunting on the Band Room Methodists.—*Life of Dr. J. Bunting*: 56.

its development, and the possibility of such acceptance taking place must be admitted as having been at least possible. It would have been almost a miracle, considering Hugh Bourne's training and the company he had been largely thrown amongst during the previous ten years, if he had altogether escaped the infection of Free-Gospelism. He had at this time, to put it mildly, no high views of the ministerial office. Even his most partial biographers admit this, and seek to account for his tendency to undervalue preaching in comparison with praying, to the fact that he had got a ply in this direction by listening to some heedless rhetoric of the popular Samuel Bradburn as far back as July, 1799. Hugh Bourne was generous as we know, and self-denying to a degree, in order that he might have the more to dispense; but, at the same time, he was scrupulous in taking from others for himself, and reluctant to tax others even for the sake of carrying on the work of God. As time went on, his scrupulosity on this score grew less, but it may be doubted whether it had altogether gone by 1811. What was true of Hugh Bourne held good also of James Crawfoot. He was rather deeply tinged with Quaker Methodism and, along with some better things, left the 'hat whim' as a legacy to our Church.

So, safely to pass this rock ahead, the Tunstall connection was already an advantage, and there was needed too, not only the pressure arising from the failure of supplies but also the good common-sense and Christian principle of the two hundred members constituting the societies, who pressed to be allowed the privilege of supporting those who "laboured amongst them in the word and doctrine." It is even affirmed that some good souls had declined uniting with the societies because such privilege was not allowed. Yielding then to the double pressure of the popular wish, and the situation created by the break-down of the financial arrangement hitherto in vogue, the assembled fathers adopted the principle that they "who preach the Gospel should live of the Gospel." One can only express surprise that they did not at once fall back upon the simply sufficient Methodist and early Christian plan of receiving week by week the offerings of the faithful. What was determined, H. Bourne tells us :—

'It was proposed that the circumstances be mentioned to the people and what they voluntarily gave should be collected by proper persons and paid into the hands of a steward, and what fell short should be made out by private subscriptions.

Question 5.—Who shall be appointed Steward? This was put upon James Steele."

Thus a beginning was made; the principle that the minister can claim support from the people, and that the people are under obligation to give it, was recognised, though the principle was fenced, and one may say qualified, by the proviso added at a subsequent meeting held October 14th, to the effect

'That all gifts and presents that may be made to the preachers are to be brought to the steward and entered in the books, and be reckoned towards the weekly allowance.' So these regulations were fixed.

Nor would Hugh Bourne, though fully devoted to the work of the ministry at present part with his individual liberty. He would be independent and bear his own charges, and William Alcock, who was found to be a man of the same mind; so also with John Benton and John Wedgwood when they shall begin their remarkable labours. But we are still in the day of small and feeble things, as we are reminded by another regulation made at the supplementary meeting of October 14th, at which Hugh Bourne was not present. It was agreed that James Crawfoot "be paid 10s. 6d. a week for the support of his family," and W. Clowes, for the reason that his house was a kind of "pilgrims' inn," and stood him at a higher rent, was to receive 14s. per week, and at that modest figure it remained for some time.

The Name 'Primitive Methodists' is Taken.

Sometimes during the course of legal proceedings a piece of paper—terra-cotta as to colour and a parallelogram as to shape will be put in, and that telegraph-form, with its brief, curt message, may prove a piece of valuable evidence. So having now reached

> Thursday February 13
> 1812
> We called a meeting and made plans for the next Quarter and made some other regulations ... In particular We took the name of the Society of the Primitive Methodists

the date of February 13th, 1812, we cannot do better than give from Hugh Bourne's *Journals* a facsimile of the entry recording what was done on that eventful day. Let the reader's eye for a moment rest on the very curves Hugh Bourne's hand once traced rather than on the angularities of printed type. Looking at this piece of script our founder's hand once penned, we are reminded of Paul's words to the Galatians: "See with how large letters I have written unto you with mine own hand." But in this case the "largeness of the letters" approaching almost to "roundhand" was not the result of defective eyesight, but rather of the writer's clear perception at the moment of writing tha

As to the name itself and its appropriateness, one or two remarks must suffice. The right and propriety of taking such a name must, of course, be based on the appropriateness of the name, duly considering the conditions and circumstances of the time when it was assumed. Was the name when first adopted an appropriate one? That is the question to be approached in the historical spirit, and not the question—so likely when discussed to wound denominational susceptibilities—whether the name as a differentiating and descriptive denominational title be appropriate now. Without prejudging this question, or even expressing at present any opinion upon it, we may suggest it to be quite conceivable that a negative answer might have to be returned to the latter question, and an affirmative answer to the former. The fact is, the two questions are quite distinct, and must be kept distinct. As to the former historical question with which alone we are now concerned. To us it seems our historians hitherto have taken too low ground, and too timid and apologetic an attitude. Unless we entirely misread the facts set forth in this book, the only impression they can make on the candid reader will be that there was but one name for the new denomination, and that 'Primitive Methodist.'

Briefly to recapitulate: the movement which eventuated in the formation of the new denomination was akin to, and one form of, the Revivalism which was endemic—one might say epidemic—during the opening years of the nineteenth century; this movement was the avowed, deliberate, enthusiastic endeavour to return to the spirit and practices of primitive Methodism; this movement was in many respects counter and antipathetic to the spirit and policy of the Methodism of the time: standing thus to each other, a clash and severance were inevitable unless, indeed, one or the other should greatly modify, and so deny itself: the inevitable happened, and the ejected discrepant fragment did not disappear in the void but persisted, and naturally took for its name what was its raison d'être—primitive Methodism. All that the meeting of 1812 did was to turn what had been a fair and honest description into a title, and to write 'primitive' with a capital P.

To us the gist and crux of the whole matter lies in the admission or non-admission of the position that primitive Methodism and modern Methodism as terms implying contrasted and conflicting ideals and tendencies, aptly describe what we find really existent and militant in North Staffordshire and Cheshire from 1800 to 1812. If this be admitted then, though the action of the Wesleyan Conference and the Burslem Circuit is explained, and in a measure justified, to the same degree is the taking of the name Primitive Methodist by our fathers also justified. On the other hand, if the fact of this antithesis—this clash of ideals, of tendencies and practices—be denied, then conclusions of a directly opposite character will follow. Then the name Primitive Methodist must be acknowledged to have been a misnomer because based on a groundless assumption; but if so, then the Conference and the minor authorities must in turn be accused of having been both blind and deaf to what was around them—so much so that they could not tell friends from enemies, or distinguish between what was Methodism and what was not. It would seem to be a somewhat bold proceeding to conclude that both the Wesleyan authorities and the primitive fathers were alike the victims of a false assumption. It were surely more reasonable to believe that neither the one nor the other was so victims.

There is a homely saying which affirms that "You cannot both eat your cake and have it." This is an old saw the modern representatives of both sides in this historical episode would do well to remember. On the one hand, we who vigorously defend the assumption of the name "Primitive Methodist" must be prepared to admit the strength of the Conference case as viewed from its own standpoint. On the other hand, those who carp and cavil and gird at the name "Primitive Methodist" must, to be consistent, accuse the Conference and all concerned of having blundered and muddled the business. As with our cake, we cannot have it both ways.

A PLAN OF THE PREACHERS
IN THE SOCIETY OF THE PRIMITIVE METHODISTS
In Tunstall Circuit.

1812.	MAR. 22 29	APRIL. 5 12 19 26	MAY. 3 10 17 24 31	JUNE. 7 14 21	PREACHERS' NAMES.
Tunstall 2 and 6	6 5	8 2 5 3	1 6 18 2 7	2 1 4	
Norton 2, Brown Edge 6	17 11	16 12 19 21	13 9 10 12 6	15 20 13	1 J. Crawfoot
Stanly 2, Badley Edge 4	20	17 10	15 21 11	10	2 J. Steel
Bagnal 2, Badley Edge 4		16 19 9	13 20 21	23	3 J. Bourne
Butt Lane 2, Talk o' th' Hill 6	10	14 15	10 17 9	16	4 H. Bourne
Roggin Row 2, Talk o' th' Hill 6		20 16 7	20 23 3	6	5 W. Clowes
Cloud 10 and 2	9	6 13	6 16 19	4	6 R. Bailey
Woodhouse Green 10 and 2	15	7 10	3 9	20 14	7 W. Allcock
Whiston 2, Alton 6	12	11 22	19 3 20	14	8 T. Woodnorth
Stanton 2, Swincore 6	3	15 22	12 14	19 12	9 E. McEvoy
Englesea Brook 9, Betley 1½	23 12	20 14 17 11	9 16 19 7 23	9 3 17	10 J. Nixon
Coppenhall 2, Weston 7	3 8	19 11 20 18	11 10 9 5 12	16 23 9	11 H. Mattinson
Stoke 10½, Cotton Work	11 10	23 9 16 20	23 4 15 16 3	16 17 19	12 T. Allcock
Caldon 10, Wooton 2, Ramsor 6		4 8	5 1 18	7 8	13 T. Hulme
Hollington 10, Boylstone 2, Rodsley 6	7	4 8	5 1 18	7	14 J. Marsh
Roston 2, Rocester 6		7 4 8	5 1	18 7	15
Cannock 2, Cannock Wood 6	5	7 4 4	8 8 1	18	16 J. Boden
Biddulph Moor 2		16 9 10 3 11 12	7 19 6 17 16	8 9 10	17 S. Broad
Rizley		1	18 5		18 •
Five Crosses		1	18	5	19 H. Wood
					20 S. Simcock
					21 M. Brown
					22 J. Buxton
					23 W. Morris

Copy of the First Printed Plan ordered to be printed by the Meeting held Feb. 13, 1812, at which the name Primitive Methodist was taken.

Churches have their process of evolution, and the antagonism between the old and new elements that showed itself in 1800-12 was but an incident in this historical process. Further stages have since been reached. What took place near a hundred years ago could not be repeated now. The old antithesis has well-nigh been overcome by a wider spiritual synthesis, destined to embrace what is valuable and worth preserving both old and new, and we must adjust our ecclesiastical arrangements to these altered spiritual conditions.

Meanwhile the name Primitive Methodist was prepared beforehand for us. We do not need the story of James Crawfoot's expulsion to account for the assumption of the name. It was inevitable. Hugh Bourne may have been drowsy at the time the name was taken, but drowsy or wide-awake it would have been the same. We got our name very much as John the Baptist got his, and presumably the Divine hand was in both name-givings. Their neighbours and kinsfolk wanted the promising child to be called Zacharias, but the mother said, "Not so; but he *shall* be called John." The father took his writing-tablet and wrote, saying, "His name *is* John." Kinsfolk and neighbours might not like the name. They might object that none of his kinsmen had borne such a name; but all the same the name was there—waiting, divinely authorised, inevitable. It had to be, or rather it was already.

CHAPTER VI.

SIDELIGHTS ON THE PERIOD 1800—12.

From the "Journals" of Hugh Bourne and W. Clowes.

THE account of the sources and origin of the Primitive Methodist Church reached its natural conclusion in the preceding chapter, which left it in possession of a name and rudimentary organisation. Hence it will be expected that we shall at once proceed to trace the course of its further history and development. Before, however, essaying this task, we will linger a little while over the *Journals* of Hugh Bourne and William Clowes (but especially of the former), tempted by the inducement that we are likely by so doing to become better acquainted both with our founders and the *milieu* in which they lived and worked. Many incidental matters that could not but be passed over when following the consecutive narrative can now, that we have reached our first convenient halting-place, be leisurely and profitably regarded. So that however impatient to get on the reader may be, we would not advise the skipping of this chapter; the pause does not mean retardment.

Bourne and Clowes both left *Journals*, so-called, but only Bourne's are really such, those of Clowes, published in 1844, being *Journals* only in name. Clowes took up the pen as seldom as he could, and when he did take it up, it did not become in his hands the pen of a ready writer, as the hard, scratchy "hand" he wrote remains to tell. His *Journals* are really autobiographic reminiscences written late in life, apparently from memory and not from written memoranda, so that they are defective in names and dates, and the right sequence and relation of events are not always preserved. Unfortunately, the important period between Clowes' coming off the plan and the amalgamation of 1812 has only fifteen small octavo pages devoted to it. Hence, as will be inferred, it does not belong to the useful class of works of reference, and is unfitted by its defects and very qualities to be in itself a sufficient guide to our early history; but as supplying collateral information and giving a vivid presentation of events elsewhere set forth only in a brief form, it has its distinct value. Moreover, as a work of religious edification it will be found difficult to match it by anything our literature can show. The style in which the *Journals* is written is easy and flowing, sometimes indeed rising into natural eloquence, and the devout, fervid spirit which breathes in the narrative cannot fail to communicate itself to the reader.

Hugh Bourne's *Journals* are just such. From the outset of his religious life in 1800 to its close, with but few breaks, he was accustomed to note down in his careful, methodical the people met with, the places visited, the thoughts that had pre-occupied his mind, even his own significant dreams or those of others are duly though tersely recorded. Each day the *Journal* is written up, with no idea the record will be seen by any other eye than his own, or some items would surely have been omitted. The psychical no less than the historical value of such a record as this needs no pointing out. What wonder that the *Journals* have been a well-worked quarry whence both biographers of Bourne and our Church historians have got their materials at first or second hand! for he still remains our chief, and in some cases, our sole authority for certain periods or events in our earlier history. But though Hugh Bourne's *Journals* have been so largely drawn upon they have never been published in their entirety, and taking into account their voluminousness and intimate character are not likely to be.

But how to describe the *Journals*? To what shall we liken them? Not perhaps, to the Journals of George Fox or John Wesley, though with each of these they have their points of likeness. Difficult, however, as it may be to class them or find their fellow, we, who are fresh from the minute reading of the MS volumes occupied with the years 1800—12, pronounce them to be amongst the strangest human documents ever penned, and make bold to affirm that both the psychologist and the religious novelist would find familiarity with their contents of the greatest advantage. Had Professor James only had access to Hugh Bourne's *Journals* when writing his "Varieties of Religious Experience," it is certain he would have enriched his pages with many a quotation; and should a second "George Eliot" arise, she might, from the materials lying here, reproduce a picture of lowly religious life in North Staffordshire that might stand a worthy second to "Adam Bede," which deals with the same time, largely with the same class, and almost with the same district.

It will be expected we shall make good this our estimate, but to do this is difficult for the *Journals* of Bourne are as complex as the man who wrote them, and refuse to be characterised or summed up in a sentence. It is the final impression left on the reader's mind as the combined, cumulative result of the typical extracts given that will be nearest the truth, for then, as by a graduated process, the reader gains his impression in much the same way as he would had he the privilege of perusing the original *Journals* themselves.

The *Journals* of Hugh Bourne are emphatically religious journals, written by one who felt called to carry on a religious and not a political or social, much less a sectarian propaganda. The great pre-occupation is religion. There is an exaltation, a dead earnestness in the writer which makes itself felt. He is bent on one thing, he is terribly in earnest to save his own soul and the souls of others. There are few direct allusions to the state of the country at the time, or any evidence that the sense of the wrongs and disabilities from which men suffered burned within him and sought expression in complaints or invective. Of course it would have been impossible for Hugh Bourne, in simply chronicling his own doings and movements during these ten years, not to have made incidental allusions to the state of things prevailing at the time he wrote, or not to have crossed the path of some people whom it is interesting, even after the lapse of a century, to recall. Here, for instance, by recorded dream and prayer and rumour we get a glimpse

"*January 17th, 1810.*—Clowes went under the transfiguration. He was exercised about the nation. We led class at Mr. Hitchin's of Alpraham, and had a good time. *17th.*—We came to Thornton. Clowes was exercised about the nation. Mourning and lamentation and woe are at hand. *February 8th.*—My brother James told me that W. Handley, a little time ago, told him that he—W. H.—dreamed that a person talked with him, and advised him to have but little business on his hand because that troubles would shortly come. Wm. H. answered that he had only the farm and looking after Mr. Adderley's colliery; and as to Stonetrough,

STONETROUGH COLLIERY AND MOUNDS.

when it was a little 'gated,' he should only have to go about once a week. The person said all business would be at a stand, and that those who had the least business would do the best, and that all who had much to do with banks would be hurt, for banks would be broken. The Lord's will be done."

"*April 11th, 1810.*— . . . I went to Warrington, where I heard the dreadful news that there were riots in London. Well, the Most High ruleth; and the Lord is still a hiding-place."

We are not allowed to forget that those were the days of imperfect religious toleration, and that the reactionary tendencies at work were threatening still further to abridge its privileges. The very month Stanley Class is formed he hears that the Toleration Act "is about to be broken in part," and that the Methodists are providing against the gathering storm by proposing to make each preacher the nominal minister of a particular church. Sometimes the holding of religious service in a particular dwelling-house has to be put off precautionary measure against the persecution which menaces. At Rodsley the licence has been secured only just in the nick of time, for the very next day they were to be informed against.

Very significant as to the manners and morals of the time are the frequent references to the local wakes and then pernicious influence. After spending the day of July 2nd, 1810, at Wootton in visiting, he tells how there was a bear-bait, and how he felt "the spirit of the wake dash upon him like a flood," as though it were one special, favourite way in which the time-spirit—"the spirit of the power of the air"—manifested itself in those days.

> "I bore the cross awhile till the cloud broke, and the Spirit said that my desire should be granted—I felt thankful. At bed-time I wandered towards the alehouse, and met with an 'earnest seeker of salvation; I went into Brown's and she was fully born again. *Tuesday 3rd.*—It rained much this afternoon. We prayed for the Lord to restrain the wake, and I believe the Lord sent rain and thunder on Sunday night, and the rain to-day to stop it. Glory be to His name for ever!"

The next year he is at Rocester at the time of the wake, sharing the hospitality of the Mace family. They plead with God to restrain the wake, and not in vain, for the bull was sent away from the town, and there were murmurings from the wake-folk "that there had been no mirth." As Hugh Bourne looks out of the window he learns a lesson. He sees a number of men in the back-yard busily engaged in 'cleansing' a man who had been fighting. 'I watched,' says he, "to see their great zeal; they appeared full of life and eagerness. *They appeared as if fighting battles in their own minds;* they seemed to venture all for Satan. If we had as much zeal for heaven we should surely reach it."

In the pages of those volumes of the *Journals* with which we have now to do, there is not a joke, scarcely a gleam of humour, to be found. It were vain to look there for the graces of literary style. Yet, though the writer is so serious and matter-of-fact, and puts things down in the plainest, homeliest, and shortest way, we do meet with occasional *obiter dicta* worth noting, on account of their quaintness, shrewdness, or 'crusty candour.' Some of these comments and by-the-way sayings could not well be better expressed or put into fewer words, and one cannot but wonder, coming upon such passages as these, whether after all this plain and rugged style was not deliberately chosen, and perhaps shall be inclined to conclude that 'he could an he would' have written just as elegantly as others who have succumbed to the temptation to sacrifice strength and clearness to fine writing. The surmise is partly correct, as one singular entry in the *Journals* shows.

> *November 3rd, 1809.*—"John Whittaker had talked to me about using the best language, as I had it in my power. He pressed it much. I told him I would pray about it. I prayed this morning, and was led to adopt the way that he recommended. Appearing to be illiterate when I am not illiterate seemed to be quite wrong. O Lord, I beseech Thee direct my soul—touch my lips. O Lord, if Thy will be that I should use fine language, give me a fine flow of eloquence; touch my lips with a live coal from off the altar. Oh may the love of Jesus flow from my lips in accents mild as the evening dew, and in beauty as the falling of the fleecy snow. Oh let the honey distil from my lips."

From this quotation we infer that the Lord must soon have made known that His will went counter to John Whittaker's well meant advice, and that He was against H B's "use of fine language," for we read of no more aspirations or efforts that way, and soon meet with evidence in plenty that the plain and forceful style of writing was the one contentedly and determinedly chosen. In striking and refreshing contrast with the poetic diction of the above excerpt, we throw together a few samples, culled from these early *Journals*, of H B's forcible way of putting things, and his aptitude at coining phrases which always remained a characteristic of his style.

"At Kingsley I had a campaign with a Deist. He proposed Universalism. I said it would not do to go to hell to try if he could not get out again."

"Mr Kersham preached. He seemed an endeavouring man, and has no objection to a stir."

"F H is become a good steady pilgrim and has nearly laid all his whims aside."

"My heart was opened, and the Word (spoken by Crawfoot) seemed to soak into me like rain."

Surprise in secret chains his words suspends,

Just so was my attention chained."

"R H is still compassed with oddities."

"They rather run wildish. O Lord Jesus bless and regulate them."

"——— is buried in shop-keeping."

"We called at Portwood, Stockport. I there saw a number of Dr Coke's 'History of the Bible.' It appears to be a badly-written whimsical catchpenny thing. Dr Coke has written six large quarto volumes to explain the Bible. He is now writing three more, and Adam Clark is writing a Commentary about as large as Dr Coke's, and all to explain the Bible ! So 'they find no end in wandering mazes lost.' O Lord, direct my soul into the plain Bible, through Jesus Christ, Amen.'

The last quotation is a good specimen of Hugh Bourne's caustic vein. Very different is the record of the way in which the old year out and the new year in was kept at Delamere Forest 1809-10. Here the words seem artlessly to fall into the simple cadence of poetry.

Sunday December 31st, 1809. —"We went to the watch-night and had a good time. We parted well with the old year, and the new year came in joyfully, and we covenanted to be more given to the Lord, and I believe the covenant was ratified in heaven." *Monday, January 1st, 1810.* —"We began this year happy in the Lord, singing and covenanting to serve the Lord unreservedly."

Not many "wise after the flesh, not many mighty, not many noble" appear before us as we read in these old diurnals—not many whose names figure in the Biographical Dictionaries of the day ; for saints are at a discount there. Yet there were some who came within sight and touch of Hugh Bourne whose characters was saintly and their lives beneficent. Amongst these was Mrs Samuel Evans, the prototype of George Eliot's immortal ' Dinah Morris" and Mrs Fletcher, the widow of the 'seraphic' Fletcher of Madeley, whose life continued fragrant to the end, which came in December 9th, 1815. Hugh Bou[rne] ... ll t W llin t n and Madeley, and he informs us he had

SOURCES AND ORIGIN. 141

listened to Mrs. Fletcher. He tells too, how he had pressed upon a Mrs. Mitton of those parts, to give herself to labouring for the Lord, but when she set about doing this in right earnest, and began to pray for the people and take their burthen upon her, she was for a period of six weeks plunged into such sore conflict and darkness that in her distress she twice sought out Mrs. Fletcher and laid open her strange case before her and got much light and help from her wise and loving counsel. Here too, duly noted down in the *Journals*, is an anecdote of Mrs. Fletcher, told to Hugh Bourne by Mr. Eli Hanley of Burslem, as the two were on their way to Eccleshall, hard by the palace of the Lord Bishop of Lichfield.

MRS. FLETCHER.

"On the way Mr. Hanley told me, that being once at Madeley, the bargemen sent a request to Mrs. Fletcher to pray for rain. The River Severn is not made navigable throughout, and therefore in time of drought the channel is so shallow that they cannot work. There had then been a long drought. She related the request in the congregation, and said, probably some of them were great sinners, and the Lord was punishing them to humble them. After enlarging a while on this head

MADELEY VILLAGE AND CHURCH.

she said, 'However, we will pray for them.' She then prayed for the Lord to send rain. The congregation firmly believed the Lord would give rain; and the next morning

It is a pleasing thought to a Primitive Methodist that Hugh Bourne was, as recorded in his *Journals*, on intimate terms with Mrs. Samuel Evans, and that once he took part with her in speaking at a service on Ellaston Green and that at another time, or times, he was a guest and probably stayed the night at her home in Derby. George Eliot, as we all know since she herself has told us all about it, found the heroine of Adam Bede in this same Mrs. Evans, her aunt by marriage. The maiden name of Mrs. Evans was Tomlinson, and she was born at Newbold, in Leicestershire. She became a domestic servant at Derby, and afterwards found employment in a lace manufactory in Nottingham, meanwhile living according to the course of this world and being fond of dress and pleasure. But she was soundly converted, threw off her gauds and gay apparel, became Quaker-like in her neatness and, it may be added, Quaker-like too in her philanthropy, for in her modest way she emulated the example of Mrs. Fry in visiting the 'sick and in prison.' She caught the contagion of prison-sickness while following her pious labours. She nerved herself to accompany to the scaffold a frail creature who had killed her own baby. While still in the fresh beauty of her youth Miss Tomlinson carried the evangel to the uplands and into the dales of Derbyshire, thus in the order of providence preparing the way for the advent of our missionaries in these parts. Two of her favourite preaching places were Roston Common and Ellaston Green—the former in Derbyshire, and the latter, just over the river Dove, in Staffordshire. Wootton, so frequently mentioned in these pages is in Ellaston parish, and Ellaston Green is the Hayslope of "Adam Bede," where George Eliot makes her heroine preach that famous sermon we have all read; and since in those early days Methodism would have none of camp meetings, we will appropriate that open-air service for Primitive Methodism, the more so since as we are about to see, Hugh Bourne and she held together what was practically a camp meeting on Ellaston Green, in 1809. George Eliot's father and uncles were born at neighbouring Roston Common, and one of the brothers—Samuel, an earnest Methodist, fell in love with the fair young preacheress whom he had heard at Ashbourne, and wooed and won her. This was in 1804. For some little time they lived at Roston, removing thence to Derby and afterwards to Wirksworth. Conference Methodism got to like women-preaching as little as it liked camp meetings; so when it was proposed—probably at the suggestion of Jabez Bunting—that Miss Barrett and Mrs. Mary Evans while allowed to take appointments should be indicated on the plan by a simple asterisk, Mrs. Evans declined the proposal, and she and her husband joined the Arminian or Faith Methodists of Derby. But, subsequently they both returned to the Church of their youth, and they are both commemorated by tablet in the Chapel at Wirksworth, where their last days were usefully and honourably spent.

And now let us learn what Hugh Bourne has to say of this remarkable woman and of his association with her.

Sunday, June 25th, 1809.—I led the class in the morning at Wootton. We were informed that Betsy Evans, Samuel Evans' wife from Derby, would speak at Wootton. He also is a local preacher. She began about two o'clock. Her voice was low and hoarse at first from having preached so much the week past and having caught several colds; but she got well into the Power. She appears to be very clear in [Scripture] doctrine, and very ready in the Scripture. She seemed to

THE PULPIT FROM WHICH DINAH MORRIS
USED TO PREACH.

DINAH MORRIS.

ADAM
BEDE'S
COTTAGE.

WIRKSWORTH CHAPEL, WHERE
DINAH MORRIS USED TO WORSHIP AND PREACH.

speak fully in the Spirit, and from the little I saw of her she seems to be as fully devoted to God as any woman I ever saw. O Lord, bless and establish her. Her husband also spoke. He appears to be an excellent man. O my Father, bless and keep him. My brother James then spoke, and then I went up, so that we occupied most of the afternoon, and we had, after, a plead with sinners near the ale-house. We had but little persecution, though it was Wake (time)."

While at Drayton, in Shropshire, on February 12, 1810, he "felt an impression to go to Derby" to see his friends, and on March 19 and 21 he acted on that impression. Of his interview with the Evans on the former date he says little, but of that which took place two days after he speaks more fully, giving the gist of what must surely have been imparted after reserve was thawed and the talk had grown close and confidential. Now that ninety years and more have passed there is no need to keep anything back or thinly to veil names behind initials.

"I came to Derby and had some conversation with Mr. Samuel Evans and his wife. He is an earnest man. She has been and is an extraordinary woman. She has been very near Ann Cutler's experience, but she met with great persecution especially from Jonathan Edmondson. She lost some ground when entering into the marriage state. She engaged this (sic) in a cloudy day while under persecution. I was much instructed by her conversation. At night I led Mr. Evans class. It was a good time. There are many of them strong in grace, yet there was much unbelief."

A few words must be given as to the evidence afforded by the *Journals* of the close association of our founders with those other communities of kindred aims and sympathies standing on the outskirts of Methodism that were struggling into independent existence. Church-formation seems to go on in much the same way as world-formation, if what scientists tell us be true. The worlds and Churches to be, at first seem to stand so close together and partake so much of the same character as to be almost indistinguishable one from the other. The process of differentiation is a gradual one, and the attainment of complete separation and independence is the work of time. So it was, at the beginning of the nineteenth century, in the contiguous counties of Yorkshire, Lancashire, Staffordshire, and Cheshire. That common movement we call Revivalism was like the whirling nebulous matter that every now and again throws off a sphere to go on whirling henceforth on its own account. To this fact we have already called the reader's attention, and it is forced upon us again as we read these *Journals*, and insistence upon this fact is all the more justifiable, because it has not, we are persuaded, had the recognition its importance demands. Our founders fraternised and co-operated with the Revivalists, the Quaker Methodists, and the Independent Methodists. They helped and were helped by them. The first camp meetings were largely supported and staffed as to preachers and praying labourers, by these same religionists, and the obligation thus incurred was paid back in full. These are the facts we cannot but recognise as we read the *Journals* alike of Bourne and Clowes.

The origin of the Independent Methodists dates from 1805, but it would seem its first Conference was not held until 1807, for just after the Norton Camp Meeting Bourne writes:—

"After the meeting I visited Macclesfield again, and was at the house of a friend who was a member of the Independent Methodists. These Methodists had delegates from different parts, and were holding a first Conference; and one of their main matters was arranging for an interchange of preachers to promote variety."

Bourne was also present at the next Conference, and evidently took part in the proceedings; for a discussion having arisen on the subject of the ministry of women, he agreed to draw up answers to certain questions which had been propounded. We all know, without reading the able brief he prepared, what side he would take in the controversy which then so heated and divided men. Though he was no "ladies' man" in the sense usually understood by that phrase, but quite the reverse, he was the convinced advocate and defender of woman's right to exercise her gifts in the public ministry of the Word. Mr. Peter Phillips, to whom he read the written statement he had drawn up, was so struck with the ability shown in his presentation of the case that he asked and got leave to send it to the press.

Of Peter Phillips, the recognised founder of the Independent Methodists (with whom were now associated the Quaker Methodists) we get repeated glimpses in the *Journals*. Perhaps the most interesting of these is that which lets us see a sort of "round table conference" going on in his house, at which were present besides himself, Hugh Bourne, Dr. Paul Johnson, the physician of Lorenzo Dow and hero of Norton Camp Meeting, and a certain Mr. Sigston. This member of the group we judge to have been the Methodist schoolmaster of Leeds, the friend and biographer of Bramwell, and the leading spirit in the troubles rising out of the organ case which led, in 1828, to the formation of the Protestant Methodists. If our surmise be correct this little gathering was a notable one. Its purpose was to consider what means should be adopted in order to carry on and extend the revival begun in the district through the agency of Lorenzo Dow, Dr. Johnson, and the Camp Meetingers. The outcome of the conference was a book. It was resolved to print and circulate as largely as possible the life of Benjamin Abbot, the American evangelist. In connection with the business of preparing and printing this book Bourne says:—

MR. SIGSTON.

"*Thursday, July 28th, 1808.*—I set out for Leeds. I took this long journey rather at the instance of Warrington friends, in order that the extracts to be added in the life of Abbot might be perfected. I went through Knutsford, Altringham, Manchester, Middleton, Rochdale, Halifax, and Bradford. There are many villages and many Methodist chapels. When I first stepped into Yorkshire, I kneeled down and prayed, and I found that the Lord would be with us in Yorkshire."

He reached Leeds a little before noon the next day, with sore feet; heard "Billy" Dawson on the Sunday, and felt himself fully paid for his journey had he done nothing more than hear him; returned by coach to Manchester, and walked eighteen miles to Stockton Heath, where a meeting was to be held by Dr. Johnson, who did his very best to convert him to Quakerism but did not succeed. Another short entry lets us see a conference of another kind, in which Peter Phillips and Hugh Bourne take their part. This time it is confined to these two, and both are in grim earnest as they confer:—

"*October 3rd, 1809.*—I had a severe controversy with Peter Phillips, he having adopted some of Mr. Law's opinions."

Other prominent members of the Quaker Methodists were Mr. and Mrs. Eaton of Stockton Heath, and Mrs. Richardson of Warrington. In the published memoir of Mrs. Eaton, it is stated she was led into peace through a conversation with Hugh Bourne. Mrs. Richardson has already been referred to. As her memoirs, published after her death, which occurred in 1848, show, she became eminent as a preacheress. One of the few incidents of this period found in Clowes' *Journals* relates to this estimable woman:—

MR. WILLIAM DAWSON.
(Known as "Billy" Dawson.)

"At Stockton Heath I preached, and also at Warrington, at Mrs. Richardson's, where I had times of refreshing from the presence of the Lord. Mrs. Richardson became a speaker amongst us, and was an acceptable labourer in the Lord's vineyard. At the first establishment of preaching in her house, I was conducting the religious services one evening, when one of the magistrates came in and demanded a sight of my licence. I put my hand into my pocket, and handed it to him. He then said he wanted to see the licence of the house as a place for preaching. One of the people told him it was above. He said, 'I must have it down.' The individual replied, 'It is in heaven.' He then began to swear and order the congregation to disperse; one man rose to obey the magistrate's order when Mrs. Richardson exclaimed, 'Sit down, my friend, and be quiet. My house is my own;' and then she cried out in prayer for God to save Justice L——. At this the magistrate endeavoured to effect his escape, but Mrs. Richardson followed him into the street, praying aloud for the Lord to have mercy on Justice L——; to convert Justice L——, and make him a Methodist preacher. He then told her he would send the water engines and blow her windows out; but she continued to raise such a storm of prayer about his ears, that he hastened his flight, leaving the Bible and hymn book in the street, which he had taken from before me whilst preaching; he, however, took my licence with him; but in a few days after I went to him, accompanied by a friend. When he saw us approaching his house, he came out with the licence in his hand, and gave it to me saying, 'Your servant, sir.' He immediately retired into the house, or else I purposed to have given him a lecture on the impropriety of his conduct." (Clowes' *Journals*, pp. 107, 8).

Finally, briefest mention must be made of the Band Room Methodists of Manchester if for no other reason than to correct the published statement that these secessionists of 1810 from the Methodists, or the better part of them, were absorbed by the Primitive Methodists. The statement is not correct, the fact being that the erstwhile Band Room Methodists merged into the United Free Gospel Churches. The *Journals* record one visit paid by Hugh Bourne on October 8th, 1809, to these lively people. He saw "many bright faces, and praying George's eyes were so bright he could scarce look at them." But his own keen eyes detected some lightsomeness, and he observes "there is much antinomianism amongst revivalists."

One thing it is impossible not to feel as we read these *Journals* in relation to Bourne and Clowes and their fellow-workers—they lived amid the marvellous and the supernatural. Wesley chronicles dreams, practised sortilege, and believed in ghosts. Ghosts, indeed, do not figure much, if at all, in these pages, but there are dreams in plenty. They all dreamed, and told their dreams, and sought the interpretation thereof; for the dreams were regarded as full of religious significance, and as having a close bearing on the day's work and duty. Faith healing and exorcism were also articles of belief as was telepathy—to use the modern term. Now and again they are convinced that some one is just then in need of them, or is praying for them. They believe in the power of the evil one as working in the children of disobedience, and often it is felt to be a serious struggle between the malign power and the power which they can exercise through faith. All alike unfeignedly believe in impressions—suggestive impulses like that which said to Philip "Go and join thyself to this chariot." Often Hugh Bourne's itinerary is modified by its being borne in upon him that he must go yonder and not there. He has wonderful openings into the meaning of Scripture. Occasionally when the testimony of the Lord as borne through human lips is rejected, especially by one who is a professing Christian, the power he had or might have had, is forfeit, and comes upon him who faithfully testified, leaving the other stripped and bare as a blasted oak on the heath. So we might go on accumulating evidence to show that to these fervid Christians the very atmosphere they breathed seemed surcharged with the supernatural. The strange mystical language they used must not be passed over. They spoke of "the spirit of burning," of "being sealed with the spirit," of having "solid weightiness," of being "in the keen cutting power," or "in the binding power," of "drawing the power," etc., etc. Now it has usually been taken for granted that this strain in the Christian life of our fathers and founders was due to their intercourse with James Crawfoot and his influence upon them. This view we confess to having shared, but closer examination has tended to modify it. It is quite fatal to the view as unmodified, that W. Clowes quite as much as Hugh Bourne and the rest talked over their deep experiences, and used mystical language of the purest water before they paid their first visit to Crawfoot in 1807.

In November, 1809, we find James Crawfoot settled in a small homestead in the Forest of Delamere near Brinn, where there was a Methodist cause largely raised and supported by him. He had also begun a monthly service on the Saturday evening at his own Forest home, at which it was not unusual in the midst of the praying and conversation-preaching and recital of experience for persons to enter into a state of trance and have visions; hence the frequenters of these services were widely known as Magic Methodists. As for Crawfoot, he was a Methodist local preacher in the Northwich Circuit when Hugh Bourne, with the cordial co-operation of his brother, agreed to give him ten shillings a week until Lady Day in order to carry on evangelistic labours on the Cheshire and Staffordshire sides on alternate fortnights. The fact that Crawfoot was in needy circumstances at this time also weighed with Bourne in making this agreement. Philanthropy joined with evangelistic zeal in sealing the contract. Crawfoot was fifty years of age when he thus became an itinerant preacher, and we gather that almost immediately after this his relations with parent Methodism—

TARVIN VILLAGE AND CHURCH.

very much strained already—reached the decisive breaking point. As we have seen, Crawfoot's genius did not lie in the direction of camp meetings, and he took part in one only. Sad to say, the *Journals* of Hugh Bourne set forth the rise, culmination, and setting of a friendship between him and Crawfoot, and 1813 witnessed the passing of Crawfoot from Primitive Methodist life. Summoned by H. B. to answer certain charges at the Quarterly Meeting at Tunstall he failed to appear, and judgment went by default. We do not know that it is necessary to go fully into these charges. Probably the fact that during his itinerancy Crawfoot had married Hannah Mountford, the long-time faithful servant of the Bournes, the visionary, and as is most likely, the person to whom H. B.

do with the breach, especially when we remember that Crawfoot had been understood to be an admirer of the celibate state, and had instilled his purely theoretic views into the mind of his patron. Then the failure of his new wife's health soon after marriage led to his omitting occasionally to take his appointments, which was a dereliction of duty that in Hugh Bourne's eyes hardly any circumstances could extenuate. Probably also Crawfoot was easy-going and lax in discipline; somewhat lax of tongue, too, it is to be feared, and at times carried out of himself by his own popularity. The truth of the matter would probably be found in an amalgam of all these explanations. So, as we have said, 1813 saw the passing of Crawfoot from the plan to the regret of some. "Howbeit a few clave unto him," and it is even said that some small societies called

TARVIN CHURCH. CRAWFOOT'S BURIAL-PLACE.

themselves after his name as late as 1831. As for Crawfoot, he died suddenly and triumphantly in 1839, and was buried in Tarvin Churchyard.

We are now ready for the question: What, Connexionally, do we owe to James Crawfoot? Along with, and probably as the result of the remarkable and in every way admirable quickened interest now being shown in the men and events of our early history, there are some signs of the beginning amongst us of what we may call a Crawfoot cult. But let us eschew extravagance, and praise with discrimination. We have in another place called Crawfoot "a rustic mystic," and the title is deserved—

the rusticity as well as the mysticism must be remembered. Our founders were mystics to begin with, but Crawfoot modified their mysticism, both for the better and also for the worse. For the better, because he helped to make it more altruistic and vicarious, so that they became less wrapped up in their own frames and feelings, and more participant in the spiritual experiences of others. He taught them much concerning the nature of spiritual conflicts. 'To explain and illustrate this matter was a main point with J. Crawfoot. His discourse was that in the exercise of faith we made war against the enemy of souls, and must expect him to make war in return, and if that could not be felt, it would be no wrestling.' He taught them all that they expressed in the oft-repeated phrases "taking the burthen" of others, "exercising faith in silence" for others, and with this clue in hand a discerning reader may find in our Connexional magazines for many successive years, plain proof how firm a hold these teachings had upon the thoughts of its leading minds.

We are still on with the *Journals*, and in them there is preserved a letter written by H. Bourne to Miss Ward, in which the writer shows himself the disciple of "the Old Man of the Forest." One might say he gives us his philosophy of the conflict of personal atmospheres. The whole letter, of which we give but a part, is remarkably accordant with to-day's trend of thought.

"It may probably be that you may bring more glory to God, and more benefit to mankind, in that line of life than in any other. It will bring you into many people's company, and give you an opportunity of doing much for God. You must look unto the power that worketh secretly—the doctrine you were teaching me when you spoke of Lorenzo. You have the fountain in you, and if you breathe your soul, the power will move upon the people you are in company with. This is all by faith. Herein is the excellency of the work of faith,—it will have its effect upon the people either in silence, or when you are doing your worldly business. Thus you may work for God at all times, and in all places and nothing can hinder you, and if there be an opening, you may also talk about religion, and offer a present salvation without money or price. But there is one point that you should be well acquainted with and it is nearly, if not quite your doctrine of two contending powers. As the power of God flows from you upon others, to enlighten convince, convert, heal, &c, so the powers of hell from others will strike upon you to hurt, wound, slay, &c. Therefore, when this is the case be not alarmed, nor think you have lost ground for *this is only bearing the burden of others*, and by faith you will conquer, and they will be very much benefited. If you do not mind this, you will be harassed and tempted that you have lost ground, and your faith will be weakened; therefore, stand fast and conquer for others.

When in company with covetous persons, I have been tempted to worldly-mindedness, and in passionate company, to anger and passion, but I never mind it, *I know it is their spirit*, and if I can conquer it the power of God will mightily return upon them, and hell will be bound.'—Stockton Heath, April 21st, 1810.

Our next quotation may be regarded as a concrete example of the taking of another's burden, only in this case the burden is that of a whole city rather than that of a single person. The quotation affords equal proof of the influence of Crawfoot, in first inducing and observing and then interpreting certain mystical forms of thought and feeling. One biographer of Hugh Bourne proffers this passage as a "racy" bit—surely a most unfortunate description. It may be grim, dantesque, quaint as though just lifted from the *Journals* of George Fox—but "racy"! It is as though one should say of a band of cut-throats that they had behaved in a most "ridiculous" fashion. It seems no lightsome matter standing with Hugh Bourne in that cathedral. The "dim religious light" looks funereal: the *Te Deum* sounds like a dirge. We too are glad to escape, feeling almost persuaded of the doom hanging over the big steeple house and the city that knows not the day of its visitation.

"I was at Lichfield, to get a licence for Mow Meeting, and I went into the minster. After the service began, it ran through my mind, 'Get thee out of this place, and beware of the woman that has the golden cup in her hand, and those that are with her; their ways are death: sin no more, lest a worse thing come upon thee.' This startled me, as I had before taken delight in their singing of the service. I saw much lightness and sin among the parsons. It seemed like gross idolatry in them to spend their time in such a manner; but then I thought 'The words of the service are good.' It then struck me, 'These people draweth nigh unto me with their lips,' &c. I prayed to God that if the impression to go out was from Him, it might increase, if not, that it might go away: it increased till I was quite miserable. I then thought to go out, and a voice came, 'Escape for thy life,' &c. They were singing the *Te Deum*. I took my hat as soon as they had done the *Te Deum*, and went out, and the burden was removed. It looked as if judgments hung over that place. I stopped all afternoon in Lichfield, and such a travail of soul came upon me as I never before experienced,—it was for the city; I mourned greatly: it seemed as if the people had almost sinned out the day of their visitation. I trembled for the place and people: O my God, have mercy on them. I asked James Crawfoot at the Forest about this. He said it was the sign of the times. It was Jesus Christ travailing in me. I might go twenty times and not have the same travail. I had found myself willing to die for them. He said something would turn up, either the gospel would be introduced, or afflictions would come upon them."

LICHFIELD CATHEDRAL.

152　PRIMITIVE METHODIST CHURCH.

OLD LICHFIELD.
Market Hall.　　St. Mary's Church.　　Town Hall.　　"Three Crowns," Dr. Johnson's Birth-place.

LICHFIELD, 19TH CENTURY.

We have intimated that James Crawfoot's influence on our fathers, though undoubtedly great, was not exclusively for good. He deepened their knowledge of the things of the spirit, but he was the means of their becoming acquainted with "vision-work," as Hugh Bourne called it, and this was at the best a very doubtful advantage. To what extent Crawfoot favoured and was responsible for those singular manifestations which earned for the frequenters of the Forest Chapel the title of Magic Methodists we cannot tell; but there is no evidence that he disapproved of those manifestations. Rather does the evidence seem to indicate that they were received as tokens of the divine favour and accepted as helps to faith. It was on their first visit to the Forest in 1807 that Bourne and Clowes got also their first experience of these strange phenomena. Both note what took place, but, rather singular to say, it is Hugh Bourne who writes most critically and distrustfully, and he is at the beginning much less prepossessed in favour of the Old Man of the Forest and with Forest ways than is Clowes. Here the matter might end were it not that the *Journals* clearly show that the time soon came when "the visionary power" was not confined to the Forest, but was claimed to be exercised by some of those who were in closest relations with Bourne and later on with Clowes. As a rule, they were the most pious and zealous females who had this experience—such as Hannah Mountford. Frequently do we meet with the entry So and so "went into vision." The word "vision" seems fitter than the word trance to designate the character of the experience professed, because however insensible to outward things the person under seizure might seem to be, she spoke on coming out of her trance, of the revelations vouchsafed. The most common form the revelations took, was to indicate the true order of precedence enjoyed by the heads of the Church. The visionary seemed to see projected on the spiritual plane the transfigured forms of these chiefs. In one hand they bore the trumpet and in the other the cup—the emblems of their office. They were not seen standing in a horizontal line, but one above the other, as though mounted on the rungs of an invisible ladder. Great significance was attached to the position they relatively occupied as seen in the vision, because it served to reveal their real status and condition in the sight of heaven and their value to the little society of the faithful on earth. Did the vision show one with his trumpet lying on the ground and his cup held crooked? then such a one was in a parlous state. Now, it is easy to see how such visionary power as this claimed to be could be abused to flatter, or to minister to envy or detraction. One or two additional remarks on this strange episode in this preliminary period may be made.

Whatever view may be taken of this vision-work—whether it be regarded as the offspring of enthusiasm and delusion, or the result of imposture, or as consisting of genuine psychical and spiritual experience, or as a mixture of some or all of these—still we can learn from these diagrams, which profess to be so many bulletins from the spiritual world, what was the current local estimate of those persons in whom we are historically interested. Well, Lorenzo Dow is always the leading trumpeter; W. Lockwood, of whom we get occasional tidings and glimpses as a noted Wesleyan preacher in these parts, and who will come before us again very shortly, stands high; so does J. Crawfoot. Clowes is always above Hugh Bourne, and James Bourne, humble soul, is always pretty near the bottom. If this is not the order of precedence in which heaven ranged these men, it certainly was the order in which they were ranged by those who knew and worked with them on earth. Nor does any one—not even Hugh Bourne—seem disposed to quarrel with the current estimate; it is accepted and recorded without demur. Whatever one may think of the vision-work these are facts worth noting.

Hugh Bourne never professed to go into vision himself, though there is abundant evidence to show that, for a time, he believed both in the genuineness and usefulness of the manifestations, and once he records his inclination to "seek after the visionary power." There are signs, too, that as time went on, the movement deteriorated in character. As the manifestations became more frequent they tended to become more extravagant and puerile. They reached their height in 1810-11, and after July, 1811, when the last bulletin was issued we hear no more of them. It only remains to express thankfulness that this mysticism run mad did not end in disaster. We suspect it was the downfall of Mrs Dunnell that ended it, for with her disappearance the visions disappeared. The heavily-laden atmosphere was purged of its vapours; the muddy waters ran themselves clear. By the time the establishment of the Primitive Methodist Connexion is completed in 1812, we seem to have got into a less romantic region, but into one more in keeping with the hard facts and requirements of the time. Hugh Bourne's native sagacity fully asserts itself, and guided and assisted by the resolute and level-headed Tunstall men the work of discipline and edification will get all needful attention.

How is it that in closing Hugh Bourne's early *Journals* the words of the Ecclesiast come unbidden to the mind and refuse to quit—"All things are full of labour; man cannot utter it"? Perhaps for one reason, because "labour" is Hugh Bourne's chosen word to denote what is done for God. He might "work" in the fields, but he "laboured" in prayer and for souls. Nature might be stingy and reluctant to yield the due returns of toil, but not so reluctant as the human heart. Our wonder rises as we try to think of the labour performed by our fathers, even in these preparatory years. As for Bourne, he was always on the move. Like Wesley he went to and fro in the earth, though, of course, his movements were confined within much more restricted limits, and were performed almost exclusively on foot. The miles he walked! In the Biblical sense he was the father of them who walk to their appointments. In these days of rapid and luxurious locomotion it is hard to grasp the truth as to the long weary trudges he was constantly undertaking in all sorts of weather—trudges varied by occasional mischances, such as losing the way or being benighted on unfamiliar roads. No wonder that, even before this period ends, there are ominous signs that his feet were cruelly wronged and that retribution would come. And what Hugh Bourne did the rest of the Camp Meeting fathers were at whiles wont to do, as the following example selected from the experience of James Bourne will show:—

"Mr James Bourne has risen early on Saturday morning and worked hard on the farm at Bemersley till noon, and then set off to walk to Warrington and sleep, which was thirty-five miles; then rise early on Sunday and go to Risley in Lancashire, preach three times, besides holding other services, return into Cheshire to sleep; then start home early on Monday, and go to hoe potatoes in the heigh-fields in the afternoon; thus doing near two days' labour on the farm besides an abunda[nce of labour on] the Sabbath, and about eighty miles' walking in the s[pace of sixty hours]."*

* Thomas [Bateman,] *[A] L[ife and] H[istory of William Cla]rke,* 1868, pp 6, 7

JAMES BOURNE.

Here is the record of another hard day's work, in which the brothers and their horse were partners:

"*Sunday, July 10th, 1808.*—Set off (from Kingsley) early to Wootton, about seven miles, to appoint a meeting for half-past two. I had then about ten miles to go to Tean, and a hilly cross-country road. However, the Lord gave me strength, and I forced my way; but was very foot-sore, and quite a stranger to the road. I arrived before James Bourne had read his text; and the power of the Lord laid hold on part of the congregation. J. Bourne had a horse; so we rode by turns, and forced our way to Wootton in due time, and we had a pleasant meeting. We then set off home (upwards of twenty miles) and arrived late."

Hugh Bourne was a working-man during the greater part of the time covered by these *Journals*. He could not live on his private means, and he would not live on the bounty of others. So we have many entries which show—sometimes in an odd way—

how he combined labouring for the meat which perisheth with the higher kind of labour. Take the following as samples:—

"I worked at Milton (Abbey Farm, the home of his grandfather), getting the roof of the barn up, and was kept in peace all the day." "Fasted, read, and worked." "Haymaking and studying Greek." "Prayed in the barn while shading." "In the afternoon I was setting up corn after three scythes, and by working quickly I often got a little time to kneel behind a 'kiver,' which was well for me. I felt nothing in me that desired anything but God."

His habits were simple, and he was most abstemious that he might the more fully devote himself to his beloved work. Mr. Thomas Steele, the son of Mr. James Steele of Tunstall, who was in a position to know, confirms this:—

"I know he used frequently to walk forty or fifty miles a day, and that under circumstances of self-denial, little practised, or even known by most. He used to put into his pocket two or three hard-boiled eggs, and a little dry bread, in the morning, and during his journey, he would sit down by a well of water and take his humble fare, and then travel on in pursuit of his great object of winning souls."*

THOMAS STEELE,
SON OF JAMES STEELE.

WIFE OF
THOMAS STEELE.
(From a miniature.)

With the almost patriarchal scene thus called up by Mr. Thomas Steele, of Bourne sitting by the well, ready, as soon as he has rested and eaten his frugal meal, to address himself to the long journey which awaits him, we may fittingly end this Book, which may be called our Connexional Book Genesis.

* Letter quoted in Walford's "Life," vol. i. p. 210.

BOOK II.

THE PERIOD OF CIRCUIT PREDOMINANCE AND ENTERPRISE

INTRODUCTORY.

THE book we now begin will deal with the history of our Church from 1811 to the year 1843, when, following the superannuation of Bourne and Clowes in 1842, the General Missionary Committee, with its Executive located in London, was established. The period in question practically covers the lifetime of one generation just as, singular to say, the next or Middle Period of our history also does. During these thirty-two years the Connexion underwent great changes, traversed two serious crises, encountered much opposition, and yet at the end had a record of progress to show almost without a parallel. What was the ground it covered in 1811 the first written plans show: in 1843 it had reached almost every county of England, and some in Wales, had penetrated into Scotland, Ireland, the Isle of Man, and the Channel Isles, and had even sent one or two of its missionaries to the United States. The 200 members it began with in 1811 had by 1843 grown to 85,625.

But the real history of a period like this cannot be confined to a mere chronological narrative setting forth the facts of geographical extension and numerical growth. Such a narrative only gives materials for history which after all has mainly to do with the interaction of causes, and especially with the play and interplay of mind. Let us, therefore, briefly indicate some of the salient features of the internal and external History of our Church (other than the progress made during this period), which will challenge our attention as we proceed.

The chief outstanding feature of the period—that which gives it its distinctive character, is the part played by leading circuits in the life and work of the Connexion. In the century's evolution of our Church we have had in turn the flourishing and energising of the Circuit, the District, the Church; just as in the order of Nature, we have "first the blade, then the ear, then the full corn in the ear." At first the Connexion was co-extensive with Tunstall Circuit. From 1816 to 1818 there were two circuits, Tunstall and Derby (the latter being superseded by Nottingham Circuit in 1817); and from 1818 to 1819 there were three—Tunstall, Nottingham, and Loughborough. Hugh Bourne may be said to have been the chief unifying bond between the circuits during this rudimentary period. He was appointed superintendent of Tunstall Circuit in 1814, and when the other circuits were formed he kept on discharging the duties of the office, holding the quarterly meetings and exercising discipline and oversight in much the same way as does a Presiding Elder of the Methodist Episcopal Church of the U.S.A. When Hugh Bourne's health failed at the beginning of 1819—as well it might, considering the physical and mental strain this general superintendency involved—there followed (*post hoc though probably not propter* how) the establishment of Annual Meetings or Conferences constituted on the representative principle. The first and not the least important of these, though called only a Preparatory Meeting, was held at Nottingham in 1819. Thus the memorable year of Peterloo may conveniently be taken as marking the end of a sub-period of our history. From this time onwards to 1843 there was little centralisation. The circuits had great powers of initiative and control, and some of them by boldly and wisely exercising these powers acquired great influence. Like the tribes of Israel they had the work assigned them of subjugating the land, and by means of the Circuit Missions, which were so distinctive a feature of the time, quite remarkable results were achieved— so remarkable indeed as to start the questions whether we have not lost as well as gained by centralisation, and whether we should not do well to revert in part to the method which was crowned with such signal success in the heroic period of our history.

But the period before us was one of striking contrasts. If it may rightly be regarded as *the Heroic Period* of our history since, with the slenderest means and appliances and in the face of difficulties neither few nor small so much was accomplished, it may also with equal truth be regarded as having been the *period of the Connexion's Lowliness and Humiliation*. Our fathers must surely have divined what was before them when they put on the first class-ticket of the Connexion the words :—"For as concerning this sect, we know that everywhere it is spoken against." The words were prophetic, and might appropriately enough have served as our motto from 1811 to 1843. It was the "Ranter" period, for by that opprobrious word we were better known than by the name that rightly belonged to us. We know nothing of all this. Even our fathers scarcely came within the range of such experience, for in the forties the denomination was emerging from the valley, winning a recognised position and seeking to minister to the enlarging needs of those whom it had rescued and elevated and gathered into church fellowship. But *their* fathers had passed through the valley and tasted of its humiliation. If therefore, we would denominationally "see ourselves as others saw us" then, it can only be done in the historical way. We must seek to catch the reflection of the current estimate of us and our work found here and there in the cyclopædias, and other books and serials of the time. These scant references are all of the same cast and tone. If they do not speak against they speak as from a higher elevation downwards. All, whether friendly or otherwise—and quite as much when they are friendly as when they are unfriendly—take for granted that our work lies amongst "the ruder of the lower class," [*] "the neglected and the forgotten" [†], that it is 'to labour on the great waste of poverty, ignorance, and crime, whose moral cultivation is to a considerable extent neglected by others"[‡] The fact that later on such statements became traditional and continued to be parroted long after they had ceased to be wholly correct or pertinent does not alter the fact that once they were true to the letter. What all men said about our mission and work, though in different tones and from opposite motives, must have been largely correct. The facts must have been as stated, and could not well have been otherwise. That we had a dispensation of

[*] Dr. Evans' "Sketches of all Denominations."
[†] John Angell James.
[‡] Dean Campbell.

the Gospel to the veriest of the poor given unto us as a people was accordant with the highest probabilities. It must have been so if we had a right to the name we bore. If we were to make good our claim to have returned to the spirit and methods of early Methodism it was to be expected that the resemblance would not stop here, but that we should be found doing as she then did—ministering to the people who were "perishing for lack of knowledge," exciting the same opprobrium and receiving the same treatment. If we inherited her spirit it was meet we should enter into her labours and be requited even as she had been requited.* Even if every line of print referring to us and our work prior to 1813 had been blotted out, any one might have known where to find us; for where else should we be but at the very foundation-beds of the national life, then so sadly out of course as to threaten ruin to the entire superstructure?

As might be expected from what has just been said, the period before us was distinctively the *Period of Persecution*. Persecution and the period seem indeed exactly to coincide, for the last two cases of the imprisonment of our ministers for preaching the Gospel occurred in 1813. But though the first period of our history seems sombre enough as we write of its humiliation, its poverty and persecution, we must remember what has been said as to the striking contrasts this period affords. One such contrast emerges here—the contrast of joy with tribulation. Our fathers were not, any more than the early Methodists were, men of sad hearts and rueful countenances, and we cannot bring ourselves to think of them as such. Their souls were "full of music," as Clowes said his was. Sometimes they might sing to keep their spirits up, and so we may now and again detect a plaintive note in their music. But nevertheless they made the valley of humiliation resound with their songs, and any one overhearing them might have made the same comment as did Mr Greatheart when the shepherd-boy was heard singing in the valley—

'Here little, and hereafter bliss,
Is best from age to age.'

"Do you hear them? I will dare to say that these people have a merrier life, and wear more of that herb called hearts-ease in their bosom, than they that are clad in silk and velvet.' In truth, the period was pre-eminently one of sacred song. Our fathers sang at their work like Adam Bede; they sang in prison like Paul and Silas, and the strains of their camp-meeting hymns floated in the air, and the echoes of those hymns have entered into literature, and to-day we are as it were present with William Howitt 'in the dusk of a summer evening the moon hanging in the far western sky, the dark leaves of the brook-side alders rustling in the twilight air, while the chorused words of 'All is well!'—'All is well!' come from the camp ground over the shadowy waste with an unearthly effect.'† Yes, "All was well!"

* 'While the successors of the Wesleyan preachers who formerly sought out colliers and miners are now faithfully preaching the Gospel to their well-established societies, the Primitive Methodists, a body already (1842) numbering perhaps 70,000 members, are principally performing the very work, so far as it is performed at all, which Wesleyan Methodism once accomplished."—Dr Dixon "Observations in Europe."
† "Rural Life in England."

We shall be ill-advised if we deny or resent or apologise for the statement once so insistently made, that we were the Church for the neglected and the forgotten. The estimate, though it looks like a reproach, is really only the obverse of a compliment. We just turn the medal and lo! we have something to be glad and thankful for. We see a new meaning in the Apostle's words. "Let the brother of low degree glory in his high estate." When men said that our special mission was to the poor, the ignorant, the degraded, perhaps going the length of intimating that for every Primitive Methodist won there was one drunkard, or profligate, or criminal the less,* they could only conclude that our mission was to do this kind of work because they saw us doing it. They had not, and did not pretend to have, any revelation from heaven as to what our mission was. What was the characteristic and the glory of our early history can be learned from others — they are our witnesses. We were down amongst the Luddites and Levellers, the oppressed and almost despairing agricultural labourers, the miners struggling for the rights of labour and the dues of citizenship. And so our history is also partially written in the history of the time.† We helped the nation to tide over its crises. For all who have written of the period before us have admitted that never was the nation in a more critical condition. They marvel that revolution was averted, that the proletariat, the unfranchised, the victims of industrial changes, heavy taxation and oppressive laws were so patient, and somehow turned aside from unprincipled agitators and chose the path of peaceful reform. They cannot understand it. It was contrary to the precedents of history—to what was happening on the Continent. All the omens were unfavourable, and yet a happy issue was found out of all these national troubles. Puzzled to account for this they fall back for an explanation on an abstraction—"the order-loving genius of the Teutonic race," but even while they are doing this they slip in some such qualifying words as "inspired by Christian teaching," words which one thinks make a considerable difference, and at once start the question. "Who were the teachers, and how did they bring their teaching practically to bear on the people?" If a new ethical spirit and direction were given to the democracy of the time who more likely to have infused that spirit and given the needful impact and guidance than that community which *then*, whatever be the case now, everybody affirmed was in closest touch with the neglected classes? If it were not so, then all that need be said is that there must be a widespread recantation and wholesale eating of words.

* Horace Mann.
† Fairburn's "Religion in History and in the Life of To-day," pp. 14, 15 might be advantageously referred to in this connection.

CHAPTER I.

CONSOLIDATION AND THE TUNSTALL NON-MISSION LAW.

JOHN WEDGWOOD.

IF we are under the illusion that Primitive Methodism entered at once upon a career of swift and uninterrupted advance, going forth "conquering and to conquer," the illusion will be quickly dispelled; for, in sober truth, the first few years immediately succeeding 1811 were not marked by any considerable geographical extension or numerical progress. In a certain way statistics show this, and a partial explanation of the fact will disclose itself as we proceed with our narrative. Our Church, like every other, has not been exempt from seasons of lassitude; it has had its periods of pause and retardment. So we have yet for a little while to do with the edification of improvement rather than with the edification of enlargement; to chronicle what the Connexion did towards consolidating and equipping itself rather than follow it in a rapid course of conquest.

There is an unaccountable break in Hugh Bourne's *Journals* from February 13th, 1812, where he records the taking of the denominational name to February 7th, 1813; nor do we get much help from Clowes' *Journal* because of its lack of chronological arrangement and the absence of dates. In his *History* Hugh Bourne briefly sums up the year thus: "The work kept enlarging [*i.e.*, within the old area], and the Connexion went on in a kind of regular way without much variation throughout the year." Reading this, one is tempted to exclaim, "What! has the reign of routine begun thus early? Day after day does nothing happen that is startling or worth recording!" Not so. We may be sure if they did no more than fulfil their planned appointments the preachers would find labour enough, and their days would not pass without incident. In proof of this we turn to the *Journals* of our chief founders where the name of a remarkable man—one of the men of special type who seem to have been raised up to do a special work—is first brought before us, and if it be true that the early part of the year 1813 saw John Wedgwood, a local preacher on trial, then something was being done for the future of the Connexion not only in the Midlands but in the Cheshire region as well.

JOHN WEDGWOOD.

As a prominent and lasting memorial of his usefulness in this latter district there stands in Crewe, that town of sudden and marvellous growth—

a goodly building, bearing on its front the inscription, Wedgwood Primitive Methodist Chapel, 1865.

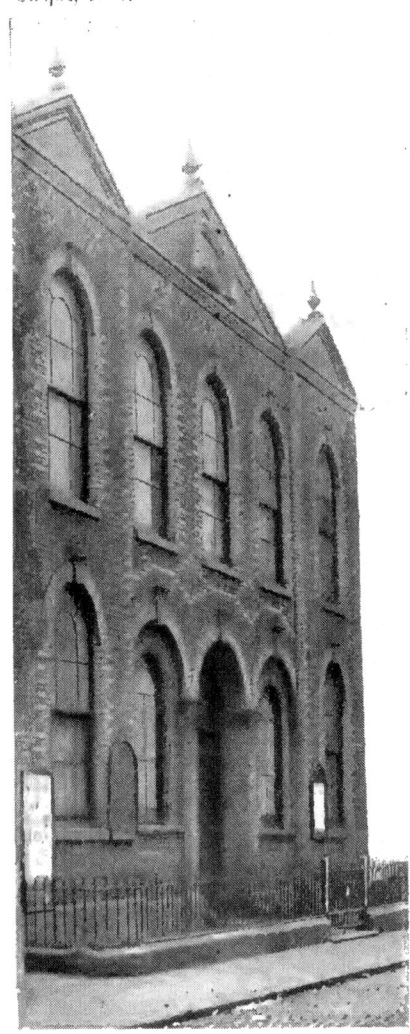

Diligent inquiry has failed to reward us with a clear outline of Wedgwood's early life, as seems to have been the case with all previous biographers. The following facts about him, gleaned from various sources, may, however, be relied upon. He was a scion of the famous family to which Clowes also belonged. As a youth he followed the potting business, becoming expert and able to earn good wages as a "thrower." His father lived "near Tunstall," and had houses and land, which, by its richness in minerals, made up for any lack of amplitude or poverty of soil. Being the eldest son, John inherited property which to the end he knew and cared little about managing either in his own interests or, as a trustee, in the interests of others. Still, being in easy worldly circumstances, he was afterwards enabled as a missionary to bear his own charges. Little is known as to the time and circumstances of his conversion. We gather that he occasionally attended the ministrations of his uncle, who was a clergyman in Burslem; but, not being a bigot, he went to hear other ministers, and amongst them Mr. Miller, under whose ministry his heart was touched. He seems to have occupied a place midway between Hugh Bourne and Clowes in relation to sinful pleasures, having for them neither the utter distaste of the one nor the relish and addictedness of the other. It is interesting to know from his own words that an earlier edition of the same little book which John Smith, the fervid evangelist of East Anglia, was so fond of and indebted to, had its influence in deepening his conviction, for he writes* :—

WEDGWOOD MEMORIAL CHAPEL, CREWE.

* Our engraving is from John Smith' own copy now in the possession of the Rev. F. B. Paston, and kindly lent.

"Oh! if I had only been mindful of the humbling power I felt when reading Russel's 'Seven Sermons' and the epitaph in Burslem churchyard, I might very soon have been brought to Christ, and have known the power and felt the blessings of conversion."

> SEVEN
> SERMONS,
> VIZ.
>
> I Of the Unpardonable Sin against the HOLY GHOST: or, The Sin unto Death.
> II. The Saint's Duty and Exercise. In two Parts. Being an Exhortation to, and Direction for Prayer.
> III The Accepted Time, and Day of Salvation.
> IV. The End of Time, and the Beginning of Eternity.
> V. Joshua's Resolution to serve the Lord.
> VI. The Way to Heaven made Plain.
> VII. The Future State of Man, or, a Treatise of the Resurrection.
>
> By ROBERT RUSSEL,
> At Wadhurst, in Sussex.
>
> A NEW EDITION, CORRECTED.
>
> York:
> Printed by and for THOMAS WILSON and SONS, High-Ousegate.
> 1814.

The reading of Paine's "Age of Reason" dropped another baneful ingredient into his cup of bitterness; then he fell under the influence of Hyper-Calvinists and was tortured with doubts as to whether he were among the elect. But at last, in 1809, when he was twenty-one years of age deliverance came, and when it did come he let all his little world know about it—

"Oh what a wonderful change! What words can express it! 'My dungeon flamed with light!' I was just like one let out of prison! My heavy burden was gone! My soul before bound with strong chains of sin and unbelief, was now completely free! Almost frantic with joy, I leaped and shouted aloud Come all ye that fear God and I will tell what He hath done for my soul Some supposed that I was beside myself but had I not given praise to my Great Deliverer might not the very stones have found a voice to upbraid me for such ingratitude?" *

Evidence as to the particular Church he united with—whether even he united with any—there is none; but certainly it is a conjecture one likes to think of as true that the Wedgwood whose name appears with Clowes' in a footnote on the Burslem plans for 1809-10, as authorised to take appointments, may be our John Wedgwood † But we have more reliable data at hand as to Wedgwood's early labours among the Primitive Methodists, for Mrs Bembridge, writing as late as 1869, records her remembrance of having, as Sarah Kirkland, heard him preach at Mereiston, her home, about the year 1812 She says —"We understood that he had met with very much opposition from his friends when seeking the Lord, but that he stood firm through it all He preached at several other villages round us, was well received, and much good was done" Hugh Bourne also under date, March 12th, 1813, notes that he had called

* Quoted in "Memoir of the Life and Labours of Mr John Wedgwood," by a Layman (Thos Bateman), 1870, p 44
† See ante

at Norton and learned that Wedgwood had "preached with good acceptance." By the summer of 1813 it is evident the Primitive fathers had learned the value of Wedgwood as a camp meeting labourer since Clowes, who is due at a camp meeting on the borders of Staffordshire, naturally thinks it will be well to secure the company and help of this new recruit to the cause. He therefore calls at the home of the Wedgwood's on the Saturday, and finds John quite characteristically praying aloud in his room for the unconverted members of his family, while the head of that family is perhaps quite as characteristically at the door of his son's chamber bidding him be quiet. The rest had better be told in Clowes' own words; to condense the narrative would but spoil it. It is a vivid travel-picture relating to the highland region in the neighbourhood of Leek, and has this additional interest for us that it was in a lonely farm-house on this same Morridge that Joseph Wood, D.D., first General Sunday School Secretary, a President of Conference, and Principal of Manchester College, first saw the light. We will only add, as we see Wedgwood and Clowes setting out, that it would have been well, considering where Clowes was going and who was his companion, if he had taken the precaution of carrying his trusty lantern, his companion on many a darksome journey.

MERCASTON FIRST PREACHING-PLACE.

MERCASTON CHAPEL.

"John and I soon started for the camp meeting; we preached to all that we met with on the road till the day began to wear away. I warned John that we ought to hasten on our journey, as we had a large common to pass over. But it was to no purpose; John's zeal for souls overcame his prudence; accordingly, as I had feared and intimated, we found ourselves utterly lost upon the common in the approaching darkness of the night. We knew nothing in what direction to

DR. WOOD'S BIRTHPLACE.

proceed, for we found we were up to the knees in the moss and ling which grow on the moor. We tried to grope our way with our sticks; but after wandering for some time we came to the edge of a large sheet of water which is called the Blackmere of Morridge. I perceived we were now in considerable danger. I therefore shouted with all my might, 'Lost! lost! lost!' Brother Wedgwood wished me to be silent; for, he said, if anybody heard us that were evil-disposed they would have every opportunity to do us mischief. I thought there was some wisdom in his advice, so I desisted crying out 'Lost.' We went on in a straight line until we came to a stone wall, and then we proceeded along until we came to a gate, over which we climbed, and there Brother Wedgwood lay down, intending to remain all night, as he despaired of finding the way till the morning. But I would not lie down, because the ground was very wet. I therefore began again to cry, 'Lost! lost! lost!' and in a short time, in the distance, we saw a light, and shortly heard the trampling of feet and the barking of a dog. I shouted again, but no answer was returned; so we began to conclude that enemies were advancing upon us; we therefore took to our heels and ran. We soon reached a wall, over which I climbed, and fell down a considerable way on the other side, and Wedgwood came after me. I arose, and as we ran we heard the dog and some persons pursuing. In a short time we came to another wall; I tried to get to the top of it, but it gave way and down came the wall and I together. However, we continued our flight until a wall or fence of some sort obstructed us again. I got over it, but on the

CLOWES' LANTERN.

opposite side there was a deep ditch; I therefore endeavoured to slide down to the bottom, and was not hurt; and onwards we ran, totally ignorant whither we were going or what dangers were awaiting us. At last, when nearly exhausted, we, on a sudden, found ourselves in

BLACKMERE HOUSE, WITH MOOR BEHIND.

BLACKMERE HOUSE.

a farmyard. We hastened to the farm-house, and having conversed with the people we found them to be relations to my wife. Never did my heart feel more thankful than for this deliverance. We were told by the people that we had certainly escaped destruction by miracle, for the precipices and moss-pits were numerous, and where we first saw the light there was a house the inmates of which bore a very bad

CANNOCK WOOD PREACHING-PLACE.

character; and as we were pursued there was no doubt but that they would have either robbed or murdered us had they caught us" (Clowes' *Journals*, pp. 112-114).

CANNOCK LANE PREACHING-HOUSE, WHERE

And this was how preachers went to their camp-meeting appointments in the Tunstall Circuit in the period when "things went on in a regular way without much variation!"

Later in the same year, July 17th, 1813, Hugh Bourne has jotted down that he set off with John Wedgwood to Cannock Wood for the morrow's camp meeting. They had a journey of thirty-one miles to do in a swelteringly hot day, and yet, though they were much fatigued and tried in mind, fearing there would be few people at the camp meeting, they threw themselves heartily into the prayer meeting of preparation held in the evening and "came into faith." On the Sunday the services opened at eight o'clock, being supported by William Clowes, Richard Weston, Samuel Simcock, and William Hollins, as well as Hugh Bourne and John Wedgwood. At night Clowes preached at John Linney's, and "had an uncommon time." On Monday the two restepped the thirty-one miles, and Bourne stopped the night with Wedgwood and "laboured much with the family;" not, he trusts, altogether in vain. We have referred to Cannock Wood the more in this connection because that place was the home of the Turners, so often tenderly referred to in the *Journals* of our founders. By

SAMPSON TURNER.   MRS. SAMPSON TURNER (IN OLD AGE).

the time the camp meeting was held, father, mother, two daughters, and a son had been converted. This son was Sampson Turner, who was to enter the ministry in 1819, and commence a career of usefulness, which was doubled after his happy marriage with Mary Edwards, herself a most acceptable preacheress. Sampson Turner became one of the original members of the Deed-poll, and he and his saintly wife survived "still to bring forth fruit," rich and mellow, in extreme age.

RULE-MAKING.

Consolidation in its application to Rules is a compound idea with which in the course of years we have grown familiar. But perhaps the most remarkable instance of rule-making and rule-consolidation that has ever taken place in our annals was that which occurred in 1813-14. The members of the new community did not want to be ruleless or a "law unto themselves." They seemed to fear the "weight of too much liberty," and to long for a freedom regulated by law. Thus as had been the case with the introduction of class-tickets and the payment of the ministers the movement in the direction of rules came from the people themselves. The desire and the demand for the drawing up of rules and regulations for the whole body found expression at the March Quarterly Meeting, 1813. Whereupon a committee consisting of James Steele, E. McEvoy, and Hugh Bourne were instructed to draft a series of regulations and submit them to the Midsummer Meeting. The committee, however, relinquished the task as too heavy for it, and the Quarterly Meeting had to content itself with grumbling that the work assigned had not been done, and to insist that it should at once be taken in hand. When October came there was no further progress to report; whereupon urgency was declared, a draft of the rules was ordered to be prepared immediately and read by the preachers to every society, and all objections and suggested improvements to be brought in writing to the next Quarterly Meeting. Thus put upon his mettle, Hugh Bourne seems to have called up his peculiar law-making ability. With

CLOUD CHAPEL.

characteristic earnestness he set to work upon the draft which unmistakably bears the marks of his hand. Not content with this, he visited almost every member of the united societies and made a note of their objections and suggested amendments. The result was laid before the Quarterly Meeting of January 3rd, 1814, and what remained after the brethren assembled had worked their editorial will upon it, was ordered to be printed forthwith and distributed. Of these Rules, which were from the people, for the people, and by the people, we feel that Hugh Bourne is perfectly justified in remarking as he does i

THE PERIOD OF CIRCUIT PREDOMINANCE AND ENTERPRISE. 171

"It is probable there never was an instance of rules being made in the way these were. They were considered as the work of the whole Connexion; there being scarce a member but gave his opinion on them before they were completed. And it is not very often that the making of rules is accompanied with so much prayer and supplication to Almighty God."

Joint productions of this kind, from kings' speeches downwards, are proverbially unsatisfactory. Many minds and many fingers often make a botch. But we are bound to say of these rules so singularly prepared, that they are well drafted, quite remarkable for their agreement with Scriptural principles, are pervaded by a liberal spirit, and lay down a broad basis for a democratic Church—in fact, the basis laid down is broader than we have been quite able to cover. This first draft of Rules remains in part a something still to be achieved. We have not space to do more than give one quotation, in which may be seen embedded a sentence from Wesley's sermon on "The Trinity," which left its abiding influence on Bourne. In this single quotation, however

MR. T. BAYLEY.

MR. ABNER DALE, J.P.
The oldest Member and Official of Cloud.

may be caught the spirit—humane, pitiful, brotherly—which breathes through the whole of the Rules; and surely it was well and of good omen that this spirit was thus early recognised as the "right spirit" for Church members to have and cultivate. For no other spirit would have availed to inspire and upbear those who had to summon to their fellowship the neglected and outcast of both Church and State.

"It is therefore the business and duty of every member in every station (3) to have the faith of our Lord Jesus Christ, the Lord of glory, without respect of persons. Putting away all bigotry and narrow-mindedness; not lightly esteeming others on account of difference in opinion; for 'it is certain that opinion is not religion, not even right opinion. And God is no respecter of persons'; but in every nation, he that feareth Him and worketh righteousness, is accepted with Him; and the Highest is kind unto the unthankful, and to the evil. Therefore walk in wisdom toward them that are without, and honour all men, highly esteeming pious people of all denominations; and endeavour to make this society a blessing unto all people. 'For whosoever shall do the will of My Father which is in heaven, the same is My brother, and sister and mother.'"

Consolidation: Bricks and Mortar.

The process of consolidation going on at this time quite naturally and of necessity took a material form, and we have to notice the erection of several chapels ranking among the first built in the Connexion. For that reason they deserve brief mention. Tunstall and Talke chapels have already been referred to, as erected in 1811 and 1813 respectively; one at Cloud in the same vicinage was soon to follow. There is indeed a tradition that Cloud can dispute with Tunstall the claim to priority of erection; but the claim must be disallowed, as the deed which bears the date May 12th, 1815, specifies that on the land given by William Clowes (no relative of the Founder) the parties "are building and erecting, etc." More reliable tradition has handed down the facts that Thomas Bayley begged the money for the chapel in three days, and that the chapel itself was built in three weeks. Cloud shares with Turnditch the distinction of being the oldest chapel now in use. The last deed of Cloud dating from 1826 has a peculiar clause:

"It vests the estate in Richard Mitchell, James Shufflebottom, Thomas Bayley, James Bayley, and

ROCESTER CHAPEL.

THE PERIOD OF CIRCUIT PREDOMINANCE AND ENTERPRISE. 173

ROCESTER CHAPEL DEED.

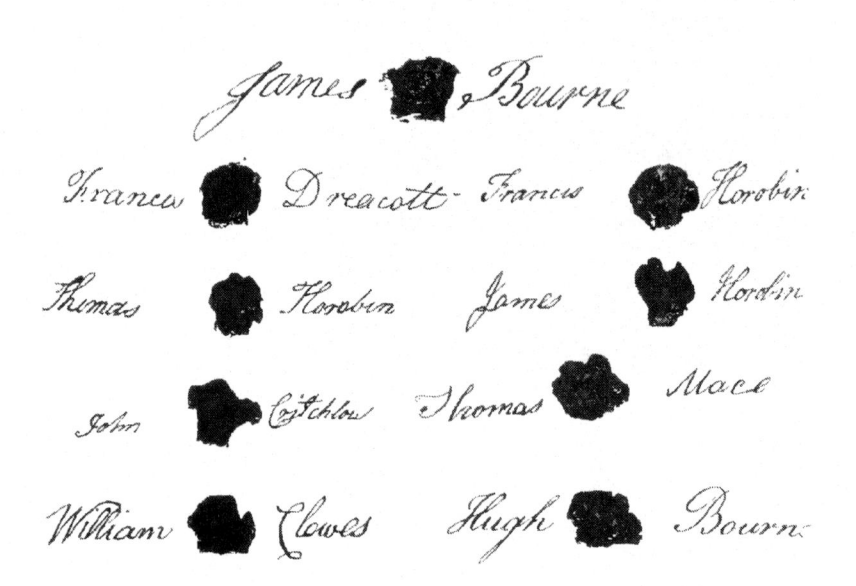

James Bourne

Francis Dreacott Francis Horobin

Thomas Horobin James Hordin

John Critchlow Thomas Mace

William Clowes Hugh Bourn

James Bourne " and all such men as do now or shall at any time hereafter reside at Cloud aforesaid or within one mile thereof, who shall be members of the Primitive Methodist Connexion, members on trial always excepted "

We now turn once more to the Churnet Valley At the lowest part of the valley between the Churnet and far-famed Dove lies Rocester with its dim memories of Roman occupation and its modern " production of cotton-yarns " When Hugh Bourne first visited Rocester on March 13th, 1811, in company with Mrs Dunnell, he pronounced it "a wicked place, we had," says he, "no acquaintance, but the Lord opened the way " After its formation the feeble society was harassed by sectarian meddlesomeness Another denomination had formerly held services in the place, but had discontinued them A person from Doveridge belonging to this denomination cast a jealous eye on the movements of the new society He got the ear of the cotton magnate of the place who was over-persuaded to prohibit the holding of services in any house belonging to him and to threaten with dismissal any of his workpeople who should persist in attending the services The society reduced to straits resorted to prayer, and in a short time the interdict was removed But the meddlesome man from Doveridge drew away a part of the society and got possession of the preaching-room Hugh Bourne himself tells the story,* and it may parenthetically be observed here that stories of sectarian jealousy and intermeddling of this kind occur with painful frequency in the early annals of our Church Opposition from professors as well as profane had too often to be reckoned with But some of the Rocester society remained firm, and amongst them Hannah Woodward, one of the magnate's employees who before had braved dismissal Through her instrumentality the daughter of Thomas Mace with whom she lodged was converted, and soon the whole of the family The cause continued to prosper, so much so, that on July 16th, 1813, the deed of a new chapel was executed As this deed is unique, being probably the earliest which vests a chapel in duly appointed trustees it is reproduced here On it will be found the signatures of several persons now familiar to us

The Derbyshire Outposts

At this time, 1813-14, a group of Derbyshire hamlets and villages is Primitive Methodistically the focal point of interest This district is that which Mrs Dunnell helped to mission and to wheedle– for that is not too strong a word for the influence which that clever but mis-guided woman exerted upon these honest and hearty Derbyshire folk The societies of the Derbyshire Mission were alienated from the Camp Meeting Methodists for a time, and are not therefore represented on the 1811 plans But the alienation was but temporary, and on the first printed plan of 1812 we find Hollington, Boylestone, and Rodsley It is now this region rather than the Churnet Valley that forms on this side the marches of the denomination Here are planted its outposts, and if advance is made it will be in this direction As we note the frequent presence of the leaders, Hugh Bourne organising from Hulland his Tract

---

* In a note attached to the Memoir of Hannah Woodward in the Magazine for 1836, Hannah Woodward afterwards removed to the neighbourhood of Hanging Bridge, and became leader of two classes

Society Mission, and starting and equipping Sunday Schools here and there amongst the villages; as we see enthusiasm rising, catch the hum of preparation, and feel that the religious atmosphere is full of expectation, we may safely prognosticate that while a good deal is already going on much more will shortly happen.

Boylestone has been mentioned. Now Boylestone is only a scattered village of some two hundred souls, and yet the new evangel found here congenial soil and gripped it. For proof, see that plain, brick chapel with its three windows, the adherents of the new cause built for themselves as early as 1811! No denominational name was inscribed on its front, for the good reason that as yet there was no denominational name to inscribe. So "1811" was all the name-plate told, until the primeval chapel was in 1846 superseded by a better one.

To Boylestone also belongs the distinction of having with Hugh Bourne's help begun, on February 27th, 1814, what was probably the first Sunday School in Primitive

MUGGINTON CHURCHYARD.

Methodism; and when in 1844 the parish clergyman refused to have at the National School those children who attended the Primitive Methodist Sunday School, these Boylestone men said: "Very good; then we'll start a day school of our own"— which they did. To make it a free school N. Tunstall and Messrs. Morley became responsible for £15 per annum, and Miss Elizabeth Smith of Derby was found willing to do the work for that sum, supplemented as it was by the gifts in kind of the appreciative parents. Such an example of public spirit and adherence to principle it is a pleasure to record.

Rodsley and Hollington are but two small townships in the parish of Longford, yet they stand side by side on the plans of this time, and are of some account in our early annals. It was in a stream near Rodsley—perhaps Shirley Brook—Clowes found the body of the old man whom, when visiting a few days before, he had urged to go to the preaching service and warned that before "the next time" came of which the old man spoke he might be in eternity. The drowning of "old Ned Carter" of Rodsley in returning from Leek Wake is said to have suggested the drowning scene in "Adam Bede."

In the neighbourhood of these two places lived and died Hannah Yeomans, one who deservedly holds a place in the gallery of "The Lowly Heroes and Heroines of Primitive Methodism." She lived in a one-storied cottage of two rooms, with a lean-to pantry; she was a plain, unsophisticated countrywoman, with ruddy face and grey hair; her garb was of rustic fashion and texture, and she spoke the dialect of the countryside. Yet she kept high company, as her prayers so reverently familiar showed; and her life, lowly placed though it was, exhaled a fragrance sweet and penetrating as the violet's. It was through her influence that the vicar of the parish and his lady were brought to the discovery that there was something in religion Hannah Yeomans had and they had not. Hannah became Priscilla to this Apollos, whose gifts qualified him for the honourable position of Chaplain to the House of Commons. But the vicar always remembered Hannah Yeomans, and counted it a privilege to pay regular visits to the cottage, and there "prayer was wont to be made." Hannah rests, we are told, in an obscure grave— a grave marked by no headstone. More is the pity it should be so. We want some "Old Mortalities" among us; not to pick the encroaching obliterating moss from the enchiselled lettering, but rather to see to it that our lowly saints shall not lack their stone of remembrance.

Mercaston and Weston-Underwood have Mugginton for their parish church; and in its ancient graveyard, with its yew-tree, there lies some "bonnie dust." Sarah Bembridge and William Bembridge, her husband; William and Mary Ride; George Warren, the subject of Rev. J. Barfoot's "Piety behind the Plough;" John and Robert Beeston; Edmund Fearns—what is mortal of these lies in Mugginton Churchyard. Of the first-named, a few words must be said. To the Connexion's first female preacher—calm, modest, capable, tender; pioneer missionary to Derby and Nottingham, and with her husband as true yoke-fellow, one of the foundation-builders of the powerful Hull Circuit—to such a woman something more is due than the mere mention of her name.

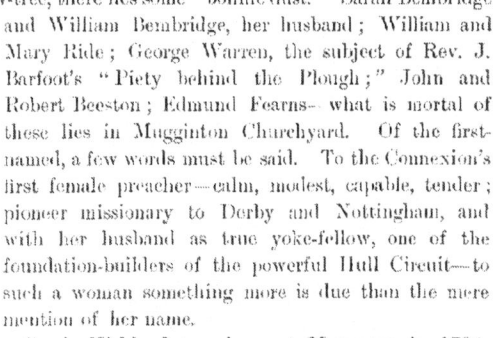

Sarah Kirkland was born at Mercaston in 1794. For some years the Wesleyans held preaching services in her father's (Rowland Kirkland) house. One of these services she had cause long to remember, for the preacher, William Bramwell, noticing the presence of children, made special mention of them in his prayers. She was impressed, even to tears, by the prayer of the man of God. But the impression gradually faded; for the services were withdrawn, to the grievous moral detriment of the place. So marked was the deterioration, and so far did it go, that Mercaston came to be known as "Hell Green." In 1811, Hugh Bourne visited Mercaston, and while at Rowland Kirkland's house, as was his way, he spoke to the girl of the home as though she too had a soul that was worth saving. Then at the tea-table he prayed for each and all. The faded impressions were revived; the habit of prayer resumed; worldly amusements forgone; her maiden finery laid aside; and before long she found peace in her own bed-chamber. She received her first class-ticket at the hands of William Clowes, and was led by him into the blessing of full salvation; was proposed for the plan in September, 1813; took her first appointment at Sutton-on-the-Hill, and had as the fruit of her maiden effort a gipsy-convert belonging to a band just then encamped in the locality. Often after this, when Sarah was missioning in the neighbourhood where the roving band happened to be, it is said the gipsy-youth would do the work of a herald for the girl-preacher. Swift-footed, he would traverse the country-side: "A young woman is going to preach at ———. I have heard her."—Here he would shortly tell what the Lord had done for him through her.—"Come and hear her for yourselves." Prior to this date, however, the Kirkland home had been turned into a house of mourning, as the following item from Hugh Bourne's *Journals* shows:—

SARAH KIRKLAND.

"*July 14th, 1813.*—At Mercaston. Since I was there last, Rowland Kirkland has died, and his two sons, of the small-pox. . . . . They were all three buried in about a fortnight. Sarah Kirkland thought that the youngest had obtained mercy. The other was brought into liberty by Mary Hawksley and died happy. The old man has been a steady pilgrim a long time; he died proclaiming 'Victory' to the last. His death has made a stop in building the Chapel at Mercaston. [There had been a movement for a Chapel, and Rowland had agreed to provide the site.] How it will be now is not yet known."

The Mary Hawksley of the foregoing extract was the wife of a soldier away in Spain at the wars. She had been brought into straits through having to quit her mother's home for no other reason than that the kind of religion she had adopted they could not away with. Hugh Bourne once more combined charity with zeal for the furtherance of the gospel. Recognising Mary's piety and her undeveloped gifts for usefulness, he made her (May, 1813,) a salaried evangelist, working chiefly at first in connection with the Hulland Tract Mission. Doubtless she is the other preacher referred to by Bourne in his *History*.

> "Two of the preachers raised up by these means [the visiting and praying companies] were women. And one of them, a middle-aged woman, laboured considerably as a travelling preacher. The other a young woman, Sarah Kirkland, . . . laboured at large as a diligent, laborious travelling preacher for a number of years with great credit and success. These were the first women-preachers who laboured regularly in this Connexion."

So let place be yielded to Mary Hawksley as second female-preacher. Soon we shall have to follow closely the purposeful fruitful movements of Sarah Kirkland.

WESTON-UNDERWOOD, FIRST PREACHING-PLACE.

Weston-Underwood was the home of John Ride, destined to become a laborious missionary in other parts. John was convinced of sin under Eleazar Hathorn, when he missioned Weston, and he at once joined the class as one who had "a desire to flee from the wrath to come and be saved from his sins." One Sunday morning, when returning through the fields from his class, he found what he had been seeking, and in the exuberance of his joy he shouted "Glory! glory!!" and flung his hat into the air. When Sarah Kirkland received her first ticket he too received his. His father became the leader at Mercaston, and William Ride, jun., the leader at Weston-Underwood. Hugh Bourne was always on the look out for fresh promising labourers. So after a full day's work at Weston-Underwood, Turnditch, and Hulland, on May 18th, 1813, he puts down :—

"I was much drawn out to pray to the Lord to raise up labourers; and I trust He will do it here as in other parts. I think John Wilson, William Warren, and the two Rides (father and son) ought to labour, even as preachers; if this be right, they would form a strong ministry, and there are others who I believe might be made useful in a public way. John Ride, for one, I think will be a preacher."

William Warren, who is mentioned in the preceding extract, and William Hickingbotham deserve a permanent place in the history of Derbyshire Primitive Methodism. Both of them were men of that special type, who, as we have remarked, were raised up to do the work of evangelists in this first period. They were men after the type of Wedgwood, Benton, and John Oxtoby; but while equally eccentric with these, they were probably gifted with a greater degree of rugged eloquence. They were in their element in the street service and on the camp ground. They knew how to address and handle the crowd; and their ready, homely wit, their quaint and sharp sayings, not only got attention, but were kept in mind, and passed round and handed down. William Warren was employed extensively to conduct revival services, and to act as supply for sick preachers as well as in the ordinary work of a local preacher. It should be added he was the father of George Warren the exemplar of "Piety Behind the Plough."

MR. W. HICKINGBOTHAM.

The Rev. John Barfoot wrote a sketch of William Hickingbotham under the appropriate title of "A Diamond in the Rough." There were a good many rough diamonds in our first period, and it is well there were, for no other kind would have been of much value. There was a time when William Hickingbotham hated the Ranters, and loved the brutal sports and ways the Ranters hated. The football match of those days was a variety of murder, and Hickingbotham referring to his former addictedness to that bone-breaking amusement was wont to describe it as "Running after wind blown up in a blether (bladder) tied up in leather." The man who could throw off such sentences as these, though couched in the vernacular, was no stolid, slow-witted, inarticulate rustic. There was in him a spark of Promethean fire, as there was in Warren and many more of that type, and it would flash out. In short there was a touch of what we call genius in these men which made their words tell with the people. Just when Hickingbotham was converted we cannot learn, but it was early in this period and during his long life of eighty-five years he preached and visited and reproved at Belper, Wirksworth, Ripley, and the adjacent villages. How he laboured let the following show. It is the Rev. W. Cutts who speaks : *

"At a missionary meeting I asked William to state to us what he did the day before—that is, on Sunday. He rather hesitated, but at length proceeded to say : 'Well, in the first place I came to the chapel at six o'clock, and when I had opened the door I knelt down and thanked God for the honour of lighting a fire in His house.' And mark, old William is eighty-two years of age. 'Then, when I had lit

* J. Barfoot's "Diamond in the Rough" pp. 85-6.

the fire, I knelt down to pray, and so I got two fires lighted at once. After I had waited twenty minutes I rapped at your shutters to remind you it was time to get ready to meet the class. At seven I went into old William's to lead the class, and he came out to the chapel to lead the prayer meeting, and mark, he always holds the prayer meetings and class meetings one hour. He will call upon the members twice or thrice each rather than give over within the hour; 'for,' he says, 'I never give my master short time, and I will not serve my heavenly Master worse than my earthly master.' 'Then,' he said, 'I came home and had breakfast, and started to take my appointment at Turnditch. I went in the morning, for I had some sick people to visit. Then I had dinner, preached at two o'clock, then had tea, visited some more of the people, preached again, had a prayer meeting (for he always had

BELPER MARKET-PLACE.
John Benton preached just outside butcher's shop in the centre.

a prayer meeting), had a bit of supper, started home, and when I got to the top of Shottle, a village two miles from Belper, I jumped and felt young again.'"

John Harrison finished his short but useful course at Mercaston, July 22nd, 1819, aged 26. Though far gone in consumption, he had on the very day he died attended a camp meeting at Brailsford. John had received a respectable education and possessed good parts and considerable natural refinement as the *Journals* he has left show. When in 1811 the new community made its entry into these parts, the servants of the Harrisons, like the rest of the folk thereabout, were talking about the doings and sayings of the new-comers, and John made up his mind to hear them for himself. An occasion for doing so soon presented itself: the preacher, who was John Benton, took his stand under a large tree in Hulland village, and shot forth his arrows. John Harrison was "pricked to the heart," but his conversion did not take place until some time after when he listened to William Warren. The youth was wishful to unite himself at once to the Hulland Society; but because of his youthful appearance, or from some other unreasonable reason, some of the members were hesitant about receiving him. But John Wilson the worthy leader was wiser than his flock, as it was fitting he should be; he brushed the flimsy objection aside, and John was admitted to fellowship. Soon his profiting appeared to all, and his call to the ministry came in 1816. He was an acceptable and edifying preacher, and though no son of thunder, like some of his brethren, there was a quiet intensity about his utterances just as effective

HULLAND CHAPEL AND GREEN—THE FIRST OPEN-AIR PREACHING-PLACE.

in its way as their stormier ministrations. Nor did the smallness of his "make," his youthful appearance, and the general impression he gave of delicacy of constitution, militate against his acceptability; rather did they serve to conciliate his hearers and prepossess them in his favour.

Enough, we think, has now been said to carry the reader along with us to the conclusion that in 1813-14 these Derbyshire villages were full of vitality and rich in promise. So thought both our founders.

"We"—who are the "we," Mr. Clowes?—"We opened Mercaston, Hulland, Turnditch, and Weston-Underwood. At each of these places much good was done from time to time as we visited them; indeed, they became much noted in what was then called the Connexion" (*Journal*, 116). "During the spring months of this year, 1813, the work flourished at Mercaston, Hulland, Turnditch, and Weston-Underwood; and a number of zealous, useful, praying labourers were raised up." (Bourne's *History*, 1823).

As to the "we" of Clowes' statement: it must not be overlooked that John Benton and Eleazar Hathorn had been and were still in these parts. It was not merely the Hulland Tract Mission or the powerful ministrations of Clowes when paying his periodic visits, or both these, that fully serve to explain why there was just now so much life and movement at this extremity of the Connexion. Have we not seen Hathorn missioning Weston, and Benton, Hulland; the former bringing down John Ride as his quarry and the latter John Harrison?

REV. T. JACKSON (1).   REV. T. JACKSON (2).   REV. T. JACKSON (3).

THE ADVANCE ON BELPER.

The fit time had now come for an advance, and the event showed the advance was to be made on Belper. Mr. Ride, of that town, Herod tells us, being at a lovefeast led by Benton at Weston-Underwood, invited Benton to mission Belper, promising if this were done to lend his house for a prayer meeting after the holding of the service in the open air. On this basis an agreement was arrived at, the day and hour probably being fixed, and a general plan of operations sketched, which was to include the co-operation of the village societies. But before the decisive day came Benton, it would seem, quietly reconnoitred the ground; for one day, as three youths were sauntering along to Belper Market Place, loudly talking and indulging in "foolish jesting," a plain man overtook them, halted, fixed them with his eye, and solemnly addressed them—

"Stop, poor sinners, stop and think
Before you further go;
Can you *sport* upon the brink
Of everlasting woe?"

This was Benton. When at close quarters with men he often used this same verse, just changing the position of the question so as to make it fit the occasion and the particular doings of the person accosted; and he often used it with such extraordinary effect as to make one wonder that such large results should follow the use of such apparently inadequate means. Goliath falls flat, and all we can see to account for his fall is the slinging of a pebble from the brook. So in this case. The two young men thus abruptly addressed were indeed "stopped" and turned about, and a new direction given to their lives by this verse slung at them in Belper streets. Both when "converted" were to "stablish their brethren," becoming early preachers, and, strange to say, destined to labour together in these parts. One, who tells the story, was Thomas Jackson (1). The figure is wanted to distinguish him from Thomas Jackson (2), who entered the ministry in 1836, and after forty-five years of faithful labour in the Brinkworth District died in London in 1879. His name and worth are handed on by Dr. Jackson, Steward

TURNDITCH CHAPEL.
Built 1813, and still standing.

of the Caledonian Road Circuit. Thomas Jackson (3), of the Working Lads' Institute, we all know and honour, and he, too, is a Belper boy, with memories going back to William Hickingbotham. The other youth smitten by Benton's versicular pebble was William Allcock (2); for if we have had three Thomas Jacksons we have also had two William Allcocks, who were for a time contemporaries.* When Belper, after being a branch of Tunstall, became at midsummer, 1821, an independent station, Thomas Jackson (1) was the superintendent, and William Allcock (2) was "called out." He began his labours, May 27th, in the Peak District by preaching at Winster, Bonsall, and Bolehill to large congregations in the open air. On June 1st he preached at Matlock to about a thousand people. Next day he is again at Matlock, when the constable, who had ordered him down the day before, again appears on the scene just as he was finishing his sermon, and made such a din by beating his staff on a watering-

* It should be observed that in early documents No. 1's name is spelled as Alcock.

can, that preacher and people were well-nigh deafened. So they sang a hymn, and the people pushed the constable away. From June 10th to 23rd Allcock was on the Ashbourne side. The treatment he and his colleague Wildbur met with while pushing forward mission work in these parts makes more significant the second resolution passed at the FIRST PRIMITIVE METHODIST MISSIONARY Meetings held at Turnditch and Belper on July 8th, 1821 :—"That it is necessary that our Missionaries carry the Gospel into the dark and benighted villages in the Peak of Derbyshire." And the gospel *was* carried ; for looking forward into the years to come we can see this country carved out into circuits—Winster, Belper, Burton-on-Trent, Ripley, Ashbourne, and Matlock. The reference to this future parcelling out of territory is not the irrelevancy it perhaps looks ; for though we have not yet got Belper missioned, its first two circuit-preachers are selected and laid hold of, and the rest will follow.

KING STREET, BELPER.

Two or three days after the above incident, what we may call the reconnaissance in force took place. Attended by contingents from Mercaston, Turnditch, and Weston-Underwood, Benton proceeded to Belper. The bridge over the Derwent was crossed, and then the band, singing as it went, moved on to the market-place, where in front of a butcher's shop Benton took his stand and began a service. But the missioners were not to have it all their own way. Opposition was to show itself at once ingenious and nasty. Benton was to be surprised from the rear. A ladder was planted at the back of the prem... and it ... proposed to cross the roof and pour down confusion upon the head of unsuspecting Benton beneath. One mounted the ladder carrying a bucket; what that bucket held we will not soil our page by telling. But God would not suffer his servant, though he had "little grammar and not much command of language," to be so shamefully mishandled; for between the caves and the ladder there occurred a slight retributive mishap, and there never was witnessed, either before or since, a more striking example of poetic justice or confirmation of the scripture—"His mischief shall return upon his own head, and his violent dealings shall come down upon his own pate."

The "Ranters."

"The Primitive Methodists were called 'Ranters' first in Belper." Belper was our

LONG ROW, BELPER.
(Showing the House, the second on the left, where the name 'Ranters' was first given.)

Antioch; the place where others named us, not the place where we named ourselves. There are variants of the story of the giving of this name, slightly differing in details, but agreeing in substance. Other visits of the mission-bands to Belper followed the one described, and they wrought their effects not only in bringing about conversions but in stirring up a good deal of excitement. One evening, after a somewhat protracted meeting, the band passed down the Long Row, singing on its way homeward. "What religion are these people?" asked a young woman of Richard Turner, who was standing at his door looking out on the processioners. "I think they must be the Ranters

I have read about somewhere," was the answer. Next day the factory-girl gave out: "Those people are called 'Ranters.' Richard Turner says so"; and so, in this foolish way, the name was given and "caught on." It will be observed that the name was no more original than was the word "Methodist," when given to the Wesleys and their Oxford friends. Turner drew on some hazy reminiscences of his reading rather than on any name-giving faculty that belonged to him. Yet we are told he was rather proud of his achievement in nomenclature, and that he lived long enough to share the honour or obloquy of becoming one of the community he had denominated.

The name is an ugly one both in its raucous sound and in what it suggests. We can afford to smile at it now; but right on through the first period of our denominational

BRIDGE OVER THE DERWENT AT BELPER.

history and far on into the second, it was quite another matter. If it be asked: "Why dwell on all that?" The answer is simple, and we think conclusive. We are not writing of Primitive Methodism as it is now, when it walks, as it were, in silver slippers and is on visiting terms with the best denominations, but of Primitive Methodism as it was regarded in the far past years. As a matter of history we are met by the facts that the name we gave ourselves was disliked by others; and that the name others gave us was quite as distasteful to us as ours could be to them. It was the name which stuck to us like a burr, as we went through the valley-period of our humiliation. There might be many of our fathers who gloried in the name, and there might be others who, while they did not wear it as a distinction were yet supremely indifferent what name was given them. But there were some, who had a degree of natural refinement and to whom even the suspicion of complicity with what was loud and vulgar was repellent, who bore the daily cross of passing as "Ranters." For this name was as a duty pellet always handy, for the bigot and the "superior person" to fling, in the hope that it might stick as a stigma and make the stigmatised wince. It is but the sober truth to say that, in this early period, there were those who habitually and on principle, ostentatiously and at every convenient opportunity, in season and out of season, passed by our rightful appellation in favour of the vulgar sobriquet. They would use no other if they could help it. This, we repeat, is part of the history of the time, and as such must be written; and Daniel Isaac's—"The Ranters have bawled themselves out of breath," is the short summation of this unpleasant side of the history of the name. But there is another side to that history, and a compensatory one.

Next to the strangeness of the fact that the name was so far acquiesced in that almost a semi-official sanction was given to it by its appearing as an alternative title on the cover of the Magazine for 1819, and as far on as 1827 on the labels of missionary boxes in Hull, is the seeming strangeness of the assertion that the name positively helped on the evangelistic labours of the Connexion—was indeed a factor in its success. Hugh Bourne distinctly affirms it was so, and others, like George Herod, who were in a position to know, confirm Bourne's statement; and indeed when examined in the light of probability and facts, there is good reason to conclude that the statement is correct. The word "Ranter" really carried with it no suggestion of religious profession or propagandism. It was vague enough for rumour to work upon and to give room for endless surmise. It might mean anything from street-singers to political agitators. It piqued curiosity, afforded a new topic. When it was noised that the people called "Ranters" had come, or were coming, into a town or village, many had very hazy notions as to who these strange people were or what was their object; some even suspected that their designs were political, that they were but Radical Reformers under a feigned name, and under that impression sought them out.

"The Tunstall Non-Mission Law."

The fuller significance of the missioning of Belper to this history needs to be pointed out. That significance is not exhausted by the fact that there we got a name we did not like. Belper was our Antioch in other and more important senses than this. Its missioning, like the partial evangelising of Antioch by them who were "scattered abroad," marked an advance; yet an advance effected irregularly and unofficially, in disregard rather than in pursuance of, the policy most in favour at headquarters. So close does the parallel hold, that what Bourne says of Benton and his mission-bands would equally apply to the scattered evangelists who carried the gospel to the city on the Orontes—

"But at length a period was put to it (the suspension of missionary labours) *by a few enterprising individuals*, who again entered upon missionary labours, and the Lord set before them an open door, which has already been a blessing to thousands. It was also attended with a present blessing: it suffused life, vigour, and zeal into the societies." (*History*, 1835, p. 72)

Moreover, neither the "pillars" of Jerusalem nor of humbler Tunstall were foolish enough to disavow the unauthorised action of their agents, or decline to take over the new slice of territory unexpectedly offered them. They had to shift their boundary-stakes, though they would rather have kept them where they were. The deputy, Barnabas, when he came to Antioch and "saw the grace of God, was glad"; so no doubt Bourne, as superintendent, was secretly glad that Benton had disregarded the "Tunstall Non-Mission Law," and that it fell to his lot to take over Belper and incorporate it with Tunstall Circuit, though some of his brethren *did* hold that the circuit was already bigger than they could well look after. This taking over took place —

"*September 9th, 1814.*— Belper. Ezekiel xlvii. 15. A good time, but I know not what to judge of this place. O Lord, direct Thy people. I then took up Belper and put things in order, and the work soon began to move in other places; and the people in Derbyshire disregarded the Tunstall law against missionarying (*sic*). And, being superintendent, I had additional labour in taking up new places, *but it was glorious labour.*"

The parallel might be followed still further; for after Belper was missioned there was a pause while, as at Antioch, the work of edification went on until the call came for a farther advance. In our case the advance was to be to the populous towns and cities lying just beyond these pleasant valleys and uplands; where the conditions of the new industrial world made life harder than here, and the task of evangelisation more difficult; where just then the haggard operative was liable to fall a prey to lying spirits, and in danger of being goaded by misery to acts of desperation.

But what was this "Tunstall Non-Mission Law" we have spoken of? Not, perhaps, a specific law passed at some one quarterly meeting and confirmed at subsequent ones, so much as it was a prevailing sentiment and steady policy. It was Bourne and Benton who gave this policy the name of "the non-mission law." To Bourne the phrase meant that the breaking up of fresh ground was discouraged, that missionary operations were suspended for a term of years, and that this policy resulting in, or associated with, a departure from the true method of holding camp meetings brought about consequences nothing less than disastrous. It is not likely that this name was given by those who favoured the policy in question. If they gave it a name at all, the one selected would, we may be sure, be a more plausible and better-sounding one. It would be a name suggesting what the policy aimed to do rather than what it left undone. Probably they would call it "the policy of consolidation," and would be ready to urge and defend it with many and weighty reasons, and not a few wise saws. "Better do a little well than attempt much and fail. Before we enclose and break up more ground let us see that the ground we have is brought under proper cultivation. Look how wide the circuit is stretching from Boylestone in Derbyshire to Rixley in Lancashire, and from Roggin Row in Cheshire to Wyrley Bank! Our local preachers are all too few for the work exacted by the plan, and as for the travelling-preachers they cannot be spared for opening fresh places. They are needed to go the regular rounds, and bring the societies under discipline, and carry on the work of edification." In short, the consolidators would appear to have reason and common sense arrayed on their side, as they certainly had the preponderance of opinion; for, as a general statement, it may be taken as true that this was the policy prevailing until the beginning of 1819 in the Tunstall Circuit. In harmony with this policy, Clowes' labours were restricted within the prescribed limits during these years. True, he made an occasional sally—notably one into Nottinghamshire in 1817, and another into Leicestershire the following year—when his progress was like that of a flame let loose among the dry stubble. He did so much during these brief missionary excursions that the mere record in his *Journals* of what he did leaves the impression on his readers that he must have been a missionary at large during the whole of this period. Probably we shall be right in concluding that the part of flaming evangelist would have been much more agreeable to Clowes and better suited to the man than that of round preacher; and that had he been freer to expatiate, the Connexion would have made greater progress than it did in these early years.

The results of this cry, "Let us consolidate," were distinctly bad, as they invariably are; for whatever reason and common sense may say in its favour, experience and history prove that the policy which postpones aggression until consolidation is complete never does anything except undo itself. And yet, because reason judges itself competent to pronounce, and experience to the contrary is limited, Churches are always committing the mistake of separating what should never be disjoined. When this is done, and consolidation is pursued as an end in itself, a process of contraction and hardening sets in, likely to prove as fatal in the result as the solidifying of a vital organ. Things never reached such a pass as this in Tunstall Circuit; for what we may call intra-aggression —missioning within the bounds—never entirely ceased. But it is noteworthy that the most considerable additions to the circuit were made in very violation of the policy advocated, and the great revival in the Midlands we have so soon to describe, was not begun or carried on by Tunstall Circuit. Furthermore, those features of consolidation previously touched upon were found chiefly on that side of the circuit where the spirit of aggression—the true missionary spirit—was most in evidence. We have no wish to exaggerate; though we do wish to make the facts clear, and to press the obvious moral. It is a pure myth that reverses and small increases are confined to our later history, and that from the beginning it was not so. Even allowing for Hugh Bourne's anxious temperament, which naturally magnified the evils viewed through its medium and made him see crises where others saw none, his estimate of the gravity of the situation is substantially borne out:—

JOHN BENTON'S COTTAGE, LOWER LANDYWOOD.

"After some time, it was found that the societies instead of prospering more [by the suppression of missionary labours] prospered less. It seemed as if the blessing of God was in some degree withdrawn from the societies; and there appeared so general a weakening that some thought the Connexion would absolutely break up."—(*History*, 1835, p. 51).

One of those who resisted the imposition of the non-mission law was John Benton who, as we have seen, after the Ramsor camp meeting of 1810, had resolved to give himself to the work of evangelisation. Having some houses and land and interest in a colliery, he was financially independent. In 1811 he had carried on mission work in London with considerable success, and it is said had his pioneer labours only been followed up, the Connexion would have gained a permanent footing in London twenty years earlier than it did. Benton returned for a time to circuit work; but going the round was not his ideal either for himself or the Connexion. He pleaded that "Primitive Methodism should be allowed to go through the nation, as it was raised up to do." As a sincere advocate of a forward policy he offered £3 a quarter towards a missionary's salary, and himself refused to be planned. His offer was declined, and he declined his plan. When it was sent after him, it is said he wrote the following lines at the back and returned it:—

"A plan from God I have to mind,
A better plan I cannot find;
If you can, pray let me know,
And round the circuit I will go."

Benton now got a thousand copies of a small Hymn-book printed at Warrington, with a view to his contemplated mission. It was soon got ready for the press. He took Hugh Bourne's edition of Lorenzo Dow's Hymn-book, omitted one or two hymns, and supplied two or three others of his own composing. The latter are not exactly metrical gems; they cannot compare with "Hark! listen to the trumpeters," or "The Lord into His garden came." Yet if one takes them, not as poetry, but as evidence of

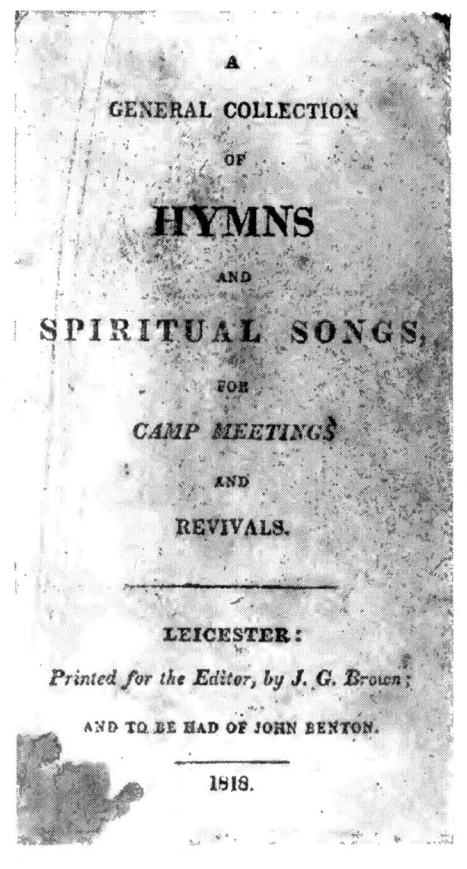

Benton's own state of mind when he broke the Tunstall non-mission law, they have their value. They have the note of sincerity, and, as we read, it somehow does not seem so strange and unaccountable that the ministrations and words of an unlettered man like Benton should produce such instantaneous and striking effects. Here are two stanzas of Hymn 23:—

> 1. The Lord gave me a special call
>   To sound the gospel news;
> My soul was willing to obey,
>   I durst not Him refuse.
> The wicked world derided me,
>   Professors join'd them too,
> For such an unlearn'd man to be,
>   A preacher would not do.
>
> * * * *

STRUTT'S MILL.
Photo. by F. Holbrook, Belper.

> 3. The Lord makes choice of foolish things
>   To confound the wise;
> Though weak the instrument may be,
>   The power in Jesus lies.
> He called me out to go by faith,
>   But where I could not tell,
> Beseeching sinners to repent,
>   And 'scape a burning hell

Benton chose for his mission certain villages in Staffordshire lying on the borders of the county of Derby. Among these were Warslow, Allstone-Field, Holme End, Fleet Green, Cow-Head, Mill-Dale, Biggin, Butterton, etc. He was aided in the mission by Eleazar Hathorn, who took part in the first camp meeting. The fact that Eleazar had lost a limb was not allowed to be a disqualification, for the loss was more than made up to him by the kindness of the people, who supplied him with a useful nag; so that he may be regarded as having been the first riding preacher—the first of a favoured few. The mission prospered; so much so, that we find Hugh Bourne, as superintendent, requested to take over "Benton's Circuit," as it was called; and so we have the following entries:—

"*October 4th, 1813.*—We had Quarter-day, and John Benton joined us. This, I think, is of the Lord."

"*October 13th.*—Came to Boylestone, and saw John Benton . . . He gave me directions for going into his circuit, and spoke of the state of the people."

After the taking over of his circuit Benton and his colleague made a "tour into the interior of Derbyshire," where some time ago we left them. So by a detour we are

BELPER PRIMITIVE METHODIST CHAPEL AND SCHOOLS, 1903.

FIRST BELPER CHAPEL.

brought back to Belper, only that on our way we have, we trust, explained how Benton broke the non-mission law and what came of it. As for Belper, the work continued to prosper. Thomas Jackson (1) tells us that at first the preaching and other services were held in his father's house, and in the summer months in the garden at its front. This becoming too small, a large room was rented, which also soon became inconveniently crowded. Now that there was a pressing call to build, the way to do so unexpectedly opened. The largest employer of labour in the town and neighbourhood was the firm of Strutt, cotton-spinners—a firm of long standing and great influence (a scion of this family in 1856 was ennobled under the title of Lord Belper). The Mr. Strutt with whom we have to do showed himself a man of enlightened mind and public spirit—one of those captains of industry who, in their dealings with our denomination and other forms of Dissent, contrast most refreshingly with some of the landed proprietors in various parts of the country. Mr. Strutt had not been unobservant of the influence for good which the labours of our people had exerted upon many of his work people; so that when approached for a site for a chapel, he generously agreed to sell as much as was required at the nominal price of one shilling per yard, and also to provide wood and stone at reasonable rates. To save expense, the wood was drawn on trucks from Mr Strutt's timber-yard to the site by willing hands. This novel mode of conveyance brought many to their doors, and others, anticipating "Mafeking night" belaboured the human teams with bladders tied to the ends of sticks! Truly the people of Belper of those days were quite as lively as the people they nicknamed. In September, 1817, Mr Clowes called at Belper on his way from Nottingham and found the Chapel progressing, and he took part in the opening services. The "writings" were signed April 16, 1818, at Duffield

CHAPTER II.

THE MOVE ON DERBY AND NOTTINGHAM.

"AFTER this" [the opening of Belper] says Hugh Bourne, "the work spread to Derby and the adjacent places." But this easy, abstract-method of writing history, although it is so common, scarcely satisfies us. It is not enough to know the bare fact that Primitive Methodism got to Derby and Nottingham, Loughborough and Leicester; we also want to know who took it there, and when and under what circumstances; for if Primitive Methodism did anything or "spread" anywhere it was no abstraction of which this is affirmed, but Primitive Methodism as embodied in certain Primitive Methodists who had their own special features and idiosyncrasies. Who, then, were the Connexion's pioneer workers in Derby, Nottingham, Loughborough, and Leicester—the first county capitals and towns of consequence to be entered by the denomination? What was the condition of these manufacturing centres when our agents first set foot in them? How did they go about their work, and what were the results which followed? Such are the questions awaiting an answer as clear and complete as the information now attainable will enable us to give. And yet when told, how simple the facts will seem to be! just illustrating as before the natural play of Christian enthusiasm. We have still to do with a movement dependent much more on individual initiative and enterprise than on official planning and support.

THE MISSIONING OF DERBY.

Robert Winfield was a small farmer living at Ambaston, a village seven miles from Derby. Until 1814 he had been a Methodist local preacher, but having in that year taken a prominent part in a camp meeting at Mercaston he had been "dealt with," and was now actively identified with the new movement, and already beginning to prove himself a missioner "with a peculiar tact for opening new places." In Sarah Kirkland he seems to have taken an interest almost paternal. Not merely did her orphaned condition appeal to his sympathy, but he seems to have discovered in her capabilities of service he made it his business to foster and direct. Winfield, we are told, had great faith in female preachers; nor is this surprising, for his faith was grounded on experience. Mrs. Taft (Mary Barrett) was one of the most successful female preachers of her generation, and it was through her instrumentality that Winfield had been led to Christ. Two future Wesleyan presidents were amongst her many converts—Thomas Jackson and Joseph Taylor; yet, although many

MRS. TAFT.

acknowledged the call of Mrs Taft and others of the sisterhood to preach the gospel, there were others who accepted the manifest election of God with ill-grace, doubtful questionings, or misplaced banter "God often works by strange instruments," said William Atherton when preaching a funeral sermon on the occasion of the death of President Taylor, "Balaam was converted by the braying of an ass, and Peter by the crowing of a cock; and our lamented brother by the preaching of a woman one Good Friday morning."*

But this convert of Mary Taft *did* believe in female preaching, and evidently he believed in Sarah Kirkland. His faith in both was justified, for his own daughter lived to become a talented and useful preacher, though in another community, and Sarah Kirkland's progressive steps of usefulness we have to follow. At the invitation of Mr Winfield she went, on March 15th, 1815, to conduct a lovefeast at Ambaston. There were some present at this lovefeast from Chaddesden who pressed her to preach at that village on her way home. She consented, and in the overflowing congregation which the novelty of the preacher's sex and youth drew together, were three persons from Derby, who, under the influence of a powerful service and the preacher's personality, besought her to visit Derby the following night. To this she agreed, on the understanding that a suitable room was found for the service. A room is said to have been hired of a barber, who himself made no pretensions to religion, and here Primitive Methodism began in Derby. Soon after this visit a society was formed, having this room for its meeting-place. A second visit to Chaddesden was the means of winning another useful adherent to the infant cause at Derby. While Sarah was conducting a lovefeast, two well-dressed men walking out from Derby, only a mile and a half distant, inquired the cause of the mild excitement pervading the village. 'It's a young woman holding a Ranters lovefeast' was the answer they got. They took their stand by the door and became riveted to the spot, as they heard one after another testifying to the freedom and power of God's grace. One of these behind-the-door hearers was Mr Robert Stone, who kept a spirit-vault in Sadler Gate, then at that time a locality of ill-repute, who was so much impressed by what he had heard, that from that time he was a changed man. He renounced his trafficking in spirits, and is said to have become a useful local preacher and a supporter of the cause for many years. In confirmation of this, two successive plans for the year 1818 are before us. These show "17, R Stone," with twenty-eight appointments to his credit for the six months. Eight of these are at Derby, four at Loughborough, and two at Chaddesden, where he had so blessedly played the eavesdropper. On what small noiseless pivots human destinies turn! Only a summer evening's saunter, a brief halt by a cottage door for curiosity's sake, and there is "a new creation," affecting the whole life of the man, including his business, domestic, and civic relations!

The next event of consequence in regard to Derby to be noted is that in 1816, probably soon after the holding of Mercaston Camp Meeting on June 9th, it was made the head of a second circuit. But it may be asked "What were the wise men of

* T P Bunting in the 'Life of Dr Bunting' (I 125), says that he himself heard William Atherton use these words 'with all possible solemnity.' The story, too, is told in *Edinburgh Review*, July 1881.

Tunstall doing to allow such an act of improvidence as this? Why, there was not a society in the proposed new circuit but was of yesterday. All alike had the rawness and inexperience of youth. Not even Belper went with the new circuit. The chick had only just chipped its egg and yet it presumes to begin housekeeping—that is the symbol for it." All this is true, and therefore all the more needing an explanation, which when found will not be wanting in significance. What if the wise men of Tunstall allowed Derby to be formed into a circuit fifteen months after the first sermon had been preached in the barber's room rather than that something worse should follow? What that worse alternative was Walford, the biographer of Bourne, tells us bluntly it was a possible secession. "It soon appeared there must either be a new circuit or a new Connexion." The "few enterprising individuals," such as Benton and Eleazar Hathorn, when, after the Mercaston Camp Meeting, the revival already spreading began to sweep over Derbyshire and Nottinghamshire, were unwilling that they and their converts, who were of the same mind with them, should be under Tunstall Circuit and its non-mission law. And never, one thinks, did the wise men of Tunstall manifest their wisdom more conspicuously than when, instead of resorting to coercive or repressive measures, they allowed the zealous spirits to have their own way in this matter. Thus the formation of the Derby Circuit may be regarded as the continuance and culmination of the mild revolt against the Non-Mission Law, of which the carving out of Benton's Circuit and the missioning of Belper and other places were also part. It seems strange that just when we had thought we had done with the conflict between modern and primitive Methodism the duality should present itself in another form—in the contrast and conflict between the two opposing ideals of Consolidation and Aggression. But so it is: by the ever renewed clash of opposite ideals, each of which contains some element worth preserving, is progress made.

All our historians, in this following Hugh Bourne, are agreed that the crisis through which the Connexion passed at this time was rendered more acute by a marked falling off in the popularity and success of camp meetings, which at the beginning of 1816 began to set in and ever grew more apparent. To Hugh Bourne, so sensitive to everything likely injuriously to affect this mode of service, the change was observed with undisguised apprehension; and he was not alone in taking an alarmist view of the situation. He pointed out the symptoms of what he regarded as a dangerous decline, laid bare the causes, and anxiously sought for a remedy. Now, allowing that Hugh Bourne was an extremist where camp meetings were concerned, and looked upon everything ecclesiastical, whether belonging to the remote past or the present, from the standpoint of a camp meeting waggon, it must still be granted that a change had indeed taken place in the character of open-air services. The old method of having a number of short red-hot appeals, interspersed as it were with volleys of prayer—a method so natural and suitable to times of awakening and revival—had given place to field-preaching of a more formal, ambitious, and edificatory kind. Nor is it hard to account for the change that every one has noted. It was but another form of that dualism which, as we have just seen, was existing in the rival policies (which ought to have been allies rather than rivals) of consolidation and aggression. The fact is, the junction of the Camp Meeting Methodists and the Clowesites was not so close but that a moderately keen eye might have detected the seam showing the line of juncture; the union had not obliterated all traces of the characteristic features of each segment. Or to change the figure, like the river formed of two confluent streams now flowing along the same bed, but rather side by side than mingling their waters, so that by their contrasted colour and other signs you may tell the one from the other—so was it with the stream of double origin we call Primitive Methodism. Indeed, we are not sure that after ninety years of movement the two types are not yet distinctly observable. There are still those who pin their faith to "good preaching," and others who think little of it as a means of usefulness. Any way, it was so in 1816. Some of the Clowesites could preach, and would preach, whether within brick walls or, as they would have said, "under the broad canopy of heaven." They had been accustomed to do their best to give good solid Methodist sermons in chapels, and when they got on the camp-ground they tried to do the same. Nor would they be stinted for time, but disdained the conductor's monitory tug behind. Even at Mercaston Camp Meeting a worthy Clowesite grumbled that he had only one hour allowed him, but Thomas Woodnorth reformed, and afterwards became, Bourne tells us, a first-rate camp meeting labourer. It is not difficult to imagine what results would follow from camp meetings so conducted. "Variety of religious exercises" would be interfered with. Where so much time was taken up in preaching there would be little time left for praying. However true it may have been of Glasgow, camp meetings would not thus "flourish by the preaching of the Word." Even had Apollos discoursed for an hour at a Staffordshire Camp Meeting he would have been listened to with weariness. The people missed the old variety, the quick interchange of exhortation and song and prayer. There would be wandering eyes, and people moving about, and the buzz of conversation on the outskirts of the crowd, dwindling companies, too, as the day wore on. We can conceive what happened as though we had been there and seen it all from the conductor's or bystander's point of view rather than from the preacher's. In short, "there were loud complaints from the societies" that camp meetings were on the down-grade and Hugh Bourne was pained and saddened. Let us just think of him for a moment amid these signs of manifest decline. In 1835 he wrote:—

"Perhaps no other Connexion for the time has suffered so much, or been so greatly injured by *the long-winded system*, as it has been called, the long-preaching and other long tedious exercises."*

In the preface to the next year's *Magazine* he remarks:—

"It is found that if a preacher sets forth the Atonement, offers a present salvation, and preaches in part to the children, he may deliver a good body of divinity in a minute and a half or two minutes; and such sermons, in some instances, produce a better and more lasting effect than sermons do of sixty minutes long." (There's for you, Brother Woodnorth!)

After these extracts, which are perhaps reminiscent of this season of trial, we can sympathise with Hugh Bourne as he noted with dismay the swelling of long-windedness and the decline of the efficiency of camp meetings.

* Preface to the *Magazine* for 1835.

It is not for us to pronounce judgments so much as to marshal facts and let the reader draw his own conclusions; but it is clear, that if long and good preaching, according to the canons, had been what was wanted at the beginning of the last century, then there was no need or justification of Primitive Methodism. Simply to have had services outside differing in little or nothing from those held within places of worship would have done little for the moral wastes of the land. Men wanted the bread of life breaking up small and well moistened with prayer. On the other hand, it was well the tradition and practice of good solid Methodist-preaching was not lost in the rush and fervour of evangelism. The Clowesite section were the custodians, and in their modest measure the exemplars, of this tradition. The time would come when it would be called for.

PETER PHILLIPS.

When things were thus in a bad way light and help came from the old quarter. Peter Phillips, his tried friend, put into Hugh Bourne's hand the *Journal* of Joshua Marsden, in which he gave an account of a particular camp meeting held near New York. After studying this account, Bourne "sketched out a plan for conducting camp meetings with praying services in companies or circles, and sent copies to different places hoping the system would take." One of these fell into the hands of William Ride, who thereupon determined to hold the Mercaston Camp Meeting, at which Hugh Bourne himself was planned to be present, on this model. The camp meeting duly held June 9th, 1816, was a notable success. John Ride, who was afterwards to be co-apostle with Thomas Russell to Berkshire, began to preach at this camp meeting.

"John Benton became like a man let loose, and the Lord, by means of the Mercaston Camp Meeting, opened out a new line of proceedings; and it was like a new founding of the Connexion. From the Mercaston Camp Meeting the Lord in His mercy set on foot one of the greatest and most extraordinary religious movements ever known in England."

But let the sequent lines of our *History* be preserved. John Benton had broken loose from the Non-Mission Law before this. He did not rush from Mercaston Camp Meeting to mission Belper; that had already been done. What he did get at Mercaston was the call to a wider field of service and a baptism for it. Mercaston Camp Meeting did not begin the mighty revival in the Midlands, but it greatly stimulated it. It generated enthusiasm and force, and then liberated them, so that Benton and others sought a wider field and entered on new ground. Thus, as we have seen, one event that can clearly be traced to Mercaston Camp Meeting was the formation of a new circuit, of which Derby was the head.

From his *Journals* we learn that Clowes visited Derby during this early period. He brings in his reference to it just after he has described the missioning of Belper and the opening of the chapel there, and Derby is introduced in such a way as to lead one to suppose that it was visited by him when he made his first visit to Belper in September, 1817, or a little later when he took part in the opening services of the new chapel. Probably he did visit Derby and neighbourhood on both these occasions; for it is clear Clowes has thrown together recollections of visits made at different times and at different stages of the society's progress. He was there when there were difficulties to perplex; when friends were few, and homes and hospitable entertainment not too plentiful. He makes kindly mention of a soldier of the Royal Artillery, who took him to his quarters in the Armoury. Properly speaking, the Armoury was the central part of the Ordnance

THE GRAVEL PIT, MERCASTON, WHERE THE CAMP MEETINGS WERE HELD.

Depôt, completed in 1805. It was a room large enough to contain 15,000 stand of arms, arranged as in the Tower of London, so as to make a fine and impressive show. On the north and south sides of this central building were the magazines capable of holding 1,200 barrels of gunpowder. The central part still stands in Ambrose Street, off Normanton Road, and is now used as a brewery, while the magazine on the south side has given place to cottages, and that on the north side to shops fronting the main thoroughfare leading to Normanton. These were Clowes' quarters for the time, and surely rather strange quarters for a preacher of the gospel of peace. At first, he confesses, he felt it rather a trial to have to clamber up into one of the bunks lying tier above tier which had to be his sleeping-place. But says he: "I remembered I was a missionary, and it behoved me not to demur about little matters of convenience and

THE ARMOURY, DERBY, WHERE CLOWES SLEPT.

comfort." We regret the name of Clowes' soldier-friend has not been preserved, for he rendered good service to the Derby cause, not only by giving the missionaries bed and board, but by helping in the converting work, and in "the getting up of the chapel"

THE OLD BARN, DERBY.

in Albion Street. Clowes' other reminiscences of Derby evidently relate to a time subsequent to this, when the headquarters of the society had been removed from the godless barber's room to the newly-erected chapel. He speaks of the chapel as crowded almost to suffocation soon after the opening of the doors. On one such evening the sight of the chapel-keeper moving about, snuffers in hand, trying to keep the dim gasping candles from going out altogether in the vitiated atmosphere, was taken advantage of by certain unruly members of the congregation bent on creating a disturbance. Clowes cried to God "to still the raging of the enemy." They rose up and rushed to the door. Had not the chapel-keeper opened the door to let them pass, the power of God, Clowes thinks, would have arrested the disturbers. As it was, they fled, but not before the poor chapel-keeper's head was severely cut by a stone thrown as a Parthian shot by one of the persecutors. The meeting broke up in confusion, and the stone-thrower was brought up before the mayor and committed. Clowes records that he also preached at several places in the vicinity of Derby, such as Willington, Boulton, Chaddesden, Draycott, Windley, Burnaston, and Normanton. At these places his labours, along with those of his "coadjutors," were blessed to the conversion of sinners to God. At Normanton, then a suburb now part of the borough, an old barn was acquired for the services at a rental of thirty shillings per quarter, which for more than sixty years was to serve as the home of a society; but in playful irony the Old Barn was dubbed and got to be familiarly known as, "The Cathedral." An iron Church, with accommodation for two hundred people, is now in use preparatory to the building of suitable premises, for which ample ground has been acquired.

The Missioning of Nottingham.

Nottingham was entered by our missionaries in the same unofficial, unostentatious way as Derby. Their coming was not previously announced by bills displayed in the windows or on the hoardings. When they made their actual entry they were not welcomed by the blare of trumpets and beating of drums, or escorted by excited sympathisers. They quietly walked into the town and mingled with the stream of traffic, and made their way to some friendly shelter to be ready for their work on the morrow. We like to think that just in the same natural, informal way the Apostles and first evangelists of the cross made their unrecorded entry into many a town and village of what we now call the nearer East. And yet, if anything, there was a trifle more of deliberation and purpose in the missioning of Nottingham than there had been in the case of Derby. We are fortunate in having a full account of this pioneer visit—

ALBION STREET,
FIRST PRIMITIVE METHODIST CHAPEL IN DERBYSHIRE, NOW COTTAGES.

how it was brought about under what circumstances it was effected and what were the results which followed—written by one who played a leading part in the affair. Sarah Kirkland, late in life, when she was no longer Mrs Harrison, but had become Mrs Bembridge, wrote the account in question of which this is the substance.

It was over the breakfast-table in Mrs Kirkland's house at Mercaston, where he was planned to preach, that Robert Winfield broached the subject of the missioning of Nottingham. As we know, he had a talent for opening fresh places, but in this instance he proposed that Sarah Kirkland should be the chief missioner. Said he, "If you will consent to go, my daughter, and I will go with you and stand by you." Then followed discussion, for the proposal was a weighty one, and not to be lightly adopted. In the end it was agreed that the attempt should be made, and that the Christmas Day ensuing should be the time for making it. The appointed time came, and the trio found themselves in the famous lace-town. But, surely, Winfield's suggestion that Sarah should open her commission in Nottingham market-place was made without due thought. The girl was barely out of her teens; she was asked to take her stand in the largest market-place in the kingdom; it was mid-winter; the year was 1815—a lawless, rowdy period, when the people had not become inured, as they have since, to the sight of young women in plain poke-bonnets singing and exhorting in the streets. No, Mr Winfield, the market-place must not be the auditorium, if you please! Sarah Kirkland put aside the suggestion as one not to be entertained. The next day (being Christmas Day, as we suppose) they found out a room in the Narrow Marsh, where a small band of secessionists, about half a score in number, with a Mr Storer for their preacher, had their meeting-place. Here they attended a lovefeast in the afternoon, and at the close readily got consent for Sarah Kirkland to preach the same evening. "An old lady shouted out that she had dreamed of a young woman coming out of Derbyshire, and told before what kind of a dress she wore." Short as was the notice, the room was crowded out. The sight of the disappointed people turning away from the door troubled the mind of a worthy dyer of the name of Sutcliff, who the next day called upon the preacheress. He was full of regrets for the shortcomings of the preaching room. But more, it was the holiday season, and his mind was made up that a more commodious building should be found, even if he had to search the town from end to end and devote a whole day to the search. Meanwhile pending the outcome of Mr Sutcliff's search for a roomier room, two or three other services were held in the Narrow Marsh under the same disadvantageous circumstances. The interest already awakened by these services increased rather than abated, and when the last one was held the names of twenty-three persons who had received good during Sarah Kirkland's visit were taken down. Before she left Nottingham Mr Sutcliff was able to report that he had found a room in every way suitable. It was the middle room of a disused factory in the Broad Marsh, large enough to hold a thousand people, and if Sarah Kirkland would promise to come and open it for worship it should forthwith be got ready. She gave the required promise, and at the opening services this capacious building was crowded, and, what was better still, on the authority of Thomas Simmons (one of Nottingham's representatives to the Preparatory Meeting of 1819) we learn that sixteen persons were converted on the opening day, of whom no less than ten subsequently became local

NOTTINGHAM MARKET-PLACE EARLY IN 19TH CENTURY.

preachers. The rest of the story Sarah Kirkland shall be allowed to tell in her own words:—

"This room was made the birthplace of many souls. The converting work so broke out that it became the talk of the market people, that if they would go to the

THE FACTORY, BROAD MARSH, NOTTINGHAM.

room in Broad Marsh they would get converted. . . . . Now, persecution arose, and crackers were let off to annoy the people. These things caused a great stir, and the Mayor of the town came to hear for himself. John Harrison was the preacher; he had a young appearance, and was a powerful preacher. The Mayor was so well satisfied that he gave orders for protection, and authorised several young men to keep the peace. One of these was the late David Musson Jackson, who became Governor of Nottingham House of Correction."*

The name Isaac gave to the last well his servants dug—Rehoboth (*i.e.*, Broad places, Room) would have been a very suitable one to have bestowed on the roomier quarters which the young society acquired in the Broad Marsh. But that name was to be reserved for Leeds, and the mother-chapel of Nottingham was to be known by a still more familiar Scriptural name. Canaan Street Chapel still stands not twenty yards from the spot where the now demolished factory stood in the Broad Marsh. The foundation-stone of the building was laid April 23rd, 1823, by the Mayor (Mr. O. T. Oldknow), in the presence of a large congregation. It was opened for divine worship towards the end of the same year—1823, the celebrated Dr. Raffles, of Liverpool, being the preacher. In 1828 a gallery on the two sides and end of the building was put in. But whence the name of Canaan Street? Did the chapel name the street, or did the street name the chapel? If the latter, then Nottingham was more fortunate than some societies we

ORIGINAL CANAAN STREET CHAPEL, NOTTINGHAM.

know, whose first chapels were planted in courts or lanes or streets with strange and not very attractive names. The Nottingham early Primitives must have turned the street, in which their chapel stood, into Canaan Street; for as to the people who inhabited this particular district at that time, we shall not be far wrong if we conclude that their thoughts would not be much occupied either with the earthly or the heavenly Canaan. It is not likely, therefore, that the name, Canaan Street, preceded the building of the chapel; nor did it, if the story communicated to the writer by the late Mr. Thomas Large be true. The story is that the chapel was built in what might be called a maze of little streets, compared with which the Maze at Hampton Court is simplicity itself. At that time there was no road running through into Broad Marsh, and many people had difficulty in finding the chapel. This was the experience of many of the delegates who attended the Conference of 1826. Some were bewildered by the intricacies of the way and lost valuable time in trying to extricate themselves from the

* Letter to Rev. J. Barfoot given in the *Primitive Methodist Magazine* for 1881, p. 227.

labyrinth. It happened just then that the hymn having for its chorus—"Canaan, bright Canaan, I'm bound for the land of Canaan," was quite new and popular, being sung at almost every service. Now, the late John Garner, then a young man full of fun and resource, had noticed that the delegates stood much in need of the guiding hand, and he resolved to supply the need. There, hard by, ready to hand, was a painter's ladder. This he borrowed and climbed, and then chalked in large staring Roman capitals the words, "CANAAN STREET" in such a position on the chapel that they could be seen at a distance over the roofs of the lower buildings. To the delegates these chalked letters were as the clue of Ariadne which guided Theseus out of the labyrinth. Before time and weather had obliterated the letters, officers of the corporation came along to name the new streets, and seeing that this one was named already, they took it over, and shortly a pair of iron plates with the name cast on them was sent and fixed.

Primitive Methodism had a good start in Nottingham. From the beginning it took hold of the people and acquired influence. It was fortunate, too, in securing the adhesion of several men of standing as well as character. Two of these have just been named—Thomas Simmons and David Musson Jackson. The latter, like the former, was one of the fifteen who took part in the Preparatory Meeting. The Rev. John Barfoot writes of him:

"For very many years he was connected with the choir of Canaan Street Chapel . . . and the picture of his fine, portly form standing erect in a prominent part of the singers' gallery by the side of his magnificent double bass violin, which he manipulated with a gracefulness that could not well be surpassed, is still fresh in my recollection."

THOMAS KING.

During the many years he was Governor of the Nottingham House of Correction, Primitive Methodist ministers found (without prejudice to their characters) hospitable entertainment at his residence. It is to be regretted that owing to his having during his later years discontinued attending his class he should have lost his membership amongst us, though his attachment to the Church of his youth experienced no abatement. During the early stirring times experienced by the society in the Broad Marsh, another man who was to become a figure of considerable note in the Connexion gave himself whole-heartedly to the cause. This was Thomas King. He was a man of more than ordinary intelligence and education, as may be gathered from the fact that he had been looked upon by the Wesleyan Methodists as one in every way suitable to serve the Church on the foreign mission field. Born in 1788, Mr King was at this time a married man, and was induced by his wife to attend the services in the Broad Marsh. After much thought and prayer he identified himself with the society, receiving his first ticket at the hands of Hugh Bourne. In 1819, when the demand for labourers will become urgent we shall find anxious discerning eyes directed to Thomas King, and that he will allow himself to be thrust out into the mission field despite the monetary and other sacrifices such a step will involve.

Such then was the manner of our introduction into Nottingham. Yet it is but fair to state that we have quite a different account of our entry into that town, given by no less a person than Hugh Bourne himself. He states that being in Nottingham (no date given) for the purpose of buying Sunday school requisites, he called at the house of Mr Weston whose wife was a zealous professor of religion. This Mr Weston was brother of Mr Richard Weston of Lexhead, near Ramsor, at whose instance the call was made. In the course of conversation Mrs Weston strongly urged that the Primitives should visit Nottingham. The request being reported Hugh Bourne goes on to affirm

"Richard Weston had a main hand in opening the town of Nottingham. My visit might have drawn some attention and was the means of his being sent for, but the Lord put on him the main work of opening that town. He laboured much at his own expense with success. R Winfield made a good impression in preaching, and had a peculiar tact for opening new places; but John Benton was, for a considerable time, a main staff. He stuck to the mode of bringing talents into action, as opened out at the Mercaston Camp Meeting, and he had great success in opening fresh places. Sarah Kirkland was managing and useful; and others laboured well."

Now this statement must at all costs be reconciled with the one already given on the authority of Mrs Bembridge. It is simply inconceivable that a woman of such transparent sincerity and candour as she was should lay claim to any honour to which she was not entitled. Her statement is "I was the first Primitive that preached at Nottingham." No words could be clearer or more emphatic. If the interval between Mrs Weston's invitation to Nottingham and her brother-in-law's visit were too short to admit of Sarah Kirkland's Christmas mission coming in, then it is easier to believe that Mrs Weston knew nothing of Sarah Kirkland's visit than that Sarah Kirkland did not know she had been preceded by Richard Weston. Nottingham was, even in 1815, a considerable town, but we cannot bring ourselves to believe that Richard Weston could "open" Nottingham and leave no trace discoverable by his successor. To us the chief difficulty lies in Hugh Bourne's apparent unacquaintance with the priority of Sarah Kirkland's visit. That difficulty, however, is a slight one compared with the difficulties created by the rejection of Sarah Kirkland's own explicit statement. It may perhaps be said that Hugh Bourne's words "Richard Weston had *a main hand* in the opening of Nottingham," may be understood to mean that he was quite aware, as superintendent, of Sarah Kirkland's visit, but that he attached little importance to it

But this explanation only makes matters worse; for it implies that not only did Hugh Bourne make light of the priority of her visit, but also failed to perceive its causal connection with all that followed. Better to think Hugh Bourne uninformed than perverse in his knowledge. In short we come to the conclusion that Nottingham and Derby alike may safely rest in the belief that Sarah Kirkland was their founder.

This is not written in disparagement of Richard Weston, or to lessen our sense of obligation to him on account of his self-denying activities. There can be no doubt that he *did* labour much in Nottingham, and "*at his own expense*," which is the fact of most significance for this history just at this point. R. Weston belonged to the Ramsor district, so prolific of useful men as we have seen. He seems to have joined the Connexion some time after its formation, if we may judge by the date when references to him begin to appear in Bourne's *Journals*. Hence his name stands No. 16 on the Tunstall plan, February—April, 1818; but No. 5 on the Nottingham plan for the same quarter. There is reason to believe that the few appointments assigned him on these plans by no means represent the work he did, but that like Benton he laboured where

SOUTH VIEW OF NOTTINGHAM.
From the Meadows early in the 19th Century.

and as opportunity offered. As a trustee Richard Weston signs the deed of Dead Lane Chapel, Loughborough (1818), and is described thereon as a "Dissenting Minister of Ramsor," which means that he had taken out a licence to preach the Gospel, though like Benton and Wedgwood and the Bournes he was in receipt of no salary. He laboured far from his home, and during the week as well as on Sundays, for on May 31st, 1819, we find him taking part in a week-day camp meeting on Round Hill near Leicester. These details are given because Richard Weston's may be regarded as a typical case: "He laboured much at his own expense." The Connexion could not have spread and rooted itself as it did during this first period of its history had it not been for the voluntary, unpaid, yet almost continuous agency of men like R. Weston and women like Mrs. Hannah Taylor, "who was wont to save as much of her earnings as she could, then go off for weeks as a self-sustained missionary . . . . and has been seen preaching in a Leicestershire village guarded by police, so strong was the feeling against the Ranter preacheress."* The number of such workers, of men and women who were real ministers, though they would not surrender their independence and freedom of movement, was much greater than any one would suspect who does not dig beneath the crust of our official *Histories*. Our Connexion was indebted for its early extension and up-building to many whose names it is now difficult or impossible to recover.

An interesting confirmation of this is supplied by the plans of the period. On these you will not find the names of any female preachers—not even the names of the female travelling preachers. You wonder at this and cannot but ask—"What have they done with Sarah Kirkland and the other godly women who did such good work?" After alternately staring at the plan and submitting it to a minute examination, it occurs to you that they must have had an unusual number of special services and collections in those far-past days judging by the capital letters so plentifully scattered over the body of the plan. At once you turn to the references for enlightenment, and turn in vain. Now quite at fault you resume your inspection, when all at once it flashes upon you that these Roman capitals mean more than collections or special services—that they mean the women you are looking for. The key fits. S. K. stands for Sarah Kirkland, M. H. for Mary Hawksley—the first and second female travelling preachers of the Connexion. But what particular labourers in the gospel may be indicated by H. P., W. A., and T. B. you cannot determine. The fact is as singular as it is indisputable, and gives rise to reflections as to man's estimate of woman, and as to woman's estimate of herself in those days—reflections which cannot be put down here; for we are in danger of forgetting Nottingham in the endeavour to show what manner of men and women they were who missioned Nottingham and the neighbouring towns and villages.

1818.	FEB.			MARCH.					APRIL.				NAMES.
PLACES.	1	8	15	22	1	8	15	22	29	5	12	19	26	1 H. Bourne
Derby 2 and 5	S K	17	8	27	45	10	9 T	7	36	28	17	19	8	2 W. Clowes 3 J. Benton
Willeton 2 Normanton 6	W A	31	14	36	46	19	37 T	9	17	31	36	8	46	4 J. Buxton 5 R. Weston
Nottingham 2¼ and 6	1	19	10 S	26	9 T	S K	15	TBL	26	18	10 S	9	19	6 J. Wedgwood 7 W Warren
Loughborough 2 and 6	19	M H	S K	17	42	9 T	44	42	10	26	H P	10	6	8 T. Hunt 9 J. Harrison 10 R. Winfield

PART OF THE NOTTINGHAM CIRCUIT PLAN FOR 1818, SHOWING HOW INITIAL LETTERS WERE USED IN THE CASE OF FEMALE PREACHERS.

NOTE. The above places do not follow in this order on the original plan. Not until after 1818 had the circuits their plans on separate sheets. From February, 1817, all the places in the Connexion were on one plan divided into two parts. The Tunstall part of the above plan had sixty-two places and sixty local preachers. The second part consisting of the places in Derby, Nottingham, and Leicester, had on it forty-five places and fifty-one local preachers. There was no week-night plan. Week-night appointments were matter of arrangement. The plan, of which a few lines are here given in facsimile, belonged to Sarah Kirkland, and her name is *written* on it, though it is not *printed* on it.

* ... ... by Rev. S. A. Barron.

Hugh Bourne was at Nottingham on August 11th, 1816, and evidently found the work in the factory going full blast. He notes down: "I spoke to a great multitude from Ephesians vi. 19. It was a glorious time; there has been a surprising work at this place." As a practical man, who carried his carpenter's foot-rule with him in his pocket wherever he went, he is interested in the workshop as well as the work done in it. He takes the dimensions of the preaching room even to an inch, and finds it "contains about two hundred and fifty-three yards six feet. Its length is sixty-eight feet eight inches; and its width thirty-three feet three inches."

And now we seem to have reached a point where a pause must be made for the

OLD MILLS IN NOTTINGHAM FOREST, THE SITE OF THE GREAT CAMP MEETINGS.

From a lithograph of the original sketch by Mrs. W. Enfield in the permanent collection of the Nottingham Art Museum.

purpose of taking in, by a sweeping glance, the general significance of what is going on. What does it all mean and portend? This: A combined and general movement on the Midlands has already begun. The statement takes, it might seem, a form more in keeping with the chronicling of military operations than the following the course of a peaceful propaganda. Yet the movement was militant, if not military. Opposition had to be met and overcome; it was a campaign that was intended, though a bloodless one, and the terminology of war best suits its setting forth. We have just seen how the two bases for this aggressive movement have been secured. Derby and Nottingham are the strategic points from which an advance will be made in different directions. From Derby the base will soon be pushed forward to Loughborough, whence an advance will be made on Leicester and other places on that side. The advance on Yorkshire and Lincolnshire will lean on Nottingham as its base. We have seen, too, something of the men and women—their enlistment and preparatory training—who will be the leaders in this forward movement. Now they are summoned: the supports are called up. Sarah Kirkland (travelling preacher since Feb., 1816) leaves Staffordshire and Cheshire, where she has been labouring, and goes Nottinghamwards, where the campaign will begin in good earnest by the holding of a great camp meeting in Nottingham Forest on Whit-Sunday, 1816, when 12,000 people, it is said, will be present. John Benton, after missioning and remissioning for a time on the borders of the old Tunstall Circuit, experiencing clerical interference at Church Broughton and Abbots Bromley, and

ABBOTS BROMLEY.
The first preacher stood opposite the old house shown in the illustration.

various minor successes in these parts, will also set off into Nottinghamshire, and John Wedgwood will be summoned to assist. Two other Johns—John Heath and John Hallsworth—will also be pressed into service, their salary for some quarters being paid by Benton. John Harrison, too, after beginning (1816) his ministry on the Tunstall side, will in 1818 proceed into Nottinghamshire and then into Leicestershire. Besides these, Richard Weston, Robert Winfield, Thomas Jackson, Thomas King, and of "honourable women not a few," will co-operate. Such is the general plan of campaign, and if its general outlines be but grasped it will save us from becoming lost in the multiplicity of detail; and though we are hurried from town to town and village to village, and seem to want as many eyes as Argus had, or the power to be in several places at once, in order to follow the shifting figures and incessant movement continually going on, still we need not get confused if we only know what is the general "idea," and what will be the outcome of it all. The details will fit themselves into their places.

But before we attempt to describe in anything like detail the course of the great Revival of 1817-18, it would seem eminently desirable that we should know something of the condition—industrial, social, and moral—of the counties of Nottingham and Leicester at the time. It will then appear that, alike in the locality it swept and in its opportuneness, there was something providential in that Revival which, as Herod truly says "Was one of the most remarkable that ever was experienced in the Primitive Methodist Connexion."

CHAPTER III.

THE LUDDITES AND THE LEVELLERS.

The Background of the Movement in the Midlands, 1817-19.

"THAT the power-loom, spinning-jenny, steam engine, and the Primitive Methodist Revival are in time closely related is, we believe, not a mere coincidence. At a grave crisis in the industrial and domestic life of the nation Primitive Methodism was instituted."*

"The entrance of the Primitives into the town of Nottingham was very seasonable or properly timed. For, two or three years previous to their visit, a spirit of dissatisfaction had reigned among the working class, which had proved detrimental to hundreds. The Luddite party had destroyed machinery to a very great amount."†

The observations just quoted show considerable acuteness, and, we believe, state a fact it is all important for us at this stage to see the bearings of. To describe the goings and doings of our missionaries from 1817 to 1819, irrespective of the industrial and social conditions amid which they worked, would be like cutting out figures with a pair of scissors and calling the result a picture. We must have the secular background or the dramatic—nay, the providential appearance of Primitive Methodism in the Midland Counties at this juncture will be missed. Besides, our missionaries were not phantoms, or even men and women so phlegmatic or etherealised as to be free from the human emotions ordinarily experienced by those whose lot is cast in times of crisis and trial. They were men and women of the people who lived and did their work amid the daily excitements of the time, and unless we conceive something of all this, the biographical no less than the historical interest of our narrative will suffer.

Here, for example, are two short extracts from contemporary *Journals*, in which, even at this distance of time, something of the original emotion under which the words were written may still be felt:

"Ev'n in our ashes live their wonted fires."

In one of these faded entries we have Hugh Bourne writing on June 10th, 1817, at one end of the district which more immediately concerns us:—

"Came and spoke at Mercaston. . . . To-day I heard that there was a mob beyond Belper, and that two men had been slain."

---
* Rev. J. T. Ecob in the *Aldersgate*.
† G. Herod: "Biographical Sketches," p. 314.

Sampson Turner writing at the other end of the same district and period, puts down in his journal

"*August 17th, 1819.*—Bro T. Jackson (1) and I both spoke at Wittenmgeroft this evening. It was now a time of public animosities concerning Radical Reform, and on our return to town (Macclesfield) at night, we had some difficulty in getting to our lodgings with safety, but the Lord preserveth the faithful. Much damage was done to people's property which was estimated at £2,000. The scene was truly disheartening to behold—so many excellent windows, casements, shutters and doors broken to shivers."

Now we want to know what all this social unrest—this popular tumult and violence means. It means that misery had bred discontent, and that discontent was seeking to avenge itself. Amongst the many causes of this wide-spread misery must be named the long war and the legacy it left of crushing debt and national exhaustion; the passing in 1815 of the iniquitous Corn Law; the wholesale enclosures of the common lands that had gone on during the war-time; the heavy taxation; the succession of bad harvests and the dearness of provisions; the abuses of a corrupt and expensive government. But over and above this formidable combination of evils there were the far-reaching effects of the industrial revolution now in full swing. In itself this revolution was no evil. In the long result it increased the national wealth and tended to the greater good of the greater number; but in the meantime, while the transition from handicraft to machinery was being effected, there were inevitably many innocent sufferers from the revolutionary changes brought in. The inventions of Hargreaves and Crompton, with the application of steam, had now largely superseded the spinning-wheel, and Cartwright's power-loom was displacing the hand-loom. The old domestic system in which the weaving was done at home or in sheds hard by, was giving place to the factory-system with its employment of women and even children of tender years in many cases brought from a distance.* The old independence, the old leisurely way of working, were becoming things of the past. Everything had to be timed to the clang of the factory bell. There was the hurried meal, the rush to the mill, the long hours of monotonous toil in which the man (perhaps formerly his own master) seemed to have become as much a machine as the machine he served. And so the gulf between employers and employed yawned ever wider, and hence J. R. Green dates from this very time ' the war of classes, the social severance between rich and poor," which, as he observes, still forms the great difficulty in English politics. Men who found themselves flung out of work, or thrust down into the ever-rising stratum of the wage-earning class were in no mood, even had they possessed the ability, carefully to analyse the causes of their own distress. Seeing their own misery reflected in the pinched wan faces of wife and children, some grew bitter and took desperate measures. "There" said they, " are the big factories and the new-fangled machines—so fiendishly clever, that inventive skill, backed by capital and enterprise, is multiplying all around ! These are at the bottom of the trouble. We will have our revenge. The hateful machines which take the bread out of our mouths

* The introduction of steam led to the Cotton Mills Act of 1819 which fixed the working age of children at nine and the working week for them at seventy-two hours !

214   PRIMITIVE METHODIST CHURCH.

and are responsible for low wages and depression of trade shall be smashed, and the masters shall learn that if the Government does prohibit workmen combining in order to better their condition it shall not prevent their combining in order to destroy." Such was the deplorable state of things and the equally deplorable state of mind of many in the Midland counties in the year 1811, when the Luddite outrages began. In February of that year, hundreds of stocking-frame makers, owing to trade depression, were employed to sweep the streets and market-places of Nottingham, Derby, and Leicester in order to earn a miserable pittance. The next month hundreds met in the market-place at Nottingham and came to the determination to avenge their wrongs; and that very night the work of destruction began which in the course of four or five years was responsible for murder and the destruction of a thousand

LEICESTER MARKET-PLACE (TIME OF GEORGE III.).

frames in the county of Nottingham, and quite as many in the adjoining counties of Derby and Leicester. The name they gave themselves was in one sense fictitious, for there was no one leader or general called "Ludd" whom they acknowledged. Some thirty-five years before, a half witted lad when told by his father to "square his needles" had in a fit of passion taken a hammer and beaten them into a heap. The witless but passionate youth's name was Ludd or Ludlam. Hence, they whose doings were marked by short-si   name of "Luddites."

It was difficult to bring the perpetrators of these trade outrages to justice. They were an organisation as secret as the Ribbonmen or Nihilists, and their confederacy was cemented by a terrible oath. This Luddite oath we venture to give in order that the reader may judge what spirit it was of.

"I—— of my own voluntary will, do declare and solemnly swear that I will never reveal to any person under the canopy of heaven the names of the persons who compose the secret committee, their proceedings, meetings, places of abode, dress, features, connections, or anything else that might lead to discovery of the same either by word or deed, or sign, under the penalty of being sent out of the world by the first brother who shall meet me, and my name and character blotted out of existence and never to be remembered but with contempt and abhorrence; and I further now do swear that I will use my very best endeavour to punish by death any traitor or traitors, should any rise up amongst us, wherever I can find him or them, and though he should fly to the verge of nature I will pursue him with increasing vengeance, so help me God and bless me to keep this my oath inviolable." *

Such was the Luddite oath of initiation, and it is not out of place here, for Luddism did its best to spread what Gospel it had in these parts, and to apply its chosen methods in dealing with the evils of the time. Primitive Methodism and it have to meet in these same parts; therefore let the reader compare their constitutive documents, drawn up about the same time—the one breathing a spirit "humane, pitiful, brotherly, with its, "Endeavour to make this society a blessing unto all people", † the other, with its, "so help me God and bless me," to work havoc and if need be to slay my brother.

The Luddites' usual mode of procedure was as follows:—They went about in bands of from six to sixty in number, each with a black handkerchief over his face and otherwise disguised. Each too was armed, and while some kept watch the rest, provided with hammers and axes, entered the buildings and smashed the frames. Then when the work of destruction was over, "General Ludd"—that is, the leader for the time—drew off his men, and at a given signal, usually the firing of a pistol, the band dispersed to their homes, removing on their way the handkerchief which disguised their features.

The outrages continuing, a large force of military was drafted into the district; two London police magistrates with their officers were sent to assist; an influential secret committee well supplied with money was busy; but still the work of destruction went on. In 1812 an act was passed making it a capital crime to break a stocking or lace frame.

The Luddite disturbances were not confined to the Midlands as readers of "Shirley" and "John Halifax" will know. In 1811-12 they broke out in Cheshire, Lancashire, and Yorkshire, where machine-smashing and what was scarcely distinguishable from political pillage went on. In 1813 eight Luddites were hanged at York. The bodies were given to their friends who showed them in the villages as the bodies of martyrs and friends of the people. The venerable Thomas Jackson was then the Wesleyan

* "Old Stories Retold" by Walter Thornbury
† See the first Society Rules *ante* pp 171-2

minister at Sowerby Bridge, and he was only just in time to prevent the chapel at Greetland from being taken possession of for a funeral demonstration and harangue, previous to the body of the Luddite being buried in the graveyard of the chapel.*

But our concern is with the Midlands, and to them we return. For a night-attack on Messrs. Heathcote and Boden's factory at Loughborough, six men were hanged in the Infirmary Square, Leicester, April 7th, 1817. Mr. Heathcote had perfected and patented his improved twist-lace frame, known as the Loughborough Machine (1809), which he had brought into extensive use in a factory he built. The attack was made in the approved fashion by men acting under strict orders armed with pistols and axes. The employees were, on pain of death, required to lie on the floor face downwards while the work of devastation proceeded. No less than fifty-five machines besides much lace were destroyed. All the windows were smashed and John Asher, the watchman, was shot, though he finally recovered. The midnight attack on Messrs. Heathcote and Boden's factory was a mad act regard it in whatever light we may. When the law had done its work, there were five widows and seventeen orphans left, when there need not have been one. The mischief wrought was a piece of sheer futility. Its perpetrators could not even plead that they were doing evil that good might come. There was no germ of goodness in it that would avail to make anything else better. To render fifty-five frames so useless that no man could earn any wages by them was a strange method of raising the rate of wages. For in this particular case the grievance sought to be avenged was "working under price," it was not, as the Luddite outrages in Yorkshire and Lancashire usually were, the work of exasperated men whose labour machinery had superseded. And yet the leader of this gang of Luddites could fatuously say to the half dozen terrified prostrate workpeople whom he had surprised—"If you know of any frames working under price, if they're one hundred or two hundred miles off, tell us, and we'll go and break them." Nor was the firm of Heathcote and Boden the chief, though they were heavy sufferers by this night's work; it was rather the town of Loughborough that suffered. For when all was over, Mr. Heathcote in a sense shook the dust of Loughborough off his feet, and removed his manufactory to Tiverton, which town he afterwards represented in Parliament. This was a blow to Loughborough from which it never fully recovered. Up to the night of the raid it had thriven and the advent of Mr. Heathcote to the town showed the way to still further prosperity. The local historian expresses the opinion that but for this Luddite outrage Loughborough and not Nottingham might have become the seat of the lace trade, and might easily have doubled its population. As it is, though the hosiery trade still flourishes, the bobbin lace manufacture has almost died out. There can, too, be little doubt that night's work was to have a prejudicial effect upon the fortunes of Primitive Methodism in Loughborough. In a way to be described more particularly hereafter, it increased the difficulties of the society. "Then Primitive Methodism had gained a footing in Loughborough by this time? You have not told us about that!" No, for the good reason that there is little to tell. Those who could have told us all we want to know have passed away and left no record. Still, by a process of inference we can

* "Recollections of My Own Life and Times," by Thomas Jackson, pp. 136-7.

approximately fix the date of its introduction. Loughborough is not found on the plan, February—April 1817, nor any place in Leicestershire. By May, 1818 a chapel had been built, and as early as January of that year, when Hugh Bourne paid his first visit to Loughborough, he found a society already flourishing there. We judge that in the Midsummer, or at the latest in the early Autumn of 1817, John Benton missioned Loughborough. So that if any one wants a convenient date-mark for the introduction of Primitive Methodism into what was to be its third circuit they may find it at a point midway between the grim scaffold scene at Leicester, April, 1817, and the one equally grim, at Derby in November of the same year, to be referred to shortly. The Luddites and Primitive Methodism are closely related in time; the vanishing of the one coincided with the entrance of the other. So, though our history-books are silent, we know as surely as though we had been there and heard it for ourselves, what the people of Loughborough were talking about in their homes, at the street corners, in the public-houses and factories. If it be true that for six or seven years the Luddites had brought in a veritable reign of terror over a large district in Nottinghamshire and Leicestershire, if they "had held possession of Loughborough by armed force in defiance of the magistracy and constabulary," if they had "even openly coerced judge and jury sitting in the Assize Court of Nottingham,"* if the factories built during this time were constructed for defence as well as work, being forts armed with blunderbusses as well as factories furnished with frames—if all this be true, which there seems no good reason to doubt, then we may be quite certain that Luddism and the doings and fate of the Luddites would be more than a nine days wonder. It would for certain be the long-lasting staple topic of conversation and discussion. The movements of the gang previous to the attack on the mill, the biographies of the members of the gang, the incidents of the night-raid and the story of the men's tardy apprehension, the drama of the trial, and the part played by judge and counsel, witnesses and prisoners, the demeanour of the condemned on the scaffold, the industrial problems associated with Luddism, and the bearing of it all on the present and future prosperity of the town—this was what men were rehearsing and discussing according to their individual bias, and with varying ability and volubility when Benton made his entry into Loughborough. It must have been so. To the public mind thus preoccupied our missionary brought a new topic—a new interest "The Ranters are come! What are they like? Who are they really? What do they do?" Men had now something else to conjecture and talk about besides "General Ludd" and his doings. Many a group would have its talk broken in upon by the lively hymn our missionary sang, and would stop and listen. Some would follow and wedge themselves into the crowd to learn for themselves what the Ranters were like and what they were after. And some few out of these we know found more than a fresh topic. The word came home with power to their hearts, or the walls of Dead Lane Chapel would not so soon have been raised. So, though we have no complete story to tell of the introduction of Primitive Methodism into Loughborough, we can with some measure of confidence fill in the background of the story. As for Dead Lane Chapel—the

* "Notes and Queries of Leicestershire."

mother-chapel of Leicestershire Primitive Methodism—though we show its picture here in advance, we will tell of its builders and its building in the next chapter. In this we are only putting in the background.

The "Levellers."

"This Luddism was mixed up with the Levelling system." So writes George Herod, and he gives the year 1816 as the date of the admixture. His statement receives striking confirmation from a competent writer, who says: "Soon the riots of the Luddites were lost sight of in the more formidable political riots which marked this period, and make the social history of 1816 little more than a catalogue of disturbances." Who the Levellers were, and wherein they differed from the Luddites, will become

DEAD LANE PRIMITIVE METHODIST CHAPEL, LOUGHBOROUGH.
1818—1837.

clear if a rapid sketch be given of the condition of the country at this time. After the crowning victory of Waterloo the spirit of disaffection previously existent became more widespread, bitter, and rampant. Men had expected so much from the peace, and their condition was worse, and their outlook gloomier than ever. So discontent tended to become anarchic, and disaffection took more and more a political colour. In the autumn of 1815 the iniquitous Corn Law Bill, designed to keep the average price of wheat up to 80s. per quarter, was passed, despite the vehement protestations of the people. Men were now just in the mood to listen to the devil's gospel, and agitators and public prints were ready to preach it. Many became the avowed followers of one Dr. Spence, who aimed at a general levelling of property. Men began to practise what they heard preached. What had been after all but trade outrages on a large scale, now became insurrectionary spirits preluding a "general rising," for this was what men secretly talked of and began to prepare for. They even fixed the date of the rising—it was to be June 9th, 1817—a date of some interest to us as being approximately the time when Primitive Methodism entered Loughborough after its successes in Nottinghamshire. A general rising too, was what the Government feared, and its hand bore heavily on all overt acts of disaffection.

But there were many who called themselves "Radical Reformers," for sturdy and sane-minded William Cobbett had fastened upon Parliamentary Reform, and energetically advocated it as the one thing needful at this crisis. The provinces followed his lead, and Radical Reform became the watchword. The more excitable Metropolis, however, got out of hand in November, 1817. After a mass meeting at Spa Fields, Islington, shops were pillaged, with the result that the Government took away the right of public meeting. Hampden Clubs had sprung up all over the country, being especially numerous in Lancashire, and the stern repressive measures of the Government exasperated the feeling already bitter enough. Secret drillings on the moors went on, ostensibly for the purpose of ensuring the orderly management of the mass-meetings, which again became legal in 1818, "the darkest year of the century." But the Government believed the intention was to overawe them by a display of force. The leaders, following the example of Birmingham, resolved upon holding a monster meeting to demand their political rights in St. Peter's Field, where the Free Trade Hall now stands. The meeting was held on Monday August 26th, 1819. Unarmed, the operatives of Lancashire, marshalled by Samuel Bamford streamed to the rendezvous where at the centre from open hustings Orator Hunt, as President, was to harangue the crowd. The magistrates determined to serve a writ upon him for some frothy talk he had indulged in 'on the butcheries of Waterloo." The constables and yeomanry were soon wedged in the crowd, and to rescue them the order was given for the 15th Hussars to charge. What followed can easily be imagined—the panic fright, the mad rush, the human welter, the broken limbs and trampled forms. Eleven persons—men, women, and children—were killed and two hundred wounded. The Sidmouth-Castlereagh Government approved the action of the magistrates and caused a medal to be struck on which the exploit of the now detested yeomanry was commemorated. By the same Government the repressive measures known as the Six Acts were passed and stringently enforced. Peterloo—as in mockery it came to be called, as though it were a contemptible travesty of Waterloo—was a decisive victory for the forces of reaction. It put an end to the "Levelling system," and opposed a dam against the Radical Reform Movement, which was not swept away until 1832.

We have anticipated the dying down of the Levelling system in 1819, but in 1817-18 it was still rife in the Midland Counties, and especially in the towns we are concerned with—Nottingham, Derby, Loughborough, and Leicester. To cope with it the Government stooped to an odious system of espionage, finding an unscrupulous tool in one Oliver, who was not only a spy and informer, but what we must go to France to find the word for—an *agent provocateur*. He pretended to be a kind of head-centre and in conversation with his dupes at the "Three Salmons" public-house in Nottingham, gave it out that the whole country was ready to rise; that he himself "could raise 70,000 in London. That the people in London would not be satisfied unless Nottingham was perfectly secured, for it was the rallying-point for Nottinghamshire, Derbyshire, and Leicestershire; and that if it was not secured the passage over the Trent would be perfectly stopped to the Northern forces. That they must proceed forward to London as soon as they could raise sufficient men against the Loyalists, and that Nottingham was to be continually occupied by Northern forces in succession." He said further: "London is now quite ripe; I am sent down to see that all is ready; they can hardly be kept down in Yorkshire and Lancashire, they are so anxious to begin." *

And so the infamous creature practised upon his victims until he got them fairly within his toils, and another gruesome scaffold-scene was the end of it all. Here is the bald entry the annalist gives us, which, bald as it is, means so much:—

"*November 7th, 1817.*—Execution of Jeremiah Brandreth *alias* John Coke, William Turner, and Isaac Ludlam for high treason. These men were the victims of an odious system of espionage, and the crime for which they suffered was occasioned and fomented in a great measure by an infamous man named Oliver, who was employed by the Sidmouth-Castlereagh Government as an agent or spy in the North Midland districts."

The misguided men were hanged, and afterwards beheaded, in the presence of 7,000 military and a vast concourse at the Old Gaol, Friar Gate, Derby (now gone), amid striking expressions of popular sympathy.

Such was the state of things in the Northern Midlands during the progress of the great revival. From the very nature of the case our missionaries were brought into closest quarters with the prevailing spirit. The gospel of salvation they carried, and the devil's gospel, which is always in its essence a destructive and "levelling system," not only eyed each other at a distance, but closed and grappled. Even if there were not a particle of direct evidence remaining to show this, we know it must have been so. Churches of long standing naturally made it their chief solicitude to keep their people from being "drawn away and enticed" by the lawless spirit abroad. They drew

PETERLOO.

* "The Datebook of Remarkable Events connected with Nottingham and its Neighbourhood

a cordon round the fold and tried to isolate their flock. But as yet our missionaries had no such necessary work to engage them. They themselves were outside the cordon, and any work they did must be carried on within the infected area. They must go right in amongst the people wherever they congregated. They might be—probably they were—Luddites or Levellers or Radical Reformers in the very act of disseminating their views and trying to make others like themselves. If so, all the better; the more need they should go. It was a providential "opening" not to be declined, but welcomed.

The very name our missionaries bore, and what was most characteristic in their

THE OLD GAOL, FRIAR GATE, DERBY, NOW CONVERTED INTO PRIVATE RESIDENCES.

methods, furthered the needed contact and helped to make it more fruitful. Hugh Bourne, when referring to the missioning of Nottingham, observes: "The term Ranter greatly assisted in opening new places. If it was given out for a 'Ranter-preacher' to preach, the neighbourhood, and often a part of the country, would usually come together." An old anecdote, that bears on it the stamp of authenticity, affords a striking confirmation of Hugh Bourne's remark:—

"Joseph W—— was a very wicked man, and usually spent the Lord's Day in wandering from one public-house to another. One day he heard a person say that the 'Ranters' were come to —— Hill. 'Oh!' said Joseph, 'it is only the Radicals under a feigned name, I will go and hear them.' And so he did on the next Lord's Day he listened very attentively, and thought he heard very little Radicalism. The preacher gave out that he should be glad to meet in class as many as would join him, at a neighbouring house. So thought Joseph, he will explain his views more clearly. 'I will go. I dare say he has some private communication to make about a general rising.' So in he went, the preacher sung, prayed, and gave his experience; Joseph's eyes began to open; the real object of the preacher was before him, and his own sins were full in view. A cry burst from him 'God be merciful to me a sinner.' God had pity on him; his soul was converted; he joined our society and became a useful class-leader."*

Fortunately we have one piece of contemporary evidence as to the successful results of the methods followed by our missionaries in the disturbed period of 1816-19. The writer—Rev George Herod—was a Nottinghamshire youth at the time and was himself among the fruits of the great revival, soon after becoming a travelling preacher. He writes of what he knew, and as his "Biographical Sketches" has long been out of print, and is now scarce and likely to become more so, we shall for this as well as other obvious reasons, give the very words of his testimony, so that it may be handed down as serving to confirm our contention that Primitive Methodism did a work in the first period of its history for which the nation had reason to be grateful

"At this juncture and crisis [industrial and political] the P. Methodist missionaries brought a counteractive influence to bear upon the masses, and in multitudes of instances destroyed the baneful virus of infidelity and insubordination. Having been raised up from among the working classes, and not having received an academical education, and their appearance and dialect being correspondent to those of the disaffected, they generally gained a patient hearing. Their manner of entering a town or village also produced great excitement; in general the missionary was accompanied with a number of warm-hearted singers, and so soon as they entered the place of their attack they commenced singing down the street, and continued so doing until they arrived at a place of rendezvous; as nearly every town and village have places where men and youths meet to discuss different subjects thither the missionaries would make their way. The Spiritual Songs which Lorenzo Dow had brought from America, with the very lively airs to which they were sung, produced a very wonderful effect upon multitudes. Had the preacher with his supporters sung a hymn or psalm to Martin Luther's favourite tune, or one commonly used in a place of worship, it would have been said—'Oh it's some Methodist preacher; it is nothing new.' But the course adopted led to a different result. Hundreds, and in some instances thousands, (and especially on a missionary's first visit to a place) were collected together through the novelty of lively singing.

"The name by which the preachers were designated—'Ranters'—was of itself a topic for general conversation, and in some instances for surmisings. For some time the people had had for a subject of conversation, Luddism and the Levelling system, and it had not been uncommon to see in the different towns and villages, groups at the corners of the streets, on a Sabbath morning, discussing political subjects; but Ranterism was a new topic. Hence the novel name was the means of causing the people to give the preacher a hearing. The minds of thousands were also excited with dis-

* "Anecdotes and Facts of Primitive Methodism," by Samuel Smith, *Primitive Methodist Itinerant Preacher*, 1872

affection towards government. This commenced in the beginning of the year 1816, and now when the preacher had collected the people in the open-air by lively singing, they wanted in eagerness to hear if he would tell them something new. And when he commenced his fervent and energetic prayer in behalf of the assembled people, deploring their wretched and miserable condition as the result of their transgressions, an influence was often brought on them that caused them to reflect. But especially when he read out his text, and began to portray the character, conduct and circumstances of his hearers, his word, by the power of the Holy Ghost often reached their consciences, and many saw the error into which they had fallen, and the danger of mixing up with infidel and political companions,—and so forsook them, and became valuable members of society. What thousands were congregated on Nottingham Forest at the Camp Meeting in 1816, and what numbers there were from both town and country that felt the glorious effects of gospel truths! Many to our knowledge, became sobered down, and were soon brought into the enjoyment of religion and became as zealous (if not more so) for the cause of Christianity, as they had been for Luddism or the Levelling system.

"We could give a number of circumstances illustrative of the great good which was the result of Primitive Methodist missionary labours at this period, but let the following suffice. At a large village, eight miles south-east of Leicester, the Levelling system took deep root in the minds of the working classes, and a sub-committee was formed, and with their frequent meetings, their correspondence with other places, their drilling for fighting and collecting for ammunition, scores of families were so reduced as to be almost in a state of starvation. A barn belonging to one of the committee was converted into a store-house for ammunition. Some time before the general expected rise, one man, possessing an unpleasant feeling against a neighbour who was a farmer, determined to have revenge, and this he sought by one night maiming a number of his sheep,—expecting that on the 9th of June, 1817, the general rise would take place, and that then he would be lawless. However, in this he was disappointed, the general rise did not take place, but he was apprehended for the crime he had committed, and examined before the magistrates, when he was committed to Leicester gaol to take his trial at the assizes. His trial lasted a considerable time, and the jury found him guilty of the offence. His lordship passed the sentence of death on him. After this his brother felt so indignant against the principal witness, that he came to the determination that if his brother were hanged he would be revenged on this man by waylaying and shooting him. The execution of the sentence was, however, delayed, and in the interim a Primitive Methodist missionary preached at a village about two miles from the place where the two brothers had resided; there the one who contemplated homicide heard the gospel, and was awakened to a sense of his situation. The night after, the preacher took his stand in C———e,* and in his discourse all the leading men belonging to the Levellers in that village were convinced of sin, of righteousness, and of a judgment to come; and such was their concern for the salvation of their souls that they resolved to hold a prayer meeting in the house of the father of the man who was under sentence of death. When the time arrived (not for a Levellers' meeting, but for what was then vulgarly called a Ranters' prayer meeting), the place was crowded to excess. The meeting was opened with singing, but when this closed there was not one to be found that could pray. However, the individual who had decided to be an assassinator recollected that there was in his

* The village of Countesthorpe, Leicester 2nd Circuit answers to description in the text.

father's cupboard a large book of prayers for every day in the year. He therefore brought it out, and as many as could kneel did, and he read a prayer, and then rose and sang a hymn, and then read another prayer, and in this way they carried on their meeting for a considerable time. But very soon after, the two principal Levellers obtained the remission of their sins, by faith in the blood of Christ, and then they were enabled to pray without a book. Soon after their conversion they became local preachers and were zealous champions for the Lord of Hosts. One of them, some years ago, died triumphant in the faith. He left a son behind, who in his youth obtained religion, and for some time was a very acceptable local preacher, and then he died happy in God. The brother of the man under sentence of death is still living, and is steady to his purpose for nearly eight and thirty years he has maintained his position in society and on the preachers' plan. His father, who was the proprietor of the barn or storehouse, was also brought into the enjoyment of religion, and many years ago he landed safely, we trust, in heaven. The barn which contained ammunition for the Levellers was converted into a place of worship and in it we dispensed the Word of Life, in our turn, for three years, a large society existed there, and now they possess a very neat chapel, and have a large Sunday school. From the society one travelling preacher has been raised up. The individual that had the sentence of death passed on him received a commutation of his sentence, and was transported beyond the seas for the term of his natural life."—Herod, *Biographical Sketches* (Introduction pp 12—15) *

* It must be remembered this was written many years ago. Unfortunately and foolishly the "Sketches" bear no date, but Herod died August 30th, 1862, and the "Biographical Sketches" would be published in the Fifties.

CHAPTER IV.

THE GREAT REVIVAL OF 1817-18.

A CLEARER idea of the course and extent of the Revival of 1817-18 will be gained if, instead of contenting ourselves with mere verbal description or tabulation, we attempt to show in some such graphic way as that adopted in the text, where the revival operated, and what it did towards the enlargement of the Connexion. As yet, we must remember, there was but one plan for the entire Connexion divided into two parts, therefore not only can we pretty accurately measure the progress made during a given time by ascertaining whether few or many fresh places have been added to the plan, but by locating those places we can also learn in what direction or directions the Connexion is extending itself. Thus, comparing the

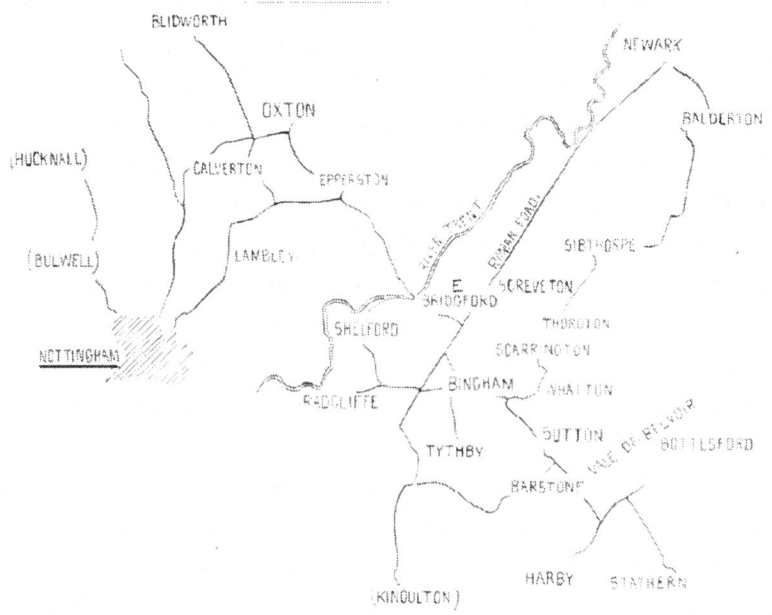

PLACES IN NOTTINGHAMSHIRE ADDED TO THE PLAN IN NINE MONTHS.

plan for February—April, 1818, with the one for the corresponding quarter of the previous year, we find that it is the Nottingham Circuit which has had by far the largest increase in the number of its preaching places, and, further, that the great majority of these new preaching places are in Nottinghamshire. Yet we note that the names of Loughborough and three or four other places in Leicestershire stand at the very bottom of the plan, signifying that already in the spring of 1818 the Connexion, after its successes in Nottinghamshire, is beginning to extend itself in that direction. None of the places shown on our rough sketch-map, drawn to scale, are to be found on the February—April 1817 plan, except Bulwell, Hucknall Torkard, and, of course, Nottingham, which is the base and centre of the whole movement. The remaining places serve to register the gains of the previous nine months' labours. We know other places besides these were missioned, but circumstances either prevented Primitive Methodism from rooting itself in them, or as yet its hold was too slender and uncertain to justify their names coming on the plan. The map, then, shows that throughout the year 1817 Primitive Methodism was specially busy in the valley of the Trent from Nottingham to Newark, in the vale of Belvoir, with an extension to Grantham in Lincolnshire; and to the north and west of Nottingham, in ancient Sherwood Forest, as far as Mansfield, though its coming on the plan will be deferred for a time.

WHERE PRIMITIVE METHODISM COMMENCED AT BULWELL.

DALE ON FOREST. Where Camp Meetings were held for many years.

HEMPHILL LANE, BULWELL. Where Open Air Services were held.

Bulwell, Ilkeston, and Hucknall Torkard, as we have seen, *have* their place on the 1817 plan, and though they were first entered in 1816, before the vigorous concerted movement in Nottinghamshire began, they may still be regarded as the early first-fruits of that movement. Bulwell was missioned by invitation just as Derby was. Sarah Kirkland had attended the famous Whit-Sunday Camp Meeting in Nottingham Forest (June 2nd), when, if we are to believe the liberal estimate given, there were 12,000 persons present at the camp meeting, and 1,500 at the lovefeast in the room in the Broad Marsh. She was quietly returning to Derby on the following day, and had got some twelve miles on her journey, when she was overtaken by a man on horseback bearing an urgent message from a Mr Turner for her to preach at Bulwell, a hosiery town, some four miles from Nottingham, that same evening. She at once turned back with the messenger and preached to some hundreds of people from a cart fixed in the middle of a field. Mr Turner, it seems, had hoped to get the loan of the Wesleyan Chapel for the service, but his application to the trustees was unsuccessful, and hence other arrangements of a rough and ready character had to be improvised. Amongst the many converts at this service was Mr Gent, a dyer, who, Herod tells us, first opened his house for preaching, and then in a few weeks got a large room prepared for worship. "Within one month from her visit sixty persons joined the Primitive Methodist Connexion." Probably the room thus "prepared" was the old barn, which continued to be the chapel of the society until about the year 1852. Though this date takes us a little beyond our period, the interesting circumstances which led to the barn's supersession by a more suitable place of worship may be touched upon.* It was felt the time had more than come for a new departure. The old barn, some twelve feet by thirty, and eight or nine feet to the wall-plates, and looking more like an entry than a chapel, had served its day and generation. But the difficulty was to obtain a suitable site, for the lord of the manor was also the rector of the parish—an ominous conjunction. The Rev. W Brownson was then the superintendent of Nottingham North, with Charles J Boden for his colleague. On these fell the task of interviewing the rector, and on the society the privilege of praying in the old barn for the success of the mission their ministers were then discharging. Said the superintendent to his colleague, as the two were on their way to the rectory, "I have not much faith. You pray while I talk." Now, a little while before this, Horace Mann, the statistician, had published his report of the various religious denominations as the result of the census of 1851. In it occurs that remarkable passage, in which Mann refers to our Church as if it were a kind of prison-gate mission and the jackal or hon-provider of the Church of England. This strange judgment, as we have already seen, has its distinct historic value, glancing back as it does on the whole of this introductory period, and showing what some well-informed people thought of us and our work. That sentence has often afforded a topic for animadversion in the days that are gone—and naturally so. But once at least, handled diplomatically, it served to wring an advantage for the Connexion. It helped to get a site for Bulwell New Chapel. Mr Boden had Horace Mann's report with him, and showed the passage to his superintendent as they went along. "That is just what we want," was the comment. During the interview the rector, of course, objected that "the Primitives were opposed to the Church of England." For answer, Mr Brownson produced the sentence:—

"They prepare people for the more refined worship of the Church of England, and for every one added to their society the country contains one criminal or immoral person the less."

* The story has been interestingly told by Rev. C H Boden in his article, 'A Momentous Mission,' Aldersgate Magazine, March, 1902. The writer and the Connexion generally are under obligation to Mr Boden for rescuing so many worthy names and deeds from threatening oblivion.

The rector read the sentence thoughtfully, and then remarked: "I was unaware of this. I will think the matter over." The ministers returned to their company in the old barn, and when they announced what could not but be regarded as the success of their mission, we are told that "a great shout of glory went up." Gent (not the dyer aforesaid) stamped his wooden leg and exclaimed, "Glory be to God!" and the sparkle in Thorpe's eyes spoke volumes. Not many days passed before the rector offered them the one site he had to give, which happened to be the one above all others they desired. Thanks, perhaps, to Horace Mann, and still more to the liberal heart devising liberal things, the Bulwell friends were handsomely treated. When they met the rector's steward for the purpose of staking out the land required, he, acting on his liberal instructions, about doubled the quantity they had ventured to mark.

Later on in the year Sarah Kirkland was again at Bulwell, for Hugh Bourne, who is evidently there for the first time, notes in his *Journals*:—

"*Tuesday, August 13th.*— I was at Bulwell: there has been a strange revival at this place. Our people held a camp meeting last Sunday, and Sarah Kirkland spoke yesternight; yet there was a huge multitude."

BULWELL CHAPEL.

Although we cannot always be making it appear by repeated quotations from his *Journals* that Hugh Bourne was quickly on the track of the missionaries, preaching, advising, "looking after the temporal concerns," adjusting disagreeables, and keeping a watchful eye on everything—such is the fact to be ever borne in mind. If he is not there at this moment, he has only just left, or is expected to arrive soon. It is not more certain that trade follows the flag, or that the representatives of law and order followed the Roman legionaries, than that Hugh Bourne will follow in the wake of Sarah Kirkland or John Benton in these parts, or wherever they may be prosecuting their mission. Bulwell not only make this plain, but are

"*May 7th.*—At Bulwell. A glorious time. They are doing well here. *June 25th.*—Finished the plan, and brought a heavy luggage for T. Saxton [who has just begun his labours as a travelling preacher] from Nottingham for Tunstall. I came to Bulwell—saw Mary Hawkesley and J. Benton. The work is going on well and rapidly; *but there is great opposition—in some places by gentlemen, in others by mobs.* O Lord, stand by them. I came to Belper—excessively hot."

We are not to conclude from the references to persecution contained in the italicised words of Hugh Bourne just quoted, that he himself had encountered persecution at Bulwell or its neighbourhood. He had no such experience there or thereabout; nor had Sarah Kirkland. And yet—and in this lies the significance of the fact—it was in this part of Nottinghamshire where there was the most disaffection amongst the operatives and miners. No: Bourne would write that sentence about persecution by gentlemen and by mobs fresh from hearing Benton tell something of the rough times he and others had experienced in the vale of Belvoir and the more purely agricultural parts of the county. It is too soon to generalise on the facts as to the persecution of our early missionaries; it is a long dark chapter as yet barely begun. But even at this point it may be well to advise the reader to note as we pass along, the particular social and industrial character of the localities where persecution showed itself most bitter. Let him be on the alert to answer such questions as these: Was persecution at all conditioned by the avocations of the people, and upon the degree of their subserviency to the influence emanating from manorial halls and snug rectories? Did persecution instinctively follow the plough, and linger about sleepy cathedral closes, and haunt steady agricultural towns? On the other hand did it flee from the sound of the pick and the whirring of machinery? Ample material will be forthcoming before we come to the end of the chapter of persecution, to enable the reader to answer these questions for himself. By that time he may find reason to conclude that there was a closer connection between mobs and gentlemen than Hugh Bourne's words may seem to imply.

Before the close of this same year—1816, and probably also in August—Sarah Kirkland missioned Ilkeston in Derbyshire, which at that time was a place inhabited chiefly by colliers, and noted, we are told, for the poverty and the roughness and rudeness of the people. When we read what Herod has to say of the manners of the people in 1816, we cannot but recall that almost the same words were used natives of Mow Cop in 1800 before the first revival began. He intimates that here too a stranger passing through the place was in danger of being pelted with filth or with language equally foul. But the missionary was favourably received, and her labours were in the truest sense remunerative. The gospel worked a reformation in many a life and home, and even when Herod wrote he could state the pleasing fact that few towns within the same time had made greater progress morally and intellectually than Ilkeston.

Hucknall Torkard, in whose church rest the remains of Lord-Byron, was another of the places near Nottingham visited by Sarah Kirkland before the close of 1816. At the time of her visit there existed much destitution amongst the people, and this was associated with widespread discontent and political excitement. "Levelling" sentiments found favouring conditions in Hucknall, and flourished as in a hot-bed. All this

HUCKNALL TORKARD MARKET-PLACE.
The place marked X is where our earliest preaching-place was.

showed the people sorely needed the gospel, and were fit to receive it; for their discontent had its justification, and hence showed it might be turned into "divine discontent," and then they would be ready to welcome the gospel of salvation and hope. Even the "levelling" sentiments that found favour with so many of the people had been adopted as promising deliverance from present evils; and they who had given ear to an imperfect or false gospel might be glad to exchange it for a better one. So in this manufacturing village, as in so many other places in the Midlands at this time, Primitive Methodism found and used its opportunity. It did not, in the person of its missionary, ... promising field, for the seemingly unfavomable

THE FIRST PREACHING-HOUSE, HUCKNALL TORKARD.

conditions showing themselves were really the very whiteness of the field ready unto harvest. Better Hucknall Torkard, with its destitution and minds saturated with levelling sentiments, than Tythby (likewise in Notts., and an addition to the 1818 plan), as John Harrison describes it after a visit paid in March, 1817.

"I walked four miles to Tithby, intending to preach at two, but when I entered the village all the people were going to the church, so I had to wait till the service was concluded. I had a large congregation, but they looked just like what they were, viz., stiff-necked professors, who had the form of religion, but were without

THE FIRST CLASS MEETING HOUSE, HUCKNALL TORKARD.

the power 'a fire was kindled round them, but they knew it not a flame burned them, yet they laid it not to heart.' I preached from the words of the Lord— 'The men of Nineveh shall rise in judgment with this generation, and shall condemn it, because they repented not at the preaching of Jonas and behold a greater than Jonas is here.' I felt barren in my soul, yet believers rejoiced *I could not move these formal professors—and to all appearance God did not—so I left them.*"

But at Hucknall many of the inhabitants *were* "moved" by Sarah Kirkland's message and appeals. A society was formed, which had for its first preaching-room the "Seven Stars" Inn Club-room. This was used only on Sundays. The week-night services were held occasionally in Mrs Osborne's cottage, Wood Lane, and also in the open-air. Then the "Seven Stars" was left, and a barn on the opposite side of the way was taken. The society grew in numbers until the membership reached between seventy and eighty. On the formation of the Mansfield Circuit, Hucknall was placed on the Mansfield plan, and its prosperity continued until 1838, when it suffered a serious reverse, the story of which must be told in another connection.* Reverting to Nottingham, Hucknall was as recently as 1901 formed into a circuit out of Nottingham III. It has now a flourishing society, and possesses valuable church property.

It would not have been surprising if Sarah Kirkland had met with opposition in missioning both Ilkeston and Hucknall, but there is no hint that she had any such experience. Nor can we recall an instance during her more than four years of continuous itinerating in districts differing widely in their industrial character when she met with insult or rough treatment. Indeed, this statement might be enlarged so as to apply to the other devoted female labourers in the first period of the Connexion's history. As a general rule they were treated civilly, and got a fair hearing. Curiosity—so keen as for the time to keep under every other feeling, their defencelessness, their trustful mien, their tact and simplicity, and the absence of everything provocative—these may serve to explain, in part, the immunity which our early female missionaries as a rule enjoyed in a much greater degree than their colleagues of the sterner and less tactful sex. There were exceptions to this rule of immunity we know but where they occurred we may safely infer we have got down to a very low human seam. The general statement made holds good for most districts of the country, and speaks much for the instinctive chivalry of the people when both the times and manners were rougher than they are to-day.

An incident of a kind, quite common in Sarah Kirkland's experience, occurred at the close of her first service at Hucknall Torkard. A stranger was introduced to the preacher, who had come from Sutton Ashfield. He had heard of the evangelistic successes of the "Ranters" so called, and had come to see and hear for himself. He was urgent that Sarah Kirkland should visit Sutton as soon as possible. The man's appearance was ill against him, for his mouth was so contorted as to give a sinister aspect to his countenance, and probably the disfigurement was also a disablement, and marred his utterance. However, after some hesitancy, the preacher gave the desired promise, and the visit was duly paid. A revival followed, and a large society was formed, which had until 1840 its headquarters in Bedlam Court. In this strangely-named locality the District Meeting of 1838 held its sittings. We are told that the barber who pressed Sarah Kirkland to visit Sutton Ashfield became the first and a most useful member of the new society there. Herod tells a story of the way in which the barber's malformation arose, which may be taken for what it was worth. When in his godless state he was much annoyed at the sight of a new Wesleyan Chapel that was rising up near his shop—so near that people would have to pass his shop to enter it. One day, as he stood surveying it, just before completion, he broke out into imprecations —and he was smitten with retribution. He repented and sought forgiveness.

Mansfield was the next place successfully missioned. Here a good society was raised, and in a few months a large room was taken and fitted up with forms and pews. The society seems to have had a continuous existence from the time of Sarah Kirkland's visit, and to have made some progress during these early years; for at the Nottingham Quarter Day, March, 1824, the following somewhat unusual resolution was passed:— "That Mansfield be a Branch of the Nottingham Circuit for one quarter *on trial*." Either the period of probation must have been prolonged, or Mansfield and the adjacent societies must have reverted to their old relation to the mother-circuit, since it is not until 1826 it entered upon its long career of circuit independence.

BEDLAM COURT, LORD STREET,
FIRST PREACHING-PLACE, SUTTON-IN-ASHFIELD.
A District Meeting was held here.

Amongst other places said to have been successfully missioned by Sarah Kirkland about this time were Cotmanhay, Codnor Park, Kirby, Lambley, Blidworth, Oxton, and Epperstone. She was the first accredited missionary of the Connexion to set foot in East Bridgford, a place that on various grounds deserves fuller reference. Yet East Bridgford is in the Trent Valley, and, therefore, geographically in that part of the county it fell to Benton's lot to mission, and her visit only by a short time anticipated his. This village is of note, as having been the home of several persons of consequence to our history: some became auxiliaries, and greatly helped to extend the revival, while others became adherents of the cause, and locally, or in the wider sphere of the ministry, were to become well known. One of the latter was George Herod. East Bridgford was his boyhood's home, and up to the last he retained a vivid recollection of Sarah Kirkland's first visit, and of the stir it made in the quiet village. She preached in a barn, with a gig for a pulpit; and here young Herod heard her as he sat perched on the big beam that spanned the barn. He had climbed to this point of vantage by he help of two poles leaning against it, and in this way he had, like Zacchæus, obviated the disadvantages of his stature: for the barn-door was so packed with people, that when he had squeezed himself among them he could see little else but the heads and shoulders of those who were bigger than himself. So he turned the beam into a gallery and the sloping poles into stairs, and from his elevation was able to see and hear everything. Benton's second visit was paid on a Sunday afternoon, when a powerful impression was made on the large company assembled in the open air. The minds of many, hitherto thoughtless or depraved, were stirred into concern; a revival broke out, and in the course of a few weeks a society of forty members was established.

Mr. William Lockwood was one of John Benton's hearers that Sunday afternoon. There is no need for us to write "*a* Mr. Lockwood," as some of our historians have done, as though he were an utter stranger to whom we are now introduced for the first

STAR LANE, EAST BRIDGFORD.—WHERE GEORGE HEROD LIVED.

time. Rather may we speak of him as *the* Mr. Lockwood, whom we heard of in the Staffordshire region in the days gone by; for is he not the Mr. Lockwood who held high rank in the heavenly bulletins the visionaries published from time to time? William Lockwood was accepted as a candidate for the Wesleyan ministry in 1800, and as such his name stands on the Minutes for that year next above the honoured name of Benjamin Gregory, the father of the able and liberal-minded late editor of the *Wesleyan Methodist Magazine*. His first station was Leek, a circuit immediately adjoining Burslem Circuit, and there is conclusive evidence that Bourne knew Mr. Lockwood so well that he could speak of him as "his esteemed friend;" that Lockwood was in these early days a noted evangelist; that he believed in camp meetings, and, but for circumstances, might have led the way in holding them; and that, even as it was, his known sentiments and example had kept alive and fed the desire of the Harriseahead Revivalists to have one for themselves. The first time we hear of Mr. Lockwood is in February, 1803. Hugh Bourne has j   l   t f   after he had with the young preacher who had recently come to the circuit, and who admired the zeal and liveliness of the Harriseahead society, whereupon—

"I told him Mr. Lockwood had been one who had aided in bringing them into that way—it being the way he carried on meetings. He said in his journey hither, he slept all night with Mr. Lockwood; but observed that if he were to exert himself like Mr. Lockwood there would soon be an end to his life."

Still more to the point is a passage in Hugh Bourne's *History* as to the influence unconsciously exerted by Mr. Lockwood in stimulating the desire for camp meetings during the abeyant period of 1806 :—

"There was a report that a meeting had been appointed to be held in the open air, upon one of the hills in the Leek Circuit of the Old Connexion, when

EAST BRIDGFORD OLD CHAPEL. NOW PUBLIC READING ROOM.

a Mr. Lockwood was a travelling preacher there [some years before]; that it was to have been carried on with various religious exercises, and to have continued a whole day; but that a short time before the day arrived the head-preacher was prevailed on to put it aside; and this was a cause of grief to many, as they believed it would have been a great means of reviving religion. This had great weight with the Harriseahead people, as they highly respected Mr. Lockwood on account of his having been useful to them in their first revival." ("History of the Origin of the Primitive Methodists," *Magazine*, 1821.)

The last glimpse we get of Mr Lockwood in Bourne's early *Journals* is in 1810, where we have the following entry :—

"*September 8th.*—I went to Biddulph Moor to hear Mr. William Lockwood. It was the opening of the chapel; there was a great congregation, although it rained; Mr. L. is much in the power. Hannah knew him; he stands between Mary Dunnell and Clowes; so now we know the fourth preacher."

This, it must be granted, is a most singular entry, and suggests a good deal, but it is quoted here simply to show that Mr. Lockwood was in Staffordshire regarded by the Camp Meeting Methodists as one in spirit with themselves; he was one of the leading trumpeters, so that if now, in 1817, he should put the trumpet to his lips, and for a time throw himself heart and soul into the evangelistic mission of the Primitive Methodists in these parts, it is just what we might expect from what we know of the man and his antecedents. His doing so will serve to give continuity to his life and to our history. Mr. Lockwood is called a well-to-do farmer and Methodist local preacher—the fact being that, after his appointment to Newark in 1802, he had married a widow lady of wealth, and settled down on his wife's estate; so that in the Minutes of 1803 occurs the entry: "William Lockwood who has desisted from travelling." His lady, whose maiden name had been Salthouse, was a thorough-going evangelical in creed and sentiment, a great change having taken place in her life as the result of her hearing Rowland Hill preach in the parish church. After this she could no longer continue to worship there, because (to use her own words) "although the clergyman preached the truth he did not know its power." So she built a chapel at her own expense, which was the first Free Church established in the village. In this building the Wesleyans worshipped until the Reform agitation of 1849, with which it seems Mr. Lockwood sympathised. Not choosing to join in this movement the Wesleyans vacated Lockwood's Chapel and built one for themselves. Mr. W. Lockwood, sen., and his wife, were by their own wish buried in the chapel, which was their own private property. Mr. W. Lockwood, jun., the son of the preceding, was a farmer and local preacher of some repute. For some years he continued to carry on services duly arranged for by plan, Methodist fashion. This went on until some twenty years ago, when "Lockwood's Chapel" was acquired for the use of the Connexion, and it is still retained for school purposes. Not only did Mrs. Lockwood make provision for public worship and the teaching of .... F. Guilford, but through her instrumentality

"LOCKWOOD'S CHAPEL."

a day-school was opened, in which free education was given to some fifty or more children by a schoolmaster paid by herself. Mr. and Mrs. Lockwood would never sit for their portraits, having, it would seem, an objection to the practice difficult for us to understand. As a poor substitute for the likeness of this worthy lady her granddaughter preserves as a sacred relic the Quaker-bonnet she was accustomed to wear.*

This, then, was the Mr. Lockwood who listened to John Benton on his second visit to East Bridgford, and thus it had come about that the Methodist travelling preacher we knew in Staffordshire had become a man of substance, and almost the squire of the village. As he took part in that afternoon's service he "received a particular manifestation of the spirit of God." The old evangelistic impulse came upon him with renewed force. "He possessed," we are told, "good natural talents, was very courageous,

KINOULTON VILLAGE AND CHURCH.

and had an independent spirit." These qualities, so essential to a successful missionary, were to receive a fresh anointing for service on that Sunday afternoon.

If we wished to show how the Revival affected the villages and towns of Nottinghamshire both at the time and afterwards, and how they in their turn reacted upon the revival, and contributed their quota to the growth of the Connexion, then East Bridgford might stand as the type of such villages and towns, and of the interaction referred to. It is a typical Nottinghamshire village that has just received the evangel brought by the Primitive Methodist missionaries, and is going to pass it on, or—better

* For some of the facts given in this paragraph I am indebted to Rev. T. W. Gooderidge, who obtained them from the granddaughter of Mr. W. Lockwood, sen.

238 PRIMITIVE METHODIST CHURCH.

still—to live it. So true is this that, according to the old saying, "From one we may learn all." Taking our stand here, we can compare the features and results of the revival in this quiet Nottinghamshire village with what can be observed in other places in the same district visited by our missionaries, and, for the most part, the comparison will yield resemblances. There is, however, one striking exception:—the almost total absence of persecution. In this respect East Bridgford presents a contrast to many places in the Trent Valley, the Vale of Belvoir, Rutlandshire, and certain parts of Lincolnshire. Whatever be the explanation, a good deal of persecution attended the introduction of Primitive Methodism into these parts. Indeed, if any were minded to show by means of tints on a map what parts of England they were in which our missionaries met with persecution, and were to graduate the tint according to the severity of the persecution encountered—just as is done to show the comparative level of a given district—then the districts in question would have to be rather heavily shaded, and there would be some specially dark patches of colour on certain places much under aristocratic or clerical influence. There was a good deal of this not far from Bridgford, as we shall see; but in its comparative immunity from persecution Bridgford compares favourably with many other places, such as Kinoulton. At this place, while Benton was preaching to hundreds of people gathered from far and near, a dangerous bull was loosed and headed for the congregation, but the beast had more sense than its master, and preferred to take the line of least resistance. On September 1st, 1817, Thomas Jackson (I), who had come to labour in these parts, was shouted out of the village; a fortnight after, while preaching at Cropwell Bishop, the parson of the parish ordered that the stocks

POST OFFICE, COTGRAVE.
Centre of Village.

COTGRAVE.

THE PERIOD OF CIRCUIT PREDOMINANCE AND ENTERPRISE.

were broken, and the constable said so. "Ought not the parish to be fined for not having the stocks in proper order?" gaily inquired Jackson. The question irritated the clergyman, who ordered the constable to detain the preacher in custody all night; and the order was obeyed. At Cotgrave all the pots and pans of the neighbourhood seemed to have been brought into requisition for the purpose of drowning Benton's voice while preaching. At Bottesford, under the shadow of the stately towers of Belvoir Castle, Benton met with a rough reception. As soon as he began worship in the open air the bells of the church were set a ringing, a dog-fight was got up, a big drum beaten, and various instruments blown and clashed. All this babel of sound and confusion failing of its purpose, rotten eggs, filth, and stones were flung at the preacher, who nevertheless stood his ground.

BELVOIR CASTLE.

When, some time after, (April 2nd, 1818) John Harrison entered Bottesford, he was treated in much the same way as Benton had been, save that there is no mention of the instrumentalists, for the beater of the big drum had followed Benton about until he had got converted, and the band by this time had been broken up. Says Harrison, of Bottesford:—

"This place may be called 'Little Sodom,' and I should be surprised if God did not destroy it, was it not for the few righteous souls that are in it. I preached at night, and met with much annoyance from the sinners of this place by their pelting us with dirt and rotten eggs

Yet in spite of High Church influence, Antinomianism, and mob violence, a flourishing society was soon gathered. A chapel was erected, and for many years Bottesford has stood as the head of a station. One of its village chapels—Thornton—has had a strange eventful history, also belonging to the chapter of persecution, but this, if told at all, must be told in a later portion of our history.

At Shelford, another aristocratic preserve, as we shall see, one after another of our adherents was evicted for allowing services to be held in his house. At Oakham, Thomas Jackson was violently opposed, and even injured, and had to stand his trial at Oakham Castle. So violent was the persecution encountered at this place that ultimately our missionaries had to be withdrawn. What happened at Newark and

BOTTESFORD MARKET CROSS.

Grantham had better be told when we come to deal with the work of Lockwood and Wedgwood.

After this short survey of the district opened up by Benton, in 1817, so far as regards persecution, the result arrived at is, that on any proposed map of persecution, scarcely any place Benton missioned, unless it be Radcliffe and Whatton, would stand on a white ground. Even Bingham and East Bridgford would show a faint tint. At the former place a large society was formed; but it was under adverse conditions. "The church party through the influence of the clergyman did their utmost to prevent the Primitive Methodists from having an interest in the place."

It is a relief to turn from such a survey as this to see in these Nottinghamshire villages a Bottesford is a good sample of the rest. On the plan, February—May, 1818, George Herod's name is found as a local preacher on trial. He was first convinced under Sarah Kirkland, still more deeply convinced under John Benton, soundly converted through the instrumentality of

MAIN ROAD, RATCLIFFE-ON-TRENT.

William Clowes, and in 1819 he began his long and vigorous ministry. He died August 30th, 1862, his last words being: "I rest, I rest, I rest on His arm," and is buried in the quiet graveyard of Christ Church, High Harrogate. When George Herod entered the itinerant ranks the work was opening out on every side. Labourers were so urgently needed that such a promising recruit as he was gladly accepted. He was indeed no ordinary man, as the books he has left testify. He had a considerable fund of information, had quite a remarkable acquaintance with our early history—although he was not free from bias in the handling of his copious materials — and he wrote in a perspicuous and vigorous style. The official memoir very justly says of him:

"He was one of the first enrolment (sic) of our successful home missionaries, when that work was most difficult and hard, and its temporal remuneration was small, and he exhausted therein one of the best of constitutions. His preaching was very energetic and scriptural, and his praying powerful. He was ... left behind him sterling works in theology and history, printed and in manuscript. He made indelible impressions on every station he occupied as a minister and superintendent, but the real results of the forty-five years of his Primitive Methodistic Christian life, and the forty-three of his itinerant ministry, can only be known in eternity."

George Herod was a married man when he entered the ministry. He married Miss Elizabeth Parrott, of East Bridgford. She was for many years an acceptable preacher, and for upwards of fifty years a class-leader, surviving till 1871. Mrs. Herod must be carefully distinguished from the Miss Parrott whom we shall soon meet with labouring in Lincolnshire.

Kinoulton has been mentioned as a place where both Benton and Thomas Jackson encountered considerable opposition. Probably the soil was found so hard and stubborn that even hardy Primitive Methodism failed to take root there. Yet it is a pleasant glimpse we get of the good which had been effected in that village, as we read in Thomas Jackson's Journals how, when he was surrounded by boys who blew horns and shouted and hustled him out of the village, "John Garner and James Bonser—two youths who had just been converted, protected me. Peace to their shade. Honour to their memory." James Bonser was a Kinoulton lad, and the churchyard contains many memorials to that family. John Garner was a native of Kegworth, but was apprenticed to a shoemaker in Kinoulton, and he tells us how on May 17th, 1817, under a sermon preached by Mr. John Benton, he was truly awakened to a concern for his eternal welfare and was on the next day enabled to believe, and in two months and three days began to exhort. The names of both John Garner and James Bonser are found on the plan, February–May, 1818, and in 1819 both entered the ministry.

MRS. HEROD (MISS E. PARROTT).

These two village youths—recruits of 1817—will be heard of again. James Bonser will thrice suffer imprisonment for preaching the gospel before he retires from the ministry in 1825. John Garner, too, will have become a prominent man in the Connexion by 1848, when he will demit the office of General Missionary Secretary, and, with a constitution broken by the privations and brutal treatment endured in the earlier years of his ministry, will seek superannuation. He will live to become one of the original members of the Deed Poll, and to figure no less than six times on the roll of Presidents; and though this distinction meant less in former days than it does now, it yet serves to show the opinion entertained by his brethren of his business capabilities and their desire to do him honour.

Besides these two, and those before named, there were other village youths won to the cause during the Revival who were "to endure hardness" and survive to be veterans. One of the earliest-won of these was James Moss, who tells us he was on the same Easter Sunday of 1816 both convicted and converted under John Benton at

Whatton. He will begin his ministry of thirty-nine years in 1819. There was Thomas Charlton, a Shelford youth, who began to travel in 1821, and laboured forty-one years in the ministry; also John Oscroft, who on January 4th, 1818, went to hear

JAMES MOSS, AGED 38.    THOMAS CHARLTON.    JOHN OSCROFT.

our first missionaries at Hucknall Torkard. There the Word took fast hold of him, and though his companions got him away to a public-house as men carry off a wounded comrade that he may not fall into the enemy's hands, he was so conscience-stricken that strong drink proved no anodyne, and he escaped from his would-be rescuers, and found relief and pardon while making his way home. He was to become one of the leading missionaries in South-East Lincoln and Norfolk. To this roll of names must probably be added John Coulson, of Calow, near Chesterfield, who, religiously inclined from childhood, will be drawn into the revival-movement and become one of the preachers of 1819, and labour thirty-five years.

The ways and training of the youth of our Churches were not made matters of such solicitude and study eighty years ago as they are to-day, and hence there remains little to tell how these young converts were handled in the brief time that intervened between their conversion and call to the ministry. Fortunately we know the

JOHN COULSON.

most—though that is not much—of the most eminent of these youths—John Garner. There seems to have been within him a spring of fun and frolic which intermittently became active. Once, his brother tells us, when as a lad of fourteen he was on a visit to Clifton at wake-time, he passed himself off among the lads, who were playing on the village green, as a French boy, and succeeded, to his own great enjoyment, in completely mystifying them. In this early delight in mystification the child was but the father of the man. Now and again all through life he would mystify his brethren—and no one likes to be mystified. The faces of the mystified bore witness to the short inward debate going on as to whether they ought to smile or frown, and it often ended by their face as   her for his

R 2

lightsomeness. Perhaps later on in life, John Garner's humour might be in danger of becoming a little too mordant, so leaving a mark on the memory. But on this we need not dwell; this was not the man in his normal condition. Some of his sallies and escapades are remembered and recounted to this day, and were we to omit all reference to them, the John Garner we are writing about would not be the veritable John Garner, who as a youth no doubt added to the gaiety of some Nottinghamshire villages. Some of his pranks had a practical purpose at the heart of them, like that one in which, in his own characteristic way, he dealt with the charge of non-visitation. Rising at an unearthly hour in the morning, he began his round of visitation by thundering at the door of the chief complainant. Presently we see the good man of the house with a guttering candle in his hand, standing half-dazed and shivering in the passage. "Eh, Mr. Garner, whatever's the matter?" "Matter, sir—matter! One cannot rest in one's bed for you and your visiting! How are you getting on in your soul, Brother ———? Let us pray a few words." And then we can see him chuckling as he departs to pay another surprise-visit.

One safeguard the newly converted youth of those days had—he was expected to attend all the means of grace, and encouraged from the first to "exercise" in public. He was not thrust into the background and condemned to silence, and sarcastically bidden to "tarry in Jericho until his beard was grown." This safeguard it was not easy for John Garner to make use of. Whether the opposition at Kinoulton, like that at Oakham, had been so violent as to forbid the establishment of a society, we know not, but certain it is that at this time there was no society there, though the missionaries paid occasional visits to the place. He tells us that—

"On the Sabbath I sometimes went twenty miles to hear a sermon by a Primitive Methodist preacher; and after I had finished my day's labour it was not uncommon for me to walk eight or ten miles to a meeting, and as no societies were formed within a considerable distance of my residence, I frequently travelled several miles to a class meeting."

Widow Garner, like Job, was the honoured parent of seven sons and three daughters. Of these the five eldest sons were away from home at this time following their callings. William, the sixth, brave lad, was at Clifton doing his best for his mother and the younger members of the family by working as a "stockinger." Hearing a great deal about the "Ranters," curiosity led him to go on June 17th, 1818, to a camp meeting at Stanton, conducted by John Wedgwood. While looking and listening, picture his astonishment when his own brother John, of whose conversion and recent movements he knew nothing, came to the front of the waggon and announced his text! He preached from the words, "O Israel thou hast destroyed thyself; but in Me is thine help." Those who knew John Garner in his prime tell us that he had a magnificent voice, and what was better still, the power of distinct enunciation, so that his voice carried far, and his words were audible even to those on the outskirts of a vast camp meeting assembly. Something of this power must already have shown itself a year after his conversion; for his brother records that "considering his youth and inexperience he preached a sermon of wonderful fluency and power," and it made a deep impression on his mind, and led up to his conversion. William Garner will begin his long and even more distinguished ministry in 1822; and in 1830 James Garner, the seventh son, will follow, and become in his turn departmental officer, President of Conference, and theologian. If the Nottinghamshire Revival of 1817 had done no more than summon forth from their village obscurity and lowly callings such men as these, and set them on the road to usefulness and honour, it was worth the toil and persecution endured.

These names by no means exhaust the list of those who, being themselves the fruit of the Revival, were hereafter to scatter the seed of future harvests in other parts. They might not be in the field as long as some of those already named, but as long as they were engaged they did good work. Jane Brown was one of these. As early as September 24th, 1818, Hugh Bourne, when on a visit to Nottingham, records:—"Jane Brown begins to travel. I took the opportunity to give her a charge. I trust she will do well." Yes, she will do well; perhaps helped in her well-doing by Hugh Bourne's charge. Her face and name are both worth remembering, not merely because she is fair to look upon and will be the first female to preach in Canaan Street, but for reasons much more weighty. Mention, too, may be made of Jacob Wilkinson, who began his life with the century, and entering the ministry in 1822 travelled till 1830, when we miss his name from the *Minutes*. After his retirement from the ministry, he was for a time actively associated with Nottingham and the Circuit, as the Quarterly Minute Books show, and then—he disappears.

JANE BROWN.
The first female that preached in Canaan Street Chapel. Her first text was John i. ver. 29.

VILLAGE SAINTS.

It is not away from the purpose of this *History*, but quite in keeping with it, to notice that the gospel our missionaries carried into these towns and villages not only rescued men and women from vice, but in not a few instances fashioned character to the finest form and issues. It is just here we touch the root of the matter, so far as Church history is concerned. Saints are the Church's chief asset, and if it cannot produce a sufficiency of these it will soon be bankrupt in the estimation of both God and man. It cannot compound for failure in fine character-building by success in fine chapel-building, or by success in anything else. Both God and the world are saying: "Never mind your ecclesiasticism. Bring out your best samples of men and women." Underlying the question whether Primitive Methodism can justify itself historically is the question whether it can justify itself ethically and spiritually. If "wisdom is justified of her children" so must our Church, like every other, be justified or condemned by the type of character it brings forth and nourishes. It has always seemed to us that the true glory of our Church has had in the lower walks of life, men and women who in this work-a-day world could win and even extort the acknowledgment "These, at any rate, are true to their religion," who in the open, and not under hot-house conditions, could bring forth the fruits of the Spirit, saints who held the plough-stilts, or stood at the wash-tub. Thank God! we have had, and still have, a goodly number of these, and we have not made enough, or as much as we shall make, of them, for it is the usual fate of saints to be passed over for what is noisy and pretentious. Yet if we only knew it, these 'living epistles" are our credentials—our denominational title-deeds.

There were—thanks to the Revival—some saints such as these,

"Not too bright or good
For human nature's daily food,"

in the towns and villages of the Midlands whom our Church can place on its roll. Dinah Maul and Eliza Richardson, of East Bridgford, may be singled out—just as Hannah Yeomans, of Rodsley, already has been—as fair samples of the peasant or artisan saints whom the Revival directly or indirectly gave our Church. "Saints" we call them, and that without scruple, for the word wants bringing back into the thick of the world's business. In the right sense, both these lowly and godly women have left a local reputation for saintliness of character and the claim deserves wider recognition, for as Thomas Arnold has said "Christianity is 'published' by the recognition of its saints. Their lives are no delusion, for they have permanently affected men, and they are all based, built on Christ and are in Him the manifestation of eternal truth among outward things." Dinah was but the wife of a "stockinger," and yet if a plebiscite had been called in the village, where everybody was known to everybody, to decide the question who was the most out-and-out Christian in East Bridgford, it is more than likely that Dinah's name, much to her own surprise, would have come out at the top. Nor would the result have been different if the votes had been counted at the public-house, with the publican sitting as presiding officer. We have classed Dinah Maul with Hannah Yeomans, of Rodsley, but her piety was of a stronger and less contemplative type than Hannah's. There was something Amazonian about her saintliness. Her prominent qualities were those of a leading and ruling spirit—"an uncommon degree of good sense, patience, decision, force of character"—so that "she swayed the rest according to her will." She championed the Sunday morning prayer meetings, and got the preacher there by having first invited him to breakfast—in this showing her womanly tact as well as zeal. She was strong for the Sunday evening procession round the village, at which it was usual for the last week's converts to take a prominent part, so that the procession assumed something of the character of a triumphal one. We think of Paul's allusion to himself as a willing captive swelling the triumphal progress of the victor Christ, as we see Dinah and the preacher at the head of the procession. They have got last Sabbath's convert between them—a poor reclaimed drunkard who happened to stray into the service. He, poor soul, goes along with streaming eyes and hands held aloft, while from Dinah's lips there comes forth every now and again her favourite ejaculation, "Bless Him! Bless Him!" As the pro

they see one who had been a terror to them when maddened with drink now so changed. Tradition loves to tell how Dinah used to pray and sing as few could, and goes on to speak of her as the efficient class-leader and a famous directress of penitents.

When people were in spiritual distress, still more when life was ebbing, the word would be, "Send for Dinah." We need no higher tribute than this to the reality of her religious experience and her skill as a physician of souls. Mark them whom the dying want to have near them. In the sincere last moments of life it is the wise virgins—they that have oil in their lamps—whose presence is sought.

Dinah had her successor. Eliza Richardson, though "born in one of the four poor labourers' cottages at the top of Trent Lane," was in the succession of the saints, and how this was brought about we learn from her own words, dictated a short time before death to her daughter:—

DINAH MAUL AND ELIZA RICHARDSON.

"I knew the people of God enjoyed something I was destitute of. So I sent for dear Sister Maul and Sister Burrows. They asked me if I would like to be saved. I said that was what I wanted. So we all knelt down on my own little hearth-stone, and then they poured out their souls to God in fervent prayer, and I prayed also; and oh, what a weight of sin I felt on my poor back! But the Lord heard and answered prayer, and I felt my load of sin was gone."

Eliza Richardson's conversion took place in 1843—the year after East Bridgford was made a branch of Nottingham Circuit—and her husband's conversion followed soon after. The prophetess has her mantle as well as the prophet, and Dinah's mantle was taken up by Eliza Richardson. She enjoyed unbroken and intimate friendship with Dinah until the latter's death, and then carried on her work. Nature had done much for her; but grace, the best of developers, quickened and enlarged her natural gifts, so that her ability as a class-leader and organiser became very marked. In her modest home hospitality was dispensed to the servants of God, and all that related to the prosperity of the cause of God lay near the heart of her and her husband, who in extreme age survives. Both showed themselves stalwarts in suffering willingly for their principles. Once their feelings were harrowed by the refusal of the clergyman to read the burial-service over their dead child in the church, because it had not been baptismally regenerated there! The intolerance of the same clergyman compelled them to send their children to a neighbouring town for their schooling, which entailed a walk of three miles each way. Do you say "How hard upon the children! What a piece of superfluous severity!" So one taking short views might have said at the time; but now that the fruits of the hardy training have had time to show themselves, it will be acknowledged, even by them who had to pass through it, that the training was greatly wise. It was better the parents should choose for their children the daily trudge imposed by conscience than that they should sacrifice their principles to save their children's legs. The children themselves honour them for the choice they made; for a blessing has followed the high-principled choice. One of those little trudgers is to-day not only a leading Primitive Methodist local preacher in the Nottingham First Circuit, but is mentioned as a candidate to contest a Parliamentary constituency against a noble lord of the house of Bentinck. Other instances of firmness in adhering to principle on the part of Mr and Mrs Richardson might be given, but let the one already cited, with its lesson for our times, suffice. Eliza Richardson, after a consistent and unbroken membership of fifty years, died in 1893, leaving others to carry on her good work.

Now, though we have confined ourselves to one village and to two persons out of that one village, it must not be thought that East Bridgford has given to our Church no other persons worthy of grateful remembrance, or that other villages in these parts visited by the Revival were barren of saintly characters. Either supposition would be utterly wrong. Indeed, as soon as you begin to examine the scanty records yet remaining, or question those whose memory is most far-reaching, you will find that almost every village where Primitive Methodism established itself had in its society some person to whom every one looked up as eminent for goodness, or unflinching loyalty, or length and activity of service. You turn to the *Journals* of Hugh Bourne and you meet with a record like this—one of many similar records—which only whets your curiosity to know more:—

"*August 16th, 1818.*—Epperstone at 2. Preached from Ruth. Renewed the tickets. Truly a good time. Miss Lealand, the leader, is a truly pious woman, and of great talents. I rejoiced to see her."

More and more are we convinced it would be a praiseworthy and pious work to rescue the memory of such as these from oblivion. It could be done by the fixing of tablets in our churches, or, still better, by the publication of local works, in which the story of their lives should be told, not in the conventional way in which the work is usually done, but by an honest attempt at description of character and the recital of authentic facts. Such memorials are not only due to departed worth, but would impress upon us the continuity of our history, and greatly strengthen Connexional loyalty. There is no lack of material, and for our own part we must forbear. One other name, however, we will mention and fit into its place as shortly as possible, because Robert Hutchinson was connected with these parts, and may well stand as the type of the sure and steady, the men who year in and year out are at their posts, and, as we once heard it put, are "like a pump-handle, ready for any one that wants them."

We have referred to the disaster which overtook the Hucknall Torkard Society in 1838. In that year, while Rev. George Herod, a strict disciplinarian, was superintendent of Mansfield Circuit, a division occurred in the Hucknall Society, most of the divisionists joining the Selstonites. If it be asked, "And who were the Selstonites?" we answer, The Selstonites were dissidents who split off from the Belper Circuit during the superintende... ...1838-9. The ... of the ... split was the action of the Quarterly Meeting in increasing the modest stipend of the superintendent from fourteen to sixteen shillings a week, and the fact that the greater number of those who were scandalised at the proposed increase of salary hailed from Selston accounts for the name the divisionists came to bear.* The Selstonites dwindled until the feeble remnant were absorbed in the greater split from Methodism in 1819. In referring to this secession, the late Dr. Gregory quite truly remarks: "It is a mistake to suppose that the younger Methodist bodies are gifted with unsplittability; the fact being that the splitting does not make such a resonant report, nor leave such a terrible crevasse." Yes, Primitive Methodism has had its splits, and a good many of them from first to last, but they have been local ones affecting a branch here at one time and there at another. They have been splitlets rather than splits. There has never been one that rived the columnar trunk, or tore off the main arterial branches—not one that affected and threatened to rend in twain the entire Connexion. The Selston split was not the first in time or in importance. There was one at Nottingham, it would seem, as early as 1821. This we learn solely from the *Journals* of Thomas Charlton, and history has no more to say about it; so soon does a vigorous Church recover from her wounds, and, like Nature, obliterate by fresh luxuriant growths the marks of former ravage. Then in 1834, during the superintendency of F. N. Jersey, Nottingham Circuit passed through its severest crisis. Feeling ran so high that Mr. Jersey was by a section barred out from the pulpit of Canaan Street. There were secessions in the societies, though these for the most part soon died out or were reabsorbed. There was one secession dating from about 1829 or 1830, which received, no doubt, some impetus from the Nottingham one of '34, and has proved more permanent than most others; for the Independent Primitive Methodists of Bingham and the adjoining villages—a Free Gospel organisation which uses our Church Hymnal—survive as a memorial of the troubles of that period. Sometimes splits seem to be a kind of self-pruning, and that which has been pruned appears to be none the worse for its enforced amputation, but rather to have gained in vitality by what it has lost in substance; so we are told that in 1835 the Nottingham Circuit generally was in a healthier condition than before, and that there was an increase of 135 on the year's working after all vacancies had been filled up, though it is admitted that Canaan Street had not yet fully recovered from the ordeal through which it had passed. Nor can we forbear saying that the Selston split may stand as a fair type of most of those that have occurred, in this one respect at least—it was "much ado about nothing." To command any respect a split must have a decent justification, or else the report it makes in its going off, however resonant, will affect the general trend and final result of things no more than the bursting of our neighbour's pneumatic tyre. So, as we have said, the Hucknall Torkard divisionists cast in their lot with the Free Gospel Selstonites.

REV. W. CARTHY.

---

* The Rev. W. Carthy, we believe, published an account of the affair, but our efforts to secure a copy of the pamphlet have proved unsuccessful.

The seven members, who alone were left, made a gallant stand against adverse conditions. They took the club-room of the "Half Moon" inn for their services, and struggled on. But what could they do? The feeling in the town, we are told, was against them, and G. Wood, the superintendent of Mansfield, 1841-2, gave up Hucknall,* but not before appealing to the superintendent of the newly-formed Arnold branch of Nottingham (1841) to take charge of Connexional interests there. The appeal was made to the right man. Edward Morton was born in 1807 at Countesthorpe in Leicestershire, where the Luddites' barn for the storage of ammunition was turned into a place of worship. He became the Primitive Methodist Town Missionary in Nottingham, and laboured indefatigably in furtherance of that forward movement in which William Antliff and John Brownson were leading spirits—a movement which more than repaired the losses sustained in 1834, and resulted in the acquisition for the Connexion in Nottingham of a second good chapel in another part of the town. This was historic Hockley Chapel, opened by Wesley and Dr. Coke in 1783; retained, and thus alienated from the Old Body, by the seceders to the New Connexion in 1797, and made the burial-place of Alexander Kilham, the founder; recovered in 1817 by the Wesleyan Methodists as the result of a Chancery suit,

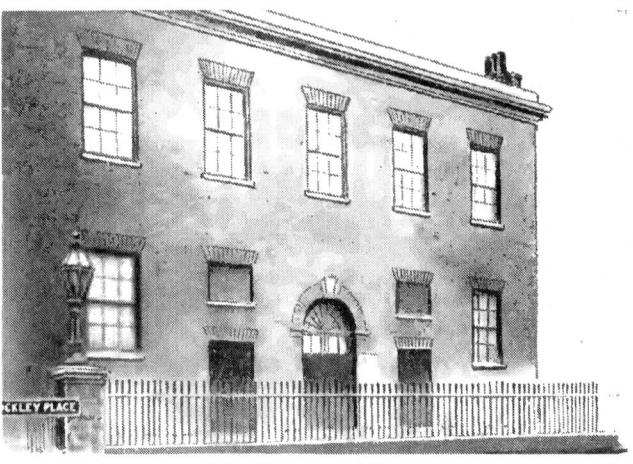

REV. EDWARD MORTON.

HOCKLEY CHAPEL, NOTTINGHAM.

and in 1839 sold to the Primitive Methodists for the sum of £2,400. Edward Morton, by his extensive labours as a town missionary, prepared the way for this notable advance, and having thus given proof of his powers, he was admitted into the regular ministry, and in 1844 we find him living at Arnold as Branch Superintendent. He at once took energetic measures to recapture surrendered Hucknall. He missioned the streets and preached on the green. At the close of the service he inquired for Robert Hutchinson and William Allen. The two were on the spot, and responded to the call. Robert Hutchinson did not fail the missionary in the time of need; he opened his house for preaching, and it continued to be the preaching-place for the society until 1848, when, now increased to thirty members, the society migrated to a room in Allen Street; and for a period of forty-six years this frame-work knitter, employé and, in later life, pensioner of Samuel Morley, M.P., of Nottingham, filled and fulfilled the offices of Leader and Society Steward.

We may seem to have mixed up village saints and Church-splits in strange confusion; but there is a closer connection between these than at first may appear. The saints are pre-eminently "the tried," and to have tried men and women you must have trials, and of all trials Church-trials are, as Paul very well knew, the most trying. It is those who have been "tried" that are to receive the amaranthine crown, and so the Church should reserve its choicest laurel-wreaths for those who stand "faithful amongst the faithless;" who do not desert their post, but calmly go on with their work in the midst of discouragements, unpopularity, and even amid Church broils and secessions. Church-life is not all rapture, or such as to evoke hallelujahs, and fidelity to truth required us to show that, not so long after the great Revival, there were hindrances and reverses, to be accounted for naturally enough, as we shall see, but only serving in many cases to bring out the finest qualities of men. It is not alone of Robert Hutchinson we are thinking or writing; he is one of a type, and we shall meet him again and again under other names and in other places, and to these life-long, tried, and trusty leaders of local Churches Primitive Methodism owes more than she can tell.

ROBERT HUTCHINSON'S HOUSE, IN WHICH SERVICES WERE HELD FROM 1841 TO 1848.

JOHN WEDGWOOD'S IMPRISONMENT.

The labours of Sarah Kirkland and John Benton, chiefly in Nottinghamshire, during 1817, have been described; but John Wedgwood, followed by William Clowes, also came on the ground, and the part these, along with William Lockwood and others, took in the work place for the holding of large open-air gatherings. The village stands hard by the Fosse Way—the famous Roman road that runs diagonally across the country from Bath to Lincoln. George Herod was present at one of these early gatherings, at which a thousand persons were computed to be present, and he tells how he saw several persons—notably a man he knew, some six feet two of stature—fall to the ground groaning and writhing under the influence of Benton's prayers and preaching. Another camp meeting, held on the same spot, was attended by some three thousand persons. This is noteworthy to us as showing Mr. Lockwood now fully committed to the revival movement, and rendering good service in stemming opposition from fox-hunting squires and their like-minded spiritual advisers. These gentry were numerous in the neighbourhood, and they watched the progress of the movement with a dislike they

ROOM, HUCKNALL TORKARD, IN WHICH SERVICES WERE HELD FROM 1848 TO 1859.

took no pains to conceal. On the afternoon of the camp meeting, Colonel Hildyard, of Flintham Hall, with a number of others, rode up and ordered the assembly to disperse. The people did *not* disperse, but if anything drew closer together. When after this the Colonel threatened to read the Riot Act, Mr. Lockwood bade the people make way, and so along the living avenue the posse of gentlemen rode right up to the waggon. Having got them there, Mr. Lockwood gave his high-class hearers "a genteel but very cutting address," and the party left the ground somewhat discomfited. The moral effect of the rebuff thus spiritedly administered was distinctly good; for it was felt that even in priest-ridden Vale of Belvoir the Ranters could and would stand unabashed before

But what brought John Wedgwood on the scene? His imprisonment at Grantham, with its associated incidents, stands out distinctly among the incidents of the time, and it was the holding of a famous camp-lovefeast in June, 1817, that led to the summoning of Wedgwood into Nottinghamshire. The idea of holding an immense lovefeast in the open-air had occurred to Mr. John Parrott, sen., when present at the Whit-Sunday Camp Meeting in Nottingham Forest in the previous year. He had been a Methodist local preacher, with strong predilections for revivalistic work, and had felt it his duty to unite with the Primitive Methodists. His name stands No. 21 on the February-May 1818 Plan, and No. 5 on that of 1827, and for a number of years he was actively identified with the Nottingham Circuit, but gradually he seems to have suffered

CAR COLSTON GREEN.
Commencement of the Green.

a change in his views and sentiments. He became dissatisfied with our discipline, and pretty frequent entries in the Quarterly Minute Books in the late twenties, referring to the missing of appointments and other matters, show that he was the cause of trouble, and prepare us for the following final entry :—

"*1829, June 14th.*—That Brother Parrott, senior's, name come off the plan according to his request by the Bingham delegate, because he cannot conscientiously continue among us."

It is singular that the secretary who penned this minute was Mr. John Parrott, jun., of East Bridgford. The Quarterly Meeting of December 30th, 1830, resolved: "That in the opinion of this meeting Bro. Parrott is an eligible person for the itinerant ministry. That testimonials to that effect be sent to the North Shields Circuit which has made application for them." John Parrott was clever; but his litigious propensities marred his usefulness, and sometimes were the occasion of trouble, both to himself and to others. He was converted at the camp-lovefeast which his senior namesake organised. The site of the novel meeting has been very precisely given as "Priest Hill," on the eastern side of Ratcliffe-on-Trent parish, on the side of the high road between Nottingham and Newark, where another road crosses the turnpike—a situation spacious and public. Over and above the direct spiritual good effected at this great gathering was the wide interest it was the means of creating. The people who came together were from all parts of the country-side. Many, in order to reach Priest Hill, had walked distances that to us, in these degenerate days of pedestrianism, would seem well-nigh incredible. The return of the people to their homes was like the scattering of brands here and there on the dry prairie; curiosity, inquiry, and enthusiasm burst into flame simultaneously at various and separate points of the country-side. The result was—and this is the historical importance of the Priest Hill gathering—John Benton received

REV. JOHN PARROTT.

PRIEST HILL, RATCLIFFE-ON-TRENT.
Site of Camp-Lovefeast.

urgent invitations to visit so many different places that it was impossible he could accept even the half of them, so John Wedgwood, John Heath, and John Hallsworth were called in to assist, and all entered heartily into the Revival.

Wedgwood must have lost no time in obeying the summons, for from a comparison of the avail... ...about the middle of August when he was pulled down from the Market Cross of Grantham, whose fine grey steeple of St. Wolfran's, towering above the rich red roofs, is familiar to all travellers on the Great Northern Railway. But there is evidence that even before this date Wedgwood must have paid more than one visit to the town. On one of these occasions he took his stand in the open space at the south end of Inner Street; for at the close of the service Mr. Bayley invited him to dinner, and his house became Wedgwood's home on his subsequent visits to the town, and the chair in which he was accustomed to sit has

GRANTHAM MARKET-PLACE.
Wedgwood was taken from the steps of the cross to prison.

found an honoured place in the vestry of our Grantham Church. A special sacredness must surely have attached to the Market Cross and its vicinity in the estimation of the civic fathers, or else why should that which was allowed at the Town End be sternly put down when attempted in the Forum? Any way, as we have seen, on or about the 15th of August Wedgwood was marched off by the constables. It was no silent, crestfallen man they dragged to the Guildhall. As far as appearances went, the constables might have been the prisoners, whose W   nds were escorting to prison; for out of the heart of the crowd, every moment becoming bigger, there arose the strains of the hymn—

"Wicked men I scorn to fear
Though they persecute me here."

The hymn with its note of defiance was the triumphant finish of their service. Arrived at the Guildhall, Wedgwood "had to sit in the prisoner's chair with a man to guard him, as though he had been a highwayman." As he sat there we may be sure he had no self-pity, nor need we pity him. He took it all smilingly and in good heart, and as he cast his eye towards the door where the crowd was surging like a rising tide against a rock, he thought almost gleefully how his arrest was throwing Grantham into commotion and how it would all contribute to the furtherance of the gospel. His attention, however, was soon recalled to his own fate as decided by the magistrates: John Wedgwood was committed to take his trial at the next Quarter Sessions, and meanwhile ordered to be detained in custody.

INNER STREET, GRANTHAM.

Tidings of what had happened were soon carried to Mr. Lockwood, who at once put horse in gig and drove straight to Grantham. The experience of Wedgwood was repeated in his case. He took his stand at the Cross and began a service, but had not got far on in it, before he too was stopped and hurried before the magistrates. His mittimus was made out, and in due course he would have become Wedgwood's fellow-prisoner; but he had no drawings towards a prison life. He had his business to attend to, and had no intention of exchanging the comforts of his own home for the inside of a prison if he could honourably avoid it; so he entered into his own recognisances to appear at the next Quarter Sessions, and probably did his best to persuade John Wedgwood to do the same, but

WEDGWOOD'S CHAIR IN GRANTHAM VESTRY.

Wedgwood's imprisonment deeply moved the Primitive Methodist community; and little wonder, for there was something in the event and its sequel that appealed to the imagination, and besides, it must be remembered, it was the first instance of the kind that had occurred. John Wedgwood was the first Primitive Methodist to undergo imprisonment; the first of a type of prisoner quite new to that generation—prisoners who were always genial in the presence of magistrates whom often they admonished and baffled, who prayed with their fellow-prisoners and exhorted turnkeys as Wedgwood did when in Grantham jail. He was the first of a goodly company of cheerful confessors for Primitive Methodism, and as such he merits recognition. The news of Wedgwood's arrest and commitment naturally excited much interest and concern at Tunstall where he was so well known. Thomas Woodnorth's feelings on the occasion sought poetic expression, as is not unusual when the public mind is greatly stirred by current events. In such times of excitement there are always some who drop, or mount, into poetry. So "precious" Thomas Woodnorth was inspired by the event to write some one hundred and seventy lines of verse in rhymed couplets in the heroic metre used by Cowper in "The Task," and by Dryden in his "Æneis." But though Woodnorth's verse is better than one might reasonably expect, it is mainly of interest to us as showing what thoughts and feelings were excited in him by the news from Grantham. The event he celebrated lent itself to poetic treatment. The humble herald of the Cross takes his stand under the shadow of the Market Cross, surely the very spot for the delivery of the preacher's message. No fitter place than this town-centre—this place of public concourse—for the proclamation of the truth that the Cross should be central and dominant in all our social, business, and corporate life. The truths the preacher enforces are just those truths the cross of stone has been bearing silent witness to through all these years, and yet the preacher is dragged down by the agents of municipal authority who ought to have protected him, and, literally, by the way of the cross, is haled to prison. How strange! and yet it is only another short act in the age-long tragedy: "He came unto His own, and His own received Him not." Some such thoughts as these seem to have been in Woodnorth's mind, struggling for expression as he took pen in hand. Though he writes of Grantham, its "belial throng," and the doings of its "grandees," what has happened there is after all only an incident—a picture in little—of the great conflict. Grantham's grandees are simply the tools of Lucifer their captain, who is fighting a losing battle against the Lord and His anointed.

JOHN WEDGWOOD.*

But Tunstall took a practical as well as poetic interest in Wedgwood's concerns. It was decided to free William Clowes from his round of circuit engagements for a time, in order that he might go to Grantham and learn for himself how it fared with Wedgwood. If this first imprisonment had had no other result than this, it would have to be considered historically an event of some importance. To put the fact

* This is a different portrait from the one given on p. 163.

strongly; the imprisonment of Wedgwood effected what was tantamount to the liberation of Clowes. It gave him fuller scope for his superb evangelising gifts. For a short time he became again a missionary at large. By this rapid visit to the outlying and promising fields of labour now thrown open, he gained a truer idea of the needs and possibilities of the Connexion; his own conceptions were enlarged and adjusted to existing facts. If it be true, as we believe it is, that in Primitive Methodism, over and above everything else, there survives and energises something of the distinctive spirit of Clowes, then it was eminently advantageous that just at this juncture the many, to whom Clowes hitherto had been little more than a name, should have the opportunity of

BUCKMINSTER HALL.

coming under the influence of his powerful personality. Until they had seen his eye flash, and had their very souls searched by the thrilling tones of his voice when in prayer or ministering the Word, they could not be said to know what Primitive Methodism really was. Good men and women were labouring in these parts; Hugh Bourne was threading his way amongst the societies, spending himself in their service; Sarah Kirkland, John Benton, John Wedgwood, John Heath, Robert Winfield, Richard Weston, John Hallsworth, and others were hard at work, but not one of these was equal to Clowes at his best. This good then came out of Wedgwood's imprisonment; it brought Clowes into contact with the great Revival, and that meant for the revival an added impetus, and for Clowes yet greater zeal and efficiency as an evangelist.

Clowes left Tunstall on August 29th, and made his way to Nottingham, where he heard rumours that Wedgwood was now out on bail. Upon this he thought it well to learn from Mr. Lockwood what had really happened. So he proceeded to East Bridgford, and was told by Mr. Lockwood that Wedgwood had at last been induced to follow his (Mr. L.'s) example, and to enter into his own recognisances to appear at the next Quarter Sessions, or when called upon. Furthermore, Clowes learned that Wedgwood had preached at East Bridgford on the Friday, and was now gone to Buckminster, near Grantham, the seat of Sir William Manners, to assist in holding a camp meeting there. It was Buckminster Camp Meeting, just about to be held, that brought Wedgwood out of prison. It was not Mr. Lockwood's example or advice, backed by that of the counsel retained for the defence, slowly taking effect that brought him to the point of giving bail. If he ever did deliberately take the attitude of "passive resistance," refusing on principle to give bail because that might seem to recognise the legality of his arrest, that attitude was overborne by the consideration that the cause he had at heart was suffering by his not altogether necessary seclusion. Labourers were scarce, and some anxiety was felt on this score as to the success of the camp meeting some time since arranged to be held at Buckminster. Such a consideration as this appealed to Wedgwood. He was no lawyer or casuist, but unsophisticated, and in some respects simple as a child. He probably felt that the Lord had suffered him to be put in prison, and that he must stay there until the Lord saw good to let him out. Meanwhile, he made himself as comfortable as he could under the circumstances. Little Sammy Bayley, aged ten, who had helped to sing him to the Guildhall, and Sammy's sister, brought him his breakfast the following morning. Others did the like, so that when a friend was about to send him four or five pounds, thinking it might be useful to him, he was told he was not in want. So during his incarceration "I felt," says he, "quite happy while I prayed and sung and preached to the prisoners." The Muses visited him too, and he wrote some prison-rhymes, which found a place in several early editions of the Small Hymn Book. Perhaps the first verse of "Wedgwood's jingle," as it has irreverently been called, will satisfy our readers:—

> "At Grantham Cross I did appear,
> The constables did then draw near;
> And from the cross they had me down,
> But could not take away my crown."

MR. SAMUEL BAYLEY.
Who, as a boy, took Wedgwood's breakfast to him in prison.

In this cheerful state of mind Wedgwood was visited, amongst others, by Sarah Kirkland (then labouring in the Vale of Belvoir). "She found him happy in God, and rejoicing that he was counted worthy to suffer imprisonment for the truth's sake." After he had been in durance a little more than a fortnight, he yielded to the solicitations of Benton, and other of his friends, "to come up to the help of the Lord against the mighty." He gave the required bond, and was liberated in time to take part in Buckminster Camp Meeting, August 31st, 1817. Now Clowes, in a sense liberated too, was at this camp meeting; for when he had heard all Mr. Lockwood had to tell about Wedgwood, he borrowed the squire's horse and made for Buckminster, though it would seem he held a service somewhere on the way. One who was present tells how he, with others, had walked fifteen miles—probably from Clipson in Rutlandshire—to be present at what was the first camp meeting they had ever seen. All the morning the people kept coming up, until there was a vast concourse. He lovingly recalls the precise features of that out-door temple which then impressed him: "The meeting was held in a fine broad green lane, sheltered by a beautiful high thorn hedge, with the spreading oaks growing thick therein; under its shade hundreds stood." Henry Sharman—for he it is who writes of his remembrances—saw Clowes draw near, make for the centre, and at once throw himself into the service with all his accustomed abandon. How the faces of Benton and Wedgwood and Heath would broaden and brighten as they saw Clowes elbowing his way through the crowd to join them! To them he was God-sent. Clowes spoke with great power from "Come thou and all thy house into the ark." Young Sharman never forgot the gracious influence which enabled him there and then to close with the divine proffer, and to dedicate himself to the service of God. Though his entry into the ministry was deferred until 1823, the resolve he made on the Buckminster camp-ground was faithfully kept. He travelled with acceptance and success for thirty-six years, beginning his labours in the Isle of Man and closing them in the Isle of Jersey, and died at Norwich April 8th, 1877.

HENRY SHARMAN.

A notable thing happened at this Buckminster Camp Meeting. During the afternoon Sir William Manners' carriage drove up, and at the close of the service Henry Sharman saw John Benton put his Bible and hymn-book into his pocket, get into the carriage, and drive off. How came it about that Benton was found in such high company—hob-nobbing with baronets, and having a footman to open the carriage door for him? The fact is, it suited Sir William's purpose to champion the cause of the Primitive Methodists at this time. He had a grudge against the Grantham "grandees" and burgesses for rejecting the Parliamentary candidate he favoured, and he meant to be quits with them, and give them a pin-prick here and a side-wipe there as opportunity might offer. One such chance now presented itself. He knew all about the arrest of Wedgwood and Lockwood for preaching at the Cross, and had got a pulpit of stone erected on his own land near the Guildhall. He was now taking Benton to Grantham to "hansel" this pulpit, and to preach for the glory of God, as Benton intended, and for the mortification of the magistrates, as Sir William hoped. It was a strange and unnatural alliance of motives, from which little permanent good was to be expected. Putting together what Clowes and Herod tell us of that drive to Grantham, it was certainly a singular one:—

"As they were going along, Sir William asked the preacher whether or not he and his brethren were inspired men. The preacher replied that his soul was full of glo... ...d that he would like to hear him preach—would he have the goodness to preach to his coachman as they proceeded? The preacher replied, that if he would stop the carriage he would preach to the people in the village through which they were passing, through the carriage window. But Sir William declined that proposal, and drew up the window-blinds.'—Clowes' *Journals*, p 129

Benton himself says —

"I preached to him the fall of man, the restoration by Christ Jesus, repentance and faith, justification and sanctification, the day of judgment, heaven and hell but while I was setting forth these truths, Sir William appeared rather restless and I have no doubt was very glad when we arrived at Grantham."— Herod's *Sketches*

On nearing the town the carriage was exchanged for a post-chaise, which carried Benton to the stone pulpit, and a servant of Sir William attended while he ascended the pulpit and preached to a large and orderly congregation

Some at least of our fathers seem to have regarded this championing of their cause by Sir William as a chivalrous and righteous act—something to be proud of and thankful for. Thomas Woodnorth, for instance, sees no incongruity or violation of principle in the co-operation of political spite with evangelical zeal. In the poetic effusion before referred to Sir William figures as a kind of crusader, so that we should not be surprised to find his cross-legged effigy in the family burial-place. The stone pulpit was in behalf of the Cross —

"Lo, Grantham's famous pulpit made of stone,
Fraught with good zeal, witness Sir William's hand
The Knight of Buckminster who made a stand
Against the sons of envy in the fight
To damp their folly and to calm their spite,
That monument he raised to Jesus' name,
To preach the Crucified and spread His fame
This was an act as brave as e'er was told
By daring warriors who in crimson rolled
Their dyed garments on the field of blood

*   *   *   *   *

'Twas done for God this makes the action shine
More bright than sun o'er equinoctial line"

This view of the case will not be endorsed now. Looking back upon the episode after all these years, one cannot but feel that it would have been better if Benton had never set foot either in Sir William's carriage or in his pulpit. What did the baronet's ostentatious patronage of the Primitives for his own ends, and his "pulpit of cut stone" do towards the establishment of our cause in Grantham? Let us see

Messrs Lockwood and Wedgwood duly surrendered on their bail at the Quarter Sessions, which came on on October 23rd. Counsel was employed on their behalf, and the jury returned a verdict of "Not guilty," so that the magistrates were beaten, and found themselves, to their chagrin, saddled with the costs. The result was a signal triumph, all the to procure a preacher's licence before beginning his missionary labours.* There can be little doubt the magistrates were mortified at the result of the trial, and were somewhat cowed by the action of their neighbour, the baronet, and the conviction that they would have to reckon with him as well as with the missionaries. Certain it is that after the trial meetings were held, occasionally at least, at the Market Cross, without interference on the part of the authorities. In proof of this we have the following entry in Hugh Bourne's *Journals*:—

"*Sunday, April 26th, 1818.*—I got to Grantham in Lincolnshire Camp Meeting. In the afternoon we stood upon the Market Cross, the place where John Wedgwood stood when he was taken up. Thus hath God wrought."

Probably the acceptance of Buckminster's "chariots and horses," like Israel's reliance on Egypt or Assyria, was of little permanent advantage to our cause at Grantham. If the alliance warded off persecution under legal forms, it did not serve to commend our work to the people of Grantham, whose suspicions were aroused by the aristocratic entanglement; and so, though there is no evidence that the people were either rowdy or truculent, they did not prove very accessible to the gospel as proclaimed by our missionaries. Be this as it may, it was not until 1835 that a permanent cause was established, though before that date several determined attempts were made, as the official records of the Nottingham Circuit show. In June, 1824, the Circuit Committee is "authorised and requested" to obtain a missionary and send him to Grantham. The December Quarterly Meeting of 1825 had the subject of establishing a mission at Grantham again under consideration, and passed some half-dozen resolutions which raise expectations that something effective will be done. "Missionary meetings are to be held at Bingham, Lambley, Barkstone, and Keyworth, and out of the monetary proceeds of these meetings a mission is to be established. Brother Whitby is to proceed to Grantham, and is authorised to expend ten pounds in the fitting up of the room. Grantham, Billingborough, Aslackley, Edenham, and Rippingale, are together to form the Grantham Mission, and Brother Brame is appointed to labour on it for three months." Then in March, 1826, the Quarterly Board authorises payment for the room, and the balance of the money raised at the missionary meetings is to be "applied to the support of a mission attached to the Nottingham Circuit;" and there, so far as Grantham entries in the circuit books are concerned, the matter ends.

A. WORSNOP.

After many disappointing failures, the set time to favour Grantham came at last. At Midsummer, in the year of the trouble (1834), Nottingham made Bottesford a Branch, and placed at its head Abraham Worsnop— a deeply pious, hard-working, successful minister, who, during his ministry of forty-three years, is said to have had an aggregate increase on his stations of twenty-three thousand members. In April, 1835, Bottesford remissioned Grantham. It was hard uphill work. Their principal preaching-place for twenty-one weeks

---

* J. Wedgwood took out his licence on September 4th between his liberation on bail and the Sessions.

was the Market Cross we know so well. But persistence had its reward, and at length a room was secured, which we take to have been the Old Granary at the Blue Sheep, standing at the corner of Harleston Road and Wharfe Road, since pulled down for the construction of the railway. To assist in the extensive missionary labours undertaken by the Branch, Robert Parks—a convert during a recent revival at Barkstone, his native village—began his missionary labours, July, 1835.* His first day's work was to mission Barrowby near Grantham, and Wolsthorpe near Belvoir. Robert Parks became one of the best-known ministers in the old Nottingham District (1836-73). He had a clear voice, an imposing presence, and was an evangelical and popular preacher and platform speaker. We see him now at the start of his ministry "enduring hardness;" for while in this district he met with a good deal of persecution, travelled long journeys, and preached scores of sermons in the open air. Bottesford and Grantham owed much to Abraham Worsnop and Robert Parks. They were well mated; for the people in their own homely fashion used to say of them: "Parks shoots the birds, and Worsnop comes along and picks them up, so that between them and the Lord they make a good bag." God's blessing was on hard work. Fresh places were missioned, such as South Sutton, hitherto "destitute of the ministry of reconciliation," and where they were discharged from their regular preaching-house, and had another immediately offered them. At Knipton, too, three miles from Belvoir, they preached three years in the open air before they could obtain a preaching-place. Then a friend, risking all consequences, opened her spacious dwelling. So the work went on until in September, 1835, Bottesford was made a Circuit with 226 members, increased by the next year to 300. As for Grantham, the cause at last took root. Before the close of the year it had a flourishing society of seventy members, and we note with interest that one of the first to join the society was Samuel Bayley, who carried Wedgwood his breakfast eighteen years before. Progress was now steady but sure, as is evidenced by the fact that on June 4th, 1837, a commodious chapel was opened by two good men—John Brownson, one of the tall pillar-preachers of the old Nottingham District, and John Middleton, a lover of peace, cheerful, conscientious, plodding, whose carefully written *MS. Journal* it is a pleasure to read. Both Brownson and Middleton were the fruit of Primitive Methodist agency in Derbyshire—the one hailing from Brailsford near Turnditch, the other from near Bradwell.

J. Middleton records in his *Journal*:

"At five I preached on the Market Cross, whence we processioned the town to the chapel. The services through the day were full of spirit and life. God was evidently in our midst making our hearts glad."

No more appropriate ending of the twenty years' story could we have than this. Grantham Primitive Methodism began at the Market Cross, and, as we have said, by the way of the Cross was it established. The "pulpit of cut stone" soon disappears—from history at any rate. Its record is the ephemeral record of Jonah's gourd. What became of it we cannot tell. Whether it found its way to the local museum, or was carried off piecemeal for the construction of local piggeries, or was spirited away in some mysterious manner, history informs us not. Its memorial has perished. But the twenty-one weeks' open-air preaching, chiefly at the Cross, left enduring results: and when Bro. John Middleton, just twenty years after John Wedgwood was pulled down from the Cross, took his stand on the same spot and preached, and then led the procession chapel-wards, both service and procession must surely have partaken of a memorial and thanksgiving character.

It only remains to be added that after continuing a Branch of Bottesford for some years, in 1864 Grantham became an independent circuit.

BRAILSFORD PRIMITIVE METHODIST CHAPEL.

CLOWES' VISIT TO NOTTINGHAMSHIRE.

Clowes' mission in Nottinghamshire and Lincolnshire was, as we have seen, causally as well as chronologically connected with Wedgwood's imprisonment. He crowded an immense amount of work into the short time at his disposal, sometimes preaching several times in the course of a day, and occasionally as early as five o'clock in the morning. Wedgwood was doing the same, profitably filling up the time between his liberation on bail and the holding of the Quarter Sessions, so that the two evangelists sometimes crossed each other's path and held joint services, or one would hold a service in this and another in that part of the same town or village in order to reach the more people. Then they would separate, each going his own way. Of course, Clowes did not overlook East Bridgford. Sooner or later all the Primitive fathers are found there; for Bridgford was just like one of those quiet villages which, because it happens to lie in the line of advance, will have billeted in its farm-houses or cottages the generals of the great armies that pass through it, and make it their temporary quarters. At Bridgford, Clowes preached—or at least tried to preach—on the green, but had to desist ; for as was remarked at the time, "the devil and the parson sent two of their underlings to interrupt the service by blowing big horns." The interruption, however, had this good result : it induced Mrs. Lockwood, who was present, to place her chapel at the disposal of the missionary and his congregation. Here the service was quietly gone through, and, "best of all," Clowes tells us, George Herod, who had been winged by Sarah Kirkland and brought down by John Benton, was now, through the instrumentality of Clowes, won for Christ and the Church, which by the time he enters the ministry will sorely need and profit by his godly discipline. If Henry Sharman and George Herod had been the sole trophies of Clowes' flying visit to these parts, the visit was worth making.

Bingham and Ratcliffe were both visited. At Bingham Clowes preached twice in the market-place, at one of the times to as many as two thousand people. At Ratcliffe

SCREVETON CHAPEL, NEWARK.

he met with Wedgwood, and after a service at five o'clock in the morning the two took their stand in the open air. Clowes preached first, and then set off to another place four miles off, leaving Wedgwood to finish the service. Clowes remarks, that when he had got a mile on his journey he could still hear Wedgwood's voice as he pleaded in prayer. It is significant in the light of what was to happen, that both Bingham and Ratcliffe thus early appear to have been honeycombed with Free Gospelism. At Ratcliffe, Clowes had an unacrimonious discussion with some advocates of an unpaid ministry, and succeeded in practically converting them ; for they not only extended to him unstinted hospitality, but sent a liberal contribution to the Nottingham Quarterly Board. At Bingham, however, it is curious to find he was not so fortunate. He notes that here one of the leaders of the two classes was a Free Gospeller, and that in the end a serious disruption took place in the society, some of the members joining the Wesleyans, others going back into the world, while a mere remnant retained their first fellowship. For Free Gospellers to cease to be Primitive Methodists in order to become Wesleyans was surely a piece of inconsistency as great as that of the man the late Rev. Thomas Smith, Governor of Elmfield, used to speak of. He left the Primitives in dudgeon because the Quarterly Meeting had authorised the purchase of a square of druggeting to lie at the side of the preacher's bed and keep his feet off the bare boards, and forthwith joined an opulent Church, whose minister's bedroom was laid throughout with the best Kidderminster! But there is some reason to believe that Clowes is blending with his own early recollections of Bingham events of a painful nature which occurred some years later—events already sufficiently described. There is no evidence

BINGHAM OLD CHAPEL.

to show that anywhere near 1817 a disruption, having Free Gospelism at its root, ever took place. The simple fact that it was at Bingham the first Primitive Methodist Chapel in Nottinghamshire was erected and opened in 1818 by no less a person than Lorenzo Dow, is sufficient to show that for some time after Clowes' visit a flourishing society existed at Bingham. At the same time, it is clear that even in 1817 Clowes was made aware, in an unmistakable and unpleasant manner, of the seed growing secretly which the years would ripen.

Clowes tells us he also visited Whatton, Sibthorpe, Thurston, Bottesford, Bulwell, Blidworth, Screveton, Calverton, Oxton, Lambley, and Great Cropwell. At most of these places ... preaching, as was usually the case wherever Clowes we... in the open air and joined five to the society.

A chapel was erected here in 1840. At Lambley, too, he admitted four to membership, preached in the open air, and speaks of Mr. G. Turner "as a succourer of many, and of me also." At Oxton, while he was speaking, a man was arrested as though struck by a rifle bullet, and would have fallen if friends had not caught him in their arms. This man afterwards declared it was one word Clowes uttered that produced this extraordinary effect. From the same meeting another went to his home to pass a night of sleepless wretchedness. He called upon Clowes the next morning, set him on his journey, disburdened his mind as they went on, and then they stopped and prayed together by the roadside until the man found peace in believing. Thus it was wherever Clowes went: so mightily grew the Word and prospered.

Newark, "the key of the north," was also one of the gains of the Great Revival, and

NEWARK OLD CASTLE.

as such its name is found on the plan of February—April, 1818. It marked the latest and farthest acquisition in a direction north-east of Nottingham. Clowes and Wedgwood both found their way here at the same time, and both preached at the same hour—the one in Northgate and the other in Millgate. Clowes remarks that his congregation was not so unruly as Wedgwood's, and that though good was done by the services, much greater results might have followed had houses only been available for the holding of prayer meetings after the open-air preachings. As the missionaries had not the use even of a private dwelling at this time, we infer that Clowes must be speaking of a very early, if not of the earliest visit to Newark; and Clowes' reference to the persecution which afterwards showed itself, tends to confirm this view. Whatever may be the case now, Newark was in former times still the seat of a rank Toryism.

Its ancient castle, in which King John breathed his last, stood and withstood three sieges during the Civil Wars. The castle was not surrendered to the Parliamentarians until the war was over; then it was dismantled, to become the picturesque ruin with which we are now familiar. It would have been a wonder if a town with such a history had given the Primitives any other than a rough reception. Newark, that had kept the forces of the Parliament at bay with its cannon, only acted like itself when it turned its engines of another kind against Mr. William Lockwood, who attempted to preach in the market-place a short time after the visit of Clowes. Mr. Lockwood's purpose had been announced beforehand, so that there had been time for opposition to organise itself. Accordingly, when he began to preach from his gig a man turned a garden-hose upon him, and then the fire-engine was brought out and

NEWARK MARKET-PLACE.
In centre of which Lockwood stood and preached when fire-engine was played upon him in 1817.

began to play on the preacher. The instigator of this watery form of persecution was the clergyman, who seems to have joined to his other offices that of custodian of the town fire-engine, which was kept on the Church premises. While others worked the manual-engine, a barber was chief fireman, and turned the hose upon Mr. Lockwood while the clergyman from the church tower watched the drenching of the intrusive missionary with evident enjoyment. But there was an unexpected diversion in the preacher's favour. Some watermen who were standing by thought persecution had gone far enough, and as Mr. Lockwood, with the water running off his person, shouted, "You can't quench the fire within," they took out their clasp-knives and cut and hacked away at the The afterwards brought an action a The magistrates asked the pertinent question "Who authorised the taking out of the fire-engine?" and when informed, they decided that as the clergyman had called the tune it was fair he should also pay the piper. But the story does not end here. Retribution of a severe kind overtook the other chief actor in this incident. The very next occasion the fire-engine was required was when it was summoned to put out a fire which had broken out on the barber's premises, for he was a manufacturer of fireworks as well as a barber, and while busy with his squibs and crackers an explosion occurred, and he was blown through the shop window, and died of his burns. This judgment by fire, following hard upon persecution by water, made a deep impression upon our fathers. They were not slow to recognise God's hand in the event. John Harrison was at Newark in 1818, and conducted the first Primitive Methodist lovefeast there on April 12th. It was held under difficulties, for the persecutors broke the windows and tried to burst open the door. When the prayer meeting began the preacher went out to expostulate with the disturbers, and "a pious young woman knelt down in the street and commenced praying for them, and she brought upon them a powerful influence, after this their rage appeared to be appeased." He remarks. "There has been great opposition against us in this town, but some of the ringleaders have had to suffer." The pyrotechnist barber was not the only one who suffered; for having described his fate, John Harrison goes on to give other instances of retribution on Newark persecutors:—

"A young man in this place, who had annoyed our people very much, had the misfortune to have a stone fall on him, which was computed to be more than three hundredweight, and it crushed him to death. Yesterday another of the ringleaders forged a ticket in order to gain admittance into the lovefeast [of April 12th before mentioned] but he was prevented from entering, and I hear to-day he has met with an accident, and has come home with a broken leg. I hope these things will be a warning to the enemies of the cross in Newark."

These instances of retribution were far from uncommon, and may be regarded as typical of the period under consideration. No mere theory of "remarkable coincidences" would have satisfied our fathers as sufficiently accounting for them. To these firm believers in an over-ruling providence, it seemed the most natural and proper thing in the world, that the God who was on their side should in a sudden and signal manner vindicate His people, and manifest His displeasure against those who sought to do them harm and hinder their work. They were on the watch for such instances of retribution, and carefully noted them when they occurred. Such was the deliberate opinion of our fathers, and the opinion was shared even by many outsiders, so that when the great bell of a village church—set a-ringing to drown the preacher's voice—cracked, the people said 'If they attempt to ring again to oppose the 'Ranters' the steeple will fall.'

Primitive Methodism has had a continuous existence in Newark ever since it was first missioned under the circumstances already described but it passed through various vicissitudes before it became, in 1862, the head of an independent station, with Paul Daykin and Benjamin Clayton as its ministers. From 1824 to 1832 Newark formed part of the old Bidderton Circuit, then in 1833 Fulbeck in Lincolnshire became the head of the circuit, and Sleaford became a mission of Fulbeck during the successful superintendency of Rev. Joseph Middleton (1834-6). He records in his *MS Journal* —

Sunday, April 5th, 1835.—I opened a large schoolroom at Sleaford for public worship. The attendance both afternoon and evening was pleasing, and I had good liberty in dispensing the Word. Thank God there is a good prospect of our obtaining a cause in this wicked town. Mr. Crosby [the missionary put down at Sleaford] is likely to be very useful here and in the villages round about.'

Though it is Newark whose vicissitudes we are following, it is interesting to note that in the Report of the Fulbeck Circuit to the District Meeting and Conference of 1836, it is stated that many new and populous villages, such as Ancaster, Welbourn,* Kirkby, Cranwell, Azeby, Navenby, and Farndon, had been opened, and many of the old places, as Balderton, Newark, Rauceby, and others, which had been low for years, had been greatly revived, and the membership which in September, 1834, was 160 had risen to 300 and upwards. "We have no doubt," continues the Report, "that this back settlement of the Connexion will yet become fruitful and yield an abundant harvest." But, adds the document: "We are sorry to say that we have been, and are still much opposed by the ministers of the Establishment, but hitherto the Lord hath helped us." Yet another change awaited Newark. It became in the early forties a branch of Sleaford; for in a document now before us, bearing date November, 1844, the Rev. Samuel Anthff, the preacher of the Newark Branch, supports the application of Sleaford that Newark may be transferred as a branch to Nottingham, which accordingly was done, and as a branch of Nottingham Circuit Newark remained until 1862. In his application Mr. S. Anthff states that Newark has a chapel for which six pounds annual rent is paid; that Balderton has a rented room, and pays its way; Claypole a rented chapel, and Dodington, Upton, and other places have their public services in dwelling-houses.

We have thus followed in some detail the fortunes of Newark until it became an independent station, because the recital may serve to show how complicated the history of a single circuit may be. Newark is a good example of a circuit that has had its several *aliases* during the course of its history.

At Shelford, a village near Nottingham, certain events occurred about this time which must be told in detail. A determined effort was made to oust the Primitives from the village in which they had succeeded in establishing a vigorous society. The persecution in the last resort took the cruel form of evicting and then levelling the cottages

---

* Welbourn had in April, 1836, its case of unsuccessful prosecution for open-air preaching. On pain of losing his farm Mr. Shepherd was reluctantly obliged to withdraw the use of his barn for public worship. Mr. Middleton then took to the open air, and Major Brown ordered him to desist, and on refusal sent for the constable. Mr. Keyworth, the constable, was a sensible man, and scrupled taking the preacher into custody. Mr. Middleton, therefore, gave himself up but preached again the same evening. The next morning his friend the constable, drove him to the Justices Meeting at Sleaford. The case was dismissed and Major Brown ordered to pay costs. Mr. Middleton returned to Welbourn, and preached in the evening from 'Pray for them which despitefully use and persecute you.' The whole story is fully and interestingly told in Rev. Joseph Middleton's *MS Journals.*

of those who had had the temerity to lend them for preaching services. But the persistent, protracted persecution—for it extended over months—using methods worthy of an Irish eviction agent—was met by a resistance just as determined and dogged as itself, and in the end more successful. It was a veritable tug of war; and now that a similar struggle for principle, though on a more colossal scale, is everywhere going on, it will be well to recall this episode in the history of village Primitive Methodism. It has a good many lessons for these times. It shows that some of our village causes have a history of which we may well be proud; that they were founded and maintained at much sacrifice by humble stalwarts. If you had talked to them of "the Nonconformist conscience" or of "political Dissenters" they would not have understood you; but their Protestantism and Methodism was so dear to them that they clung to it at all

VICKERSTAFF'S COTTAGE, SHELFORD,
Where services used to be held in the cottage on the right-hand side.

costs. The poet bethought him of village Hampdens: so we have had our village Vickerstaffs and Woodwards—

"..... that with dauntless breast
The little tyrant of their fields withstood."

We have had them, and are anxious to keep up the breed, and recent events in the neighbourhood of Wirksworth and elsewhere show that the breed is not extinct. Over the whole of this story is broadly written: "Don't forget your village causes. When tempted to leave them, think what it cost to found such as they." But the story? Clowes tells it, but he tells it incompletely, as if from partial knowledge or imperfect recollection. But Clowes was at Shelford while the first part of the story was being enacted, and naturally it made a deep impression on him, so that when he came to write his reminiscences he speaks of little else save that he records how a persecutor was "removed by being drowned in the river;" and he ends his references to Shelford by this enigmatical sentence: "But I left this place with some hopes; I resembled a bark tossed with the tempest and exposed to the yawning gulf."

The completest account we have of the Shelford tug of war is furnished by a contemporary observer—with every detail duly noted and in its place—so that for result we have a true story with its proper beginning and end. The writer was John Parrott, jun., of East Bridgford, and the narrative, though relegated by Mr. Herod to the foot of his pages and printed in small type,* deserves to be given *in extenso* here as an authentic document—the more so as it is written in a lively and graphic style, giving one a very favourable opinion of the writer's literary ability. Says Parrott:—

STOKE FERRY, RIVER TRENT.

"Directly after the Camp Lovefeast of June, 1817, an opening presented itself in Shelford—a village in the vicinity, displaying some rural beauty, and of some note as the family burying-place of the Earls of Chesterfield, whose hereditary estate stretches far away round the village, in which is only one plot of ground, about some half acre, not belonging to that valuable estate. In this village one Joseph Vickerstaff opened his door for preaching. His house stood on a strip of waste land by the roadside leading to Stoke Ferry. Many souls were converted to God beneath its very humble thatched roof, and a living Church sprang up within this domicile of 'stud and mud,'† which faced the rather imposing and substantially built parish church. This upstart (as some designated it) primitive Church gave unpardonable offence to the National

* Herod: "Biographical Sketches," &c., footnote on pp. 347–50.
† "Stud, the upright in a lath and plaster wall." Wright: "Dictionary of Obsolete and Provincial

THE PERIOD OF CIRCUIT PREDOMINANCE AND ENTERPRISE. 273

Church party, and a very hot persecution followed. As a cover to their real design, the enclosure of this waste land was determined on—Vickerstaff paying no regard to threats and entreaties to 'turn out the Ranters.' A regular discharge was then sent to him, which produced no more effect; then came an ejectment; still the services of religion were continued in his house as usual. Ultimately workmen were sent who pulled the house down, and the family and their furniture were shown the way into the street.

"This door shut, another was opened in time for the next religious service. Henry Fukes welcomed beneath his thatched roof 'the Ark of God,' and all its attendant blessings, for 'he was a devout man, and feared God with his house.' His domicile was of the same material and tenure with that of his friend Vickerstaff, and it stood in the midst of the village, adjoining the orchard, and at the back of the under-steward's house. Vickerstaff's had been an eyesore in front of that officer's house. For a short while the infant cause was allowed a home herein, and souls were converted, and the Church prospered and multiplied. But the unrelenting spirit of persecution and cruel hatred to dissent soon raged with redoubled fury. The banishment of the people from the village was determined on. Fukes was threatened with the fate of Vickerstaff if he did not 'turn those noisy people out.' Henry heard all with respectful calmness without yielding to the intolerant mandate, or wavering in the face of the threatened annihilation of his 'stud and mud' habitation, where he lived rent-free.

COTTAGE REBUILT ON SITE OF
HENRY FUKES' HOUSE, SHELFORD.

"For a number of years the Wesleyans had had a society in this village, whose preaching services were held in the house of Mr. Nathan Bailey, a respectable farmer of good report. It was now currently said he had received orders to allow no more preachings on pain of being turned out of his farm. Preaching services ceased in that house, and were now confined to the National Church and Fukes' cottage, 'made of unbaken clay and straw-thatched roof.' There, at this period, we often worshipped with delight, amid saving power, streaming glory, and flowing tears, in the closely packed congregation inside, and among those standing without on the high road unable to gain ingress, while the preacher in the nook or the open doorway was pouring forth in simple eloquence the simple truth of God with all the fervour of

T

a heart full of its saving energy and power. It was not uncommon then to see numbers present from East Bridgford, Newton, and other adjacent villages and hamlets; for the conflict for principle, and the determined retention of the village by this infant cause of Christ, was noised abroad and brought together sympathisers, scoffers, and the curious.

"As threats proved powerless on pious Henry Fukes, our modern Obed-Edom, a regular discharge was sent to him, but with no more effect. Then followed an ejectment, which was equally unable to make the desired impression; but one evening afterwards, on returning from his labour as a husbandman, he found the spoilers had pulled down his house, and had turned his pious wife and their furniture on to the high road. God, however, provided them both with shelter and a home in the house of friends; and although thus plunged into trouble for some time, in the end they suffered no loss. He overruled this wrath of man and made it praise Him. No sooner

SITE OF WOODWARD'S GARDEN, SHELFORD.

was the house of our Obed-Edom levelled with the ground than another door was opened for the Ark of God in the house of Matthew Woodward. His was also 'a parish house,' but it stood within a garden, a few paces from the public street, and was withal a much better fabric. Under its roof we have often worshipped, and felt it to be the gate of heaven.

"No plea could be urged about improving the village streets by removing this house, as had been done in the two former cases; so that the chasing of the Church from house to house was brought to a standstill. But the persecuting spirit now acted without a mask. Woodward was threatened and brought before a bench of justices. Matthew was of unpolished and stern material, and in reply to the threats of these higher powers, said: 'Mine is a parish house, and if you turn me out of it you must find me another; and as soon as I get into that I shall have the preachings there.' This is said . . . . offence to those sitting professedly to administer justice; and one of them now swore openly. Woodward seized the moment, and turned it to good account, showed the impropriety and sin of the swearer, and contrasted it with the object and practices of himself and fellow-worshippers. This procured him a hasty dismissal from the council-room, whence he returned home in triumph. It was then said 'It is of no use tormenting ourselves with these incorrigible Ranters—we may pull half the village down and not get them out at last.' 'Then had the Church rest,' and took root and grew. A change of stewards for the estate about this time had also a favourable effect. Mr Hassell commenced his stewardship in the spirit of religious tolerance much to his credit.

"Subsequently, the society not being able to obtain a plot of land on which to build a chapel, purchased the waterman's floating chapel at Nottingham, swam it down the river Trent, drew it into Woodward's garden, and there fitted up the amphibious sanctuary and worshipped in it. Many efforts had been made to purchase the fractional part of an acre of land (the only plot in the village not belonging to the earl's estate), but without effect; nor could the Primitives secure a piece of it although they often tried. At length, however, in answer to continuous and fervent prayer, the Lord changed the heart of Mr Girton, the owner of that little freehold. He granted them an eligible building site, on which they soon erected a neat, suitable, and substantial brick chapel; and there it stands, in the very heart of the Earl of Chesterfield's estate, as a memorable trophy and worthy fruit of prayer, and of indomitable perseverance in the work of faith and labour of love for the cause of Him of whom it is said, 'the earth is the Lord's and the fulness thereof.'"

Mr Parrott paints no fancy-picture; his narrative receives incidental and independent confirmation from the *Journals* of both Hugh Bourne and John Harrison. Writing on February 14th, 1818, the former remarks —

"At Shelford the man who takes in the preaching is thrown out of employment, and is likely to be thrown out of the house. O Lord appear for him and undertake his cause."

When John Harrison followed some six weeks afterwards, what seemed likely to happen had become matter of certainty, for on March 30th he writes —

'I came to Shelford, and in this place I found the family, in whose house we preach, under trying circumstances; they had received notice from the Earl of Chesterfield's steward to quit their house the next week. But in the midst of difficulties they could say with the prophet 'Although the fig-tree shall not blossom, neither shall fruit be in the vines; the labour of the olive shall fail, and the fields shall yield no meat; the flock shall be cut off from the fold, and there shall be no herd in the stalls, yet I will rejoice in the Lord, I will joy in the God of my salvation.''

Probably Vickerstaff was the humble confessor referred to, for the persecution was long drawn out; and this was but its beginning. A good many years had to pass before the "amphibious" chapel was superseded by the brick building standing on its own freehold; for 1840 is given in the official documents as the date of the erection of Shelford Chapel.

We leave Nottinghamshire for a time, glad to know that in the towns and villages Primitive Methodism has secured there a men and women to the last is to come may be relied upon to do their best for the Church which has done so much for them. It is almost invidious to select from the number of such, names that even after this lapse of time occur to the memory. We cannot, however, forbear, as we think of the circuit town, mentioning the name of James Barker, who was an early member of Nottingham's famous Circuit Committee, and frequently its secretary, and an able one, as the neat and carefully written records in the circuit books attest; also John Spencer, given to

JAMES BARKER.    JOSEPH BAILEY.    DAVID MUSSON JACKSON.

hospitality, and the frequent entertainer of Hugh Bourne, who often mentions his name. Mention may also again be made of David Musson Jackson, as long and close search has at last been rewarded by a discovery of his portrait and the following data:— He was born February 11th, 1794; made Governor of the House of Correction May 30th, 1833; died December 12th, 1862.

As we think of Ilkeston we think of "Friend" Joseph Bailey, as Hugh Bourne with reason called him, who will sign the *Conference Journal* of 1853 as President. He will also become a deed-poll member, and as such attend many Conferences, and by his intelligence and goodly presence and geniality win many friends.

Thinking of Mansfield, who can forget good Joshua Rouse, wire-worker, model superintendent, logician, and an expert and yet sympathetic examiner of probationers, and a familiar figure at Conferences. So we might go on; but duty calls us to another part of the mission-field, and we must obey.

THE GREAT REVIVAL IN LEICESTERSHIRE, 1818.

The progress made by the Connexion in the years 1817–18 was, geographically, not in one direction only. It was not the result of a linear but of a centrifugal movement. The Connexion grew as a tree grows; it spread like a series of constantly enlarging water-rings. If you take Nottingham as your centre you will have to keep shifting your circumferential line further and still further back. Progress does not stop in the east

JOSHUA ROUSE.

and north because you want to follow its course in the west and south. It is difficult to .... and yet it must be conceived if it cannot be written. Therefore, although our attention must now for a time be turned to Leicestershire (with Loughborough as a new centre), we must remember that progress in the direction we have hitherto been following has not rounded itself off and stopped because we cannot for the time attend to it. Unfortunately, the official documents of Nottingham Circuit prior to 1824 are no longer available to prove this, and the convenient system of "branches" was not adopted till 1819; yet there is abundant evidence of an incidental though unofficial kind to show that while Bourne (and for a time Clowes), Benton, Wedgwood, Heath, and other leaders of the main movement are hard at work in Leicestershire, what may be called a skirmishing movement is going on in Lincolnshire and elsewhere, which will in due time prepare the way for an advance on Lincoln, Boston, Sheffield, Chesterfield, Scotter, Grimsby, Hull, and even more distant Norwich and other places in East Anglia. The story of this advance, however, belongs to 1819 and onwards. We have still to do with the Great Revival of 1817-18, and with the Plan of February-April, 1818, which marks the beginning and course of that Revival. We have already seen how the places—chiefly in Nottinghamshire—which for the first time stand on this plan, register the progress of the Revival in these parts; and we have also seen by whom and under what circumstances of trial and persecution they were missioned. We have glanced, too, at what the future had in reserve for some of these gains of the Revival, and have seen that by 1843 they had become branches, or even circuits, in their own right.

These earliest plans are of considerable historical value, because places were, as a general rule added to them chronologically—in the order of their acquisition. Thus almost at the bottom of the plan which ends April 26th, 1818, we find Loughborough followed by Seagrave, Switcherland, and Barrow—places in its vicinity. This, of course, means that quite recently a footing had been gained in these places. The very next plan shows that twelve fresh preaching-stations have been added, including such well-known names as Quorndon, Sileby Syston, and Markfield. Leicester does not occur on this plan, though it will be found on immediately subsequent ones, so that we can quite distinctly read such facts as these. Towards the close of 1817, Loughborough Seagrave, and Barrow had been reached; that for a time our missionaries were shy of entering Leicester, and confined themselves to the evangelisation of the busy villages round Loughborough, and to that fine well-marked district, so rich in natural beauty, historic associations, and under-surface wealth known as Charnwood Forest recently by the Inclosure Act of 1808 brought under cultivation, and by means of good roads made accessible to the outside world, and its quarries of granite, slate, and limestone exploited to the great advantage of the once secluded inhabitants of the district. All this will be plainer if we give the last and purely Loughborough section of the May-July Plan.

Then for the purpose of comparison, and to deepen and complete the impression thus gained, we give a document of great historic interest—a Plan of Loughborough Circuit for 1822. This plan is worth, and will repay, close study. This plan has on it' forty-two places situate in five several counties; for though the bulk of the places are naturally in Leicestershire, the counties of Derby, Notts, Northampton, and Warwick are also represented on the plan by one or more places. What may have been the precise geographical area covered by this plan we have not calculated, but

LOUGHBOROUGH CIRCUIT.

Lord's day Plan of the Preachers,
CALLED
Primitive Methodists,
KNOWN ALSO BY THE NAME OF RANTERS.

"O Lord revive thy Work".—Habakkuk, iii 2.

LOVE-FEASTS.
Belgrave Oct. 27, Mountsorrell and Barleston Nov. 3. Sheepshead, Quorn and Markfield Nov. 10. Anstey, Wigston and Hinckley Nov. 17. Loughboro', and Seagrave Nov. 24. Countesthorpe Dec. 1. Ratby, Dec. 8. Leake Dec. 15. Thurmaston Dec. 15. Mousley Dec. 29. Kegworth, and Enderby Jan. 5. Croxton Jan. 19. Barrow, Dec. 26.

CIRCUIT COMMITTEE.
Richardson, Handford, Bishop, Jerram, C. Jarratt, Attenboro Simons, Shevington, Richards and Snow.
N.B. The Circuit Committee, meets at Quorndon, Nov. 4 h. Dec. 2 and Jan. 6. Every person on the Committee desiring to meet, without a sufficient reason, shall pay 6d. for each neglect.

1822 & 1823.	OC	NOVEMBER.	DECEMBER.	JAN. 1823.	PREACHERS.
Places & times of Preaching	27	3 10 17 24	1 8 16 22 29	5 12 19	1 Alicock
Loughborough,	2&6	1 8 8 44 20	16 5 7 21 3	10 16 25	2 Robinson
Sheepshead	2&6	53 51 16 32	3 20 8 44 25	20 36 4	3 Woolley
Castle Donington	2&6	44 26 25 41 5	46 17 31 39 47	32 20 36	4 Timms
Kegworth	2&6	22 5 16 2 35	24 39 44 26 51	61 39 P3	5 Shevington
Diseworth	2&6	11 30 40 47 16	25 39 P 31 32	46 43 3P	6 Handford
Sutton Bonington	2&6	24 29 31 35 30	44 20 32 25 11	20 35 46	7 Bishop
Leake 2, Costock	6	17 21 43 36 35	39 23 41 10 20	44 26 32	8 Richardson
Hathern	2&6	25 16 35 46 47	43 41 39 11 28	31 17 44	9 Markham
Hoton	2&6	6 44 17 24 39	7 8 43 P29 16	2P 40 20	10 Goodrich
Walton	6	40 35 29 20 24	5 36 P 35 29	3 25 43	11 Simpson
Barrow	2&6	7 7 20 5 4	6 42 16 56 111	23 49 7	12 Sutton,
Sileby	2&6	56 8 23 7 10	11 J 5 17 26	43 4 24	13 Williford
Seagrave	2&6	53 42 6 58 11	13 17 35 2 8	56 15 11	14 Ward
Mountsorrell	2&6	49 50 40 17 8	18 24 17 42 38	37 57 JP	15 Simons
Roadley	2&6	42 6 15 43 17	58 59 37 7 28	27 10 2	16 Jarratt
Quoradon	2&6	10 1 12 20 40	20 29 10 4 5	7 6 15	17 Richards
Woodhouse	2&6	15 17 24 52 49	27 46 41 3 7	8 97 42	18 Sims
Leicester 10, Belgrave	2&6	16 10 5 42 50	53 11 30 14 28	P 2 17	19 Palmer
Leicester	2&6	1 15 31 6 10	8 4 3 14 7	5 56 9	20 Kendall
Thurmaston	2&6	13 30 38 9 15	32 5 42 39 37	24 19 49	21 Kenny
Syston	2&6	43 13 11 3 36	42 30 24 68 21	19 6 30	22 Pike
Quemboro' 2, Kearsley	6	30 58 20 38 13	30 39 30 43 6	13 42 8	23 Phipps
Croxton 10&2. Quemboro'	6	38 4 50 13 33	30 30 20 9 43	40 23 61	24 Bayless
Ashfordby	2&6	9 23 13 16 25	49 43 42 23 15	11 55 40	25 C. Jarratt
Anety	2&6	3 49 28 11 48	10 34 12 15 52	P 27 33	26 T. Woolley
Groohy 2, Ratby	6	55 27 18 37 22	6 15 48 53 57	P 53 21	27 T. Nuttup
Markfield 2, Shaw Lane	6 8	53 41 34 5	52 57 19 32 1P	2 12 47	28 Burley
Barlestou	2&6	52 38 12 18 58	22 37 27 P 30	55 34 41	29 Attenboro
Bagworth 2, Newbold	6	3 37 53 27 12	18 22 52 57 34	22 P 18	30 Thornton
Enderby	2&6	9 19 19 30 21	18 33 1P3 52 37	12 1 50 22	31 Astle
Thurlston	2&6	10 9 19 21 30	17 27 3P 35 22	28 52 50	32 Halford
Wigston	2&6	53 14 50 15 10	16 23 21 26 33	24 11 39	33 Jeffery
Oadby	2&6	19 21 52 56 14	23 P 33 38 P	1P 50 58	34 Kirkland
Countesthorpe	2&6	21 50 55 19 26	40 56 14 P 42	30 33 105	35 Marshall
Hinckley	2&6	1 22 14 41 17	53 55 34 51 P	34 22 27	36 Sleath
Mousley	2&6	50 33 21 38 10	14 19 9 10 41	P 25 14	37 Neal
Warwickshire Coventry Mission,	2&6 6	12 17	63 45	51	38 Measures

ON TRIAL.
41 Slack
42 Barfoot
43 Webster
44 Garner
45 Bambury

EXHORTERS.
46 Bears
47 Mitchell
48 Geary
49 Histon
50 Loveday
51 Heydon
52 J. Hastle

WOMEN.
53 R Sutton
54 H. Taylor
55 M. Peat
56 H. Simpson
57 A. Geary
58 R. Tacey

N. B. Quarter day at Leicester, December 9th.—Preachers to meet at 9 o'clock.
SACRAMENTS.—Barleston, Nov. 3. Loughborough, Nov. 24. Wigston, Dec. 8. Thurmaston, Dec. 15. Hathern, Dec. 29. Sutton, Jan. 12.
It is requested that every Preacher will conduct his own appointments, and if unable...
All Letters to be directed to J. Rawson Quorndon, near Loughborough.

some idea of its extent may be gathered from the fact that what was Loughborough Circuit in 1822 has been carved into eleven existing circuits! No wonder our fathers used the word "circuit" rather than the word "station" in designating their spheres

LOUGHBOROUGH SECTION OF THE NOTTINGHAM CIRCUIT PLAN.

MAY–JULY 1818.

1818. PLACES.	MAY. 3 10 17 24 31	JUNE. 7 14 21 28	JULY. 5 12 19 26
Loughborough 2 and 6	19 10 5 49 56T	40 L SK 17	43 9 22
Quorndon 2 ...	43 P 55	44T P	40 P
Quorndon 6 ...	44 54	41 56	41 42
Thrusingt. 2, Segrave 6	9 54 56 66 P	42T 55 41 P	54 56 43
Switcherland 6 ...	55 56	9T 43	42 43
Barrow 2 ...	P 57	9T P	57 66
Barrow 6 ...	54 43 41	66 54	44 41
Sileby 2 and 6½ ...	42 57 9L 43 56	66 41 41 41	56 43 P 42
Rai. 10½, Qbo. 2, Sys. 6½	41 43 42 44 9T	55 56 66 57	42 41 55
Markfield 2, S. Lane 6½	55 41 57 P 42	43T 9 55 42	P 41 57
Hoton 2, Burton 6½ ...	52 55 44T	57 43	55 52
Costock 2 ...	66 55	P 42	44 55
Mount Sorrel			

43.	G. Hanford
44.	J. Rue
45.	J. Barker
46.	J. Bouser
47.	T. Woodward
48.	T Mounteny
49.	T. King
50.	W. Ashby ON TRIAL
51.	T. Simmons
52.	J. Garner
53.	G. Herod
54.	R. Bishop
55.	E. Frier
56.	R. Bent
57.	P. Richardson
58.	J. Slack
59.	W. Doughty
60.	W. Ward

NOTES.—The preachers for Loughboro' are: W. Hind, R. Winfield, R. Weston, T. King, W. Ashby, J. Skevington, representative to Preparatory Meeting, Sarah Kirkland, R. Stone, (vid. p. 195), G. Hanford, J. Harrison, W. Dakin. Truly a good plan!

Of the few preachers whose names are given above no less than six became travelling preachers.

of labour! We need no further evidence to show that the Great Revival in the Midlands left its enduring impress on our history, and that Loughborough has good reason to be ranked among the fruitful mother-circuits of Primitive Methodism; and it was also one of the earliest circuits formed, for if we exclude Derby—that in a time of crisis was prematurely made the second circuit, and held that position for a short time only—then Loughborough takes the third place in the order of circuit formation. September, 1818, is the date usually assigned for Loughborough's attainment of circuit independence—and this assignment of date is made on the authority of a passage in Hugh Bourne's *History*; but in his private and contemporary *Journals*—from which, in our judgment, there is no appeal—March 23rd is given as the date. On Monday, the 18th, he comes twenty-one miles from Huckuall Torkard to Loughborough, and finds the society "flourishing very much." The next day he holds a quarterly meeting, and adds "It was proposed to make Loughborough into a separate circuit." On the 23rd of the same month of March we have the entry —

Quarter Day.—Hastened to Nottingham. A deal of business. Temporal concerns tolerable; made arrangements for forming a new circuit, Loughborough to be the central place."

Then on September 15th Hugh Bourne records his being at Sileby and making the plan for Loughborough Circuit nearly a week before the Nottingham Quarterly Meeting, when the work was found to be going on well, but "the temporal concerns" to be "very bad." Besides, in another passage from a later *Journal* Hugh Bourne distinctly says —

"*December 26th, 1818.*—Set out for Derby, then to Ashbourne, came to Leek, stayed at Mr. Alcock's, Latheredge. *Monday, March 23rd, 1818.*—Nottingham Quarter Day Board formed a new circuit in Leicestershire, and made Loughborough its head. Having to superintend the three circuits caused me a deal of trouble, and I had a deal of travelling to attend the three quarter days each quarter, and the travelling was almost uniformly at my own expense, but then I travelled chiefly on foot, my feet were often sore, but this I endeavoured to bear patiently. From Nottingham to Tunstall is about fifty-four miles, from Loughborough to Tunstall about fifty-five miles, and from Nottingham to Loughborough is about sixteen miles. When we became strong it was almost impossible to prevent improper persons from getting in among us [let this be carefully noted for its bearing on after events], and this caused serious troubles, but still the converting work went on rapidly, hardly anything could stand before it. At Nottingham we were blessed with an active leaders' meeting, and I believe it was long the only leaders' meeting we had in the whole Connexion, and the active Nottingham leaders' meeting attended to the general affairs of the circuit between quarter days. But in September, 1818, they laid before me an official statement to say they would still continue to give due attention to the general affairs of the town of Nottingham, but it was too heavy upon them, and took up too much of their time to pay attention to the general affairs of the circuit, and this part they must therefore give up into my hands. I was quite in a dilemma, but at the Quarter Day Meeting, held September 21st and 22nd, 1818, brother Thomas King and others were formed into a committee to arrange the temporal concerns, and with much entreaty and persuasion I prevailed on this committee to attend to the general concerns of the circuit till the ensuing quarter day. At the Quarter Day, December 21st 1818, it was found that the circuit, through the exertions of the committee, was beginning greatly to recover itself, and their attending to general concerns had been so valuable and useful to the circuit, that every one saw the propriety and necessity of appointing a committee for the like purpose for the next quarter. This was the origin of the Circuit Committees— a measure which has since become a permanent part of the discipline of the Connexion. *Nottingham had made* Loughborough into a circuit, and others of its out-stations were becoming large and powerful."*

We have given these extracts from the *Journals* of Hugh Bourne for various reasons, chiefly because they do not in the least bear out the idea that Loughborough was formed into a circuit in order to relieve Nottingham from embarrassment, occasioned or heightened by the incompetence of two unnamed preachers who are reflected on in the *History*. On the contrary, the extracts rather compel the view that the step was taken before the embarrassment was felt, and at the initiative of the Loughborough Society. The step was felt to be a natural one in view of the rapid spread of the Connexion in the locality, and the desirability of having a nearer centre of management than Nottingham. Even amidst the troubles of the Nottingham September Quarter Day, Hugh Bourne could thankfully write: 'The Lord has brought among these people some men of talent,' and Loughborough's bid for circuit independence evidently commended itself to the judgment of these far-seeing men. Incidentally the last extract is interesting, as giving a clear account of the natural way in which Circuit Committees had their origin. As with other features of our constitution, they were not the outcome of theorising, but of a business-like endeavour to meet a practical difficulty. For years the Nottingham Circuit Committee elected quarter by quarter wielded considerable power, and, as a general rule, wielded it wisely. The same extract again brings vividly before us the serious view Hugh Bourne took of his office of general superintendent, and how strenuously he set himself to discharge the duties of his office as he understood them. What a real thing his superintendence of the Connexion was at this time, and how much care and labour it entailed! As we see him with sore, or even bleeding feet, arms and back aching under the load of plans and magazines and school requisites, trudging from place to place to adjust disagreeables, and to deal with the increasing number of "improper" characters, who crept in to disturb the harmony and interrupt the true work of the societies—one cannot but admire, and yet be glad for his sake, that by the end of the year the heavy burthen will be somewhat lightened. He was a true bishop—overseer: so much so that the frequency of his visits to a place or neighbourhood becomes a gauge of the importance of what is happening there. Where most business is going on there the overseer is sure to be. Applying this gauge, and with the *Journals* before us, we gain another piece of evidence as to the growing importance of Loughborough and the neighbourhood to Primitive Methodism. Hugh Bourne paid his first visit to Loughborough on January 24th, 1818, and he revisited the town at shorter and still shorter intervals during the year; but it is significant that he did not enter Leicester until September 16th. Between these dates Hugh Bourne is several times at Segrave, Quorndon, Barrow-on-Soar, Sileby, and Loughborough—the places which formed the nucleus of the Loughborough Circuit. A glance at the map will show that these were just the places John Benton, Heath and Wedgwood were likely to take in their way when, towards the fall of 1817, they faced round to begin the self-same work of itinerant evangelisation in Leicestershire they had been pursuing in Notts and Lincoln. They had no tempting railway facilities to modify or determine their choice of locality, and they carried their Master's general commission, so that their itinerant movements were almost as natural as the movement and direction of flowing water. They simply walked on and lifted up their voice and evangelised Hugh Bourne came on his first Loughborough round, it was to prune and water the new and vigorous societies planted by others who had moved on, going further into the country to break up the fallow-ground.

An incidental verification of these views of our origins, so far as they relate to Barrow-on-Soar, is supplied by the very first article in the first number of the monthly *Magazine*, 1819. In the memoir of Elizabeth Ainsworth there given, it is stated that she, her mother, and two brothers were religiously awakened under a sermon preached by John Hallsworth at Barrow "about the beginning of the winter" of 1817–18. We should hardly have expected to meet with John Hallsworth, of Mercaston's name as

BARROW CHURCH. THE FIRST PREACHING-PLACE WAS JUST OUTSIDE CHURCH GATE.

a pioneer missionary in these parts, as his sphere is supposed to have lain farther east, and chiefly in Lincolnshire; but the evidence is indisputable, and all the more interesting because unexpected. We may safely conclude that ever since John Hallsworth's visit there has existed a Primitive Methodist Society in good Bishop Beveridge's place of nativity. Bourne visited it on January 26th, 1818, and under rather unfavourable circumstances: for in hurriedly passing out of Loughborough he walked full against a post and hurt himself very much. But this accident did not deter him from preaching, and he "had a glorious manifestation." The converting work was still going on in 1821, as the *Journal* of Robert Bent shows. Bent's name will be found on th   *Pryor*

THE PERIOD OF CIRCUIT PREDOMINANCE AND ENTERPRISE.   283

Richardson—a most singular collocation of names. The circuit books show that at this time R. Bent was receiving salary as a hired local preacher. Bent records in his *Journal* how, just as he was finishing preaching at Barrow, a woman fell down and cried for mercy—and then another, and as soon as they had found deliverance two men cried earnestly for mercy. *

Barrow was for a considerable number of years the residence, as it is now the last resting-place of John Mayes, one of the worthies of Loughborough Circuit, whose name deserves to be held in remembrance, not only by Leicestershire Primitive Methodists, but by a still wider circle of his co-religionists. The introduction of his name compels a reference to Woodhouse Eaves Camp Meeting. This notable gathering took place in the twenties, and if tradition counts for anything, Woodhouse Eaves

WOODHOUSE EAVES VILLAGE, CHURCH ON THE LEFT.

Camp Meeting must take its place amongst the half dozen admittedly greatest camp meetings of Primitive Methodism. Those who had been there talked of the glories of that day, and their children still love to tell the story as of something the like of which was never seen before, and will never be seen again. Traditional estimates are not always commensurate with the real historic importance of events. Tradition is apt to be impressed with the big and the grandiose, and has not—and small blame to it—a very clear perception of the bearing of events. Judged by this severer standard, Woodhouse Eaves Camp Meeting cannot rank with the first and third Mow Hill, or with Norton Camp Meetings, though it may well be allowed to take its place along with Wrekin and Nottingham Forest (1816), Priest Hill and Buckminster Camp

Meetings as having stirred a wide district and led to something. Its site was admirably chosen, lying as it did within the limits of Charnwood Forest. Its surface was diversified by rock and bosky dell. Here quarries had been opened in the slate-beds, and there the rock thrust itself up into caverned cliff, like the one at the end of the single village street, that since 1837 has been crowned by its picturesque church and parsonage. Within half a mile was Beaumanor, the ancient home of the Herricks, and not far away, in another direction, Bradgate and its spacious park, once the residence of Lady Jane Grey—

> "Most gentle, most unfortunate,
> Crowned but to die, who in her chamber sate
> Musing with Plato, though the horn was blown,
> And every ear and every heart was won,
> And all in green array were chasing down the sun."

WINDMILL HILL, WOODHOUSE EAVES. (SITE OF CAMP MEETING.)

But why dwell on these things? The power to appreciate natural beauty is largely a taste acquired within the last eighty years, and even if it were not so the bulk of those who flocked to Woodhouse Eaves Camp Meeting had something else to think of than the natural beauty and historic associations of their surroundings—though these, rich as they were, may have tended unconsciously to idealise the tradition of that day's proceedings which still survives. Scenery cannot save the soul any more than it can satisfy the hungry stomach. It was a Salvation-meeting that was held at Woodhouse Eaves; for our fathers knew both the name and the thing itself long before the Salvation Army was thought of.* Some were bursting to declare the good news, and

* Resolu... ... ... Quarterl... M...tin... p...—d S...pt...mb...r 23rd 1839; "That a Salvation M... ... ..."

others came to catch the stimulus, and taste the excitement the presence and impact of the crowd would afford. If they did not put it clearly to themselves that it was personal and social salvation they wanted, we may well believe in a dim vague way they hoped that by attending the Ranters' Camp Meeting that day their lives would somehow be lightened and brightened.

As things went then, Woodhouse Eaves was a convenient centre for a camp meeting. It was four miles from Loughborough, eight from Leicester, seven or eight from East Leake, twelve from Ashby, and eighteen from Nottingham. There were contingents from all these places present. It must have been a vast multitude that came together that day. Tradition, disdaining figures, falls back on hyperbole, and as though it were describing the course of some devastating army that "licks up all that is round about

WOODHOUSE PRESENT CHAPEL.

as the ox licketh up the grass of the field," it goes on to tell how on the day of the Woodhouse Eaves Camp Meeting the village wells were drunk dry, and the food supply gave out! In sober truth, the company that came together on this great field-day must have been immense. It was not difficult to reach the people in Leicestershire during these early years; they had the "spirit of hearing," and the villages were fairly populous, so that it was often true to the letter that "listening thousands gathered round." Nothing strikes us more than the size of the congregations John Harrison notes as everywhere listening to him during the three months he spent in Leicestershire while the Great Revival was in progress; and though it is easy to over-estimate numbers, we cannot think of John Harrison as prone to exaggeration of this kind. At Hoteby, "May 12th he preached to a large congregation, the people behaved well," and hundreds accompanied him on his way to Leicester. At Quenborough he had three hundred to hear him at half-past five in the morning. At Thrussington some hundreds were gathered together in the street. At Coleorton, Sheepshead, Segrave, Elstone, Whitwick—wherever he went—it was the same; there were crowds—not hostile, but curious and eager to see and hear.

The spiritual results of that day's labours it is impossible to tabulate. Three hundred adherents are said to have been won for Loughborough and its village societies, besides the willing captives the more distant contingents took back with them, and the gleanings made by other Churches. John Mayes was one of the substantial gains of Woodhouse Eaves Camp Meeting. When he fell under the power he was carried to one of the praying circles, where, we are told, he remained unconscious for a long time, and then woke up with the language of praise on his lips. When young he worked at a hosiery-frame; after his marriage he became a small shopkeeper in Barrow, and such he continued until that day in 1866 when the village was in mourning at his burial. As we read his history[*] it shows us nothing great, but the greatness of simple goodness—the cumulative greatness of numberless acts of kindness rendered out of pure love to the deserving poor, and those who "suffered in mind, body or estate." The widow and the fatherless knew him, and respected him; so did the hard-worked poorly-paid ministers of his own Church. He was their very good friend. John Mayes' methods of doing others a good turn were sometimes peculiar and ingenious. He seems to have read to some purpose the Biblical narrative which tells how Vizier Joseph put his divining cup into his brother's sack, and one might almost imagine this narrative had prompted him to act on the same lines of surprise with the materials his shop gave ready to his hand. He would return the widow's money wrapped up in the pound of sugar or rice her child took home. One day a hard-working local preacher walked two miles to return two half crowns he had found, to his amazement, in a packet of oatmeal. This J. M. had put into his hand the night before, when the local preacher had looked in on returning from his appointment. Parcels of groceries would sometimes come by the carrier to distant manses just when and where they were needed. Yet, though John Mayes dispensed with a liberal hand, and his books might show a fairly long column of bad debts, his little business prospered. He had friends amongst the well-to-do and highly placed, who appreciated his character. But all this did not spoil him. "He was na pricked-eared," as an old local put it. He did not despise the queer structure that served for purposes of worship in Barrow,[†] and when a better one was a-building he would, when troubled with insomnia, betake himself there in the small hours to pray. He loved the Church which took him in and sheltered him so long—its sanctuaries, its doctrines and practices, its ministers and literature. And all this can be traced back to Woodhouse Eaves Camp Meeting. The poet Wordsworth

[*] See Rev. C. H. Boden's article "A Precious Son of Zion," *Aldersgate Magazine*, 1900, pp. 670-3, to which we are largely indebted.

[†] This chapel is said to have consisted of two houses thrown into one by Mr. William Cryless. One day in 1818 John Wedgwood being at Barrow took his stand upon a stone by the side of the churchyard [...] Wedgwood asked if any one would afford him shelter. Mr. Cryless [...]

THE PERIOD OF CIRCUIT PREDOMINANCE AND ENTERPRISE. 287

thought the recollections of his visit to Tintern Abbey some years before might have

"had no trivial influence
On that best portion of a good man's life;
His little, nameless, unremembered acts
Of kindness and of love."

For Wordsworth put John Mayes; for Tintern Abbey put Woodhouse Eaves, and the acknowledgment of indebtedness may stand.

CAMP MEETINGS AT WAKES AND LANTERN-LIGHTED SERVICES.

The Switcherland of the first quarter's plan for 1818 is probably Swithland, now

THE GREEN, SEGRAVE.
Where first Open-air Services were held.

famed for its woods and slate-quarries, and a popular holiday resort. When our denominational fathers first came this way they found themselves in the midst of most picturesque scenery. Their eyes rested on some of the oldest rocks in England—the granite of Mount Sorrel and the compact slate of Swithland and Woodhouse Eaves. They stood not far from the highest land in the Midlands—Beacon Hill and Bardon Hill. But though it is interesting, and may help the imagination to know these things, we do not linger, but pass on to Segrave, which, unlike Swithland, *has* had a permanent cause ever since it was missioned, before the close of 1817, by some one unknown. Hugh Bourne visited it on January 28th, 1818, and he says: "They are doing well here." John Harrison soon followed; on Sunday evening, March 3rd, the chapel was crowded from pulpit to doors. The chapel referred to was the private property of a farmer, and was lent for the occasion; it was not until 1845 a Connexional chapel was built at Segrave. As the first article in the *Magazine* for 1819 recalls Barrow, so the third article in the same number furnishes an interesting reference to Segrave. The article in question states that a camp meeting was held at Segrave on November 8th, during the wake or yearly parish feast, and was continued on the Monday, "when a novel scene appeared: there were two nearly equal companies, and they were in view and within the hearing of each other. One company, or party, was engaged at cricket-playing, and the other in the solemn worship of Almighty God. And this striking scene continued nearly the whole of the day." The purpose of the article is to show that camp meetings at wakes "have a peculiar beauty and propriety," and Segrave is instanced as a case in point. "Wakes are seasons of much leisure, and camp meetings by their diversity are well calculated to fill up that leisure." Then the article closes by laying down rules for providing the needful variety. No one but Hugh Bourne could have written this piece; and this is said in the full knowledge that the first eight numbers of the *Magazine* were "edited by a person at Leicester." The piece has all the distinctive marks of Bourne's style. What is more, the view taken of camp meetings, and the enthusiasm shown in relation to them, are still more characteristic of the man. He had all the tactician's delight in fresh combinations and movements that gave promise of effective results.[*] But of all combinations, the camp meeting was Hugh Bourne's favourite tactical formation in presence of the enemy, because it afforded scope, such as no other formation afforded, for variety of exercises—for setting all to work for a common purpose. Moltke himself did not give more thought to the strategy of his campaigns than did Hugh Bourne to the ordering of camp meetings down to their smallest minutiæ. The true military tactician must have in him something of the inventor and the artist. He must be endowed with a considerable measure of imagination in order to anticipate the chess-like moves of his opponent, and to provide against them with the forces at his disposal. So do not call Hugh Bourne a matter-of-fact faddist where camp meetings were concerned. Let us rather call him a practical idealist—a tactician in camp meetings, who honestly believed he had come upon the secret of how to deal effectively with the prevalent conditions of his time—which conditions, be it remembered, may be very different from those obtaining now. There is the joy of the discoverer in the zest with which he will publish to the world some idea that has come to him—an idea that has been found to work well on the camp-ground. Such a glad "Eureka" we have in the same first volume of the *Magazine*, in the piece entitled, "On Celebrating Divine Worship in the Open Air by Candle-light." During the Leicester campaign of 1818, a camp meeting

[*] "The various movements, ingenuities, and improvements that rise when the work of God is proceeding are admirable. The Conference religious services had a walking prayer meeting, and a walking preaching, and such things as these may be of service in various instances. The re-missioning processions have much useful variety, and are considerably improved. And the minute or minute and a half, or two minutes' sermons are not among the least of the improvements."
Hugh Bo

was held at Hinckley on November 18th. The night was dark, and "a man stood on a bench holding a lantern to light the preacher." This struck out the thought that with some improvements it would be easy to hold meetings in the open-air by candle-light. The experiment was tried on the following Thursday night at Burbage, when a number of lanterns, tied to sticks, were held aloft in different parts of the congregation that no building would have held. "The meeting looked brilliant and dazzling, and the whole had a solemn and striking appearance." There is quite an imaginative glow about the picture of the American Forest Camp Meetings this lantern-lighted service calls up before the mind's eye of the writer:—

"The night-scenes at the American Camp Meetings are grand and sublime. The surrounding darkness; the lights of numerous lamps and lanterns suspended

PREACHING IN THE OPEN-AIR AT NIGHT WITH THE AID OF LANTERNS.

to the boughs of trees, &c., accompanied by the voice of solemn prayer, powerful preaching, or sacred singing, together with the solemn appearance of the whole assembly, present a scene of sublime grandeur that is not often equalled." (p. 15.)

As though by touch of magician's wand we can see and hear it all. Those who say Hugh Bourne had no imagination will have to reckon with this paragraph. Their cheap judgment will split on this piece of "imagination all compact."

The happy thought that occurred to somebody at Hinckley that dark November night "caught on," and many a scene was to be enacted during the years that were to follow, quite as weird and striking as that chronicled in the first number of the *Magazine*. Henceforward mere darkness need not deter preacher or congregation. Here, for instance, is a rapid glimpse of a lantern-service got from the journal of one who bears honoured name—John Woodhouse, of Hull:—

"September 27th, 1820: Went to Howden and borrowed a lantern and a chair. I hung up the lantern against a wall, and began to sing, pray and preach in the open-air. A large company soon gathered together, and were very serious, excepting one or two. I had a good time."

But to return to our immediate subject as suggested by Segrave—the tactical value of camp meetings, especially as the deliberately designed counteractive of wakes. What wakes were in those days we have in a previous chapter tried to show,* and there can be little doubt that Hugh Bourne had good reason for regarding them as a favourite and formidable device of the devil. Quite as certainly he believed camp meetings on his model to be the most effective method of counter-attack known to him; and there is no lack of evidence to show he was right in both opinions. Camp meetings during the time of wakes had been held in Staffordshire with most encouraging results, and some

THE GREEN, BARLESTONE, WHERE OPEN-AIR SERVICES WERE HELD.

with the same specific character and purpose, that were held in Leicestershire, proved no less successful. Of such, the one held at Barlestone, in the month of September, stands out historically above the rest, and the reference to it here is relevant because the article in which it is described is a continuation of the one before referred to in which Hugh Bourne lays down the principle that "Camp meetings at wakes have a peculiar beauty and propriety." Of that principle Barlestone is intended to supply the illustration and confirmation, as it fully answered its purpose in restraining the wake and also began a considerable revival.

Primitive Methodism was introduced into the village of Barlestone in the June of this year, but nothing specially remarkable occurred until the holding of this protracted camp meeting that began on Sunday, September 13th, and continued until the following

Friday. On the Sunday, Pryor Richardson and his inseparable companion, Brother Bishop, took a leading part; on Thursday, Hugh Bourne, R. Culley, and Brother Harcott were present; and on Friday—be it noted as a fact of historical interest—no less a person than Lorenzo Dow was at this Barlestone camp meeting. But after giving due weight to all these names, it still remains true that the chief labourer at these services was Ruth Simpson. She was "in labours more abundant." After the Sunday open-air services were closed an adjournment was made to the house of Brother Sutton, and when the prayer meeting ended at one o'clock on Tuesday morning, it was found that sixteen persons professed to have found salvation, and there were still others mourning on account of sin when they reluctantly retired to their homes. The early volumes of the denominational *Magazine* furnish valuable incidental evidence as to the lasting good accomplished during this wake-week's labours of love; for they contain the memoirs of several persons whose conversion is directly attributed to the prayers and exhortations

SEGRAVE. FIRST INDOOR PREACHING PLACE.

of Sister Simpson. After this we are not surprised to come across the following entry in Hugh Bourne's *Journals*:—

"Thursday, September 17th. At Barlestone Camp Meeting. A good time. I spoke from John iii. 3. At night meeting; some saved. Yesterday I saw Ruth Simpson. She stands up to speak with good acceptance. O Lord, be with her! She appears to be a gracious young woman. To-day I had much conversation with her."

All this gives us the highest opinion of Ruth Simpson's character and ability and makes us almost resent the fragmentariness of our knowledge concerning her.

The wake camp-meetings of Segrave and Barlestone are representative of numberless others that took place during this period. That from what we call a tactical point of view, Barlestone camp meeting was a distinct success is proved by the following testimony, and in its influence and results Barlestone is also representative of many others:—

"This Camp Meeting was held at the time of the wake or annual parish meeting. The wake there had been uniformly attended with great improprieties, and the camp meetings were intended to prevent these improprieties, and to counteract the bad effects of the wake. And, through the tender mercy of God, this was accomplished. Nearly the whole of the inhabitants were constantly engaged in religious exercises until Thursday in the wake-week, by which means, drunkenness and quarrelling were almost set aside, families were comfortable, and the village was peaceable." *

Neither the wake nor the camp meeting may have retained just its old influence: the one has not the power to hurt nor the other the power to heal it once possessed. In a sense the poet never meant, it is true—"The old order changeth giving place to new." Battles are not lost or won by employing or misemploying the exact tactics of Marathon or Agincourt, but warfare remains, and the study of strategy and tactics is more urgent than ever. So in the spiritual warfare methods may and must change and our success, as a Church, will depend, not on slavishly imitating the precise methods of Hugh Bourne or any one else, but in seeking to have his spirit of practical idealism, his openness to suggestion, his readiness to adapt his methods to suit current conditions and demands.

In leaving Barlestone it should be added that in the thirties it became a branch of Leicester Circuit. In the forties it was included within newly-formed Earl Shilton, now known as Hinckley Circuit. Samuel Antliff began his ministry at Earl Shilton.

Providing for the Succession

The facts as to the introduction of Primitive Methodism into the border villages of Leicestershire, and the after-history of the denomination in these villages, suggest the thought that Carlyle so stoutly insisted on. That history is mainly concerned with the call of select souls to fulfil their vocation, and must largely occupy itself with the recital of what these select souls have done for the many. So true is this with regard to the history of our own Church, that we can best follow that history by marking the series of select souls; by following up the succession of men and women of fire, who had the zeal and the power to kindle other souls, and who, after they had run their illuminating course, could, like the runners in the Greek torch-race, pass their torch on to others, and so leave the succession sure.

It was not enough that camp meetings were held that stirred Leicestershire villages into temporary excitement, and were a nine days' wonder; nor even, as was the case at Woodhouse Eaves, that the concourse should be so vast, and the enthusiasm so great, that the gathering is talked of to this day. It was not enough even that, as at Seagrave and Barlestone, camp meetings were held which exerted a wholesome restraining influence, and tended to the softening of manners, or brought men and women to lead "godly, righteous, and sober lives." It was so, and the fact is soon stated, though its implications are vast. For the perpetuity and the spread of the Connexion something more was wanted, and the present position of the denomination in the county prepares

* *Magazi*... ... Barleston Camp Meeting in this volume. As ...

us to find that this "something more" was supplied. It was needful to secure the future by providing for the succession of men and women who belonged to the true order of evangelists, who could not stay at home to enjoy religious quietism, but must "run to and fro" to spread knowledge, and to infect others with their own enthusiasm. Even Woodhouse Eaves did in this way take seizin of the future and provide for the succession. From the day that John Mayes was illumined to the day he laid down his torch and "devout men carried him to his burial" in Barrow Churchyard, there was not wanting a true witness for God in those parts, or a true propagandist of our Church. But even more striking examples of this providing for the succession are supplied by others of these Leicestershire villages which were opened towards the end of 1817. Take Quorndon. This place was visited by John Heath who was a native of Derbyshire, and thus, by him, we are linked on to the Revival in Derbyshire of an earlier time. Heath was a man of only slender abilities, but he was very much in earnest to explain and enforce the great verities he understood so well by practical experience. He was a man of much prayer and strong faith, so that we do not wonder at being told "a particular influence attended his preaching." His health gave way under the strain of continuous and arduous labour, and in 1820 he was compelled to retire from the ministry.

With the materials supplied by tradition we can picture to ourselves the appearance John Heath would present on the day he entered Quorndon in pursuance of his evangelistic mission, and began the service amid an excitement which grew as the service continued.

'His face, we are told, was short and broad, with projecting lower jaw, strong close-set teeth, through which a loud voice finished its natural climaxes with a hiss. His eyes were strong and piercing. He was a small man attired in a blue swallow-tail, corduroy smalls, blue stockings, and well-nailed, well-oiled boots.'*

Pryor Richardson, a Rearsby youth, but now a butcher's apprentice at Quorndon, was one of those who heard him, and at the lovefeast in the Wesleyan Chapel which followed, he underwent a remarkable religious experience. He joined the infant society and became its leading spirit. His zeal and power of utterance soon marked him out for a local preacher, and he became one of the Connexion's best-known and most indefatigable labourers in these parts. Pryor Richardson had as bosom friend one who bore the name of Bishop, and the two, though men of very different type, were often companions in travel and associates in missionary labour. The Pryor and the Bishop got on well together, as is not always the case with the "regulars" and "seculars" of the Romish Church who bear these names. Pryor Richardson, we take it, was intense and somewhat narrow in his views. Honest doubt he could not understand. Anything savouring of scepticism was an offence to him. He believed as firmly in the devil as did Martin Luther or Parkinson Milson, and often talked of his wiles, and recounted his own struggles with the great adversary. He was strongly of the opinion that the hours immediately following conversion were amongst the most critical of life, for that then Satan employs his subtlest devices. Hence he was accustomed to take the new convert to his home for the night in order to ensure his indoctrination and enrolment, and after that he felt much easier in his mind, and had good ground for his assurance. From all this it will be seen Pryor Richardson was what men are accustomed to call an "eccentric." Yes, he was eccentric, as were Crawfoot and Wedgwood, and Bourne and Hickingbotham. They were all more or less eccentric, and the denomination they founded was itself a piece of eccentricity in the current estimate of the world. So Pryor Richardson ran his course until 1856, when the end came, and as he was one of those who helped to make and mould Loughborough—itself a missionary circuit—we may also claim that he in his measure was one of the makers of Primitive Methodism.

But though 1856 carries us some way beyond our first period, Pryor Richardson's influence comes down much further than that. At Quorndon in the year 1852, a camp meeting was held at which a young man of twenty-two was sorely smitten. For some weeks he was miserable; so much so that he had about resolved to throw himself into the Soar. But one of the camp-meeting preachers revisited the place, and with the help of preacher and Pryor Richardson, the youth struggled into liberty and joy. Pryor took him home for "confirmation," better than that bestowed by bishop's hand. After some years of useful service in the Loughborough Circuit, John Wightman became town missionary in Nottingham, and did a work of beneficence in many respects similar to that done by the well-known and much-respected Westminster Police Court Missionary, Mr. Thomas Holmes. He died with startling suddenness in the house of a lady on whom he had called. "I deem it a great honour," said she, when condoled with on account of the shock and inconvenience such an event must have involved—"I deem it a great honour that God should have allowed so good a man to find my home the entrance-gate to heaven." That was on June 4th, 1882, and we may rest assured that the flame he bore, before he passed hence, had lighted other torches.

JOHN WIGHTMAN.

Quorndon was also, until the thirties, the home of Phœbe Smith, who rightly takes her place among the noble band of women who graced this early period of our history. She afterwards belonged to the society at Dead Lane, Loughborough, and was "the religious genius of the church." * The mention of Quorndon will at once remind a privileged circle of the famous "Quorndon hunt" † ; to Primitive Methodists the place

---

* The phrase is Mr. Tucker's, the Steward of Loughborough Circuit, who is enthusiastic in speaking of Phœbe Smith's good works and the fragrant memory she has left.

† "Quorn is still the headquarters of the hunt, the horses and hounds being kept here. On these, it is said, that the late Sir R. Sutton spent ten thousand a year, keeping here and at Oadby,

will ever be associated with the names of Pryor Richardson, Phœbe Smith and John Wightman. We may add, the chapel at Quorndon was purchased in 1826.

Illustrations of this "providing for the succession" abound. Almost every pioneer place in the new Loughborough Circuit furnishes its example. Two others may be instanced. During his two months' successful labours in these parts, John Harrison—with a young man out of the Vale of Belvoir named George Herod to assist him—came to Grooby and preached to about three hundred people. After the service he met those who were wishful "to give in their names," and ten responded. One of the ten was Mr. Thomas Sutton, whose name stands No. 12 on the plan of 1823. Mr. Herod, who knew him well, has recorded this testimony to his character and loyalty:—

"He has been one of the most diligent and laborious local preachers we ever met with. He is always at his post when health permits; with him there is no parleying about long journeys, dark nights or bad weather. We query whether any local preacher has travelled more miles or preached more sermons the last thirty-five years than Thomas Sutton. Moreover, his house has been a home for the preachers more than thirty years." ("Sketches," p. 358).

REV. JOHN WOOLLEY.

Thomas Sutton was a frame-smith, and had apprentices in his house. The Christian atmosphere in which they lived so influenced some of these youths that they in their turn became decided Christians and adherents of their master's church. Michael Billings, a Leicester local preacher and Sunday school worker of great repute, was one of such apprentices, and there were others who for their lasting good came early in life under Thomas Sutton's quiet but wholesome influence.

Syston, missioned on January 18th, 1818, affords our final example. By the service on the Green—to be described in the next section—John Woolley was arrested and brought to God. He was a native of Hathern, but at that time resident at Syston; became a local preacher in 1819, and was called into the ministry in 1822, by his native circuit. The wear and tear of the ministry was heavy in those days. Many retired broken in health; others died early, and John Woolley was one of these; travelling only eleven years. His last circuit was Fulbeck, where he died July 20th, 1833, after labouring there but one week.* The official memoir says of him: "He possessed good talents, and his piety was of a high order and his conduct remarkably correct."

SILEBY AND THE PRESIDENT OF THE FIRST CONFERENCE.

The reference to the missioning of Syston at once suggests Sileby, the home of George Hanford, who was the chief missioner on the occasion referred to and became

---

* Rev. Joseph Middleton preached a funeral-sermon at Fulbeck for Mrs. Sarah Walker, December 15th, 1835. "For many years she had been a mother in Israel. It was under her roof that the late Mr. John Woolley gave up the ghost and went to the immediate and uninterrupted presence of God."

President of the first Conference at Hull in 1820. Precisely when and under what circumstances Sileby was first entered we are not informed; but it already had, in 1818, a vigorous society, and Hugh Bourne, W. Clowes, J. Wedgwood, and J. Harrison all visited it during the first six months of the year. On March 20th, Hugh Bourne was at Sileby "about a chapel," and the chapel must have been erected soon after, for the second and last number of the Quarterly Magazine (July, 1818) says: "A new chapel has been opened this quarter at Sileby and another at Queniborough, both in Leicestershire." Hence it appears that Sileby must have run Loughborough pretty close for the honour of having the first chapel in the county. At Sileby, too, the September quarterly meeting of the young Loughborough Circuit was held. The strength and importance of this society was no doubt largely owing to George Hanford's connection with it. As a

FIRST PREACHING PLACE, SILEBY.

"lace manufacturer," he must have occupied a fairly good position, and his contributions to the early Magazines and the prominent part he subsequently took in Connexional affairs all indicate that he was a man of considerable ability and force of character. He signs as a trustee of Loughborough new chapel; is one of the representatives of the Circuit to the Preparatory Meeting of 1819; is President of the first Conference; is at the second and fourth Conferences, and though not expressly named, was probably a delegate to the third, held at Loughborough. He is the second local preacher on the 1823 plan, delegate to the Nottingham District Meeting in 1825, and then he disappears—whether as the result of his withdrawal or death there is no evidence to show. Alike in his first appearance and his disappearance there is a singular, and rather disconcerting, abruptness, perhaps accounted for by the paucity of our information. We conjecture he belonged originally to some other Church, and that he transferred himself and his influence to the Primitives on their first appearance in these parts. When we first meet with him he is alre... ...Hugh Bourne a practised speaker, and possessing both the instinct and the qualifications of an evangelist, as his circumstantial account of the missioning of Syston gives sufficient proof.

Hanford tells us that on Plough Monday, January 12th, he was accosted by some mummers fantastically dressed, who hailed from Syston. They looked for money, but he gave them good advice instead, whereupon they intimated he must be a "Ranter" by his talk. This led him to ask whether they had any "Ranters" at Syston. "No," said they, 'and if they ever come there we will kill them.' Mr Hanford's half-formed resolve to mission Syston, which had been encouraged by consultation with one of the ministers, slumbered until the Sunday morning, when, under the stimulus of a tragic incident, it at once matured and took action. A young woman by his side was called out of the chapel because her father had dropped down dead. "If anything is to be done in a transitory world like this, it must be done at once. There is no time to be lost. I will go to Syston this day." So thought—so resolved George Hanford. Twenty-six persons of varying degrees of courage went with him. At first they stepped out resolutely and kept well together, but as they got near to the 'large respectable, and populous village" a hymn was struck up, "one deserted to the right, another to the left, some stopped behind, others ran before; till they all left but six." The Green reached, George Hanford and his half-dozen stalwarts found hundreds assembled, and the service began with praise and prayer. Presently, amid cries of "Make way! make way!" the clergyman, the lawyer, and "a gentleman"—a triumvirate familiar to our early missionaries—pushed their way to the front, and a colloquy began. From the part he took in this wordy encounter, Mr. Hanford showed that he had other qualifications for the position of premier President besides evangelistic sympathies and gifts. It is scarcely too much to say that he taught the clergyman theology, the lawyer law, and the 'gentleman' good manners. With the first he discussed such high themes as "the forgiveness of sins the witness of the Spirit, and the sensible perception of the love of God in the heart." He joined issue with the second on certain points of law relating to the licensing of preachers and places, and wrung from his opponent the rather damaging admission "This is a point of the law on which I am now not fully acquainted." As for number three of the party—if the tradition be correct, which says that this was farmer Parr who threatened to thrust his stick down the preacher's throat—by giving him the courtesy-title of a gentleman Mr Hanford showed an example of good manners. From words they proceeded to pull the preacher about a little, while a "local" standing on an eminence cried "Mr Hanford, stand him!" and then the three went off—the lawyer, with a curse, muttering "Oh —— he knows the law!" Mr Hanford preached, and felt very happy. 'Every soul seemed inspired with courage, and we sang down the street. 'Turn to the Lord and seek salvation.'" The singing of this hymn was used for the conversion of brother Webster whose memoir is found in the *Magazine* of 1823.

Ten days afterwards, Hugh Bourne was the guest of Mr Hanford, and "conversed much with him about discipline." Considering that the one was shortly to write "A Treatise on Discipline," to which the other, as President of the Conference of 1820 will give his official imprimatur, the discussion was well-timed and appropriate.

The mis...... ge Hanford

"The signal power of God that rested upon the people that day induced them to give us pressing invitations to Rearsby, Queniborough, Thurmaston, Leicester, and other places at which we now have large societies." To Leicester then, the proud capital of the county, we must now direct our attention.

VILLAGES versus TOWNS

Herod, in referring to the Revival which began in Leicestershire under the labours of John Benton Hallsworth and Heath, and after mentioning several places in that county which profited by the labours of the missionaries, goes on to say:—"*But Leicester he felt reluctant to enter.*" Why this reluctance?—if indeed it were really felt. Herod's words should hardly be passed over without remark, coming as they do from one whose testimony as to matters of fact relating to Primitive Methodism in his own particular district at this time, we have every reason to regard as trustworthy. Herod's statement is interesting, not so much because it professes to admit us to the secret workings of Benton's mind—the play of feeling, the struggle between preferences and dislikes going on within—which had its effect in shaping the course of the evangelistic movement. Even so regarded the statement is interesting. But it may do us the further service of putting us upon the inquiry whether this "reluctance" to enter upon evangelistic labour in the larger towns and cities was not in a sense characteristic of the movement as a whole up to this time. Had not Primitive Methodism hitherto shown itself to be, in fact and by preference, a rural rather than an urban movement? The question, stated thus generally must be answered in the affirmative. Primitive Methodism was rural in its origin; it took kindly and naturally to the villages, and lingered amongst them lovingly. Village evangelisation became its habit—one might even say its passion so much so that what was its chief distinction and glory had in it the element of danger it might fail to respond to the demands of the rapidly growing towns, and like Reuben of old, continue to sit "amongst the sheepfolds to hear the pipings of the flock." This temptation—the reluctance to adjust itself to the marvellous changes brought about in this industrial age—was only tardily overcome. But it *has* been overcome, until now the danger lies in an entirely different direction. Formerly the temptation was to neglect the towns in favour of the villages; now the temptation is to abandon the villages and concentrate on the towns.

But when we think of the antithesis between town and country as it presented itself about 1820, we must remind ourselves that the contrast was not by any means so striking and glaring eighty years ago as it is to-day. The population of the country, far less in its aggregate then than now, was much more evenly distributed. It was not agglomerated and concentrated in what we call "the great centres." The system of domestic manufacture had not died out, though it was declining, and the whirr of the spinning-wheel and the rattle of the frame could still be heard as you passed along the village street. Towns were more rural and villages more town-like than now. The movement to the large towns had begun but it had not yet become a rush, leaving the villages depleted and depressed. Towns had not yet fully entered upon that process of abnormal growth which statistics register—a growth so rapid that even the middle-aged man who spent his boyhood in any of these great centres, when he revisits it after

THE PERIOD OF CIRCUIT PREDOMINANCE AND ENTERPRISE.

the lapse of years, almost fails to recognise the once familiar spots. If we take the towns in which we are now specially interested—Nottingham and Leicester—we see that eighty years have had the effect of intensifying the contrast between town village. In 1801, the population of Nottingham was 28,801, and that of Leic 17,005; in 1881 it stood at 186,575 for Nottingham and 122,251 for Leicester. even in the first decades of the nineteenth century the words "town" and "cou represented strongly marked differences other than that of comparative densi population. Amongst these differences those that related to religion were perhap most observable. Towns such as Leicester and Northampton, Bristol and Bath, the strongholds of evangelical piety, both within and without the fold of the Esta ment. This evangelicalism was very orthodox, very respectable, very correct, ambi to preserve the proper tone, and quite disposed, in keeping with the spirit bequea from the preceding century, to resent the introduction within its borders of a for Christianity that was fervid and demonstrative and unconventional in character, like our fathers believed in and practised. Now Mr. Herod, in seeming to explain John Ben "reluctance" to enter Leicester, tells us that a Methodist preacher had informed B "that he would be taken up if he made an attempt to preach there." We do not

LEICESTER ABOUT 1800.

an intimation such as this of what awaited him, would at all have discomposed hi acted as a deterrent had he really wanted to enter Leicester. Of mob-violence or per tion veiling itself under legal forms he would have said: "None of these things move But the avowed thorough-going opposition of those who are utterly different ourselves does not gall us half so much as the sneers and censure of those with v we are in general agreement and sympathy. So when the Methodist minister we further to tell Benton how in several stationers' windows in Leicester there exhibited a caricature of himself "in the act of preaching, with a red handker tied round his head, while a multitude of people surrounded him and stared in the face"—we are not so certain that he would preserve the same equani "Boanerges" Benton was not the typical Revivalist preacher of some novelists v we see pictured as a man with lungs of leather and forehead of brass, and no nerv manners to speak of. Unless we are very much mistaken, he knew his limitations was sensitive to his own defects. We think we see indications that he had a m

His work. He knew he was not learned, and that foolish caricature in the Leicester stationers' windows would suggest to him that he had not only to reckon with the open opposition of the ungodly, but with the disfavour of the truly pious and orthodox, who did not want him and his irregularities in Leicester, and would let him know that he was not wanted. What Benton divined, was really in the minds of sincere but prejudiced men, and the prejudice was allowed to distil in speech, and to drop from their pens. It was in Leicester, some time after this, that the Rev. Daniel Isaac, "the Polemic divine," wrote from Leicester in a letter to a friend: "The Ranters have bawled themselves out of breath in this neighbourhood, and I think are losing ground. . . . . They have chanted till the people take no more notice of their noise than the Quaker's stillness." *

RUSSELL SQUARE AND THE LOWER END OF WHARF STREET, WHERE OPEN-AIR SERVICES WERE HELD.

Whether facts and considerations like the foregoing help to explain Benton's personal "reluctance" to enter Leicester, while he continued to hang on its skirts and to mission the villages in its neighbourhood, we shall, of course, never know. But whether they do or do not, such considerations, personal to Benton, do not touch or explain that deeper denominational reluctance to fasten and concentrate its strength on the chief towns which marks the course taken by Primitive Methodism in the early years—a reluctance that was the outcome of habit and of preference, if not of deliberate policy. The explanation of this is what we want to see a little further into if we can. We have glanced at the towns regarded in their religious aspect; what of the villages of the same period?

We have seen that, relatively, the villages were of far greater importance eighty years ago than they are to-day. That fact does in itself go some way towards explaining and justifying the amount of attention bestowed on their evangelisation. But absolutely, and not merely relatively, their need was greater than that of the towns; for they had been too much neglected by existing religious agencies. Here and there, especially in the manufacturing villages of the West Riding and other districts, and in East Anglia, the older Nonconformity might be represented; but in how many hundreds of villages and hamlets throughout the country was there no Baptist or Congregational Church to be seen. The evangelical clergy of light and leading were mainly in the towns. The Church, as by law established, did little for the people of the villages. The Oxford movement was still in the future. It had not yet pervaded the land, planting in almost every village a hard-working clergyman resolutely bent on outworking and outgiving Dissent. Instead of an aggressive, resourceful, ever-active Anglo-Catholicism, there was absenteeism, or the indifference, incompetence, or worse, of those who had 'the cure of souls.' True, numerous Methodist societies kept piety alive, but even many of these societies had lost somewhat of the old fervour and aggressive spirit, and had not yet gained the new evangelic and evangelistic fervour. The spiritual need of the villages was great. A rousing out-door evangelism was called for. The need of the villages was our Church's opportunity, of which it was not slow to avail itself, and the effort to supply the need coincided entirely with the desires, the training, the habits, and the special qualifications of our missionaries, who, with scarce an exception, were village-born and village-bred.

Let us recall the history of Primitive Methodism so far as we have come, and it will be admitted that the narrative given, unless it altogether belie the facts, bears out the view that Primitive Methodism put its chief strength into village work, and had its reward in so doing. The tide of village evangelisation never reached a higher point in the districts with which we have been, and shall for some time be, concerned, than in these years. Since then, indeed, the wave has somewhat receded. There were villages and hamlets missioned in these years, and had societies established in them, which were afterwards abandoned. Does any one point to Derby and Nottingham to prove that the towns were not neglected? True, but these examples of successful work in the towns does not invalidate the statement that our Church did, by choice and preference, put its main strength into the work then most urgently needed—the work of village evangelisation.

The Entry into Leicester

John Benton's reluctance to enter Leicester yielded at last under the force of the assurance that some, at any rate, of the good people of Leicester were anxious that the Primitives should mission the town, and had preferred their request at the service recently held at Syston. Whether John Benton had been specially asked for or not we do not know, but he was evidently regarded as the best man available for undertaking this important business. Arrangements were accordingly made for the attempt to be made on Sunday, March 1st, 1818, which arrangements became matter of common rumour in Leicester itself and the neighbourhood. Even in taverns and other places where men congregated and gossiped, the forthcoming invasion was freely discussed, and opinions condemnatory and otherwise of the Ranters and their proceedings frankly expressed. In proof of this, we are told that on the eve of this Sabbath, William Goodrich was at the 'Pied Bull' public-house, and heard the news there. As this is the occasion of our first meeting with a man who afterwards became of note in Leicester Primitive Methodism, and who left his impress on our early literature, and made himself felt   may not be out of place. But what doest thou here, William Goodrich, in the sanded parlour of the "Pied Bull"? we may well ask; for we are told that his father had been for many years a faithful and acceptable Wesleyan local preacher, and his mother was now a sainted spirit; and yet, despite all this, that surely should have given advantage to virtue and prepared the way for grace, he had become a constant frequenter of this same tavern called the "Pied Bull," and much admired there for his open-handedness, his sprightly talk and convivial turn. As he was sitting there on this particular Saturday night, his attention was arrested by a heated discussion two other habitués of the place were carrying on respecting the merits and demerits of some strange people called "Ranters," who had recently visited Syston and Ratby. He learned that they visited the villages, singing lively hymns, preaching sermons in the open-air, and that they drew much people after them; furthermore, he learned that they were due at Leicester on the morrow, and his curiosity was greatly stirred to know more about these exciting and excitable people. He remarks:—

"I began to inquire into the lives and doctrines of these men, and I soon learnt enough of them to induce me to interpose a word or two in their favour."

Then comes a passage which curiously reminds one of a certain maid's recognition of Peter by the light of the fire, and who, looking stedfastly upon him, said, "This man also was with Him." But he denied, saying, "Woman, I know Him not." So, when William Goodrich spoke up for the miscalled people,—

"The landlady turned and looked at me in a peculiarly striking manner, exclaiming: 'And you, Goodrich, will be a Ranter, too, directly!' This I denied with all my power, but my heart said a different thing."[*]

BELGRAVE GATE AND THE OLD CROSS AS IT IS TO-DAY.

According to report, and in keeping with the arrangements made, John Benton entered Leicester on the following day, being Sunday, and with him came a goodly number of persons from Thurmaston, Syston and the adjacent villages. They came, we are told, along the Melton-Mowbray turnpike, singing as they came:—"Turn to the

[*] Quoted in the Memoir of Mr. W. Goodrich by Rev. Robert Parks: "Primitive Methodist Magazine," 1874, p. 4.

Lord and seek salvation." Now, just here, unfortunately, authorities differ in their statements as to the precise spot chosen by Benton for opening his commission in Leicester. But William Goodrich, who was there, says—and the Leicester tradition accords with his view—that Benton and his host made for the old Roman Cross in Belgrave Gate.* Floating traditions blend with sober records in giving us a vivid impression of the excitement the advent of the Primitives created in Leicester that day. The news spread like wildfire—"The 'Ranters' have come!" From all points the people came pouring into Belgrave Gate. At one time, Herod tells us, Benton was carried off his feet by the surging crowd. In their excitement men did strange things. One ran out half-shaved to see what was to be seen. Another man, named Farmer, climbed a lamp-post to watch the proceedings, and was pierced to the heart and came down "a new man." He was a moulder, and shortly after his conversion a mighty work of God broke out in the foundry, and many of its workmen were brought to the Saviour. All accounts agree that Benton's sermon on "Let me die the death of the righteous, and let my last end be like his," was one of marvellous power, they are at one, too, in noticing admiringly the rare quality of Benton's voice. It was "stentorian," "ringing," "clear as a clarion, and carrying far." Tradition hints that there was an attempt at opposition—one man beating a drum for the purpose of drowning the preacher's voice, but he might have been Benton's own drummer beating the "assembly," for the only effect of his drum-beating was to assist in making the congregation still larger. Meanwhile, as Benton lifted up his voice like a trumpet William Goodrich stood there—an islanded soul—in that vast crowd. After he left the "Pied Bull" he had passed a troubled night, tempered however with resolves to begin to lead a better life. As he stood there in the gutter, heedless alike of the crowd and of the falling rain, "the great transaction" was effected within his soul.

This notable service was literally the "opening" of Leicester so far as Primitive Methodism was concerned. From that time it was as though the Lord had said "Behold, I have set before thee a door opened, which none can shut." Leicester would now be regarded as belonging to the Loughborough Circuit, and although the plan for May–July was issued in the April number of the quarterly Magazine, too early to admit of Leicester's appearing thereon, yet arrangements would meanwhile be made for supplying it with preachers resident in the neighbourhood; and soon and frequently the leading missionaries would pay their visits. These visits were looked forward to with high anticipations, and were made the subject of prayer by the new converts, so that we are not surprised to learn that the labours of the missionaries told mightily for good in the town. Leicester duly appears on the next plan—that of August–October

---

* The main authorities for this site are Memoir of William Goodrich, 'Primitive Methodist Magazine,' 1871. Herod's 'Sketches,' p. 298; Petty's 'History,' p. 75 (who cites Rev. J. Brownson is his authority) and Mr. Thomas Lawrence's 'Primitive Methodism in Leicester,' p. 5. Other authorities amongst which may be named that of Rev. C. H. Boden, name Coal Hill where the memorial Clock Tower now stands, as the site of this first service, and instead of "an adjoining lamp-post," they make Farmer climb the town pump. As the two sites are separated by no great distance, the question is not of much practical importance, especially as those who differ in their opinions as [illegible]

The name is found twice over at the very bottom of the plan, without reference to building or street, from which we infer that as yet two public open-air services were held simultaneously in convenient places; while prayer meetings and class meetings would be held in the houses of friends or adherents. Amongst these regular and occasional open-air preaching stations were Belgrave Gate Cross, Orchard Street, Foundry Square, Frog Island, West Bridge, Russell Square, Coal Hill, Old Haymarket, Turner Street, &c

Owing to the regrettable absence of dates, the chronology of the visits of Wedgwood and Clowes to Leicester is difficult to trace; but it is clear that Wedgwood soon followed Benton. His first service is said to have been held in Foundry Square, near the door of Mr. Bennett, who is described as "a gardener and Sunday salesman." But such a description soon became inappropriate, for he ceased to be a Sunday trader; his house became a rendezvous for the young converts; here the first class was formed, of which W. Goodrich

FOUNDRY SQUARE, FROM BELGRAVE GATE.

FOUNDRY SQUARE, FROM ARCHDEACON LANE.
Showing a part of St. Mark's Church.

was one of the earliest members, and Mr. Bennett and his wife "got that good which they never lost."

William Clowes, as we know, made a missionary tour into Leicestershire in 1818, although his account of this mission found in the *Journal* is strangely mixed with

THE OLD HAY MARKET.
The open space is where the Primitives used to hold meetings.

1818.	August.	Sept.	Oct.	Preachers.
Places.	2 9 16 23 30	6 13 20 27	4 11 18 25	4. R. Weston
				5. J. Wedgwood
Leicester 10½ and 6	...	13 18 4 13T 4	18 13 4 18	13 4 18 13	13. R. Culley
				14. J. Skevington
Leicester 2 and 6	...	26 24 21 14	26 19 14 24	26 17 5	17. G. Hanford
				18. J. Rue
				19. T. King
				24. R. Bent
				26. C. Villiers

LEICESTER'S FIRST APPEARANCE AT THE BOTTOM OF THE PLAN
AUGUST 16TH, 1818.

the account of his visit into Nottinghamshire paid the previous year. Clowes' first experience of Leicester and its people, as recorded in the *Journal*, must have occurred before the end of April, and after the first visit of Wedgwood just referred to.* Once more, as our quotation shows, we find the two labouring conjointly, and once more, curiously enough, Wedgwood, overwrought, wants to lie down while Clowes will go on — †

"On Sunday we proceeded to hold a camp meeting at Croxton Lane Ends, near Barsby, here the Word of the Lord prevailed, and many experienced the converting power. From this place we went onwards to Leicester the same evening. As we went through the villages thither, we sang the high praises of our God, the people flocked after us, and appeared moved with astonishment. When we arrived in Leicester we were very weary, and it was very late at night. In the morning, however, we marched forth and hoisted the gospel standard in Belgrave Gate. It was supposed that about two thousand people gathered themselves together on this occasion. We both preached. Wedgwood from Job xvii. 21, and I from Rev. iii. 20. Just as I was rising to address the congregation, a person whispered in my ear that an alderman and one of the magistrates were present, but I did not feel any fear on that account. I felt my soul impressed with a consciousness of higher powers—the value of immortal souls, and the necessity which lay on me to cry aloud and spare not, regardless of the trifling distinctions of earthly rank and power. The multitude on this occasion were exceedingly well-behaved; a deep solemnity reigned over the meeting, and all was still and quiet as if we had been in a chapel. [Be it noted—one Mr. Richard Woolhouse, of Hull, was one of Mr. Clowes' hearers at Belgrave Gate.] We terminated our proceedings about twelve o'clock, and at half-past one we held a prayer meeting in Orchard Street, in a friend's house. The gathering together again was very numerous. Vast numbers stood on the outside, many were powerfully affected, and cried for pardoning mercy, and their cries were not in vain. It was supposed that about twenty souls found the Lord and rejoiced in sins forgiven; the prayer meeting continued till six o'clock in the evening. When I came out of the house I found my clothes were as wet as thatch on a very rainy day. After partaking of a cup of tea we set out and walked seven miles to Sileby. We felt ourselves so much exhausted on the way that Wedgwood was inclined to lie down in a meadow, but I opposed this, as we should have endangered our lives by such a course. After a good night's rest and breakfast we departed from Sileby, to walk a distance of seventeen miles; we then took leave of each other, that we might preach at different places."—*Journal*, pp. 139-140.

We get one other glimpse of Clowes at Leicester during this same spring of 1818, for William Goodrich speaks of Clowes' preaching in Orchard Street in the evening, and Mary Hawksley in the morning of the same day. Orchard Street figures a good deal during the beginnings of Primitive Methodism in Leicester. In that street Wedgwood

* Our data for this conclusion are these. Hood speaks of Clowes' Leicestershire mission as a fortnight's one. Probably it occupied a little longer time than that. At the end of the mission he called at several places in Derbyshire and preached. He mentions, too, the visit he paid to the widow of Samuel Simcock, who was then near death. Hugh Bourne hears of her death on May 3rd

† See *ante*, p.

usually stayed when in the town at the house of Mr. John Cross, to whom spiritually he had been of service. In Orchard Street, too, were three other adherents of the new cause—Messrs. Pool, Markham, and Andrews—whose houses were thrown open for the holding of prayer meetings. The first two became leaders of the second and third society classes, which met in their respective houses, while the last-named is described as "an eccentric character, but a sterling jewel, who lost his status as a Wesleyan in consequence of breaking out into bursts of praise during the time of service." *

John Harrison spent close upon two months on what may be called the Leicestershire Mission—from May 3rd to June 20th—and from his *Journals* we get a vivid view of the eager crowds that followed the missionaries, and hung on their words "like a bee upon a jessamine flower." We cannot condense without defeating our own object, which is to see the crowds as the writer saw them, and to breathe the very atmosphere of this time of refreshing and Revival, when men's sorely-tried souls were stirred by a new hope. As we read, let us try to take in what is said of the mere bulk and numerical strength of the crowds he everywhere met with in this town of but moderate size, as we must reckon it to have been, judged by present standards of populousness. Unless John Harrison wilfully exaggerated, or we have to credit him with a fatal incompetence to estimate numbers, we can come to only one conclusion: that the congregations were quite extraordinary, and that the people must have been hungering for the gospel.

WYMESWOLD CHAPEL.

"*May 7th.*—I preached at Wymeswold, in the street, without much opposition. *May 8th.*—I came to Leicester. . . When I entered the town an influence and thoughts similar to Jonah's came, and I felt as if I should like to take shipping and go to Tarshish. But in the midst of my difficulties and temptations the promises supported me—'In Me is thy help': 'Lo I am with you alway, even to the end of the world.' . . . I preached at half-past ten on the next morning in Orchard Street, and stood on a table for a pulpit in the middle of the congregation, which consisted of several thousand souls. I never preached to such a number that behaved with such seriousness. At half-past two in the afternoon I was in the open-air in Horsepool Street, and was favoured with a table for my stand. It was computed that I had not less than five thousand of a congregation to hear the Word of Life, although two of our brethren were preaching in other parts of the town. The people gave great heed to the Word, and many scores are seeking the Lord. I gave it out that I should preach in Frog Island at six o'clock in the evening; and I was again favoured with a table for

* Letter of William Goodrich quoted in Ridgeon's *Life of W....*

a pulpit. When I ascended it, and took a view of my congregation, I was like Moses—'I did exceedingly fear and quake' for the number of hearers appeared to have doubled. I preached with great liberty, and the Lord was present and precious. It was said that not less than eight thousand were present. *Monday 10th.*—I preached near the West Bridge to the largest congregation I ever had. There were many deeply wrought on by the Word and Spirit. When I had concluded, a woman came to me weeping, and gave me a very pressing invitation to go and preach where she resided, which was fourteen miles from Leicester. She said, 'Do come, for we are all sinners.' I told her that was just the class of persons our Lord came to seek and save. *On Tuesday, the 11th,* we held a prayer meeting at one of the friend's houses, when the Lord was pleased to pour His Spirit out, and many souls found peace. In the evening a stranger was expected to preach, but I had my fears he would not come, and that I should have to preach. However, a little before the time a female from Derbyshire came, and we entreated her to take up the appointment. She complied with the request and I never before heard her speak with so much liberty and power."

John Harrison was bashful even before his own *Journal* therefore he does not tell us that the "female from Derbyshire" was none other than Sarah Kirkland, who, in less than two months, will become his wedded wife and "a help meet for him!" Her, too, still bearing the old name, we welcome this way: glad to know that she bore her part in the Leicestershire as she did in the Nottinghamshire Revival.

It will doubtless have struck the reader, as it strikes the writer very forcibly in the retrospect, that we have heard and seen very little of persecution while we have been in Leicestershire. True, we heard something like the beating of a drum while Benton was proclaiming the Gospel at the Cross in Belgrave Gate, and we have met with allusions in contemporary *Journals* to "mild stone-throwing," which we take to mean that stones were sometimes thrown that never seemed to hit any one. We remember, too, the occasion when "the clergyman, the lawyer, and the gentleman" set out with the intention of intimidating George Hanford, and retired feeling that they had not persecuted him so much as he had coerced them. The fact is, there was no persecution experienced in Leicestershire worth speaking of. One swallow does not make a summer, nor one snow-flake a snow-storm; neither does a solitary instance or two of horse-play or outbreak of spite, or bad manners such as the attempt of the post-boy or farmer (probably bemused with drink) to drive his horses through a quiet, out-door congregation —warrant us to write of the persecution met with by the Primitives in Leicestershire in 1818. A chapter under this heading would be as short as the famous chapter on snakes in Ireland.—"There are no snakes in Ireland." And thus far there was very little persecution in Leicestershire. How does this absence of the persecuting spirit from Leicestershire contrast with what we saw in Rutland and in parts of Nottingham and Lincoln, where it was continually manifesting itself in the most diversified ways! The fact is creditable to the county and to be borne in mind. But as yet the full significance of the fact cannot be dwelt upon; nor are we at present yet prepared to attempt an explanation of this extraordinary difference in the treatment of our pioneer missionaries by neighbouring counties. That explanation must await the ac..how it will fare with the propagandists of Primitive Methodism in other parts. We will only again hazard the opinion that in a very true sense Persecution is "racy of the soil"; that, in proportion as men are tied to the soil which is not their own freehold, there are the conditions most likely to be found favourable to the propagation of the persecuting spirit.

But while persecution as ordinarily and quite properly understood was rarely experienced by our pioneers in Leicestershire, they were not unacquainted with it as manifested in less tangible and more subtle forms. They could not and did not escape the reproach of the Cross or the usual fate of those who turn aside from beaten paths. There is much to be met with in life that is not called persecution that is intrinsically of the same character, because it is designed to punish—"to let a man know," "to make him feel"—to deter or to coerce. It can manifest itself in numberless small but unmistakable ways—in the supercilious look; in the voice touched with scorn; even in the curl of the lip, or uplifted eyebrow. We see it in the disgust shown by the tepid soul on any display of enthusiasm; in the displeasure visited upon those who dare to violate some of the smaller conventions whether of social or religious life.

It was probably the dim perception that he would be leaving the more congenial atmosphere of village-life and be exposing himself to persecution of this unsubstantial bodiless kind which, as we have seen, made Benton reluctant to enter Leicester. Probably there were persecutors in grain of this kind in the county capital, and he was surely one of them to whom incidentally we owe that vindication of our people and of our work by Robert Hall, that broad-minded Christian man and prince of preachers—which vindication has become almost a classical piece amongst us and cannot be omitted from this history.

ROBERT HALL.

Robert Hall was at the time Benton entered Leicester the minister of Harvey Lane Chapel, to which people from all parts of the country found their way, breaking their journey here and travelling by a subsequent coach in order that they might avail themselves of the opportunity of hearing this eminent divine. Robert Hall, we are told, was on his way to a village where he occasionally preached on a week evening just at the time Benton was preaching in the open-air. He stopped and for a time listened attentively to the preacher, whose zeal he admired as well as the command he evidently had over his congregation. The rest of the story shall be told in the words of George Herod:—

"An individual who had a taste for decorum, felt himself annoyed with street preaching, and said to Mr. Hall:—

"'What do you think of the "Ranters," sir? Don't you think they ought to be put down?'

"'I don't know enough of their conduct to say that,' was the reply. 'What do they do? Do they inculcate antinomianism or do they exhibit immorality in their lives?'

"'Not that I know of, but they fall into very irregular practices.'

"'Indeed! What practices?'

"'Why, sir, when they enter a village, they begin to sing hymns, and they go on singing until they collect a number of people about them, on the village green, or in some neighbouring field, and then they preach.'

'Well, whether that may be *prudent* or *expedient*, or not, depends upon circumstances, but as yet, I see no criminality.'

"'But you *must* admit, Mr Hall, that it is very *irregular*.'

'And suppose I do admit that, what follows? Was not our Lord's rebuking the Scribes and Pharisees, and driving the buyers and sellers out of the temple, *very irregular*? Was not the course of the apostles and Stephen and of many of the evangelists very irregular? Were not the proceedings of Calvin, Luther and their fellow-workers in the Reformation very irregular—a complete and shocking innovation upon all the quiescent doings of the Papists? And were not the whole lives of Whitefield and Wesley very irregular lives, as you view such things? Yet, how infinitely is the world indebted to all these! No, sir, there must be something widely different from mere irregularity before I condemn.'"

This dialogue shows us Robert Hall in a very favourable light. We see a man, highly placed and richly endowed, honestly striving to gain an understanding of the times in order that he may "know what Israel ought to do." At the outset, when confronted with novel methods of evangelisation, he is studious to keep his mind dispassionate and free from prejudice. He will not prejudge the case, or condemn hastily, without the due weighing of evidence. God and time will show. While he thus puts in a plea for suspension of judgment, he is not prepared on summons to pronounce off-hand that this work is of God, and these men the servants of the Most High. Yet he hopes that it may be so, and he will not be surprised if the event should prove that God is in both the men and their work; for then this much-discussed movement would be seen to be quite in line with other so-called "irregular" movements of the past that were condemned of men but owned of God.

In all this, Robert Hall offers a striking contrast with his fellow-citizen and ministerial neighbour, Rev. Daniel Isaac, who was resident in Leicester from 1820 to 1822. What strikes us the most in Daniel Isaac's phillipic against Primitive Methodism is not the splenetic character or bad taste of the outburst, so much as the confused, and one might say, cross-eyed view taken of the progress of the body in his neighbourhood. He says and unsays at the same time and of the same thing. He casts a slur upon camp meetings ("the Ranters have bawled themselves hoarse"), and then immediately goes on to reflect on the wisdom of the Primitives in suffering their zeal for camp meetings to slacken—"They have got chapels, and are neglecting field preaching. *We mean to take it up.*" Here the writer, who begins with a fling at camp meetings, ends by allowing their usefulness, and by preparing us for the historical fact that within a dozen years after the Wesleyan Conference had pronounced against camp meetings, the practice of holding them had been introduced in various parts of the Wesleyan Connexion; so that Hugh Bourne could say as early as July, 1818 * "The utility of camp meetings has so fully appeared to the wise and good, that our respected friends of the old Methodist Connexion have begun to hold them in Nottinghamshire and in Leicestershire." Furthermore, Hugh Bourne states "It is understood that in 1820 their Conference adopted such meetings, only requiring them to be called by a different name."* So that the Conference of 1820 blessed what the Conference of 1807 had banned. It could scarcely be expected that Daniel Isaac would look upon the movements of Primitive Methodism with the same unbiassed mind as his great townsman—Robert Hall. Nor did he. Yet we are glad to find him a convert to the belief in the utility of camp meetings.

Robert Hall convinced himself that the Primitives did not deserve to be "put down," but rather helped on. He removed to Bristol in 1826, but so long as he remained in Leicester he continued to be their vindicator, and on one occasion at least showed his kindliness in a practical way by lending his church for the preaching of a funeral sermon by one of our missionaries; he himself attended the service, and expressed his satisfaction with the sermon he heard.

As for the other interlocutor in the dialogue we have given, he is of no importance whatever, except as he was one of a type, a representative "man in the pew," one of the many who professed to be shocked at the "irregularities" practised by our fathers, and who half frightened, half angry, put their question. "*Don't you think they ought to be put down?*" We wonder how many of our readers know that the question here so timidly put was in 1820 proposed in good earnest to a noble lord, high in office, by a Lincolnshire clergyman. He wrote a letter to the noble lord, in which the latter was adjured by all that was sacred to put down the "vociferating Ranters' and their pestilent and seditious camp meetings. This remarkable open letter was printed in the *Christian Remembrancer*, and in the columns of the same Christian publication there appeared a communication from another writer, who observed —

"That as far as private influence could interfere, it has been exerted on some occasions to prevent their assemblies (*i.e.*, the camp meetings), but it is surely desirable that the *authority of Government* also should in some way interfere to prevent the degradation and debasement of that holy religion, which is so essential to the present and future welfare of the nation." He would welcome any restraints "which would defend pure and undefiled religion from the injuries it sustains by the rude assaults of enthusiasm and fanaticism'

But let us turn from those who merely looked on the Revival—it may be with doubt, or apprehension, or hostility—to glance again for a moment at the Revival itself, and at those who were in the midst of it. We can form some idea of the rapid growth of the Church at Leicester under these revival conditions, from what William Goodrich tells us of the society classes. Members were added in such numbers that soon it became difficult to find experienced leaders. Where were officers to be found for all these volunteers of the rank-and-file continually pouring in? At one time William Goodrich was the leader of four society classes, the combined strength of which was 297. One of these had belonged to Mr Pool, who on account of failing health was obliged to lay down the leadership. When Mr Goodrich took over this class there

* "History of the Primitive Methodist Connexion," 1823, footnote p. 19.

were one hundred and seventeen members on its roll. But we cease to be surprised at the numerical strength of these classes when we are told that, at one service, twelve or thirteen persons experienced the forgiveness of sin, and at once joined the class.

All those with whose names and doings we have got to be familiar have by this time been at work in Leicester. Besides Benton, Clowes, S. Kirkland, M. Hawksley, Harrison, and Wedgwood, who laboured much in Leicestershire in 1818, and whose converts, we are glad to learn, are almost invariably distinguished for their seriousness and steadfastness, we must, in addition, mention Robert Winfield, ' whose appearance was singular, and his preaching peculiar, so that he drew large audiences every night, and the fruit of his ministry was abundant", Richard Weston, too, "Dissenting minister of Ramsor," is much in evidence at Leicester and its vicinity from this time forward, so that one thinks he must either have removed this way or, what is more likely, have become a recognised leading labourer in these parts. He has four appointments at Leicester on the August-October plan. Others who also have appointments are something more than names, as R. Bent, who becomes a hired local preacher, J. Skevington, of Loughborough, a member of the Preparatory Committee, George Hanford, of Sileby, and Thomas King, of Nottingham—two other members of the same committee. Yes, they are all here, sooner or later, and it was meet that Hugh Bourne last of all should come to oversee all, and be as it were the visible 'sign and seal" of the complete establishment of the Leicester Society. One other thing only was wanting to round off the Great Revival and make it ideally complete, and that was that Lorenzo Dow should come and give the Revival his blessing. This, too, did really happen, and what might have seemed a wild chimerical idea became a veritable historical fact. Let us, because of the interest that attaches to the man and his appearance in Notts and Leicester at this time, throw into a paragraph a few rough, rapid notes of our own summarising his movements :—

Dow landed in the Mersey on his third visit to England, July 18th, 1818. Hugh Bourne at once hastened to Stockton Heath to meet his friend. Dow spoke at a camp meeting at Tunstall the next day, and at five o'clock on the morning of the 20th Hugh Bourne had his disagreements with L. Dow, probably because the latter was travelling with Dorothy Ripley the Quakeress, who had 'crossed the Atlantic more than a dozen times to preach to the Indians.' The differences, however, were adjusted, or some working arrangement was hit upon, for we find the trio as remarkable a one as was ever brought together—afterwards closely associated in Nottinghamshire and Leicestershire. Before this, however, be it noted, Hugh Bourne preached the annual sermons of the Tunstall Primitive Methodist Sunday School in the Wesleyan Chapel, 'kindly lent for the occasion.'* Next followed a week or two of labour in Lancashire, and then we find our trio in Nottingham, where each one preached. The same week Dow visited Basford, Hucknall, Bulwell, and Lambley. At the last-mentioned place George Herod met the trio with a vehicle to carry them to East Bridgford. En route Dow preached at Burton Joyce and Gunthorpe from his vehicle. At East Bridgford he preached in the open air. At Bingham, September 13th, he and Dorothy opened the new chapel at Bingham. Thence he left for Leicestershire, visiting Sileby, Ratby, and

Ansty, and on the 16th and 18th September, he took part in camp meetings at Leicester and Barleston. After this he made again for Lancashire and Ireland, to return in the spring of 1819 to America—never to return.'

These notes may have other uses; but they are mainly designed to show that Lorenzo Dow in 1818 *followed the track of the Great Revival*. He in his rapid swallow-flight way goes over the same ground we have gone over, and touches at some of the same places we lingered at. He begins with us at Nottingham and ends at Leicester. As the other preceding workers had poured themselves into this revival movement, so now he who had something to do with the origination of the Staffordshire Camp-meeting Movement also traverses the district where its latest and greatest successes have been won, and gives to it something of the quality of his strange personality.

CHAPTER V.

SOME EARLY CHAPELS AND THEIR STORY, WITH OTHER LEICESTERSHIRE MATTERS.

Dead Lane, Loughborough.

DEAD LANE is a good example of a Primitive Methodist Chapel which must have been a busy centre and of considerable note in its time, and yet is not known even by name to any save the smallest number of Primitive Methodists of the present day. This is easily to be accounted for from the fact that, as a building its career was short. Unlike Canaan Street, Nottingham; West Street, Hull; Bethel, Sheffield; and others that might be named, it was not destined to preserve its identity through change and improvement in form, and privileged to become known as one of the historic chapels of the Connexion. Dead Lane had finished its course by 1837. Could it speak from the grave it might with Jacob say of itself: "Few and evil have the days of my life been and have not attained unto the days of the years of the life" of some favoured structures that yet remain. No contemporary picture of Dead Lane is known; the one appearing on an earlier page of this book * has been put together—created one might even say—from written data, helped out by the recollections of Mr. John Moore, the only member of the Dead Lane society who yet survives, and who at eighty-three years of age can vividly recall the old structure.

"If this be so, why, then," it may be asked, "trouble to resuscitate such a building? Why not let Dead Lane Chapel remain among the dead and gone edifices of the past?" The answer is: Dead Lane was the head of the third circuit of the Connexion—a circuit at one time extending into five counties; it was the first Connexional chapel built in Leicestershire; it was built by one member of the Preparatory Meeting, and four others who attended that meeting were either members or trustees of Dead Lane or circuit officials; the third Conference of 1821 was held within its walls, and several district meetings; Hugh Bourne and the rest of the fathers frequently came here; such ministers as S. Atterby, J. Garner, W. G. Bellham, W. Allcock, T. Sanders, T. King, J. Brownson, J. Tims, ministered from its pulpit; and last, but not least, item in the plea for revived remembrance:—it was the home of such saintly souls as Phœbe Smith and Hannah Taylor, whose piety and good works would consecrate the memory of any building which sheltered them. We think the plea must be sustained, and that Dead Lane must be ranked as one of the historic chapels of the first period of the Connexion.

The site chosen for the new chapel was in a street which got its ill-omened name,

* See ante p. 218.

tradition says, in the time of the great plague, when at first, perhaps, its victims were borne along this way, though in quicker and quicker succession, to the churchyard for burial. The alternative tradition which connects Dead Lane with the former existence of plague pits may date from a later stage of the visitation when such pits were dug here for the wholesale and more expeditious disposal of the dead. In this connection one cannot but think of another Primitive Methodist chapel which also has a mortuary suggestiveness about its name. We refer to St Sepulchre Street, Scarborough, which, despite its name, has persisted in living and flourishing under improved conditions, having, as had Dead Lane, a Friends' Meeting House for its near neighbour.

From Hugh Bourne's *Journals* it is clear that, at the beginning of the year 1818, the new society at Loughborough had no chapel, nor had it acquired one even at the date when it was elevated to the dignity of a circuit-town. Hugh Bourne and John Wedgwood "preach abroad" or "in the street" but meetings are held in "the room," and Hugh Bourne speaks of being at a prayer meeting "in the coach-yard" which probably means a *room in* the coach-yard. This is the state of things prevailing as late as Good Friday, March 20th. But it is clear also from the *Journals* that during this time important business is on foot, and that steps are being taken to supply the need, that must have been keenly felt, of suitable Connexional property to serve as the headquarters of the movement in Leicestershire. Thus, on January 26th, Hugh Bourne records "We had a meeting for consultation. They are young at this business", and, on the 30th, he writes:—"We viewed the intended place of the new chapel at Loughborough."

By the aid of extant documents we are able to supply the facts at the basis of these allusions. Two plots of land, originally belonging to the Earl of Moira, containing altogether 382 square yards, were acquired by William North. On January 18th, he contracted for the consideration of £95 to build—before payment or conveyance—a chapel or meeting-house for the use of the people called Primitive Methodists. The course of procedure adopted in this case may not be one with which we are now familiar, but it was by no means uncommon in the earlier days of chapel enterprise. Sutton Bonington, and other chapels, were acquired in this way.

The William North referred to was one of the famous fifteen of the Nottingham Preparatory Meeting. He was, therefore, no mere outsider employed in this specific work, but one of the most substantial members and officials of the Loughborough Society. The department of Church-work for which he was best fitted, would, we judge, be that of administration, more especially on its financial side; accordingly, for some years his name is found in the circuit books in connection with its business transactions. Unfortunately, we cannot trace his course beyond the year 1834, as the scribes of those days, when they did their work, had no eye to the probable requirements of the historians of these later days.

And now, under the direction of William North, the chapel is nearing completion, and arrangements must be made for its formal opening; and nothing will serve the friends but some one from London shall be brought down for the occasion. This we gather from a most characteristic non-committal entry in Hugh Bourne's *Journals*:—

"*April 26th*. Here [at Loughborough] they have a .... with the

London Primitive Methodists One is to come down and assist to open the chapel Whether this acquaintance be of the Lord or not the event must determine" And on April 29th he writes—"Saw W Jefferson the preacher from London [at Nottingham] At night he spoke'

Of course, the W Jefferson here referred to could not be "the Thomas Binney of Primitive Methodism," for in 1818 he would have been but thirteen years old So it seems we have had two William Jeffersons as well as two William Allcocks and three Thomas Jacksons, and the same number of John Pairotts But the real significance of this entry lies in the quite unexpected evidence it affords of the existence in London at this time of unattached Primitive Methodists So that it appears there was something to show even yet for John Benton's labours in London in 1811

Next came the appointment of trustees for the newly-opened chapel We learn that it was on June 9th the selection of trustees had to be made, for John Harrison records —

Thursday — I came to Loughborough, and preached at night in the chapel My mind was much exercised that we could not have a prayer-meeting after the sermon, on account of a meeting that was called by the leaders and stewards, that the society might choose trustees for the chapel But it is well to pay attention to such things in their season—as saith the apostle—'Let all things be done decently and in order'"

The deed of Dead Lane Chapel, executed 27th May, 1819, supplies us with the names of the trustees chosen on the night John Harrison was present, and lamented the supersession of the invaluable prayer meeting The list has its points of interest, and hence may be given here —

1 Edward Wells
2 Pryor Richardson
3 William North
4 John Benton
5 Joseph Skevington
6 Thomas Attenborough
7 Richard Weston of Ramsor, Dissenting Minister
8 William Wells
9 Benjamin Dawson
10 George Handford

The deed is in some respects peculiar and Declaration of Trusts, all in one It is a deed of Conveyance, a Mortgage Deed, It contains one proviso, which historically possesses most significance for us, as it gives the trustees under certain contingencies the power to sell without having first secured the sanction of any other authority— Conference, of course, as yet there was none But what were these contingencies? Just as the building of the first chapel at Tunstall in the house-form argued a measure of doubt in the minds of the builders as to the perpetuity of the Connexion, so this proviso of the Loughborough Chapel Deed remains to show that the men who signed the deed still felt that all ground for doubt as to the perpetuity of the Connexion had not been removed They evidently did not believe that all the talk about "putting down the 'Ranters'" meant nothing, and that under no conceivable set or combination of circumstances could the wish be realised or the threat made good To us this proviso, drawn up within three months of the drafting of our constitution, and signed by three of the shapers of that constitution, is most illuminative as to what was the condition and apparent prospects of this country in the year 1819—the year to which we have now come. Let the proviso, with all it suggests, now speak for itself:—

"That in case at any time the laws or statutes of the Realm should prohibit the religious worship of the said Primitive Methodists, or the use of the said Meeting House for these purposes, or in case it should appear to the trustees for the time being acting in the exercise of the trusts hereby created that there shall be no occasion for the use of the said Meeting House—then the trustees are empowered to sell."

The time came, unfortunately, when the trustees felt themselves driven to use the powers vested in them, and in 1837 they surrendered the property. This is the unpleasant fact stated in its barest, shortest form. The story is a painful one, but it is a story of misfortune and trial—national and Connexional, as well as local—rather than a story of wrong-doing or incompetence.

When, in 1819, the deed of Dead Lane was executed, there remained a consolidated liability of £250 which John Benton undertook to meet, and he thus became mortgagee. Let it be told to his credit that next to the brothers Bourne, he was in the first years a financial stay and help to the Connexion. He came to the help of Belper Chapel and supplied the means for fitting up the Broad Marsh Room in Nottingham. So now he finances Dead Lane. Meanwhile, and largely as we saw, as the result of the Luddite outbreak of 1816, the prosperity of Loughborough declined. The hopes cherished in the early years of the century that it was destined to become the chief seat of the lace-trade, and a formidable if not successful rival of Nottingham, were not realised. Moreover, Loughborough fully shared in the terrible national reaction which followed on Waterloo. It was not a large town: in 1821 its population was but 7,494. The society at Loughborough came within the chilling influence of this wave of depression. Few in the society were in easy circumstances or able to render anything but insignificant monetary assistance. Yet again, there is no doubt that the industrial depression—national and local—in part synchronised with a Connexional one, for it is one of the outstanding facts of our history that the years 1826-8 formed a crisis for the Connexion; and we have every reason to believe, that in no part of the Connexion was this crisis more deeply felt than in Notts and Leicestershire. Men unaccountably disappear—whether by death or secession we are not told, but "David's seat is empty." William North disappears, even George Hanford disappears, we know not why or whither. Now was the time, if ever, one thinks, to sing the plaintive verses of the old hymn:—

> Where are those we counted leaders
> Filled with zeal and love and truth,
> Old professors tall as cedars,
> Bright examples to our youth?
> 'Some in whom we once delighted,
> We shall meet no more below;
> Some, alas, we fear are blighted
> Scarce a single leaf they show.

The causes of this temporary but general decline will naturally have to be investigated when we have reached a farther stage. At present the fact of this decline is simply stated as it was called to pass. As the result of alterations effected in the fabric some twelve years after erection, and of arrears, the entire indebtedness reached £450. No evidence is forthcoming to show that John Benton, as mortgagee, was any other than considerate; but though successive ministers, and especially Jonathan Tims,* struggled desperately to retrieve the situation, the end came at last; and John Benton was requested to sell the chapel with all speed. This was done and Dead Lane was demolished; but the society, undiminished in numbers, kept together and worked on in lodgings for a few years until, under the superintendency of William Jefferson, in 1848, the present Connexional property in Swan Street was acquired. This takes us into the next period.

Chapels have very varying fortunes. Some seem to be prosperous from the very beginning. The only changes they know are changes for the better. Some have had their little romance of stone or brick; others have had their vicissitudes—it may be their tragedy. The Circuit chest of Loughborough contains the faded-ink reliquiæ of several such stories of struggle and loss besides the one we have told of Dead Lane. Here, for instance, is a resolution relating to Sutton Bonington written in September, 1844, passed at a Quarterly Meeting, of which Robert Parks was the president. Though properly it relates to the next period, it may well be given here, as it could not have been written except at the end of a long and wearisome struggle. The entry comes down to us like a message in the bottle desperate mariners flung out to let it be known that their water-logged vessel is about to go under. All is lost! It is about the most dismal and hopeless resolution we have come across in a Circuit book :

SUTTON BONINGTON PRESENT CHAPEL.

"That the District Committee be informed that it is the opinion of this meeting that every effort which the gigantic machinery of Primitive Methodism can put forth has been brought to bear on Sutton (Bonington)—such as open-air preaching, revival meetings in the street, band meetings, visiting, etc., for the last three or four years; but all has proved ineffectual and abortive."

* Jonathan Tims was called out by the Loughborough Circuit in 1823, and was still further linked to that Circuit by his marriage with Miss Rachel Tacey, whose name will be found in the list of women at the bottom of the 1822 Plan. He has been described as "methodical, industrious, plodding." The mother of John Barfoot was Rachel Tacey's sister.

As a postscript it may be added that since the story of Dead Lane Chapel, as given in the text was written, a farther reference to Loughborough Circuit and its first chapel has come to light. This is valuable as establishing beyond doubt the view as to the earlier date and cause of the formation of the circuit expressed, ante, p. 281. Hugh Bourne notes on the cover of the quarterly Magazine for April 1818: "At Loughborough, in Leicestershire, a chapel has been erected in a central part of the town. Our friends here have experienced a loss of £25. Their chapel was covered, when a strong wind arose and blew it down. The work in Leicestershire has been so strong and rapid, that arrangement ... circuit of which Loughborough is intended to be the head."

And yet this despairing cry was premature. Under the pilotage of Robert Parks the vessel escaped the fate that threatened. Sutton Bonington Chapel, that in 1844 was in such financial straits that its loss seemed imminent, was preserved to the Connexion, and is now debtless. The chapel was built in 1832 under the superintendency of Thomas King, at which time there were thirty members in society.

MARKFIELD.

We turn now to Markfield—an ancient village, as its Saxon name—the Field of the Mark attests—lying seven miles from Leicester, and nine from Loughborough, on the outskirts of Charnwood Forest, and on the edge of the Leicestershire coal-field.

FIRST PREACHING PLACE, MARKFIELD.

When it was first missioned during the Great Revival, and visited by Benton, Wedgwood, and the rest, it was given up to agriculture. Now the adjoining mines and its quarries of syenite, yielding stone in great request for the paving of streets and the macadamising of roads, give employment to a considerable population.

The Primitives were bidden welcome to the house of Mr. Hugh Lauder, who with his wife were amongst the first adherents of the society. Mr. Lauder was a stocking-maker, living in a quaint thatched cottage his own property, which was the preaching place until 1823 or 1824. One of the earliest members of the society was Mrs. Esther Read, whose

Mr. William Read still survives as the oldest member of the Markfield society. Subsequently, services were held in the house of a Mr. Webster until, in the early twenties, a chapel was built, which continued for no long time to be the home of the society. A trustee named Wildbur, we are told, "got hold of the writings," took possession of the building, and turned it into a public-house! So says tradition; and it is certain that the chapel was lost to the Connexion, and perverted to the uses of a licensed house, though it has now been turned into cottages.

Markfield was the home, though it was not the native place, of another Wildbur, who no doubt belonged to the same clan as the appropriating trustee just named. William, of that name, was originally a Wesleyan, and joined our Church in 1818. He was soon taken out to travel by the Nottingham Circuit, and laboured both on the home branch and on the Lincolnshire and Norfolk Missions. Mr. Petty says: "He was a man of feeble powers and of superficial piety." This severe judgment seems fully justified. Herod also tells us he was a man of weak abilities, and was "much in the habit of neglecting his appointments." We might have passed him by without the mention of his name, in harmony with that conception of writing history which studiously avoids reference to those who cannot be named without seeming to reflect on their character. But those who marred, as well as those who made, helped to make the history what it really is. So it was with William

MR. READ.

MARKFIELD OLD CHAPEL; NOW COTTAGES.

Wildbur. He was one of the two alluded to by Hugh Bourne, whose doings and, still more, whose non-doings led to the establishment of the Nottingham Circuit Committee. One good thing Wildbur did was the organisation of a society at Ashby-de-la-Zouch, although it consisted only of some fourteen weeping children. The story is worth telling, both for Wildbur's own sake, and because it also allows us to watch the humble beginnings of Ashby, which became the head of a circuit, formed out of Loughboro

Ashby-de-la-Zouch was first visited by John Harrison and a friend on Saturday, June 16th, 1818. They entered the town singing the usual battle-hymn: "Turn to the Lord," &c., and soon had hundreds of people after them. They had expected arrest, but not a dog moved its tongue against them. The people gave great attention to the Word, and showed the missionaries no little kindness. They left the place as they had entered it, singing the praises of God, and were attended out of the town by more than a hundred people, who could not be persuaded to go back until he had given a promise to come again and preach to them. Evidently acting under instructions, Wildbur visited the place in July, to test whether those who had received good from the occasional visits of the missionaries were willing to form themselves into a society. The account of what took place on this visit, as found in the first volume of the *Magazine*, betrays the hand of Hugh Bourne; and reflects his well-known views with

ASHBY-DE-LA-ZOUCH.

regard to youthful piety, and the practical interest he took in all plans and efforts for laying hold of the young "for Christ and His Church":—

"He spoke much at large on the subject [of joining a society], and showed if there were no prospect of good it would be best to give it up, as there were so many other places which were anxiously waiting for their coming. He put the matter upon issue, saying he should go into a friend's house at hand, and if any came forward to encourage the preaching they would continue to come, if not, they would decline.

"He went into the house, but neither man nor woman followed; in a few minutes a few children came in with tears in their eyes, requesting to be taken into society. The number increased, and fourteen names were at length entered upon a ____ paper. He took the children into ____ and ____ them into a circle round him. It was a truly affecting sight to behold fourteen babes in Christ (and comparatively babes in age), weeping upon their knees, while our Brother Wildbore was bearing them up in prayer before a throne of divine mercy. Some of our friends from Coleorton were present, and in going away they visited a family or two, and showed how necessary it was for grown-up people to start for heaven, since children had started on the heavenly course. Next morning (Monday) Brother Wildbore assembled his little flock in the open air, and, forming them into a circle, he prayed with them. Another affecting melting season took place: adult persons became alarmed for the sake of their immortal interests; the work of God broke out immediately, a numerous society was formed in a short time, and we have the happiness to say, the work still continues to prosper." *Magazine*, March 1819, pp. 70-1.

In 1833, while William Antliff was the superintendent of Ashby Circuit, a chapel costing £450 and seating 250 persons was erected. At that time its membership stood at only twenty-four members; by 1845 it had increased to fifty. In 1842—the end of our period—the membership of the circuit was 510.

The interesting incident thus recorded must be allowed to stand to the credit of W. Wildbur. What remains to be told is by no means so creditable. In 1821, while on the Norfolk Mission, he became dissatisfied with the Nottingham Committee and made a division in the society at Lynn, carrying off with him some seventy members. But he proved himself as incapable of ruling as of obeying, and the secession came to nothing.

"Wildbur" or "Wildbore," as the name is spelled in the extract just given, only thinly disguises "Wildboar," and seeing the change brought about by the Markfield bearer of this name, it was, perhaps, natural enough that tradition should so play upon the name as to remind us of the language in which the Psalmist speaks of the Lord's vineyard as wasted by the boar out of the wood. But probably tradition may have been a little hard on Mr. Wildbur. The facts are obscure, but it is likely enough the chapel was in an embarrassed position and that, on the strength of a proviso similar in character to that in the Dead Lane deed giving the trustees power to sell, Wildbur took over the chapel along with its liabilities. We say the facts are obscure, but they are capable of being so construed: and it is certain that at a circuit-meeting it was concluded not to follow up the chapel case. What is much more difficult to understand is why the society thus put to the street should have been deserted by the authorities. With such men as Thomas King (1830-1) at the head of affairs, there must surely have been some reasons unknown to us for apparently casting the society adrift in this way. Still, the members were not lost to the Church of Christ. The bulk of them, we are told, united themselves with the Arminian or Faith Methodists of Derby—the community which afforded a temporary home to "Dinah Morris" and her husband. In 1844 Markfield was revisited by our people, and in 1842, during the superintendency of Thomas Webb, a new Connexional Chapel was erected for the congregation and the society of forty members.

THOMAS WEBB.

The regulation establishing District Committees was made in 1828; but District Building Committees, as distinct from these, are first provided for in the Conference Minutes of 1835. We judge the propriety of establishing a Committee of such a kind had been forced on the attention of the authorities by various warning examples of recklessness and mismanagement. When what has hitherto very largely been an evangelistic movement, carried on in the open-air or in houses and hired rooms, begins to consolidate itself; when it has to acquire property, and to raise and administer funds for the maintenance and management of such property,—then the time will soon come when the need will be felt for some central, independent, expert authority to oversee this important material side of the united societies' work. From an inspection of the Minute Book of the Nottingham District Building Committee, beginning in 1836, it is quite clear that some of the societies and circuits were, in Hugh Bourne's phrase, very young in the business of chapel-building, and much needed the guiding hand.

MARKFIELD PRESENT CHAPEL.

Occasionally, leave to build would be asked when leave had already been taken; or a proposal would be submitted, satisfactory in most respects, save that it contained not even the most distant allusion to the delicate subject of ways and means. Sometimes, the Committee would be asked to give its sanction to an application to build that gave no information as to the situation, site, or estimated cost of the building proposed to be erected. We are told that in the time of the South Sea Bubble the public were once asked to come forward and liberally to subscribe its capital in favour of "A certain project to be made known afterwards." This was what the Nottingham Building Committee of 1842, composed of T. Morgan, W. Carthy, J. Spencer, J. Barker, and A. Worshop, at one of their sederunts were virtually asked to do; and one can conceive the quiet satisfaction with which its secretary transcribed and dispatched the Committee's answer to this singular application.

324   PRIMITIVE METHODIST CHURCH.

"To the Boston Circuit, October 18th, 1842.

"Dear brethren:—Be so kind as to inform us where you intend building your chapel. You have not informed us whether it is to be on sea or land, in Lincolnshire or Norfolk, &c. Say whether it would not be better to place the pews at the end, one above another with about nine inches' rise on a boarded floor; and say whether one-third of the money cannot be obtained by begging, &c.

"Yours, &c., A. WORSNOP."

The somewhat important items of information lacking in the application from Boston Circuit seem to have been supplied without any great loss of time and to have proved

GEORGE STREET, LEICESTER, WITH GROUP OF OFFICIALS.
FROM AN OLD PHOTO CIRCA 1866.*

satisfactory; for at the next meeting of the Committee, held a week after the preceding, Boston Circuit was informed that sanction was given for the erection of a chapel at Kerton Skeldyke, in Lincolnshire, to be a solid structure and not a floating chapel.

GEORGE STREET, LEICESTER.

Within one year and eight months after John Benton held the first Primitive Methodist service in Leicester, George Street Chapel was opened for worship by James Bourne. The chapel was situated at no great distance from Belgrave Gate Cross, where

* On the back row, beginning from the door—George Hefford is No. 4; William Goodrich, No. 5; Rev. C. H. L

Benton took his stand, and in that thickly-populated quarter where our first missionaries had won their earliest triumphs, so that George Street stood on what Primitive Methodists must ever regard as classic ground. The opening services of that Christmas Day of 1819 marked an achievement and a fresh departure. By dint of toil and God's blessing on faith and prayer, a long-desired object had at last been attained. The services were also in very truth, for the Church, the "opening" into a fuller life and into wider possibilities of usefulness. Right through and beyond this first period of our history, George Street was to be familiarly known in our Zion as the centre of a remarkably live and aggressive Church. On sentimental grounds, perhaps, we may regret that it does not still stand on the same site and bear the old name. True, it may be said to live on in Belgrave Gate Chapel, which is its successor and the inheritor of its traditions, as well as supplying by its name a closer link with the historic first service. All this is so, and yet Belgrave Gate is not the same as George Street, we cannot claim for Belgrave Gate practical identity with the sanctuary that was such a figure in the early days. A community such as ours, which in the short space of some eighty years passed rapidly through all the intermediate stages between a Revival movement and a fully-equipped Church, changed too fast to leave many unchanged buildings on which sentiment can fasten. The structures that satisfied our fathers, that suited their purpose and were such only as they had the means to command, soon became inadequate to enlarged requirements, out of keeping with ampler resources, and objectionable to a developed and more exacting taste. They have been superseded—ruthlessly swept away by the march of improvement. Unlike the older Nonconformist denominations, and yet more unlike the Establishment, we have not, and from the very nature of the case cannot have, many buildings that go back even to our not very remote beginnings—which stand where at first they stood, and have preserved their identity through all the years. That we have few chapels like West Street, Hull, is only the loss of our gain—the negative condition of rapid progress and advance in social influence.

Until the erection of George Street, the main centres of our work in Leicester, we are told, were Orchard Street and a chapel in Millstone Lane, formerly belonging to the Wesleyan Methodists, in which John Wesley occasionally preached. This fact shows that the Wesleyans also have gone the way of Connexional progress before us, and that with them, as with us, out-of-date, disused chapels strew the path traversed. The structures which served them in the beginning were vacated for better ones. Like certain crustaceans, they cast their now too-narrow shell and acquired for themselves one better adapted to their size and growing importance. Sometimes, as at Millstone Street and Hockley, we came along and found temporary accommodation in what they had discarded.

One sentimental advantage, however, the poorer of the Free Churches have over the more opulent ones, or as against the State Establishment. If the Ecclesiastical Commissioners decide to devote part of their revenue to the building of a district church, or a millionaire, out of the abundance of his wealth, decides to do the same— then a church will rise almost "like an exhalation," or as if called up by the wand of a magician.

the counterfoil of the millionaire's cheque-book, or in the transactions of the Board of Commissioners. That church has all its history to make. But it is quite otherwise with the churches built by the poor. They have their history to begin with. Not only has the building its story, but almost every brick or stone could tell its tale. No better example of the truth of this could be supplied from our history, so far as we have yet come, than the building of George Street. If Dead Lane had its tragedy, George Street had its romance; one might even say (thinking also of the companion instance of Belper) its touch of sacred comedy. Our local Connexional historian, who naturally is fully conversant with the traditions centring round old George Street, tells us:—

"Unless the members of our first Society had possessed almost supernatural energy, courage, and faith, they could not have triumphed over their difficulties as they did. . . . . To build the Chapel the members practised much self-denial. Few of the members were in a position to give any but small sums. Perhaps not one member was able to give five pounds in aid of the Building Fund. Many of the bricks were begged. The methods adopted to secure help were certainly ingenious. Instead of letting out the contract as a whole, an arrangement was made with the builder, which enabled the trustees to find much of the material required. When they had enough money to buy a thousand bricks they would visit a brickmaker and place the order, and having bought one thousand they would beg another, so making the bricks come at half-price. In this way, probably all the brick-yards for miles around were visited, and made to contribute some of the material needed to raise the walls."

Who does not know the story of how George Street Chapel got some of its windows? We have seen Hugh Bourne working at the window-frames of the first Tunstall Chapel, and the Belper Primitives drawing timber through the streets for their intended chapel, but at Leicester the time came when their rising chapel wanted windows, and they had neither windows, wood, nor money to supply them. In this dilemma William Goodrich and another put their case before Squire Day, of Thurmaston. He seems to have been a gentleman of a humorous, if not of a roguish turn, and made a proposal which no doubt was intended as an ingenious device for at once saving his pocket and his credit. "There is an ash-tree lying on my farm. You can have that if you like. Only you must yourselves drag it to Leicester." The squire for once had miscalculated. His offer was gladly accepted. Friends were found in the village willing to lend a helping hand. The tree was placed on wheels and dragged to Leicester, some three or four miles distant. But first the tree was made both pulpit and text, for as it lay in front of Squire Day's house, one of the brethren (we presume W. Goodrich) stood upon it and preached from—"And now also the axe is laid unto the root of the trees; every tree, therefore, which bringeth not forth good fruit is hewn down and cast into the fire." The ash-tree was sold to a builder for £7, and the money went towards putting in the windows of George Street Chapel. Mr. Day, we are told, became the mortgagee of the new chapel, ... will.

JOHN THORNTON.
One of the men who drew the tree.

We can form some idea of the burthen of anxiety pressing upon those who were mainly responsible for the erection when we learn that, in addition to monetary anxiety, there was the fear lest the work done during the day should be overthrown in the night by mischievous or unfriendly hands. To guard against this danger, the friends took their turn as night-watchers. Truly George Street was built in troublous times, just as were the second temple and the walls of Jerusalem. One of these volunteer night-watchers was John Briggs, one of the early converts—trophies one

THURMASTON.
The spot on which W. G. preached, from the tree as pulpit.

THE HOUSE AT THURMASTON, WHOSE OWNER GAVE THE TREE.

might even say — of Primitive Methodist agency in Leicester. "From a drivelling, penniless drunkard," says his memoir, "Christianity raised him to the position of a respectable tradesman, and led him in time to the acquisition of considerable property. From being an associate of the vile and abominable, it elevated him to an honourable status in civil society and to important offices in the Church of God." Not only was John Briggs an efficient class-leader and local preacher, but he became widely known throughout the Midlands as a popular temperance advocate. He had a fine play of humour and great readiness of speech, so that his services were in great request, and his round ruddy face, and short portly person, became very familiar and welcome to various congregations and audiences. In 1855 he was elected a permanent member of Conference, but held that position only a short time, dying at Ruddington, near Nottingham, August 5th, 1856. John Briggs serves to link together the two great Midland towns which rightly have had so much of our attention; for, some eight years after his conversion, he removed from Leicester to Nottingham. The infant society at Old Radford found in him an efficient leader; and it was largely owing to John Briggs that the efforts of the society to secure a suitable place of worship were crowned with success. Eight years later he removed to Ruddington, where also "his services greatly conduced to the preservation and extension of our Connexional interests, at a most critical and important crisis in their history in that village."

JOHN BRIGGS.

Let the reader receive a few facts, shortly stated, respecting George Street, gleaned from official documents. The building is stated to have cost £1,500, and to have had on it after completion a debt of £650. The membership, at the time of erection, is given as 500. It is said to have been built during the superintendency of "Mr. Richard Wesson, since deceased." The person evidently referred to is Richard Weston, whom we have already met with several times; and this item is interesting as confirming what was advanced as probable—that even before his name is found on the *Minutes* he was still fully given up to the work. Resuming our inspection of the documents we learn that in 1825 a gallery was erected at the cost of £150. In 1832 two schoolrooms were built at an outlay of £170. In 1838 the chapel roof was raised at a cost of £100. Finally, in 1846, £180 were spent in painting, repairing and flooring the chapel.

Now these facts may appear dry indeed, but if we could only closely question them we might find that these items, relating to the enlargement or improvement of the fabric, would also yield their story. And it would not be difficult to get into the confidence of these items and extract their story. The first item to wit—that relating to the putting in of the gallery would say: Yes: I remember the trustees were in some little difficulty about a loan to meet the expenditure incurred; but one night William Goodrich and some others were called in by a gentleman who was much disturbed by strange noises, in order that they might investigate the matter. They discovered and exposed the ghost, which was no ghost, and the gentleman and his wife, under a feeling of relief tinged with gratitude, very willingly lent the trustees one hundred pounds, to be repaid by instalments. *

WILLIAM GOODRICH.

William Goodrich, who is mentioned in the preceding paragraphs, has many

* See the story with all names fully given, told in the *Magazine* for 1872, p. 748 and *Aldersgate*,

claims on our remembrance. We have seen him at one time a leader of four strong classes; he took an active part in the missionary labours of the Connexion, having, it is said, while so engaged travelled 28,266 miles and delivered 3,163 sermons; he was an intelligent man, well versed in the Scriptures, and a most acceptable local preacher. At the time of his death, which took place November 27th, 1871, with him there passed away the last trustee of the old George Street Chapel. It is also advanced in behalf of W. Goodrich that for a period of some seven or eight months he acted as Editor of the first Primitive Methodist monthly *Magazine*. Let us see how far this claim can be justified.

THE BEGINNINGS OF CONNEXIONAL LITERATURE.

As early as January, 1818, we find Hugh Bourne "planning a small magazine" and busy writing for it. On March 26th he gets an estimate for the printing from J. Tregortha, a Burslem tradesman. There is disappointing delay: it is not until April 16th he receives at Derby 340 copies, instead of the 2,000 he had expected. Next day he distributes the Magazines and receives 800 more. On the 18th he carries three hundred Magazines and some other things seventeen miles to Loughborough. This Magazine is called 'A Methodist Magazine for April 1818. Conducted by the Society of people called Primitive Methodists. To be published quarterly." It was added at the bottom of the title-page: 'Price Twopence, to be sold for ready money only." This, our first Quarterly, consists of twenty-four pages, six of which are taken up with the Circuit Plans for the quarter. From the somewhat long "Introductory Address" with which the Magazine begins, we can form some idea of the purpose sought to be accomplished by the new venture, and the expectations formed of its probable success.

> "A new channel of usefulness is opening: it appears now to be the will of God that our body should enter upon a Magazine. And there is so peculiar an opening of Providence for its commencement, that it may be begun and carried on almost without any additional burden to the Society. It may, at present, be considered simply as an improvement in the mode of publishing the plans, as it will perform the same service, and its circulation and disposal will be the same. A Magazine of this description will be suited to the present state of the body, and if it can be supported, is likely to be useful in every respect.
>
> "This work is intended to be conducted in a regular series of quarterly numbers, and so soon as it shall be large enough to form a handsome volume, a supplement will be published containing an index and a title-page. The numbers may then be bound and will make a very valuable book; and in future times, the early volumes will be valuable indeed, as they will in a great measure show the infant movements of the body, with the rise of camp-meetings and other important matters. Such are the views, and such are the prospects with which this Magazine commences."

Yes, but such were not the views and prospects with which this Magazine ended. The prospectus was one thing, the retrospect quite another. The 'handsome volume' of the quarterly never got itself materialised. The venture was not a success. The Magazine did not pay; and Hugh Bourne, who practically made its appearance far on in July. This contains the plans of the three circuits for the ensuing six months, and on its cover there is an intimation that, although the Magazines for the last quarter have not paid their way, yet "so soon as a proper opening shall appear, and a sufficient number of subscribers shall be obtained, it will be expedient to undertake a Magazine on a larger scale." This looks as though the idea of a threepenny monthly Magazine had already presented itself to Hugh Bourne as something eminently desirable. Yet in the autograph letter reproduced he allows the credit of the suggestion

> Dear friend
>
> At Leicester on thursday Nov. 5th 1818 one of the travelling preachers at Leicester, said that this friends in this circuit want a Magazine at 3 a number to be published monthly. He said the difficulties of circulating it might be easily surmounted, that it was much wanted, and would be a blessing to the people, that it might be begun with a small capital and would bring in income that returns. I said if 500 subscribers could be obtained it might be undertaken. I laid the matter before one of the stewards and he thought it should be spoke to on. We are now getting subscribers and if you think proper it may be well if you do the same among you and direct the places around to do the same and let the names be prepared for Nottingham or Tunstall Q. day
>
> Yours &c
> H. Bourne
> (over)

to "the friends at Leicester, who indeed may well have brought such a proposal before him on some previous visit, to be fructifying in his mind until November"

By means of the *Journals* we are fortunately able to supplement the particulars contained in the letter. R. Culley was the travelling preacher who voiced the desire of the friends at Leicester, and Joseph Skevington was that Loughborough steward who thought "they had acted rightly," and encouraged them to push forward the business. That night Hugh Bourne wrote a letter to Nottingham on the subject—though this one was written to R. Stone of Derby; on the 26th of the same month he and R. Culley secured two hundred and sixteen subscribers for the intended Magazine. Finally, on January 11th, 1819, he put the manuscript of the Magazine and the plans into the hands of the printer. On the Sunday following Hugh Bourne was taken seriously ill, and was removed to Leicester, whence he was taken by his brother James to Bemersley. This illness closed the general superintendency of Hugh Bourne, which had extended over four years, and one of its minor effects was to render it necessary that some competent person should see the first number of the new Magazine through the press and be responsible for the editing of the successive numbers. Who was that person? William Goodrich distinctly affirmed that it was he, and Hugh Bourne states in the preface to the Magazine of 1841 that the first eight numbers were "edited by a person at Leicester." There is no further mention of Robert Culley in connection with the Magazine in which he took so practical an interest. It might be interesting to know why. He is called a travelling preacher, and as on the Loughborough Circuit Plan ending January, 1819, he is planned thirteen Sundays—four of them in Leicester—he deserves the title, and as given by Hugh Bourne, it was strictly correct. R. Culley was a travelling preacher as was R. Weston. After this we cannot trace R. Culley, nor is that surprising if he be the Robert Culley who died at Shelton, near Nottingham, on January 8th, and whose memoir appears in the first volume of the Magazine. From the memoir itself we can glean little concerning its subject. It is one of those factless biographies which tell you nothing, and tantalise you as you read, and finally leave you with a sense of injury and vexation. The most striking thing in the memoir is one of the dying man's own sayings —' I have been lost for two or three days, but found myself in the twenty-third Psalm, verse four, 'Yea, though I walk through the valley of the shadow of death, I will fear no evil, etc.'" If R. Culley had been compelled by sudden illness to relinquish his work and return to his home only to die (and his illness is said to have been of short continuance), then all is clear. With R. Culley gone, who more likely than William Goodrich to undertake the duties of Editor of the new Magazine? He was intelligent, a man of considerable education, a solicitor's clerk, who later in life when he had become less prosperous in his circumstances, frequently wrote letters for those who were poor scribes. We may safely conclude, we think, that W. Goodrich was the man we are in search of. All the internal evidence is accordant with this view. Each number bears the imprint of 'Fowler, High Cross, Leicester.' By far the larger part of the matter relates to this district. On the cover it is advertised that preachers' licences can be obtained from W. Goodrich, Leicester. His editorship does not nullify the fact that Hugh Bourne prepared the first number and that there is much from his pen in subsequent numbers. Still, it must be remembered that this venture was after all a private one. There was as yet no Connexional Magazine or officially appointed editor. There could not well be, for as yet no court existed with the requisite power of appointment.

This Monthly Magazine met with little better success than the Quarterly one. Its publication terminated with the August number; but 1820 came to the help of 1819. At the first Conference Hugh Bourne was appointed editor, and he was desired to complete the first volume. So we have "A Methodist Magazine, published June 1820, intended as a Substitute for September 1819." It consists mainly of a Treatise on Discipline and Minutes of the first Annual Meeting. Two other complementary or substitutionary numbers were issued in August and November—one from a Burslem the other from a Derby press—making vol. I. of our Connexional Magazine which came out to the world under the strange title:—"A Methodist Magazine for the year 1819, conducted by the Camp Meeting Methodists, known by the name of Ranters, called also Primitive Methodists." Thus did the Magazine struggle into existence.

Here it may be convenient to chronicle certain facts of a kindred character relating to the changes made in our humble Connexional organs during this first period. At the beginning of 1825, the Magazine was enlarged by twelve pages, and began to be sold at fourpence. In 1830, its size was changed from a 12mo. to an 8vo., and it became a sixpenny Magazine. In the autumn of 1824, a Children's Penny Magazine was started, which in a few months reached a circulation of between six and seven thousand.

After an interval of some years, a second chapel was acquired for the use of the denomination in Leicester. It was situated in Alexander Street, but because it stood in that ancient district in which, centuries before, the Dominicans, or Black Friars, had established themselves, it was popularly known as "The Friars." The Friars was a building "with a past." Before its completion it was blown down, and when completed it was burdened with debt. The Independent Methodists, to whom it belonged, were not at peace among themselves, and, finding some difficulty in securing a minister to take the place of the one they had asked to resign, the chapel was sold to the Primitives. But the usual ill-luck of the building seemed to follow it after its change of ownership: a temporary gallery justified its character by giving way, though fortunately the accident does not appear to have resulted in loss of life or limb. The importance of Alexander Street did not lie in the character of the building or in the strength and influence of the society; for in 1834, we are told, its members were but forty-three in number and its quarterly income only £3 6s. It was not what it was, but what it gave the promise of becoming, that made the acquisition of the Friars a notable event. It gave the Connexion a foothold in another part of the town, and provided the nucleus which time and change would develop into the powerful Leicester 2nd Circuit. "The Friars" has gone. Like many another building thereabout it has been demolished to make room for the Great Central Railway. Yet associated with it were some good men like William Key, one of its earliest officials, and long and honourably known in connection with Leicester Primitive Methodism. Here, too, Elijah Jennings was early won for

W. KEY.

the Connexion, and began his useful course. That course may more fittingly be traced when we come to deal with a later period of our Connexional history; but however far the stream may have travelled, and however beneficently it may have flowed, it broke out in old Alexander Street.

Leicester, too, had its season of trouble culminating in a secession. Its experience in this respect was curiously parallel to that of Belper, Hucknall, and especially to that of Nottingham, with which it almost synchronised. And yet, perhaps, the parallel was not so curious after all, as the several troubles are distinctly traceable to identical conditions prevailing about this time. Moreover, the conditions were just such as one would naturally expect to find in a rapidly growing community which is seeking to settle down and organise itself. The analogue to all this is found in those subtle physiological changes which explain the crises through which human beings usually reach adolescence. So our Church had its infantile crises. There was morbific matter of which it had to be purged: there were adjustments required to which some could not adapt themselves. The truest word the Rev. Daniel Isaac wrote about Primitive Methodism in 1821 was: "They want discipline." Well; all in good time. They will get what they want at Leicester as they did at Nottingham, only wait a while. George Herod, the strict disciplinarian, was at Leicester 1833-6, and his hand was felt to be too heavy for some who were brought under discipline. A secession of some sixty-five members took place which was known as "the Denmanite split," from the locality of the building which the divisionists made their headquarters. The date is approximately fixed by a resolution of the March Quarterly Meeting of the Loughborough Circuit, 1834: "That we disapprove of any of our preachers going to preach for the divisionists at Leicester or of any of their preachers coming to preach for us." That the discipline administered was wholesome may be inferred from two facts: that some of those who came under it found their way back and became loyal adherents of the cause; and that the disciplinarian himself left seventy-three more members in the Circuit than he had found in 1833 on entering it. George Herod was followed by Thomas Morgan, whose superintendency of three years was marked by vigour and material and numerical success. We do not stay to note what he did in chapel building and improvement, but must point out the significance of the statement that in 1839 "a third society was raised in the town." We judge the reference is to the missioning of the York Street district, and the establishment of a cause there which, in 1841, resulted in the building of York Street Chapel. Four names are closely associated with this forward movement—Messrs. Thomas Stevenson, Thomas Lawrence, Samuel Cheeney, and Mrs. T. Lawrence, the wife of the second-named and the mother of our respected African Missionary Treasurer. Though all were worthy, fuller reference is due to Mrs.

THOS. MORGAN.

THOS. STEVENSON.

us a woman of rare excellence, who by her character and service did much for Leicester Primitive Methodism.* At a time when it meant much to belong to the sect that was "everywhere spoken against," she, when but a girl, united herself with the struggling band worshipping in old Alexander Street, and for more than sixty years she continued loyal to her early choice, dying December 2nd, 1893.

The formation of Leicester Second Circuit in 1852; the building of Curzon Street as an extension or offshoot of George Street in 1860; and the supersession of both Alexander Street and York Street, and the building of Nicholas Street in 1873 by the joint societies, are events which, for the sake of giving a complete view, may well be foreshadowed here, though the history of these movements belongs to a later period.

THE CHARTISTS.

York Street was built in the thick of the Chartist agitation which, like Luddism, had misery as well as political disability at its root. From this bare statement one might rightly infer that Church-work, both on its spiritual and material side, would be carried on under very difficult and discouraging conditions. If any one should wish to know what was the state of things prevailing in Leicester and the neighbouring hosiery towns of Loughborough and Hinckley at this particular time, let him read "Thomas Cooper's Life." Cooper entered Leicester in November, 1840, to take up journalistic work in connection with the "Leicestershire Mercury." In the discharge of his duties as a reporter he was brought into touch with Chartism, and, by force of sympathy with the suffering and oppressed, he was soon drawn within the vortex of the movement. He found broken-spirited men who, after working a whole week, had only as the net result four and sixpence to live upon, so many were "the petty and vexatious grindings" of which they were the victims. He tells us "the poor framework-knitter was worn down till you might have known him by his peculiar air of misery and dejection if you had met him a hundred miles from Leicester." Thomas Cooper became a follower of O'Connor and the recognised leader, and in many cases the succourer, of the starving Chartists of Leicester.

YORK STREET CHAPEL, LEICESTER.

We are concerned with Chartism only so far as it affected Primitive Methodism for good or ill. That it did affect it the traditional account of the origin of the

* See Memoir by Rev. James Pickett, "Aldersgate," 1895, pp. 941-2.

hymn—"The Lion of Judah"—remains to show. That story bears all the marks of authenticity, and it has no point except as it afforded another example of successful tactics in the warfare the Church has to wage—another example of generalship retrieving the drooping fortunes of the day. To us the six points of the Charter may appear innocent enough; so much so that one finds oneself wondering that all the six points together were able to stir men's minds so deeply; and yet when we transport ourselves into the midst of the conditions prevailing in 1840, we shall cease to wonder at the enthusiasm evoked by the Charter. It was put forward as a new gospel, and was proclaimed as the one thing needful for bringing social salvation to the suffering working classes. There was danger lest the Charter should so preoccupy the minds of men that there would be no room for anything else; so excite them that even the supreme concerns of religion would stir but a languid interest. Leicestershire Chartism had its camp meetings, its hymns, its singing processions, and as our ministers saw their congregations distracted and their young people drawn away, it looked as though the Primitives were going to be outdone and beaten by their own weapons. Remember that Thomas Cooper began, as Joseph Barker ended, a Primitive, and we shall the better understand the methods of propagandism he adopted:

MRS. LAWRENCE.

"During the summer of 1842," says Cooper.* "I often led the poor stockingers out into the villages,—sometimes on week-day evenings,—and thus we collected the villagers of Ansty, and Wigston, and Glenn, and Countesthorpe, and Earl Shilton, and Hinckley, and Syston, and Mount Sorrel [all places by this time familiar to us], and inducted them into some knowledge of Chartist principles. One Sunday we devoted entirely to Mount Sorrel, and I and Beadham stood on a pulpit of syenite, and addressed the hundreds that sat around and above us on the stones of a large quarry. It was a *Gwennap*—Wesley's grand Cornish preaching-place on a small scale. Our singing was enthusiastic; and the exhilaration of that Chartist 'camp meeting' was often spoken of afterwards. Now and then, I preached Chartist sermons on Nottingham Forest, where at that time there was another pulpit of rock; but it was seldom I had meetings there, though I liked the place, the open-air, and the people, who were proud of their unenclosed 'Forest'—unenclosed, now, no longer—but thickly built upon.

THOMAS COOPER.

"As the poor Leicester stockingers had so little work, they used to crowd the street, around my shop door, early in the evenings; and I had to devise some way of occupying them. Sometimes I would deliver them a speech; but more generally, on the fine evenings, we used to form a procession of four or five in a rank, and troop through the streets . . . chanting 'The Lion of Freedom,' which began as follows:—

* The "Life of Thomas Cooper," written by himself, 1872, p. 174.

"'The Lion of Freedom is come from his den;
We'll rally around him, again and again;
We'll crown him with laurel, our champion to be;
O'Connor the patriot; for sweet Liberty!'"

It will be seen from this that, under the leadership of Thomas Cooper, the Chartist movement borrowed the tactics of the camp meeting Methodists. The procession that swept the streets chanting "The Lion of Freedom" produced much excitement, which William Jefferson marked with anxious eye. Were the Primitives to be beaten on their own ground and by methods which they had made peculiarly their own? Who was Feargus O'Connor that the streets should ring with his hymned praises? William Jefferson was much exercised in his mind at the look of things, but as he lay one morning mentally canvassing how best to stem and turn to account the prevailing excitement, a happy thought struck him:—he would write a hymn in the same measure as "The Lion of Freedom." The tune could not be beaten but it might be borrowed, as the Israelites borrowed of the Egyptians.* "And it shall," said he, as he sprang from his bed. The hymn was written, and appeared on the plan. It took. The hymn with its well-known refrain was sung in the processionary services, and "The Lion of Judah" was successfully pitted against "The Lion of Freedom"—Christ against Feargus O'Connor.

If Thomas Cooper gained such an ascendency over the pale-faced operatives of Leicester as to be familiarly known amongst them as "the General," an ex-Primitive Methodist travelling preacher acquired similar ascendency over the operatives of Loughborough, and, by virtue of the display of similar qualities. Thomas Cooper and John Skevington were the two most noted and trusted Leicestershire Chartists, and we now refer to the latter because he has received but scant justice, and deserves Connexional rehabilitation. John Skevington was the son of that Joseph Skevington of Loughborough, who was one of the representatives of the third circuit at the Preparatory Meeting. Beginning to preach when in his teens, John was known as "the boy preacher," and would have John Garner as his contemporary on the Loughborough plan. Next, he became a travelling preacher, and in 1822-3-4 travelled

W. JEFFERSON.

JOHN SKEVINGTON.

* Thomas Cooper denied being composer of either words or melody of "The Lion of Freedom." He says "the song first appeared in the columns of the 'Northern Star,' and was understood to be the composition of a Welsh female Chartist. A Leicester working man (Valentine Woolley) first set it to an air (or rather a fragment of the melody of a glee). See letter of Cooper in Appendix to Gammage's "History of the Chartist Movement." So if the Primitives borrowed the tune the Chartists h[...] in The Mission Hymnal

successively at Halifax, Barnsley, and Bradwell. He then ceased "to travel," mainly, perhaps, because his lameness rendered the work of the regular ministry difficult, if not impossible. Obviously, his retirement was not due to any decline of zeal, for, back in his native circuit, he filled the offices of leader and local preacher, and as the books show, his services were in frequent requisition for recording minutes and drafting resolutions of importance for the District Meetings. Unfortunately, however, he was severed from the Connexion in 1836. Into the details of that severance we do not enter, suffice it to say it was led up to by the troubles of Dead Lane—he being trust-treasurer at the time; further, on reviewing all the circumstances of the case, we are bound to say, he ought not to have been allowed to leave. In 1837, the year after his severance, the People's Charter was formulated and adopted, and John Skevington became a convinced Chartist. For years he had been an ardent "friend of the people." "From early life," he says, "I advocated the rights of the many." By his ready command of telling language, his sympathetic nature, and not less, by the sanity of his judgment, he was fitted to be the leader of those of his fellows who were not equally endowed. At election times, we are told, though he had no vote, he would mount the hustings to voice the grievances of the working classes. We say he was a convinced Chartist,—and he was this to the end; for, as he was consciously nearing the verge of life, he wrote :—"As an advocate of the principles of the People's Charter, I found nothing on inspection to condemn in them, nor in my advocacy of the same, but a firm conviction that though a man may be a Chartist and not a Christian, a man cannot be a Christian and not a Chartist unless through ignorance."[*] In 1839 the first great Chartist National Convention was held in London, and the historian of the movement records that "The democrats of Loughborough sent John Skevington, another *veteran* in the Radical cause, to represent them."[†] His enthusiasm in the cause of the Charter, and his personal likings, were shown in his naming his son John Feargus after the idol of the hour. He retained his place in the respect and affections of the men whose cause he championed, for, in 1848, they commissioned Mr. J. Boden (the brother of the Rev. C. H. Boden) to paint his portrait in oils, and this was publicly presented to him by Thomas Cooper.

Yet, though a democrat, John Skevington was no demagogue. He did not pander to those below him, or only astutely follow where he seemed to lead. He was no Physical Force Chartist, but to the end ranged himself on the side of the advocates of Moral Force. He could, and did, withstand those who hankered after swifter and more violent methods of obtaining their rights. In proof of this we are told that, during those tumultuary days, the men came to him and said 'Skevington, only speak the word and we will tear up every stone in the Market Place.' But that word was never spoken.

[*] Where J. S. himself speaks the quotations are from a short MS. account of his views and feelings written when he believed rightly that he had not long to live. The same sentiment is found in an eight-page tract 'A Letter by the Rev. John Dudley, and in Answer by John Skevington,' Leicester 1818.

[†] Gammage 'History of the Chartist Movement, p. 68.

After his severance from the Connexion John Skevington did not unite with any other Church as did his wife and family "Still I revere it," are his words when he writes of the Church in whose ministry he had served. He never drifted into doubt or infidelity as Thomas Cooper did. He never ceased to fear God or forget to pray. Yet, as the years went on, it came home to him that he had lost somewhat the fervour of his first love, that "he had not always served God as earnestly as he had served men." In his MS account, he feelingly quotes Hosea ii 7—' I will go and return to my first husband, for then was it better with me than now." And he *did* return. In the presentiment of death's stealthy approach, he repented of all his shortcomings and earnestly sought and found the Lord, and in his recovered joy shouted—"Glory!" Then *heimweh*—homesickness—came upon him, and he desired to be re-united to the Church of his youth. But alas! his overtures were coldly received. But another Church welcomed him, and he died a happy death January 4th, 1850, aged 49.

Now, looking back upon these transactions of John Skevington's life, one cannot but regret that he was not allowed to retain his status as a local preacher and to die in full communion with that Church he had never ceased to love, and to which he turned at last. Because some one blundered, we refuse to be robbed for all time of our Connexional rights in John Skevington and John Benton. We claim them both. Had the former been living now, it is not difficult to predict the line he would have taken. He would have been on the Town or County Council—it may be the colleague of John Wilson, Thomas Burt (whom also in his own despite, we claim), Charles Fenwick, H R Mansfield—in any case, honoured by his own community as resolutely taking up the duties of Christian citizenship. We look upon John Skevington and Joseph Capper—to be referred to directly—as the first and most striking instances we have so far met with, of men who may, Connexionally, have been a little before their time, but who were only carrying out explicitly those principles of Christian Democracy which from the beginning had been implicit in Primitive Methodism. And this is why we have at some length recalled the story of his life, and tried to vindicate his memory and reclaim him for the Connexion. Primitive Methodism began by being neither avowedly political nor avowedly non-political, but purely evangelistic; but seminally it had in it the life-principle of a democratic Church. If it grew at all it was sure to grow in much the same way as it has grown or else we must conclude that all that it has done for the elevation of the miner and the manumission of the agricultural labourer has been after all of the nature of a sport or misgrowth rather than a natural, legitimate development—which is not to be thought of for a moment. Whether it be an organism or an institution that is in question, what it is can best be ascertained by marking its maturer outgrowth—its efflorescence and fruitage, rather than its foliation. Little wonder, then, that Primitive Methodism should have grown—we speak not of mere size—to be a bigger, more comprehensive thing than was conceived of by our fathers, who saw it only in its beginnings and were not gifted with preternatural insight to divine the Democratic developments that were wrapped up in those beginnings.

If John Skevington was a little before his time, surely that cannot be said of the attitude taken by our senior founder with regard to the political and social movements of the day. He ..... George IV for having signed the

Act of 1812, his nervous desire that the Connexion should keep on friendly terms with the Government lest camp meetings should be put down—these feelings surely culminated and found singular and dramatic expression when Hugh Bourne invaded the Conference Chapel at Tunstall—which happened to be his own—and demanded the expulsion of a delegate on the ground that he was a "speeching Radical." And because Hugh Bourne was master of the situation he had his way. We can easily see *now*, that this act was as irrelevant and futile as the brandishing of Mrs. Partington's mop, or, lest that should seem too undignified a comparison—let us say—as futile as Canute's rebuke at Gainsboro' to the advancing tide.

Who the "speeching Radical" at the Conference of 1821 was, cannot now be ascertained. It could not well be John Skevington, who was then but nineteen years of age. But we are not so sure, after all, whether Hugh Bourne had not a hand in the

"THAT MAN SHALL NOT BE IN THIS CHAPEL."

keeping out of John Skevington. It may be a mere coincidence, or it may be of such significance as to furnish a clue, that the resolution which was Loughborough Circuit's answer to John Skevington's application for redress and reinstatement, was written by Hugh Bourne himself. But why? Well; if in 1838 Skevington was already a "veteran Radical," he must in 1836 have been for some time known as that most objectionable of characters—a "speeching Radical." Hugh Bourne's assured knowledge of this fact, coupled with his well-known views, and his ascendency in Loughborough Circuit's councils, may have been largely responsible for the refusal to open the door for readmission. "The door is shut: it is well; let it remain shut."

Staffordshire, as well as Leicestershire, had its sturdy Primitive Methodist Chartist, whose story by an honoured minister of a sister community who knew Joseph Capper well.* We shall only presume to borrow one interesting quotation from this book. To do more would be unfair to the author, whose book, abounding as it does with information as to the condition of things in Tunstall and Burslem in the Chartist period, and the kindliest references to the work of our own Church, should be read for its own sake. Our single quotation shall introduce us to the Primitive Methodist local preacher, blacksmith, and Chartist whom "an Old Potter" evidently regards as a hero :—

'Joseph Capper was born near Nantwich, in the year 1788. In early life he came to Tunstall and was destined to make it famous in a famous crisis in his country's history. He had had but little schooling, but he had learned to read his Bible, the sole lesson-book of so many poor people in that day. It has been said that he was almost a man of one book. But this one book happened to be the greatest, even as literature, in our language. Capper seems to have loved its storied pages, its sacred counsels, and its revelation of Divine love. Whatever he was as man and citizen, as patriot and Christian, he was made so by the teachings of his Bible. His ordinary speech got its quaintness and unction and force from its pages. His imagination was stirred and illuminated by its imagery. Neither the schools nor society had tinctured his strong nature. He was a Bible-made man in every function and activity of his life. He was made, as the humbler Puritans were made, without any knowledge, perhaps, of their literature, excepting probably the 'Pilgrim's Progress.' He was as stern as the Puritans were in their love of righteousness and their hatred of tyranny. With less of gloom in the tenets he held, he had broader conceptions of liberty. Perhaps this was because of the Methodist leaven which entered early into his life, for we are told he was one of the first converts in the great Primitive Methodist camp meeting held on Mow Cop in 1807. He afterwards became a local preacher in the same denomination. Primitive Methodism at first was a demand for wider liberty in evangelical methods in preaching out of doors. While it cherished all the fervour of the early Methodists, it resented the restrictions of what were believed to be the hardening and narrowing respectability of the parent body of Methodists. Joseph Capper found in the Primitive Methodist Society an atmosphere in which he could breathe more freely and a sphere of labour he loved. He travelled many miles on Sundays, preaching the Gospel of Jesus Christ. He was one of the noble band of men in all the Methodist bodies who made heroic self-sacrifices in carrying the Gospel to outlying districts, where but for their labours, it would hardly ever have been heard, and certainly not heard with the fervour and simplicity with which they preached it. This habit of life was the reason why, in later days, finding the clergy among his bitterest political opponents, he so strongly girded at them and told them to preach for nothing as he did. He was the leading spirit of many Chartist meetings. His vigour was perennial, and, in spite of advancing years, he gave himself to the cause which carried the promise of political redemption." (pp. 143-4 and 146)

Like John Skevington, Joseph Capper was no believer in, much less an advocate of, violent measures. He was not numbered with the Physical Force Chartists. Yet a vindictive government was not careful of nice distinctions. It was only too glad to avail itself of any chance that offered to strike a blow at Chartism, regardless of the particular tenets—moderate or extreme—held by its victims. So Capper—than whom "no purer and more loyal patriot lived in the Queen's realms," was pounced upon and made to suffer. On Monday, the 14th August, 1842, he spoke with Cooper at an open-air meeting at Hanley, and then went home to his blacksmith's anvil and forge. Though, doubtless, he heard, during the week, of the wild work going on at Hanley, and also at Burslem, where maddened men marched along to the strains of—

"The lion of freedom's let loose from his den;
And we'll rally round him again and again,

to commit arson and pillage; yet Capper quietly and sadly went on with his work. But on the Sunday evening, after he had taken part in the services of the sanctuary and family devotions were over, four men broke in upon the peaceful household, and Joseph Capper was led away. He stood two trials for "sedition, conspiracy and rioting," and endured two years' imprisonment in Stafford gaol. He came out of prison broken in health, but unshaken in conviction and unsubdued in spirit, and to be held in respect and reverence until the end, which came January, 1860. His biographer, who has so nobly revived his name and vindicated his character, has written this final word of him:—"I have never met a man who did more to enrich England with simple ideals of progress, freedom, and goodness. . . . He was a citizen who saw the greatness and glory of his fellow-country must spring from its freedom, its industry, and its character." Such an estimate as this, unsought, unbiassed, amply justifies us in placing Joseph Capper side by side with John Skevington as men who exemplified and illustrated in a troublous time that sane, balanced, humane yet strenuous Christian democracy which Primitive Methodism tended, and yet tends, to foster.

We have briefly outlined the course of events until 1842 so far as Loughborough and Leicester are concerned; but nothing has been said as yet of the mission work undertaken by these two circuits during the same period. For this rapid survey the year 1819 must be taken as the starting point. In the February of this year, John Garner began his labours in the Loughborough—his native—Circuit, under somewhat unfavourable circumstances; for Robert Winfield, of whom more anon, had just made a division and the societies were unsettled. John Garner was a valuable acquisition to the ranks of the itinerant ministry, although he was barely twenty years of age. He brought "a comely person, a cheerful temper, agreeable manners, a fine voice, ardent zeal, and a vigorous constitution." Some of these qualities—especially the cheerful temper and the vigorous constitution, were soon severely tested. Neither his comely person nor his agreeable manners availed to save the stripling from being the victim of persecution of the very worst kind—that

JOHN GARNER.

of personal m

342   PRIMITIVE METHODIST CHURCH.

we have yet had to chronicle, unless it be the treatment Thomas Jackson (1) met with at Oakham, of which we have no details. In the case of John Garner, he himself has left a description of what he passed through at Sow, near Coventry, on the confines of the Loughborough Circuit, where in May, 1819, he had gone to do pioneer work. This moving description ranks as a historical document and calls for preservation. He begins his narrative by saying:—

"At this place (Sow) we had preached several times, but to little purpose, the inhabitants being vile persecutors, and the parish clergyman conducting himself towards us in so vile a manner that prudence forbids it being published. No sooner had I entered the village than stones were flying in every direction. I made haste to the house of Mr. ——— where a few people were assembled to hear the word of life. The mob followed me, surrounded the house, broke the windows, and compelled me to

SPOT ON RIVER SOW, AT WALSGRAVE-ON-SOW, NEAR COVENTRY.
Where Rev. J. Garner was ducked in February, 1819.

stop the meeting. Seeing no probability of the persecution abating, I was necessitated to expose myself to the malicious rage of the wicked, by whom I was furiously driven out of the village with stones, rotten eggs, sludge, or whatever came first to hand. The friends who accompanied me seeing the madness of the mob, became afraid, and endeavoured to effect their escape by taking a footpath. The rebels followed me out of the village, and some of them seized me; others propped my mouth open with stones, while some were engaged in attempting to pour sludge down my throat. The cry was raised, "Kill the devil! d——— him!" Immediately a man knocked me down, and after I had been shamefully beaten with the hands and feet of my enemies, and with divers weapons, I .... to a pond, around which they gathered, hoping soon to be gratified with my death. At this juncture of time I had not even a faint hope of ever being rescued from them alive; hence I committed my body and soul into the hands of the Lord, and most earnestly wished for death to put an end to my sufferings, which were almost insupportable. However, 'the thoughts of the Lord are not as our thoughts, neither are His ways as our ways,' for, contrary to my expectations, He made a way for my escape. One of the vilest persecutors rescued me from the fury of his companions, and some of them pursued my friends, who had at first escaped. Then the rebels were withdrawn from me. After having walked a few hundred yards, I perceived a woman much affected, tears were rolling down her cheeks; she kindly invited me into her house, and then assisted in washing my head and face. Being somewhat recovered, through the hospitality of my hostess, I returned, with the assistance of a friend, to walk to Bell Green, a distance of perhaps two miles, and by my kind friends at this place I was cordially entertained and taken care of. They lent me what clothes I wanted, for my persecutors had also torn my clothes, of a portion of which they afterwards made a scarecrow. After being carefully nursed at Bell Green a few days, I was enabled to attend to my usual labour."

We have hitherto met with nothing quite so dark as this picture of the reception Warwickshire gave our missionaries in the person of John Garner. And yet, dark as the picture is, its blackness is here and there relieved by gleams of brightness—the promise of better things to come. Witness the chief persecutor turned into a protector; the mother's heart of the woman crying over somebody's bairn as she washes the filth from his comely face and laves his bruises; the freely offered shelter with bed and board and wardrobe. Nor is the picture without its touch of grim humour, as we see these Warwickshire persecutors, in their severely practical way, making the preacher's torn garments, useless for anything else, do duty to frighten the blackbirds from their currant-bushes. When September came, John Garner left this part of the country and moved off to Tunstall Circuit, as Hugh Bourne and John Wedgwood had done before him, to take his part in the wonderful revival which will make Cheshire another famous Connexional centre.

Meanwhile, Loughborough Circuit held on tenaciously to this tract of country. In 1820 we find William Jefferson (1) labouring on the Welton branch, and then he passes from the stations and we know not what becomes of him. But where is Welton? It may perhaps help us to locate this village which, until 1841, stood as the nominal head of what began as the Warwickshire Mission, if we say it is a village in Northamptonshire, lying in what may be called the "Naseby country," midway between Daventry, whence Charles I marched to his last fight, and Market Harborough in Leicestershire. The boundaries of this mission in two counties have been shifting, its very constituents variable, and its fortunes fluctuating, though never mounting high at any period. And yet, though villages and even towns of some size, like Daventry and Lutterworth, have been abandoned, the labour spent on this apparently niggard soil by good men has not been wholly in vain. Parts of the old circuit still remain under other names and in other combinations. John Woolley, Robert Bent and W. G. Bellham were amongst the early workers on the Welton branch. The latter began his labours there in 1823, and met with a rough reception at Daventry. Cries were raised—' No bacon preach .. . . . street and back again—he all the while clinging to the chair on which he had first stood to preach. Then they "Jonathan Barneyed" him; that is to say, they treated him much in the same way as oranges in a bag are treated, when a couple of costermongers roll them backwards and forwards; only in this case the bag was represented by a ring of rough men who, when Mr. Bellham tried to get out at one rim of the circle, pushed him back to the other, and he was so battered and hustled that at last he fell, and expected nothing else than that he would part with his life under the feet of his tormentors. But the Lord mercifully preserved him, and he came out of all this "with the loss of his hat and one lap of his coat;" nor does he omit to mention that, even here, "the people generally were sympathetic." A society was formed at Daventry, and here most frequently the preacher resided, but the society was never other than feeble. Welton became a circuit in 1824—the same year as Leicester—but in 1830 its membership, through some cause, had sunk to ninety-three, and it was in contemplation to attach it to Leicester Circuit; especially as the young man put down to it was just entering the ministry, and wished to be under a superintendent rather than be one himself. But John Brownson was put down for bare-pastured Welton after all, and did his best; and the reason his very natural wishes were overruled is no doubt to be found in the following letter, which we have pleasure in giving, not only because it affords evidence of the humane, paternal interest taken in young preachers by the General Committee of that day, but also because it casts an interesting sidelight on another honoured name which will come before us—that of John Petty.

W. G. BELLHAM.

"Dear Brethren:—Welton Circuit being united with Leicester Circuit arose entirely from the difficulty of its present situation, and from Brother Brownson's reluctance to travel except under a superintendent. But as that reluctance appears now, in some degree, done away, and as he thinks the circuit not hopeless, the difficulties are removed. We have therefore put it down as a circuit separate from Leicester Circuit, and Brother Brownson as preacher.

"Derby Circuit was once reduced to a similar situation, and G. Appleby was called out to travel in it, and he brought it about, and became a good superintendent.

"Haverfordwest, in Pembrokeshire, South Wales, was in a manner a complete wreck. And John Petty was called out and sent to it. He was young, and they thought him a mere boy. However, he stopped there, and soon began to bring things about. He laboured there two years and fully brought up the work, and now he is one of the best superintendents in the Connexion. His being so appointed at Haverfordwest, made him expert in the office of superintendent.

"And we have no doubt of Brother Brownson's being able, with perseverance, to bring up the circuit. We believe him to be of a harmonizing turn, and that he will by degrees succeed in harmonizing the whole circuit. But there is one thing we wish, and that is that he do not labour beyond his strength so as to injure his health; but that in prayer meetings, after preachings, and at other times, he gets others to labour chiefly, he only conducting the meetings. And, too, he must get them to be short in their exercises.

"In behalf of the General Committee,
"DAVID PAISLEY,
"Assistant Corresponding Member."

Address:—
"Mr. CHAMBERLAIN,
"Grocer,
"Market Place,
"Daventry,
"Northamptonshire."

On the Welton Circuit plan for July-October, 1824, we find both Northampton and Coventry. The former had only a temporary place on the plan; it is not found on the next one, and it was not until ten years later that Northampton became a mission of the powerful Burland Station with James Hurd as its first missionary. The connection of Welton with Coventry was longer and closer. The poet tells us how he

"waited for the train at Coventry:
He hung with grooms and porters on the bridge
To watch the three tall spires; and there I shaped
The city's ancient legend."

JAMES HURD.

There is a simple Primitive Methodist legend of how W. G. Bellham once shamefacedly walked these streets. He was a young man of twenty-six, and his top-coat was very shabby, so he carried it over his arm in order to hide its imperfections. But thinking that he had allowed pride to get the better of him, he resolved to do penance for his weakness. He retraced his steps, put on the shabby coat, and went over the ground again indifferent to prying eyes. When, in 1849, Coventry makes its appearance on the stations as an independent circuit, it will be through the agency, and as part of Tunstall District.

Besides the five counties that are represented on the 1823 plan, Leicester, the offshoot of Loughborough, has the credit of breaking ground in a sixth county—Oxfordshire. Scarcely had it achieved circuit independence for itself, than it commissioned William Allcock to take his travel-staff and set it up in "the most eligible locality he could find." He fixed upon Witney, the blanket-town, and the surrounding villages, and, certainly, if spiritual destitution constitutes eligibility, his choice could not have been bettered; for many of the villagers had not heard a sermon for twenty or thirty years, as though they had been living in Patagonia rather than within easy distance, and almost in sight of the spires and towers of Oxford's churches and seats of learning. As we read the story, one cannot but feel that in 1825 some "Oxford Movement" or other was sorely needed to pierce the gross darkness that covered the people. Before the end of the year 1824, W. Allcock had W. Shimwell to share his toils and privations—literally priva̶ ̶ ̶ ̶ ̶ ̶ ̶ ̶ ̶ ̶ ̶ ̶ ̶ ̶ ̶ ̶ ̶ ̶ ̶ lter them.

Yet they persevered. Some notorious sinners were converted, and ere Christmas-day came, the two missionaries were able to report 135 members, of whom ten were local preachers and exhorters. In May of the following year, W. G. Bellham, with three local preachers, set off one Friday to assist at the first camp meeting ever held in Oxfordshire. Preaching on their way, they reached Witney, where a mile and a half out of the town the camp meeting was to be held. The usual processionary service to the ground took place, which for noise must surely have beaten the record; for forty horns, we are told, were blowing at once as they marched on. The whole town was moved, and hundreds followed the procession. One of the two waggons used as a preaching-stand was upset by the roughs; yet, despite turbulence and opposition, fifteen or sixteen persons were crying for mercy at one time. Next day, one of the

COVENTRY IN 1820.

brethren stood up in the Market Place to preach, while all sorts of missiles—chiefly rotten eggs—were flying.

Being in tolerable force, it was deemed a fitting opportunity to "storm Oxford." So the same evening (May 24th), they entered the city, and Mr. Bellham stood up against the walls of the City Prison, and the service began in quietude. But presently the gownsmen came out carrying eggs in their handkerchiefs, which were freely applied. One student got himself knocked down by an indignant citizen, and a town-and-gown row ensued. The missionaries were so besmeared with eggs and filth that they "took a wisp of straw to a pump and cleansed themselves as well as they could." The hardly-bestead me......... .... shelter and entertainment in the home of a pious

Baptist family. The attempt on Oxford may be said to have failed, but Witney and the villages around received the Gospel. In 1826 Witney stands as the head of a circuit, with John Hallam as its preacher. By 1827, the circuit, with its judicious

BUTTER CROSS AND TOWN HALL, WITNEY.
Where Open-Air Services have been held for many years.

and every way excellent superintendent, was transferred to the Tunstall District, with which we leave it for the present.

Rugby may be regarded as the heir and representative of Welton Circuit, which Connexionally deceased in 1841. "Rugby Mission" stands connected with Nottingham Circuit on the list of stations for 1842; and the circumstances which led to our establishment in this town of Public School fame make an interesting story. As far back as the beginning of the second decade of the last century, a blacksmith, named Flavel, lived at Newbold-on-Avon in Warwickshire. He had a wayward, drunken son, who gave him much concern. In his solicitude, he was anxious that the Primitives, of whose doings in Staffordshire and elsewhere he had heard, should visit Newbold, if haply they might be the means of rescuing his son from his evil courses. He declared that should they come, they should have his horse-block

JOHN HALLAM.

to preach ... and ... to Newbold

RUGBY OLD CHAPEL AND MINISTER'S HOUSE.
Now turned into three Cottages.

and did preach from the horse-block—but the father "died without the sight." The son, however, respecting whom he was so solicitous, got converted, and his name is found in the list of "Exhorters" on the plans of 1824. He became a zealous local preacher, and wherever he lived—at Newbold, Coventry, Long Lawford—made himself useful in the cause. But the years went on, and Rugby continued to defy attack. The *chevaux-de-frise* of respectability and churchy

THE PRESENT RUGBY CHAPEL.

exclusiveness had not as yet been partially levelled by the advent of the railway, and seemed difficult to overcome. W. Flavel saw where the difficulty lay and what was wanted. So in 1839 he took the decisive step of offering to go and live at Rugby, in order that his house might serve as the base of operations. He went and

W. FLAVEL. HY. FLAVEL. MRS. MARSON.

had his prompt and rich reward, for the first convert was his own son. For years the names of W. and H. Flavel were on the plan together, and then Henry emigrated to New Zealand, where he died in the faith. William Flavel's daughter—Mrs. Marson—still survives as the oldest member of the Rugby Society. After being a mission Rugby became an independent station in 1884. The first chapel of 1841 was superseded by the present excellent chapel in 1878, and recently the Sabbath school has been greatly enlarged.

Lutterworth and Rugby have had very dissimilar histories. While the latter accepted the railway in the beginnings of the railway movement, Lutterworth rejected it. It seems strange that when it was in question to take the London and North Western *via* Northampton, landowners and graziers should have fought against the proposal, on the ground that the smoke of the passing engine would seriously discolour the wool of the sheep, and that the continuous rush of the locomotive through the meadows would so disturb the cattle as to interfere with the process of their fattening. So the line was diverted from the course originally marked out for it by the engineers, and was made to pass eight miles or so to the left of Lutterworth. Rugby became Dickens' "Mugby Junction"—a noted railway centre, while Lutterworth was left to its bovine sleepiness for a term of years, until the Great Central came along. Lutterworth does not seem to have taken to Primitive Methodism much more kindly than to the railway. Its name stands on the Leicester plan of 1827-8 with the letters O. T. against it; which we conjecture to mean "on trial." If so, the trial resulted in failure, for in

MELTON-MOWBRAY.
Showing the Market Place, where the first Open-Air Services were held.

1839, during Mr. Morgan's term as superintendent, another attempt was made to mission the town. A camp meeting was held near the spot on which Wycliffe's exhumed bones were burned, and near "the Swift which was to convey his ashes into Avon, Avon into Severn, Severn into the narrow seas, they into the main ocean, so that the ashes of Wycliffe became the emblem of his doctrine which now is dispersed all the world over."* A society was formed, and in 1841 a chapel built, but the cause remained feeble, and, after some years, finally flickered out, and Primitive Methodism is not represented in Lutterworth to-day.

Melton-Mowbray was missioned by Loughborough. Though Wedgwood had preached at Melton in the open-air in 1818, no permanent society was raised until 1834. In the July of that year Loughborough sent three local preachers to hold two services in the open-air, and by the end of the year there was a society of thirty members in the pork-pie town. There is a record in the Loughborough Circuit books relating to Melton, which goes to show that the first General Missionary Committee established by enactment of the Conference of 1825, was not quite the dead letter it is sometimes thought to have been. The Quarterly Meeting of October 1834 resolved:—"That application be made to the General Missionary Committee for a donation of £10 to assist us in our mission at Melton." The application was so far successful that a grant of £6 was obtained. During the year 1835 societies were formed at Nether Broughton, Clawson, and Frisby, and chapels built at Melton and Scalford. The outlook seemed so promising that a preacher was put down to Melton-Mowbray, and in 1836 it became a separate circuit. In 1842 it had 214 members.

The Silencing of John Benton.

Three events happened in 1818, or soon after, that have all the appearance of being

MELTON-MOWBRAY FIRST CHAPEL.
Now private house.

MELTON-MOWBRAY PRESENT CHAPEL.

terminal and prelusive of change. These events are of similar character, and have their parallel in the retirement of James Crawfoot just after the establishment of Primitive Methodism in Staffordshire. The reference to these will appropriately close the present chapter, in which the development of Leicestershire Primitive Methodism until 1842 has been sketched. These three events are, (1) the retirement of Hugh Bourne from the office of general superintendent through illness, (2) the discontinuance of John Benton as a labourer in the mission field, and (3) the separation of Robert Winfield.

The first event has already been touched upon in another connection. Here it is referred to because it ended the system of giving unification to the Connexion which had obtained ... 1821. Hugh Bourne ... Tunstall

Circuit, and though Nottingham had its Circuit Committee, and Leicestershire was not without its capable officials, there was left "a gap in discipline" which the Preparatory Meeting of 1819 was intended to supply. As to the separation of R. Winfield, growing out of his refusal to accept his appointment to Hull—that will more appropriately be dealt with in our next chapter.

The retirement of Benton must detain us a little while. Had he died, or emigrated, or seceded, our task would have been a simpler one. But he lived for thirty-eight years after his retirement; and yet he became in a sense dead to Primitive Methodism. This is the fact that needs explanation. We are not specially prepared for this retirement by anything we have met with or observed. We might, possibly, have predicted the retirement of Crawfoot; scarcely that of Benton. The event comes upon us somewhat as a surprise, and we are almost ready to bring in the verdict—Silenced by the visitation of God.

ROUND HILL CAMP MEETING SITE.

In the month of May, 1818,—two months after the opening of Leicester—a great camp meeting was held at Round Hill—a popular site for such gatherings. With characteristic precision Hugh Bourne thus describes the position of Round Hill. "It is an elevated piece of ground, about three and a half miles from Leicester, and is situated at the junction of the Roman Fosse Way with the Melton Turnpike Road." Time and place were favourable for a large gathering; and there was one. From every direction people came, on foot and in vehicles of all kinds, until it was computed there were ten thousand persons present. The meeting was well supported by preachers and praying labourers. The morning service had been powerful, yet marked by decorum. At noon the converting work broke out, and the cries for mercy were loud and continuous. Benton was in great force; and as he spoke on "the great day of God's wrath," and the feelings of some of the people were much wrought upon,—a panic ensued. This is how we prefer to state what really occurred. Herod says that a gentleman's horse that was right in the midst of a mass of people began to rear and "squeal"; that some thought the day of judgment in very truth had come; others that, like Korah and his crew, the Primitives were offering unhallowed fire, and that the earth was about to open and swallow them up; that some fell upon one another in heaps, while others fled, not daring to glance behind them. It is a strange and, one cannot but think, an over-coloured picture of what really happened. There was a panic —that is clear; and it is the very peculiarity of panic fear that it can give no reasonable account of itself or of what is done under its influence. We may never know what the people thought or whether, indeed, they thought at all. But there was panic fear and confusion, a human welter, danger to life and limb; and Benton did the only right

COSTOCK FARM-HOUSE, THE RESIDENCE OF MR. W. WOODROFFE.

thing under the strange unforeseen circumstances. He lifted up his voice and spared not. He shouted until he seriously injured his larynx—some say, less probably, he burst a blood-vessel. Whichever it was, it is evident he seriously injured himself; for on the 25th May, Hugh Bourne, who is at Wyrley, writes:—"Heard yesterday that John Benton was still unwell—perhaps dangerously."

Assuming injury to the larynx, the medical prognosis agrees with the evidence available as to the course of events that followed. Benton lost his voice for a time— probably for a considerable time. On August 8th, Hugh Bourne called at Costock and notes—"John Benton's voice is low; he cannot preach." He may not have been able to speak above a whisper for some months, but he did not permanently lose his voice; for there is the evidence afforded by his own family, and of those still surviving who in their yo... regained something of its old power. This evidence is quite sufficient, but it finds additional confirmation from his signing himself on the deed of Dead Lane as "Dissenting Minister," whereas, in 1837, he is described as "Farmer."

The former description would seem to imply that, if in 1819 he were not actually preaching, he had not yet relinquished the purpose of doing so, regarding it still as his main business in life; whereas the later description would best be explained by concluding that in 1837 he had ceased his missionary labours in order to enjoy a restful eventide. The frequent change of residence that marked the earlier years is also confirmatory of the view that he was still missioning. Again, there is before us one of his hymn books, printed by W. Ordoyno, Cross Street, Nottingham, bearing the date 1834, which contains the notification "These hymns are the private property of John Benton, having originated from him; therefore this is to warn all people against printing them." This piece of evidence, also, fits in with the view that after recovering his voice Benton resumed his old course of life.

On the other hand, the evidence is equally indisputable that, after July, 1818, John Benton's name never stood on a Primitive Methodist plan, and that he was never officially active in our Church. Yet there is not, as far as we know, a shred or particle of reliable evidence to prove that he fomented a division or set up another community. He financed Dead Lane fifteen months after his retirement; its pulpit was open to him; and his relations with that Church seem to have been forbearing and friendly to the end. There is no hint of any breach of friendship with his former colleagues; on the contrary, H. Bourne was occasionally his guest.

But the strongest evidence is that supplied by Benton's own family, in that his own wife and son who both outlived him, died in communion with our Church. John Benton was married to Miss Elizabeth Woodroffe, December 3rd, 1817, she being then thirty-seven and he thirty-four years of age. Miss Woodroffe was the daughter of a well-to-do yeoman farmer of Costock, whose social standing rather than his gentle blood is indicated by the word 'Gent" inscribed on his tombstone, and who, if not in circumstances of the greatest affluence, was yet able to give or bequeath a thousand pounds to his daughter. His marriage with the staid daughter of such a house has in it a touch of romance. John Benton might be the first, though certainly not the last, of the early preachers to take a wife from a good home against the consent of parents or guardians to share the inevitable privations of his migratory life. In this case we cannot add—to share his poverty; for in a worldly sense John Benton was as well off as Elizabeth Woodroffe, though he was probably less refined in manner and speech, and had still less of the tincture of learning. She was his convert, won, it may be, about the time when Loughborough was missioned, from which town Costock was not far distant. Acquaintance speedily ripened into friendship, and friendship into a still warmer sentiment. But, as was not unnatural, the father disapproved of the match. He was a staunch, old-fashioned Churchman, accustomed to be waited upon and to have his own way, and now, that he had turned his three score years and ten, it was not likely he would readily consent for his daughter who had become necessary to him to be carried off by an itinerating Primitive Methodist. The old man's refusal to sanction the marriage wa

THE PERIOD OF CIRCUIT PREDOMINANCE AND ENTERPRISE. 355

a romantic episode. Elizabeth Woodroffe had made up her mind; so she rode on a pillion behind John Benton to Broughton Sulney where the marriage was solemnised; nor have we any reason to believe that either of the contracting parties ever repented of that day's doings, or that the wife grew tired of the inconveniences incident to their manner of life. Her husband was ever her hero; "she worshipped the ground he trod." Let it be noted that it was after his marriage, and when the shadow of bereavement rested on his home, that John Benton missioned Leicester; and when Round Hill camp meeting stopped him he was in the full career of missionary work. Mrs. Benton, as the saying is, "made a good Primitive." She encouraged her husband in his work, and herself occasionally conducted house-services. To the end she exemplified that plainness in dress that characterised the old Primitives. Mrs. Benton survived her husband some years, dying October 13th, 1862; her son, W. J. Woodroffe Benton, was for some time the steward of Loughborough Circuit, and died (1889) in communion with our Church. Are the facts thus related compatible with the belief that John Benton headed a schism or that he even identified himself with some other community?

No wonder that Rumour with her many tongues should voice contradictory opinions respecting the facts of which it had but a partial knowledge; that now it should say that, like W. Lockwood, John Benton had married a rich wife and settled down, and then again should assert that, like Robert Winfield, he had gone off with some grievance in his mind and set up for himself. Both these statements cannot be true together; and in point of fact neither of them is true. The only theory that explains all the facts, so far as diligent research has recovered them, is that John Benton ended, as he began, by being an unattached Primitive Methodist. When he had so far regained his voice as to be able to preach, Primitive Methodism was fast organising itself. With that necessary inevitable process John Benton had little understanding or sympathy. He reverted more strongly to his old position; more than ever he became an individualist; and as we watch his reversion we are reminded of the words of Dr. R. W. Dale:—

BENTON'S TOMB, BARROW-ON-SOAR.

"The Evangelical movement

undenominational temper. It emphasised the vital importance of the Evangelical creed, but it regarded almost with indifference all forms of Church polity that were not in apparent and irreconcilable antagonism to that creed. It demanded as the basis of fellowship a common religious life and common religious belief, but was satisfied with fellowship of an accidental and precarious kind. *It cared nothing for the Church as the august society of saints.* It was the ally of Individualism.'

John Benton was not one who could lend much help in the harmonisation of the ideas of the Church and the Evangel, which harmonisation was very much needed in 1819. John Benton did not try to harmonise them. John Wedgwood had something of the same temperament and cared little for the business side of Church life; but in 1819 he was transferred to the Cheshire Mission of Tunstall District, and threw himself heart and soul into the revival movement. Here he found his true vocation and he ended by becoming—for a short time at least—a salaried and duly recognised minister. But John Benton never *did* adapt himself to the changing conditions. Temperament, training, habit, all conspired to make and keep him an individualist. Yet, he was too much an individualist to be able to become an avowed undenominationalist. If he were any 'ist at all, he continued to be a Primitive Methodist. Such his own people declared him to be, but they likewise said: "he would not be under any one." He had once declared he got his plan from God and would take no other. Many John Bentons would have rendered the crystallisation of Primitive Methodism impossible; for all that, he was a good man whom God had remarkably owned, and of whom we may and ought to speak with respect and gratitude for the pioneer work he did. If perplexed by his later attitude, let us remember Christ's words, "He that is not against us is on our part." John Benton died in peace, February 5th, 1856, and his mortal part lies in the graveyard of Barrow-on-Soar.

CHAPTER VI.

INTRODUCTION OF PRIMITIVE METHODISM INTO HULL.

General Forecast of Events until 1824.

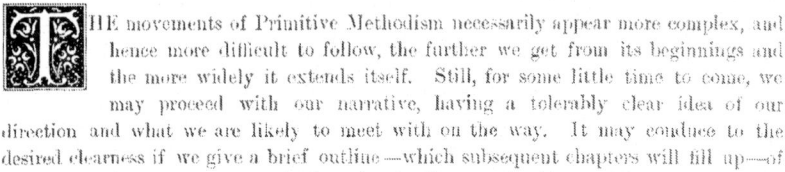

THE movements of Primitive Methodism necessarily appear more complex, and hence more difficult to follow, the further we get from its beginnings and the more widely it extends itself. Still, for some little time to come, we may proceed with our narrative, having a tolerably clear idea of our direction and what we are likely to meet with on the way. It may conduce to the desired clearness if we give a brief outline—which subsequent chapters will fill up—of the course of events up to and after the Conference of 1824.

Hull was reached in January, 1819, and, at midsummer of the same year, Hull became the fourth circuit of the Connexion. It looks as though it had been written in the book of destiny, or were the result of some pre-established harmony, that King Edward's town on the Hull and Humber should be won for the Connexion. Like the Trent, Primitive Methodism had been steadily making for the sea through all these years. It had its source in the Trent country, and like that river, was formed of two branches which effected their junction at Tunstall. Like the Trent it made its way through Staffordshire, Derbyshire, and Nottinghamshire, and when we left it in the last-named county, it had got as far as Newark. It is a generalised historic fact—so true and graspable as materially to aid the memory—that up to this time, Primitive Methodism had done its main work in the country watered by the Trent and its affluents. Not even excepting Leicester, all the chief towns that we have followed Primitive Methodism into, stand either on the Trent or on one or other of its tributaries. The onward striving which carried our missionaries as far as Newark, was not likely to end there, any more than the water which flowed from Biddulph Moor or Mow into Trent was likely to stand still when it got to Newark. We expect the seaward movement to continue, and to find our missionaries at Gainsborough, the next considerable town on Trent, and then at Hull, Barton, and Grimsby. The expectation is fulfilled to the very letter. Gainsborough was entered late in 1818, and Hull and Grimsby in 1819; and the Preparatory Meeting signalises the approximate completion of the movement, and shows that the country from Trent-source to the sea had been traversed. At that meeting the representatives from the four circuits—Tunstall, Nottingham, Loughborough, and Hull—attempted to give some cohesion and unity to the various societies which had been established between Mow and Hull on the line of the Trent.

These and similar facts are chronicled in the *Minutes of Conference* for 1820 and still more in those for 1821. It is to these annual *Minutes* we have now to look to find the gains of the year registered, just as heretofore we had to look to circuit plans, only now the unit of gain is the circuit instead of a society. At the first Conference of 1820, the Connexion was reported to consist of eight circuits, the additional ones—the increment on the year's working—being Scotter, Sheffield, Darlaston, and revived Derby. So that after Hull, we have to glance at the introduction of Primitive Methodism into these places and neighbourhoods, Scotter, be it remembered, representing Gainsborough, which was first a branch of Nottingham. Prior to the Tunstall Conference of 1821, several new circuits had been formed, and as the principle of direct circuit representation to the annual meeting still obtained—three delegates from each circuit—

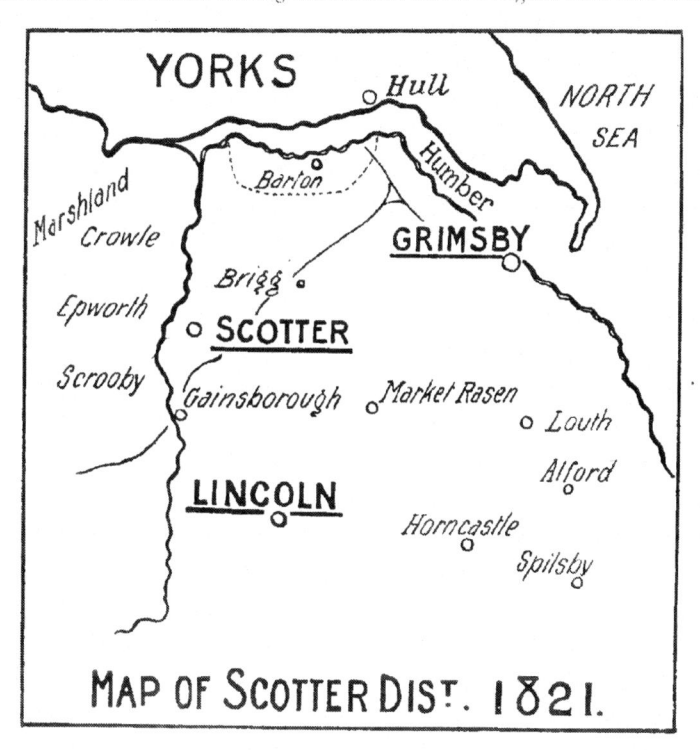

MAP OF SCOTTER DIST. 1821.

there should have been upwards of forty delegates to that Conference. This was the Conference from which Hugh Bourne got the "speeching Radical" expelled. The delegates assembled were unable to cope with the difficulties of stationing, and business was brought to a dead lock. H. B. had not been appointed a delegate to the Conference held in his own chapel, and like Achilles had retired sulking to his tent. But his hour of triumph came. Being brought to a stand, the delegates sent for Hugh Bourne to help them out of their difficulties. He did so in a way that proved his possession of statesmanship spot by the delegates of contiguous circuits resolving themselves into committees and proceeding to station their preachers by mutual arrangement. The committee-stage over, the whole meeting made the necessary adjustments. As early therefore as 1821, the original system of direct representation of circuits to the annual meeting broke down under its own weight. It was plain that if circuits continued to be formed as rapidly as they had been, it would soon be impossible—on the score of expense, if for no other reason—to continue to send three representatives from each circuit. So the arrangement improvised by Hugh Bourne was henceforth adopted: circuits were grouped into districts, and the direct representation of circuits was henceforth limited to district meetings, which court alone was to have authority to send district representatives to the annual meeting. In 1821, then, circuits were first grouped into districts. But not then or in either of the two following years was a workable system of grouping hit upon. It was only in 1824 that the whole Connexion was formed into four districts which should be empowered to send nine delegates to Conference, irrespective of any addition or loss of circuit during the year. This was the principle of representation that obtained until the numerical strength of a district was made the basis of representation—the system at present in vogue. The four districts created were Tunstall, Nottingham, Hull, and Sunderland, and out of these all the existing districts have been carved. In order that facts of the same class may be kept together, how one district was evolved from another may be shown from the case of Norwich District. In 1824, Norwich, Fakenham, Lynn, and Cambridge are included amongst the circuits constituting Nottingham District; in 1825, these circuits, with the addition of Yarmouth and Upwell, form the Norwich District. Manchester District was formed in 1827 and Brinkworth in 1833, so that at the close of the period with which we are now dealing—1842—the Connexion was a Heptarchy—a federation of seven districts.

But to return to the important year of 1821 and the district arrangements then formulated: the new districts created at this time were Scotter and Sheffield. The former included Grimsby and Lincoln, and it is interesting to note that to these three circuits the whole of North and Mid Lincolnshire was assigned, with the exception of Barton, which belonged, as it still belongs, to Hull District. This old Scotter District, then, may be considered to represent the present Grimsby and Lincoln District, the creation of recent years. Though the latter was in great part formed out of Hull District, with which it stood connected so many years, it had, as we shall see, its origin in the labours of missionaries sent out by Nottingham, so that its separateness from Hull is a reversion, and justified historically as well as geographically. Sheffield too, with Barnsley as its one circuit was made a district, showing that pioneer work was being pushed on in this part which would soon result in Chesterfield, Halifax, Wakefield and other towns appearing on the roll of circuits. Nottingham alone stands without any new circuit to its credit, but some of its many branches will soon become independent. Tunstall with Darlaston, Macclesfield and Manchester, attached to form the Tunstall District, show that the mother-circuit has, in good earnest, resumed the work of aggression, and Burland, Oakengates and Ramsor are branches almost ripe for independence. Hull District comprises Pocklington, Brotherton and Hutton Rudby (soon to be .... discern the promise not only of the present Hull District, but also of Sunderland and the Leeds and York Districts. From these facts we may gather that, until 1824, we have to watch the progress of circuit propagation, and even after the country has been allotted among the four districts—Tunstall, Nottingham, Hull and Sunderland—as though with a view to the four points of the compass, we shall find that the relative advance of the several districts will very largely be conditioned by the work done by the prolific mother-circuits which do not take rank as districts, of which Scotter and Burland may be taken as the type.

W. Clowes' Entry into Hull.

Hull may be called the Thessalonica of Primitive Methodism. It was the first sea-port reached by the accredited agents of the denomination; and though its population, at the time of their entry, was but 42,000,* yet it was already a mart of nations, and a busy

SOUTH-EAST VIEW OF KINGSTON-ON-HULL.

distributing centre, from which, as from Thessalonica of old, the word of the Lord was to sound forth, not only in the East Riding of Yorkshire, but also in Northumberland and Cornwall, Cumberland and Kent, London, both sides of the Solent, and the United States. Such a record of early missionary achievement on the part of one circuit, is quite enough in itself to lend perennial interest to the questions relating to the origins and success of Hull Primitive Methodism. But when to its missionary record there is added its later and equally remarkable chapel-building record, such questions become doubly interesting, and almost press for an answer. In their search after causes and explanations, the thoughts of many thus shape themselves: Hull has long been spoken of as the "metropolis of Primitive Methodism." You yourself have just called it our Thessalonica, and elsewhere have likened it to Venice, the city-state, that once set fleets and armies in motion. We do not deny the fitness of such comparisons; we only want

* The estimate given needs an explanation. The population of Hull, in 1821, was 28,591. But it would be incorrect to regard this as the population at that time of the area which now constitutes Hull. Sculcoates, Drypool and part of Sutton are now included in Hull, but this was not the case in 1821. The area which now constitutes Hull would contain about 42,000 persons in 1821. This information has been kindly communicated through the Rev. C. C. Henn.

to know the facts which explain, and are supposed to justify, their use. Let us turn then to the facts, in which, perhaps, lies, latent, the explanation desired.

Primitive Methodism had a good start in Hull, a town which, ever since the days when King Charles tried in vain to wrest it from his Parliament, had been the stronghold of evangelical religion and liberal sentiment; so that the *genius loci* may be said to have smiled upon our advent. Moreover, Primitive Methodism went to Hull by invitation, and found auxiliaries ready to help for a time, while some were even ready to give themselves permanently to the movement which they had welcomed. These facts strikingly illustrate, and are best explained by, what was strongly insisted upon in an earlier part of the history—the prevalence during the earlier years of the nineteenth century of Revivalism, which was not so much an organised system as it was an impelling spirit—a tendency and aspiration. There were some in all the Churches—but more especially in the mother-Church of Methodism—who had sympathy with ardent aggressive evangelism, and who found neither sufficient scope nor encouragement in the societies to which they belonged. So had it been in Staffordshire; so was it to be in Yorkshire—in both Hull and Leeds. Primitive Methodism grew out of Revivalism, and as it had drawn to itself sympathisers and helpers like Winfield in Derbyshire, and Lockwood in Notts, so had it already attracted the attention, and won the sympathy, of an ardent band of Revivalists in Hull.

Amongst these were Mr. R. and Mrs. H. Woolhouse, who had much to do in introducing Primitive Methodism into Hull. It is said they were both class-leaders in the Wesleyan Methodist body. Mrs. Woolhouse was evidently a woman of much zeal and of considerable ability for public labour. Mr. Woolhouse was a sack and sail-cloth manufacturer, carrying on business in an old factory, still said to be standing, the end of which abuts on North Street near Garden Street. The requirements of his business frequently called him to visit Nottingham and other towns in the Midlands. One such visit was paid to Nottingham in 1817, when he chanced to meet Mr. R. Winfield in the Marketplace. The latter was quite full of the revival which had begun under Sarah Kirkland's ministry, and he gave Mr. Woolhouse a pressing invitation to go and hear her. He went and received much good, and caught the contagion of the revival. He observed to Mr. Winfield that "he should like the Primitives to visit Hull: that he and his wife were class-leaders in the Methodist Connexion; that Mrs. Woolhouse had a great

WOOLHOUSE'S FACTORY, HULL.

desire to preach, but that she had no encouragement from the people at Hull, and that he believed she would be in her element if she had the privilege of attending such meetings as those in Broad Marsh." On his return, Mr. Woolhouse told his wife what he had heard and seen and felt amongst the people (vulgarly) called "Ranters." The information was deeply interesting to her. Her curiosity was excited to know more, and she determined to visit Nottingham at the first opportunity. The opportunity soon presented itself, and before the end of 1817 Mrs. Woolhouse, accompanied by Miss Healand, went to Nottingham. They engaged lodgings that they might remain some time, so as to form a correct opinion of the religious movement going on. They threw themselves heartily into the work, and were abundant in labours. Having seen a considerable number converted both in town and country, they returned to Hull and spoke at large respecting the great work the Primitives were carrying on. The classes led by the Woolhouses experienced the benefit of this visit.

Mr. Herod in his "Sketches" tells us that in the summer of 1818 Miss Healand, in company with the celebrated Ann Carr, the Revivalist, paid a second visit to Nottingham. They laboured at camp meetings and at other open-air services, and saw much good effected. On their return to Hull it is said they commenced to preach both in town and country, and that great results followed. According to Mr. Herod they united with the Primitive Methodists, and for two or three years were very successful in the converting work. Miss Healand was subsequently married to a Wesleyan minister. As to the other members of this group of preaching and praying women, Miss Carr and Miss Williams while zealous, were irregular in their movements and, as we shall see, subsequently made a division in our Leeds societies.

The next stage in the evolution of events was reached when Mrs. Woolhouse personally appeared before the Nottingham December Quarterly Meeting of 1818, to urge that a travelling preacher should be sent to Hull. This she did, not only in her own name, but in the name and on behalf of the other members of the Revivalistic sisterhood already referred to. Mrs. Woolhouse also asked that the two young men who accompanied her might be constituted travelling preachers. This request was granted, but as John Hutchinson and Samuel Atterby were at that very time members of the Methodist Church, they had first of all to be received as members, then made local preachers, and lastly appointed travelling preachers. This quick dispatch of the necessary formalities clearly shows that in December, 1818, there was no Primitive Methodist Society existent in Hull. Of the two travelling preachers thus expeditiously made, Samuel Atterby was to render the more effective service. He was a native of North Somercotes in Lincolnshire, and was a shoemaker by trade. He travelled for a considerable number of years with credit to himself and with advantage to the community he served. Plain in his mode of preaching, and in his general habits, he yet knew how to lead souls to Christ. He was distinguished for an even peaceable disposition, largely induced by careful Christian culture, for he himself has left it on record that he early formed the resolution that neither men nor circumstances should disturb the patience of his soul. John Hutchinson also laboured with acceptance and usefulness for a few years, but trouble of some kind overtaking him, he severed himself from our Church and joined the New Connexion.

Mrs Woolhouse was favourably listened to when she pleaded for the sending of a missionary to Hull, and at a subsequent stage of the proceedings Robert Winfield was appointed. He was present when the appointment was made, and was understood to acquiesce and to agree to enter upon his important duties in three weeks' time. But at this same long Quarterly Meeting, Hugh Bourne preferred a series of charges—of a vexatious, if not of a serious character—against Robert Winfield. One of these was that he had got an edition printed of the "Hymns and Spiritual Songs" Lorenzo Dow had brought over, and was making merchandise of them. There were other complaints of a like sort. At the close of the discussion, though each party appeared to be satisfied, there seems to have been left a sense of injury rankling in Winfield's memory; for a day or two after the meeting he sent a letter to Mr King declining the mission. Instead of going to Hull he went into Leicestershire, and, whether intentionally or not, was the means of that unsettlement of the societies in the Loughborough Circuit amidst which John Garner began his itinerant labours. He seems to have had the design of founding a distinct denomination, and was so far successful in carrying out his purpose, that a community, some thousands strong and employing several travelling preachers, was the result of his labours. His talented daughter itinerated as preacheress, and became very popular. But Mr Winfield's gift for converting sinners was much greater than his gift for governing saints, and his sect—the "Revivalists"—was at last brought into confusion and disruption. He took refuge with the New Connexion and remained with them until his death.

The letter of declinature was addressed to Mr King, and came to hand on the Friday of the same week in which the appointment had been made. Mr King remarks:—"I took his letter to the prayer meeting in the evening, held in the long-room, and at the close desired the local preachers and class-leaders present to remain, when I laid Winfield's letter before them, and they decided that some person should go to Tunstall Quarterly Meeting to be held the following Monday." But who was to go? Mr King could not, for he *had spent four days that week at the Quarterly Meeting*, and there was work waiting for him to do which was as good as ten shillings a day to him. So he went in search of some one who could discharge the duty of delegation, and at eleven o'clock at night he engaged Thomas Simmons, who went to Tunstall and secured Mr Clowes as a missionary for Hull in behalf of Nottingham Circuit, whence it will appear that Hull Circuit—with all that came of it—was the joint *protégé* of Nottingham and Tunstall.

Mr Clowes arrived in Hull on Friday the 15th January 1819. If, as was most likely, Nottingham Quarterly Meeting was held from the 10th to the 15th December, a month or so would intervene between the appointment of Mr Winfield and the arrival of Mr Clowes. Was any one sent to Hull during this month to labour there until the next was officially sent, as a matter of fact, Jane Brown went to Hull unofficially, and preached both in the town and in the adjoining villages, prior to the arrival of Mr. Clowes. She, it ought to be said, had been appointed by the Nottingham Circuit to labour in South Lincolnshire. While there she had formed an acquaintanceship with Mr. George Nicholson, and it was under his escort, and probably at his suggestion, that she made her way to Hull. The late Mr. John Brown, who was a native of Hessle, remembered Jane Brown's visit to Hessle; how she stood upon his stool while preaching; and how he accompanied Mr. Thompson and eight or nine others to Hull on the following Sunday to hear her preach in the old Penitentiary near High Flags, Wincolmlee. Moreover, Mr. Clowes recognises, and even Mr. King does not deny, the priority of Jane Brown's unofficial labours in Hull. The former records that the first Sabbath he spent in Hull, Jane Brown preached in the afternoon, while he, himself, preached morning and night. So let us unite with Mr. Clowes in giving due recognition to Jane Brown's pioneer, though it may have been unofficial and stop-gap work in Hull, as we have recognised Sarah Kirkland's pioneer labours in Derby and Nottingham.

JOHN BROWN, HULL.

The George Nicholson who is mentioned above and became the husband of Jane Brown, figured very prominently as a revivalist through the greater part of the first half of the last century. He was a native of North Lincolnshire, belonging to a family that filled a very good position in life; but George thought little of worldly prospects, and preferred preaching to farming. When our Church was providentially called into existence, he had much sympathy with its spirit and enterprise. Though a Wesleyan local preacher, he cast in his lot with the Primitives, and in companionship and toil with kindred spirits—such as John Oxtoby, Robert Coultas, and others—became remarkably useful as an itinerant revivalist. There can be no question but that during his life he saw many hundreds brought to Christ. In the end he was again more closely identified with the Wesleyan Methodists, but during the Reform agitation of 1850 he joined the Wesleyan Reformers in Louth. In this community he laboured till the time of his death, which took place about 1856. Mr. Nicholson was the first person interred in the Louth cemetery.

Mr. Clowes, as we have said, entered Hull on Friday, January 15th, 1819. He had been three days on his journey, but he is silent as to the route he took, and recounts no incidents that may have diversified his journey. His thoughts were divided between the endeared home and friends he had left, and the arduous post of duty that awaited him. Arrived in Hull, he at once made his way to the residence of Mr. Woolhouse. What followed, Mr. Clowes shall himself tell us:—

"As soon as I entered the house, Mrs. Woolhouse and John Oxtoby, commonly called 'Praying Johnny,' fell down upon their knees and returned thanks to God for my safe arrival. This act of devotion was very encouraging to me, and became a prelude to greater things. On the very day of my entering into Hull I preached in the evening in an old factory in North Street. Vast numbers of people attended, many influenced by curiosity, others with an intention to create disturbance, having heard of the arrival of the 'Ranter preacher'; however, God was present in my first effort to make known the riches of His mercy, and the wicked were restrained, so the meeting terminated in peace and quiet. On the day following, I took a walk down to the pottery by the Humber-side, where I had worked upwards of fifteen years before, when I was in the old olive tree, which is wild by nature; but I found the working of the pottery had been discontinued. I, however, entered the place, and proceeded to the room in which I formerly laboured, and kneeled down and praised God for the great change He had wrought in me. I then returned, and took a walk up and down the streets and lanes in which I had formerly wrought folly and wickedness. It brought to my recollection the time and place when captured by the press-gang, and other circumstances of dissipation and riot. Oh, what gratitude filled my soul when indulging in the contrast!—instead of reckless and brutal conduct throwing the reins upon my passions, neither fearing God nor regarding man, I am now a sinner saved by grace, and a missionary of the cross.—*Journal*, pp. 146-7.

Mr Clowes had another reason for thankfulness as he musingly perambulated these streets; he had honourably paid the debts contracted during the period of his wildness and excess, and could look any one in the face as he passed along without fearing to encounter the glance of an unsatisfied creditor. "How majestically he walks!" said a man who heard him at the Old Factory. "Yes, and his conduct is as straight as his walk!" was the reply of one who knew whereof he affirmed. *

"Praying Johnny" and other Preparers of the Way

One of the first and most pressing duties that called for Mr Clowes' attention on beginning his Hull ministry, was to meet those who were desirous to be united in Church-fellowship, to form them into classes, and to bring them under 'principles of discipline in conformity with the general character of the Primitive Methodist Connexion." Accordingly, at the close of his first Sunday evening's service in the Old Factory, Samuel Atterby, the newly-made travelling preacher, being present, he formed two classes, set leaders over them, and appointed a society steward. Again, the following Tuesday evening in the same way he formed a society at Hessle, where "the prospect bore a cheering aspect." Such records as these are worth pondering. Those gathered in were not the converts of the day, but the fruit of labours of other days. Where Clowes was, the converting work always went on; but in this case, it looks as though the ready-ripe fruit had got to be housed before Clowes could give full proof of his evangelistic ministry. He had to garner others' fruit before he had time to gather his own. Another fact of similar import worth following up because of the explanation it yields is, that John Oxtoby was found waiting to welcome Clowes, and that he already was known as "Praying Johnny." Where and when had that name been bestowed? We have not met with John Oxtoby before, and yet his bearing such a name implies a Christian experience of some length and of such a character that it had struck the public mind. It was not "Praying Johnny" who called himself by that name, we may be sure. It was a section of the religious public, familiar with Oxtoby's work and ways, which noted the characteristic and marked it by the name. Now, the explanation of these facts will serve to reconcile the traditionary account of the state of things existing at the time of Clowes' entry into Hull, with the current historical account. Tradition tells of fully organised Primitive Methodist Societies flourishing at the time William Clowes first set foot in Hull: our biographies and histories write as though he entered on virgin soil, that he began from the very bottom, and, as though in this case, we have to do with—that rarest of all things in nature—an absolute beginning. Thus sharply put, neither of these views as to our origins in Hull is correct; the true view will be found in a combination of the truth in each. The late Mr John Brown, a native of Hessle, was a thorough-going traditionalist and stoutly maintained that there was a society at Hessle *before* there was one in Hull. There is nothing antecedently improbable in this assumed priority; on the contrary, were it proved it would simply be another illustration of Primitive Methodism's early predilection for village evangelisation. But the view is untenable. There was no organised Primitive Methodist Society at Hessle or anywhere else north of the Humber, prior to William Clowes' arrival as the duly appointed missionary; but there was material waiting—asking, one may say—to be organised, and, as we have seen, to this work of organisation William Clowes immediately addressed himself. It was not virgin, but prepared soil Clowes entered upon; but he fenced it round, and wrought in it, and planted and watered it, until, God giving the increase, it became as the garden of the Lord for fertility. This view fits all the assured facts. It does not detract from the honour due to William Clowes who was not second to any man as a breaker-up of the fallow ground; while it redounds, not less but rather more, to the credit of Hull as compelling us to see in them "a people prepared of the Lord." Instruments of such preparation were the band of earnest women already named, one of whom—Ann Carr—was invited by the Hull Quarterly Meeting, of 1820, to enter the itinerant ministry. By their occasional visits to Nottingham these women found refreshment and such stimulus as enabled them on their return to persevere in their chosen mode of Christian service. Yet more avowedly and of set purpose was Jane Brown a preparer of the way of Clowes, by her three or four weeks' unofficial labours in Hull and the neighbouring villages. John Oxtoby, too, in his own way and measure, was another preparatory worker. We left him in Mrs Woolhouse's kitchen and we will now show how he came to be there as the welcomer of Clowes, and how he got his name of "Praying Johnny."

Little Givendale, a hamlet near to Pocklington, claims to be the birthplace of John Oxtoby, though he was brought up at Warter. He was born in 1767, so that he would be fifty-two years of age when William Clowes came to Hull. Misled, no doubt, by some self-accusatory references of Oxtoby's, some accounts allege that he led a boorish and profane life before his conversion. But so far from this having been the case, he was a good liver, and so regular a church-goer that when, through sickness of soul rather than of body, he was missed from his accustomed place, the clergyman called to see what had kept his model parishioner from church. The clergyman pooh-poohed the idea that aught ailed Oxtoby but his sins, and promised to send a bottle of wine that would soon put him right. Then he read the prayers for the visitation of the sick, and went his way, having done his poor best to "minister to a mind diseased."

Oxtoby found salvation amongst the Methodists, and soon became a "general family visitor." At Warter, then a benighted place, he at first met with much opposition in going from house to house. But nowise deterred by this, he went on visiting and praying wherever he could gain admittance, until in the end he was everywhere welcomed. Did he but pass a house without calling, the inmates would cry after him, asking—"What they had done that he did not call and pray with them." Soon the people at Warter wanted a chapel, and Oxtoby gave the land required for the purpose, and ten pounds towards the building fund. And yet he was not a man of means, as commonly understood. He was only an agricultural labourer; but, being a bachelor with few wants, and frugal and thrifty in his habits, he was able, even out of his small wages, to accumulate savings, and, like Hugh Bourne and John Benton, be master of his own movements.

Some time after his conversion (which took place about 1804) Oxtoby obtained the blessing of entire sanctification. Now his usefulness was redoubled, and his efforts to do good took a wider range. But he must always have a colleague, and so we find him in association now with Robert Coultas of Acklam, another "devoted, antique, and capricious man," going on religious excursions as a rustic evangelist; and then, in 1818, taking part with George Nicholson—a man of much larger mental calibre—in a great revival in North Lincolnshire, which no doubt prepared the way for the success of Thomas King and his colleagues in the immediately following years. Still more important is it for us to know that on leaving Lincolnshire, Oxtoby, still in conjunction with Nicholson, laboured at North and South Cave, Newbald, Elloughton, and other villages in the neighbourhood of Hull. Oxtoby must have heard of the Primitives and their doings when in North Lincolnshire, for they were already at work in the county, and as near as Gainsborough and Scotter; and in Hull he was evidently acquainted with Mrs. Woolhouse and her circle, to say nothing of George Nicholson and his friend Jane Brown. No more is needed to explain his welcome of Clowes, and the fact that he at once cast in his lot with the new community and became Clowes' auxiliary, accompanying him on his mission to Swanland, Elloughton, Brantingham, Ellakar, and North and South Cave, at three of which villages Oxtoby had recently laboured in

VILLAGE CHURCH AND ELM-TREE UNDER
WHICH OXTOBY HELD MEETINGS.

But the man? We should like to "see him in his habit as he lived," and to know the man as well as the circumstances of his life. Take, then, a pen-and-ink likeness of Oxtoby, which, though imperfect, is accurate as far as it goes. Picture to yourself a man a little below the average height, broad-set, features a little sharp, his garb plain and unpretentious to a degree, brown coat, small-clothes and gaiters, chocolate neckerchief, and unclerical hat, his hair seeming to belong to one living in a world where the *coiffeur* is unknown, and all the arts of perfumery and adornment have still to be invented. The marks of care and taste in "outward adorning" are to him symptoms of worldly pride and vanity, to be shunned, spurned, and denounced.

Intellectually, Oxtoby must be acknowledged to have been a man of slender abilities, nor were his obvious deficiencies compensated, as they sometimes are, by a pleasing manner or natural eloquence. Such a man was not likely to make his mark as a preacher; nor indeed was he a "pulpit preacher" when he became acquainted with Clowes, but only a 'conversation preacher"; and though he soon ventured to use his talents, such as they were, in the pulpit, yet beginning so late in life, he never shone in the pulpit—and it would have been almost a miracle if he had shone. Like his friend, R. Coultas, he contemned carefully prepared sermons, designating them "paper-pellets," and he committed himself to a text, trusting to the Divine Spirit to aid him in what he should say.

Many are the stories preserved by tradition revealing the mingled simplicity and shrewdness of Oxtoby's character. On one occasion Mr. Flesher, inclined to a little innocent banter, asked Oxtoby 'why the results of their preaching were so different?' "Oh," said John, "thou leads the people to the tree of knowledge, and I leads them to the tree of life.' It is scarcely possible to conceive two good men so dissimilar in all respects as John Flesher and John Oxtoby. One was a Sévres vase, the other an earthenware jug; but in this case our Connexional Chrysostom met with a retort which was not wanting in appositeness and point. Another story belongs to the time when Oxtoby and his friend Nicholson were co-workers in Lincolnshire. One day they were at Kirton Lindsey, and, while sitting in the house of a friend Nicholson was singing in a low key,—"'Prone to wander, Lord, I feel it,' etc. 'You do not sing, Oxtoby!'" said Nicholson. 'No, and I am not going to sing that,' replied Oxtoby, "if I were to sing that I should tell the Lord a *lee* (lie)! I none feel prone to wander, not I. My heart is fixed." Pascal, in his "Thoughts," tells us that even a philosopher may argue a little incoherently if a fly be buzzing at his ears. So small a thing as that may disturb that sovereign understanding which gives laws to cities and kingdoms. It would seem we have another illustration of the greatness and weakness of man in the case of Oxtoby, for there were times when the normal action of his faith was disturbed by small things. On one occasion, at North Cave, he was seeking to lead a person into a state of salvation when R. Coultas came near and placed his hand on Oxtoby's shoulder. The person did not find conscious pardon. In the evening Oxtoby said, 'Brother Coultas, don't put thy hand on my shoulders any more when I am praying with inquirers; that person would have been saved but for thee."

Yet there must have been something—nay very much—in Oxtoby to account for what he ac— — — — — — the — — — — of our people. Our history affords no better illustration of the striking contrast there may be between the earthen vessel and the treasure it holds. We are jealous lest we should be so pre-occupied with the oddity of the vessel as to overlook the preciousness and divinity of its contents. We may dwell as much as we choose on the commonness of the clay, the plainness and even grotesqueness of the vessel's pattern, if we only go on to the Psalmist's blessed "nevertheless,"* and clearly recognise that this saved agricultural labourer had in a remarkable degree the gifts of faith and prayer. Were there no other

A STREET IN NORTH CAVE.

incident in Oxtoby's life than that which shows him wrestling and prevailing with God on behalf of Filey, he would stand confessed a spiritual giant—though it may be an intellectual weakling. We cannot help but smile at Oxtoby sometimes, but Oxtoby on Muston Hill is no more a subject for cheap pleasantry than Jacob at Peniel, but rather a sight to be regarded with silent reverence.

S. BOTTOMLEY.

The New Testament recognises the truth that Christ has dispensed a variety of gifts to His Church. One of these is the gift of faith. Oxtoby's faith gave reality and life to the doctrines which he proclaimed. His creed might consist of but few articles, but these his faith vivified, so that they no longer lay "bedridden in the dormitory of the soul." He was, too, a man possessed by the prayer-spirit. The Rev. Samuel Bottomley, one of our early worthies, a man of sober speech, and who knew him well, says: "He generally spent six hours each day upon his knees, pleading earnestly with God on behalf of himself, the Church, and sinners, whose salvation he most earnestly desired."

"John Oxtoby finished his mortal career January 19th, 1830,

at Londesborough, in the house of his sister, where twenty-six years before God had blessed him with a sense of His pardoning mercy." His remains were interred in the beautiful churchyard of Warter. A memorial headstone, the cost of which was met by subscription, was placed over his grave, having on it the following lines written by the late Rev. W. Howcroft :—

" 'Tis not on marble, nor on gilded page,
To print thy worth—thy charity display!
For chronicles like these may in an age
Be lost, and in oblivion pass away.
Eternity itself will best unfold
The souls led by thee to th' heav'nly fold."

Through the good offices of the Rev. W. Hayton, a service was held at the grave in 1887, and the stone and grave piously attended to. *

HULL A LEADING CIRCUIT.

So swiftly and satisfactorily did the cause progress in Hull and neighbourhood, that at the March Quarterly Meeting Mr. and Mrs. Harrison were appointed to labour on the mission as Clowes' colleagues. At the June Quarterly Meeting Hull was made into a separate circuit, as the plan appearing on the opposite page will show.

OXTOBY'S GRAVE.

Old plans are not history, but they throw considerable light on history: they are documents *pour servir*. Given a modicum of knowledge to start with, there is a good deal to be learned from the study of an old plan like this first one of the Hull Circuit. For example, we already know something of the Woolhouses, and so we notice that no less than three members of this family have their place on this first plan. Mrs. Hannah Woolhouse's name stands, appropriately enough, immediately after that of Sarah Harrison, whom we knew as Sarah Kirkland. Hannah Woolhouse, therefore, takes rank as the first local preacher. But Richard Woolhouse, her husband, who seems to have been more anxious that his wife should preach than that he should preach himself, has been induced to try his modest gifts, and his name is first of those who are local preachers on trial. John Woolhouse has his place next after his mother, but in 1821 we miss his name; the fact being that in that year he commenced his labours as a travelling preacher, and is on the stations for Grimsby. His itinerant course was only a short one, but while it lasted it seems to have been marked by considerable energy and success. We have already seen him preaching by the light of a lantern at Howden,

THE PERIOD OF CIRCUIT PREDOMINANCE AND ENTERPRISE.   371

and in November, 1820, we find him at Knottingley along with Sister Armstrong. Says he in his *Journal*: "Having spoken a little on what the damned souls would have to endure in hell, I sat down for two or three minutes for them to consider whether

[Illustration: Hull Circuit preachers' Sunday plan, 1819]

they would go to heaven or hell." From this brief record we may gather that John Woolhouse was a man very much in earnest, and no stickler for stereotyped methods of conducting religious services. Obviously there is a limit to what the study of old plans

—as a kind of fossilised history—can teach us, and so we often rise from our study of them feeling that we would like to know more. They pique our curiosity only to tantalise us. We would, for example, like to know more about the Woolhouse family, and how it fared with them in the after years. Hitherto, research in this direction has been baffled, but it is just possible that another old plan furnishes a useful clue. On the Leicester Circuit Plan, for 1827–8, we find, side by side, the names of R. and H. Woolhouse and we cannot but conclude that the earliest befrienders of Primitive Methodism in Hull had removed to Leicester, with which town we know Richard Woolhouse had business connections, and from the position of the names on the plan —Nos. 23 and 24 in a list of 55 names—we infer that the removal must have taken place some considerable time before 1827. There was yet another member of the Woolhouse family who made herself useful in the early days. Mrs. Woolhouse, junr., was a class-leader, and is said to have conducted a class for children at her own residence. The class was held on Thursday afternoons, at three o'clock, that being the hour when children were loosed from school.

On the plan are the names of other embryo travelling preachers besides John Woolhouse and John Oxtoby, such as Samuel Laister and John Hewson. Laister was a native of historic Epworth, though at this time at Market Weighton. "He was fully in the doctrine of a present salvation, and had a great love for the souls of men." At the September Quarterly Meeting, 1820, he was stationed to Leeds with Thomas Nelson for his colleague; and at December, Malton becoming a branch of Hull circuit, he was appointed to labour there. Then we meet with him labouring at Darlington, which in its turn had also been made into a branch, and here his all too-brief course terminated.

Our plan contains the notification that the Quarterly meeting would be held on September 13th. Now the "preachers' meeting" of that board brought two of its members under discipline. One of these was John Oxtoby, upon whom, as yet, the preaching harness sat uneasily. So the following resolution was recorded:—"That John Oxtoby be reproved by R. Woolhouse for neglecting his appointments, and that he have only one or two on the next plan." W. Ricketeson also was "to be spoken to by W. Clowes for long preaching and praying, and for talking about philosophy and astronomy, etc." Imagination may range at will over this *et cetera*. All the ologies may be wrapped up in it. It was not Bro. Ricketeson, but another Yorkshire local, who fell under the same condemnation of introducing astronomy into his discourse. After he had expatiated at some length on stars and systems, an old steward called out: "Let them alone. They'll go reet, and thee come down and talk to us a bit."

Turning from the preachers to the places on the plan that were within the borough, we notice that Mill Street stands first, having already superseded the Old Factory in North Street. But we note, further, that no provision is made for services in Mill Street until September 19th. The fact is, the growing requirements of the new-born society and congregation rendered a more commodious building indispensable, so that in three months from the time W. Clowes entered Hull, the society was in the throes of chapel building, and in September, Mill Street Chapel was opened.

MILL STREET CHAPEL.

A piece of ground at the end of Mill Street, on which some old buildings were standing, was purchased of Mr. Edward Taylor, Waterhouse Lane, rag-merchant, for the sum of £345. Eleven pounds more were spent in clearing the ground for building. The foundation-stone was laid on Friday, the 12th April, and of course W. Clowes and his colleagues took part in the services; but it was Ann Carr who laid the chief stone, and who seems to have given the principal address. Some who were present remember the excitement produced in the neighbourhood by the fact of a woman's preaching in the open-air, and they tell of the impression her powerful voice, commanding manner, and her individualising mode of address made on the audience.* The chapel was in

MILL STREET CHAPEL.

an unfinished state when opened, as the pews lacked doors, and the building throughout was unpainted; and even when all was done that had to be done, and the last finishing-touches had been given, there was a studied absence of the attractive and even the convenient, about the building. Architecturally, our fathers did not aim very high. They set before them no lofty ideal of what a place of worship should be. The one problem they cared to solve was this: how to enclose so many cubic feet of space with weather-tight walls and roof, so that sitting (not lounging) room might be found for a given number of men and women to hear the everlasting gospel. No

* See "Rem'... ... ... Garbutt.

fewer than three sermons were preached on the opening day, which was Friday, September 10th. The preachers were Thomas King, of Grimsby, W. Braithwaite, of Scotter, and John Dent. Messrs. King, Dent and Sarah Harrison occupied the pulpit on the following Sunday, while "sisters Carr and Healand each gave an exhortation." John Harrison remarks of the chapel-opening. 'Through all the services we had humbling and weeping times." Now, it is said, a great revival broke out. Some of the outcasts of society became reformed characters, and so great was the alarm felt by some persons about the sinful lives they had led, that it was no unusual thing to continue the Sabbath evening meeting until midnight. These were "protracted services" indeed! As the result of this revival a large increase of members was reported at the Quarterday following the opening.

The total cost of the Mill Street undertaking is given as £1,604 18s. 9d. To us this sum may seem to represent an outlay by no means extraordinary, but we must recollect that eighty years ago the purchasing power of money was greater than it is to-day, and further, that amongst those by whom the work was projected and carried out, there was only here and there one who had any other source of income than the returns of his own labour week by week. Amongst the items of expenditure in connection with the building of the mother-chapel, we find four shillings put down for the hire of four constables for the night. The item is significant. It suggests that those who came together to the new chapel opening, were not all models of order and propriety, and it gives incidental confirmation of the realistic pictures W. Clowes occasionally draws of the difficulties under which public worship was conducted at the beginning by him and his colleagues—difficulties arising from the rowdiness of some of the populace. Here is one picture which may serve as a sample of the rest:—

"On Sunday, 24th February, I preached morning, afternoon, and evening, in Hull. We had a gracious visit from on high; but the wicked lifted up their hands against us, and were very violent and fierce in their conduct, and excited the people to such a degree, that they imagined the place was about to fall upon us. Alarm and consternation overwhelmed the multitude in such a manner that they attempted to make their escape from the place. The scene presented an indescribable picture at this crisis,—some crying for help, others forcing their way to the door, whilst some threw up the windows and jumped out; but, as the building was but one story high, there were none seriously injured. At the evening service we got the police to guard the door, to keep out the most furious of the rabble; and when we commenced our meeting, they shouted and bellowed on the outside, and threw up stones and broke the windows. The battle then became very hot, both inside and outside; however, 'the battle was turned to the gate', for many of the jack-tars who had persecuted us and fired whole broadsides into us, struck their colours, and came aboard of the 'Ranters'' ship, to sail with us along to the port of glory. It became a necessary course likewise (to protect the great number of anxious inquirers after salvation from the violence of the mob) to apply to the mayor; by his exertions in our favour, three of the sons of Belial were imprisoned."—*Journal*, pp. 149-150.

After such a description it would be a bold thing to assert that our fathers met with no persecution at the beginning of their labours in Hull. All that can be affirmed is that, as distinct persecution. What Thomas Binney says of the Thessalonica of Paul's time, was true of the Hull of Clowes' time: "Thessalonica was a sea-port, and these 'lewd fellows of the baser sort' were of the set you always see loafing about decks, quays, and wharves,—a kind of 'long-shore men,' who can always be hired for a pot of beer and a shilling."* Remembering this, and also the educational advance of the people since 1819, and the remarkable softening of manners that has followed, one cannot but wonder that our fathers did not encounter even greater opposition in Hull than they did encounter.

Their comparative immunity from persecution must in part be put down to the credit of the town. Hull, on the whole, was true to itself; and if there were any exceptions, the magistrates, acting in consonance with the noble traditions of their borough, did not "bear the sword in vain," but took care that the pioneers of our Church should not be at the mercy of any low-bred, drunken fellow, who thought the "Ranters," as they were vulgarly called, were fair game for insult and annoyance.

There were two or three small houses in Chapel Court contiguous to Mill Street Chapel, belonging to the trustees, which at one time were occupied by our ministers. They were the temporary and humble residence of many men of ministerial power and influence. William Sanderson was the last of his brethren to live in Chapel Court, but such men as Suddards and Hewson, Verity and Hutchinson, had preceded him as ministerial occupants of the trustees' property. Here, too, William Clowes had lived prior to his removal to Spencer Street. Subsequently, however, they were let to other people, and, in 1835, we find one Luke Green became a tenant at a rent of £4 5s. per annum.

CLOWES' HOUSE, HULL.

Green was killed by a steam-packet explosion at the South Pier, June 9th, 1837. By this untoward event several persons were hurried into eternity with awful suddenness. Mr. Green had removed from Hull a little time before, and had been over to Hull to attend the camp meeting on the previous day. Fearing he was late he ran to get

* "St. Paul: His Life and Ministry," p. 222.

on board, and in a moment or two the explosion occurred by which he was killed on the spot. From his *Journal* we learn that W. Clowes had fully intended being on board the Gainsboro' packet that very morning. Mrs. Clowes had arranged to go by it, and he intended seeing her off; but he had lingered so long at his devotions the night before, that he overslept himself, and was thus unable to be at the pier in proper time to catch the packet. Possibly his drowsiness saved his life. Jacob Dawson, another of our ministers, was on board when the catastrophe occurred, but escaped with a slight wound on his arm and the loss of his hat.

Mill Street was not the first chapel built north of the Humber; that distinction belongs to North Cave—also found on this same plan—whose chapel was opened by John Harrison and his wife and John Woolhouse, on July 26th, 1819. Yet, though Mill Street just missed this distinction, and cannot claim to be the oldest Connexional chapel still in actual use, there is no existing chapel of equal size and importance still

JACOB DAWSON.

THE FIRST CHAPEL, NORTH CAVE.

occupied; and as the prolific mother of chapels, and in the richness of its historic associations, it admits of no rival. It is such considerations as these that justify the recording of details which, in the case of a modern structure, would be felt to be out of keeping with the purpose of this history.

The fact that Mill Street Chapel came to be known about 1849 as West Street has, no doubt, tended to obscure the identity of the one building. The account of the structural alterations and improvements which gave the original sanctuary an approach from another and a better street, belongs to the next period, in which Hull became as famous for its enterprise in chapel building, as it was in this first period famous for its missionary achievements

SOME HULL WORKERS AND THEIR WORK

We have described the acquisition of Hull's workshop, a few words must now be devoted to some of its workers and the work they did. One would naturally expect to find some of the earliest and best available workers amongst the twenty persons who composed the original trust of West Street. We find such to be the case, but, unfortunately, here as elsewhere, some who seem to have been both locally and Connexionally prominent in the years immediately following 1819, afterwards disappear. In the absence of information we can only put—"missing" to their names, and wonder whether death removed them from their posts, or whether they went out from us in some time of trial and sifting, such as we know was experienced in other parts, and was responsible for so many disappearances.

Of the thirteen laymen who were trustees of West Street, E Taylor, Richard Jackson, G Gill, and M Scafe figure on the first Connexional Committees. What this means, as a gauge of Connexional influence, had better be explained here once for all. In 1822 a General Committee, with one of its two branches located in Hull and the other in Tunstall, was established. To the Hull branch was also assigned the duty of administering the Contingent Fund established the same year. The Contingent Fund, it may be said, was the precursor of what we know familiarly as the S W P and O Fund. This arrangement continued until 1825, when the Hull branch of the General Committee was abolished, though it was still allowed to manage the Contingent Fund. This same year, 1825, too, saw the establishment of a General Missionary Committee at Tunstall, with Auxiliary Committees at Nottingham, Hull and Sunderland. In 1831 the Contingent Fund became "The Circuits Assistant Sick Preachers' Fund," which name of portentous length was shortened into "C A S tr prs Fund," and the executive of this fund was fixed at Tunstall; so that, with the unimportant exception of a branch Publishing Committee allowed to Hull, all the Committees as well as the Book room were located at Tunstall, which was thus the official centre of the Connexion until 1843, Hull and the other districts having to be content with their own District Committees.

For a short space Edward Taylor appears to have been one of the most conspicuous figures in Hull Primitive Methodism. From him the land on which Mill Street Chapel stood was bought, and he gave a donation of ten pounds towards its building fund. His name is found on the first plan next to that of Hannah Woolhouse. We should take him to have been a man of some worldly substance, plain in his dress, serious and even severe of aspect, and rigid in his views as to the proprieties demanded of Christian people; for it was he who was entrusted with the delicate duty of admonishing John Oxtoby, and he was set as a watchman by the September Quarterly Meeting of 1820 to prevent, if possible, the intrusion of worldly fashions into the singers' pew of Mill Street. The resolution authorising his appointment is too good to be consigned to oblivion and ran as follows:—" E Taylor to take care of the singers' pew, and let none in except those who appear no frills, no bunches of ribbons, and no superfluities whatever. All the preachers and leaders are requested to get a plain dress as soon as possible, that they may insist upon plainness in all the society." Edward Taylor's Connexional standing is witnessed to by his being one of the earliest members of the Hull branch of the General Managing Committee and still more by his sharing the honour with William Woolhouse and R. Woolhouse of being a representative of Hull Circuit at the Preparatory Meeting at Nottingham, August, 1819, and at the first Conference of 1820 held in Hull.

Even at the risk of keeping some Hull worthies waiting, this would seem to be the time to refer to the doings of the Nottingham Preparatory Meeting. The reference need not detain us long, as all those amongst the fifteen representatives of the four circuits to that meeting, of whom information is available, have already been mentioned, and as far as possible described. All that need now be done is to give a complete list of the representatives, and to add a few remarks on the historical importance of the meeting.

The following is the list of delegates sent from the four Circuits to the Preparatory Meeting:—

1. TUNSTALL CIRCUIT
Hugh Bourne
James Bourne

2. NOTTINGHAM
Thomas King
Thomas Simmons
W. Guy
Samuel Bailey
James Rudd
D. Musson Jackson

3. LOUGHBOROUGH
Joseph Skevington
George Hanford
William North
William Goodrich

4. HULL
William Clowes
Richard Woolhouse
Richard Jackson

The meeting, which commenced on August 10th, "and continued by adjournment till the Saturday evening following," was much more than a Preparatory Meeting. It was also, as Mr Petty remarks, "a legislative assembly, and that to an extraordinary extent." It laid down the basal principles of our Church polity, in harmony with which the evolution of the denomination has ever since proceeded, so that this Nottingham meeting might with strict propriety be regarded as our first and most important Conference, had not usage decided that it be known as the Preparatory Meeting. Only in one or two respects has limitation been imposed on what was then enacted, as, for instance, in the composition of the Quarterly Meeting which was made "the seat of authority, the source whence all power was drawn," as it still remains. The Quarterly Board had to be composed of "travelling and local preachers, leaders, stewards, and delegates, and such other persons as the several General Quarterly Meetings shall think proper." The Circuit Stewards were to be three in number, and the principal steward was to be the custodian of the books and property of the circuit. The appointment, and not merely the nomination, of the Society Steward was with the Leaders' Meeting. The printed proceedings of the Preparatory Meeting are in the form of question and answer, and the last question asked is "(43 Q.) Shall a person be appointed to attend to the general concerns of the Connexion?" To which the brief answer is "Yes." Now this affirmative answer might be so construed as to favour the creation of the office of a General Superintendent of the Connexion, such as Hugh Bourne had been from December 1814 to 1818, or the appointment of Chairmen of Districts or Presiding Elders. But even these advances in the direction of episcopal government were declined in favour of the more Presbyterian form of the appointment of "managing committees" of various kinds with their "corresponding members" or secretaries. Instead of concentrating authority in the hands of one man, or few men, Primitive Methodism has preferred to take the more democratic line of distributing authority amongst committees freely elected.

It was at the Preparatory Meeting that the question of delegation to the first Annual Meeting had to be considered and decided; and it was decided in the way we all know. Three delegates were to be sent from each circuit in the proportion of two laymen to one travelling preacher. This arrangement was arrived at only after considerable discussion. If any credence is to be given to floating traditions, we must conclude that what was finally agreed upon was largely due to the suggestion of James Rudd, one of the Nottingham delegates, who gave as his reason for urging the two-to-one arrangement, that in another community where the representation was one and one, there had been some dissension which had not been easily allayed; that, in fact, despite the flattering picture of the working of equal representation found in the early cartoon given on the other page, the minister and the layman did not invariably walk together arm in arm. On the other hand, it was objected that, if one in every three delegates was to be a travelling preacher, that arrangement would give the travelling preachers a larger numerical representation in the highest court of the Connexion than they enjoyed in the lower courts. But the suggestion of James Rudd (if indeed it were his, and not George Hanford's or William Goodrich's, as some hold) took with the meeting, and was, we are told, acceptable to Hugh Bourne. When we remember that only two out of the fifteen delegates to the Preparatory Meeting were travelling preachers, we can only express surprise that so large a proportion of representation was conceded to the ministerial element. The delegates to that Nottingham meeting of 1819 were broad-minded and far-seeing men, and though they did not profess to claim any Scriptural sanction or divine inspiration for the working arrangement they hit upon, yet the history of our Church shows that the arrangement has worked well.

The Richard Jackson who went from Hull to the Preparatory Meeting was, until 1828, Connexionally very much to the fore. He came, he tells us, as a volunteer from the Wesleyans, in May, 1819. He was the principal Steward of Hull Circuit for some years, and as such from time to time sent to the *Magazine* short but enthusiastic letters—veritable war-bulletins—recounting the progress made by the circuit. He was the corresponding member of the Hull Branch of the General Managing Committee while it lasted, and then treasurer of the Contingent Fund until we miss his name from the records.

Thomas Newsam and Thomas Lascelles, among the laymen who were trustees of Mill Street, survived the longest, and died in communion with our Church. The latter,

380 PRIMITIVE METHODIST CHURCH.

EMBLEMS OF THE POLITY OF METHODISM.

especially, long played a useful part. He filled the offices of local preacher and class-leader. He plied the trade of a shoemaker, and his house in Bond Street was long a home for the single preachers. Many a minister, afterwards to grow grey and infirm in the ranks, would to the end cherish grateful recollections of the hospitable and quiet abode of Thomas Lascelles.

> "The sweet remembrance of the just
> Shall flourish when they sleep in dust."

Mrs. Beecroft is referred to by W. Clowes in his *Journal* as one of his early converts at the Old Factory, and in the sermon preached by him on the occasion of her death, he speaks of her fourteen years' unbroken connection with our Church; her liberality in supporting the cause of God, the sick, and the poor; her custom of devoting half-an-hour twice each week in praying and singing with her servants and work-people. Her house was a "Pilgrim's inn" where Clowes and Oxtoby, and the early preachers constantly resorted for comfort and refreshment. The name and family traditions were worthily continued for many years by her son, Samuel, and her nephew, Charles Beecroft.

SAMUEL BEECROFT.

CHARLES BEECROFT.

William and Jane Holliday's tombstone stands hard by that of William Clowes' in the "Primitive-corner" of Hull general Cemetery. For some years they gave themselves to missionary work, labouring separately, though in contiguous circuits, chiefly in the Dales of Northern England. In 1828 they settled in Hull, and both became local preachers and class-leaders. Mrs. Holliday was a noted visitor of the sick and neglected; and during the visitation of the cholera in 1832, she fearlessly and unsparingly, by night and by day, tended those who were stricken by this fell disease. She died in 1838, while her husband survived until 1863.

What Hull Primitive Methodism owes to the various members of the Hodge family it would be difficult to tabulate, though a better idea of the extent of this indebtedness will be gained when we reach the chapel-building era. The family came from Kilnsea near Spurn Point, in Holderness, a district which has suffered, and is still suffering, severely from the inroads of the sea. W. Clowes went on a mission into Holderness—then a most benighted part of the country—in 1820. "At Kilnsea," he says, "I preached in the house of Mr. W. Hodge, who had a large family of children, of whom many were converted; and some became preachers of the Word. Here I was kindly entertained." He visited one of the lighthouses on the Point, and as he returned by the shore, washed by the German Ocean, "I saw," says he, "that the ocean had gained upon the land; the sea was breaking against a churchyard, and the bones and coffins of the dead were visible. What an awful sight! What hath sin done!" As Clowes passed along that day he would see Kilnsea Church standing on the edge of the cliff, unroofed and the haunt of sea-fowl. Soon the walls and tower, which pious hands had reared centuries before, fell into the engulfing sea.

Of William Hodge's four sons, John, Samuel, William, and Henry, the first two on their removal to Hull became actively associated with our cause in another part of the town. Mrs. Jane Garbutt, a very competent authority, thus tells the story in her interesting little book of "Reminiscences of the Early Days of Primitive Methodism":—

"Previous to the erection of Mill Street Chapel, and in addition to the Old Factory, the disused Penitentiary in Church Street, Wincolmlee, was rented; this was continued by services at six o'clock, and it was still a great medium for the conversion of sinners, and by means of the classes and other meetings, strengthened the faith of believers. When it was no longer available for our purpose, the meetings were held at a house tenanted by Mrs. Harper on the opposite side of Church Street, a little further down. About this time Mr. John Hodge came to reside in a commodious house in Church Street, which was offered for our use and gratefully accepted. Many, many times has the converting glory been felt, and the power of the Holy One has rested on the ark. A small chapel was built, either on the site of, or near, the above-named house. This was afterwards enlarged, or rebuilt, with class and school-rooms and other conveniences, in 1846. *This was the second chapel and second society which was raised up*— a band of men and women whose hearts the Lord had touched, and who ardently worked for Him. This society was afterwards removed to Lincoln Street, the present chapel, named after its benefactor, 'The Samuel Hodge Memorial Chapel.' This gentleman (as also his son the lamented Alderman George Hodge) has since entered into his rest, beloved and esteemed by all those who knew him. He laboured in our midst as a class-leader and local preacher, and sustained with commendable efficiency the various offices of the Church."

KILNSEA CHURCH, HOLDERNESS.*

When the Hodge family resided at Kilnsea, gainsayers who witnessed their hospitality to the servants of Christ, were used scoffingly to predict that the "bacon-preachers would soon eat them up." But God's blessing was on the industry and thrift and integrity of the sons of the household, and they prospered in the world, sufficiently, one thinks, to shut

* The view of Kilnsea Church in its dismantled state, here given, is from a sketch taken in 1826, by Mr. W. Little, of Patrington, afterwards reproduced in Poulson's "History and Antiquities of

the mouths of all gainsayers; but the higher they rose in the social scale and the more affluent their circumstances became, the more did the Church of their choice benefit by their social and temporal advancement. From the earliest times, the policy of "scattering their fire" was pursued by our fathers in Hull. Prayer meetings, well supported by organised praying bands, were held in various parts of the town; tract distributing bands were hard at work; a sick visiting association, formed in 1830, by three young men, Samuel Hays, William Bentley, and John Parrott, afterwards of Leeds, at one time had 330 members in its ranks; open-air services were stately held in the most neglected and degraded parts of the town, and in these mission services William Hodge, Jun., who twice came to occupy the position of chief magistrate of the borough, took an

TOWN HALL, HULL.

active part when a young man. Leadenhall Square was one of the districts thus missioned, and with good reason it was regarded as one of the most disreputable quarters of the town. This squalid rookery was cleared away for the purpose of erecting the present Town Hall. While mayor of the borough, it fell to Mr. Hodge's lot to open this fine building, which covered the site of his own early missionary labours, and in which the Conference of 1902 was to be the recipient of civic generous hospitality.

Henry Hodge's name is familiar as "household words" in the mouths of our people, but fuller reference to what he did for Hull Primitive Methodism, and the Connexion generally, will more appropriately be made when we come to speak of Hull chapel extension, and the educational and missionary movements of the next period.

His friend and relative by marriage, John Sissons, was another village contribution to Hull Primitive Methodism. North Cave was his home, where his parents were early adherents of the cause, and where he was converted during his apprenticeship. About 1832, he came to seek his fortune in the big town, and by dint of hard work and strict integrity, he became a leading, and at last, the oldest established tradesman in the old Market Place. Beyond serving as a guardian of the poor, he did not take an active part in public life, but gave all his available time to his Church. He identified himself with Mill Street, and retained his connection with it until his death, in 1882. He was Circuit Steward during those early years when the Quarterly Meeting lasted four or five days, and was of the dimensions of a District Meeting. His house was the home and gathering-place of the ministers. He was the close friend of John Flesher and William Clowes, and the latter was accustomed for many years to spend every Thursday with him in social intercourse and prayer. For several years he served as Connexional auditor, and very frequently represented his district in Conference. He was a man of intelligence, and, within a limited range, a considerable reader. He read and re-read Young, and Pollock, and Milton until his own vocabulary became greatly enriched. John Sissons was in many respects original—some would say eccentric—in his ways. He had a rich vein of kindly humour, and, both from principle and natural bent, was cheerful and disposed to look on the brighter side of things. Never would he admit that a service had been to him wholly barren; if the sermon had been poor, the hymns had made up for it all, or the preacher had got near to God in prayer, or the Scripture lesson had come home to him with unusual sweetness and force. One of his characteristic sayings was that he had three reasons for always being found in his pew on week days as well as Sundays. The first was, that he went to the house of God for his own profiting; the second, that he went to encourage his minister; and, finally, that he went to set a good example. He was a firm believer in systematic and proportionate giving, and had what he called "the Lord's bag." The worthy poor experienced his bounty, and when he died, which was a few hours after his return from the week-night service at West Street, his weekly pensioners had good reason to lament his loss.

JOHN SISSONS.

WILLIAM GRAY.

CHARLES BOWMAN.

Since William Gray began his business life as the apprentice of John Sissons, and was his .... for himself somewhat late in life, their names may well be linked together. For some years he was an instrumentalist in the singers' pew of the mother-chapel, and afterwards a leader and official of Spring Bank. He was intelligent, considerate of the feelings of others—a gentleman by nature and grace. All who knew William Gray will readily acknowledge that he gave dignity and character to the official life of the Church he adorned.

A man in many respects of a very different type was Charles Bowman. He was unmistakably eccentric, narrow in many of his views, blunt, the sworn foe not only of tobacco, but of the moustache, of musical instruments employed in the service of the sanctuary, and of everything else which seemed to him to approach to conformity to the fashions of the world. But he had many estimable qualities, and it was by virtue of these, and not of his eccentricities, that he won the regard of his brethren, and was appointed a permanent member of Conference. He was punctual, untiring in labours, intensely loyal, and capable of strong attachments, as was evidenced by his profound reverence and affection for William Clowes. Nor was he without a grim humour of his own, which made some of his sayings live in the memories of men. When, in order to keep moving with the times, it was proposed to bring a harmonium into West Street chapel, Charles was asked for a subscription. He complied with the request of the daring collector, and when twitted with his inconsistency gave as his answer: "Well; if we are to have the Devil in the singers' pew, we may as well have him in one piece as in many."

MRS. J. CHAMBERS.

Brief mention only can be made of other of the early worthies—of J. Brown of "The Retreat," and John Wallis; of John Chambers, originally of Yarmouth, and his wife; of Mrs Temperton, who became the second Mrs. Clowes, and her daughter Charlotte, who was married to John Davison, the biographer of Clowes; of the families of the Beckworths, the Blakestones, the Normans, the Medds, the Southerns, the Wilsons, the Halls of Sutton, the Charlesworths; of Clara Chaffer, who became the wife of Jeremiah Dodsworth. Other names of early workers and supporters of the varied interests of the Church might be given, and others belonging to a later period will come before us; but these will suffice as a sample, and be enough to indicate that Hull's vigorous church-life and far-reaching influence were not only due to its succession of able and devoted ministers, and to the presence in its midst, for so many years, of the holy Clowes, but were also largely due to a remarkable band of active Christian workers and capable officials.

J. CHAMBERS.

W. BLAKESTONE.

In 1825, the society in Mill Street, Hull, being now large and adapted to various kinds of Christian labour, the friends determined to try to organise a Sunday school. But at the very threshold of the undertaking, they were to find that, "Where is the school to be taught?" For a time they were brought to a stand, as no place suited to their purpose formed any part of the trust premises. But Mr W. Rodgers thought he knew of a room in every way adapted to their requirements, and the matter was put into his hands. He hired the schoolroom of Mr. Ledell, in Roper Street. Then an appeal was made from the pulpit for voluntary labour, for subscriptions, and for books, and in fourteen days from the first meeting which was called to consider the subject, the school was opened with seventy-six scholars. Among the first scholars were three of Mr. Ledell's children, one of whom was to be one of the heroes of the "Birkenhead," while George became an official of the church, of a very useful and meritorious type. Among the first officers of the Sunday School we may name Messrs Rodgers, Gill, Newsam, Day, Locking, Bowman, W. Hodge, and R. Fisher. The last laboured long and conscientiously in the school, and passed away in peace from his toil and sorrow in 1873. Though it was a good step from West Street to Roper Street, the schoolroom there soon became filled every Sunday. Five years later, the topmost story of a building in Chapel Street was taken. As there was a passage from Chapel Street to West Street, the room was very conveniently situated, and it, like the one before it, soon became strait enough. There was at one time a branch Sunday school in the old town. In 1833, the trustees of the old chapel resolved to build schoolrooms adjoining the chapel, and to alter the chapel itself. They were encouraged to take this step, in part, from the fact that the debt had been considerably reduced, as well as from a desire to meet a felt want. The new schools were opened in the spring of 1834, and the speedy multiplication of both teachers and scholars showed that the trustees had not missed the mark they aimed at.

Mill Street Society prospered so greatly, that at length it was deemed desirable to provide additional accommodation, and, if possible, to provide it in such a locality as would suit the convenience of those members and adherents who lived on the Holderness Road, Drypool, the Groves, and other more distant parts of the town. Hence, in 1841, Mason Street Chapel, built in 1822 for the use of a Calvinistic congregation, was acquired as a "relief chapel." This made the third chapel possessed by the denomination in Hull. In January, 1839, a town-mission was established, one minister being set apart to this work, and the results of the appointment were gratifying. Subsequently, schools were built behind the Mason Street property, and the growing interest here led afterwards, as we shall see, to the building of Clowes' Chapel in Jarratt Street.

CHAPTER VII.
HOME BRANCH OF HULL,
And its First Three Circuits.

IN June, 1820, Hull fell into line with the other Circuits, and divided its inconveniently wide missions into branches. This was done by a committee consisting of W. Clowes, J. Verity, S. Laister, and R. Woolhouse. Its territory was carved into seven branches, of which Hull itself, with its four preachers, was called the Home Branch; the labours of fourteen other preachers were apportioned amongst the remaining six branches as follows: Pocklington, three; Brotherton, two; Ripon, three; York, three; Leeds, two; Malton, two. At present we have only to do with the Home Branch, and Pocklington, Brotherton, and Hutton Rudby, which were the first circuits made from Hull, and along with it constituting the first Hull District of 1821.

Even after this arrangement was made, the Home Branch covered a wide stretch of country, including that part of North Lincolnshire represented by the present Barton Circuit, the district of Holderness in its widest sense, as including Beverley, and the fringe at least of the Wolds. At the Conference of 1820, held in Hull, three great camp meetings were held on Conference Sunday, instead of one, as is the custom at present. One of these was held across the Humber, at Barrow, and served as a rallying centre for Barton, Goxhill, Ferriby, and other villages which had already received the evangel through the agency of our missionaries. This district became a stronghold of Primitive Methodism, and long retained a close connection with Hull; Barton not becoming an independent station until 1852.

Holderness.

Another of the three Conference camp meetings was held at Keyingham, in Holderness. This last name, strictly speaking, designates that triangular tract of country which has its apex some few miles to the south of Flamborough, and its base stretching from Spurn to the mouth of the Hull. The word "Holderness" epitomises the physical geography and earliest history of this district: it is the "Promontory of Hollow Deira." Many of its villages have their names ending in "ea," as Kilnsea, Hornsea, etc., which tells us that, formerly, the places so named must have stood on sites largely surrounded by water. Lakes such as Hornsea Mere—the only one of the kind remaining—would fill up the numerous depressions in what was itself a "hollow" —a saucer-like depression: hence its name. It was, indeed, an out-of-the-way corner, and, in much earlier days, its inhabitants must have been largely shut out from the larger world, living, as they did, hemmed in between the ocean, the Humber, and the vast Wold Forests beyond the river Hull. All this remoteness and isolation are things of the past; but even as late as 1819, a gifted retired Wesleyan minister, who had a good house and property in Holderness, proposed that he become an unsalaried minister in order that he might labour in "this dark benighted part." The Rev. Thomas Galland's words as applied to Holderness were at that time quite correct. It stood very much in need of Methodism, as he knew, and probably there are few parts of the country which, more than Holderness, have been dependent on the ministrations of Methodism. The other branches of Evangelical Nonconformity seem to have left this corner of the land to the Wesleyan Methodists and ourselves; and it is but the sober truth to affirm that our Church, as represented by Tadcaster, Hornsea, and partly by Hull Circuits, has not played the secondary part in the evangelisation of Holderness.

John Harrison was the pioneer missionary of Holderness; for as early as April 17th, 1819, he records in his *Journal*:—"I left Hull, and went into the country, and

KEYINGHAM.

continued for one week. There were many awakened to a sense of their duty towards God, and several united with us. God has opened our way in a wonderful manner in this part of Yorkshire [Holderness]; four barns have been emptied by their proprietors, on purpose for us to preach in them."

So the holding of the Keyingham camp meeting was a piece of wise strategy. It served as a rally for the newly formed societies, and a further means of spreading the Gospel through the district. That village subsequently became the head of a Branch of Hull, and so continued until, in 1841, Patrington, as being more central, took its place.

As illustrative of the change for the better in the manners and morals of the district, brought about through the labours of W. Clowes and his co-workers, the story must be

HEDON-IN-HOLDERNESS.

told again of the camp meeting held at Preston on Maudlin Sunday and what came of it. From time immemorial it had been the custom for a football-match to be played on St. Magdalene or "Maudlin" Sunday between the villages of Hedon and Preston. The two villages stood for the respective goals, and the object of each village-team was to kick the ball through the windows of the first public-house they came to that had not its windows guarded by shutters. The ball was urged hither and thither, amid the

PRESTON-IN-HOLDERNESS.

partizan cries of the onlookers of both sexes, and the oaths and shouts of the contestants, many of whom were bruised and maimed in the struggle, from the fact that some of the players had their boots tipped with hard leather or steel in order to make their kicks more telling. Blood flowed freely, and so did strong drink. The whole countryside was stirred, and vocal with the rival cries of, "Now Preston!" "Now Hedon!" Preston Church has been known to empty as the ball drew near, and the parson, after hurrying through the service, would "stand treat" to the victors. True to their principle of meeting vice on its own chosen ground, the Hull friends determined to hold a camp meeting on Knowl Hill on Maudlin Sunday (August), 1820. Preston had been visited for the first time but a short while before by preachers who were returning from a camp meeting at Keyingham, and who preached from the cart in which they had ridden. Some person drew out the linchpin from one of the wheels, by which mischievous act they were placed in considerable peril. This was but a tame rehearsal of what awaited the Hull Primitives on Maudlin Sunday. On this occasion, "a number of the rabble strove to the utmost to upset the waggon, and got under one side of it for the purpose. The friends did their best on the opposite side to prevent it. Between the two parties, the waggon was for some time rocked like a cradle, or tossed like a vessel in a storm. The wicked, however, failed to upset it, and the brethren succeeded in holding a camp meeting according to their purpose, though one of the preachers had his coat-laps torn off, which were thrown high into the air. Many were convinced of sin, and a good work broke out in the neighbourhood."

THE HOUSE FROM WHICH THE FAMOUS FOOTBALL MATCH STARTED AT HEDON.

These particulars were given to Mr. Petty by the late Peter Jackson, a popular local preacher of Preston who was present that day and witnessed all that took place. Billy Rattle was a ringleader in these football-matches, but he was converted under Clowes, of whom, and of that day's proceedings, he often spoke."

Though W. Clowes says nothing in his *Journal* of this famous camp meeting which checked and prepared the way for the abolition of these unseemly practices, he visited Preston a short time afterwards and records an amusing incident which then occurred:—

"At Preston I preached in the open-air, from the words: 'If any man thirst, let him come unto Me and drink; he that believeth in Me, as the Scriptures hath said, out of his belly shall flow rivers of living water.' It having been a dry summer, and there being a great want of rain, an old woman who was standing by when

THE PLACE WHERE THE CAMP MEETING WAS HELD AT PRESTON-IN-HOLDERNESS.

PRESTON-IN-HOLDERNESS, SHOWING OLD CHAPEL

I delivered my text, when she heard 'rivers of living water' mentioned, ran down the town, and told the people that the waters had broken out against old Pallister's house, and everybody might have some. On this, the people flocked up to see the wonder, but they found that the waters that had broken out were 'living waters,' and at that time they were flowing very freely. Several were under conviction, and one man, lying on a heap of stones just by, was crying to God with all his might. We soon had a blessed work in the place, and sixty souls joined in church fellowship."

The first chapel at Preston was built in 1822, at a cost of £200, and was capable of seating 174 persons. For several years Preston, Burstwick, and Rimswell Chapels were a source of great anxiety, especially so as they were not originally Connexional chapels, but private property. The Hull Quarterly Meeting of 1827 directed that Brother William Brining "should get Preston and Rimswell Chapels painted without cost to

BEVERLEY MARKET AS IT APPEARED 100 YEARS AGO.

the funds, or, if he painted them himself, paint should be found him." During the course of its history Preston has sometimes been attached to Patrington, sometimes to Hull. A Society was formed at Hedon in 1840.

BEVERLEY.

Primitive Methodism was introduced into the ancient town of Beverley in 1820, by John Verity, who, on the afternoon of August 20th, preached in its spacious market-place to a very peaceable congregation. Some short time afterwards W. Clowes preached in the same place to "a huge multitude"; and though he seems to have preached under the anticipation of arrest, the service went on without interruption, and at its close he had the joy of adding six members to the society. William Clowes had some ground   just the kind of town in which opposition both from the authorities and the freemen might be looked for. Indeed, at a date subsequent to this, W. Driffield—another of the preachers of the Home Branch—was forcibly pulled down from his stand while preaching in the street, by constables acting under the orders of the Mayor, and taken before the magistrates. After examination, however, he was courteously dismissed.

Cherry Burton, a village some three miles from Beverley, was visited at the same time by Hull's leading missionary. The infamous Bonner, afterwards Bishop of London, was presented to the rectory of Cherry Burton in 1530, by the Canons of Beverley. Here W. Clowes found the people so "callous" that, at the close of the sermon, he declared his resolve to shake the dust off his feet as a testimony against them, and take the Gospel to others who would receive it with greater readiness of mind. This

BEVERLEY. THE UPPER ROOM IN THE FISH SHAMBLES, SHOWING THREE WINDOWS OVER THE TWO SMALL SHOPS IN CENTRE OF PICTURE.

declaration had a rousing effect upon several. They came forward offering to take in the preachers and assist the cause; whereupon the preacher relented, the threatened interdict was recalled, and Cherry Burton continued to be visited as usual. In 1840 a chapel was built here under the superintendency of George Lamb, capable of seating seventy-seven persons, and in 1851, a second and improved building was erected.

Returning to Beverley, we find as the winter of 1820 drew on, with its cold and storms, a large upper room near the Fish Shambles was taken. This was effected mainly through the liberality of two pious widows—Mrs. Copling and Mrs. Rogers—both Wesleyans, who made themselves responsible for the rent. In this first meeting-place a chair did duty as a pulpit, which is still preserved as an interesting relic of the early times. A plain bench, capable of seating some six persons was all the room offered in the way of seatage for the whole congregation, yet the people gladly attended and contentedly stood to hear the word of life. Many more were added to the growing Church meeting in the unpretentious "upper room," and it soon became too small. A more commodious room was then hired in Turner's Yard. In this new home the infant church had for a time to contend with a good deal of opposition from the baser sort of the populace, and even from those who made pretensions to respectability. One evening a person entered the room with two constables for the purpose of breaking up the meeting. But, notwithstanding this unseemly interference, the service of praise and prayer went on until the usual time of closing. Mr. John Jenkinson, however, having been recognised as one of the worshippers, was summoned on the following morning before the magistrates of the borough on a charge of "making a riotous noise." He was required to find security in a bond of £20 for his appearance at the next Quarter Sessions. When the Sessions came Mr. Jenkinson duly appeared in court; but it would seem the magistrates had got a little more light during the interim, and they wisely omitted calling for the case.

THE OLD CHAIR.

Another instance of magisterial interference is worth recording because it relates to Captain Robertson, the father of the famous "Robertson, of Brighton," who was Mayor

BEVERLEY CAMP MEETING SITE ON THE WESTWOOD.

THE PERIOD OF CIRCUIT PREDOMINANCE AND ENTERPRISE   395

of Beverley at the time the incident occurred. Beverley has always been famous for its camp meetings held on the fine stretch of ground known as Beverley Westwood. At one of these historic camp meetings—that of 1824—William Locking, of Hull, was deeply convinced of sin, and at this same camp meeting two well-known characters who were present from no religious motive, by the breaking of the fence on which they sat, were suddenly thrown into a pond, from which they emerged well soused and bedrabbled, to the great amusement of the bystanders. Some mock verses were written on this incident, which now lie before us. It was to another of these great Westwood camp meetings our people were making their way in the usual style, by singing through the streets, when they were met in the Old Waste by Captain Robertson. He appeared to be shocked and made angry by the apparent irregularity of the proceedings, and peremptorily ordered the singing to be stopped. His behest was obeyed, and the

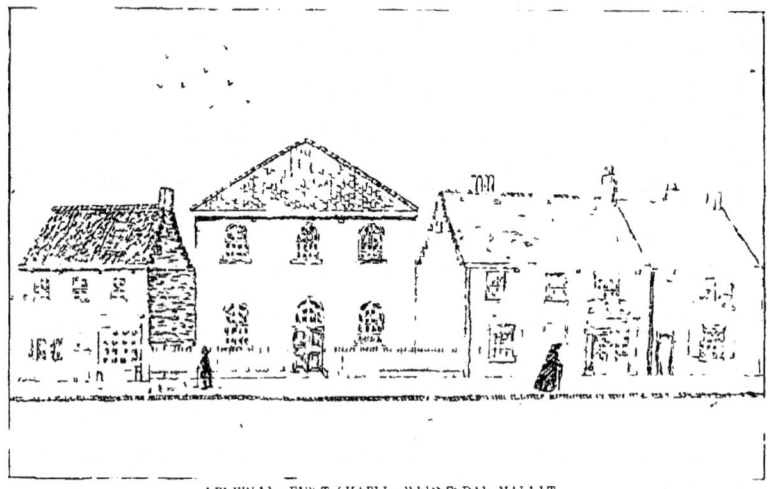

BEVERLEY, FIRST CHAPEL, WEDNESDAY MARKET

procession moved forward to the camp-ground in comparative silence. We are told that this was the last instance of opposition on the part of the authorities our people encountered in Beverley.

On the 1st May, 1825, the new chapel was opened in Wednesday Market by John Flesher and Thomas King. The cost of the erection was about £800—a large sum in those days to be faced by a new and poor society and ten trustees, who, with one or two exceptions, were working-men. Only about £100 was raised towards the outlay, and the trustees were soon involved in pecuniary difficulties. Many were the plans devised to reduce the expenses and the liabilities of the trust, and to put it in a financially sound and workable position. The Quarterly Meeting instructed that each superintendent should make   t Beverley, and forward the proceeds as quickly as possible. Then, the pressure still continuing, it was arranged that Brother J. Flesher should go on a preaching and collecting tour on behalf of the chapels at Beverley and Cottingham. Mr. Flesher's commanding presence, courteous bearing, captivating and suasive conversation, and silvery and often pathetic pulpit address, always ensured him great popular acceptance. Not forgetting William Sanderson and others, John Flesher must be pronounced to have been the most considerable pulpit and platform orator Primitive Methodism has produced. No wonder, therefore, he should have succeeded in obtaining, after all expenses had been met, some sixty pounds, which were divided between the two burdened trust-estates. Fortunately, despite all their struggles, the trustees did not act upon the advice given them in high quarters—to sell the vestry and the land behind the chapel belonging to them. The retention of this land was to be of untold advantage to them in the days to come.

JOHN FLESHER.

In the *Journal* of W. Clowes there is one other entry relating to Beverley of some interest. He tells us that on a certain Sunday, probably in 1831, he preached anniversary sermons for Beverley Chapel; that in the morning he had liberty of soul, but was in partial bondage in the evening; that R. M. Beverley, Esq., a celebrated polemic, was present, and put a half-sovereign in the collection-box; and that after the service he took supper with his sister, who was not ashamed of the cross of Christ. Miss Beverley was at this period identified with our cause. She was both gifted and devout, and devoted her time and substance to religious and philanthropic purposes, holding services in her own house and sometimes preaching in our Beverley chapel. Her brother, mentioned by W. Clowes, published a pamphlet on the abuses of the Church of England, which excited considerable attention at the time. In 1830, or a little later, Mr. Flesher, at the Hull Quarterly Meeting, recommended for our ministry a Mr. Carlyle, then of London. Mr. Flesher, in his effective way, spoke highly of his qualifications, and the upshot was that Mr. Carlyle was written to and engaged. Being appointed to preach at Beverley, he soon made himself known to Miss Beverley and married her. It was not long before he left our ministry, and though he made considerable stir in the religious world, we need not pursue his career further.

R. MACKENZIE BEVERLEY.

The society at .... experiencing the vicissitudes of alternate adversity and prosperity. At the latter end of 1838 the Hull Circuit was favoured with much spiritual prosperity. Mr. Clowes remarks:—"Several places besides Hull were partakers of the soul-saving baptism. Beverley arose in spiritual power, and extended the borders of its society." In 1868, after much discussion, deliberation, and prayer, the old chapel was pulled down, and the present handsome and commodious one, more in harmony with the progressive spirit of the age, took its place. The foundation-stone ceremony was the last service of the kind Mr. W. Hodge, of Hull, was privileged to attend.

MATTHEW DENTON.

Matthew Denton, Francis Rudd, and W. Edmandson should have honourable mention in any account, however brief, of the early history of Primitive Methodism in Beverley. The first-named joined the Church as far back as 1826, and lived to be appointed in 1886 a Deed Poll Member, and to attend several Conferences in that capacity. In the midst of many difficulties and discouragements, he, as a youth, gave himself assiduously to the cultivation of his mind. It has been claimed for him that he was the first Primitive Methodist layman to publish a book. Whether this priority can be established or not, his four volumes of "Anecdotes—Religious and Moral," attest the range of his reading and his intellectual activity. Francis Rudd was converted in 1828. "For fifty years he was a class-leader, and local preacher, very popular, and in oft demand for special services. His religion was not occasional but habitual." * J. Edmandson joined the society on coming to Beverley in 1835, and was a pillar of strength in that society until his death, which took place October 6th, 1867.

POCKLINGTON CIRCUIT.

We have now reached a point when, in harmony with the design of this work, the scale of narrative may very properly be reduced. We have traced in detail the formation of the first four circuits of the Connexion out of which all the rest, in one way or another, have been formed. No materials exist for writing the history of the many and oft-changing branches which the leading circuits were forming, but for a time, the geographical extension of the Connexion on its different sides may be noted by the new circuits formed. If we cannot go into all the out-fields, white unto harvest, where labourers are at work, we can, as long as may be needful, take our stand by the gate, and watch the waggons roll in with their load of golden grain.

Pocklington is, next to Hull, the oldest circuit in the Hull district, and stands on the stations next to the circuits of the parent-town. The circuit embraces a portion of country of unusual ecclesiastical interest. Goodmanham is within the limits of the Pocklington circuit; and Godmundingham—"the home of the protection of the gods"—will ever be famous as the spot where, in A.D. 626, Edwin, king of Northumbria, with his court and people, destroyed the heathen temple and accepted the Christian faith.

* "Piety among the Peasantry: being Sketches of Primitive Methodism on the Yorkshire Wolds," by the Rev. Henry Woodcock, p. 155.

At the village of Sancton, two miles from Market Weighton—as Wesleyan Methodists will remember—the venerable Father Jackson, so called by his admirers, and his two brothers, Robert and Samuel, were born. Jackson Wray's "Nestleton Magna," we may be quite certain, was somewhere within the radius of the Pocklington circuit, and Primitive Methodists should know that Warter stands on its plan, with its memories of William Sanderson, John Oxtoby, and Thomas Wood, "the little shoemaker," hereafter of Driffield.

There is a slight conflict of evidence as to the person to whom belongs the honour of having first missioned Market Weighton and Pocklington. Herod, in his "Sketches," claims for Sarah Harrison that she "opened" both these places, as well as Warter,

"RANTER CHAPEL LODGING-HOUSE." THE OLD CHAPEL, MARKET WEIGHTON.

Elvington* and Riverbridge, in the early part of May, 1819. But Herod does not quote Sarah Harrison's own words, or give the precise dates, and, moreover, his bias against, rather in favour of, Clowes' priority in a given case must be borne in mind. On the other hand Clowes' words are perfectly clear and the claim made unmistakable: "The next day (May 27th,) I made my way to *open* Market Weighton. I preached in the

* On a large farm at Elvington, resided George and Alexander Bond, who "joined our society at that village, and became great helps in spreading Primitive Methodism throughout the whole of the Ouse and Derwent division of the East Riding of Yorkshire. They also rendered great help to the infant cause in the city of York, by becoming responsible for the rent of the first chapel we took. They afterwards emigrated to Canada West, and laboured, during life, in connection with our missionaries in that part of the world."—Rev. S. Smith, as quoted by Herod in his

market-place to a well-behaved people, who were very courteous and friendly in their conduct towards me. The good work of God broke out at Market Weighton, and a lovely society was formed, and the cause still progresses." The last words must be regarded as anticipative, since a month afterwards he writes: "I again stood up in the market-place, and cried: 'Behold the Lamb of God, which taketh away the sin of the world.' The presence of the Most High carried the communication to sinners' hearts. I afterwards formed a society of six members." The *Journal* contains distinct references to two other visits, and it is clear from one of these references, that W. Clowes had come to look upon the market-place as his "pitch." At the September Quarterly Meeting, Market Weighton is reported as having nineteen members. The meetings, we are told, were first held in a cottage which has since been converted into a model

MARKET-PLACE. THE SCENE OF CLOWES' FIRST SERMON IN POCKLINGTON.

lodging-house, and the house is known to-day as the "Ranter Chapel Model Lodging-House," and is inquired for by pedlars under that designation.

Pocklington, on the Derwent, appears to have been missioned by Sarah Harrison, and to have been visited some months after by W. Clowes. If the reader will look back to the first plan of the Hull Circuit, given on p. 371, he will see that on Sunday, October 3rd, Clowes was planned at South Cave, Newbald and North Cave. Now in his *Journal* he duly describes this day's doings, and then goes on to say:—

"I held a prayer-meeting next morning, and good was done. Onwards I proceeded, and spoke at Riverbridge, Market Weighton, Melbourne, Seaton,

Bishop Wilton, and Bugthorpe. At the latter place I called at a public-house, and asked liberty to pray with the family, which was granted; and I left the inmates weeping. At Bishop Wilton I preached in a croft belonging to Dr. Meggison. I then made my way to Pocklington, and preached in the market-place to a vast multitude; in the evening I spoke in a barn, the property of Mr. John Moore: here the prospect of success was very promising. In the neighbourhood of Pocklington I spoke frequently, and the stir among the people was considerable. I then directed my attention towards Beilby, Newton, Millington, and other places, God confirming his word by signs and wonders and mighty deeds" (p. 168).

Through the kindness of Rev. G. Ellis we are enabled to give views taken from old prints, showing the stepping-stone, formerly in front of the "Black Swan Inn," on which Clowes stood to address the people gathered in the old market-place; also a view of the barn (long since pulled down to make way for a modern mansion) in which the night service was held. As recalling some vanished outward features, then before the eyes of Clowes and his hearers, these views are not without their interest.

During 1820 and 1821 the Hull Quarterly Board called into the ministry several men and women whom we shall shortly have to refer to, such as John Verity and Samuel Smith, who were foremost in securing the introduction of Primitive Methodism into Leeds, and Thomas Johnstone, who was to become a troubler of our Israel. It was Samuel Smith, the second of these, who, in 1821, was placed at the head of the newly-formed Pocklington Circuit, having for his colleagues T. Jackson (1), the devoted Ann Armstrong, and M. Martell. But before the year 1821 closed, a young man, destined to become more eminent as a preacher than they all, was borrowed from Scotter Circuit, in which he had just begun his labours. We speak of William Sanderson. As a motherless lad he had been apprenticed to a worthless tailor and draper, who tried to make up for his thriftlessness by taking a public-house. That boded ill for young Sanderson, who had already taken a few steps on the primrose path; and it was well for him that Primitive Methodism was brought to the neighbourhood, and that Thomas Wood, his companion, had got religion before him. He attended a camp meeting in the Gravel Pits at Market Weighton in the summer of 1819, and in February, 1820, he found salvation in the Wart

THE BLACK SWAN PUBLIC-HOUSE. STEPPING-STONE FROM WHICH CLOWES PREACHED HIS FIRST SERMON AT POCKLINGTON.

afterwards they were discharged therefrom. On his way home he shouted through the street—"He has pardoned all my sins; I am happy." His nights were now given, not to fiddling and dancing, but to prayer and reading. One December night he was locked out, and had to pace the streets for hours because he had become engrossed listening

THE BARN, POCKLINGTON, WHERE CLOWES PREACHED.

to some one's reading aloud Russel's "Seven Sermons."* It was in Pocklington Circuit William Sanderson tried to preach for the first time, an experience which he has described in his own inimitable way, thus: "As soon as I opened my mouth I shut my eyes, and when I opened my eyes I shut my mouth." And yet this timid, stumbling novice in the art of speaking, became second only to John Flesher as a preacher—if indeed he were second. For such a competent judge as the late George Race, of Weardale, regarded him as Primitive Methodism's greatest living preacher, and would gladly journey to Newcastle to hear Sanderson when he paid his annual visit to Nelson Street. Both in speaking and writing his sentences were pointed and sparkling with brightness. That was a most apt characterisation passed on his preaching by the aged sister of John Oxtoby. Passing through the village after some years of absence, Sanderson and his friends met the aged woman. "Do you know who this is?" said

W. SANDERSON, AGED 30.

See also p. 165 for a facsimile of the title of this book.

D D

one of the visitors "Yes," said Betty "It's Wilhe, he's come to give us a 'glister'" (a brilliant or sparkling sermon, she meant) "Glister" is a good, expressive word, reminding us of the "white and glistering" transfiguration-raiment of the Christ. We, whose own boyhood's remembrances go back to the days when William Sanderson led the devotions by our father's hearth, can see now how well that word hits off the originality and brightness which impressed us, as we listened to the prayers of this great and good man. He was superannuated in 1852, yet in the thirty-two years which made up the term of his active ministry, he has recorded with humble thankfulness that he, with his colleagues in labour, had seen 1330 added to the societies, and he claims as his children in Christ, W. Lonsdale, J. Holroyd, and C. Kendall.

BROTHERTON CIRCUIT

The fact that Brotherton, a large village in the vicinity of Pontefract, was made the head of Hull's Second Circuit, shows that in the early days a place was frequently chosen to be the head of a circuit, not because of its size or importance, or even because of the strength of the cause thereat, but it was chosen as a centre round which the ministers could conveniently itinerate. Brotherton Circuit roughly speaking, included the country lying between, and even beyond, the lower reaches of the Aire and the Ouse, so that its occupancy gave the promise of a speedy ascent to Leeds and York, to Wharfedale and Nidderdale, and the other dales watered by the tributaries of the Ouse. We have said—the country lying between "the lower reaches" of the Aire and Ouse, not "the lowest reaches." For there lies before us, as we write, a plan of the Marshland branch of Scotter Circuit for 1822, which shows that Scotter must for some time have been hard at work in the marshy country lying in the angle between Goole on the Ouse, and the Trent. This old plan has on it the names of twenty-five places, including such well-known ones as Goole, Swinefleet, Thorne, and Crowle. But, though the Brotherton Circuit did not at first include any of these places, it did reach as far as Howden; for in the year 1825 Howden was made a circuit from Brotherton, and continued such till 1827.

Sarah Harrison reached the geographical limit, in this direction, of her evangelistic labours when, in May, 1819, she made her way from Pocklington to Ferrybridge. In connection with her visit here, we have the first mention of Mr John Bailey, who kept a boarding-school of some repute in Ferrybridge. Mr Bailey rendered valuable service to the cause of Primitive Methodism during this period, as will be evident as we proceed. It was in Mr Bailey's schoolroom that Sarah Harrison preached, and as the result of her labours a revival is said to have broken out. Tidings of this revival reached earnest souls in Leeds and led to further extension. Next, Mrs Harrison proceeded to Brotherton and preached in the open-air to several hundreds of people. Then we find her at Knottingley where, to secure partial shelter from the cold, she took her stand under a hedge to preach the Word.

Within two months after Sarah Harrison's visit to this frontier of the Hull Circuit, William Clowes followed. In his *Journal* he speaks of his being "affectionately received." I   on Sunday, July 23rd, he preached at nine o'clock in the morning, standing by Mr. Bailey's door; then he made his way to Knottingley, and preached in the open-air. On a subsequent visit, while holding a prayer-meeting in Mr. Bailey's schoolroom, a stone was violently thrown at the door, and a piece of parchment was blown in, on which was written some foolish words—which incidents encouraged him to think that the devil felt his power shaken, and that "the iron sceptre of his enchantment had begun to tremble in his hands." On a third visit, an attempted wife-murderer was converted one day, and his intended victim the next. In November, Mr. Bailey accompanied him on his mission to Leeds. In December, he found the work still "rolling on," and describes how some fantastically-

KNOTTINGLEY CHAPEL AND SCHOOLROOM, PONTEFRACT CIRCUIT.
Rebuilt on the Site of probably the oldest Chapel in the Circuit. There were formerly two Societies in this Village.

dressed men, calling themselves "ploughmen," invaded Mr. Bailey's house, asking for money, but beat a precipitate retreat when W. Clowes bade them get on their knees and cry for mercy. His last recorded visit was in March, 1820, when he speaks of having visited the misions he "had opened," among which are included Ferrybridge and Brotherton. The claim to having opened these places may perhaps be reconciled with the statement in Sarah Harrison's *Journals*, by understanding Clowes to mean by "opening," the formal establishment and organising of societies.

Brotherton has not stood on the roll of our stations since 1833 and, though as a circuit designation the name may be obsolete, Primitive Methodism has never let go its hold of the country first missioned by Aire and Ouse in 1819; and both Brotherton and Ferrybridge are to day societies in the Pontefract Circuit, which, since 1831, has taken Brotherton's place as head of the circuit. It would be an intricate business tracing the history of the Brotherton Circuit from the beginning through all its changes. Given the tract of country already indicated, it would almost seem as though every possible arrangement had been tried before the present one had been arrived at. This will appear from the following tabular setting-forth, which the reader can skip if he choose, although it may have its value as a permanent record illustrative of circuit evolution. It will be seen that Pontefract and Swinefleet Circuits, with Goole, Selby and Howden as offshoots of the latter, represent the old Brotherton and Marshland Circuits.

MARKET-PLACE, PONTEFRACT, A.D. 1777.

CIRCUITS AS PER CONFERENCE MINUTES.

Years.				
1821-2	Brotherton	...	Marshland Branch.	
1823-4	Do.	...	Marshland Circuit.	
1825	Do.	Howden	Do.	
1826	Pontefract	Do.	Tadcaster and Ferrybridge Union Ct.	Thorne.
1827	Brotherton	Pontefract	Howden	Do.
1828	Do.	Do.	Swinefleet	Do.
1829-33	Brotherton and Swinefleet Union Ct.	...		
1834 &c.	Pontefract		Swinefleet.	

HUTTON RUDBY CIRCUIT

The *Journals* of W. Clowes, as given in the *Magazine* for 1821, show that the account of his remarkable mission to the North Riding of Yorkshire is, in his published *Journal* of 1844, chronologically misplaced. This mission was entered upon soon after the last visit to Brotherton already related. On May 18th, 1820 Clowes left Hull on a missionary tour, and after preaching at Ripon and several other places in the vicinity, he, on the 20th July, came to Hutton Rudby, not knowing a soul there, and bearing no letters of introduction, or having any well-grounded hope, except what his faith supplied, that he would find friends and a shelter for the night. It is probable that some of our readers might have a little difficulty in precisely locating Hutton Rudby, and hence may naturally wonder why a place so little known was made Clowes' objective. The answer is, that Hutton Rudby is near the small market-town of Stokesley on the slopes of the Cleveland Hills, and that Clowes pushed his way there because it seems to have been fixed upon as the base of the purposed mission. And yet the tract of country to be covered by the mission was so extensive that it might as well have been called the "North Riding Mission" or "The Vale of York and Cleveland Mission." As for Hutton itself—it was more than a geographical expression, or a convenient central point; one of the very first chapels in these parts was built in the village, and though it stood as the head of the circuit for one year only, being superseded by Brompton, there is a society in Hutton Rudby to this day belonging to Stokesley Circuit.

Several notable incidents occurred during this North Riding Mission, such as the conversion of Henry Hebbron in his father's barn at Potto, and the holding of the famous camp meeting at Scarth Nick—a wild mountain gorge between Swainby and Osmotherley. There would be a pleasure in recalling these incidents, but the circuits now comprised within the tract of country missioned by Clowes, will waive their natural desire to hear these stories once more, while we take the story of the mission generally, and use it as proving incontestably that W. Clowes possessed all the qualifications, to a supreme degree, of a pioneer; that he could break up the fallow ground as well as reap what others had sown; that, in short, he was, as we have heard it put—"an unmitigated missionary."

But is it necessary to insist on this at this time of day? We think so. In following events up to this point we have had occasionally, because of the evidence, to assign the first opening of certain places to others rather than to Clowes, whom, perhaps, tradition had credited with the pioneer visit. Herod, too, in his "Sketches," though usually careful and precise in his statements, does, as we have hinted before, write with a certain bias when W. Clowes is in question. Herod had a theory that he—Clowes—was not adapted to be a leading or pioneer missionary; but that he did his best work—which was excellent indeed—when he followed in the track of others. Herod himself was one of Clowes' converts, and he writes from his heart in saying of Clowes :—

"He was instrumental in bringing many souls to God. We believe no man in the Connexion was the means of raising up more local and travelling preachers than he; and perhaps no one comparatively successful ever had so backsliders from among his converts. Perhaps this may be account [...] the fact of his

MARKET-PLACE, THIRSK.

living in a great glory, by which he was the means of bringing a larger amount of the Holy Ghost upon, and into, the souls of his converts."—(p. 443.)

This is high praise indeed; yet this eulogy is qualified, in one direction, by its being preceded by a statement of Herod's theory:—

"But he could sail the best where the ice had been broken for him: and he generally planned a harbinger to go before him. He visited but few places where some move had not been made previously to his entrance."—(*Ibid.*)

But the theory shatters itself against the simple record of what Clowes accomplished in this brief Hutton Rudby mission. We can see now that, even if hitherto the facts do seem to lend countenance to Herod's theory, it is because circumstances did not permit it to be otherwise. Now circumstances have altered, and opportunity is given for a test-case—a case standing out, clear of all embarrassing side-issues and conflicting claims put forth on behalf of others. When Clowes went to Hutton Rudby, no one had gone before to prepare his way; to break the ice; to be his harbinger. As far as we can learn he went uninvited, unannounced, unexpected; and he went alone. Once more he would remember "he was a missionary," when at the outset he had no

BROMPTON CHAPEL, BUILT 1821.

friendly shelter except that afforded by a public-house; though, even then, he acted as the man of God and talked of spiritual things and prayed with the family. The country he "opened up" was then, more than now, considered remote and wild, though beautiful in its wildness. It was just the kind of country, and the work he had to do, and the conditions under which the work had to be done, were just such as to test his physical endurance, his patience, his zeal. He had long journeys; he was drenched to the skin; he was benighted when crossing into Bilsdale, and had to climb the steep by pulling himself up by the ling which clothed its sides. He was ready to drop from physical exhaustion, and yet he rallied his almost spent powers that he might preach to the waiting people. He stood up in the ak in the name of Jesus, and also in that of Stokesley, under Roseberry Topping, where a drunken man tried to disturb the service, but "God put a hook in his jaw."

Such were some of the conditions under which Clowes did his work in this district; and yet his faith, his tact, his personal magnetism gave him power with men. Houses and hearts were alike thrown open to him; and, in the short period of eight weeks, he created a new circuit—or rather laid the foundations of three circuits and what came out of them. Here is Clowes' own unadorned statement of what he did on this mission:—

"After making a plan to direct my colleagues in this mission, in which I opened many places and travelled four hundred miles on foot, my whole expenses amounting to thirty shillings, I set off for the Hull September Quarter-day, 1820, travelling by way of Thirsk, Ripon and Leeds."

STOKESLEY.

Hutton Rudby—now Brompton—Circuit, was destined to show too, that W. Clowes could not only build on his own foundation, but also re-build what others had thrown down. There lies before us the evidence of this, in an unpublished MS., written in Clowes' own crabbed hand, in which he simply, yet pathetically, describes his experiences as a repairer of the breach. Thomas Johnstone, a Hull Circuit preacher, had resigned because he could not meet certain grave charges that had been preferred against him; and, marking his opportunity, had entered the Brompton Circuit and sought, with some degree of success, to alienate the societies and get hold of the Hutton Rudby Chapel which had been willed to the Connexion. In this critical state of affairs the Leeds Conference of 1823 requested the Hull Circuit to send down W. Clowes to save the circuit from total wreck. So he went down, with what feelings we can imagine, "to take up the heavy and tedious task, and to gather the people that had been   they were the children I had begotten in Christ, and gathered together; for I had before opened all that country." Into the details of the struggle we shall not enter. Suffice it to say, Brompton Circuit was saved and soon "regained its feet." For five years, it stood as the first station of the Sunderland District, and even when Sunderland took that position, Brompton stood next to it. Guisborough stood on the stations from 1822 to 1826, inclusive; in 1827 we find "Whitby and Guisborough circuit." We miss it for some years, and then it re-appears as a branch of Stockton-on-Tees, and becomes an independent station in 1864. Stokesley was a mission of Brompton for a series of years, attaining circuit independence in 1854.

Brompton was visited at the earnest entreaty of Thomas Ramshaw, who had been led to Christ under Clowes' ministrations at Hutton Rudby. Brompton was an old-time weaving village where the weavers plied their craft in their own cottages. They could think for themselves and act an independent part. There was no persecution at Brompton. At the sound of Clowes' voice they would leave their looms and stand at their doors to listen as he preached on the village green. The society, originally composed of seven members, flourished, and in 1821 a galleried chapel and cottage were built. These premises are still in use, but the seatage has been largely increased by the taking in of the cottage.

In adjoining Northallerton, Clowes is said to have preached in the market-place to an orderly congregation of a thousand people. William Carver, James Foster, and the few others associated with them, at first worshipped in a room near a tan-pit; after a time a disused theatre was purchased; now we have a splendid block of church and school property with a flourishing society. At Swainby,

JOHN DELAFIELD.

Potto, and Osmotherley, too—all places visited by Clowes—we have societies and Connexional property.

Associated with Brompton Circuit have been many whose names it would be a pleasure to record. We think of Joseph Wrigley, of Northallerton, and his generous hospitality to the servants of God; of the saintly Robert Walker, who afterwards removed to Hendon, Sunderland; of John Delafield, who lived and died at Appleton Wiske, and was for sixty-eight years an active and useful local preacher, and who occasionally conducted successful evangelistic missions in Allendale, Alston Moor, Shildon, and Middleton-in-Teesdale. The intellectual calibre of the man may be judged from the statement that amongst the few select books he prized and studied, that fed his mind and made his sermons "meaty"—were George Steward's "Mediatorial Sovereignty" and Butler's "Analogy." In his own village he battled for the right of Nonconformists to bury their own dead; and in his station he was to the last respected as "an exemplar ministry of his Church."

CHAPTER VIII.

SCOTTER CIRCUIT AND SCOTTER DISTRICT.

GAINSBOROUGH.

HITHERTO, our *History* has had much to do with the Trent; and it is at Gainsborough the Trent attains the dignity of a tidal river. This dignity has its own special drawback, for at times, the tidal wave, like a wall, sweeps up the Trent, making the vessels rock at their moorings, flooding the staithes and low-lying lands, and sometimes swamping boats, whose owners have either not heard or heeded the warning cry—"'War' eagre," *i.e.*, beware of the "eagre." It is the Trent which has made the history of Gainsborough such as it is. Lincoln was the port of the Romans: they dug a canal to connect it with the Trent, and at Torksey, the point of junction, they built a castle for defensive purposes. Gainsborough was built from the ruins of Torksey, and in such a position as better suited the bolder, sea-loving genius and habits of the Saxons and Danes. Its position was a strategic one. It was, and is, the most inland port navigable to sea-going vessels of three-hundred tons or thereabouts; and not far from it, too, were the lowermost fords of the river safely passable under ordinary conditions. Next to the Thames, it afforded the

GAINSBOROUGH BRIDGE.

best haven for fleets. Here they were comparatively safe from attack, while the vessels could easily slip down on the ebb-tide and reach the open sea within the twenty-four hours. Historically Gainsborough was the most northerly town of importance belonging to the ancient Kingdom of Mercia, and so we have the feeling that when Primitive Methodism reached Gainsborough, the first stage of its history was rounded into unity. Primitive Methodism was Mercian in its origin and early progress, and when it reached Hull, it set foot in a country with a different history, and its course lay open to an position, Gainsborough has memories of our Saxon and Danish forefathers. Sweyn landed here; Canute was born in the ancient palace that preoccupied the site of the Old Hall; and here the captains of his ships acclaimed him king. Here, too, King Alfred was married to the daughter of the Ealderman of the Gainas, and later memories are associated with the names of John of Gaunt and Cromwell.

In 1818, Gainsborough was a busy and, relatively, a much more considerable place than it is to-day. Its position, not far from inland waterways—such as the canalised rivers Don and Idle—brought it into touch with Rotherham and Sheffield. In the Napoleonic war-times tons of shot and shell were weekly shipped at Gainsborough; and from it the old bridge at Vauxhall was in 1815–16 conveyed in twenty-seven vessels.

GAINSBOROUGH HALL.

Thanks to the graphic descriptions of some who spent their boyhood-days in Gainsborough, eighty years ago, we can picture the old town and the life that went on in it.* Even yet there are touches of old-time quaintness about it, but in 1818,—what with its fluted tiles, its yellow-ochred doorsteps, its green outside shutters, and especially the sight of spars and masts standing out above the corn-fields—it was the most foreign-looking town in England.

Gainsborough has other memories making a still more powerful appeal to Free

---

* See Thomas Mozley's "Reminiscences chiefly of Towns, Villages, and Schools, 1885." "The Life of Thomas Cooper, Written by Himself." Thomas Miller's "Our Old Town."

Churchmen. In its ancient Manor Hall, standing on the site of a still earlier building, lived the Hickmans who befriended the cause of religious liberty in the days of the Stuarts. Probably the Separatist Church, founded in 1602, and presided over by John Smyth would occasionally meet in this historic building. For three or four years this church served not only Gainsborough, but the villages for miles around. William Brewster, of Scrooby, and William Bradford, of Austerfield—who became governor and historian of New Plymouth colony—were members of this Gainsborough Church, and travelled to Sabbath worship some ten or twelve miles, crossing the river by ferry where now it is spanned by Weston's famous bridge. For the convenience of the scattered members, a second church was founded at Scrooby, of which Richard Clyfton was the pastor and John Robinson the teacher. Puritan sentiments were fermenting

THE TRENT AT EAST FERRY, SHOWING PART OF OWSTON FERRY.

strongly on both sides of the Trent in those days, and fines were levied on the more prominent leaders—amongst the rest, on Brewster. Desiring for themselves fuller freedom to worship God these sturdy Puritans made two attempts to reach the coast of Holland. The first was unsuccessful, but the second, which was made in the spring of 1609, met with a measure of success. This time the place of embarkation was a lonely spot on the salt-marshes, somewhere between Grimsby and New Holland. The men went to the rendezvous by land, and the women and children with their goods went by water down the Trent and Humber. Each section of the emigrant party, it is interesting to know, would skirt one of the sides of the early Scotter Circuit—the men probably t   Keadby, Epworth, and thence to the

Humber banks.* Ever since the men of the "Mayflower" took their memorable journey this north Lincolnshire district has been a stronghold of Puritan sentiment. The author vividly recalls how this fact of Lincolnshire's inveterate proneness to "heresy and schism" was bitterly dwelt upon in the parochial school of Scotter close upon fifty years ago. Our teacher proved his allegation up to the hilt. No lack of illustrative examples! This exodus of Gainsborough and Scrooby Puritans to the freer air of Holland, was an instance in point. Was not Epworth, the birthplace of the Wesleys and of Alexander Kilham, but a few miles away? And, as though that were not enough for one county, a whole 'army of aliens' has since then been called into existence by General Booth, another Lincolnshire man! Even in 1854, village Methodist Chapels were as plentiful in the parts of Lindsey and Kesteven as blackberries in the hedges; and that our teacher knew right well. Were statistics only

GAINSBOROUGH MARKET-PLACE IN 1838.

available, they would show that scarcely a village in North Lincolnshire but has sent forth some of its sons to recruit the ranks of the Methodist ministry. No district has been more fertile for the raising of Primitive Methodist ministers than this, though we judge the East Riding of Yorkshire runs it close.

In the light of such facts as these it was a notable event when William Braithwaite and Thomas Saxton, as missionaries sent out by Nottingham Circuit, entered Gainsborough on a certain Sunday in December, 1818. They opened their commission in the approved way by singing along the street as they passed to the market-place. Thomas Cooper, then a lad of fourteen, was one of the many who ran out to see what

* Their probable course is indicated on the Map of Scotter District .....

the unwonted sounds meant. It was soon evident that these two decently-clad, middle-aged men were no mendicants singing for coppers.

'They were called "Ranters" by the crowd,' says Cooper 'but I soon learned that they termed themselves "Primitive Methodists."' These men remained in the town for some weeks, and preached in the open-air, and held meetings in houses, and the crowd, young and old, were greatly affected. Soon a society was formed, and they began regularly to preach in the very small chapel which John Wesley himself caused to be built, in a small square, in Little Church Lane, but which had been occupied as a warehouse for some time. I became a member of the society, in company with at least a dozen other lads, some of whom were older and some younger than myself. I cannot describe my anguish and sorrow for sin. And, apparently, it was an equally serious case with each of the lads. My grief continued for many weeks, until I could find no delight in my books or drawing, or dulcimer, and could read nothing but the Bible, and was getting into secret places twenty times in a day to pray for the pardon of my sins. Many lowly earnest preachers came and preached in the little chapel, and prayer meetings were prolonged till midnight, often. And many up-grown sinners professed to find the pardon of their sins. The change of heart and life was real in some. I remember well an elderly man, an inveterate cock-fighter being humbled, and becoming a true penitent. This man lived, for many years afterwards, a consistent Christian life. Nor was his case a solitary one."—"The Life of Thomas Cooper," pp 37-8

One can only speculate what might have been Thomas Cooper's career had his connection with Primitive Methodism been more lasting; certainly it would have "saved him from a thousand snares" and many bitter regrets. But another adherent was early won to the cause of Primitive Methodism whose connection with it was to be life-long. This was W. G. Bellham, who at this time was a young man of three-and-twenty, and a Wesleyan local preacher and class leader. Though a native of King's Lynn, he had removed into Lincolnshire, and, being in Gainsborough, he was induced, on October 23rd, 1820, to hear a Primitive Methodist preacher for the first time. He has himself told us what he thought of the preacher and the service. "I thought," he says, "I never saw so much of God in a man before; he was all love, and every word he uttered was to my soul like honey dropping from the honeycomb. I felt so happy in my own soul, that I thought I could live and die with this people." And he did live and die with this people. After a struggle, he honourably resigned his offices and membership with the Wesleyans, united himself with the Primitives, and in May, 1821, began his labours as a travelling preacher in the Scotter Circuit. The first four years of Mr Bellham's whole-hearted and successful ministry were spent on the Scotter, Loughborough and Welton stations; the remaining twenty-eight chiefly on the stations of the Norwich District, where we shall meet him again. He died at Ramsgate, January 24th, 1854

The name of George Rex, and equally that of his excellent wife, is closely associated with the early history of Primitive Methodism in Gainsborough and Retford. He came to the former town soon after the formation of the Scotter Circuit, and took his share in the labour which fell to the lot of local preachers, travelling—chiefly

THE PERIOD OF CIRCUIT PREDOMINANCE AND ENTERPRISE. 415

on foot—to Messingham, Austerfield, Epworth, Ferry and other places. When Gainsborough became a separate Branch he was one of its leading officials. Largely through his instrumentality a chapel was erected in Spring Gardens, and a Sabbath school established. George Rex, too, it is said, was the first person in Gainsborough to sign the total abstinence pledge. About 1847 Mr. Rex removed to Retford and became of great service to the Carol Gate Society and to the Circuit generally, sustaining many important offices and often being sent to represent his Circuit at the District Meeting.

While residing in Gainsborough Mr. Rex had a house built for himself which he called "Joppa." He was probably led to give it this name from the fact that he was of the same occupation as Simon the tanner who lodged Peter in his house hard by the seashore at Joppa. In the Gainsborough "Joppa" many of the servants of God through the years found rest and hospitable entertainment. But if the story we took down from the lips of the venerable Sampson Turner be true, the parallel between the two tanners' houses holds still further. At Joppa "Simon Peter" had his didactic vision; at Gainsborough Sampson Turner and his colleagues were troubled in the night-watches by what they firmly believed to be ghostly visitants. Such a story might of course be easily omitted; just as an expurgated edition of Wesley's Journal might be published in which all references to ghosts and the supernatural might be left out—and some might think the book improved by the omissions. But we prefer Wesley's Journal just as he left it—ghosts and all. Its historic value as a picture of life and a chronicle of the times is depreciated in proportion as it is tampered with. Now, we who knew the fathers, also know that some, even of the most hard-headed of them, such as Thomas Southron and John Sharpe, would occasionally in their confidential moments, allude to certain experiences in their lives which in all seriousness and good-faith they credited to the occasional impingement of the supernatural on the ordinary natural round of life. And so this one story, linked as it is with George Rex and his "Joppa," may stand to testify to our fathers' belief in one segment of the supernatural that has been cut off from our circle of thought; and to suggest that they may have had apprehensions, and whispered confidences, and wrestlings that we who claim to be their emancipated children know little of. We neither justify nor condemn their beliefs; we only want to know what the beliefs were that lurked at the back of their minds. It was on January 5th, 1874, that Sampson Turner drew forth his recollections of the past and spoke as follows:—

GEO. REX.

MRS. REX.

"It was in the years 1835-6 I travelled in Scotter, having come there from Oldham. We lived at Kirton, and I had William Sanderson and Abimelech Coulson for colleagues. We preached at Gainsborough, twelve miles from Kirton, and lodged there at the house of George Rex, tanner. The room we slept in was a room over a passage leading to the tannery and separated from Rex's room by a wainscot or wooden partition. This room had a bad reputation. William Parkinson, who travelled here and went to America but soon left us, had been disturbed. . . . My turn came. It was Sunday. There was an eclipse of the sun that day, and I had to preach afternoon and night at Gainsborough. I laboured hard, and sleep was sweet and sound. But, as the church-clock, which was near, sounded three, I lying on my face, a great weight as though of a calf came flat down upon me. I sat up as though a secret spring had been touched, and in the name of the Blessed Trinity adjured the something—whatever it was—to declare itself 'Who art thou? O God, drive away the powers of darkness.' Rex heard me, inquired what was the matter, struck a light, came in and we searched the room, but found nothing. He went back and we lay talking some time until

HARDWICK HILL, WHERE EARLY CAMP MEETINGS WERE HELD. THE HOUSE JUST ON THE HILL IS WHERE MANY OF OUR MINISTERS OFTEN STAYED. *

* When "Poet" Sanders travelled the Scotter Circuit in 1834 he was inspired to write some lines on this preacher's home, on Hardwick Hill, beginning thus:—

"There is a pleasant Pilgrims' Inn,
By Hardwick Hill you'll find it.
Persons who walk the downward road
Pass on and do not mind it.
This house to many is well known;
The Lord with bliss hath crowned it.
Comfort and Peace within it reign,
And hills of sand surround it.
The ministers of Christ call there,
Though sinners may despise them,

I became drowsy and began to sink into sleep. Then the 'call' fell on me again. I went through the same form of words and once more Rex came in with the light, but we found nothing. Abimelech Coulson changed his quarters after being troubled once. As for Sanderson and myself, I don't think we were much troubled after that."

From the indisputable evidence of old plans it is clear that the Gainsborough Branch of 1819, became, in 1820, Scotter Circuit, and that from 1821 to 1823 Scotter stood at the head of a district. On the plan—May–October, 1821—there are forty-four places and six travelling preachers, viz., S. Bailey, W. Wombwell, W. Curtis, M. Bell, W. G. Bellham, and J. Oxtoby. By March, 1822, Marshland has been made into a Branch with W. Wombwell and W. G. Bellham as its preachers, and with twenty-six places, none of which, save Butterwick, are included in the forty-four places on the Scotter Plan of the preceding year, so that we have a total of sixty-nine places stately served with preaching by fifty preachers. Hence the remarkable fact emerges that, from 1819 to the beginning of 1822, a tract of country had already been missioned, which in the course of years was to be divided up into nine circuits, viz., Scotter, Gainsborough, Swinefleet, Goole, Selby, Epworth, Winterton, Crowle, and Scunthorpe. In this enumeration Howden is allowed to Brotherton. The astonishing progress made in this short time makes us look with the more interest on the first Gainsborough plan, for it is certain that much of this progress must have been due to the pioneer missionaries.

With the first modest sheet before us we note the announcement: "All preaching to be given up on the 13th of June, as there will be a Camp Meeting on Hardwick Hill, to begin at 10 o'clock, a.m." This camp meeting was duly held, and was so great a success as to entitle it to rank amongst the historic camp meetings of Primitive Methodism. We note further that there are only seven preachers on the plan, of whom three are travelling preachers—William Braithwaite, John Manuel and Hannah Parrott. On the Sundays these are planned at what may be considered a reasonable distance from Gainsborough, but on the week-days they are planned further a-field—as far as Kirton and Bishop Norton. What little we know of William Braithwaite relates almost entirely to his pioneer work in the old Scotter Circuit. When we first see him singing along the streets of Gainsborough he has just emerged out of twilight obscurity, and when he leaves the Scotter Circuit we are baffled in our attempts to trace his after movements. The last time his name occurs in the Minutes of Conference is in 1831, when at the end of the stations, we have this note: "Under the direction of the General Committee. W. Braithwaite." And yet, despite the paucity of our information respecting him, William Braithwaite made his record. If he did nothing else, he fairly earned the distinction of being the apostle of north-west Lincolnshire. As such the popular tradition of the locality holds him and loves to recount his doings, and as such his name will be handed down to posterity. Scotter Circuit has been favoured with the labours of many greater men than William Braithwaite—and it does not forget them; but it is no disparagement of William Sanderson and the rest, to affirm that in this region the fondest traditions of the early times gather round William Braithwaite. as he was more often called, was an oddity in his way. He travelled a few years, but trading with a very small capital, and being withal very erratic in his movements, he soon found himself without a circuit. For some time he had an authorised roving commission. Like the captain of a privateer, holding letters of marque, he steered his course where the most spoil was to be taken from the enemy." In the gist of it this statement is correct enough. William Braithwaite had his oddities, as had the three Johns with whom he must be classed—Benton, Wedgwood and Oxtoby. They were all men of similar type; men "thrown up," or rather, providentially given, to do rough pioneer work in a decadent time. Like them, Braithwaite preferred to go where he listed and do his work in his own way; like them he had, there is reason to believe, some private

C. KENDALL'S BIRTHPLACE, BISHOP NORTON.

means, and therefore could afford to take his way. But though we do not retract the statement just re-written, there is one phrase of it we must qualify—that which speaks of his trading with a very small, *i.e.*, intellectual, capital. He must have had considerable capital of some sort, or he could not have carried on the trade he did. A preacher is not mainly one who peddles intellectual wares. His capital is his sanctified personality. It is this which tells; especially in such times as those in which these men had to do their work, when the intellectual modes of presenting truth favoured and fashioned by the schools, would have been about as effective as a razor would be effective for the backwoodsman's purpose.

What kind of capital William Braithwaite was endowed with, may be gathered from certain incidents, in which he bore a leading part, that were connected with the introduction of Primitive Methodism into villages whose names stand on the first plans. Here is one incident concerning East Stockwith, on the banks of the Trent, which shows him drawing on the infinite resources of God, and reveals the main secret of his power. One day a farmer while at work in his field was surprised to hear a voice raised in expostulation or entreaty. He left his horses and peeped through the hedge. Instead of seeing two persons as he expected, and being made privy to an ordinary ignoble human quarrel, he saw but one man on his knees, pleading with an invisible Power. The tears were running down his cheeks, his eyes were closed, his hands were clasped, and he was saying "*Thou must* give me souls. I cannot preach without souls. Lord, give me souls or I shall die." Awe-struck, the man withdrew to his ploughing. When loosed from labour he told his wife of the strange occurrence. "Why," said she, "he must be the man who has been round saying that he is going to preach at the sluice-head." "Then let me have my things,' said he, "for I'm going to hear him." That farmer became a member of the first class, a useful official for many years and died in the full triumph of faith.

Bishop Norton, the birthplace of Charles Kendall, though a long stretch from Gainsborough was missioned and regularly visited on the week-days, by W. Braithwaite and his colleagues. George Smith, a Wesleyan local preacher, had been praying that the Lord would send some person to arouse the people and spread the doctrines of the cross, and when he heard Braithwaite on his first visit to the village, in 1819, he involuntarily exclaimed "Bless God, that man's God is my God." We at once recall W. G. Bellham's similar expression of feeling as he listened to the preacher at Gainsborough. Taken together, the two incidents suggest that Braithwaite's power with God meant also power with men; that the man put men in love with the message; that he 'so" let his light shine that men were moved to take his God as their God, and his people as their people. George Smith merits an additional word. As the newly-gathered flock was without a shepherd, he volunteered his services until a suitable leader could be found. This arrangement however was not satisfactory to the Wesleyan authorities, and his name was erased from the official roll. And so what was intended to be merely a *pro tem* arrangement went on for the long space of fifty-one years. For forty-four years he was a local preacher, and for the same length of time his house was the home for the preachers, both lay and itinerant, who supplied the village pulpit. He was a trustee, steward, and treasurer of Bishop Norton chapel, built in 1833, and he lived to see it enlarged and free of debt. He supported the cause even beyond his means, as many thought; since his household of twelve had to subsist on a labourer's weekly wage. His church loyalty was severely tested, as it often was in Lincolnshire in those days; for Sir Montague Chomley, his aristocratic master, by expostulation and even by threats of dismissal from his employment, endeavoured to detach him from Methodism, but without avail. George Smith died January 24th, 1870, aged 84 *

William Braithwaite was not always tender and persuasive; he often preached

---

* See his Memoir *Primitive Methodist Mag* ~ February 1872 also "Life of Parkinson Milson" by Rev George Shaw pp 196-7 where stories of his loyalty are given

"rousing" sermons, and sometimes could denounce as sternly as a prophet of old. Indeed, the late Robert Ducker, who was a native of Burnham in the Isle of Axholme and began his long ministry of forty-nine years in Scotter Circuit and Gainsborough Branch, has written of Braithwaite: "He seemed to me more like one of the old prophets than a man of his times." This feature of his character comes out in the story of the missioning of Appleby, in June, 1819. Appleby is a pleasant village of Winterton Circuit, lying between Brigg and Winterton. The Wesleyans had discontinued holding services in the village, probably because of the quiet pressure—not to be distinguished from persecution—brought to bear upon the householders by those of higher social standing. Braithwaite took his stand on the basal stonework of the old village cross, and began to sing. While the service was proceeding, the steward of

APPLEBY CHURCH.

the estate came up, and in an imperious tone ordered the preacher to desist. His order not being at once obeyed, he tried to pull the preacher down, and not succeeding in his attempt, he fetched a crowbar from the blacksmith's shop, and, with the help of two men, began to prize the stones from under the preacher's feet. At last, to save himself from falling, Braithwaite had to step on to the road. But when every one deemed him effectually silenced, after pausing a moment with closed eyes, he shot a glance at the three persecutors which transfixed them, and said in solemn tones:—"People of Appleby, mark my words, if any one of these three men die a natural death, then God never sent me to preach here to-day. They think they have prevented the truth from bein   cause in this place, and a prosperous one too." This was no splenetic outburst; for, strange to say, both the doom foretold and the church-prosperity promised came to pass. One day there was a dinner-party at the Hall, and the steward accompanied some of the guests to the top of the old church tower, whence a fine view can be gained of the Humber and the Yorkshire Wolds on the one hand, and of Broughton Woods and the Lincolnshire Wolds on the other. Perhaps unduly stimulated by the wine he had taken at dinner, the steward clambered up one of the pinnacles. It yielded under his weight, and he fell from the tower, and when the rest had made their way with all speed to the churchyard, there lay the steward with his neck broken. The late George Shaw visited the spot in 1855 and he avers that, though the accident had occurred fifteen years before, the spot was quite bare as if the grass had been worn away by the trampling of innumerable feet, though, in fact, few sight-seers visited the spot on which a curse seemed to rest.* This is not all, Mr. Shaw asked an old man what became of the other persecutors. One, he was told, was gored by a bull, and the other, a few months after, was drowned in a shallow dyke. It is all very strange, and we leave it thus, without venturing an opinion as to whether it were a singular triple coincidence, or a threefold retribution. As to the facts themselves there can be no reasonable doubt, and the facts could easily be paralleled by other incidents in our earlier history.

JAMES KEIGHTLEY.

The brighter side of William Braithwaite's prophecy concerning Appleby has been fulfilled to the letter. God did raise up a prosperous cause in the village, although it was not until 1894 that a chapel was secured. For more than fifty years services were held in the cottage of Mr. Richard Keightley and his devoted wife. God's blessing was upon them and theirs because of their faithful service and ungrudging hospitality, and they lived to see two of their sons, James and R. W. Keightley, take an honoured place in the ministry of their Church.

Brief mention must be made of adjoining Broughton, if for no other reason than that it was the place of Parkinson Milson's nativity.

"The house in which my nativity occurred," says he, "was a portion of what was known as the Old School House, and was situated near the corner of the East Wood. The position is remarkably pleasant, bounded as it is by the East, North, and West Woods. The village lies near the fine chain of hills known as the Wolds, the sides of which wear a sylvan loveliness, particularly when steeped in the cloudless splendour of a summer's sun, in its first post-meridian altitudes."

R. W. KEIGHTLEY.

Broughton was missioned in 1819, and its name is found on the early plans of the Scotter Circuit. At first, the services were held on the village green and in the cottage of Mrs. Mally Allgarth. At her death, the society was left with the open-air for its only sanctuary, until William and Ann Neal proffered the use of their cottage which continued to be the recognised preaching-place until the building of the chapel in 1841. William Neal touched the lives of many for good. It was at a prayer meeting in his house when, in July, 1843, Parkinson Milson knelt as a penitent and " wept much, though he did not pray audibly." Neal, too, was the leader of the class with which, three days after this, Milson united himself ; so that he began his Christian course just as the first period of Primitive Methodism was closing. It was amongst these Broughton Woods he worked and prayed, and thought out his Sunday sermons, and where he experienced a remarkable deliverance from death which helped to decide his career. When, one day busy in the woods he was buried beneath a tree which another tree had unexpectedly crashed down upon, and William Neal was weeping under the impression that Milson was crushed to death, he crept out from under a big branch whose fracture had made a small arch of protection for him, exclaiming—"I am Thine by preservation." One of his workmates voiced the general feeling by saying: "I'll tell thee what, lad, the Lord wants thee to do better work than felling trees ; and if thou does not do it, the next tree that falls will kill thee as sure as thou art born." So Milson himself thought; and within the month (June, 1846), he left his woodman's tools for ever, and began his ministry of flame. As for William and Ann Neal, they both were spared to reach a patriarchal age. William dying (a triumph) in 1878, aged 81, and Ann surviving three years longer. "They have been devil-fighters all their lives," was Parkinson Milson's brief and characteristic tribute to their character.

Atkinson Smith put off the harness three years after Parkinson Milson put it on. He was only fifty years of age when superannuated by the Sunderland Conference of 1849, and yet, as the poet wrote of him:—

> "The scars were on thy flesh—
> The marks thy body bore;
> The spirit still was strong and fresh,
> The clay could fight no more."

Like Parkinson Milson, he was a North Lincolnshire man, being born at Scotterthorpe; and though he died at Goxhill, where he settled on his retirement, his remains were interred in the churchyard of Scotter, his native parish, by his own request. It was only in 1829, eight years after he became a member of the Church, that Atkinson Smith showed any indications of what he afterwards came to be. Up to that time, religiously he enjoyed little and did little; but he now experienced a deeper work of grace which made him tenfold more useful than he had been before. He was borne into the ministry on the crest of a revival-wave, which in the spring of 1830 swept over the whole of Scotter Circuit. "It is probable," says his biographer,

HOUSE IN WHICH PRIMITIVE METHODISM COMMENCED AT BROUGHTON—W. NEAL'S HOUSE.

"that the revival which then took place was one of the most powerful and extensive that was ever experienced in that part of the county of Lincoln. The country was baptised. Nearly every house was a house of prayer. It was truly interesting, as well as profitable, to take your stand in the streets of some of these villages at the time when the curtains of evening, like the doors of a sanctuary, were shutting the people up with God. The voices of praise, sometimes from the family alone, at others from collected neighbours, could be distinctly heard ascending at the same moment from many a family hearth. The reformatory power of religion was soon strikingly manifested. That which civil laws and magisterial authority had failed to effect, after many a trial, was accomplished by the religion of Christ. A great number of the pests and plagues of a large neighbourhood were converted to God; and several of them, to our knowledge, after having lived for years as becometh the gospel of Christ, have been gathered to their rest in heaven, and many others continue in well-doing to this day.

"In all this the village of Messingham appeared to be the most favoured spot. Hundreds of people journeyed thither to witness the strange things which had come to pass, and not unfrequently some returned home in tears, making the roads and lanes vocal with the song of praise. All classes of society were excited. On the village-green, in casual intercourse, or among the busy scenes of the market, the usual topic was the great revival in Scotter Circuit."*

It is a pleasing picture the writer draws of what he himself had seen and known—a picture which almost involuntarily starts the prayer—" Haste again, ye days of grace !" Equally pleasing is the biographer's description of Atkinson Smith's absorption in this great revival. He was happily circumstanced both for furthering and enjoying it, being at the time foreman on a large farm at Messingham, occupied by a Wesleyan local preacher who, like himself, was fully in the spirit of the revival. Master and man would often take the lead in services held in the large farm-kitchen, in the presence

SCOTTER CHURCH. THE RESTING-PLACE OF ATKINSON SMITH.

of the numerous children and servants who, in patriarchal style, lived under the same roof. Once, praise and prayer were still going on, with the blinds drawn and the candles burning, while the sun was already up and climbing the eastern sky. It was nothing to them that the struggling angel said, "Let me go, the day breaketh." It might, break and dawn and shine ; they said, " We will not let thee go except thou bless us."

When Atkinson Smith travelled in Hull, in 1833, he was known as "the young sanctification preacher." The description was accurate, fastening as it did upon that feature of his ministry which distinguished it to the last. The compulsion which gave this bent to his preaching grew out of a definite outstanding fact in his own experience. With this behind him, he might have said, "Woe is me if I preach not" the full privilege of believers. But in seeking the perfecting of saints, he did not forget the saving of sinners. So far from that, the saving of men became the chief concern and the main business of his life. His solicitude on this score drove him to his closet and kept him on his knees for hours together, and urged him to efforts beyond his strength. "The zeal of God's house" consumed him; like the lamp which burns with so ardent a flame that it uses up too fast the oil within the vessel. It is no ideal man but the actual Atkinson Smith we are depicting, as we may be assured of, if for a moment we leave general statements and come to particulars supplied by his contemporaries. "I called upon him one day," says one of his leaders, "and on entering the house, I heard him in his study in a vehement agony of prayer. Mrs. Smith was in tears; she said: 'Oh, brother W., if the Lord does not revive his work soon I shall lose my

MESSINGHAM, PRIMITIVE METHODIST CHAPEL AND STREET.

husband.'" William Lonsdale, one of his colleagues, a man like-minded with himself, has written of Atkinson Smith: "He was a man of much fervent prayer. I remember him saying to me one Friday (I think at Gainsborough), 'Lonsdale, I have prayed two hours before breakfast every morning this week.' He seemed in a flame of holy zeal for souls, and the glory of God." Again, George Wakefield, an influential official of Scotter Circuit, has left it on record: "The influence which accompanied his prayers, while only young, was extraordinary. Doubtless he and his brother Edward were two of the mightiest men in prayer ever raised up in these parts."

Enough: it was an incalculable good that such a man as Atkinson Smith was permitted for nineteen years to fulfil his ministry in the circuits of the old Hull District. Doubtless, during those years, many a scene must have been witnessed like that fondly recalled by one who was present in old Mill Street. Atkinson Smith was preaching on Ezekiel's vision of the waters which flowed from under the altar. A powerful influence rested on the congregation, reaching its climax when the preacher recited, with much feeling, the lines of Richard Jukes:—

> "When first in this river I ventur'd my soul,
> The waters of life to my ankles did roll,
> But still persevering my Saviour to please,
> I soon found the river was up to my knees:
> A thousand is measured, and then I go in,
> 'Tis up to my loins,—'tis freedom from sin.
> And then I go on to prove it a river,
> So deep, and so wide,—I swim in't for ever."

PARKINSON MILSON.

"The sun was setting in its splendour, and his full soul was swimming in the fountain of rich redeeming love what time he led the praying host into the fulness and sinners to Calvary."[*] At the close of his ministry when seeking superannuation, he could modestly claim that, through the labours of himself and his colleagues, one thousand two hundred and four had been added to the membership on his various stations.

What has been said of Atkinson Smith might, with little modification, be said also of Parkinson Milson. They had both passed through the same crisis of experience, and lived and preached the same truths; and in both, the intense spirit "o'er-informed the tenement of clay." And yet Milson was very human, in the best sense—loving and loveworthy, intermeddling with knowledge, and possessing considerable imagination and poetic sensibility. We are apt to forget this, and to think of him *merely*, instead of mainly, as the red-hot revivalist and preacher of holiness. Atkinson Smith and Milson, along with Thomas Proctor, John Smith (I), George Warner, and others who have been given to our Church, must be classed with William Bramwell, David Stoner and Thomas Collins. Their reputation will tend to increase

WILDSWORTH CHAPEL.

rather than diminish as the years go by; for, after all, it is the record of saintliness and usefulness that lasts the longest, and which brightens as it lasts, as though even here

[*] "Read ... Methodism in Hull. By Jam. Garbutt.

the promise were beginning to have its fulfilment—"They that turn many to righteousness shall shine as the stars for ever and ever."

The villages of old Scotter Circuit are full of memories. Here, for example, is Wildsworth, a little village on the banks of the Trent where, in 1821, a curious little chapel was built on a piece of waste ground near the river. With this village cause, the family of Airy, so well known throughout the circuit, was early associated. At West Ferry and Kirton Lindsey chapels were built before the close of the year 1849. It was at Kirton, lying under the brow of the Lincolnshire Wolds, where William Sanderson, to use his own phrase, "nestled down" after his superannuation. Here he spent in an almost idyllic manner the remaining twenty-two years of his life, cultivating his ample garden, enriched as it was with flowers contributed by friends in the various

W. SANDERSON'S COTTAGE, KIRTON.

parts of the country he visited for special services; for, until 1865, it was true of him as he said, that "his speaking parts were as good as ever, but his going parts were disabled." Then when the seizure came, it took the form of aphasia, and the once ready and eloquent man would smilingly look at you, hopelessly lost for the commonest word. With his garden, a few good books, as long as might be the means of grace, and not forgotten by his friends, he quietly awaited the summons which came April 3rd, 1874, only some six weeks before, John Flesher, his closest friend, also received his call. It was here, or hereabouts, too, that the shattered William Lonsdale, the Weardale convert of Sanderson, came to die (1863), and where William Bywater, ex-Missionary Secretary, and latterly Chapel builder, spent the last years of his life.

though he died in 1869, at Cote Houses, the hospitable home of the Harsleys—a family which, ever since the time Thomas Harsley's name stood as first local preacher on the first plan, has been honourably associated with Scotter Circuit.

Reference has been made to Messingham and the great revival of which it was the centre. Messingham stands next to Scotter on the early plans, and there is an incident connected with its missioning in 1818 of some interest, at least to the writer. At that time there lived at the hamlet of Ashby one Thomas Kendall, a cottage-farmer and carrier who for many years drove his cart every Tuesday to Gainsborough, and "put up" and dined at the Black Bull hard by the Old Hall. Going to Messingham one evening on business, he heard that a party of mountebanks was there, and

MESSINGHAM, SHOWING THE TREE UNDER WHICH THE SERVICE WAS HELD.

determined to witness their performance; but his purpose was frustrated in an unexpected manner. William Braithwaite was that evening conducting a service at Messingham, and Thomas was somehow drawn to the place, where he heard part of the sermon preached, and the old hymn—"Turn to the Lord," etc., sung. We quote from the memoir of Thomas Kendall as to what followed.

"Conviction for sin seized him while he listened, and it was of so powerful a nature that he often declared his hair rose up upon his head and displaced his hat. A similar effect is not unfrequently produced by strong fear. . . . For several weeks he remained in an awakened state, and then entered into gospel liberty as he stood against the doorstead of a barn at Crosby, listening to a sermon preached by Miss Hannah Parrott, afterwards Mrs. Smith of Goxhill. This was in the spring of 1819. A class was soon afterwards formed at Ashby, which he joined. Its first meeting was at his house. He co-operated with the rest of the members in the erection of a chapel. This chapel, not being properly secured to the Connexion, was in a little while sold by the person on whose land it stood, and the infant society was scattered. For a time the Primitive Methodists did not preach at the village. They, however, revisited it; a society was again formed, of which Thomas Kendall became a member [afterwards a leader and chapel steward] until his decease. There was a revival of religion not long afterwards in the Scotter Circuit.

MISS PARROTT,
(Afterwards Mrs. Smith.)

THOMAS KENDALL'S HOUSE, ASHBY.

It reached Ashby, and the cause there was established. A second chapel was built, of which he became a trustee, and some improvement which he had effected in its financial state was a source of satisfaction to him on his death-bed."

Just before he expired, February 22nd, 1854, he spread his attenuated arms and exclaimed: "Learn to die, my dears!" As a memento of this dying charge, one of his sons wrote a verse which was inscribed on his tomb-stone in Bottesford churchyard, where devout men, headed by William Sanderson, laid him to rest.

"With daily energy supplied
His task through life he sought;
'Oh Lord, I'll hold Thee by thy hand,'
He said, 'do come to me.'"

430   PRIMITIVE METHODIST CHURCH.

Thomas Kendall was a plain man of few words, but these sharp and decisive as pistol shots. He was independent in sentiment and action, prompt, and so true a time-keeper, that the carrier's punctuality was a proverb in the village. While his character thus showed something of Puritan ruggedness and austerity, Fanny Dennis, his wife, had all the vivacity and fluent speech of her Celtic race. Some at least of their eleven children who survived, must have derived largely from the maternal side; for, of the

BOTTESFORD CHURCH.

ten sons, six were at their father's death preachers of the gospel. These all began their course as Primitive Methodists, but three subsequently entered the ministry of other Churches, while, Charles, Thomas and Dennis fulfilled a long and useful ministry in the Church of their youth. Charles carved his record deep in the Hull District. He was a capable administrator, a good manager of men, a careful and prayerful superintendent; a powerful preacher, with an unusually large vocabulary at command, from which he knew how to select the right word, as the books he has left testify. He was the biographer of Atkinson Smith and William Sanderson, in conjunction with the latter the originator and editor of the first series of the "Primitive Pulpit"; and in collaboration with his brother Henry, the author of "Strange Foot-leps, or Thoughts on the Providence

THE PERIOD OF CIRCUIT PREDOMINANCE AND ENTERPRISE. 431

of God," besides being the writer of various pamphlets. He was elected President of the Conference of 1881, held at Hull, and died during his term of office, May 5th, 1882. Thomas Kendall was converted at Gainsborough, and began and ended his thirty-four years' ministry in his native circuit. By his genial, kindly disposition and pastoral diligence he endeared himself to his people. His soul was full of music so that he sang as well as preached that gospel which he illustrated by his life. He died at Doncaster January 24th, 1878. Dennis Kendall began his successful ministry at Swinefleet in 1847. His ministry of forty-four years was chiefly spent on Circuits in

CHAS. KENDALL.

THE KENDALL MEMORIAL CHAPEL, ASHBY.

the South of England where, as we shall see, he proved himself an efficient superintendent. How much good resulted from those two open-air services which shaped the life-course of the humble village carrier!

A further though not the final stage in this story of village Primitive Methodism was reached when, in 1885, a removal was made from the old site in Bottesford Lane to the High Street of Ashby, and the "Kendall Memorial Chapel" was erected at a cost of £1050, and opening services conducted on four consecutive Sundays by members of the Kendall family. The cause in the village continues to prosper, and bearers of

CHAS. KENDALL.

the old name are still doing good service, the Nestor of whom is James Kendall who occupies the old homestead, while Leeson Petch survives as a veteran official.

Favoured, no doubt, by its more central position, Scotter soon superseded Gainsborough as titular head of the Branch, and in 1820 was formed into an independent circuit. It speedily took rank with the leading circuits, becoming strong and aggressive, and having at the close of this period, 1842, no less than sixteen travelling preachers labouring on its eight branches, three of which were the distant Norman Isles—Jersey, Guernsey and Alderney. A new chapel was built as early as 1819, the opening services being conducted on September 5th, by John Harrison and Hannah Parrott, the latter being one of the station ministers. Miss Parrott was a woman of excellent character and abilities, who was made extensively useful in the early days. In his

SCOTTER CHAPEL.
In which the Deed Poll was read and approved.

"The Female Advocate"—which perhaps still remains the best apologia for female preaching we have. John Stamp says of Miss Parrott: "She has spiritual children in the ministry. I am one." As Mrs. Smith, of Goxhill, this pioneer preacher survived many years, honoured by all who knew her. Scotter Chapel, which with its adjoining preacher's house was built "on the site of an old duck-pond, given by Mr. R. Ducker," was ultimately lost to the Connexion, as so many of the early chapels were. One who wrote near the time and knew all the persons and circumstances connected with the alienation of the property, does not hesitate to attribute it to

"a factious movement for a cause that had always passed for trustees of the

THE PERIOD OF CIRCUIT PREDOMINANCE AND ENTERPRISE. 433

Scotter Chapel, and were found in the end to be proprietors, having caused to be inserted in the deed of conveyance certain clauses empowering them to dispose of it as they might think proper. The society had contributed towards its erection, and twice afterwards to its enlargement under deceptive representations. The proprietors refusing to sell it or lease it to the Connexion, it was abandoned, and through the gracious interference of Divine Providence, and the sympathies of the public, a new chapel, in easy circumstances, was soon erected [on Gainsborough Road]. Many wondered to see a chapel and two preachers' houses springing up in the very best part of the village, but the brother of Atkinson Smith and a host of his old friends were praying, and the long-tried, earnest, and loyal friends of Primitive Methodism in Scotter and its neighbourhood were giving; and what difficulty, associated with the maintenance and diffusion of God's cause, can stand before praying and giving?"—"Life of Atkinson Smith" (pp. 88–89).

GENERAL VIEW OF SCOTTER.

The old chapel (vacated for the new one in 1849) still stands, though its outward aspect is not quite the same as when the delegates to the Conference of 1829 carried on their deliberations within its walls; for to Scotter belongs the distinction of being the only rural village at which a Primitive Methodist Conference has been held. We say "*rural* village" advisedly, to distinguish it from Tunstall, which was little more than a manufacturing village when the second Conference, of 1821, was held there. No clearer proof is needed of the higher *rôle* played by villages in the early period of the Connexion's history, or of the standing and influence of Scotter as a circuit at the close of the last century's third decade. At this time, though Scotter is the head of a good country station, and is a large, clean village pleasantly situated on its little

F F

tributary of the Trent, it is no busy centre, as one may gather from its being unserved by any railway line, and gives small indication of its former, almost diocesan, importance. The Conference of 1829 was noteworthy in several respects, and first and chief of all, because then there appeared various signs not to be mistaken that the Connexion was at last emerging out of that period of depression and crisis which, like a malignant shadow, had rested upon it from 1824 to 1828. True, during these four years the borders of the Connexion were very considerably extended, especially in the North and West, but this extension was coincident with stationariness or retrogression in other parts. We have already had occasion to anticipate this painful fact in writing of the Midlands. And when we turn to the numerical returns for the period, there is proof, plain enough, that something was wrong. The increase reported for 1825 was only 75, and no returns whatever were issued for 1826 and 1827; then when the muster-roll was again taken in 1828, the membership of the Connexion was found to be 31,610, or 1,897 less than it had been in 1824, four years before. In addition to this, many of the circuits were found to be unable to pay their way, and were in debt to their ministers. The outlook was so dark that many good men—and especially Hugh Bourne—began seriously to dread that the Connexion was on the down-grade and would soon cease to be.

To what causes must this period of reverse be attributed? Mr. Petty has we think put his finger on two of the main co-operative causes in specifying. First, the too rapid increase of travelling preachers, rendering it inevitable that a good many unsuitable men would be employed to the grievous detriment of the circuits. Second, a certain number of restless, turbulent spirits crept in from other churches and, turning the Connexion into a cave of Adullam, ultimately wrought mischief. Both these causes must be allowed due weight, and a moment's consideration will go to show that in the case of a denomination like ours, beginning from the ground, increasing and extending itself so rapidly, and doing its chief work among the poor and less-instructed class, it was inevitable that the causes already specified would operate, and sooner or later a time of trial and crisis be reached such as that which was traversed from 1824 to 1828; and, with Mr. Petty, one can but wonder the crisis was traversed with, what must after all be regarded as, comparatively little loss.

Mr. Petty finds his third cause contributing to the Connexional crisis in "the great commercial distress" which prevailed at the time in the manufacturing districts. As to the existence of this distress, with all the social unrest to which it gave rise, there can be no manner of doubt. But while this is fully admitted, it may be doubted whether, had the other causes been inoperant, the state of the country would have proved other than the Church's opportunity. In the time of distress and disorder which obtained in the Midlands before 1819, when the Luddites were at work and "Levelling" principles were rife, the Great Revival took place and, as we have tried to show, men lent a willing ear to the message of good-will and consolation our fathers brought to them. Again, in the disappointment which fell upon the people after the passing of the Reform Bill, Primitive Methodism could more than hold her own during the excitement which attended the advocacy of the Charter. And further, when, by resorting to drastic measures, our Church had got rid of the elements which disturbed her peace and robbed her of her power with men, then her strength came back to her, and there is no more fear of issuing numerical returns, and no decrease to report until 1845. And yet, though the Connexional crisis was over, the state of the country grew worse rather than better, until, in 1830, publicists and clergymen and men of all schools, were in dread that a revolution was at hand. Our own deliberate opinion is that Primitive Methodism was no inconsiderable factor in averting the revolution that so many feared was coming,* also that she has done her best work when and where, by reason of unequal laws or industrial changes, social distress has seemed to create difficulties in her path, whether that path has taken her amongst the operatives, or miners or agricultural labourers of this our land.

The Scotter Conference stands out in refreshing contrast with some of the Conferences immediately preceding, especially those of 1821 and 1825 held at Halifax and Sunderland respectively. Looking at the state of the Connexion as it then presented itself, and looking at it by the light of the journals, official documents and letters of the time, we are again forcibly reminded of Daniel Isaac's dictum,—"They want discipline." Hugh Bourne was the stern, pitiless prophet of the time. He lifted up his voice, vibrating with passionate anxiety, in exposing and denouncing the evils that threatened the very existence of the denomination. There were hot debates in those two early Conferences, and yet at the end of them, Hugh Bourne found himself in a minority. Many of his brethren regarded his judgments as harsh, and his proposals more severe than the occasion bad as it was, demanded. But in 1826, the situation was if anything worse than ever, and his sterner counsels prevailed. Though, strange to say, his name never stands as President of any Conference, his spirit pervades the *Minutes* of those years and there is no mistaking his pen. At this time the circuit debts amounted in the aggregate to some thousand pounds—a widely distributed cause of anxiety and embarrassment. The preachers on these stations were roughly divided into "useful" and "running-out preachers." This latter term, evidently of Hugh Bourne's minting, denominated the preachers who ran the circuits into debt. It was these drones or inefficients who were aimed at by a regulation of the Nottingham Conference of 1826. In answer to the question, 'How shall the Connexion be preserved?' it was enacted "No circuit, already in debt, shall be allowed to run any further in debt, and no circuit not now in debt shall be allowed to run in debt." The course taken was suggested by the self-denying ordinance adopted by the Hull preachers in 1822 when, faced by a circuit deficit, they proposed to forego a portion of their quarter's salary, until, by hard work and the blessing of God, there should be an improvement in the circuit finances. This temporary bye-law was now made a Connexional statute. "It was found necessary for all preachers to be put on beginning to make proof of their ministry." The regulation worked as was expected and desired. In the course of twelve months thirty of these "runners out" made good their name by quitting the ministry. The new regulation bore hardly for a time upon some of the "useful preachers", so much so, that a Charitable Fund was started in order partially to recoup them for the

---

* For further illustration of this position see the chapter on "The Kingdom as Salt," in "Christ's Kingdom and Church in the Nineteenth Century."

losses they had sustained. In other ways the bands of discipline were tightened. The system of Circuit and ministers' pledges was begun: the creeping into the societies of unprincipled men from other Circuits or Churches was sought to be frustrated: entrance into the ministry was more carefully guarded. The action of the Conference of 1826 was a piece of relentless surgery; but the patient's condition was too serious for mild treatment. By 1828 the worst was past, and although the returns showed a decrease of 1907 on the returns of 1824, there was an actual increase of 1610 on the year, and in nine years the membership of the Connexion more than doubled itself, the rather less than 30,000 members of 1827 having by 1836 become 62,306. No wonder that inspired by the brightened aspect of affairs in 1829, Hugh Bourne should write:—"This was allowed to be the best Conference ever held in the Primitive Methodist Connexion . . . and is likely to be remembered with a degree of satisfaction for years to come and to be spoken of by children yet unborn."

RUTH WATKINS.

Two notable things were done at the Scotter Conference, both of which showed that at last the Connexion had come clear out of the shadow of her temporary eclipse:— the establishment of a mission to the United States, and the presentation and passing of the Connexional Deed Poll.

The desirability of following the numerous Primitive Methodists who had crossed the Atlantic had for some time been keenly felt by the authorities of both the Hull and Tunstall Circuits. The proposal to send missionaries to the United States emanated from these two circuits, and the enterprise was jointly theirs. The Scotter Conference gave its sanction to the scheme and commended it to the prayers and sympathy of our people in the first Conference address. Four missionaries, W. Knowles and Ruth Watkins from Tunstall, and W. Summersides and T. Morris selected by Hull Circuit, sailed for New York on June 19th, 1829. There is extant an old letter which brings their departure before us in a realistic way and shows William Clowes figuring in a new character —that of an energetic man of business. The letter is addressed to John Flesher, and is written from Manchester.

"Through much fatigue I got the missionaries to Liverpool last Wednesday afternoon, sought a vessel, paid their fare, £24 15s., bought their sea-stores and bedding, got their luggage to lodgings and from there to the ship and them on board, according to orders by nine o'clock the next morning. The ship is called 'The New York.' The wind being against them they did not sail till the next morning. They cleared the docks about five minutes past eleven, at which time t . . . . bade me adieu. A good wind and all in good

WILLIAM KNOWLES.
Went to America, June 19th, 1829.

THE PERIOD OF CIRCUIT PREDOMINANCE AND ENTERPRISE. 437

spirits, with the exception of Sister Ruth. She sate pensive and wept. You will observe they all sailed in one vessel, bound for New York. I felt bound with them in spirit. Brother Flesher! without a spirit of enterprise there is no glory."

Such, as brought back by this old letter, was the leave-taking of our first over-sea missionaries. Now enthusiasm, when it takes the form of missionary enterprise, is an admirable thing; but looking back now upon this American mission, one may well doubt whether it were wise to undertake such a mission. But even granting that it was, one can easily see now, with the documents before us, that our brothers under-

---

THE Primitive Methodist Connexion TO THE INHABITANTS OF NEW YORK AND OF THE UNITED STATES OF AMERICA IN GENERAL, SEND GREETING.

Friends and Brethren,

THE LORD having in his Providence raised up the Primitive Methodist Connexion, in Old England, and made it an instrument, in his hands, of turning thousands and ten thousands unto righteousness, and many of its members having emigrated to the United States, it was judged providential to appoint a regular Mission. We have accordingly sent over our respected Brother and faithful Minister, the Rev. WILLIAM KNOWLES; as also our respected Sister, RUTH WATKINS, who has laboured much in the LORD. And we trust they will be made useful in the Gospel of our common LORD, and will meet with that kindness and respect among you, that you, under similar circumstances, would expect from us.

Signed in behalf of the Conference of the said Connexion,

James Bourne, President.
Hugh Bourne, Secretary.

rated the magnitude of their undertaking, with the result that the mission was but inadequately equipped both with agents of the right kind and with means. The handbill which the missionaries took with them for distribution looks as though what the United States might be was hardly understood. There is a certain insular simplicity about this bill which surely needed the counteractive of larger maps.

After the arrival of the party, W. Knowles and Ruth Watkins began their labours in New York, while the Hull missionaries proceeded to Philadelphia where, as also at Pottsville, some ninety miles distant, societies were formed. The United States mission did not fulfil the sanguine expectations of its promoters —must indeed, so far as its earlier history is concerned, be regarded as having been a comparative failure, and at the annual Conference held at New York, September 16th, 1840, it was— "Resolved that we consider ourselves from this time distinct from and unconnected with the English Conference." In harmony with this resolution the united societies were legally incorporated under the title of "The American Primitive Methodist Church." The severance, however, was not final: for, in 1843, overtures were made to the English Conference with the view of resuming closer connection. The result was the opening of a new page in the history of Primitive Methodism in the United States which will have to be glanced at when we come to look at the missionary movements of the next period.

MR. ROBERT WALKER, CANADA.

Primitive Methodism was introduced into Canada by loyal and zealous laymen from the Home-land, and, under the old flag, met with greater success than in the United States. Mr. William Lawson, who had been a local preacher in Carlisle, began to preach in the streets of Toronto, then called Little York, in July 1829, just before our missionaries landed in New York. The first Primitive Methodist class in the Dominion was organised in September of the same year in the house of Mr. Lawson, who acted as leader, having that excellent man —Mr. R. Walker as his assistant. Mr. N. Watkins entered the country as the first duly appointed missionary, August, 1830. Two years after, the Conference entrusted the Canadian missions to the care of Hull Circuit, and with them they continued until in 1843, they were taken over by the General Missionary Committee.

THE DEED POLL.

The Scotter Conference of 1829 should also be remembered as the Deed-Poll Conference. Alike in the origin of this legal instrument, and in the delay which attended its execution, we may see a reflection of that Connexional crisis of which we have spoken. On the authority of the late venerable Thomas Bateman we learn that the precarious tenure on which our places of public worship were held had been so borne in upon the mind of Hugh Bourne by one painful incident after another that, as early

MR. WM. LAWSON.

as 1823, he had become anxious for the preparation of a Deed of Settlement for the Connexion similar to that Mr Wesley secured for the Methodist Societies He paid several visits to Burland for consultation with Messrs T Bateman and G Taylor (who afterwards became one of the twelve original permanent members of Conference), and sought to interest them in his plans The proposal of a Deed of Settlement "to legalise the Connexion and secure its chapels," was brought before the Conference of 1823 at Loughborough, and a committee of five persons appointed "to see after the execution of the Deed' Nothing, however, seems to have been done, and before the Deed was really executed several members of this executive committee had disappeared —another proof of the unsettledness of the times Again, in 1825, the necessity of the Deed of Settlement was reaffirmed, and a fresh committee appointed to see after its execution, consisting of H and J Bourne, W Clowes and James Steele This committee seems to have carried out its instructions, for, "an eminent attorney '— probably Mr John Ward, of Burslem—was employed to draw up a deed which was presented to the Conference of 1826, and in the main approved, though various modifications were ordered to be made Then we hear no more of the Deed of Settlement until the Scotter Conference of 1829 What is the explanation of the delay? Mr Bateman is ready with the answer —

"A first draft was prepared, and the opinion of men learned in the law sought thereon But before the end of the year the Connexion was found to be in such a state that no one could tell whether it would be entirely broken up or not So the deed was left in abeyance to await results When the happy change came and prosperity returned, the necessity for the deed became more than ever apparent It was again taken up and completed by the Committee, and finally it was examined and passed by the whole Connexion, through and by their representatives legally elected in Conference assembled at Scotter, and a Mr Wilks, of London, very generously undertook to put the matter into legal form without charge " *

The Mr Wilks referred to in the preceding extract was a man eminent in his day, and interesting to us from his family connections and his associations with our Church John Wilks was the son of Matthew Wilks, minister of the Tabernacle, and father-in-law of James Parsons, of York When the Protestant Society was formed in 1811 for the protection of religious liberty he became its secretary, and "Wilks and Liberty' was the battle-cry of his supporters at the contested Parliamentary election at Boston in 1830, in which he proved successful Such was the public-spirited man whose legal eye scanned and weighed every clause in the Deed-Poll For that he deserves mention here, and not only for that, but because afterwards he was the adviser and befriender of Thomas Russell in the time of persecution, giving his professional services without fee or reward

The Deed Poll was duly "signed, sealed, and delivered," by Hugh Bourne, James Bourne, and William Clowes,† on February 5th, 1830, in the presence of John Ward,

---

* "Observations on, and Explanations of, the Deed Poll of the Primitive Methodist Connexion," by Thomas Bateman

† James Steele who would have been one of the signatories died in 1827 See p 407

Attorney at Law, Burslem and his clerk, and after enrolment was presented, read and approved at the Leicester Conference of 1831. This should have been done at the preceding Conference, but there had been some "delay in London," and the document did not arrive in time for presentation. It does not belong to the purpose of this History to analyse the provisions of the Deed Poll, which from first to last was some eight years in the making. It may, however, be well to place on record the names of the four ministers and eight laymen standing on the original document as "permanent members of Conference"; for this and not "Deed Poll Members" is, throughout, their legal designation.

Hugh Bourne,
James Bourne,
William Clowes,
Sampson Turner,
John Garner,
John Hancock,
Richard Odlin,
George Taylor,
David Bowen,
Thomas Sugden,
Ralph Waller,
John Gordon Black.

Grimsby Circuit and its Offshoots.

The history of Primitive Methodism in north-east Lincolnshire has had many features in common with its history in the north-western part of the county. If Market Rasen be substituted for Gainsborough and Grimsby for Scotter, the course of events relating to the four circuits has Connexionally been much the same. Market Rasen began as a branch of Nottingham; it soon yielded the headship to Grimsby, and until it achieved circuit independence for itself, continued a branch of Grimsby—the place to which it had served as a stepping-stone. In these respects the parallel between Market Rasen and Gainsborough seems complete. In other respects the history of Scotter and Grimsby Circuits offers a contrast rather than a parallel. Grimsby has not been such a mother of circuits as Scotter, nor did it sustain, or help other circuits to sustain, distant missions in the early period, as did Scotter. Yet Louth (1823), Market Rasen (1854), Tetney (1868), besides Grimsby, second and third circuits, have been formed directly from it, and Alford indirectly through Louth (1860).

GRIME THE PIRATE.

And yet, though this is no despisable record, Grimsby's distinction as a circuit rests on other grounds. It is a good example of a circuit-town in which our Church has conserved its gains. Amongst the towns we have considered, it stands almost alone in having had no division or serious loss. With very few exceptions, the old families, gradually rising in the social scale, have remained with us to the second and third generations, so that our Church has struck its roots deep into the social and civic life of the town. Related to the preceding both as cause and effect, it has made a vigorous attempt to meet the needs of a rapidly growing population. Not only has it planted its chapels betimes at strategic points, but it has made them so attractive that none of its own people has cause to be ashamed of them; and it has made them so commodious and well-furnished that no one can justly complain of lack of facilities for carrying on the spiritual and educational work of the Church. We should have some difficulty in finding a town which, for its size, has put forth so much well-directed enterprise in chapel building. In this respect Grimsby leaves little to be desired. It was not until the middle of the last century was well turned that the need began to press to which the building of Victoria Street Chapel in 1859 was the response. Since then, Grimsby

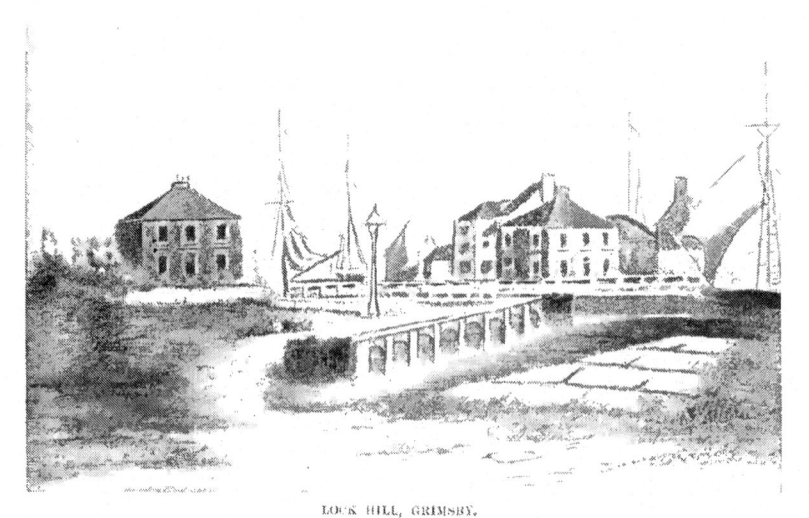

LOCK HILL, GRIMSBY.
From which Clowes sailed to Hull, and T. King and others afterwards. A favourite site for open-air services.

has grown by leaps and bounds, and so has Primitive Methodism in the borough on its material side, as the views of its many fine chapels, given on a later page, sufficiently prove. Scotter Circuit had done much of its best work when Grimsby was just about beginning the work which has given it distinction. The two circuits are almost coeval and contiguous, yet historically the contrast between them is marked. Scotter shows what a rural circuit did for the Connexion in the first period; Grimsby is an object-lesson as to what Primitive Methodism can do for the towns of even abnormal growth.

We begin, then, with Market Rasen, as it was to this place—already, or in anticipation, a branch—that Thomas King made his way when he began his ministry in August, 1819, just after the Nottingham Preparatory Meeting. had been a lay-member. The success already reported in Scotter Circuit would naturally suggest the desirability of missioning the adjacent part of the county, and there were good reasons for making Market Rasen the first objective of the mission. Once more there had been "preparers of the way." According to Herod, Ann Carr and Miss Healand had preached at Market Rasen, Caistor, Tealby and Walesby in the summer of 1818. This may have been the reason why John Harrison, shortly after his appointment to Hull, spent some ten days in preaching at some of these places. He crossed to Grimsby by packet on the 18th of May, and walked the twenty miles to Market Rasen after four o'clock! Next day he formed a society of eight members—the nucleus of the Market Rasen branch and all that was to come out of it. During these ten days

MARKET RASEN MARKET-PLACE.

John Harrison visited Middle Rasen and Nettleton, but especially Market Rasen and Caistor, where the most interesting incidents occurred. It was at Market Rasen where persecution of the rough and rowdy type seems to have played itself out so far as north Lincolnshire is concerned; for we do not meet with anything further north in the county quite as bad as the scene witnessed in the market-place on May 25th. There had been mutterings of the coming storm at the service held in the same place on the previous Sunday morning. Timid friends, aware of the threatened interference, tried to dissuade John Harrison from carrying out his announced intention of preaching on the same spot on the Tuesday evening. But he was not to be intimidated, and taking his "little ... One ruffianly fellow soon made himself particularly troublesome. He came up, making a "horrid noise," shook his fist in the preacher's face, and tried to pull him off his chair; but another man constituted himself the preacher's champion and knocked down the persistent disturber. It was not until he had been knocked down three times in succession that the man at last desisted and turned upon his assailant. While a set fight was going on between the two, Mr Harrison carried his chair a little distance away and proceeded with the service. When the fight was over, the man with the horrid voice returned and once more tried to pull the preacher off the chair, but only to meet the same fate as before. Then, and not till then, did he pick himself up and slink away. During the service sticks and stones and *shot* were flung, though without doing much damage. Finally, the clergyman gave orders for the church-bells to be set a-ringing, a proceeding that led Mr Harrison to make some plain observations on the use and misuse of church-bells and parsons. Despite these annoyances, the vast congregation listened intently and was deeply impressed.

Caistor also was twice visited by John Harrison during this mission-round. Each time, be it noted, he was accompanied by Miss Healand, whose home we judge to have been in these parts. On their first visit they sent the bellman round to announce that a service would be held in the middle of the market-place. Their reception was all that could be desired. The people ran together "as if to a bull-baiting," until some five-hundred persons were assembled who, while John Harrison preached, were as "still as though he had been promising them an earthly inheritance on terms of their obedience that night." Amongst those who listened were three clergymen and a dissenting minister; the latter acknowledging that open-air services might be useful to many who would not attend either church or chapel. This was on the Friday, and on the following Wednesday, May 26th, a congregation double that of the former one assembled in the same place to hear the two missionaries. The clergyman of the place was present to hear and judge for himself, thus showing that he had the true Berœan spirit and was "more noble" than he of Market Rasen. At the close of Miss Healand's exhortation he shook her hand, remarking, he thought it an honour to do so. "I heard," said he, "such an unfavourable account of the 'Ranters,' I thought I would come and hear for myself, and I must say I heard nothing but the gospel from your lips. I wish you every blessing."

Naturally it was deemed desirable to follow up the success already gained, and hence from June 7th to 11th, we find W. Clowes and J. Harrison in Lincolnshire purposing to pay another visit to Caistor. But between them and their goal lay other villages which were anxious to hear the Word of Life from their lips and would not be denied; and so they got no nearer than Limber. Here Lord Yarborough's lodge-keeper told them the villagers had long been expecting them, and they had reluctantly to forego their main purpose.

The June Quarterly Meeting of Nottingham Circuit almost immediately followed this short excursion. By this time experience had shown both the desirability of prosecuting the Market Rasen mission and the impracticability of Hull's undertaking the work. Clearly the missionary should be located in the midst of his work and not have to keep crossing and recrossing the Humber and then going twenty miles afoot in order to reach it. These considerations would have weight, and the same June Quarterly Meeting which made Hull a Circuit urged Thomas King to enter the ministry and probably assigned him the Market Rasen neighbourhood as his sphere of labour.

It is significant of the changes the years have wrought that Thomas King went to the scene of his future labours on foot. He spent some days at Market Rasen visiting and preaching, and then did the same among the dwellers in the "moors, wolds, clays and marshes." While so engaged he "*heard of Grimsby*," we are told. There seems something odd in this way of putting it, as though Grimsby had been an obscure place in some out-of-the-way corner that he had got to hear of by the merest chance. The idea suggested is in the main a true one; for the Grimsby of 1819 *was* an obscure place. In days gone by it had been famous. It had its legends of Grime the pirate and Havelok the Dane. It had been favoured by kings, and given birth to famous men: but it had fallen from its high estate. Its natural haven had silted up; it had no manufactures to export and no means of forwarding imports. We can form some idea of the obscurity into which it had sunk by the casual references made to it by those who chanced to

GRIMSBY PAST.

GRIMSBY PRESENT.

know it in its low estate. Thomas Mozley, speaking of North Lincolnshire as he knew it in 1819, intimates that nobody went there except on business, or to take the ferry for Hull, or "to go to the most dreary of all watering places near what I remember as the miserable little port of Grimsby."* Wilkie Collins makes one of his characters fly to Grimsby to be in safe hiding. William Cobbett, in driving from Louth to Barton, changed horses and breakfasted at Grimsby. Wishing to recall something that happened there he imagines his readers exclaiming— "What could you find there to be snatched from everlasting oblivion, except for the purpose of execration?"† When Thomas King heard of it, its population was barely 3,000, though that was an improvement on the 982 at which it stood in 1790. In short the local historian says: "Grimsby was so obscure that it probably owed its place in maps and topographical dictionaries to its privileges as a parliamentary and municipal borough." The worst was past and Grimsby's fortunes were on the rise in 1849, when

* Mozley's "Reminiscences," etc., vol. ii. p. 11.
† Cobbett's "Rural Rides" vol. ii p. 322. Edition of 1855.

the foundation-stone of the Royal Dock was laid by Prince Albert. But even then the "Times" correspondent on the occasion could write of Grimsby as "one of those places that few of our readers have heard of, and a less number have seen, but which I can best describe as a place which a London contractor would cart away in three weeks." What the Church of England did for it may be gathered from the fact that so recently as 1828, "it had service but once a day, and the minister served Clee also." *

Such was the Grimsby Thomas King heard the rumour of and determined to visit. How different is the Grimsby of to-day we need not stop to point out. All the world knows of its spacious docks, its famous water-tower, its timber-yards and unrivalled fishing-trade. We can follow

DEANSGATE BRIDGE.
Thomas King entered Grimsby by this road.

THE OLD MARKET-PLACE, GRIMSBY (SHOWING OLD TOWN HALL).
Thomas King preached here in afternoon of October 31st, 1819, first day of his visit.

all his movements on the day he carried his determination into effect, which was the last day in October, 1819. He had slept on the Saturday night at Barnoldby, and left for Grimsby four miles off, accompanied by two men to show him the way. But when they were within two miles of the town they left him to enter alone. Keeping his eye on the tower of the church, he pushed on—for the morning was cold—and presently the church and adjoining town-hall and the market-place were passed; then Clayton Hall in Baxter Gate (now Victoria street), and tradition says he drank at the pump then standing only a few minutes' walk from the spot where he preached his first sermon. This was on a piece of waste ground not far from where the present Victoria Street Chapel stands. Thomas King stepped into a wheelbarrow waiting to be ennobled by serving as a pulpit; pulled a sevenpenny hymn-book out of his pocket; sang, prayed and preached without interruption or the occurrence of any particular incident, save that the grandmother of George Shaw was present, ready to become the first convert. The house where she and her husband lived became the home of Thomas King and many of the early preachers, and served as an occasional meeting-house.

A second open-air service was held in the "old town" in the afternoon according to announcement. At its close "Farmer" Holt stepped up to the preacher, warmly

NORTH SIDE, BAXTER GATE EAST, LOOKING WEST.

grasped his hand and invited him as his guest to Old Clee. Incidentally we gather that this was not the first time Farmer Holt had acted in a Gaius-like way to the missionaries of the Connexion. Some time before, at his invitation, one such missionary whom he had heard preach in a certain village, had visited Clee, preached on the Saturday evening, and next day accompanied by his host had gone to Grimsby to hold an open-air service. This fact, we may be sure, does not stand alone though our records may often be silent. It would have been hazardous to affirm of any village in Lincolnshire at any point between 1818 and 1820—"No Primitive Methodist has ever come this way and delivered his message here." Skirmishers preceded the main body, preaching whenever and wherever they found opportunity—like the unknown one who anticipated Thomas King at Grimsby and Clee.

THE PERIOD OF CIRCUIT PREDOMINANCE AND ENTERPRISE. 447

When Thomas King reached Clee he found another service awaiting him, and the congregation already assembling in the farm-kitchen; but first he was shown by the thoughtful housewife into the dairy and urged to help himself to anything it contained. She, good soul, remembered that the dispenser of the bread of life could not himself dispense with the bread that perisheth. But when, a little while after, Farmer Holt put his head into the dairy to see how the preacher was faring, he found him on his knees.

For a day or two Thomas King occupied the guest-chamber of the farm which for many years was proverbial for its hospitality. William Holt was one of the makers of Grimsby Primitive Methodism. His biographer, the Rev. Joel Hodgson, says of him: " In the day of small things it was no doubt a recommendation of the new society that Farmer Holt united with it. His social position, force of character, and religious zeal,

HOUSE OF MR. WILLIAM HOLT, OLD CLEE.
In which Mr. King preached on the first evening after visiting Grimsby.

placed him for many years in the front rank of the local preachers and leading officials of the Grimsby Circuit." He and Thomas King became fast friends, and were often companions in travel. Once they walked to Tunstall to attend the Conference of 1821, and when the sittings were over they walked back again to Grimsby. After this we can easily credit the statement that after preaching at Grimsby one Sunday evening, Thomas King supped on bread-and-milk and set off to walk to Nottingham, arriving in time for the opening of the Quarterly Meeting at ten o'clock next morning. William Holt lived to see wondrous changes in the position of the Church he helped to found in Grimsby and the neighbourhood, since he attained the ripe age of eighty-seven years and died in the triumph of faith.

It was on Wednesday, November 3rd, 1819, the first society was formed in Grimsby. Thomas King had spent the day in visiting, and at night he preached in a room procured by Farmer Holt "up the town." The society formed that night consisted of eight members of whom W. Holt became the leader. The cold weather had already begun, so that a shelter was essential, and yet the society had for a time to be content with a stable, that being the best place obtainable. By September, 1820, however, a room in a warehouse that stood back of the spot where Thomas King preached his first sermon was secured. This was afterwards vacated for a disused chapel in Loft Street, which, undergoing several alterations and enlargements, continued to be the society's principal place of worship until the building of Victoria Street Chapel in 1859.

The plan of the Grimsby Branch, beginning October, 1st, 1820, with the side-lights cast on it from other sources, is instructive. When he made it, Thomas King had just returned from the Nottingham Quarterly Meeting which had reappointed him to the Grimsby Branch. He was strong to labour and in a very hopeful frame of mind; and indeed as we follow his incessant movements, and notice his unfailing tact and courtesy, his buoyancy of spirit and how he never seemed to spare himself in labour, he seems to us to have been one of the most considerable figures of this early time, and a veritable missionary bishop; so that we are not surprised the Nottingham Quarterly Meeting of 1828 should have seriously urged his appointment as "District Superintendent." Thomas King's colleagues on the Branch were George Herod—who had been appointed some six months before to assist him in missioning Louth and its neighbourhood—and Thomas Blades, who after being appointed to Belper in 1835, passed off the stations. George Herod began his ministry as a married man. An early usage made a distinction between preachers who could be interchanged between circuits by any Quarterly Meeting, and those who could only be stationed by the Annual Meeting. The former were really "hired local preachers," whose tenure of office was very insecure. This, those concerned, who were chiefly married men, were fully aware of. As is shown by a circular now before us—of which Herod, S. Cookman, J. Brantfoot (*sic*), R. Hawcroft, and J. Hutchinson are the signatories—they convened a meeting of all the "hired local preachers" at York on the 28th May, 1822, for the purpose of discussing their grievances,

FIRST PREACHING PLACE, GRIMSBY.

which were soon redressed by all preachers being placed on the same footing of a four years' probation. Herod, we remember, had married Elizabeth Parrott of East Bridgford, so that in his appointment the Grimsby Branch really acquired two preachers. There is a touch of pathos in the account of the way husband and wife went to their mission :—*

"A friend took care of their child. There being no railways, and unable to afford a conveyance, they, luggage in hand, trudged many a weary mile till they were benighted and knew not where they were. She sat down on the luggage and wept as she thought of her child and circumstances. Her husband climbed high ground to look for a light. One was descried which they made for. It proved to be a farm-house where lived a Wesleyan local preacher who fed and lodged them for the night, and afterwards assisted them in their work. The child was well-cared for, the mission a success, several souls being saved under her first sermon on that missionary journey."

GRIMSBY FIRST CHAPEL, NOW COTTAGES.

Louth, on its little river Lud, at the foot of the Wolds, was then as now a clean well-built, municipal town of considerable size and importance, boasting the possession of one of the noblest spires in England, and an ancient Grammar School where, at the very time our missionaries entered the town, the brothers Tennyson (whose father was vicar of adjoining Somersby) were getting their grounding in the classics. Louth holds second place on the Grimsby plan of 1820. Thomas King was appointed to preach twice there, and once at Legbourne, on its first Sunday. He tells us he entered the town "with very great concern of mind," for, though they had a society of "from twenty to thirty lively souls," the good woman who had allowed them to preach in her dwelling-house could do so no longer, so that he had the task before him of securing a place to preach in and a home for the preachers. Before he left the town he had succeeded in securing both.

J. F. PARRISH.

J. HODGSON.

Louth prospered so much that in 1823 it became an independent station, and as such has ever since continued. Its area comprised not only the pleasant villages in the undulations of the Wolds, but also the marsh country extending from Louth to the sea, with its dikes broad and deep doing duty for hedges. It was not until on in the forties that the Alford part of the circuit stood on the stations as a Branch. The Rev. Joel Hodgson who, with J. F. Parrish, Daniel Moore, Jabez Wood, F. W. Atkin and a host of ministers, too numerous to name, is a native of this part of the old Louth circuit, tells us that in 1835, when Elizabeth Rowbotham was stationed at Scotter "first six months" and Louth "last six months," with J. Wright as superintendent, each would on alternate fortnights walk on a Saturday from Louth to Hogsthorpe, some twenty miles, preaching at night in the kitchen and taking their Sunday appointments next day. "Mrs. Sutton, of Addlethorpe Cottage, near Hogsthorpe," says Mr. Hodgson, "a lady of independent means, entertained the preachers. I once heard her say, 'she did not care if they chalked "Ranter" on her back.' Mrs. Sutton became the wife of W. Briggs, a young travelling preacher who settled at Hogsthorpe, then lived at Leeds and died at Skegness." Mr. Briggs was in his day a prominent official.

The early history of Primitive Methodism in Alford affords an illustration of the influence a domestic servant, who is a consistent Christian and loyal to her Church, may set in motion. One of the members of the Alford Society was Sarah B——, servant with Squire Young. Occasionally the minister called at the Hall to see this member of his flock and to leave her magazine. After one or two such visits had been paid, the squire intimated his desire to see her minister and to show him courtesy for her sake. This was done; the courtesy was received and reciprocated. Acquaintanceship gradually ripened into the intimacy of Christian fellowship. The result was that, in the most natural way, important and far-reaching changes were effected. Alford, instead of Hogsthorpe, became the preacher's more convenient residence. At that time houses were difficult to obtain in Alford, but the squire housed the minister in one of his own dwellings. The chapel and other interests of the society were benefited. Squire Young became a regular contributor to the missionary funds of the Connexion;

ALFORD CHAPEL (PAST).

broke bread with the humblest in the Alford Chapel, and in a hundred delicately thoughtful ways befriended the servants of God and the Church they represented. The story is true; for the writer has recollections of the squire's benevolent face, and can recall how his own child-life was enriched by the changes brought about by Sarah B——.

For some years Louth Circuit made but slow progress numerically, so that in 1835 it reported but 204 members to Conference. By 1838, however, the number had risen to 610. We get some details of this notable advance in a course of cases "approved by the Circuit Committee and signed, John Stamp," which appeared in the Connexional Magazine for 1839:—

"During the three years that Father Coulson and myself have laboured in this (the Louth) circuit we have built sixteen chapels, enlarged one, bought another, and fitted up a large room, and have had an increase of twenty-five local preachers, and four hundred and sixteen members; and our last quarter's income was sixty-five pounds more than the first; and we have called out three additional travelling preachers, and have fitted up a preacher's house. I have walked more than ten thousand miles; have preached upwards of one thousand five hundred sermons; and have visited near six thousand families; and through the blessing of God, I feel more strong to labour than when I first began, which I attribute in a great measure to total abstinence from intoxicating drinks, and the blessing of Almighty God."

That part of this roseate report which relates to chapel enterprise sets forth a prosperity largely fictitious and radically unsound, as after events soon showed. Some of these "sixteen chapels," etc., were built without money—or what amounted to the same thing—with other people's money; some had no title deeds or legal trustees, and the inevitable day of reckoning soon came.

ALFORD CHAPEL (PRESENT).

It was well for Louth Circuit that at this critical time it had connected with it some men of substance and tried loyalty such as John Maltby and William Byron. The latter, especially, did much to relieve the circuit from its embarrassment. In his unostentatious way Mr. Byron rendered, at various times, many valuable services to ⋯ ⋯ and Mr. J. Maltby were joint Treasurers of the

THE PERIOD OF CIRCUIT PREDOMINANCE AND ENTERPRISE. 453

General Missionary Fund from January 1856 to 1862. He was elected a permanent member of Conference, and at the Yarmouth Conference of 1872—the last he was privileged to attend—he and "his excellent lady" received the thanks of the

J. MALTBY.   MRS. BYRON.   WILLIAM BYRON.

Conference inscribed on parchment for their gift of £559 10s. to various Connexional funds. Amongst all the other services he rendered to the Connexion Mr. Byron's decisive action in purchasing some of these recklessly built properties must be

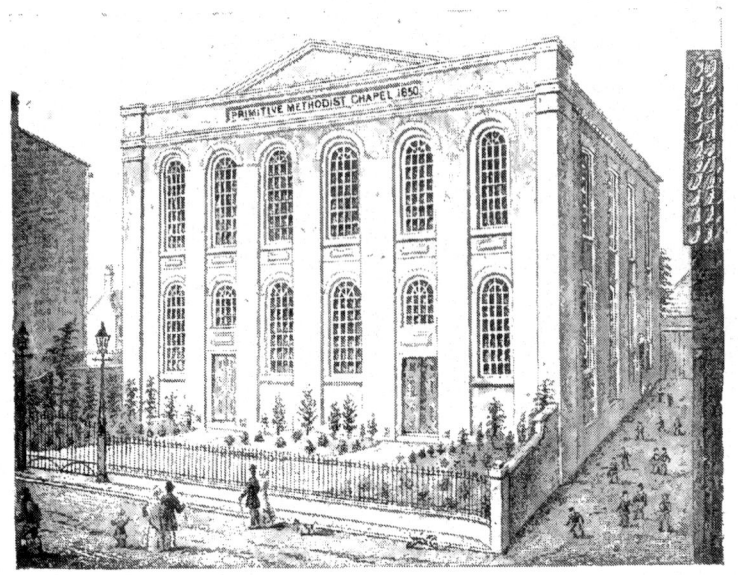

PRIMITIVE METHODIST CHAPEL, LOUTH.

regarded as not the least valuable. His prompt action preserved the buildings to the Connexion and helped the circuit to tide over its difficulties. Still, an unfortunate experience like this could not fail to react on the genuine spiritual prosperity which had been enjoyed; so we find that in 1850 the membership of the circuit had been reduced to 422. During the next ten years, under the labours of Messrs. Knowles, Campbell, C. Kendall and their colleagues, steady progress was made. The membership of the circuit more than doubled itself, and Louth Chapel was rebuilt on a greatly enlarged scale and provided with schoolrooms, and all else needful for the requirements of a vigorous working church. In following the history, and giving any estimate of the present standing of our Church in Louth, there are one or two facts needing to be borne in mind. One is, the almost inappreciable increase of population which took place during the last century. Unlike Grimsby, Louth was about as large and important years ago as it is to-day. A second fact is that, for many years, Louth was a stronghold of Wesleyan Methodism. In 1848 there were 2,600 members in the circuit, more than a thousand of them living in the town. During the troubles of the "Reform agitation" twelve hundred members seceded from the parent body, since which, Louth has been one of the strongest circuits of the Methodist Free Churches.

BURWELL CHAPEL, LOUTH CIRCUIT.

JOHN STAMP.

John Stamp's name is now fairly before us, and this seems to be the right time to refer to him more at length; since he was a native of Louth Circuit, as was also his pious and gifted wife; he spent the first three years of his ministry in Louth Circuit, and afterwards was closely associated with Hull Circuit, and was the main cause of the troubles which marked the close of the first period of our history in that town. Though his more active association with our Church lasted only from 1835 to 1841, he yet filled during those six years a considerable space in the eye of the Connexion, and was much in the thoughts of its responsible advisers. He looked upon his appointment by Hull to its Sheerness Mission, in 1838, as a sentence of banishment on account of his ardently avowed "Radical teetotalism." For all that he loyally took up his appointment, and threw himself into the work of evangelisation with his accustomed enthusiasm and success. All the old revivalistic methods were adopted, and some that then appeared novel, but are so no longer. "Protracted Meetings" were one of such novelties re   , from America. The first meetings of the kind in the Connexion are said to have been held at Sheerness in July, 1838. Each day, for near a fortnight, services were held at five in the morning and at three and seven o'clock; and at the close it was found that twenty converts were the fruit of this protracted effort.* By 1839, the 112 members of Sheerness Mission had become 310, and it was formed into an independent station with three ministers. In 1840 it was transferred to Brinkworth District, and its reported membership was 410. John Stamp affirms that at one time Sheerness employed seven preachers; but never more than three appeared on the stations, and the rest must have been called in by Stamp to assist him. There can be no question that in 1838-40 the northern part of Kent was the scene of a remarkable revival, and that Primitive Methodism reached and made itself felt in some places in this lovely county, from which, alas, it has long since receded. We have before us an interesting letter, dated August 18th, 1840, written from Ashford, by John Stamp's colleague—Henry Thomas Marchment. For various reasons it will be well to quote from this letter which has never been published:—

"It is with the feeling of deep-toned gratitude to Almighty God I inform you that in this town (Ashford) we are doing well. I came for the first time a stranger to every one in the place on Saturday, July 11th, and on the Sunday preached three times in the open-air. I was taken to the "Cage" by two constables but was soon liberated, as perhaps you read in the paper. I continued persevering, rejoicing that I should be counted worthy to suffer shame. We have now twenty in society, and a place to worship in, and good openings in four adjacent villages. On Sunday I preached five times: in the open-air at nine, in our room at ten-thirty, two-thirty and six, and in the open-air at a quarter before eight in the evening, when about a thousand were present. We are getting some saved and added every

JOHN STAMP.

* At the Hull September Quarterly Meeting Brother Summersides, lately returned from the American Mission, gave an account of Protracted Meetings as conducted in America, and the propriety of adopting them was discussed. It was, in the end, resolved that a beginning should be made in October at Barnard Castle.

week and the discipline of Primitive Methodism (which I have strictly enforced) takes well. God is with us. We shall do valiantly.'*

This is a fair picture. Would there were no other! Then would Primitive Methodism in Kent have had a less chequered history, and its present condition would have been more prosperous than it is—hopeful though its condition may be as compared with that of some previous periods. But there *is* a reverse picture of which the fact that neither in Ashford—a large market-town, an important railway junction, and the seat of the South Eastern railway-shops,—nor in its adjacent villages have we any connexional interest, may be taken as the type.

In the Sheerness Circuit there soon arose troubles—some unpreventable, others plainly occasioned by mismanagement and the reckless incurring of liabilities there was no reasonable prospect of discharging. At Ramsgate a chapel was bought for £1100; at Margate a play-house was turned into a chapel. One of Stamp's colleagues died of fever, another proved a failure, a third assistant—Joseph Eden—was confined nine weeks in Canterbury jail for refusing at John Stamp's instance to be bound in a hundred pounds not to sing through the streets of the city. Stamp's own excellent wife, and also a child, died during these troubles, and he shocked the propriety of some of his friends by himself preaching her funeral sermon. Finally, on his being removed to the Canterbury Branch, dissension arose in the Circuit, and Thomas Holliday came down to hear and report to the authorities on certain charges which had been formulated against the superintendent. This report found its way by the usual channels to the Reading Conference of 1841, which left John Stamp without a station.

Now the scene shifts to Hull, whither Stamp had made his way. It was alleged that he had been expelled for his Teetotalism and without being heard, and that the Connexion was in his debt. These allegations were sounded forth from public platforms in Hull, received currency in the local "Temperance Pioneer," and the London "Temperance Weekly Journal," of which latter Jabez Burns, himself an ex-travelling preacher, was one of the editors, and the friends of justice and temperance were in the columns of these prints invited to subscribe to a Stamp Defence Fund. John Stamp himself rushed into print with a "Defence" of sixty-four pages, in which at times the language used approaches scurrility. Messrs Clowes and Flesher are styled 'Pope William and Pope John," and as for certain laymen who stood by them throughout this trying time—they are called names which we will not repeat. To John Flesher was assigned the duty of vindicating the Connexion through the medium of the press—a duty which it is hardly necessary to say, he discharged in a most satisfactory way. A secession of some score or more of John Stamp's supporters took place from the Hull societies. Some of these were well parted with, while others were good and sincere. Fetter Lane Chapel and Moxon Street School-room were the first quarters of John Stamp and his friends, and at the end of the year 1841, a chapel in South Street was

* The letter was written to John Frisken, 33, John Street, Bedford Row, London. Marchment afterwards left the Connexion, probably as the result of the Sheerness troubles, and became we believe a Congregational

opened. Here history repeated itself. What had happened at Louth and Sheerness happened here also and afterwards at Leeds. The wheel went round full cycle and revival and enthusiasm went under while dissension and embarrassment were uppermost, and at last South Street Chapel had to be sold. Many of those who had left our Church returned to do good work, and as West Street was crowded, a room was taken in Nile Street and a school established in Wilberforce Rooms—these the nucleus of the Thornton Street that was to be. As for Sheerness Mission, it had no local William Byron to stand by it in the evil day. It was taken again under the fostering wing of Hull Circuit and in 1843, when the Missions were transferred to the General Missionary Committee, four Kentish stations were occupied—Sheerness, Ramsgate and Margate, Maidstone, and Canterbury.

John Stamp was a remarkable man in whatever light we view him; remarkable for gifts which ensured success, and equally so for deficiencies by which failure in another direction was no less ensured. He had remarkable declamatory powers. One passage of impassioned rhetoric in which he denounced intemperance has, one may say, gone, and is still going, round the world. It was plagiarised to the last letter and comma by Col. Robert C. Ingersoll, and delivered as though an extemporaneous outburst before the Supreme Court of the United States. As so given, it electrified that assembly. It was copied into newspapers, did duty in many a temperance campaign, ran from press to press all over the American continent; and yet what made all this sensation was just a piece of a letter addressed by John Stamp to the Reading Primitive Methodist Conference of 1841. But John Stamp was more than a rhetorician or Temperance orator,—he was a doubly-born evangelist; endowed by nature and qualified by grace to convince and convert men. This was his call, his forte, his business, and he should have been kept to it, and kept from having anything to do with bricks and mortar, and promissory notes and balance-sheets. Instead of that—and therein lay the tragedy—he was sent into distant Kent, made superintendent of a station that embraced half a county, allowed to build chapels, hire rooms and engage a little corps of helpers who continued, spite of all, to believe in him, so great was his magnetism. In short he was put into just such a position in which his talent for mismanagement, which was quite as remarkable as his other talents, could be put out to usury. Even in Louth, with "Father" Coulson as his superintendent and Messrs. Byron and Maltby as circuit officials, we know what happened. If such things were done in the green tree, what would be likely to be done in the dry? The tragedy worked out its own sad inevitable denouement. And when the catastrophe came John Stamp's gift of declamation swiftly passed, as it easily can do, into vituperation, and bitter things which it were best if possible to forget, were spoken and written of the men who had wished him well. There can be little doubt that at this day our Church would be glad to have a half-dozen men with the evangelistic gifts of John Stamp; and one may hope that if it were to be so blessed, it would have the wisdom to let the evangelist by God's election evangelise. But we are not so sure that it would; so prone are we to assume that a man richly endowed in one direction must necessarily be a man of "all the talents."

The sum and the best that can be said for John Stamp has been said by Rev. Joseph Odell. Mr. Odell believes in the principle of spiritual breadth and claims to be the direct spiritual descendant of John Stamp. The claim, so far as it relates to the possession of remarkable evangelistic gifts may readily be admitted. Beyond that the claim must not go, for, certainly, Mr Odell has not inherited his ancestral hero's talent for mismanagement as we beg leave to call it. This last and best word for John Stamp may suitably find place here, since we find ourselves in general agreement with its writer. It will, however, be necessary to refer to the attitude of our Church to the new altruistic movement of Total Abstinence which began in this country about 1830—a movement of which John Stamp himself was the erratic child as he was one of its most advanced representatives and spokesmen. These remarks will best come in a separate section at the close of the present chapter. Meanwhile Mr Odell shall speak:—

"The Rev. John Stamp was certainly ALL ALIVE. We think him very much alive still. It is very many years since his name appeared on the list of our ministers. He forfeited his position we quite believe. He was rash enough for that. But what was rashness then, appears heroic now. He lived at least fifty years before his time, and was the victim of a transition period. He blundered in chapel-building and battled for Temperance, when "Gospel Temperance" was thought to be rank blasphemy in the Churches. But the great fact about the man appears to be this: his remarkable talents, his resources of intellectual and spiritual wealth were of that unique order, that required a definite line of labour—the line of the evangelist. Instead of that, he found himself in chapel-building efforts and financial straits. Added to this was an apparent extravagance of language upon the drinking habits of Christian men, and proposals of a kind entirely too drastic. These things deprived him of his place amongst us as a minister. Were he living now, and such as he are needed now, we should see him the first Evangelist of Primitive Methodism—the man our Churches need. His portrait is before us. The face is finely classic; his form and features seem breathing with life and vital with irrepressible energy. This is a man who could not die. He is all alive. We have his writings also. They are all alive. How they stir the readers! We know of more than one minister who has been made by them. If the writings prove so potent, what must the preaching have been? We are able to tell. His sermons held people for God and eternity. Hundreds were converted as he preached. We knew a man—our own Professor of Theology, and the only college tutor we ever had, who used to drive thirty-three miles one day and back the next, in order to hear John Stamp preach. In a missionary meeting in Kent, we mentioned John Stamp's name incidentally in a speech, and all the old people rose involuntarily as they heard the name of the man who led them to Christ. This man cannot die. His triumphant life was crowned with a translation rather than a death. His departure took place at his own little residence, "Teetotal Cottage," Deansgate, Manchester, and he lies buried not far from our Higher Ardwick Church. *

To return to Grimsby Circuit and its first plan, it is interesting to notice that Caistor, Middle Rasen, Grasby, Usselby, and Holton-le-Moor—all places in the Market Rasen district—are on this 1820 plan; and further, that Ann Carr's name stands on

* "All Alive! A Revival Letter by John Stamp, reprinted by Joseph Odell." Primitive Methodist

the plan next after the travelling preachers. As we have seen Market Rasen attained to Circuit independence in 1854. Grasby is the village of which Charles Tennyson-Turner was so long the vicar, succeeding to the living on the death of his uncle Turner, whose name he assumed. In a volume of interesting reminiscences of the Tennyson family recently published, we are told how the poet, whose fame has been overshadowed by that of his greater brother, would stand on his lawn on a summer Sunday afternoon and listen with the keenest interest to an open-air service—doubtless a camp meeting—that was being held close by; "though his innate shrinking from publicity used to set him wondering as the preacher would shout in a stentorian voice—"Now, brethren, let us count up how many the Lord has saved at this service."* The type of Christianity from which, in some of its manifestations, the vicar of Grasby might shrink, has kept on all through the years helping men and women to live and preparing them to die, exerting, too, a searching wholesome influence on village life, as even the poet himself would have been the first to grant. One cannot but be impressed with this as we read the memoir of a Grasby worthy who recently passed away after forty years' active association with the village society. Mrs. Barkworth we are told was "upright, generous, devout, trustworthy;" "a Dorcas indeed."

Tetney, too, which was "Wesley's favourite village in Lincolnshire," is also found on the first Grimsby Circuit plan, and remained associated with that circuit until 1868, when it attained independence. Here on his farm near the famous "Blow Wells"—traditionally regarded as bottomless—lived Mr. R. Surfleet, for many years a stay to the society and a befriender of the Grimsby Victoria Street Chapel trust-estate.

MRS. BARKWORTH.

Thus the result of our inspection of the first Grimsby Circuit plan goes to show that already in 1820, we have the cadre of the seven existing circuits with their combined membership of 3,703. Looking forward just a quarter of a century and examining the Grimsby plan for 1845, amongst the six places not on the plan of 1820, we find Cleethorpes which has taken the place of Clee. Yet how small and feeble Cleethorpes was at its beginning is clear from the fact that it had but one service a Sunday, the hours of service being 9.30 one Sunday and 2 p.m. the next. Cleethorpes' advance as a watering-place has been almost as rapid as Grimsby's advance as a port. What has been said of the remarkable material progress made by our Church in Grimsby may with equal truth be said of Cleethorpes which has now come to be almost the sea-side suburb of Grimsby.

Amongst the names of the fifty preachers having place on the plan of 1845 there are several that merit a word of recognition. No. 3 on the list is Elizabeth Lingard, who was known throughout North Lincolnshire, and had, as John Stamp states, "spiritual children all around her, and not a few of them preachers and class-leaders." Then there is Sarah Moody, "whom the Rev. G. Austin once announced as the Rev.

* "Glimpses of Tennyson and some of his Relations and Friends," by Agnes Grace Wild. In C. Tennyson-Turner's "Small Tableaux" there is a sonnet entitled—"Fanaticism: a Night Scene in the Open Air."

Sally Moody," and if goodness and faithfulness entitle a preacher, whether male or female, to reverence and respect, then Mrs. Moody was worthy of the style and title thus humorously accorded her. She preached the gospel with great point and force, in a way calculated to make sinners tremble and saints rejoice, the lukewarm to bestir themselves and the backsliding to retrace their steps." Such is the testimony to Sarah Moody borne by a venerable minister who knew her.[*] There is, as No. 16, Thomas

OLD CLEETHORPES.

Barkworth who was pronounced by George Shaw to be one of the most gifted preachers he ever heard. Lower down on the list is the name of Henry Smethurst, born in 1819, at Newark, and converted when about twenty years of age at Grimsby. His father had settled at Grimsby after (from 1820) serving as a travelling preacher for a few years, travelling successively at Bottesford, Nottingham, Scotter, Grimsby, and Louth—all circuits that have come under our notice. His retirement was rendered necessary by the demands of his large family for which the small stipend then received was found quite inadequate. By virtue of his own sterling qualities young Henry gradually won his way to a good position. He was closely identified with the town's staple trade and with the social and corporate life of the borough. He became a member of the Town Council, an alderman, justice of the peace, and was for many years chairman of the School Board.

ALDERMAN H. SMETHURST.

[*] Rev. Joel Hodgson in "Christian Messenger."

THE PERIOD OF CIRCUIT PREDOMINANCE AND ENTERPRISE. 461

GRIMSBY CHAPELS

For two years in succession he was elected Mayor of the Borough, and on the occasion both of his election and re-election, he was accompanied by the Corporation to the Flottergate Chapel. Henry Smethurst was an ardent temperance advocate in a town which very much needed such advocacy. One of the cherished schemes of his life was within sight of realisation when he laid the foundation stone of the present Temperance Hall. When in his prime he was a vigorous gospel and temperance out-door speaker, a hard-working local preacher, and an "aider and abetter" of our Church in its efforts at extension both in Grimsby and the adjacent villages. He died August 7th, 1892, only three days after his faithful wife who had sympathised with all his efforts to do good. His fellow-citizens marked their appreciation of Henry Smethurst's worth by erecting a marble memorial in "The People's Park." As the lifelong friend of Henry Smethurst, and probably the only witnesser of his conversion still surviving, respectful mention must be made of the veteran official—Joseph Robinson, in whose society class the writer began his association with the people of God. To the roll of Grimsby worthies must now be added the names of Alderman J. C. Wright, J.P., J. W. Emmerson and George Shaw, who have just passed away. Each, like Paul, "served God from his forefathers," and by their inherited and ingrained attachment and loyalty to our Church their lives illustrate that "continuity" which has been so pleasing a feature in the history of Grimsby Primitive Methodism. What each did in his own way and measure cannot be told here, but their portraits are given to recall them to remembrance. Without such officials of the type of Henry Smethurst, J. W. Emmerson, J. C. Wright, and others like-minded who remain, the goodly chapels figured on the preceding page could never have been built. In a true sense these are their monuments.

THE SMETHURST MEMORIAL.

LINCOLN CIRCUIT.

There is no one name so definitely and exclusively associated with the introduction of Primitive Methodism into the ancient city of Lincoln and the parts adjacent as is the case with most of the circuit towns we have thus far had before us. It was in

September, 1820, Lincoln was formed into a Circuit, but for some time before this, Hugh Bourne tells us, it had been familiarly known as "Lincoln Circuit," though only as yet a branch of Nottingham. Much of the country around had been traversed by John Hallsworth and others, for when stationed to the new circuit in 1820, Hallsworth

JOSEPH ROBINSON.    J. C. WRIGHT.    J. W. EMMERSON.

records his thankfulness at finding the position of things so much improved since he laboured in these same parts years before; he recalls the fierce persecution he and his fellow-labourers then endured, and notes the retribution with which former persecutors had been visited—as notably at Fulbeck, where the ringleader had since lost his reason and "had to be shut up in a madhouse," while others had suffered the loss of their cattle.

Thus Lincoln had probably been entered by our missionaries prior to the famous visit of William Clowes and John Wedgwood during Clowes' Leicestershire campaign of 1818. We speak of Clowes' mission as "a campaign"; and such he himself evidently regarded it, if we may judge by the warlike spirit and phraseology of the extract from his *Journal* which follows. It is clear he felt himself engaged in a veritable "Holy War." Having announced a fortnight before that they would "lift up their banners in that city"; they proceeded to do so on a spot "between the Minster and the new Gaol."

G. SHAW.

"We began the labours of the day about nine in the morning, and terminated them about nine at night. About eleven o'clock in the forenoon, the conflict with the powers of darkness was very hot. A goat which some sons of Belial procured, was run in among the congregation with a shout of three times three, and throwing dust in the air. But we remained in firm phalanx amid this storm, and returned upon the legions of the devil a powerful discharge from the big guns of Sinai, whilst at the same time we unfurled the ensigns of the cross of Jesus, inviting the enemy to ground his arms, and surrender upon the terms of peace and reconciliation offered in the gospel. Many that day did accept of offered pardon; the solemn stillness, and the tears which stood in the eyes of numbers, were evidently indicative of this. Generally the work of conversion went on well during the day, and as a division of the grand army of Emmanuel we that day took the city and we have not been driven out of it to this day. Hallelujah!"

William Clowes did not come scatheless out of this spiritual conflict. Some coward hand threw a stone which cut his face and drew blood. But Clowes meekly bore the wrong and prayed for his persecutor. The sight of the blood trickling down his cheek and, still more, the bearing of the preacher under this assault—so Christian in its calmness and dignity—made a lasting impression on one who was standing by. The man thus impressed came from Eagle, a place some seven miles from Lincoln, and it is said he afterwards showed our people great kindness. The next day the missionaries pushed on to Waddington where a farmer, who had been at Lincoln the day before,

THE OLD NEWPORT ARCH, NEAR NORTHERN ENTRANCE TO CITY OF LINCOLN.

lent them a waggon from which they preached to "a vast multitude, most of the heads of the town being present"; and this was followed by a prayer meeting in the farmer's house. Wellingore was also visited by Clowes and Wedgwood, but whether just at this time is not clear. Here a camp-meeting was held amid a good deal of turbulence. One passage from the *Journal* is significant:—"I turned my eye upon some of these Philistines, and God accompanied my glance with an arrow of conviction, and two or three of the rebels fell into the rear as if utterly powerless, and remained quiet during the remainder of the meeting." Let these words be noted and remembered. W. Clowes was quite aware that his eye at times had the power to pierce and quell the defiant, just as he was aware that under certain conditions his voice had the power to search and thrill the souls of his hearers.

Information respecting the early history of Primitive Methodism in Lincoln Circuit is scant; and what little there is has had to be gleaned from scattered sources. The first chapel or room in the city occupied by our Church, we are told, was erected in 1819, in Mint Lane, though the building was known as Hungate Chapel. In 1823, there are no less than six preachers on the stations for Lincoln Circuit, and the membership for that year is reported as six hundred and sixty-four. By the next year the preaching staff and the membership have both been reduced by one half. How is this? It looks as though the boundaries of Lincoln Circuit in this early period were shifting ones and had contracted between 1823 and 1824. Nor must we forget that Balderton Circuit first appears on the stations of 1824. But even allowing for some transference of territory, there is good reason to believe that the Connexional crisis of which we have so often spoken made itself felt even here; for it is certain that some of the places that were missioned as early as 1818 and 1819 had to be remissioned some years after. In the absence of all numerical returns from the stations from 1824 to 1829 we cannot tell how it fared with Lincoln Circuit in the interim, but in the latter year it reports two hundred and twenty-one members.

Many of the Connexion's leading ministers laboured in the Lincoln Circuit during the first period of our history. With all its drawbacks the old system of stationing ensured this. No matter that the circuit was wide and laborious, and the city itself only

CASTLE HILL, LINCOLN, WHERE CLOWES AND WEDGWOOD PREACHED IN THE OPEN AIR.

chill and unkindly soil for Methodism to work—as are most places where the cathedral casts its long shadows—still the men of light and leading had to take their turn. So in 1825 we find William Sanderson here, his circuit extending from Willingham, near Gainsborough, to Ashby beyond Horncastle, from point to point a distance of about thirty-five miles, and, he significantly adds:—"I was expected to superintend."

Robert Atkinson was the superintendent of Lincoln Circuit in the years 1829 and

1830. He was a native of Owersby in what the Bible calls the "coasts" of Market Rasen. He began his ministry in 1820 and died at Thirsk in 1859. "He lacked imagination and mental opulence" says Mr. Petty, but again "he was respected for his meek and gentle spirit, and his upright and consistent walk;" and the official memoir of him records that "he was a plain, earnest, faithful and earnest preacher of the gospel." These solid, wearing qualities were recognised by his appointment as a permanent member of Conference in 1856 in the room of John Garner.

Mary Birks travelled the Lincoln Circuit in 1823 and again in 1829 as the colleague of Robert Atkinson. She laboured in Hull and in several of the stations which, after 1824, belonged to the Hull District and, as John Stamp says, she laboured "with credit to herself, and honour to the Connexion, and died in full triumph shouting 'Victory.'" Physically she was an uncommon woman, being quite six feet in stature. What she was intellectually and as a minister may be gauged from the fact that at the December Quarterly Meeting (1829) of the Hull Circuit, Mary Birk's name was under consideration as a suitable person to reinforce the staff of the American Mission, and W. Clowes was deputed to cross over to Grimsby to interview her on the subject. She declined the proposal. Parenthetically it may be noted that from the same Quarterly Meeting a letter was sent to Belper to inquire whether W. Bembridge, to whom Sarah Harrison (whom we knew as Sarah Kirkland) had been united in marriage, would make a suitable missionary for America, and if so whether both would go. We do not hear anything more of this proposal. After travelling fifteen years, Mary Birks located at East Stockwith, and at her death a modest sketch of her life was published by John Davison, the biographer of Clowes, who, in 1842, was the superintendent of Scotter Circuit.

REV. ROBT. ATKINSON.
Aged 37, 1831.

During John Garner's superintendency of the Lincoln Circuit in 1835-6, considerable numerical and some material progress was made. Chapels were built at Horncastle (1835), and Hogworthingham (1836), and Horncastle was made into a Circuit with two hundred and two members. Tradition relates how John Garner made Elizabeth—familiarly known as Betty Swinton—his Circuit Steward and got her to supply his pulpit in his not infrequent absence from the Circuit for special services; she invariably appeared in white and attired in Quaker bonnet, and how, when she did thus officiate for him, no complaints were made because she was so well received by the people. Betty was a remarkable woman with a strange history. She had belonged to a gipsy clan and been addicted to the telling of fortunes. When converted she settled for a while at Fulbeck, and was made very useful there as a local preacher; but after her marriage she and her husband removed to Lincoln.

Without adhering strictly to the order of years short reference may here conveniently be made to one or two other Lincoln worthies who are still remembered and whose "works follow them." Elizabeth Ingleton is still spoken of as a woman mighty in prayer. She was afflicted with deafness but made no trouble of it, but rather a cause of thankfulness "seeing there were so many things not worth hearing."

Edward Chapman was a highly valued official of the early days—local preacher, and

E. CHAPMAN.   JOHN OLIVER.   J. BROADBERRY.

for many years, the leader of a large class having for a time John Oliver as his assistant leader. He was a convert of that useful preacheress Ann Tinsley, who travelled in Lincoln Circuit during the second six months of 1828. Of Mr. Chapman it was observed that "literally as well as spiritually he lived on the hill, and often, to avoid strife, declined to descend in the valley." At the time of his death, which took place in 1871, he was the oldest member of the Lincoln First Circuit.

It is fifty-two years ago since Joseph Broadberry left Grantham for Lincoln. He was emphatically a strong, though cautious, man and made his mark both in the Church and in the city of his adoption. To him belongs the distinction of having been the first working-man to climb to the city magisterial bench.

Resuming the chronological thread of our narrative, we have to chronicle the opening in 1839 of the first Portland Street Chapel, Lincoln. Though this date brings us near to the close of the first period, we must take a glance beyond; for in the case of Lincoln Circuit, as in that of Grimsby, 1842 gives no fitting terminal point. In 1844, when Lincoln Circuit was transferred from Hull to Nottingham District, it had only one hundred and seventy-eight members, and other indications are not wanting that our cause in the city at this time, and for a year or two after, was feeble, and the circuit generally in a depressed condition. But during the term of Messrs. J. Hurd and W. Price circuit prospects gradually brightened. Some of the village interests were revived, especially that of Metheringham, where a new chapel was built. The employment of a city missionary to work in the very haunts of vice led to a remarkable reformation

FIRST PORTLAND PLACE CHAPEL, LINCOLN, ERECTED 1839.

and redounded to the enlargement of the Church's borders. The story is interesting and worth outlining, since it proves that the Gospel fearlessly applied just where it is most needed is the best curative of the vices which are the curse and almost the despair of our cities.

It was well known at this time that certain districts of the city had been taken possession of by the "strange woman whose house inclineth unto death and her paths unto the dead." There were three quarters of the city that deservedly lay under this imputation, differing from one another only in the graduated presence or utter absence of sham respectability. The authorities must surely have been very supine to suffer such a reproach to sully the fame of their fair city. But be this as it may, the state of things weighed heavily on the heart and conscience of some Christian people. Already they had attempted something. A Reformatory had been built at Burton, a suburb of the city, but the class for whom it was designed showed little disposition to enter its precincts. At this point a public-spirited Wesleyan—Mr. Warrener—made a proposal to the effect that, under the direction of our Church some suitable person should be engaged to preach in the open-air and visit and work right amongst those whom we euphemistically call "unfortunates," promising if this were done to bear most of the expense. Whereupon, Jabez Langford, an unpolished agricultural labourer hailing from the borders of Donnington and Sleaford Circuits, was engaged and carried on his mission with most gratifying results. Some remarkable conversions took place. The stigma of ill-fame which had attached to certain houses ceased, and the Reformatory now went on with its Christianizing work. Rasen Lane was in one of these cleansed districts, and here a new Connexional interest was begun which ere long had its centre in Rasen Lane Chapel, and in 1870 became the head of Lincoln Second Circuit. "It was so fully recognised that our work had led to the reformation that, although it was two miles from the Reformatory to Portland Place Chapel, several of the inmates, along with the matron, used to attend the Sunday morning services." *

Thus, as Hockley Chapel was acquired through the Nottingham Town-mission, so Rasen Lane grew out of the City-mission of Lincoln. After labouring for a year or two in Nottingham District, Jabez Langford was sent out in August, 1854, to assist John Sharpe, the veteran Australian missionary, and subsequently left the denomination.

From this time Lincoln Circuit continued to make considerable progress. In 1853, at the close of the term of Messrs. W. Jefferson, W. R. Widdowson and J. Eckersley, it reported seven hundred and three members. In 1854 Portland Street Chapel was enlarged and a piece of land bought from a Mr. Bunyan, said to be the lineal, if not the last surviving descendant of John Bunyan; and in 1874 the chapel was entirely rebuilt.

* Comm.   .   .   .   .   For the reference to Hockley Chapel, see ante, p. 250.

"The Rising of the Temperance Star."

The simplest way of dealing with the allegation that John Stamp was expelled because of his teetotalism would be flatly to deny it, as John Flesher did. He maintained—and rightly—that it was not true, and could not possibly be true; that in face of the attitude taken by the Connexion as a whole to the Temperance question, such an allegation was preposterous; that any one who could believe it would go on believing it, despite all proofs adduced to the contrary. So let us leave this particular allegation on one side for a moment, while we consider the gradual advance in the Temperance sentiment of the Connexion which, beginning about 1830, had by the middle of the century become very pronounced. Here we have a question of fact resting on evidence; and when the evidence shall have been brought forward there

SECOND PORTLAND STREET CHAPEL.

will be no need to trouble much further about the allegation aforesaid. It will have died of inanition.

The growth of Temperance sentiment through the Nineteenth century was a long, slow process. It was a growth from "moderation" as the accepted position of the generality of Christian people, to the acceptance of total abstinence as the right rule of life. Time was when drunkenness was regarded as being only a sin by excess, like gluttony or incontinence. But science has changed all that. It has cut the ground from under the feet of Moderatism, which now stands self-condemned.

The most eminent members of the medical faculty have pronounced one after another that alcohol in all its forms is not only useless but positively harmful, that it does not permanently exhilarate, that it does not feed or strengthen, that it is a poison and as such ought to be labelled and shelved, and only used homœopathically, in those very rare cases where one poison may legitimately be employed to expel a still more deadly one. So science has reacted on morals. What our fathers might do, in all good conscience, we cannot permit ourselves in without a sense of condemnation; for we know we have no right to sin against our own bodies and souls by imbibing, even in carefully regulated doses, what science by its high priests declares to be poison. But these consentient pronouncements of medical science are but of recent date—that is to say as uttered *ex cathedra*, by those whom everybody must acknowledge as having the right to speak, and from whose judgment there can be no appeal.

Now the relevancy of all this to the early history of our Church is obvious. There were a few who were ahead of their time, who were wiser than the faculty, and had an inkling of the truth as to the physiological action of alcohol. But they were a small minority indeed. The great bulk were under the prevailing delusion—a delusion encouraged by the medical opinion of the time—that the moderate use of intoxicating drink was innocent, and that beer was as bread. Hence there was no consciousness of wrong-doing in the habit of moderate drinking. Say we are touching on delicate ground! Surely the time has come calmly to look upon the process of evolution that went on in our own as well as in other Churches, and by so doing justify our fathers, while at the same time we cannot exalt or take any special credit to ourselves for not sinning against the light which science, in these last days, is shedding. It is all very strange when we come across entries from the old Minute Books authorising brewings for the Quarterly Meeting dinner, or find that men who believed it wrong for a Christian professor to wear a double-breasted coat, or cried out against the sin of wearing a topping, should have felt no scruple in being moderate drinkers.[*] Connexional sentiment on the drink question surely reached low-water mark when, at the Manchester Conference of 1827, legislation was brought forward to the effect that the trustees of chapels should be desired or required "to provide wine for the use of the preachers, either before preaching, to give them a little spirit for their work, or after preaching to revive their exhausted energies." Hugh Bourne, who was in advance of the opinion and practice of the time, strenuously resisted the proposal both on economical and moral grounds, and the legislation was rejected. The account of the turning of the tide deserves a fresh paragraph.

At the Conference held at Leicester in 1831 a notable thing happened—much more

[*] At the Sheffield Conference of 1837 a charge was brought against W. Clowes for suffering John Flesher to be appointed a delegate, on the ground that Flesher wore a double-breasted coat. The charge was based not on the result of an actual inspection of the coat, but of Flesher's portrait, which we take to have been the identical portrait shown, *ante* p. 396. It turned out that the incriminated coat was not a true double-breasted coat but simply one with two rows of buttons. The charge was withdrawn and John Flesher was permitted to keep his seat as not 'guilty of the crime' imputed. As for the "topping" we have this entry in John Harrison's *Journal*—"How alarming to see ... he ... pulpit with a topping, and a shirt-ruffle shown in his bosom."

notable, one thinks, than the declaration against "piece-sermonising"* or the imposition of a ten-shilling fine for long preaching, which were also *memorabilia* of this Conference. Hugh Bourne brought the subject of Temperance before the assembly and dwelt on it at some length, with the result that "the editor was instructed to devote a portion of the *Magazine* to articles on the Temperance Question." It is probably more than a mere coincidence that within the leaves of the Tunstall District reports for the year 1831, there has lain undisturbed until now, a four-page Temperance tract which was no doubt referred to and quoted by Hugh Bourne during the course of his deliverance. This tract, issued under the auspices of "The British and Foreign Temperance Society," founded in 1831, contains a form of Temperance pledge which it will be well to give. It will be noted that the pledge proposed is what is known as "the moderate pledge."

"We whose names are subscribed, do voluntarily agree, to abstain entirely from the use of ardent spirits, except for medicinal purposes; and although the moderate use of other liquors is not excluded, yet as the promotion of Temperance in every form is the specific design of the Society, it is understood that excess in these necessarily excludes from membership."

We have spoken of the action taken by this Conference in relation to Temperance as "notable." So Hugh Bourne evidently regarded it. Taking into account the vested interests, the customs and the opinions obtaining at this time, he says:—

"It might have been deemed almost a miracle for any religious community to take up this new Temperance movement. Such miracle was, however, accomplished, for in May, 1831, the Primitive Methodist Conference, at Hugh Bourne's instance took up the self-denying Temperance movement, and made or enacted a law or rule for the promotion of Temperance."

He calls the years 1831-8 "seven Temperance-law years," and claims that the twenty-six thousand three hundred and eighty-four increase of these seven years more than the increase of the seven years immediately preceding them, affords a signal demonstration of God's approval of the new movement which had been accepted by the Connexion, as evidenced by the Minute of the Conference of 1832, and incorporated in the Consolidated Minutes of the same year as the permanent expression of Connexional opinion.

Q.— "What is the opinion of Conference in regard to Temperance Societies?"

A.— "We highly approve of them and recommend them to the attention of our people in general."

Hugh Bourne's use of numerical returns, in this instance, is employed here only to show that the advance in Temperance sentiment was incontestable and notorious, or he could not with any show of reason have made use of the fact to point his moral. We have already found reason to conclude that the remarkable numerical progress made by the Connexion after 1829 was largely the result of the preservative measures taken

---

* "Piece-sermonising" was Hugh Bourne's name for the practice of bringing out a sermon in numbers as it were, when a preacher full of matter was unable to finish his discourse and promised to complete it on his next occupancy of the pulpit.

during the critical period preceding that year. At the same time it may be readily conceded that the Temperance movement was another factor in that progress. Its influence must have been of the most salutary and conservative kind; and an inspection of Church-records would go to prove that there was much less wear and tear in the societies after the inception of the movement, than in the ante-teetotal days when the antecedents of many of the converts made lapses from the strict line of temperance perilously easy. In this respect, at least, we do not well to say the former times were better than these; for they were not.

As for Hugh Bourne, he became more and more enthusiastic in the cause of Temperance, until he almost got to believe that he was the father of teetotalism as well as of English camp meetings. When Mrs. Shafto, of Bavington Hall, asked him if he had joined the Total Abstinence Society, his answer was: "No; they have joined me; I was a teetotaler before the teetotalers began their society." There is a similar suggestion conveyed in the following more serious passage in which he speaks of himself in the third person: "When the total abstinence system rose he had still more cause to thank God and take courage, as the Lord was then *raising up many to stand much on the same ground he himself stood on for so many years.* And he believes the teetotal system has been, and is, a great handmaid to religion." Many of the leading ministers of the Connexion became pledged abstainers and zealous advocates of the cause—men like George Lamb, the brothers Antliff, S. Smith, T. Morgan, and others too numerous to mention. Laymen too, of whom George Charlton and George Dodds in the North, and John Briggs and Richard Horn in the Midlands, may be taken as samples, were using their gift of popular address in the same cause. Even in 1841 the leaven of the new movement had so far spread in the Connexion that, in a circular addressed to the stations by the General Committee, it was but a mild statement of the truth to say: "It is well known that our Connexion approves of Teetotalism, and recommends the prudent advocacy of it."

THE LATE ALDERMAN GEORGE CHARLTON.

After Hugh Bourne's superannuation in 1842, Walford, his biographer, tells us:—

"He became a teetotal preacher [sometimes taking as many as a half-dozen texts for one sermon to show that the Scriptures were full of it]—visiting, writing, preaching, and lecturing on teetotalism, in different parts of the Connexion. He had for years been a man of temperance and great self-denial; and having watched and witnessed the good effected through the agency of teetotalism in the Primitive Methodist Connexion, and now being at full liberty to dispose of his labours as he thought best, and invitations pouring in from different parts of England, he entered into this field of labour with all his accustomed zeal and activity; and as he considered this branch of religious temperance calculated to promote the cause of religion and the interests of Primitive Methodism, he threw his whole soul into the work."

A letter of Hugh Bourne's, hitherto we believe unpublished, bears witness to this enthusiasm for "religious temperance." The letter was written in March, 1843, to Thomas Morgan, and it gives an account of a two months' tour of visitation amongst various circuits, chiefly in the North. In this long letter there is not a single allusion to camp meetings or processions, and not a single fling at long preaching or piece-sermonising. True, it was winter and therefore not the season for camp meetings; still, had Hugh Bourne written a letter as long as this thirty years before, he could not, we may be sure, have kept camp meetings out of that letter, even though it were written in the middle of a seven weeks' frost. This letter of 1843 is alive with all the old passion for reaching men by the gospel, and he cannot but express his joy that wherever he goes men are being so reached. But it is also perfectly clear that new methods of applying the gospel and furthering the interests of the Church are now in the ascendant. So he alludes once and again to "Protracted Meetings" but recently introduced, and to the "golden system," from which system much was expected, and above all to "religious temperance."

GEORGE LAMB.

He arrived at York on January 3rd, and the same evening he says:—

"I had the opportunity of hearing our brother, George Lamb, and other great speakers at a great teetotal meeting. A speaker of the name of Whitaker turned his speech into a religious view. I was much taken with this, as I myself had before been contemplating teetotalism in a religious view. This meeting was held in the Concert Room. I think teetotalism stands high at York."

He preached at Brompton, and "we introduced 'the golden system.'" "Teetotalism," he remarks, "is strong here." He had liberty in speaking at a teetotal meeting at Hartlepool and "felt the presence of God." When he gets to Newcastle he notes:—

"I understand that all the travelling preachers in the Sunderland District are zealous teetotalers; and you will be aware that the Lord owns the labours of the teetotaler. I am told that Sunderland, Berwick, Westgate, and Newcastle-on-Tyne Circuits are going on powerfully. The Lord owns the labours of the teetotalers in the conversion of souls. To Him be glory and dominion for ever and ever. Amen."

Then before folding his letter he adds a long postscript to say that he has good news out of Cornwall from Joseph Preston, who "is a zealous teetotaler"; and at Durham, where he is writing, they had a meeting the night before when "teetotalism was advocated in a religious way" which "gave great satisfaction." The letter does get finished at last by an interesting reference to Preston: "I think they will, like our brethren at Preston in Lancashire, go into the way of holding their own teetotal meetings and holding them in their own way."

JOSEPH PRESTON.

Hugh Bourne was very impressionable to new ideas which he had the knack of appropriating and exploiting as though he himself had discovered them. In this, as in other respects, he presents a striking contrast to William Clowes who could not so readily throw off the old and put on the new, and modify the convictions and habits of his prime. Temperance as a specific movement was one of the manifestations of that altruistic spirit which now in the thirties began to breathe upon society and the Churches, softening the hard outlines of individualism and beginning its work—now going on with accelerated rapidity—of blending men together in a conscious community of interest. Hugh Bourne caught the early fannings of this movement, and, as we have seen, with the years it got increasing power over him. But Temperance in its original crude form, as expressed in the "moderate pledges" of the early societies, was still largely individualistic and more akin to stoic morals than to Christian ethics. But Total abstinence was nothing if not altruistic. While as yet Science delayed her decision on the question, men lent a readier ear to the high teaching of Paul—that the strong should be considerate of the weak, and abstain for their sakes if not for their own. This was not only Temperance but "religious Temperance." And now Science has at last mounted her rostrum, and pronounced in her high pontifical way that the teetotaler while deserving credit for his self-sacrificing intentions, has after all taken the line of enlightened self-interest and has benefited himself while seeking to benefit others.

PROVIDENCE CHAPEL.
The Old Independent Methodist Church, Stockton Heath, Warrington.

Whence came the new spirit and how did it find out Hugh Bourne? The answer is it came from America, *via* Ireland and Warrington; and it is impossible not to be struck with the remarkable similarity between the origin of the camp-meeting movements and the Temperance movement as each affected Hugh Bourne and our Church. Both these movements were Transatlantic in their origin.[*] With both Irish Quakers and Warrington and Stockton Heath Independent Methodists had much to do. We became very familiar with the names of Peter Phillips and Thomas Eaton in dealing with the origin-period of our history. Now these names recur once more; for we shall assume that recent historical research has demonstrated that the first Total Abstinence Society was founded at Stockton Heath in 1830. As Mr. Mounfield in his recently published brochure says:—

[*] "The light of this new movement shone across the Atlantic and enlightened England and Scotland." *H. Bourne.*

"Thomas Eaton was a local manager of the Bridgewater Canal, a member of the Independent Methodist Church, and a close friend of the founder of that body, Peter Phillips. . . . The Church to which Thomas Eaton was attached had been formed in a barn as the result of the preaching of Lorenzo Dow, but a new building called Providence Chapel had just been erected. In this building on April 4th, 1830, George Harrison Birkett and William Wood [members of the Society of Friends from Dublin] held their first meeting and formed the first Total Abstinence Society." *

At Warrington the "battle of the pledges" was fought, having for one of its results the formation in 1834 of a second Total Abstinence Society which had its head-quarters in old Friars Green Chapel. Here we will quote again :—

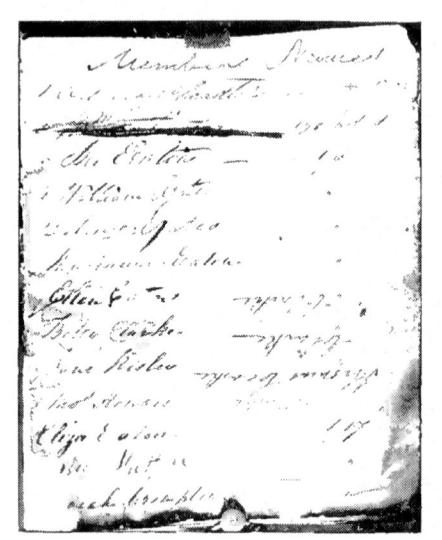

PAGE FROM ROLL BOOK OF THE STOCKTON HEATH SOCIETY, COMMENCING DEC. 23RD, 1830.

"From that time [December, 1830] forward, Friars Green became the scene of a succession of stirring and historic meetings which grew in interest and influence as the years went by. Peter Phillips and his family joined in the work and gave the weight of their influence, and henceforth the doors of the Church were ever open to the teachers and advocates of Total Abstinence. It became a recognised centre and witnessed some of the finest efforts of Joseph Livesey and his eloquent co-worker Henry Anderton. 'Next to the cock-pit at Preston,' says Edward Grubb in his Memoirs of Henry Anderton, 'the old Friars Green Chapel deserves to be associated with his name as one of the places where he displayed that mighty eloquence that touched all hearts and filled every eye '" (p. 29).

It seems, therefore, that the claim of "the seven men of Preston" to have been the first Total Abstinence Society will have to be surrendered; though the story of the origin of the word "tee-total" from Richard Turner's emphatic utterance of the word "total" has not, as far as we are aware, been disproved. It may have been challenged, but it still holds the field. As now told, however, the true story of the origin of the Total Abstinence movement should, if anything, prove more interesting to Primitive Methodists than the story it displaces, since it takes us back to the very neighbourhood of our origins, and brings us once more in touch with some worthy people who in the

* "The Beginnings of Total Abstinence The Warrington Societies of 1830." By Arthur Mounfield, 59, Fleet Street.

Connexion's infancy were, in Scripture phrase, its "nursing fathers and mothers." It was for preaching in Friars Green Chapel that W. Crawfoot got into trouble. It was the Eatons who helped him financially when he paid his visit to London along with Hugh Bourne, and theirs was the home Clowes pronounced a "pilgrims' inn" and "the best ordered family he had ever seen."

"This was like the rising of a new star, and its light was brilliant." Such are Hugh Bourne's words in speaking of what happened at the Conference of 1831, when the Temperance movement was recognised as making for righteousness and beneficence. But this star did not rise in the east but in the west and, if one may say so, it came and stood over the spot that owed its existence to the visit of the meteoric Lorenzo Dow.

As still further indications of the spread of Temperance sentiment in the Connexion, it may be stated that at a great Temperance Conference of ministers, held at Manchester in 1848, there were present twenty-eight ministers of our Church, a number exceeded only by the representatives of the Congregationalists and the Baptists, who numbered forty-seven and twenty-nine respectively.

CHAPTER IX.

THE SHEFFIELD GROUP OF CIRCUITS.

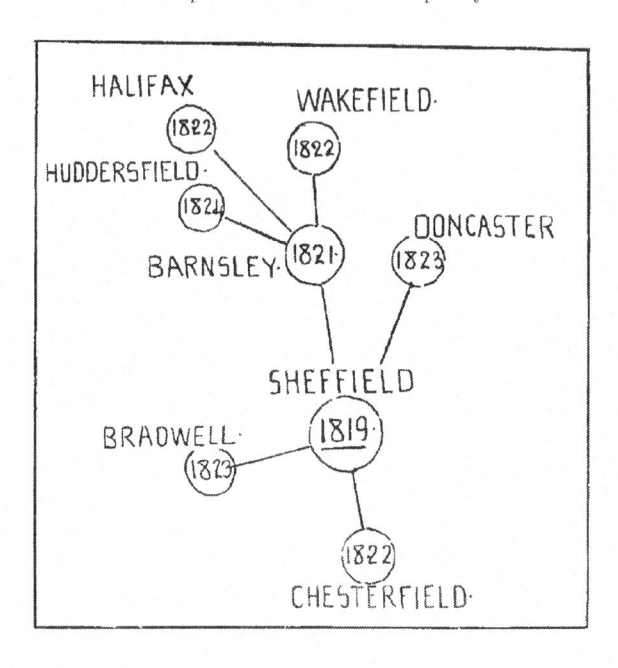

THOUGH we speak of Sheffield Circuit, that name from 1820 onwards for a year or two, does not so much designate Sheffield with its adjacent towns and villages as an extensive tract of country which was rapidly evangelised by our pioneer missionaries. Though there might be extensions into Nottinghamshire this tract mainly consisted of the northern and eastern parts of Derbyshire from Chesterfield to the High Peak, and the West Riding of Yorkshire from Doncaster to Huddersfield, so that the missionaries here joined hands with those who were labouring in Leeds and its neighbourhood. By 1824 this wide area was broken up and formed into no less than eight important circuits, viz., Sheffield, Barnsley, Chesterfield, Halifax, Wakefield, Doncaster, Bradwell, and Huddersfield. The way in which these important circuits were so quickly formed affords a good illustration of what—borrowing from organic chemistry—we may call the cellular method of circuit propagation, as distinct from distant circuit missions or branches of which Hull affords the best type. The third method—that of circuit-division, belongs to the later era of consolidation—and of this method—multiplication by division—no Connexional centre offers a better instance of late years than does Sheffield. It is therefore not so much with the local extension and consolidation of our Connexional interests in Sheffield this chapter has to do, as we have to show how in little more than four years an area equal to that of a province was visited by our missionaries, and the foundations well and truly laid for others to build upon.

The process of Circuit propagation that went on during these years is attempted to be shown in the accompanying diagram.

Who were these hardy, indefatigable pioneers! That name specially belongs to four persons, each of whom suffered hardship and imprisonment—Jeremiah Gilbert, William Taylor, S. Perry, Thomas Holliday. To Jeremiah Gilbert belongs the honour of being the pioneer of the Connexion in Hallamshire, while to William Taylor was assigned the task of breaking up the ground in Barnsley and its neighbourhood. Thomas Holliday was won by Jeremiah Gilbert, so that, although he was quickly pressed into the service and was inferior to none of his colleagues in efficiency and zeal, yet priority belongs to them as first in the field.

JEREMIAH GILBERT.

William Clowes was indirectly concerned in the establishment of the Sheffield mission. There were two persons present at the March Quarterly Meeting of the Nottingham Circuit who would not have been there but for his invitation. One of these was S. Atterby whom the meeting appointed to Retford Mission; the other was he who afterwards came to be affectionately known as "Father Coulson." Early in the century Mr. Coulson had removed from Chesterfield to Sheffield, and was now desirous that the Primitive Methodists should begin a mission in this important industrial centre. When on a business visit to Hull he had brought the subject before William Clowes who suggested that he should attend the next Quarterly Meeting and there personally plead the cause he had so much at heart. The result was that, probably by the appointment of the Nottingham Circuit Committee, Jeremiah Gilbert was designated to the mission, and set out for his sphere of toil assured of the help and sympathy of John Coulson, who had now identified himself with the denomination. Both S. Atterby and Jeremiah Gilbert seem to have

T. HOLLIDAY.

respective missions, and both were shut up in Bolsover Round House for preaching abroad. Eight days after, Atterby tells us, he was again taken into custody at Tickhill in Yorkshire. As for Gilbert, the first Sabbath of his ministry was made ever memorable to him by his experience in the Round House, where he had "neither bed nor straw," but where "God took possession of him—body, soul, and spirit."

We have a pretty full journal of Jeremiah Gilbert's labour in the mission after May, 1820, by which time it had become a circuit; but precise details of the first nine months' labours are wanting. One early record in his *Journals* conveys a vivid idea of the work that could be crowded into one Sabbath, and by it we gain a glimpse of some Sheffield localities associated with our humble beginnings in the hardware city:—

"*Sunday, May 14th :*—At Sheffield. Preached at six o'clock in the morning, in Young Street; a good time. At eight, preached at Water lane, which I suppose

BOLSOVER CASTLE.

to be the wickedest place in Sheffield; but many appeared to be greatly affected, and came in the evening to the chapel. Preached at half-past ten in the chapel; and at two administered the sacrament of the Lord's Supper. It was a solemn time. Preached again in the chapel at six, and in the park at eight. It was a blessed day to many souls.

Eight days after the preceding entry, Jeremiah Gilbert notes that he preached a funeral sermon in the chapel and afterwards renewed the tickets to three classes. All this indicates that a considerable society had already been established in Sheffield. But Gilbert was essentially an itinerant missionary and one of the most devoted and successful the Connexion has ever had. Hence the references to Sheffield are only occasional. The greater part of his time was taken up with carrying the gospel to various towns and villages comprised within the extensive area of the Sheffield Circuit. He visited amongst other places Rotherham, Greasborough, Bradgate, Clown, Doncaster and even Retford. He does not seem to have had much experience of rough handling by the mob, but he had rather more than his share of clerical persecution. Many of the clergymen of the district were bitterly hostile, and did all in their power to prevent open-air preaching in their parishes. So zealous were they that sometimes, when the constables felt their task distasteful and hung back, the clergyman would himself pull the preacher down. When, at Balber, the constable did lay hands on Jeremiah Gilbert who thereupon began to sing, "Wicked men I scorn to fear," etc; the clergyman tried to put his hand before the preacher's mouth: but

The first preaching place, Bolsover, was in this upper room.

BOLSOVER CROSS,
Where first open-air services were held and where Gilbert was arrested (?)

says Gilbert, "I told him my tongue was not to be tethered; and as the Almighty had imparted unto me such a gift as my tongue, it should be employed in praising Him." And here, perhaps, one should put in a good word for the old time parish constable into whose hands our early missionaries so often fell. These men were often unwilling agents, hating the work which they were compelled to undertake. "I had a deal of conversation" says Jeremiah Gilbert "with the constable on the way to Chesterfield. He wept very much and said, he hoped it would be the last time he should have a job of that sort;" and, as they drove along, the constable confessed that "he was so timid, that he was forced to go and get a glass or two of ale ... pull me down

There is one passage in Gilbert's *Journal*, written in July, 1820, which reminds us of that noble passage in which Paul enumerates the sufferings he endured on behalf of the gospel. One item in that heavy account is—"in prisons more frequent." So, quite in Paul's spirit and manner is Gilbert's statement: "Although within the last fifteen months I have been taken before magistrates six or seven times for preaching the gospel, I have never lost anything but pride, shame, unbelief, hardness of heart, fear of man, love of the world, and prejudice of mind. I have always come out of prison more pure than I went in."

It is a fair inference from these words that, although Jeremiah Gilbert gives us in detail only one of his prison experiences, there were several such experiences he might have given; and it has always seemed to us that the description of what happened to

ROUND HOUSE, BOLSOVER.

him in the "damp and doleful" prison at Eckington, in Derbyshire is, because of the cheery spirit it breathes, and the quaint, naive way in which it is written, worthy to be reckoned with similar narratives in the lives of the early Quakers or Baptists. As John Garner was allowed to speak for himself in describing the sufferings he underwent at Sow some fourteen months before this, so here we must let Jeremiah Gilbert tell his own story in his own way. Sow and Eckington make good companion, though contrasted, pictures. There is here no brutal rabble, only a timid constable that must prime himself with ale for the disagreeable work he has to do, and the inevitable clergyman in the background:—

"*Wednesday, 12th July.* At Eckington, Derbyshire. Got upon a chair, sung and went to prayer, sung again, and gave out a text. Then a constable came and desired me to come down. I asked him two or three times where his summons was, and began to preach again as if nothing had been amiss. He then called out for assistance, but not one would engage to help him. He then got hold of my coat and pulled me down. I then began to sing:—

'Christ He sits on Zion's hill,' etc.

It caused the people rather to smile to see me take hold of the constable's arm, and walk with him. He took me to a place which seemed to be as complete a prison as I had ever seen. The window had strong bars. The door appeared to be full of great nails. I looked through the bars of the window and there was a great many people. I exhorted them to flee from the wrath to come; and those who feared

YOUNG STREET, SHEFFIELD.
Where Jeremiah Gilbert first preached in the open-air in Sheffield.

the Lord to glorify Him; and many sang the praises of God without, while I sang His praises within. After some time the gaoler came and conversed with me. I persuaded him to go down on his knees in the prison; and prayed with him. I afterwards wrote a part of my *Journal*; and at midnight I prayed and sang praises to God, and then retired to rest. I had blocked up the window as well as I could to keep out the cold; for it was a wet, damp, doleful prison. I had neither bed nor straw, but lay across some laths, and had a besom for my pillow. It was afterwards remarked to me that my prison was a deal worse than Derby dungeon; but the Lord converted it into a paradise."

Next day for the second time Jeremiah Gilbert was driven to Chesterfield to go before the justices. He would not walk; for, as he said, he had to walk quite enough when he preached the gospel, and when he was taken up for preaching it it was his intention to ride. There is a tradition that, as the constable was driving along with his prisoner, he good-naturedly dropped the hint that Gilbert might slip into a wood they were passing at the time, and make good his escape. But the hint was not taken; for Gilbert meant seeing this business through. Whether it be true, as is sometimes affirmed, that the fox may even get rather to enjoy being hunted, we know not. But be this as it may, we cannot suppress the feeling that some of our early missionaries such as W. R. Bellham and Jeremiah Gilbert, rather enjoyed the evident perplexity of the Justice Shallows of the period to know what to do with their prisoners when brought before them. They secretly chuckled as they saw the magistrate, helped by

PARADISE SQUARE, SHEFFIELD.
Where the first room was secured for Primitive Methodist Services.

his clerk and the parson, referring to musty precedents, fumbling with law-books and getting mixed with the statutes of different reigns. So it was at Chesterfield on this occasion. The magistrate opened his law-book and began to read. "Is that Queen Elizabeth?" asked the clergyman who was Gilbert's accuser. "No, Sir, it is King Charles the Second" was the answer, at which the prisoner put in his word:—"You must try to get to another place if you please; turn to King George the Third—the Fifty-second year of his reign." The interview—for trial in any real sense it was not—lasted between two and three hours, and at the close the clergyman, and constable seemed glad to get rid of the business with any kind of formality

484   PRIMITIVE METHODIST CHURCH.

of imposing a forty pound fine was gone through! Jeremiah Gilbert at once made his way back with all speed to Eckington and finished the discourse which had been interrupted the night before.

However much the history of Primitive Methodism in Sheffield prior to the year 1836 may involve—however much conscientious labour, struggle, and self-sacrifice—the main facts of its history up to that date can soon be outlined. It is with the process of circuit ramification, from Sheffield as the original root, that went on in the

GROUP OF OLD OFFICIALS, SHEFFIELD FIRST CIRCUIT.

early years that this chapter has to do. The remarkable extension of our denomination in the city of Sheffield, the story of its chapel-building enterprise, beginning with the opening of Bethel Chapel in 1836, and the division and sub-division of its various circuits that has gone on in late years, is quite another and a later chapter. It will be enough to say here, before passing to other places once included in the original Sheffield Circuit, that for fifteen years after the formation of that Circuit the society in the town had ... preaching room, we are told, was secured in Watson's Walk, through the amalgamation with the mission of a small congregation worshipping there. Better accommodation was afterwards secured in Paradise Square, Brocco and the Park followed, and finally in Coalpit Lane, now called Cambridge Street, possession was taken of a chapel previously occupied by the Baptists, and in 1835, the present Bethel Chapel was commenced, and completed in the following year, under the superintendency of the Rev W Carthy."*

Never perhaps did a band of men and women, 'poor as to the world,' attempt a more formidable task than did the Sheffield Society when it set about the building of Bethel Chapel. The audacity of faith could surely go no further, nor could faith have proved her sincerity by a greater degree of self-sacrifice and cheerful toil, not wanting in resourcefulness. "The total expenditure, including the purchase of the old leasehold property, and the erection of the new premises was, we are told, £4,460, the whole of which was borrowed.' In order to keep down expenditure as much as possible, the trustees undertook to pull down the cottages standing on the intended site, and to prepare the land for building. In our group of old Bethel officials are a few of those who took their share in this self-imposed labour. Joseph Hunter is one of these. His connection with the Sheffield Society began some years before the erection of the chapel. He and his wife were famous class-leaders, and at one time had one hundred and thirty members under their joint care whom they carefully shepherded. Mr Hunter became a trustee for the new chapel. He helped in the demolition of the cottages and in the digging out of the foundations, and as he had his own day's work to do, this extra labour had to be put in before his own work began or after it was finished. His wife seconded his efforts in her own way. She made butter of the domestic cream she contrived to save, and gave the proceeds to the chapel-fund. Like Mrs Dale, whose portrait is also in the group, and others not represented, she dressed the bricks of the demolished buildings so that they might be used again. Edwin Machin and William Wright, two other trustees, are also in this group. They, too, wheeled barrow and handled spade at the digging out of the foundations. For some time the former lived in daily expectation of a visit from the bailiff because of his chapel responsibilities, but he lived to see the brighter days that followed the erection of the chapel in Coalpit Lane, afterwards known as Cambridge Street. An interesting reference to the opening of this historic building is found in the *Journal* of W Clowes, and with this we leave Sheffield and its workers for the present.

"On June 19th [1836] I accompanied brother J Flesher to Sheffield, to assist in the opening of a commodious chapel in Coalpit Lane. Brother Flesher preached in the morning and evening, and I officiated in the afternoon. The congregations were very large and respectable, and as I listened in the morning to the beautiful and powerful reasoning of brother Flesher, and witnessed the effect of his appeals on the large assembly, I felt humbled in the dust, and wondered how it was that I had ever been received as a preacher, and been continued such for more than twenty years. With these views of myself, I fled to the throne of grace and implored divine help for the service of the afternoon. The Lord granted my request, and as I addressed the audience His glory filled the house, and appeared to be felt by all present. On the morrow as brother Flesher and I journeyed homewards, I told him what my feelings and views were as I heard him preaching on the previous morning; and to my astonishment, he stated that as he was hearing me in the afternoon, he had just the contrary views to mine of my preaching and of his; and that the fear of spoiling my sermon, were he to pray after it, induced him to leave the pulpit and retire into the vestry, to prevent my asking him to pray. Thus the Lord frequently humbles us, to prevent any flesh from glorying in His presence, and to show us that he who glorieth should glory in the Lord."

BARNSLEY.

To revert to the beginnings of the Sheffield Mission: just about the time the prison-scenes already described were being enacted, William Taylor was sent out as an additional labourer into this wide mission-field. He was a native of Tunstall and his name had stood on the Tunstall Circuit Plan. Slackness of trade in the Potteries had led him to obtain employment in Sheffield, but he had not as yet taken up his duties as a local preacher in the Sheffield Mission. A visit to his native place, however, and the faithful admonishment of a Tunstall friend, led him on his return into Yorkshire to engage heartily in aggressive Christian work. He soon became the leader of three classes and the missioner of Hough, Newhill, and other neglected places. When the June Quarterly Meeting of the new Sheffield Circuit found itself in want of two preachers to "break up fresh ground," it was but natural that the eyes of the brethren should turn to William Taylor as a man in every way likely to make a useful missionary. The officials had not mistaken their man, nor did they commit an error of judgment in thrusting him forth in July, 1820, into the mission-field. For twenty-nine years William Taylor did useful work in various parts of the Connexion, dying August 11th, 1849. From his *Journal* as given in the *Magazine* we find him labouring at Barnsley, Penistone, Wakefield, Horbury, Silkstone, Cudworth, Huddersfield and many other familiar places in the West Riding. When the Branch Quarterly Meeting was held it was found that four hundred persons

BETHEL CHAPEL, SHEFFIELD.

WILLIAM TAYLOR.

had been added to the societies during the quarter, and the success of the mission in this part was so encouraging that, during this same year, Barnsley was made into an independent station. According to a well-authenticated tradition, it was Mrs. Tamar Hall (the grandmother of Rev. T. Markwell) who opened her house to the first Primitive Methodist missionary in Barnsley, and in this house the first money was given towards a chapel. Amongst other early befrienders of the cause respectful

FIRST PRIMITIVE METHODIST CHAPEL, BARNSLEY.

mention should be made of J. Pollard, a local preacher of fifty years' standing, who died in 1873, and J. Glover. When in 1832 the official addresses of the stations first have place in the Minutes of Conference, we find the superintendent preacher of Barnsley Circuit living in Rymer's-row, Barebones! Such eminent men as Dr. W. Antliff and J. Brownson lived in this oddly named locality. In 1842 we find Charles Lace housed in Castlereagh Street. In the later as well as the earlier period of its history Barnsley Circuit has continued to be the fruitful mother of circuits as the successive formation of such circuits as Horbury, Clayton West and Hoyland shows.

JOSEPH POLLARD.

JOHN GLOVER.

HALIFAX AND WAKEFIELD.

Another notable missionary was called out by Sheffield Circuit to do pioneer work in Halifax and its vicinity. Now, though Thomas Holliday gets only three poor lines in the *Minutes* of 1858, which record that his "end was peace," for all that, he was a man possessed of considerable vigour both of body and mind, and in the early days his strength and force of character were freely expended in the service of our Church. Holliday began his labours in the spring of 1821 by preaching at Elland and other places in the neighbourhood of Halifax. So much success attended his labours in this district, that he appeared at the Adjourned Quarterly Meeting at Barnsley, April 28th, with the request that another preacher might be appointed to assist him in the Halifax Branch. His request led to the appointment of a helper called Revel whose name, however, does not appear on the stations.

The foundations of Halifax Circuit were laid in persecution; and Thomas Holliday, like Jeremiah Gilbert and William Taylor, had his "baptism of fire." The circumstances were these. On the 27th May, Holliday and his colleague were holding a service in the Butter Market. While the former, with closed eyes, was in the act of prayer, some one shook him by the arm and bade him desist. Without heeding the interruption Holliday continued and reverently finished his devotions, and on opening

WESTGATE CHAPEL, BARNSLEY.

his eyes found himself face to face with the constable. The preacher readily gave his name when it was demanded, but expressed his determination to go through with the service unless prevented by force, and gave some reasons for his determination. What was alleged to be a summons was then produced, and Holliday and Revel were led off to the constable's house. Here, after a time, the constable left them, and in his absence, Holliday from the window preached on "the New Birth" to the crowd that had gathered, and which seemed reluctant to disperse when the sermon was over. "The people seemed much troubled about us," says Mr. Holliday "but we told them we were h   ... "cursing and swearing," made his way into the house, he threatened to knock the preacher down if he did not come down, tried to thrust his umbrella down Mr. Holliday's throat, and ended by dragging the two into a lumber room which did duty as an "inner prison."

Next day, Justice Horton came to what was evidently regarded as Police Court as well as prison, and had the two missionaries arraigned before him. When they refused to find bail to appear at the Bradford sessions, or to give an undertaking not to preach in the streets of Halifax, the magistrate committed them to Wakefield House of Correction there to await the sessions. They praised God for counting them worthy to suffer in His name, and the Justice bade them "cease their blasphemy!" Next day the preachers sang the praises of God as they passed through the streets of Halifax and through the villages on their way to Wakefield.

Messrs. Holliday and Revel remained in durance only from Tuesday to Saturday evening when they were liberated through the interposition of friends who thought fit to give bail for them. They were liberated just in time to enable them to take part in one of the largest and most memorable camp meetings ever held in these parts. Jeremiah Gilbert makes special mention of six camp meetings held in Sheffield Circuit during 1821. The first was at Wolfstones, near Thong, on April 29th, when ten thousand people are said to have been present. To get to another held on Heenly Common on July 29th, Gilbert walked twenty miles, he being at that time on the Halifax Branch. A third, held on August 5th, on Greetland Moor, was attended by thousands, amongst whom were many members of the Old Connexion who threw themselves heartily into the services of the day. This camp meeting was the precursor of a great revival at Greetland. Others were held during the year on Stain Cross Common near Barnsley, Heath Common near Wakefield, and Skircoat Moor near Halifax. But none of these equalled in magnitude the Sheffield and Barnsley Union Camp Meeting held on Mexbro' Common, June 3rd. At one time during the day there are said to have been sixteen praying companies engaged, and the newspapers of the district reported the number present as upwards of twenty thousand. It is only fair to say that Hugh Bourne in his *History* gives the much more moderate estimate of ten thousand.

The presence at this camp meeting of the missionaries just released from prison would naturally lend additional interest to the proceedings, and the persecution so cheerfully borne by them would make a powerful appeal to the high-spirited and liberty-loving Yorkshire people. No surer method of winning the people to the new movement could have been found than trying to stop it with the constable's staff. What with the zeal of the missionaries and the sympathy in their favour aroused by persecution, the Halifax Branch was almost from the first self-supporting, and in 1822 both Halifax and Wakefield became independent stations. It should be added that when the Bradford sessions came on, Messrs. Holliday and Revel duly surrendered themselves and were honourably acquitted. Finding themselves in Bradford our missionaries began preaching in the streets with the view of annexing that town, but they were in this forestalled by the Leeds Circuit.

HALIFAX.

The first class-meetings of the Halifax society were held in the house of Mrs. Halstead, and the first meeting-house, now a printing-office approached by outside steps, stood in John Street. In 1822, Ebenezer chapel was built at a cost of £2,206, and here, just as at Sheffield, women as well as men, counted it an honour to give their personal labour, and assisted in getting out the foundations and clearing the ground for the builders. The original schoolroom below the chapel, low and dark, and therefore ill-adapted to its purpose, is now a store for ironmongery; and in 1884, a fine suite of schools and class-rooms was erected at a total cost of £4,460. Connected with the chapel is a burial ground, wherein lie the ashes of many of the early adherents of the Church.

From the beginning Ebenezer has been a centre of earnest, aggressive work. Four circuits have resulted from the missionary enterprise of the Church, and the old spirit still lives. Ebenezer has a further claim to remembrance as having given accommodation to the fifth Conference—1824. Of this, as of the rest of the early Conferences, it is surprising how little we know. We do not even know the *personnel* of some of them. The official records are meagre in the extreme, and as yet the *Minutes* do not give the names of those who attended the preceding Conference. We have no descriptive reports, no sketches of the principal figures, no piquant notes and comments on the proceedings to help us to realise what went on day by day. The privilege of admission to the Conference was jealously guarded, as may be gathered from the fact that, at the Sunderland Conference of 1833, Hugh Bourne demanded that John Flesher pay down on the table sixpence as a forfeit for proposing that brother Aspinall, the superintendent of Sunderland Circuit, should be the Conference door-keeper. Hugh Bourne we........ felt that such an irregularity was likely to

FIRST PREACHING PLACE, HALIFAX.

EBENEZER CHAPEL, HALIFAX.

produce. But his brother, who was in the chair at the time, was of a contrary opinion, and J. Flesher had his sixpence restored to him.*

The second Conference was attended by about forty delegates; the third by fifteen; the fourth by forty-four, and Hugh Bourne, writing shortly before the holding of the fifth, anticipated that as there were now near seventy circuits, there would probably assemble at Halifax, on Whit Tuesday, 1824, upwards of seventy delegates. He foreshadows the plan, then adopted, of dividing the Connexion into four large districts, so that an assured basis of representation might be found, and the fluctuations in the number of delegates, from year to year, be obviated. At the Conference, W. Clowes preached in the chapel in the morning, and Brother Bowen (probably David Bowen of Darlaston) in the evening. We read in the *Magazine* that "a peculiar unction attended the services of worship;" but this was a very critical time, and the discussions that went on in Ebenezer were not only animated but at times acrimonious. As strikingly confirmatory of what we have more than once said of the crisis now reached, let the reader take the following from the private *Journal* of Thomas Bateman. He himself was not present at Halifax, but writing in September, 1824, he says:—

"Mr. Hugh Bourne came over again for another consultation as to the almost hopeless state of the Connexion, and the best means to adopt to save it if possible. Poor man he is nearly heart-broken, and well he may. . . . Some few fancy that since the last Conference at Halifax they see a rift in the dark cloud. Oh, that it may prove to be correct. At best the struggle will be sharp and long. I trow the pruning-knife will have to be used with an unsparing hand. Many dead branches will have to be lopped off if the tree must live and thrive."

That this crisis—which nearly broke the heart of Hugh Bourne and the hearts of

JOHN FEARNSIDE.    WILLIAM PARRY.    MRS. HOOSON.

others besides him—was safely overpassed, was not entirely owing to the enforcement of discipline and the excision of dead branches. It was rendered possible, mainly, because, up and down the Connexion, there were found a sufficient number of those who daily were content to be faithful in the local fields of inconspicuous service. It is right that those who were forgetful of self should not be forgotten by us. Amongst

* Unpublished MS. of W. Clowes in the author's possession.

the faithful workers at Halifax in the early years let a few be named. John Fearnside, a deeply pious and successful class-leader and family visitor; Timothy Schofield, an "ideal chapel-keeper" and earnest school-worker; William Parry who rendered valuable service for many years; Mrs. Hooson, mother of the late Rev. Stewart Hooson, "a saint indeed;" and Mrs. Driver, mother of Mrs. J. Brierley, a most devoted woman and liberal supporter of the Church. Mention too must be made of W. Gledhill, formerly a missionary in Canada, who, after his superannuation, settled down in his native town and rendered much useful service.

MRS. DRIVER.

W. GLEDHILL.

That intra-aggressive movement in Halifax itself, out of which resulted the formation of Halifax second circuit, is an interesting though later story, and must be told at a later part when we come to speak of the Bradford and Halifax District.

HUDDERSFIELD.

William Taylor was, no more than his colleagues, exempt from persecution, in the form of arrest by the constable and imprisonment. As early as July 16th, 1820, he found his way to Huddersfield, and there met with Sister Perry, another devoted labourer in the mission. As usual, they sang along the streets to the market-place and began to preach. Then "the constable came in a rude manner and took them into custody," and under his escort they went along singing the hymn consecrated to such an experience—"Wicked men I scorn to fear." They were thrust into a dirty prison and locked up for the night. But the day's work was not done. They sang praises in their cells, and to the people assembled outside—many of whom were weeping —Taylor spoke concerning the doctrine they preached and for which they suffered. Some kindly souls "put victuals through the bars." The people lingered near the prison till midnight, and "cried, shame! shame! on the constable for putting us in with nothing to lie on. The constable then sent two blankets and took sister Perry

THE FIRST PRIMITIVE METHODIST CHAPEL IN HUDDERSFIELD.
Removed from its original site for Railway purposes, and rebuilt in Northumberland Street from the old material in 1847, precisely as it stood on the old site.

out." Early in the morning a prisoner in an adjoining cell, who had been imprisoned for house-breaking, cried to Taylor to pray for him, and "himself began to pray likewise, and was in sore trouble." The picture is almost a replica of that drawn by Jeremiah Gilbert of his experience in the damp and doleful prison at Eckington, only that in this case we have the darker detail added, of a gentle woman treated as though she had been one of the vilest of her sex. Next day the two missionaries were taken before a magistrate who, after vainly trying to extort the promise that they would not preach anywhere in the town, dismissed them. Such was the manner of Primitive Methodism's introduction into Huddersfield. Yet "the word of God was not bound," and in 1824, Huddersfield became an independent circuit with Thomas Holliday as its superintendent.

We get an interesting side-light on Thomas Holliday's habit of way-side sowing from an incident told in a local history of Methodism—an incident that must have occurred when Thomas Holliday was itinerating the district round Huddersfield. This dropping a word in season as they passed along was a common practice with the first race of preachers. It was conversation-preaching in its simplest but most difficult form. Two souls, like two ships, cross each other's path, perhaps never to meet again. To bid the passing stranger "good day" were not enough. The one sentence possible must be a message—a rousing inquiry. Some of our fathers were adepts at this single-sentence-preaching, and we suspect that Thomas Holliday was one of these. But the incident! "Young Squire Brooke was out shooting on Honley Moor and got shot. The plain and pointed words of Thomas Holliday,—'Master, you are seeking happiness where it will never be found,' were well aimed and well meant, and did more execution than all the sermons he had heard preached." For over forty-five years he was a popular Wesleyan Methodist salvation-preacher, and, as once more confirming the view that "Like father, like son" is a principle that holds good of spiritual as well as of natural filiation, we are told that—

"Squire Brooke had a wonderful way of speaking a word in season, and still more wonderful way of speaking a word at times apparently to many out of season. The manner and the message roused sympathetic interest, awoke sleeping memories, and often resulted in sound conversion. To a card-player he said, 'Young man, you have a mother praying for you.' On journeying through a village he inquired the way to 'Paradise.' The man said he had lived in that village forty years and had never heard of such a place. 'What! never heard of such a place as "Paradise"? I am going there.' 'Ah, master, I understand you now.' . . . . He never forgot that the word spoken to him on Honley Moor by the humble yet earnest Thomas Holliday was the means, under God, of his conversion, and believed that under the same Divine blessing a stray word or a direct appeal might mean salvation to others." *

We give portraits of one or two of those who did much to establish and consolidate Primitive Methodism in Huddersfield. First must be named its first circuit steward, Mr. John North, who also was a well-known Connexional man and filled for some years the office of Treasurer of the General Chapel Fund, receiving the thanks of the Conference of 1862 on his retirement from the office. James Rayner joined the society in 1830, and was a member for the long period of sixty-eight years, filling the offices of local preacher and society steward. The brothers Samuel and Alexander .... were amongst the earliest local preachers and prominent officials.

* History .... Hoqqton and Denby Dale, by Rev. Joel Mallinson,

CHESTERFIELD.

The tradition that Primitive Methodism was introduced into Chesterfield by Messrs. Gilbert and Coulson is undoubtedly authentic; but no details survive as to the circumstances which attended its introduction into a place ranking next in importance to the county-town. The open-air preaching and lively singing of the missionaries would be sure to create a stir amongst the five-thousand inhabitants of the town, yet no echo of that stir has come down to us, and tradition is silent as to any persecution having been met with.

Our records begin with the statement that a cottage in Froggatt's Yard was the first head-quarters of the society. This soon becoming too small, a remove was made to an old paint-shop in Silkmill Yard, which in its turn was superseded by the first connexional chapel built in 1827, when Jabez Woolley was superintendent and the society numbered but thirty members. As no site could be obtained within the borough (now greatly enlarged), the building was planted just outside the borough boundary, in the parish of Brampton. Here was rebuilt, in 1866, Mount Zion Chapel, now standing as the head of Chesterfield Second Circuit. But even eighteen years before this, Brampton had taken second place, yielding the position of circuit chapel to a new building erected within the borough proper; for, by 1848, the accommodation available was inadequate to the requirements of the society, now numbering two hundred and thirty-five members. In that year, therefore, a chapel was built in Wyatt's Yard, Beetwell Street, which served until 1881, when the old School of Industry was bought, and Holywell Cross Church built under the superintendency of Rev. John Wenn.

We have not space, neither is it necessary, to detail what has since been done in Chesterfield in the way of Church extension. The ninety-three pounds that in 1827 represented all that the society of thirty members had been able to raise towards the eight hundred and three—the cost of the first chapel, points to the small and feeble beginnings of Primitive Methodism, contrasted with its latest developments as set forth in our illustrations of its present chapels.

SAMUEL GLENDINNING.

ALEX. GLENDINNING.

First Preaching Room in Froggatt's Yard, Chesterfield.

The society at Hasland in the Chesterfield Second Circuit has had a long and interesting history which is thus outlined by the competent pen of Dr. G. Booth :—

"The first preaching services at Hasland were held in Mrs. E. Widdowson's cottage (my grandmother's house, also my own birthplace), and this was the place of entertainment for the preachers for many years. The house became too small for the number of worshippers, and, after many anxious deliberations, two female lay-preachers rented, cleaned, and caused to be fitted up, an empty shed formerly used for storing wool-pack waggons. This was afterwards turned into a blacksmith's shop. These two zealous and active members—Miss S. Webster and Miss B. Cooper—were destined to fill a wider sphere of action; for the first-named became the wife of the Rev. G. Booth, and the latter the wife of Dr. William Antliff. The

THE OLD CHAPEL AND PREACHER'S HOUSE, BEETWELL STREET, CHESTERFIELD.

WHERE PREACHING SERVICES WERE HELD.

THE PERIOD OF CIRCUIT PREDOMINANCE AND ENTERPRISE. 49

CHESTERFIELD CHAPELS

HOLYWELL CROSS SCHOOL

HOLYWELL CROSS

BRAMPTON MOOR

WHITTINGTON MOOR SCHOOL

WHITTINGTON MOOR

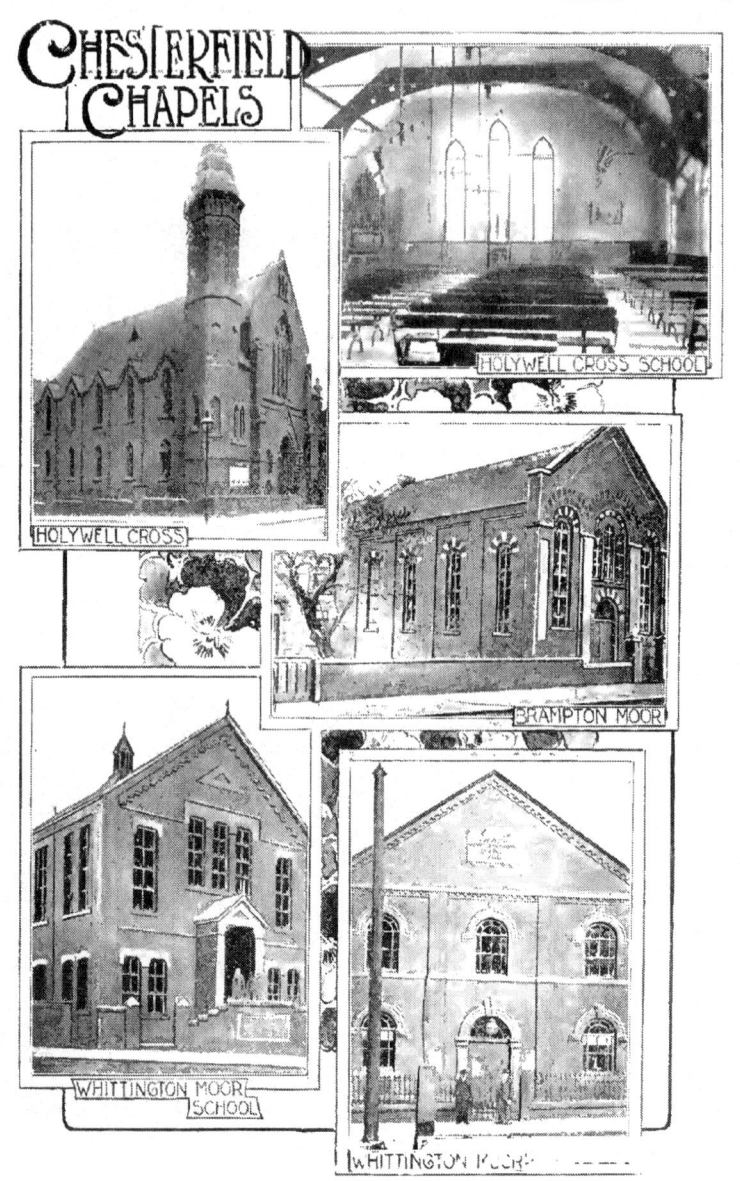

K K

first chapel was built [1842] during the time when Mr. Booth travelled in the Chesterfield Circuit. He designed the plans, drew up the specifications, and laboured thereon with his own hands. As this was the only Nonconformist place of worship in the village, some years after, increased accommodation was required, and then the son took up the task and the chapel was enlarged. Again the sanctuary became too small for the worshippers, and another chapel was erected [1880] by the side of the old building which was used as a school-room, etc. Lastly, the handsome Gothic church now used was erected in a prominent part of what has now become a populous township [1890]. The intimate connection of the Booth family with the Primitive Methodist cause in Hasland was kept up by the laying of a foundation-stone of each of the last-named structures by the editor of the Hymnal Tune Books."

It was in Chesterfield the veteran G. W. Armitage, Dr. S. Antliff and George Booth began their ministry. The last-named was born at Emley, near Barnsley, in 1805, began to travel in 1832, and died at Winster, April 9th, 1854; the twenty-two years of his useful and laborious ministry all being spent within the limits of the old Nottingham District. He was

BARBARA COOPER OF HASLAND.

HASLAND CHAPELS

FIRST & SECOND CHAPEL

HASLAND FIRST PREACHING PLACE

THE NEW CHAPEL

a plain, practical preacher, a diligent pastor and a man of deep and unquestioned piety. Excessive labour broke down a naturally strong constitution and laid it open to the inroads of disease, and George Booth died at the comparatively early age of forty-nine years. From certain entries made in his diary we may see something of his unsparing labour.

"*January 3rd, 1849*:—Visited more than forty families, and prayed with them when I had an opportunity. . . . *January 5th*. Walked fourteen miles. I was not very well; but I visited a few families, and preached with power. . . . *January 6th*, Walked twenty miles and rode fifteen. The weather was cold and frosty, and snow was falling; but I found the presence of God on the journey. The Lord brought me safe to East Shilton Circuit, where I saw three persons converted to God on the Sabbath. . . . *January 15th*, I was not very well; but after visiting a few families and exhorting the officials to love one another, I preached at Melton. *January 16th*, I visited sixty families ; and in every house prayed with the inmates and exhorted them to serve God."

Thanks to the care and training of a wise mother—the before-named S. Webster of Hasland—George Booth's only son was to find his way to Chesterfield, to make his mark on the civic life of the town, and greatly aid in that development of our Church in this busy centre which has gone on in these later years. To Primitive Methodists generally, Dr. Booth is chiefly known from his connection with our excellent Hymnals, to which fuller reference will be given. But in Chesterfield he is known not only as a medical man in large practice, but as a veteran educationalist, a magistrate, an alderman who has passed the chair (Dr. Booth was Mayor in 1887), and as a loyal Primitive Methodist, whose musical taste and interest in Christian education have largely contributed to give to the particular church he belongs the distinction of having the largest Nonconformist Sabbath School in the town, and the most effective service of praise in connection with its public worship.

DR. GEO. BOOTH.

In 1829 the Chesterfield Circuit was reported as having only two hundred and sixty-six members. In 1842 the membership stood at four hundred and twenty-one, and by 1863 it had increased to one thousand and seventy-three. In that year Clay Cross and Belsover branches were formed; these latter in 1869. In 1879 the Staveley Circuit was formed. Thus it will be seen that, including the three Chesterfield Circuits, what was originally part of Sheffield Circuit, and then one of its branches, has by a process of division and subdivision become six Circuits. The local historian intimates that "Chesterfield has re-awakened to vigorous life: especially during the past half-century." It is gratifying to have to conclude from the facts already cited that the same statement might be made of Primitive Methodism in the town and district For the future the omens are favourable; so much so that the words with which the same local historian concludes his survey of Chesterfield's past, by a hopeful prognostication for the years to come, may very well be appropriated by us:—"There is every probability that with intelligent municipal government, etc., Chesterfield will continue to expand, and in greater extent and prosperity, thoroughly realise the estimate of the historian who described Chesterfield as 'Ye fayrest towne in ye Peake countrie.'" *

DONCASTER AND BRADWELL.

Doncaster was within the radius of Jeremiah Gilbert's missionary labours. He held a camp meeting on Ravensfield Common on June 2nd, 1820, and another at Doncaster on July 2nd. Of the latter he says:—"We had not many people, nor many preachers; but the Lord was there." In the *Journals* of Messrs. Brooks and Ingham, there are sundry references not only to Doncaster but to Balby, Adwick and other places in the neighbourhood, and it is clear from the

SCHOLES YARD, HALLGATE, DONCASTER.
Old Dancing Room to the left, front half now turned into cottages.

reference to Doncaster that, by 1821, there was a society there worshipping in its own hired room. Doncaster was formed into an independent station in 1823, and in the redistribution of circuits made the next year, it was included in the Hull District. Right through the first period Doncaster had a chequered history. In 1829 its membership had fallen to 129; it lost its circuit independence and was re-incorporated with Sheffield Circuit; then it was promoted to be a branch, and it was such when John Garner, who had for two years been on the Sheffield Station, was appointed to take charge of it He found the society in a feeble and depressed condition: "worship was conducted in a room inconveniently situated adjoining a public-house." This would be the old dancing-room in Scholes Yard, Hallgate, which was the second place occupied by the society, the first having been a cottage in Fishergate. The Sheffield authorities despairing of their ability to carry the burden much longer, got it transferred to the shoulders of Scotter Circuit which

* "Meder   †   ‡   B. John Pendleton and William

accepted the responsibility with some misgivings. Under the new arrangement, to which John Garner was more than a consenting party, a vigorous policy was entered upon—an additional preacher was called out! "The appointment was a happy one. Mr. Garner and Thomas Kendall, his colleague, laboured together with fervent zeal and affection, and God blessed them and their combined efforts with abundant success. In Doncaster, Providence put them in possession of a commodious chapel. The country places improved rapidly, and in the course of a few months the station in regard to its numerical, financial and moral strength occupied an honourable position." The chapel thus providentially acquired in 1839, was one in Duke Street, belonging to the Methodist New Connexion, from whom, after some negotiations, it was purchased. Duke Street now stands officially as the head of Doncaster second station.

It would have been unlike John Garner if there had been no touch of originality even in his methods of conducting the routine work of the circuit. His biographer tells us that once, at Balby, John Garner "preached to himself," and thereby largely increased his after congregations. He had gone to the village to fulfil a week-evening appointment, but had not a single hearer. This, however, made no difference. He went on with the service as though the chapel had been full of people, and the fact was duly reported by one who had put his head within the door while the strange service was going on. The next time Mr. Garner came to Balby, and many times after, the curious came in numbers to see and hear the man who "preached to himself."

INTERIOR OF DUKE STREET CHAPEL, DONCASTER II.

So marked was the improvement made by Doncaster while under the wing of Scotter that, in 1853, it was again granted circuit autonomy. At this time it had three preachers—T. and R. Cheeseman and H. Woodcock, some fifty-six local preachers and twenty-nine preaching places, amongst which were Mexborough (now the head of a circuit) and historic Austerfield, and 541 members were reported to the Conference of 1854. Another step in advance was marked by the opening in October, 1854, of Spring

Gardens Chapel, justly regarded at the time as one of the best chapels in the Connexion. Under the successive superintendency of the brothers Cheeseman the circuit continued to increase in strength and influence. The holding of the Conference of 1858 at Doncaster to some extent registered the local progress made. Doncaster's first camp meeting (held soon after the close of the first Conference) with its "not many people, nor many preachers," was in striking contrast with the thirty-ninth Conference camp meeting, held on Doncaster race-course, as described in a few pen-strokes by one who took part:—"Processioning very large; much excitement, approaching that on the St. Leger day; two stands." *

SPRING GARDENS CHAPEL, DONCASTER.

There was one man present that day who would appreciate the change the years had brought, and who himself had been no mean instrument in bringing about the change. This was Richard Wadsworth, who was a delegate to the Conference held in his own town. He joined the society in Hallgate in 1828, and finished his course in 1897, in the ninetieth year of his age. For sixty-five years he was a local preacher, and is said to have walked some twelve thousand miles in fulfilling his long ministry. He was a class leader sixty-three years; attended eight District Meetings and five Conferences as a delegate. But this record, remarkable though it be, pales before the record of what he did, week by week and year by year, in visiting the sick and dying. We have read and re-read his private journal. We read it first from duty; we read it a second time for love. The reading leaves an impression, distinct and clear, of a man to whom religion was the main concern of life. Amongst the spiritual children of Richard Wadsworth are Dr. Reynolds Trippett, who after being on the Doncaster plan in 1845 entered the ministry of the M. E. South, and James Shaw, now in our own ministerial ranks.

It has been the good fortune of Doncaster to be chosen by several veteran ministers as the place wherein to spend the quiet evening of life. William Leaker, who died September 26th, 1878, was one of these. Two years of his ministry—1857-8—were spent in the Doncaster Branch, during which he married the daughter of George and Martha Harring, of Wormsworth, whose cottage from a very early date was the preaching place and the home of the servants of God. His declining days were spent in "visiting the aged, the suffering, the poor, and giving comfort to the sorrowful." He may well be remembered here; for, when the Balby

RICHARD WADSWORTH.

Road Chapel could not pay its way and the trustees and superintendent were greatly concerned, Mr. Leaker came to their help. His gifts, amounting to £400, meant self-denial for him but salvation for the cause. The last one was so opportune and so unostentatiously and graciously bestowed as to enhance its value, and the Conference of 1872 quite properly acknowledged it by a special resolution. In Doncaster cemetery also lies the dust of T. Kendall, William Saul, a native of Doncaster Circuit and son-in-law of Richard Wadsworth, who after serving the Church for forty years died at Doncaster 1889; and J. T. Shepherd, for forty-one years an able and successful minister of the Hull District, who died September 5th, 1897. The name of George Taylor should be chronicled in connection with the Hatfield Society, Doncaster second circuit. He was converted through the instrumentality of George Lamb on his first visit to the place, May, 1834. The society at Hatfield owed, and still owes, much to the fostering care of Mr. Taylor who, from the time of the opening of the chapel in 1835 up to the time of his death, was class leader, society steward and school superintendent.

BRADWELL.

Bradwell in the High Peak, though it is one of the oldest circuits in the Manchester District, genealogically can be claimed by Nottingham. It, like Doncaster and the rest, was one of the fruits of the Sheffield mission begun by Jeremiah Gilbert. The first clear, dated reference to Bradwell Primitive Methodism we can find is in a communication to the *Magazine* by James Ingham, describing a camp meeting held there on October 7th, 1821. The date was late enough for a full day's services in the open-air in that high region. Indeed, "many expected it would be a wet day," says the reporter of the proceedings: "But God can answer prayer. It was a fine day, and the wicked were heard to say—'See, they can change the weather.'" Ingham is explicit enough as to this being a pioneer camp meeting: "Six of us [from Sheffield] were there to hold the meeting, and I believe we had not a member in the town. Well might we say: "What are these among so many?" He is equally explicit in giving us to understand there were quite a score of converts ready to be enrolled as members at the close of that Michaelmas camp meeting.

The first services were held in the house of George Morton, who became the first circuit steward; and a chapel was opened in 1822 by Hugh Bourne. This we learn on the authority of Joseph Middleton, who tells us that, from the time of the Primitive Methodists coming to Bradwell, he had generally attended their meetings, and in this same year, when a youth of seventeen, joined the society. He soon after entered the ranks of the ministry, and was followed by his brother, the present governor of Bourne College. Joseph Hibbs, John Hallam and John Morton, were also sent forth from this circuit.

Joseph Middleton kept a full diary, from which we learn that he was born at Smalldale, adjoining Bradwell. Quite excusably for a native of this interesting district, he boasts of the natural wonders to be seen near his birthplace;—Mam Tor, or the Shivering

FIRST CHAPEL, BRADWELL.

Mountain, of the well which ebbs and flows, of the stream which disappears in unknown depths, of the natural caverns which, sparkling with crystals and roofed with stalactites, look like fairy palaces. It will keep us in touch with Hugh Bourne's early friend to know that these very wonders were looked on admiringly and speculated about by Peter Phillips, when traversing this district on foot to attend the Annual Assembly of his denomination at Sheffield.

The outside of the first Bradwell chapel may be judged of by our engraving: but inside, the chapel had its own special distinction, derived from the riches of the adjoining lead-mines. True, the chapel had no porch or vestibule; its seats were movable forms without backs, and its floor was unboarded. But for all that, the said floor was out of the common order. According to the veteran, Rev. Jesse Ashworth—who began his long ministry here—the ground was covered with what was called "small feith," or spar from the mines, which sparkled and glistened with little particles of lead ore; this was renewed every year. John Verity travelled on the Bradwell Circuit in 1831, and he was wont to describe this time-honoured structure in his own peculiar fashion. "My chapel," said he, "is floored with sparkling gems..sliding up an it, coming in or going out;..paring it down on the floor to play with the diamonds. If I want any one to engage in prayer two or three forms from me, I take up a handful of gems and throw them at the person's back."*

In this same year—1822—another camp meeting of note was held at Bradwell. Jeremiah Gilbert, who conducted it, tells us that it was held "upon a very high hill," and that thirty persons were "truly converted to the Lord." Let the date be remembered, for May 19th, 1822, was a famous camp meeting Sunday in our annals. At Congleton, Oakengates, and especially at Oldham, camp meetings on a large and impressive scale were being held during these very hours when Jeremiah Gilbert and his band were making the high hills vocal with praise and prayer.

Bradwell was made a circuit by Sheffield in 1823, and had for its first preachers Thomas Holliday and J. Hopkinson, whom we shall meet again in the North Country. John Skevington, the future Chartist, spent half a year of his short itinerancy here, and Thomas Blaides was one of its early preachers. In 1845, during the superintendency of that remarkable man, David Tuton, a new chapel was built at Bradwell which has since been enlarged. His two years' ministry in this circuit were very successful, so much so that he earned for himself the honourable title of the Apostle of the Peak. His name and fame still live in the district. We give the portraits of two of the early worthies of the Bradwell Circuit each of whom served the Church as a local preacher —John Backing Darwent for nearly fifty years, and Rebecca Edges for more than that number. What that involved in the early days may be guessed, when we know that in 1826 the Bradwell Circuit had something like fifty-eight places on its plan, and covered the ground now occupied by New Mills, Glossop, Marple, Newton and Hyde, and Buxton stations. New Mills Branch was made a circuit in 1827, and was annexed to the Manchester District; and the next year Bradwell itself was transferred from Nottingham District to Manchester.

There is some significance in this transference. When the Sheffield missionaries reached these high altitudes, Primitive Methodism had circuitously returned to its sources; for the High Peak is part of the Pennine range of which Mow Cop is also a part. The Peak country is a watershed feeding the Mersey on one slope, and the Dove, the Derwent and the Don, tributaries of the Trent, on the other. Primitive Methodism from Bradwell spilled over the water-parting somewhat, and mingled itself with the movement from Manchester and Stockport. A similar process went on from Macclesfield on the other side; for from that Cheshire town now aflame, earnest men and women crossed the ridge to evangelise some of the Derbyshire villages. So the point we have reached marks a stage in the geographical extension of our Church. When Bradwell Circuit was formed, the Trent basin, and especially that portion of it lying in the county of Derby, was earmarked for the Connexion. It was formally taken possession of and mapped out, and what remained to be done in the years that followed, was to divide and subdivide the territory into smaller and more easily workable areas.

CHAPTER X.

THE TUNSTALL FORWARD MOVEMENT.

END OF THE "NON-MISSION LAW."

WE have now to chronicle a notable advance on the part of Tunstall Circuit. In 1819 it fell into line with the newer circuits, and was not a whit behind any of them in missionary enterprise. Prior to 1819 this could not have been said; but from that date a stirring chapter in its history begins.

The facts have already been noted that, in December, 1818, W. Clowes was given up to the Hull Mission, and that in January, 1819, Hugh Bourne's illness led to his resignation of the office of General Superintendent. Up to this point the mother circuit had not materially enlarged its area, or even greatly increased its membership; for in December, 1818, the number of members reported was but 690, as compared with the 200 of the year 1811. But during the next fifteen months a remarkable change for the better took place. An extensive tract of country was missioned, and so successfully, that one slice of it was deemed ready for circuit independence. An increase of 1,013 for the fifteen months was reported. A circuit debt of some thirty pounds was wiped off, and a balance remained available for mission purposes. Better still, a spirit of enterprise and hopefulness took the place of languor and depression.

Hugh Bourne had diagnosed the disease and applied a remedy to which he attributed the pleasing change. In his view the decline of the circuit had been coincident with the decline in camp meetings, and the advance of the circuit had kept step with the reform in camp-meeting procedure. The lesson of Mercaston Camp Meeting had been lost; the circuit had fallen into the old groove and stuck there all through the years 1817–1818, when the great revival was going on in Nottinghamshire, Leicestershire and Lincolnshire. But with "the sweeping away of the long and tedious exercises, the restoring of the praying services, and the bringing of the talents of the people generally into action," new life and vigour had been infused into the circuit. These new regulations for the ordering of camp meetings were made at the March Quarterly Meeting, 1819, and printed on the back of the plan. A camp meeting on the new, or rather the restored, model was held at Wrine Hill, nine miles from Tunstall, May 23rd, 1819, and, as an event marking a forward movement, an account of it was inserted in the *Magazine*. With the signs of circuit improvement everywhere in evidence, Hugh Bourne's own health rapidly improved. He intimates that it was mental anxiety even more than labour that broke down his health. He was "wounded to the quick" by the "camp meeting ruin," brought home to him by the findings of a committee of inquiry that sat at Alton soon after the December Quarterly Meeting. He does not hesitate to say that "the Spirit of God was grieved," and that "the system

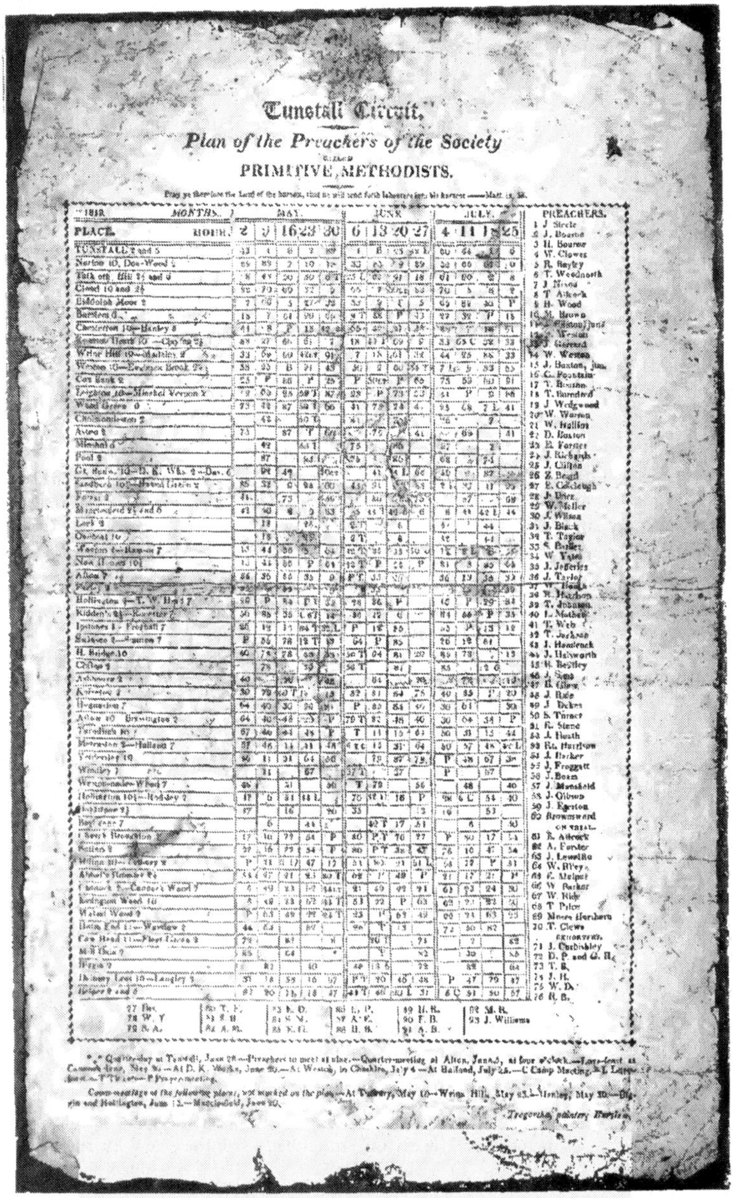

Tunstall Circuit.

Plan of the Preachers of the Society

CALLED

PRIMITIVE METHODISTS.

Pray ye therefore the Lord of the harvest, that he will send forth labourers into his harvest.—Matt. ix. 38.

1818. MONTHS. MAY. JUNE. JULY.

PLACE. HOUR. 2 9 16 23 30 6 13 20 27 4 11 18 25

TUNSTALL 2 and 5

Norton 10, Dee-Wood 2

Clowd 10 and 2½

Biddulph Moor 2

PREACHERS.
1 J. Steele
2 J. Bourne
3 H. Bourne
4 W. Clowes
5 R. Bayley
6 T. Woodnorth
7 J. Nixon
8 T. Alcock
9 H. Wood
10 M. Brown
14 W. Weston
15 J. Buxton, jun.
16 C. Fountain
17 T. Bourne
18 T. Barnsford
19 J. Wedgwood
20 W. Warren
21 W. Hollins
22 D. Buxton
23 R. Forster
24 J. Richards
25 J. Clifton
26 Z. Boyd
27 E. Colclough
28 J. Dier
29 W. Meller
30 J. Wilson
31 J. Black
32 T. Taylor
33 S. Barber
34 W. Yates
35 J. Jefferies
36 J. Taylor
38 R. Harbon
39 T. Johnson
40 L. Mathew
41 T. Web
42 T. Jackson
43 J. Hemlenck
44 J. Halsworth
45 H. Bentley
46 J. Sims
47 R. Glew
48 J. Rile
49 J. Dykes
50 S. Turner
51 R. Stone
52 J. Heath
53 Rt. Harrison
54 J. Barker
55 J. Froggatt
56 J. Beam
57 J. Mansfield
58 J. Gibson
59 J. Egerton
60 Brownsword

ON TRIAL.
61 S. Alcock
62 A. Forster
63 J. Lewellin
64 W. Riley
65 E. Malpas
66 W. Barker
67 W. Ride
68 T. Price
69 Moses Hershorn
70 T. Clews

EXHORTERS.
71 J. Corbishley
72 D. P. and G. H.
73 T. B.
74 J. H.
75 W. D.
76 R. B.

93 J. Williams

Quarter-meeting at Alton, June 8, at four o'clock. C Camp Meeting.

of holding camp meetings with "continuous preachings" had continued another year, the circuit would have been ruined. While bowed under the stress of such convictions and forebodings as these, the sight of the havoc caused in Leicestershire by the secession of R. Winfield came as the last straw, and what seemed like complete physical collapse followed as the joint result. Hence, at March, Hugh Bourne was left unplanned; but reviving prosperity acted like a medicine, and he soon found himself able to assist his "boys," as some rather contemptuously called his young but willing labourers. By June, he tells us: 'It was found that the circuit was rising out of its crippled state, and that it had begun to revive in almost every part. During the next quarter, the regulations began more fully to take effect, and the circuit rose very fast. The Lord graciously made bare His arm in the conviction and conversion of great numbers; the praying services at the camp meetings, and the prayer meetings at the close of preachings, were crowned with very great success.'

Such is Hugh Bourne's version of the history of the decline and rise of the Tunstall Circuit, from 1816 to 1820—a version which gives a theory of the facts as well as the facts themselves. There can be no question that the new camp-meeting regulations were a considerable factor in effecting the improvement which showed itself in an increase of one hundred per cent in the membership on the labours of fifteen months. But Tunstall had annexed a good deal of territory during this same period, and it is in the policy of expansion by which its borders were enlarged that we shall find the real explanation of the improvement made. It was not merely the resumption of the praying companies, but the resumption of missionary labour, the return to the old-time method of pushing forward and breaking fresh ground that had proved so successful in the origin-period of the Connexion, and was even at that very time carrying Primitive Methodism from county to county,—in other words, it was the virtual annulling of the 'non-mission law' which was opening for Tunstall a new and eventful chapter of history. It is only when an army leaves its cantonments and enters upon an active campaign that the special correspondent finds his work cut out for him. Our difficulty is that we cannot be with three army-corps at one and the same time. While we follow the advance of Tunstall, the missionaries of Hull are pushing on to Leeds and Newcastle, and the missionaries of Nottingham are breaking ground in the Eastern counties. Events that really happened together can only be described in succession. We must recognise the disability narrative labours under, and make the best of it.

A Recapitulation and Forecast

In one of his not infrequent historic generalisations, Hugh Bourne gives a useful retrospect of the ground we have gone over, and an indication of that which has next to be traversed:—

Before the year 1819, we never had any opening to spread the work to any extent from Tunstall. But from Bemersley the work got to Ramsor, Wootton, and Lexhead, and so on to Hollington and Boylestone in Derbyshire, and also to Mercaston, Turnditch, and Hulland; and from there to Belper. And then from the camp meeting held at Mercaston, June 9th, 1816, the work by the good hand of God opened out and in two years and a half extended to Derbyshire,

Nottinghamshire, Leicestershire, Lincolnshire and Yorkshire. And this year, 1819, the work in Tunstall Circuit opened out in Cheshire, and a foundation was laid for what are now Burland and Preston Brook Circuits."

This passage needs little comment or qualification. Note well, for it is very significant, that Bemersley and Tunstall are distinguished from each other, as though each had its own particular history, and represented a somewhat different policy. Further, it may well be that in this passage Hugh Bourne suggests his own dissociation from the non-mission law. But the third factor in our history must not be forgotten. The extension to Belper and the Midlands was brought about by Benton, Wedgwood, and the more active and irregular workers, with whose doings Hugh Bourne undoubtedly sympathised, though he followed rather than led. Thus qualified, the passage may stand as a useful summary of our history thus far. We are told that James Steele was in favour of the reform of camp meetings and had witnessed their worsening with pain and disfavour. That may well be; but we have reason to believe that he was a strong believer in the policy of consolidation. That policy was now happily to be balanced by the policy of aggression, and of this new policy Wrine Hill Camp Meeting supplies the symbol and the date-mark. As Mercaston Camp Meeting had presaged and heralded the great revival in the Midlands, so Wrine Hill, looking out over the Cheshire border, inaugurated the Cheshire Revival with all that sustained and heroic effort that succeeded in evangelising the country watered by the Mersey, the Dee, the Ribble, the Wye and Severn.

In consequence of the extension of Tunstall Circuit during the year 1819, certain important changes were made. First, as the work had spread so rapidly in what we call the Black Country, Darlaston was in March 1820, made the head of a new circuit. Then, as the result of anxious deliberations, the remaining part of Tunstall Circuit was divided up into six branches—the Home Branch, Ramsor, Belper, Burton-on-Trent, Burland and Preston Brook. The circuit had become so unwieldy as to be difficult to work. Only think of Sampson Turner in the course of two short months having to walk to his appointments at places so far removed as Cannock, Burton-on-Trent, Macclesfield, Talke and Northwich in Cheshire! It was time some method of economising the time and strength of the preachers should be devised, and perhaps no better arrangement could have been hit upon than the system of branches under the general supervision of the Home Branch, and with frequent interchange of the preachers thereon. Each branch in its turn became a convenient centre for further advance, and with this end in view one preacher at least was usually employed in purely mission work—opening fresh places.

HOW THE CHESHIRE MISSION BECAME BURLAND BRANCH

We have first to look at the beginning and development of the Cheshire Mission which, as Thomas Bateman says, "in its grand results has perhaps but seldom been exceeded." Quite properly it was called a "mission," since it was started, and for a time carried on, without the direction or supervision of the Tunstall Circuit authorities.

there as invitations came, or as openings presented themselves. As was the way with him, he filled the day with labour, often carrying on the meetings until late, and rising from a short night's rest to hold a five o'clock morning service. He ate but sparingly, so that anxious hosts wondered how he could do the work he did on so meagre a dietary and remonstrated with him—all to no purpose. In short, we have in the Cheshire mission a repetition of the methods adopted by Benton and Wedgwood at the beginning of the great Revival in the Midlands.

The Cheshire mission began in a very simple and natural way. In the spring of 1819, the Tunstall Circuit had certain outposts on the Staffordshire side, including Englesea Brook, Coppenhall, Leighton, Wood Green, and a few other places. Mr. George Chesters, who had taken a farm at Wolstanwood, having heard John Wedgwood preach at Leighton, was desirous that his parents at Ridley Farm, near Bulkeley, and the other friends he had left there, should have the opportunity of seeing and hearing this remarkable man. With some difficulty arrangements were made for John Wedgwood to preach at Bulkeley Four-lane-ends, on Easter Sunday night, 1819.

Wedgwood could not pass Nantwich without bearing his testimony and delivering his message. Years before it had driven out John Wesley; and though many trials had been made, our people had as yet gained no permanent footing in the town. So Wedgwood took his stand and preached on the Snow Hill near the bridge in the High Street, and Richard Ikin, who had gone into Nantwich to spend that Sabbath afternoon at the ale-bench, was seized with conviction as he listened to the preacher. When afterwards he found rest, he joined the Ravensmoor Society, and his name is mentioned here because he may be regarded as having been the first-fruits of the Cheshire Mission."

THOMAS BATEMAN.

From this point, we are fortunate in having the copious *Journals* of Thomas Bateman, of Chorley, by the help of which we can follow the succession and correlation of events. But though we have the *Journals* as a salvage from the wreck of time, little of a pictorial kind survives, so that it is impossible to give, as we should have liked to do, portraits of some who have strong claims to remembrance.

Thomas Bateman was yet six months from his twentieth birthday at the time of Wedgwood's visit—a fact we have difficulty in taking in as we read these *Journals*. They are written with the sense and gravity often hard to find in a man of forty. He had been accustomed to attend the services of the Church of England, and had even taught in its Sabbath school. Occasionally he attended its services still, but he was more frequently found on the Sabbath morning and afternoon at the Faddiley Wesleyan Methodist Chapel. But he was neither a communicant-member of the Church of England nor was his name down in any Methodist class-book.

It was the talk of the country-side this Easter, that "a great gentleman out of the

* Richard Ikin died July 1822, and Thomas Bateman wrote his memoir in the *Magazine*.

Potteries" was going to preach at Bulkeley, and Thomas Bateman was asked by his friends to go hear him. But there was preaching at Faddiley that night, rather singular to say, and there was also a little prejudice in Thomas Bateman's mind, and he declined. But from those who were present at Bulkeley he afterwards got a full description of the service, which was probably the first held by the Primitive Methodists in West Cheshire. First-hand reports of what took place in those early stirring times are too rare and valuable not to be used when available, especially when penned by so keen an observer as Thomas Bateman. The descriptions he gives of Wedgwood's public services, and the effects they produced, bear the stamp of actuality, and out of the shadows of the past bring the events and the people right before us. Hence we make no apology for quoting freely.

"My special friend and companion C. W. came to tell me about the Bulkeley meeting. He described the preacher as having a very strange appearance, and his manner as strange as his look. At the prayer-meeting after the preaching, he said there was a strange scene—singing, praying, shouting, weeping—many professing to get converted there and then. This was no strange thing to me. I had seen revivals before and was often saying 'Haste again ye days of grace.' He said the meeting continued very late, and the preacher said he would preach again at the same place at five next morning. This was considered strange and new. No, no, not very new. Did not Wesley usually preach at five in the morning? Are the old days and scenes of Methodism going to return? Why not? I see no reason why it should not be so."

He heard John Wedgwood for the first time, April 26th, on Egerton Green, 'standing on something behind a chair, with an Indian handkerchief tied round his head." He remarks on his "solemn look and manner of giving out the hymn and his sermon altogether strange and out of the ordinary way of sermonising", and his twice striking up the verse of a hymn in the course of his sermon. On May 16th, Thomas Bateman heard Wedgwood nearer home, for his brother John had succeeded in getting Wedgwood to preach on Chorley Green. Quotation is here indispensable, because George Taylor is for the first time brought before us:—

"The meeting was held under a large oak-tree on the north side of the green and what a congregation and what a time! Scores in distress, and among them my old friend G. Taylor. I spoke to him, and he told me how he felt—very doubting. I said 'You don't need to despair. Only believe and yours is heaven.' As I moved in the congregation I felt constrained to speak to some about their souls. But timidity and prejudice kept me back. The number professing to get converted that night was not small. Amidst all this I felt an impression steal over my mind, for the first time, that I should one day become one with this people. And after all my former purposes I should never join the Wesleyans. This impression I felt disposed to shake off. Oh, for divine direction! I would do right whatever the sacrifice or cost."

But he did not shake off the impression. Almost unwillingly, for he knew that from a worldly point of view it was not to his advantage, he yielded to what seemed to be his destiny. If one may put it so, he got into the swim of Primitive Methodism gradually...

He attended class some time before he would suffer himself to be counted a member. He took up the same non-committal attitude with regard to the plan. He would be known on the plan by a mere "star," and not have his name thereon in plain black and white. But all the time, though he did not realise it, he was being drawn further and further in, becoming more and more immersed in the movement, until with his friend George Taylor, he gave himself whole-heartedly to it. And then his friends the Methodists, with whom he continued on the best of terms till the day of his death, would have made him a minister—a missionary—anything in reason. But it was too late. He had taken the irrevocable step, and was not the man to draw back. So with George Taylor. There was a brief space when he too was undecided whether to join the Old Body or the new. To each he was greatly indebted. But a repulse from a love-feast at Nantwich, with the ungracious words "You cannot enter here, you are Clowesites," decided his future once and for all. He joined the society and became its leader, and remained such to the day of his death in 1837; he was also steward of Burland Branch, and then of Burland Circuit, as long as he lived.

"*June 7th*—Yesterday was a day that will not soon be forgotten. Mr W preached again on the green. He took his stand at the side of a brick-kiln at the south-west corner [he never pitched on the same site twice together]. The congregation was very large for a place so thinly populated; much larger than before; not less than two thousand being present. Many were in distress, and many got blessed with a sense of pardon—how many could not be told. The meeting commenced at ten in the morning and continued until afternoon. There were several remarkable conversions took place this morning. One especially fell under my own notice in going round among the mourners. A respectable man whom I knew, stood looking down on a company of mourners who were down on the ground crying out for mercy. On speaking to him of the necessity of securing pardon for sin before it was too late, he said—'Before I would demean myself as these people are doing there I would have my hand cut off.' I thought 'You had better beware, my friend; the fire is catching if you come too near.' It was not long before he was on the ground crying earnestly for mercy like the rest. Mr Wedgwood went to preach for the Wesleyans at Barbridge at night. I went there also. This cost me a twenty miles walk that afternoon."

There were those present at the June Quarterly Meeting of Tunstall Circuit who had come straight from witnessing such scenes as these, who like Barnabas had "seen the grace of God and were glad." It was determined that arrangements should be made for supplying a certain number of places on the Cheshire Mission with preaching. When the new arrangements began to take effect, John Wedgwood, as was customary with him, left the work of organising societies to other hands and moved farther north, extending the mission to Huxley, Burton Hall, Tarvin, etc. He even entered Chester, but not meeting with much success there, he pushed on into the peninsula of Wirral, opening the way for what are now the Chester, Wrexham and Buckley circuits.

We cannot follow John Wedgwood any further on his Cheshire mission, full of incident and successful though that mission continued to be. How he worked and with what results may be gathered from the samples already given, but the subsequent career of so interesting a personality to whom Primitive Methodism was so greatly

L L

indebted, may be briefly outlined. In 1829, probably induced by a change in his circumstances, he became, by his own request, a recognised travelling preacher for three years, two and a half of which were spent amongst his old friends of the Burland Circuit, and six months in Prees Green, one of its offshoots. This short period over, he revisited the scenes of his former labours and triumphs in the Midlands and elsewhere. He was gladdened to find strong churches in many places he helped to mission, and, in this connection, he makes special mention of Bottesford and Grantham. Then, as it is the impossible that often happens, in 1840 he married, and for seventeen years was a householder at Boylestone. But it would be a mistake to suppose that he was a constant resident of this pleasant Derbyshire village. His wife might be but he was not. The old instincts and habits were too strong to permit of his settling down in one place, and he continued to be much from home, visiting among the churches. In 1857 he removed to Crewe, chiefly induced by the greater facilities it afforded for travelling.

JOHN WEDGWOOD'S HOUSE, BOYLESTONE.

Here he found a congenial church and a home in a district where he was well known and much respected. That respect took tangible and enduring form in the Chapel bearing his name, figured on a preceding page.* As far as declining strength would permit he made himself useful, until he quietly passed away, March 20th, 1869, aged 81 years.

When the day of interment came, the funeral cortege had to go fourteen miles to the place of sepulture which was Brown Knoll Cemetery. Crowds witnessed the setting out of the long procession of vehicles; throngs gathered at various points along the route as well as at the grave—a "new tomb," presented by the trustees of the Cemetery. Such a funeral as this had never been known in that neighbourhood. It was remarked that the road taken by the cortege led through the centre of John Wedgwood's mission, and passed the spot where just fifty years before he had opened his commission in that district, now testifying in this striking way to the genuineness and lasting influence of his work. One simple incident that took place as the crowd turned away when the last rites were over, may serve as John Wedgwood's not unworthy elegy. Says his biographer :—

"To an old man that tottered away from the grave, and sat down on a stone wiping eyes that were not dry, we said, 'Well, friend, what makes you look so sad?' Casting a look towards the grave he had just left he said 'Sad! who can help looking sad?'

"'Why so? did you know Mr. Wedgwood? What did he ever do for you?'

"'Do! Why I owe the use of all my comfort in this life, and all my hopes of a better to his teaching through Christ.'

"'But why weep? Ought you not rather to rejoice when the righteous are taken away from the evil to come? Are there not plenty of preachers left now he is gone?'

"'Plenty! but where will you find another like him?'

"'Don't despair,' we said, 'if God sees it right to take away His workmen, He can still carry on His work, rest assured of that.' So saying we left him. Oh, what a cloud of living witnesses! What a number of such testimonies might have been collected that day."*

"He was just the man for the work Providence had called him to do." So wrote one who visited John Wedgwood in his last hours. The verdict is just, just to the man himself, without being unjust to others who were, and could not but be, unlike him. The same verdict—shall we not rather say, the same encomium—must be pronounced on Benton, Braithwaite, Oxtoby and others of their type.

John Wedgwood was a preacher on Tunstall circuit plan (No. 19) while he was prosecuting his Cheshire Mission, and therefore that mission formed a kind of *hinterland* naturally falling to Tunstall. Not only was the circuit enlarged by the addition of this huge cantle of country, but in other directions its area was being rapidly enlarged, so that we are quite prepared for the following brief entry in Thomas Bateman's *Journals*.

"*February 1st 1820.*—The good work still spreads rapidly. Tunstall Circuit is become too large, and it is intended to divide it at the next quarter-day. George Taylor and I have had several consultations as to the best division."

Accordingly, at the March quarterly Meeting the Cheshire Mission became a Branch of Tunstall Circuit. It had on its first plan thirty-three places, for the most part in Cheshire, though there were a few in Wales and still more in Shropshire, in which county there was a splendid prospect if only more labourers had been available. As it was, the staff of labourers consisted of three travelling preachers—John Garner, John Platt a native of Faddiley, near Burland, and Thomas Brownsword "the boy-preacher" —and twenty-three local preachers, two of whom were females. In fact, places were being multiplied faster than preachers, so that most of the places had to be content with preaching once a day every other Sunday, and once in three or four weeks on the week-day.

* "Memoir of the Life and Labours of Mr. John Wedgwood." By a Layman (Thomas Bateman) 1870

So now that Cheshire Mission has become an integral part of Tunstall Circuit it shares the fortunes of the latter. Its preachers are the same as those who are working—now here, now there—in other parts of the same unit, at the task of still further enlarging its borders and preparing its branches for circuit independence. Let us glance at some of these Tunstall preachers, and then go on to look at their pioneer labours on the various extensions of the Tunstall Circuit.

SOME ENLARGERS OF TUNSTALL CIRCUIT AS REFLECTED IN T. BATEMAN'S JOURNALS.

The already rapid extension of the Tunstall Circuit created a demand for more labourers, which could only be met by pressing into service the young and comparatively inexperienced of both sexes. The critics with a turn for sarcasm, who complained that the circuit was being worked by boys fresh from the plough, might just as truly have added—and by girls fresh from the milk-pail; for some of the most acceptable and useful workers in these parts during the next few years were young women scarce out of their teens. True; there were in the circuit at this time Thomas Jackson (1), a seasoned veteran of thirty, and Sampson Turner, quite mature at twenty-three, and John Garner, no novice though only twenty years of age. These three we know; but we now meet with others for the first time, whose names will frequently recur as we chronicle the growth and ramifications of the Tunstall Circuit. To some of these we will introduce the reader.

THOMAS WEBB.

Now that the Cheshire Mission had become part of the Tunstall Circuit, it was visited by all the preachers in turn; and even when the Burland Branch had been formed, there were such frequent interchanges, that almost every quarter saw a fresh staff of preachers. In his *Journals*, Thomas Bateman notes the coming and going of these workers, and sometimes adds a brief characterisation that may be helpful for identification and remembrance.

After the departure of John Wedgwood the first new-comer was Thomas Webb, who, "from his appearance, might have been just taken from the plough, like the son of Shaphat, very earnest and loud, but more methodical in his preaching than John Wedgwood." Then came on his round Sampson Turner, sedate, practical—"a plain, good preacher, but not so noisy as some," who looked well after the organising and due ordering of the societies. Thomas Jackson came along from Preston Brook way, and it is recorded of him that his tongue was like a pen in the hands of a ready writer, and that "he had scarcely ever heard a preacher so fluent." The diarist appears to have been particularly interested in the advent of William Sanders, the poet. The first impressions were decidedly disappointing: "From the first look at him you could not well expect either good poetry or ought else worth notice from him. But who may not have felt agreeable surprise to have music soft, smooth and sweet from what appeared a rough, unready instrument? None who had any mind for rhyming could listen long to him without perceiving poetry in his prose."

A para[graph] diarist heard

as early as October 29th, 1819. Brownsword was then only "a boy, comparatively. However, I heard him with profit. But I felt terribly ashamed of myself. I believe I am twenty years old this day; and for what purpose have I lived? What good have I done? I have purposed much and I fear done but very little. I still feel as bashful and timid as ever." So wrote this youth of twenty, whose life was almost to span the century, and who was to crowd into the more than three score years and ten still remaining to him an amount of labour truly astonishing, as if to show that grace is the best discipliner, and hard work healthful, and friendly to length of days. Thomas Brownsword and his sister are figures that scarcely stand out in such sharp relief as they deserve to do, and hence we will recall the singular, primitive method of his call to the ministry.

WILLIAM SANDERS.

Worthy Thomas Woodnorth, while doing duty as a preacher in these parts fell ill, and, deeming that his preaching days were over, wanted to get back to his home. So he asked friend Darlington, of Burland Green, to let his son take him on horseback as far as Englesea Brook, and bring back some one who could enter into his work. Accordingly this was done. The preacher named—the son of a small farmer-innkeeper at Goisty Hill—happened to be at work in the harvest-field, where young Darlington found him amongst a number of rough fellows. The message was no sooner delivered than the youth threw down his sickle, called at his home to change his clothes, mounted behind young Darlington, and went into Thomas Woodnorth's preaching-round. Such was Thomas Brownsword's call to the ministry in which, for a number of years, he did good service. He was soon followed by his sister, Ann Brownsword, who by her respectable appearance and more than ordinary preaching talent, was made very useful in opening out the mission in Cheshire, Staffordshire and other counties. She afterwards became the wife of Mr. Abraham, of Burslem.

Besides the Brownswords, Englesea Brook sent out other travelling preachers from its numerous "locals," such as Thomas Webb and William Newton, the blind preacher. Its productiveness in this respect, which, with its geographical position, almost made it the key to the Cheshire Mission, was largely owing to Sarah Smith, who kept a dame's school for a number of years and served God and the Church in her calling. She used to pray with the children; take the little ones on her knee and teach them the old hymns. She began a prayer meeting on the Sunday evenings, and got the elder children

JOHN SMITH.

to pray, and encouraged the more promising among them to exhort; so that, under her influence, Englesea Brook came to be a kind of normal school for the training of evangelists. We suspect Thomas Bateman never had any particular love for "Institutes," and hence there may be veiled sarcasm in his suggestion that our first Institute was at Englesea Brook and that Sarah Smith was its first tutor, as well as its theological and divinity professor. She did what she could: a professor of divinity could do no more.*

Two other persons whose careers are of consequence to this history are repeatedly mentioned in the *Journals*. John Smith (1) had been a scholar in Thomas Bateman's Bible-class. He came on the stations in 1824, and until 1829 laboured at Burland, Chester and other parts of the old Tunstall Circuit, and then moved off to East Anglia, to be written down by his old friend and teacher as "the bishop of Norfolk." John Ride's appearance in these parts came about in a somewhat singular way. When last we saw him, he had just begun to preach at Mercaston Camp Meeting. In 1820 he emigrated to the United States, but his wife dying shortly after his arrival, he soon found his way back to Derbyshire and engaged in evangelistic labours with all his old ardour. Some of the inhabitants of Ashbourne, not relishing his proceedings, set a cunning trap for him. A respectable householder offered his doorstep as a stand for an open-air service, and when the offer was accepted in all good faith, steps were taken for the issue of a summons against him for having preached on private premises unlicensed for public worship. Urged on by his friends, John Ride travelled all night to Bemersley to ask counsel of the Bournes; and they, at the end of the fortnight, sent him to Burland with the request that a place might be found him on the Cheshire Mission—a thing by no means difficult to do, as the Mission's sphere of influence practically extended from Liverpool to Shrewsbury in one direction, and from Tunstall Circuit to beyond the borders of Wales on the other. So John Ride went into the northern part of the Mission, following John Wedgwood and Thomas Brownsword, opened Wrexham, and found his way to Liverpool, where he was put into Bridewell for preaching in the open-air, but was soon liberated as the result, it is said, of a letter of remonstrance addressed to the magistrates by Dr. Adam Clarke. In this way was John Ride thrust forth into the ministry. He laboured in these parts until 1823, when he was stationed successively at Tunstall, Oakengates and Darlaston, and then he, too, moved off, to become one of the pioneers of the Brinkworth District. We have, in the *Journals* so often referred to, a thumb-nail sketch of John Ride, taken June, 1822, after the holding of a love-feast. "Oh, how he did labour! His zeal seemed to have no bounds." Here we have the man as he was to the end.

These then were some of the preachers—most of them mere striplings to begin with—who pushed forwards the boundaries of Tunstall Circuit in different directions, and carved it into circuits that became the Tunstall District of 1821 and the larger district of 1824. And there were others—Sarah Spittle, Ann Stanna, Joseph Preston, of Bronington in Flint, and William Doughty, a Lincolnshire man, and James Bonser, of Kinoulton, both of prison-fame, who did their part.

JOHN RIDE.

* Sarah Smith's memoir is in the *Magazine* for 1823. See also the *Magazine* for 1881, p. 551. It was Sarah   En-----'s Brook in June, 1811. See

Darlaston Circuit.

Only six months intervened between Darlaston's coming on the plan and its being made into an independent station in March, 1820. Like Hull, it shot up rather than slowly grew to maturity; and in its case as in that of the town by the Humber, quick growth did not mean either quick decay or slow death; for Darlaston Circuit was destined to become one of the most powerful and procreative circuits of the Connexion.

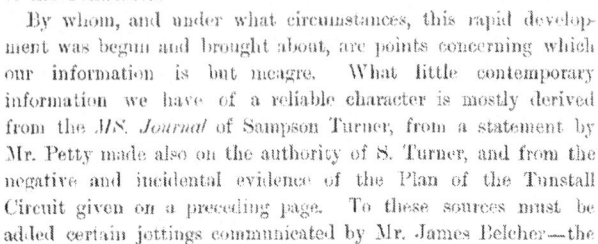

By whom, and under what circumstances, this rapid development was begun and brought about, are points concerning which our information is but meagre. What little contemporary information we have of a reliable character is mostly derived from the *MS. Journal* of Sampson Turner, from a statement by Mr. Petty made also on the authority of S. Turner, and from the negative and incidental evidence of the Plan of the Tunstall Circuit given on a preceding page. To these sources must be added certain jottings communicated by Mr. James Belcher—the oldest local preacher in the Darlaston Circuit—whose mother's name stands third on the Roll-book of members for 1827, and who lived a long and honoured life.

MRS. N. BELCHER.

Sampson Turner, it will be remembered, lived at Cannock Lane, and was converted in 1812. Cannock Lane, Cannock Wood, Essington Wood, and Walsall Wood are all on the plan of 1819, and the societies at these places would afford a base for missionary efforts in the populous district we know as the Black Country. In his *Journal*, S. Turner tells us that he and others had missioned Brownhills, Pelsall, Walsall Wood and other places, and that in the early spring of 1819, he devoted some four days to missioning Bilston, Wolverhampton, Willenhall and Darlaston.

At Bilston he spoke, "amid quietness, in a space in the centre of the town," but at night he was put into a small room in a common lodging-house along with tinkers, cadgers and chimney-sweeps, and was glad to slink away very early next morning. When at Wolverhampton he took his stand in the market-place, before he got to the end of his discourse he was hustled and howled at; nor did the mob cease its unfriendly attentions as he made his way to the south-west end of the town with a gentleman who had rescued him from his persecutors and invited him to be his guest. As they went along, the mob followed them, using abusive and menacing language. At Willenhall he was stoned out of the town, but found shelter at New Invention, where he met with great civility and kindness. His brief mission over, he returned to his home on the Thursday before Easter, and awaited in some suspense his call either "to missionary" or be a travelling preacher—that is, either to raise societies where none existed, or visit those already formed. Through some mischance, there was delay, but at last the official letters from Tunstall arrived, informing him that he was to be a travelling preacher. He began his duties on the first Sunday on the plan and the reader can if he chooses,

JAMES BELCHER.

follow No. 50 on his round through the Circuit. On the last Sunday of the plan, he fulfilled appointments in his own neighbourhood and amongst his own acquaintance. He says:—

"*July 25th :*— Preached in the morning at Essington Wood, in the afternoon at Cannock Lane, and in the evening at Cannock Wood. This day J. Benton heard me for the first time. He lost his speech some time before and has never been able to preach since. There seems to be a greater prospect than ever of a revival of religion in this neighbourhood. *Three preachers have lately joined us, and Darlaston is put on the plan.*"

This entry seems to explain Mr. Petty's statement, made from information supplied by the diarist: that Mr. W. Carter, being present at a service at Walsall Wood, offered the use of his large room at Darlaston for services; that some few weeks after, the offer was accepted, the large

BLOCKALL, DARLASTON.

room occupied, and that Messrs W. Carter, Humpage, and others joined the society, and a little later, Mr. D. Bowen. This incident must have happened while S. Turner was on his round, and it put a new face on things. Not only was the revival spreading, but the acquisition of the preaching room,

THE BULL STAKE, DARLASTON.

and still more the adhesion of three preachers—men of standing and business ability, added to those there already were, would seem to justify making Darlaston thus early the head of a West Midland Circuit, desirable as that arrangement was on the ground of convenience.

The regulation of the Preparatory Meeting requiring travelling preachers to furnish their Circuit Committees each month with extracts from their *Journals*, soon bore fruit in the *Ma* . . . . like dispatches from the seat of war.

The first reports of this kind relating to Darlaston we meet with, were written by Thomas Brownsword and James Bonsor, who both began their labours in the circuit almost immediately after its formation. They tell us of the places they visited Bilston, Tipton, Wednesbury, Darlaston, etc., of the open-air services and house prayer-meetings they held; of the varying spiritual results which followed. It is a record of hard and successful evangelistic labour, told in the briefest, barest way, and quite wanting in those details which would justify quotation here. But each preacher had an early experience of legal persecution to report, which varies his journalistic summary of work done, and demands our notice.

Thomas Brownsword might be a boy-preacher, but he was evidently a man in courage; and he tells his story in such a modest and even reticent way that Hugh Bourne feels it necessary to supplement his narrative. On July 8th, T. Brownsword preached at Round Oak in the morning, and then went to Stourbridge in Worcestershire, where one of the mission-band preached without interruption to a large congregation. Brownsword's own turn came in the evening, when he had about a thousand people before him. He had sung and prayed and got a short way on in his discourse, when he was taken into custody by a constable, as was also one of his companions who tried to continue the service after Brownsword's arrest. The next morning, the brother who had preached without molestation "stood up" again, and was led off, so that three were taken before the magistrates, and, because they would not give their word to cease from preaching in the open-air, they were committed to the County Gaol at Worcester. Even during their more than a week's imprisonment they cannot be said to have suspended their work, but only to have carried it on under different conditions. How it was that our imprisoned preachers of those early days were allowed such facilities of intercourse with their fellow-prisoners, we know not. But that they often had such facilities, and made good use of them, is certain. The evidence is too abundant and clear to admit of doubt. "Praise God!" writes T. Brownsword, "He was with me, and we spared not to preach Christ to the poor prisoners. We preached or exhorted every night. A great reformation appeared among the prisoners; those who had been accustomed to curse and swear and sing, began to read and pray. The Lord was with us in a powerful manner."

The event created quite a stir in the district. Popular sentiment was with the preachers in prison, and not with the magistrates who sent them there. The new denomination, struggling to gain a footing in these parts and carry on its beneficent work, shared in the sympathy that was evoked, and profited by it. It was seen that the Black Country of 1820 was not the Black Country of Wesley's days, and that Wednesbury riots were no longer possible. It was determined to use every effort to win a favourable verdict at the approaching trial. Tunstall Circuit pledged its

WILLIAM CARTER.

DAVID BOWEN.

assistance. The Dissenting ministers came nobly forward with proffers of help. Contributions were freely offered, nor was prayer forgotten. On the 11th June, after suffering ten days' detention, the prisoners were taken to the Shire Hall and—dismissed.

'The same day in the evening," says Hugh Bourne, "they held a vast meeting on the race-ground at Worcester. Multitudes flocked in to see and hear those who had been in prison. There were others also who had gone to attend the trial: four of the preachers spoke, and hundreds were in tears. This was the introduction of the Primitive Methodists into Worcester.'

James Bonsor had visited Brownsword while in prison, but his own turn soon came, and in time he got to be "well known to the police." After a camp-meeting at Bilston Wake on July 31st, he, with a few to help, went to Wolverhampton to hold an evening service in the market-place, but he was "interrupted by a policeman and then led away by a magistrate." He continued, during the night and morning he was in prison, to pray with the prisoners and even preach to them. "Many people," says he, "came to visit me and brought me food. I read them several chapters, and the prisoners wished me to stay with them!" The next day at noon he was brought before the magistrates. As he was wont to do, he argued the case with them, and assured them that as long as men swore, told lies, broke the Sabbath, and did other bad things, "he meant to preach as long as the Lord gave him strength, and as soon as he was at liberty he should preach again." He was bound in two sureties to appear at the Stafford sessions, and when the time came duly surrendered. For decency's sake the Justices inflicted a nominal fine, but as he would not pay it but told them he thought they should rather give him something for his trouble, they dismissed him, and—"So I went away, and at night preached at Cannock Lane." *

We are almost tempted to conclude that the persecution undergone by the newly formed Darlaston Circuit was opportune and a blessing in disguise. It tended to the furtherance of the Gospel. Not only did it publish the movement and rally popular sympathy in its favour, but it served also as a wholesome tonic to those who had the task before them of carrying the old gospel by new methods over a wide district, stretching from Cannock to Worcester, and from Wolverhampton and Birmingham to Presteign in Radnorshire. Already Darlaston Circuit was the present West Midland District in embryo. For a brief while we leave the young circuit just entering upon its much needed work, while we look at the extensions Tunstall Circuit was making in other directions.

BURTON-ON-TRENT

Burton, in East Staffordshire, with extensions into South Derbyshire, was another of the branches formed at the important March, 1820, Quarter-day of the Tunstall Circuit. And yet the head of this new branch has no place on the plan of 1819, given on the preceding page, though some of the villages not far away had long been visited. Some of these, with whose names we are familiar, now stand connected with one or another of the Burton Circuits. Such are Tutbury,—where the famous fasting-girl lived in 1810, whom James Crawfoot and Hugh Bourne and W. Clowes all visited and believed in,—and Church Broughton,—the home of the Salisburys, early befrienders of the cause,—and, above all, Boylestone. The brewery town, therefore, must have been opened during 1819, with such a degree of success as to justify the resolve to make a more determined effort to mission it and the surrounding villages. Sampson Turner was designated for this work, which he began in May, 1820. He seems to have had a special interest in Burton, for he spent a week there just before he began his labours as a travelling preacher. "I preached" says he "to as many as could get into a Baptist chapel. It seemed to give general satisfaction, and they desired that the 'Ranters' might come if it were the will of God." Then, on the 5th October, he hears that they are getting on well at Burton, and he adds "I still believe that the Lord will carry on His work, and that, in spite of all worldly opposition, if believers are faithful," and on the 21st of the same month, he justifies his faith by walking twenty miles to Burton where, he says, "We held a prayer-meeting at night, the house was full, and souls were crying for mercy. There is at present a very bright prospect at Burton." Then in March, Burton is made a Branch, and a month after, we find Hugh Bourne spending three days there, busy with the plans, and preaching in the afternoon of Sunday, April 23rd, in the street, and at night in the room.

In going to his new sphere of labour, S. Turner took Lichfield on his way, and on Whit Sunday preached on Green Hill among the caravans that were there for a show. He returned during the week for another service, but such a din was made by the beating of kettles, tambourines and other noise-producing instruments that were handy, that he removed to another place nearer the centre of the city and there, standing under a tree, he finished his sermon in peace. He informs us that a 'blacksmith's penthouse' was afterwards secured as a place of worship. But not even was the slender footing furnished by this humble conventicle long retained. Burton Circuit made several attempts to regain its hold of that city in whose cathedral, as we remember, Hugh Bourne had a strange experience, but these attempts were not attended with any great measure of success. In 1836, however, Darlaston and Birmingham Circuits combined to maintain two missionaries to concentrate their labours on Lichfield and the surrounding villages. For a time they preached in the open-air, then an old malt-house in a back street was rented, and in 1848 a small chapel was opened. Ten years before this, Lichfield had been made an independent station with the laborious Richard Ward as its superintendent.

But to come back to Burton and the "missionarying" of Sampson Turner. In returning from Lichfield in the evening of Whit Sunday, he visited Alrewas and held a service on the Green. The public-houses emptied, and the news ran that the "Radical Reformers" had come. A society was formed, out of which, we are told, several local and travelling preachers were raised up, and the society continues to this day. At Barton-under-Needwood, he was greeted on his first visit by the ringing of bells and a general tintinnabulation; but despite the opposition met with, a footing was gained in the place. Accompanied by two friends he went to Tattenhall, and began to preach in a large open space not far from a large house, out of which came two persons, one of whom—the worse for drink—pulled him off his chair, to the detriment of his clothes, and ordered the constable to take him in charge. S. Turner and his companions were kept that night at a public-house but unprovided with a bed, and the next morning were taken before a magistrate. Our missionary refused to pay the costs the magistrate imposed, and, being let go, they went to the same place as before and held a service. Here from S. Turner's *Journal* is the record of a full Sunday's labours:—

"Early one Sunday morning I preached in the open-air at Tutbury, and then proceeded to Stretton to preach in the forenoon. On entering the village several rotten goose-eggs were thrown at me and so besmeared my clothes that I was obliged to borrow another person's coat, in which I preached in the street while my own was rinsed and dried. In the afternoon I preached at Horningham, and in

WOOD MILL CHAPEL.

the evening at Burton-upon-Trent. Persecution raged in several of the places we visited; but the word of the Lord ran and was glorified, and many sinners were converted to God. To Him be all the glory."

It was by labours and amid difficulties such as these, that the Burton Branch was so extended and established as to justify its being made into a separate station as early as 1822. It belonged to the mother district of Tunstall until 1827, when it was transferred to Nottingham, and now quite properly has its place next after Loughborough on the stations of the Nottingham District. We deal here with the missionary period of Burton-on-Trent's history, rather than with its later development by which it has become the arrangement of the circuit varied from time to time. For four years Alrewas ranked as a branch, and Uttoxeter also stood on the stations as such from 1849 to 1860, when we judge it was transferred to Ramsor. With a word as to the early chapels of the circuit, we pass on. Boylestone excepted, the oldest chapel in the original circuit of which we have any record is Wood Mill, built in 1823 by G. Parsons, at a cost of sixty pounds! The deed of this building, which was non-connexional, is a curious document. The original chapel was superseded by a Gothic structure, built in 1870, to which a burial-ground is attached; but the old building still does occasional duty for the holding of tea-meetings. As far as can be ascertained, the first chapel in Burton was built in 1829, and the shell of it is still in existence serving as a hardware shop.

SITE OF FIRST CAMP-GROUND, WINSTER.

BELPER BRANCH EXTENSIONS.

As a result of the vigorous mission carried on in the Peak of Derbyshire by Belper Branch—made such along with the rest in 1820—many fresh places, in what was then a secluded and benighted part of the country, were visited, and a number of new societies established. These, along with the older societies of Hognaston, Kniveton, and Brassington, were, in 1824, grouped in order to form a new circuit of which Winster was the head. The very fact that only three out of the twenty places standing on the first plan of this circuit are found on the Tunstall plan of 1819, shows that the missionary spirit expressed itself in hard successful work near home, as well as in passing resolutions at the first missionary meetings at Turnditch and Belper.

We have already referred in another connection to the missioning of Winster by W. Alcock in 1821, and little more need now be added except to note the fact that a chapel was built in 1823 and enlarged in 1833.

Hognaston, already named, was missioned by Belper as early as 1817. It was the home of Philip Bown, a leader and a local preacher, whose name stands first on the first plan of the Winster Circuit. It was he who gave the ground for the village chapel, while another friend, Richard Wheeldon, by his will left £50 for the same purpose. Philip Bown was a noted evangelist whose fame lingers amongst the Derbyshire hills to this day. He did a good day's work when, at the direction of the circuit authorities, he re-missioned a village nine miles from Winster called Monyash. The village is not

MONYASH CHURCH.

large:—it has not more than four hundred inhabitants. It cannot be said to be beautiful, though it is not devoid of a certain austere attractiveness. It can, indeed, lay claim to the possession of an ancient church—restored without being spoiled—and to a crumbling village cross. There is, too, the druidical circle of Arbor Low in the neighbourhood, ranking next in importance to Stonehenge. Within the enclosure of Arbor Low a famous camp meeting with three stands was once held. But to Methodists of all sections, Monyash will always be associated with the names of John Nelson, who was pulled down by the clergyman while preaching at the cross; and of Dr. Bunting, whose mother, Mary Redfern, got lasting good from hearing a sermon by Richard Boardman. 　　　　　　　　　　　　　　　 was more honourable than his br   to the future law giver of Methodism.

When Richard Boardman preached that sermon, he was on his way from the Leeds Conference to Bristol, there to embark as the first Methodist missionary to America. He travelled across the country—old Methodist-preacher-fashion—on horseback, with the indispensable saddle-bags. To all Methodists the story is interesting, and instructive too, since it shows the vitality and fecundity of the seed of the Word. It was right and fitting that in 1869, the Wesleyans should commemorate Richard Boardman's visit to Monyash and what came out of it. But to Primitive Methodists the village has an additional association of interest; for here Joseph Wood, Sunday School Union Organiser and General Secretary, President, and Principal of Manchester College, spent

REV. J. WOOD.

ten years of the most formative period of his life, only leaving the Whim Farm in 1851 to become a travelling preacher in Hull Circuit.

When Philip Bown took his stand by the remains of the old cross in the year 1828, both Wesleyan and Primitive Methodism had died out of the village. His coming was the means of opening a fresh and not unworthy chapter in the history of village Methodism. Among those who stood listening to him that day, was a burly young quarryman named Joshua Millington. No apparent effect seemed to have been produced in him by the service; but some time after, being in the tavern with his companions, the devil inspired one of them to vent the most horrible curses and blasphemy, and by so doing the devil overshot the mark; for, as Joseph looked upon his companion's livid and distorted face, he saw depicted there, sin in its most hideous guise and hell in its terrors. Alarmed, he then and there cried out for mercy; and when next Philip Bown came to the cross, and at the close of the service invited seekers to follow him into a certain house, Joshua shrinkingly followed, and enrolled himself a member. We have no space to write his life further—that has already been done—suffice it to

BACK.

FRONT.
The Whim Farm where Dr. Wood was brought up.

* "Historic Villages of Methodism." By Rev. J. Wood, D.D., p. 1. June, 1897.

say, he became a champion of the cause, and, for the long period of sixty years, preached far and wide, in all weathers; led his class, and lived to a patriarchal age, honoured for the goodness and usefulness of his life.

With the year 1835, another page was turned in the history of Primitive Methodism in Monyash. So much had the Winster Circuit prospered under the labours of its ministers—David Beattie and T. Hobson— that in this year a third minister was appointed, and special attention was directed to aggressive Christian work. Monyash shared in the general prosperity of the station. One evening, when Mr. Hobson the missionary was sitting in the house of Mr. Palfreyman where he was to spend the night, a woman rushed in uttering loud cries. She had been at the service, and sought relief for her anguished, burdened heart. The little company fell to prayer, and Mary Critchelow found peace. Her conversion was speedily followed by that of her husband, their two eldest sons, and other members of the family. When we know that Daniel and Mary Critchelow were the parents of seventeen sons and daughters, fifteen of whom reached maturity, we are not surprised that it was deemed desirable to build a chapel, which accordingly was done in the same year—1835. This building served its purpose until 1888, when a more commodious structure was erected with school attached. The descendants of this worthy couple are exceedingly numerous, and though many of these have left their native village, it is pleasing to know our Church in different parts still reaps the advantage of their loyalty and service. Bakewell, not far from Haddon Hall and far-famed Chatsworth, is all the better for the conversion of Daniel and Mary Critchelow; for it is largely owing to the enterprise and liberality of Mr. Charles Critchelow, their grandson, that Bakewell has at last, after its chequered history, a neat and commodious chapel. We allude to an event that happened so recently as 1895, simply to continue the story which illustrates the far-reaching, ever-expanding results of village evangelisation.

JOSHUA MILLINGTON.

As Bakewell, which stands on the first plan of Winster Circuit, has been lost and won several times, so have several other places in the Peak of Derbyshire. For example, Flagg, a village not far from Monyash was first visited in 1821 by preachers from Macclesfield, and afterwards relinquished. Two years later, Bradwell took it up, but after a time withdrew. Then Winster Circuit re-missioned it; and finally it was incorporated with Buxton Circuit. The mere physical difficulties of distance, rough and steep roads— difficulties made harder under wintry conditions—rendered it almost impossible to serve and conserve some of the village societies which had been established.

Mainly as the result of these causes, even Buxton, important a circuit as it now is, was not founded without repeated reverses and efforts more than once renewed. As to this we will let the late Dr. Wood speak; for as a 'ih ,he circuit's early

C. CRITCHELOW.

"Thomas Hobson's first duty was to mission Buxton and Chelmorton. The former place had been missioned and given up some years before by a neighbouring circuit. Notwithstanding this discouragement, conversions took place, a society was formed, and the work prospered for several years, but again had to be given up, principally for want of a suitable room for the services, together with the difficulty of reaching the town owing to its distance (sixteen miles) from most of the preachers. But some seed remained, and was ready to spring up, when another and a better effort was made, and Buxton is now the head of a flourishing circuit, and has the best chapel and society in this part of Derbyshire, and is supplying its villages with some of the most efficient local preachers in the Connexion."

SITE OF THE JUBILEE AND ANNUAL CAMP-MEETINGS, WINSTER.

Precisely similar was the history of the village of Chelmorton now belonging to Buxton Circuit. It had been a famous place for Methodism. John Bennett had preached here with marvellous success, and amongst his converts were the forebears of the Marsdens and the Lomases. But Methodism had died out of the village before our missionaries from Macclesfield visited it in 1821. A society of twenty members was soon established, but it had become extinct by 1834, when Thomas Hobson remissioned it. The years passed, and once more the same work had to be done over again; for though Thomas Hobson's mission was not without success since, among his converts were Mr. and Mrs. Grindy, who became useful local preachers and left descendants wh

Connexion—still, in course of time, Primitive Methodism died out of Chelmorton. Then, yet a third attempt was made. Three devoted local preachers of the Winster Circuit—Walter Wood (the brother of Dr. Joseph Wood), John Hibbert, and Henry Prime missioned the village, and the effect of their work, we trust, will abide.

We allude to these things—Connexional minutiæ though some may regard them—simply to make good one point we think of some historic value. The mission-period of our history was, it will be admitted, a remarkable one. The enthusiasm of evangelism, like a tidal wave, rose high and went far. The missionaries of the Connexion found their way into remote villages, and startled the villagers as did the ubiquitous Uhlans in the Franco-German war, when they drew up in market-places and on village-greens to the surprise of the inhabitants. To take concrete examples; it was a great thing for the missionaries from Macclesfield to climb into the Peak country and carry the gospel to Chelmorton; and for the missionaries from Bradwell to cross the Derbyshire Wye and mission Monyash. This was the order of the day all round Tunstall Circuit in 1819-21. Say that the wave was somewhat a refluent one; that if the missionaries came they also in some cases retired. That this should be so was to be expected. In the older parts of the Connexion we hear less of missioning of the old type in the 'Thirties, 'Forties, and 'Fifties, though it was still going on elsewhere; and because this was so we think that period a somewhat drab and prosaic one in comparison. But during this period there was, as we see, a great deal of *re*-missioning done, and that in its way was quite as remarkable and heroic as the missioning at large of the earlier period. When, by the sure working of change and death, old village-causes had died out, it wo... in the world to have let them die and not to have troubl... Winter might... have kept "looking

KNIVETON PRIMITIVE METHODIST CHAPEL.

FARMHOUSE, FIRST PREACHING-PLACE, KNIVETON.

on its own things," and not have minded what had once belonged to Macclesfield or to Bradwell. But the facts cited prove that it did mind, and in this, Winster Circuit was not alone during the "drab and prosaic" period. It is well for us now that it was so. We may have lost ground in the villages, but we should have lost much more if a great deal of re-missioning had not then gone on of which little record remains. In short; if it was a great thing for Macclesfield to mission Peak villages in 1821, it was just as laudable a deed for Winster to re-mission the said villages in 1834, and repeat the process still later.

KNIVETON AND WIRKSWORTH.

Kniveton, a village eight miles south-west of Winster, was missioned as early as 1817 by a zealous band of Primitives from Weston Underwood. In 1827, it was the tenth place on the plan, with preaching services appointed for Sunday afternoons and Friday evenings. In 1832, what was at the time considered to be one of the best chapels in that part of Derbyshire was erected, and some time later the old Wesleyan chapel was acquired for school purposes. Kniveton is of interest from the fact that, though it is but an inconsiderable village, it was in the 'Forties made the head of a new circuit and so continued until 1860, when the headship of the circuit was given to Wirksworth, in which town, through the remarkable exertions of J. T. Neal, a spacious and comfortable chapel, with schoolrooms and vestries, had shortly before been secured. Mr. Neal is said not only to have secured the land, superintended the erection, and seen after the completion and due conveyance of the chapel to the Connexion, but to have also "worked in the quarries getting the stone, to have begged the leading of all the materials, and often fed the workmen from his own humble larder."

WIRKSWORTH CHAPEL.

Apart from the fact that Wirksworth will always attract attention from its association with Mrs. Evans—the "Dinah" of "Adam Bede"—who lived and died here, it has other claims on our regard. Since 1820, when it was first missioned, it seems to have been favoured with a succession of loyal and sturdy adherents. Joseph and Hannah Frost opened their house for the first preaching-services as well as for the entertainment of the ministers. One of the first converts was their daughter, of whom a well-written memoir from the pen of Philip Bown appeared in the *Magazine* for 1822. The account there given of Temperance Frost is not without a certain biographical interest, inasmuch as this young woman of thirty-two was deaf and dumb, and yet seems not only to have been very intelligent, but to have had quite remarkable power in expressing her religious emotions to the edification of others.

Ible, which stands on the first plan of the Winster Circuit and is now connected with Wirksworth, has a chapel with a history. "In the year 1824," says an old document now before us, "God put it into the hearts of the inhabitants to build an house for Him. They employed their horses, also on the work; the stone and lime were brought together, free of expense; consequently only a debt of £40 remained when it was completed." Previous to the erection of this little Bethel, the same document informs us, a shelter had been provided by W. Buxton who, "when the chilling winds which sweep over these hills became too severe for the people to endure the open-air service, opened his house, and a society was formed." Here we have the beginnings: what of the after history of the little sanctuary? When Ible was missioned in 1820, the brothers John and Samuel Rains were amongst the first hearers, and they, along with Hannah Rains, the wife of John, joined the infant church on the hill "just above splendid and ever flowing water-springs." John and Hannah were class-leaders and workers for over thirty years. Ten of their sons were converted in the early days, and became prominent and valuable officials in the Nottingham and Manchester Districts. One of these sons was the late Mr. Samuel Rains, for more than half-a-century a local preacher and a furtherer of the interests of our Church in the City of Manchester; another—Henry Rains—is making his presence felt in the Buxton Circuit; a third, the late James Rains of Kirk Ireton, circuit steward of the Ashbourne Station, who kept open house at Alton Hall for all Primitive Methodists for over thirty years; and his children are following in his steps. Yet another son is John Rains, whose connection with our Church dates from 1820, and who has filled various official positions to the great advantage of the Wirksworth Circuit.

MR. JOHN RAINS.

The "little church on the hill above the water-springs" is an emblem of the far-reaching influences for good that have gone forth from our village chapels. It is partly the design of this book to make this clear by concrete examples, which Derbyshire is not alone in supplying. We are persuaded that a master-key to the proper understanding of our history is put into our hands by the recognition of the great part played by the villages in founding and extending our Church. It was the villages that missioned the towns in the first instance; and right along, and especially till the 'Fifties, rural Primitive Methodism has been the water-shed and collecting ground of urban Primitive Methodism.

ASHBOURNE.

Though Ashbourne was the last circuit formed in this part of Derbyshire, it yet includes some of the very oldest societies in the Connexion. Borrowing a term from geology we may call Ashbourne a conglomerate circuit; for it holds together and encloses not a few primitive fragments. The conglomerate boulder has

GENERAL VIEW OF RIGGIN.
Showing Old Farm-house where Preaching Services were held.

PRESENT-DAY CHAPEL, RIGGIN.

embedded within it water-worn fragments of the oldest rocks. We have told the story of Hulland and Hollington and Brailsford, and need not tell it over again, so that when we say these three places form part of the Ashbourne Circuit, it is clear that some components of the circuit are ninety years old. There are also within the limits of the circuit two places on the borders of Staffordshire, first missioned by Eleazar Hathorn and John Benton, which formed part of the "Circuit" Benton handed over to Hugh Bourne in 1814. We refer to Biggin and Mill Dale, to both of which places there are repeated references in the early *Journals*. Biggin has a chapel built in 1896, now debtless, and at Mill Dale, romantically situated at the end of Dovedale, there is also a chapel built in 1834. These two places are on the Tunstall plan of 1819; afterwards they belonged to Ramsor, and, still later, probably to Leek Circuit. Three places that were component parts of the original Winster Circuit are also on the Ashbourne Circuit plan—Hognaston, Kirk Ireton, and ex-circuit-town Kniveton. When Ashbourne was formed in 1890 the old and the new touched each other.

MILL DALE PRIMITIVE METHODIST CHAPEL.

STEPPING STONES OF DOVEDALE.

Ashbourne itself must have been missioned early, since its name will be seen on the Tunstall plan of 1819. Hugh Bourne and the rest of the Tunstall preachers must have been far If   often have rested on the "pride of the Peak," as its citizens call the towering spire of Ashbourne Church. It was here Hugh Bourne bought the tracts for the Hulland Tract Mission, which he causally connects with the raising up of the first two female travelling-preachers. Nor must we forget John Ride's hurried flight from Ashbourne to escape arrest for preaching from some one's doorstep. It requires an effort to think of John Ride as running away from anything, but—

"... those that fly may fight again,
Which he can never do that's slain,"

and we remember how Paul made a somewhat hasty flight from Damascus before he began his ministry.

But we have not yet quite done with Belper, for the simple reason that its missionary energy was not confined to the early years, even to suit the exigencies of a theory. So,

ASHBOURNE CHURCH.

just when the era of consolidation was opening, it renewed its youth and began again. And yet it is but fair to say, many other circuits would have been glad to do the like, only they could not. There was no "hinterland"—not any piece of "no-man's land"—for them to annex. They had got the portion of territory that naturally fell to them, and so were circumscribed and hemmed in, and, perforce, had to make the best of it. But, while most other circuits were settling down to the founding of schools and the building of chapels, and were dividing and sub-dividing themselves in order the better to consolidate their local interests, Belper Circuit had both the opportunity and the will to do a little more real mission-work. There was a bit of unopened country lying away on the borders of Notts, and, by laying hold of this, the geographical hiatus would be filled up and the borders of Belper Circuit march with those of Chesterfield and other offshoots of Nottingham. The facts have been succinctly stated by Mr. Petty in his *History*, and we reproduce them here, just observing that the "unhappy division" referred to was the "Selston split" we have already described as affecting Hucknall Torkard, where also Edward Morton did such good work.*

"Belper Circuit reported 664 members in 1840; but in 1842 it was reduced to 601. Selston, Normanton, and Portland Row, having, probably during these two years, been transferred to another circuit. In the following year they were restored to Belper Circuit, and with Somercotes and Golden Valley, they formed the nucleus of a mission station [at first called Somercotes Mission], to which Mr. E. Morton was appointed in April, 1843. It may be proper to remark, that the three former places had been greatly injured by an unhappy division, three or four years previously, and were now almost a wreck. It is to the honour of Mr. John Smith, of Golden Valley, that we have to record that his fidelity to the Connexion in this time of trial, and the influence of his respectable character and position, were of incalculable service. A better day now began to dawn upon these suffering places; and Mr. Morton also succeeded in establishing societies at Crich, Swanwick, Green Hillocks, and other places, where chapels were in due time erected. In 1850, this mission contained 283 members; and in the following year was made into an independent station, now called Ripley Circuit, a very compact and comfortable station. It is gratifying to add, that notwithstanding the formation of this station, Belper Circuit reported 811 members in 1850, 147 more than 1840" (p. 415).

It should be added that, in 1880, Alfreton Circuit was made from Ripley, which partition would, one think, tend to make the latter even more comfortable and compact a station than it had been before.

This account may be supplemented by a few reminiscent jottings communicated by the present Ripley Circuit Steward—Mr. John Henshaw, the worthy successor of the good men he recalls. At the beginning of its history, the Ripley society worshipped in a small room in a malt-house reached by steps. Mr. John Smith, mentioned above, was colliery manager under the Butterley Colliery Company, and though in a good position was noted for his Christian simplicity and his devoted labours. He could, and did, visit every house in Golden Valley, save one. Here he was refused admission; but he prayed on the door-step. As a local-preacher he was in great request for special services and, on these occasions, often had as his travelling companion Thomas Hardy of Ironville, who contributed £100 at the stone-laying of Ironville chapel. Some of the traditional accounts of John Smith's journeyings as a local preacher almost pass belief. It is said he has been known to preach at Derby in the morning, go on to Little Eaton for the afternoon, and to Belper for the evening service, reaching home at midnight. When in the Peak district, he would not get home until two o'clock on Monday morning. On the Sunday mornings when not preaching he led the class at Selston, four miles away. Little wonder that such a man was humanly speaking the stay and saviour of the societies. At his death he was succeeded in the Circuit Stewardship by

MR. JOHN SMITH.

Mr. Charles Shelton, and subsequently by Mr. Edwin Cox, who is described as a man of strong evangelical sympathies and "one of the best stewards any circuit could have."

In leaving Belper—for we cannot return to it—we are struck with the continuity of its history. In that history we do not find two or more clearly defined periods such as we find elsewhere; and that is the reason we have followed up its development. Primitive Methodism has taken kindly to the soil and become hereditary in families, so that its representatives to-day are the descendants of those who stood by it in the days gone by, only—for the stock is a vigorous and prolific one—there are more of them. Nor is the old sturdy spirit dead. The fact that Mr. Thomas Charles Smith—the first "Passive Resister" who is a member at Ashlehay in the Wirksworth Circuit,* and that a retired minister—Rev. W. Sharman—spending the evening of a well-spent day at Weston-under-Wood, has undergone imprisonment in the same cause, show that the air of freedom blows over these hills, and that the yeomen of Boylestone, who began a free day-school as a counter-stroke to clerical intolerance, have their living representatives. In leaving Belper, we give the portrait of its late worthy Circuit Steward, who not unfittingly bears the name of Jackson; and we do so the more readily because he has interested himself in recovering the fast-perishing *memorabilia* of early Derbyshire Primitive Methodism.

Ramsor, Leek, and Cheadle.

Still working round the circumference of Tunstall Circuit, we next come to that part of North Staffordshire which embraces the country lying between the Dove and the Team, stretching from Leek and Warslow on the north, to Rocester on the south east, and taking in the rugged elevations of Morridge and Weaver, and the pleasant valley of the Churnet. This tract of country was made a branch of Tunstall Circuit in 1820, and two years after a circuit, having Ramshorn or Ramsor, near Weaver, as its head. We have already described the very early missioning of this interesting district, and little more need be added, especially as the circuit did not greatly extend its borders. Nor can we wonder at this when we consider its wide area, together with the semi-mountainous character of much of its surface, and its scattered population. Two internal administrative changes must be chronicled.

* It was on May 28th, 1903, Mr. Smith, accompanied by his minister, the Rev. J. Pann, appeared in Belper Court [illegible]

In 1838 Leek—another composite circuit—was partially made from it, and Cheadle entirely so in 1872. Both these changes, though they tended to reduce its area and facilitate its working, have still left it one of the widest circuits in the Connexion.

In or about the year 1831, during the superintendency of Edward Foizey, the last two societies that had clung to James Crawfoot and held aloof from Primitive Methodism, sought union with the Ramsor Circuit. The societies were at Waterfall and Caldon, and their co-lay-pastors were Thomas Mottram and Joseph Bratt. The event, interesting in itself as the healing of a breach, is still more so, because it gave to the Connexion Thomas Mottram, no ordinary man. For one thing, he was the grandson of Samuel and Elizabeth Evans, better known as Seth and Dinah Bede, so that he was half-cousin to George Eliot. But Thomas Mottram scarcely needs this adventitious distinction, though it is worth noting. The memoir of him, written by his son, makes one think what treasures of Christian biography are buried in the old *Magazines* that might very profitably be brought forth. For more than half-a-century Thomas Mottram taught in Sunday school, led his class, climbed the rugged hills, and trudged the lanes of the extensive Ramsor Circuit—"no journey too long, no night too dismal, no weather too severe," to preach to the village congregations. He maintained his Free Church principles, took part in parochial business, and yet had the respect of those who differed from him in politics and Church government. We have had, and unfortunately shall have again, to present many Church clergymen in no very pleasing light; but in their treatment of Thomas Mottram they are seen at their best. In one case he was called upon to visit a lady during a long and painful illness, who had three clergymen among her immediate relatives. One of these was her son, who, on meeting him there, would say: "Now, Mr. Mottram, just do your duty, and pray with my dear mother as you would if I were not here." At his largely-attended and impressive funeral, Mr. Sargent, the vicar, prayed in the little chapel at Waterhouses in a way to melt all hearts, gave out at the grave side the hymn from the Primitive Methodist Hymn Book, and preached his funeral sermon in the parish church. Thomas Mottram died 1874, in the eightieth year of his age. Others of the family remain in the old homestead to dispense the accustomed hospitality, and to carry on the father's work.

REV. EDWARD FOIZEY.

MR. THOMAS MOTTRAM.

Macclesfield, Congleton, and Sandbach.

Macclesfield, as also Congleton and Sandbach, are not on the Tunstall Circuit plan ending April 18th, 1818, but they are found on that beginning May 2nd, 1819, so that the date of their missioning may approximately be fixed somewhere between these two points. Nor are we left entirely to inference; for Hugh Bourne distinctly says that Macclesfield was entered early in the year 1819, and that "Congleton was opened by the exertions of our Macclesfield friends." When Primitive Methodist missionaries crossed the hills and opened their commission in these two towns they were but paying a long-standing debt; for we do not forget the visits of the Stockport Revivalists to Congleton which led to the Harriseahead revival, and how the earliest camp meetings could scarcely have been held but for the help of men from Macclesfield and Knutsford. So these towns were to feel the warmth of the fire they had helped to kindle.

Hugh Bourne intimates that though a society was soon raised up in Macclesfield, "in its infant state, it had to contend with many difficulties; the burden of it was heavy;

BEECH LANE CHAPEL, MACCLESFIELD.

and the circuit was obliged to make great exertions to keep it on its feet." As confirming this general statement, S. Turner records a particular experience of his: how he and T. Clowes went about Macclesfield to beg a little towards the debt incurred in that place, and got three shillings and sixpence. But the collectors were unfortunate in their selection of a day; it was August 18th, the day after a destructive Radical Reform riot in Macclesfield, and eight days before Peterloo, so that, perhaps, all things considered, they did not do amiss. For some time before this, the society had the use of "a large room near the old church;" and though in December, Hugh Bourne speaks rather dubiously of the proposal to build a preaching-room, he notes with evident satisfaction that "there is preaching every Sunday night at eight o'clock near the new church and at Hurdsfield." But, difficulties or no difficulties, the converting work rolled on in a remarkable manner, as is evident from the space given in the first volume of the *Magazine* to the encouraging reports sent in by the preachers who successively laboured in Macclesfield—T. and Ann Brownsword, John Garner, Thomas Webb, and others. There was at this time a large and flourishing Sunday School, and, in order to provide Bibles, Hugh Bourne, in his usual thrifty managing way, bought twelve Bibles in sheets for thirty-six shillings, and then had every sheet of the twenty-seven each Bible contained, stitched in stiff paper covers, costing twelve shillings more ; "so that they got three hundred and eighty-four books for forty-nine shillings, which would have cost them twenty pounds had they got whole Bibles." Much activity too was shown in the raising of classes, class-papers being put into the hands of those who seemed to have in them the making of leaders. By March 20th, 1820, Thomas Webb could report that: "the work of the Lord is in a prosperous way; there are one hundred and eighty-one in society, eight leaders, and six preachers."

Macclesfield was one of the new circuits of the Tunstall District made in 1821 ; but it remained such only for twelve months.

As yet, it seems, it was not able to walk alone, and it reverted to Tunstall, and, though fourteen long miles away, continued under its governance until 1834. Then we have "Macclesfield and Congleton Union Circuit." In 1835 the two were separated and, as part of the Tunstall District, have so remained. Surely something must have occurred to cripple the young circuit's energies; for, at the beginning of its course, its missionary zeal carried it to Flagg and Chelmorton and Burbage near Buxton; to Stockport, H. B. tells us, to Congleton and, what was even more, to Manchester; and there we shall have to follow it as soon as we have skirted the North Western segment of Tunstall Circuit and noted the advance made in that direction. From information received, we learn that the first preaching-place at Congleton was a turning-shop in Canal Street, afterwards perverted into the "Horse and Jockey" public-house, and now a private dwelling. This room, which has played so many parts, is doubtless referred to by James Bonsor in his *Journal*:—

FIRST CHAPEL AT CONGLETON, BUILT 1822. DESTROYED SEVERAL YEARS AGO.

members. At eleven I preached in the open air. At two, Elizabeth Dakin preached, and opened the room they have taken. It was a good time. It was full, and the room above was nearly full. The Lord poured His Spirit down. Sinners were awakened, and cried for mercy."

FIRST CHAPEL IN BURSLEM.
As it was, now a public-house.

The Elizabeth Dakin of the above extract, was of Ashmore House near the Cloud. She was one of the early protégées of Hugh Bourne, who notes in his *Journal* the preaching of her first sermon—April 30th, 1814. The initials of her name may be picked out from those of the rest of the anonymous sisterhood at the bottom of the 1819 plan. But in 1835 her name is first on the list of local preachers on the plan of the Macclesfield and Congleton Union Circuit. She continued for many years a successful local preacher and, in 1837, was married to Mr. George Harvey. On their removal to Oak Farm, Broomhall, in 1845, they were numbered among the influential families of the Burland Circuit.

At Congleton we meet with several leading personages of the Tunstall Circuit of the early days. Thomas Steele was one of these. Born in 1801, he was, like his father, already giving proofs of strong individuality. He was a trustee of the first Burslem Chapel [opened December 24th, 1822, by David Delany] and in the deed he is designated "preacher." About this time he removed to Congleton, and had much to do with the strengthening of the cause there and the building of its first chapel, for which also he was a trustee. The site for this chapel was given by Mr. John Andrew, sen., a man of considerable means, who died in 1826 and bequeathed one hundred pounds to our mission funds—probably the first testamentary benefaction of the kind. His son, John Andrew, jun., was, until 1827, one of the select few who formed the Book Committee, and the Tunstall General Committee. In the 'Forties he was twice mayor of Congleton and, probably before this, left our Church for the Wesleyans. As to Thomas Steele, he

MRS. ANDREW.

MR. J. ANDREW.

married for his second wife the sister of John Andrew, the younger, a gifted preacheress whose name stood on the same plan. He was a man of fine physique and of much alertness and determination, as his portrait would suggest.* He is described as having been a powerful singing-preacher and a noted pioneer worker of the early days. From 1843 to 1847 he was postmaster of Congleton, but he seems to have had a passion for evangelistic labour, and, in 1857, he became a colporteur in Buenos Ayres. His diary—of quite exceptional calligraphy—is without the taint of commercialism, though it is the diary of a man whose daily business it was to sell Bibles. As a colporteur he did sell more than thirteen hundred copies of the Scriptures in Spanish, French and Italian, but it is evident he was more anxious to save souls than to sell Bibles, or rather he pushed the sale of his Bibles that men might "buy the truth." We get the same impression of him from the record of his unpaid evangelistic labours in Canada and the Channel Isles. Whenever and wherever the way was open he endeavoured to rouse the Churches and to promote revivals of religion. Some looked on him askance and thought him "queer," but yet more appreciated and were profited by his labours. This was shown when, on leaving for England in 1864, the ministers assembled at the Ottawa District Meeting (Wesleyan) thanked him by resolution for his disinterested labours. He felt himself driven by Divine impulsion to engage in these over-sea labours just as did Lorenzo Dow—of whom he somehow reminds us. Thomas Steele was a man of more than ordinary education and with special evangelistic gifts, of whose activity to promote the interests of our Church in the early years we get glimpses in the *Magazines* and in unpublished diaries and letters; and this is the reason he is referred to here. True, like his brother-in-law and others about this time he left our Church, precisely when and why we know not. We suspect that with all his father's ability and with more than his father's push, he had also inherited a certain masterfulness and impatience of rules and restraints not self-imposed, and possibly there may have been commercial troubles. Ultimately, he left the Wesleyans, on the allegement that they had departed from primitive simplicity. His final relations with our Church were cordial and sympathetic, he died March 24th, 1885.

Later workers, true and faithful to the end, were Samuel Oakes, of Mow Cop, Mrs. Brassington, afterwards Mrs. Graham and James Broad, who preached the last sermon Hugh Bourne was privileged to listen to, carried his dying message to the Conference, and preached his funeral sermon at Congleton. Of these the Rev. Charles Smallman, who knew them well, has said:—

"As it regards Samuel Oakes, I never expect to look upon his like again. He was without exception, the best all-round man I ever met with. He was very pious, by no means boastful or talkative, but there was very little he could not do.......James Broad was a remarkable worker. He walked thousands of miles to preach in the Congleton and other circuits. He was in this way the most remarkable man I ever knew.......Jane Brassington was very pious and very useful as a local preacher. She had the honour of witnessing the first conversion that took place at Mow on the occasion of the great revival."

THE PERIOD OF CIRCUIT PREDOMINANCE AND ENTERPRISE. 543

The great revival referred to in the preceding extract, began soon after Mr. Smallman entered upon his station at Congleton in 1856. The Mow Cop Society had ineffectually agitated to be re-attached to Tunstall Circuit, and were sore in consequence of the failure of their efforts. "We want to have sinners converted, and we can get none converted as we are," was the reason assigned by Samuel Oakes for the prevailing dissatisfaction. But a revival came, in which the Rev. James Shenton and other members of his family were converted. Not only were those who were just outside swept into the Church, but also those apparently afar off—poachers, whom neither gamekeepers nor magistrates could tame, and even one who had just been let out of Knutsford Prison, where he had been confined for killing his antagonist in a prize-fight. We refer to this revival because it took place just on the eve of the great Jubilee Camp Meeting on Mow Cop, and showed that the old evangel could repeat on the old ground the triumphs of fifty years before.

MR. SAMUEL OAKES.

MR. JAMES BROAD.

Mrs. Brassington became the wife of Rev. John Graham, and survived until 1887. "Jane Graham," says the local annalist, "was a bright, happy Christian, full of hope and joy. She was known as a peace-maker and comforter, and sick-visitor through the town of Congleton." Her husband was the superintendent of the Tunstall Circuit in 1840. One who knew him well at that time says:—

"John Graham was an earnest and successful soul-winner. This was his aim and joy in preaching and in family visiting. As a preacher he might not satisfy the critical, but he had fruit. J. Hallam heard him preach one Sunday at an adjoining place, when he became somewhat embarrassed in his sermon, but extricated himself by breaking forth: 'Glory be to God; we had a number of souls saved when I was preaching the other Sunday.'" †

Sandbach, in Cheshire, was missioned a little earlier than Macclesfield and Congleton. On and between August 9th and September 18th, 1818, Thomas Jackson held half a dozen services at the Town Cross, amid much excitement and opposition, which largely showed itself in the throwing of apples, potatoes, and stones at the preacher and his congregation. The last date mentioned was Sandbach Fair, and on that day he and his friends sang from the Cross to Scotch Common, where there was to be a bull-baiting. The bull was driven in the direction of the preacher with the view of

MRS. JANE GRAHAM.

REV. JOHN GRAHAM.

---

* Those who are on the look-out for glimpses of the supernatural in our Connexional History may be interested to know that Mrs. Graham is credited with having had a remarkable dream, by which she was assured of the death of Hugh Bourne before any one in Congleton knew of the event.

† The late Rev. T. Bayley

dispersing his congregation but, when some two or three hundred yards off, the bull would persist on kneeling down as if to do obeisance, and the would-be disturbers were glad to get it away. On the evening of this day a society of seven or eight members was formed in a cottage. After this, Hugh Bourne paid occasional visits to Sandbach and other places in the neighbourhood, and on November 22nd he records "there are twenty in Society." Sandbach appears on the stations as an independent circuit in 1840, and Thomas Jackson lived to take part in the Jubilee Services held at Sandbach in August, 1868, to commemorate the introduction of Primitive Methodism into that town.

Preston Brook.

We have now to glance at the missioning of that part of Cheshire, lying contiguous to the original Burland Circuit which, in 1820, took the name of Preston Brook Branch, and three years after became an independent station. This tract of country forms the last section—the last felloe of the big wheel—of Tunstall Circuit as it was before its partition. It must not be forgotten, however, that some parts of this district had frequently been visited by Hugh Bourne and his fellow-labourers amongst the Camp Meeting Methodists. Within this district are Warrington, the home of Peter Phillips, the welcomer, and sometime host of Lorenzo Dow, and early associate of Hugh Bourne; at Warrington, too, is Old Friars Green Chapel, erected 1802, for preaching in which James Crawfoot brought himself under censure. Historic Delamere Forest is also in this district, and Budworth and Barnton, places that were frequently visited by Hugh Bourne during his early itineraries. Brynn Chapel, too, with its original inscription: "Primitive Methodist Chapel. Built 1819. Prepare to meet thy God," still preserved in the re-constructed building, is included within the present Northwich Circuit. Brynn Chapel is situate about a mile from the former residence, long since demolished, of the "old man of the Forest." A year ago it was re-floored and re-pewed, and now, over and above the historic interest attaching to the building, it is one of the neatest and most comfortable country chapels in the Connexion.

THE HOME OF PETER PHILLIPS, SHIP YARD, WARRINGTON.

But it was not as Primitive Methodists that Bourne and his coadjutors had first visited these parts. It was not until 1818–19 that a combined, determined effort was made to win North-West Cheshire for the new denomination founded in 1811. The honour of .... belongs to

Thomas Jackson, though there were very soon in the field other of the Tunstall Circuit preachers. In July, 1869, he took the leading part in a series of Jubilee Services in celebration of his having, by his missionary labours, laid the foundations of the Preston Brook Circuit. Two particulars may be noted in connection with this jubilee: W. M. Salt and T. Spooner, who were amongst the first-fruits of the mission, took a prominent part in the celebration; and the jubilee itself was kept at Runcorn, which, though missioned by T. Jackson in 1819, was afterwards abandoned. It was remissioned in 1823, but again adverse circumstances led to its abandonment in 1828. Once more it was remissioned by Mr. R. Turner, who volunteered to do the work without extra cost to the circuit. He succeeded, as he deserved to do, and in 1838 the first chapel was erected.

Writing of the Preston Brook Branch in the first volume of the *Magazine*, Hugh Bourne says:—

"This branch was opened chiefly in 1819: and, it takes in Delamere Forest,

OLD FRIARS GREEN CHAPEL, WARRINGTON.*

Weaverham, Northwich, Great Budworth, Bartington, Crowton, Kingsley, Norley, Frodsham, and other places, all in Cheshire. Thomas Jackson and John Hallsworth held several camp meetings with great effect; particularly one at Bartington on Sunday, June 6th."

Now, Sampson Turner was present at this camp meeting, as also at one on the Sunday preceding, in the same neighbourhood, and he has described both in his unpublished *Journals*. The first entry is specially interesting, as affording clear proof

---

* The valuable views of Peter Phillips' house, and Friars Green Chapel, have only recently been secured, and we have been allowed to reproduce them by the courtesy of Mr. A. Mounfield, the editor of the "Independent Methodist."

that Mrs. M. Richardson, of Warrington, the West Indian proprietress who freed her slaves, was still associated with our founders in aggressive work. It shows that W. Clowes' words "Mrs. Richardson became a speaker amongst us," were quite true as late as 1819, at least. Indeed, there is every reason to believe that the initials "M. R.," at the bottom of the plan for that year, are hers, and that she was a recognised auxiliary preacher, taking regular appointments in the Tunstall Circuit. The Ann Egerton referred to by S. Turner in his *Journal*, was another prominent female preacher in the early times. Her initials will also be found on the plan amongst the rest.

"*Sunday, May 30th, 1819*—I was appointed for a camp meeting at Dunkirk Works, in the vicinity of Northwich, with Brother T. Jackson from Belper, Sister M. Richardson from Warrington, and Sister A. Egerton from Wood Green. The meeting was numerously attended by all ranks, it being a novelty in that neighbourhood to hold such a religious meeting out of doors. I judged there to be two thousand present at least. Believers were much in the spirit of their duty, and life and zeal animated the meeting most of the day. I believe much good was done. To God be all the glory. Another camp meeting was given out at the above, to be held next Sabbath Day on Bartington Heath. Spoke nine times this week. May the Word be sent home to every heart.

"*June 6th*—I was planned at Weston and Englesea Brook, but by some means it was supplied another way, as I had to speak in the street at Halford, near Northwich, and then attend the camp meeting that had been given out as above. Great numbers attended from all parts, and it was very manifest that much good was done. Much was said about us, and of our eccentric proceedings; but they were compelled, in a sense, to acknowledge that we were men of God, for God was with us. I spoke at Northwich at night in the street. The Lord was present."

To these graphic details of a week's labours, may be added a summary of results condensed from Thomas Brownsword's *Journal*, inserted in the first volume of the *Magazine*.

"In December, 1819 there were forty-five members in society at Delamere Forest, twenty-two at Weaverham, seventeen at Frodsham and forty-one at Preston. In the February following, there were thirty at Crowton, and thirty at Kingsley. Messrs. Jackson and Hallsworth, and Turner and John Garner, and T. and A. Brownsword, appear to have been rendered very useful in this district and to have been the means of turning hundreds of souls from darkness to light, and from the power of Satan unto God."

Other events as yet remote, but directly traceable to these pioneer labours, were the making of Warrington Circuit out of Preston Brook in 1837, and of Northwich in 1855. Beyond this date we need not further follow the process of circuit subdivision. Nor must it be forgotten that Preston Brook was for a time, as will be shown hereafter, a kind of foster-mother to Liverpool, and that it closely followed Shrewsbury in sending —April 20th, 1832—a missionary to Ireland. F. N. Jersey, the agent selected, had intended to concentrate his efforts on Dublin, but finding on his arrival that the city was in a state of political ferment he deemed it prudent to choose another field. He fixed upon Newry in the north of Ireland, as his centre, and soon met with a measure of success. In 1839, the Lurgan Mission, as it was then called, embraced a considerable district in the counties of Down and Armagh, some twenty-six Irish miles in length and fourteen in breadth, and including within its radius four towns and some twenty villages. In 1842, at the end of the circuit mission period, the Donoughmore and Lurgan Mission, as it was now called, was still under the care of Preston Brook, and had for its ministers J. Judson and Jesse Ashworth.

CHAPTER XI.

CHESTER CIRCUIT.

WE have in this chapter to try to show how, from Burland as a centre, Primitive Methodism reached Chester and the surrounding district, there securely planting and ramifying itself. From Chester a beginning was even made in populous Liverpool; and it also extended itself into Shropshire, forming the "Shropshire Mission," out of which grew Prees Green Circuit, with its numerous offshoots.

CHESTER.

To trace the beginnings of Primitive Methodism in the city of Chester, it is necessary to go back to the time when Burland was still a branch of Tunstall. At first, the branch was more successful in extending itself in the north-western parts of Cheshire than it was in Shropshire, and this from various causes. For one thing, John Wedgwood had gone in that direction, and the regular preachers of Tunstall Circuit soon followed in his track. Then, as yet, the preachers were too few to admit of the vigorous prosecution of the mission in more distant Shropshire. Yet another and a very sufficient reason of the earlier success realised in Cheshire, lay in the number of respectable families who early identified themselves with the cause, and became its stay and support. Messrs. Taylor and Bateman have already been referred to, and the latter plainly states of the former and his family, that, without them and their influence, it is not easy to see how there ever could have been a Burland Circuit at all. There might have been a circuit in these parts, but that it should get the name of Burland, was simply owing to the fact that the Taylor family lived there, and made any other name out of the

CHESTER TOWN HALL AND MARKET-PLACE.

question. But besides these families, there were others of influence, such as Mr. Dean, of Walk Mills, and Warburton, of Burton Hall, who opened their houses for preaching, and extended hospitality to the preachers. And, farther north, there was Mr. Ephraim Sadler, of Huxley, and his brother William, of Tiverton. The former, who was born at Burland in 1773, was for some years a Wesleyan. In June, 1819, Sampson Turner, while on his long circuit-round, came into John Wedgwood's mission for some three weeks. Supported by a volunteer helper named Job Gibson, he took his stand near to Mr. Sadler's farmstead. He was courteously invited to preach in the farm-yard, and did so, standing on a stout stool planted under the shade of a clump of elms, and exhorting the people from, "Enter ye in at the strait gate."* Young John Sadler was convinced at this service, and when a class was formed by Thomas Brownsword he, together with his father, mother, and other members of the family, joined the society. S. Turner was at Huxley again on September 22nd, and notes in his *Journal* that "many desired that Huxley should be put on the Preachers' Plan in order that they might have regular supplies, as there are many hearers, and a prospect of much good being done." The farm-house became the home of the preachers and the sanctuary of the society, of which Mr. E. Sadler became the first leader. The next step in advance was taken when in March, 1822, Huxley was made a branch of Burland Circuit. The branch comprised twenty-five places, including Tarporley, Tiverton, Wrexham, and Chester; it had three travelling-preachers—T. Sugden, W. Sanders, and Ann Stanna, and twenty local preachers, with ten auxiliaries belonging to Burland Circuit.

Chester had been attacked as early as December, 1820, but it would not surrender. A second attempt, however, which proved more successful, was made in the spring of 1821. Thomas Brownsword, having hovered round it for some time, just as Benton did round Leicester, preaching in the neighbouring villages, made a descent on Chester in the manner and with the results described in the following historic record:—

"*Sunday, March 18th.*—I went to Chester, and at eight o'clock preached on the Cross to about five hundred people. Many seemed much affected. We then went into Watergate Street, and held a prayer-meeting in a yard. Here I gave an exhortation; it was a good time. I then went to

ST. PETER'S CHURCH CROSS, CHESTER.

* On September 17th, S. Turner spoke from a table at Hampton Heath in Mr. Davis' croft, and remarks: "A table or a stool has been my pulpit, and the open air my chapel, most of this summer."

Hanbridge, and preached at ten to a large concourse of people. I believe good was done. I then visited some sick, and while praying, two women were much affected, and began to cry for mercy. I intended to preach in Boughton. A large company assembled, but the weather was so unfavourable that we were obliged to divide into companies and go into three houses, and hold prayer-meetings. I then gave an exhortation. I believe much good was done; many were in distress, and some obtained pardon. When we had done in Chester I went to Tarvin, and preached to a many people."

By this full good day's work Primitive Methodism got foothold in Chester, and it is worth noting that both Nantwich and Chester came on the Burland Plan beginning

CASTLE GATES, CHESTER.

April 29th, 1821, together; as the latest additions their names standing at the bottom. Chester's reception of Primitive Methodism was anything but cordial—indeed it was rough. The rowdy element invaded the preaching-room in King Street, shouted "Amen," hooted, howled, and sometimes ran up against the worshippers as they left or went to the services, in a way hardly distinguishable from "assault and battery." To make matters worse, the disturbers were emboldened in playing their godless pranks by the chilling response of the magistrates to their appeal for protection: "No; it serves you right. Why don't you stop at home, and not come here disturbing the peace of the ———." M———— ——t, d—t their wor—t, and began to mend when John Ride visited the ———— ———— ———— for his presence in this region, and

THE PERIOD OF CIRCUIT PREDOMINANCE AND ENTERPRISE. 551

observed that he opened Wrexham in March, 1821. On April 21st, soon after Brownsword's visit to Chester, Ride was present in the room, into which some unruly spirits, bent on mischief, had thrust themselves. They mocked, with their "Make way for the parson!" When the devout sang a hymn they started a song. While the preacher prayed they shouted. But the preacher, who at times was very mighty in prayer, rose into faith and prayed, until he prayed some of the ringleaders to their knees and others out of the building. After this outburst the sky cleared, and the atmosphere became less thunderous and electric. Thomas Bateman noted the pleasing change that had taken place, when next he fulfilled his appointments in the city in October. He was agreeably surprised to find the congregation large and pretty well-behaved, and that even the rabble in the streets did not insult him in any way as they had done others. "Surely," he adds, "the bitter persecution will now drop." Two months later (December 8th) he found the outlook still brighter. He rose "a great while before it was yet day," ate a little dry biscuit, and walked to the city—a distance of some eighteen or twenty miles, and at the close of a day of toil, he records:—"The work prospers much in this ancient city now. Thank God! After a storm there comes a calm."

Between these two visits (October 27) Huxley Branch had become Chester Branch. Mr. Ephraim Sadler had now removed to Saughall near the city, and other persons of respectability and influence had become connected with the society. Hence the change.

LICENCE FOR PREACHING-HOUSE, BOUGHTON, CHESTER.

But when Burland, two months after, was made a circuit, there still remained the somewhat delicate question: What particular circuit is Chester now a Branch of—Tunstall or Burland? This was a moot point, especially at Chester. "What! have we, the Palatine city, just got released from Huxley to be tied to Burland?" We can hear the fireside debates of those dark December days. The question came before the Tunstall Quarterly Meeting for settlement, and the fathers very wisely left Chester to choose its own head. On January 5th, Thomas Bateman walked to Chester to meet the Branch Committee which met in Bold Place, at the house of Captain Howie, who was master-gunner at Chester Castle, "and quite a leader among our people." This gentleman proposed a resolution to the effect that ... from Burland than from Tunstall, they would belong to Burland." This resolution was seconded by Mr. E. Sadler, "who seemed to have much influence," and carried *nem. con.*

Though the King Street room had been the scene of unseemly disturbances and opposition, it had also been the scene of many manifestations of divine grace. Among the converts won in this room were Edward Davies, the first Sunday School Superintendent, and some whose descendants are numbered with the Church of to-day. Besides the room in King Street, the house of Thomas Ellis, in Steven Street, Boughton, was, in 1821, licensed and used as a place of worship. This house-sanctuary was the precursor of the first chapel in Steam-Mill Street. Thomas Bateman was present at the opening of this chapel on May 2nd, 1824, and speaks of it as "a plain building and nothing wasted in useless ornament, though it was a great effort for the society to raise

FOLLY FIELD, WHERE CAMP MEETINGS WERE HELD, CHESTER.

it. I went over several times," he adds, "to assist my friend Mr. M'Millan in collecting money and in other ways."

A month after this (June 1824), Chester was made a circuit with three travelling preachers and thirty-eight places, with a good prospect of success, which its history has not belied.

The Chapel in Steam-Mill Street—which owed much to the liberality of Mr. E. Sadler[*]

---

[*] We are in..... the ..... Chapel was given by Mr. Sadler. He died January 5th, 1853. See a sh..... of him in the *Magazine* for 1854, p. 330.

—served the purposes of the Chester Society for a goodly number of years. The Church had its vicissitudes like other churches. Though we have no evidence that it was weakened by dissension or rent by secession, it had its seasons of depression and decline, and it was while it was passing through such an experience that the thought and purpose of building another chapel came as a sudden inspiration. Open-air mission services in various parts still continued to be held in the city and its suburbs—the Castle Gates, Boughton, Machine Bank, and a new suburb called Newtown. After an unusually successful mission at the latter place, several of the workers retired to the house of Mr. James Adams, and, after conference, resolved at once to form a committee to look out for a suitable site in that district for a new erection. The result—a result achieved only after much prayer and self-denial—was the erection in 1863 of the first

MACHINE BANK, BOUGHTON, CHESTER.

George Street Chapel, now the Temperance Hall. Among those who constituted the first committee may be mentioned the names of Hulse, Fletcher, Vernon, Moore, and Adams. The ambition of the projectors of George Street Chapel did not look beyond this building. At the time it was looked upon as the *ne plus ultra* of Primitive Methodism in Chester. It was thought it would meet all requirements for a long time to come, if not for ever. But twelve months had scarcely passed before it was found to be almost ludicrously inadequate to its purpose. The teachers and scholars of its school were themselves quite sufficient to fill it, without any other congregation, so that services had to be held in the chapel and the school at the same time.

If any one with the mind's eye had seen "finality" written on the front of the first George Street Chapel, the time came when they saw it no longer. A growing

FIRST PRIMITIVE METHODIST CHAPEL, CHESTER.

church, like a crustacean, is sure in time to outgrow its accommodation, and to have to look out for a bigger shell. So it was with the George Street Church. The time came when its old habitat no longer sufficed, but was felt to be cramping and inadequate. Once more the church had to put forth a strenuous effort to provide roomier quarters.

GEORGE STREET CHAPEL, CHESTER.

HAMILTON ST.

TARVIN RD.

GEORGE ST.

Chester Chapels

HUNTER ST.

affording greater facilities for many-sided church work. The result was the erection, at an outlay of some £7,500, of the present goodly pile of buildings, which already are felt to be none too large and only provisional. The story of Chester's enterprise in chapel-building cannot be further told in detail, but it may be summed up in the statement that we have now three chapels in the city, and one in the suburb of Hoole, in course of erection, the aggregate cost of these erections being little short of £16,000.

Regarded Primitive Methodistically, Chester reminds us of Grimsby. True, the latter was missioned a year earlier than Chester, has more chapels and a larger membership, but in both there has been commendable activity shown in the erection of places of worship, and in both our Church has a recognised prestige, and wields considerable local influence. In Chester our adherents are found on the City and Hoole District Council, the Board of Guardians, and associated with every local organisation of a philanthropic kind. The reason is not far to seek. In Chester, even more markedly than in Grimsby, Primitive Methodism has become hereditary in families. In some towns we look and look in vain for the direct descendants of those who were leading officials fifty years ago. The old families have no living representatives in active communion with the Church. But in Chester many of the old names are still to be found on the church-roll, and the new blood is nothing but the old blood enriched, as it should be, by inheritance and the benison of heaven. Take in proof of this the following facts:—On the trust deed of George Street are to be found thirteen names of those who are the children of former trustees and officials. Amongst the officers and teachers of the school there are children, grandchildren, and great-grandchildren of former superintendents, and there is one scholar who is at once the grandchild of the present superintendent and the fifth in descent from a former superintendent. At the seventy-fifth anniversary of the school a portrait-group was taken, in which were included thirteen who figured in the group taken twenty-five years before. It is this hereditary attachment—this continuity of service, which gives cohesion and strength to a Church.

Two Conferences have been held in Chester—those of 1866 and 1894. The former held its sittings in the Music Hall, and it is noteworthy that of the eighty-four representatives present that year, only one—a layman—was found amongst the one hundred and ninety-four who assembled at the Conference, held twenty-eight years after, in George Street Chapel. So true it is, that while the Conference as to its form and functions may be permanent, its *personnel* may in less than a generation be almost entirely changed. It is like a river or waterfall in its permanence; like a river, too, in the flux of the particles which compose it. And yet, singular to say, there were still living in 1894, though in age and feebleness extreme, two men who were not only coeval with the beginnings of Primitive Methodism in the city and county of Chester, but active participants in those beginnings. One of them had been among the earliest missioners of Chester, while the other had been one of its very first travelling preachers. John Smith (1), the superintendent of Chester Circuit on its formation in 1825, had been in his grave forty years in 1894, but Joseph Preston, who spent the first six months of his ministry in Chester, still survived, though in his ninety-second year, while Thos. l . . . 1 b 1 Joseph Preston tells us that he had not been at Chester more than six weeks before Burland Circuit wished to have him in exchange for another preacher. John Smith, with the letter of application in his hand, said to his young colleague: "Let us go and pray about it." They went upstairs and fell on their knees. John Smith began: "O Lord, Thou seest they have sent for Joseph to go to Burland. Don't let him go. Don't let the devil part us:" and they were not parted. Thomas Bateman spoke at the chief public meeting of the Chester Conference of 1866, and according to the local report of the day, "related the difficulties which Primitive Methodism had to contend with when their system of religious worship was first introduced into Cheshire nearly fifty years before."

There are many scenes in our history which would form fitting subjects for the artist's pencil. One such would be the picture of the two veterans already named, sitting musing in their chairs, what time the seventy-fifth Conference Public Meeting is being held in Chester. In their clairvoyant vision they see the great congregation, and witness its enthusiasm. The thought of that Conference, and where it is being held, carries the memory back to the toils, struggles, and successes of the far-back pioneer days. Vanished forms reappear; scenes of which they were part are re-enacted. Then the mind reverts to the present, swiftly crossing the gulf of seventy years, and reverie passes into the anticipation of the Master's "Well done!" and the last quiet resting-place. In 1894 those two silent figures were the sole remaining links with the earliest days of Cheshire and Shropshire Primitive Methodism—links soon to be sundered. Both were born and died within the area of the old Burland Circuit, which they lived to see embracing some fifteen circuits. Both had a long working day; their sun took a wide circuit, but at last it sank to the horizon amid its own lengthening shadows:

REV. JOSEPH PRESTON.

THE BATEMAN MEMORIAL.

"Be the day weary, or be the day long,
At length it ringeth out to evensong."

FROM SEA TO SEA.

We have now reached a point when, for a moment, details may be lost sight of, and a wider survey taken of what has already been accomplished.

In a lecture on Mow Cop, once delivered by James Broad in Mow Cop Chapel, he referred to the famous Corda Well, situate not far from where he stood, that never ran dry even in the severest drought of summer. He stated how the desire took him to ascertain where the overflow of this well made its way. The stream, he found, soon divided, each part taking its own course, turning mills and making itself generally useful as it flowed. One streamlet made its way by Smallwood, to Sandbach, Wheelock, and Middlewich. But the two came together again at Northwich, and with other streams "flowed into the great canal to carry the great boats and flats to Winsford and other places, and then they flow on to Runcorn and help the packets to Liverpool, and there helped to swell the great ocean whereon merchandise was conveyed to almost every nation under heaven.

> "For the little rill keeps running still,
> Which first began on Mow Hill."

All this is a parable; for the significance of the formation of Preston Brook and Chester Circuits consists in its showing that Primitive Methodism, which had its origin hard by Corda Well, has now reached the Mersey and the Dee as it has reached the Humber and the Wash. For, by this time, the missionaries of Nottingham have reached South-East Lincolnshire, as the *Journals* of Francis

Birch testify, and have visited Boston, Sutton, Holbeach, Spalding, and Donnington. In 1821 Boston became a circuit, and Spalding was made a branch of Nottingham; but Boston retained its independence for only one year, and did not permanently regain it until 1826. Much activity was shown in the building of chapels in this district during the following years, twenty-one chapels being reported to the Nottingham District Meeting of 1848 by the two circuits of Boston and Donnington. The mission into this corner of Lincolnshire led the way into Norfolk as is shown by the following statement of John Oscroft :—

"When I commenced travelling [in May, 1821,] Boston was then a branch of Nottingham Circuit. In a fortnight after beginning to travel, I was sent to labour in that branch. About six weeks afterwards Boston was made a circuit, and Spalding Branch became a branch of Nottingham Circuit. I was appointed to labour in this branch with five other preachers, though at this time there was not sufficient work for two. We therefore opened a mission in the county of Norfolk, where the work of the Lord spread rapidly, and hundreds were soon converted to God."

FIRST WRITTEN PLAN AFTER THE AMALGAMATION OF THE SOCIETIES, JUNE 1811.

END OF VOLUME I

FLETCHER AND SON, LTD. PRINTERS NORWICH

Lightning Source UK Ltd.
Milton Keynes UK
UKOW04n0611010716

277449UK00006B/69/P